D1037098

Primitive Mental States
and the Rorschach

Primitive Mental States and the Rorschach

Edited by

Howard D. Lerner, Ph.D.

Paul M. Lerner, Ed.D.

INTERNATIONAL UNIVERSITIES PRESS, INC.

Madison   Connecticut

Library of Congress Cataloging in Publication Data

Primitive mental states and the Rorschach.

   Includes bibliographies and index.
      1. Rorschach test. 2. Psychoses—Diagnosis.
3. Borderline personality disorder—Diagnosis.
4. Narcissism—Diagnosis.   I. Lerner, Howard D.
II. Lerner, Paul M. [DNLM: 1. Personality Assessment.
2. Personality Disorders.   3. Rorschach Test.
WM 145 P952]
RC473.R6P75   1988   616.89′075   88-2935
ISBN 0-8236-4295-X

Manufactured in the United States of America

Contents

Contributors

David Arnow, Ph.D.
   Private Practice, Scarsdale, New York

Susan Bram, Ph.D.
   Assistant Professor of Clinical Psychology, New York State Psychiatric Institute, College of Physicians & Surgeons, Columbia University, New York City
   Private Practice, New York City

Vera Campo, Ph.D.
   President, Sociedad Española del Rorschach y Métodos Proyectivos
   Honorary Member, Asociacion Argentina de Psicodiagnostico de Rorschach
   Member, Society of Personality Assessment, The British Society for Projective Psychology and Personality Study, Société Française du Rorschach et des Methodes Projectives, International Rorschach Society

Mary S. Cerney, Ph.D.
   Staff Psychologist, The Menninger Foundation, Topeka, Kansas
   Section Psychologist, C.F. Menninger Memorial Hospital, Topeka, Kansas

Susan Coates, Ph.D.
   Director, Childhood Gender Identity Project and Child Psychology Training, Child and Adolescent Psychiatry, Roosevelt Hospital, New York City
   Associate Clinical Professor of Medical Psychology, Department of Psychiatry, Columbia University, New York City

Steven Cooper, Ph.D.
Instructor in Psychiatry (Psychology), The Cambridge Hospital, Harvard University Medical School

James Eyman, Ph.D.
Staff Psychologist, C.F. Menninger Memorial Hospital, Topeka, Kansas

Michael A. Farris, Psy.D.
Staff Psychologist, Fair Oaks Hospital, Summit, New Jersey
Private Practice, New York City and Springfield, New Jersey

Barbara Fibel Marcus, Ph.D.
Assistant Professor, Department of Psychiatry, Cornell University Medical College
Assistant Attending Psychologist, New York Hospital–Cornell Medical Center, Westchester Division

Risto Fried, Ph.D., ABPP
Acting Professor of Family Therapy, University of Jyväskylä, Jyväskylä, Finland
Director, Cape Matthias Dream Laboratory
Training Analyst, Therapeia Foundation, IFPS

Mary M. Gallagher, Ph.D.
The Children's Guild, Inc., Baltimore, Maryland

Odile Husain, M.A.
Clinical Psychologist, Outpatient Psychiatric Institution, Lausanne, Switzerland
Assistant in Differential Psychology, University of Geneva, Geneva, Switzerland

Marja-Helena Huttunen
Staff Psychologist, Parikkala Mental Health Center, Parikkala, Finland

Lee S. Jaffe, Ph.D.
Staff Psychologist, Child and Adolescent Unit, Mesa Vista Hospital, San Diego, California

Richard L. Karmel, Ph.D.
　Staff Psychologist, Montreal General Hospital
　Lecturer, Department of Psychiatry, Faculty of Medicine, McGill
　University, Montreal, Quebec, Canada
　Member, Canadian Psychoanalytic Society

Martin Leichtman, Ph.D.
　Director of Psychology, The Children's Division, The Menninger
　Foundation, Topeka, Kansas

Howard D. Lerner, Ph.D., ABPP
　Assistant Clinical Professor of Psychiatry (Psychology), The Uni-
　versity of Michigan Medical Center, Ann Arbor, Michigan
　Private Practice, Ann Arbor, Michigan

Paul M. Lerner, Ed.D.
　Assistant Professor, Department of Psychiatry, Faculty of Medi-
　cine, University of Toronto, Toronto, Ontario, Canada
　Teaching Faculty, Canadian Psychoanalytic Institute, Toronto
　Branch, Toronto, Ontario, Canada

Ronnie Levine, Ph.D.
　Director, Doctoral Psychology Internship Program, Rockland
　Psychiatric Center, Rockland County, New York
　Assistant Professor, Department of Psychiatry, College of Physi-
　cians and Surgeons, Columbia University, New York City
　Supervisor of individual and group therapy in the Clinical Psy-
　chology Internship Program, New York State Psychiatric Institute,
　New York City
　Teaching Faculty, Department of Psychiatry, New York Univer-
　sity Medical Center, New York
　Graduate Member, New York University Postdoctoral Program
　in Psychotherapy and Psychoanalysis, New York City
　Private Practice, New York City

Christopher G. Lovett, Ph.D.
　Staff Psychologist, Westwood Lodge Hospital, Westwood,
　Massachusetts

Pamela S. Ludolph, Ph.D.
Lecturer, Department of Psychology, University of Michigan, Ann Arbor, Michigan

Elina Malkavaara-Kallinen
Staff Psychologist, Kajaani Public Health Center, Kajaani, Finland

Colette Merceron, M.A.
Clinical Psychologist, Outpatient Psychiatric Institution, Lausanne, Switzerland

Judith Meyers, Psy. D.
Senior Clinical Psychologist, Forensic Evaluation Unit, County of San Diego, California
Assistant Clinical Professor of Psychiatry, University of California, San Diego, San Diego, California
Adjunct Lecturer in Women's Studies, San Diego State University

Randy S. Milden, Ph.D.
Visiting Assistant Professor, Department of Psychology, Haverford College, Haverford, Pennsylvania

Niva Piran, Ph.D.
Associate Professor, Ontario Institute for Studies in Education, Senior Consultant, Eating Disorder Program, Toronto General Hospital, Toronto, Ontario, Canada

Eero Rantasila
Staff Psychologist, Central Finland Mental Health Center, Jyväskylä, Finland

Matti Reinikainen
Staff Psychologist, Inner Finland Hospital, Suohahti, Finland

Frieda Rossel, M.A.
Clinical Psychologist, Outpatient Psychiatric Institution, Lausanne, Switzerland
Teacher in Projective Techniques, University of Geneva, Geneva, Switzerland

Arnold H. Rubenstein, Ph.D.
Consulting Psychologist, East Metro Youth Services, Huntley Youth Services, Jewish Family and Child Services, Toronto, Ontario, Canada

Sandra W. Russ, Ph.D.
Associate Professor of Psychology and Assistant Provost, Department of Psychology, Case Western Reserve University, Cleveland, Ohio

Barbara R. Slater, Ph.D.
Professor of Psychology, Towson State University, Baltimore, Maryland

Kim Smith, Ph.D.
Associate Director, The Menninger Clinic of Albuquerque, Albuquerque, New Mexico

Alan Sugarman, Ph.D.
Clinical Associate in Adult and Child Psychoanalysis, San Diego Psychoanalytic Institute, San Diego, California
Associate Clinical Professor of Psychiatry, University of California, San Diego, San Diego, California

Steven B. Tuber, Ph.D.
Assistant Professor, City University of New York, Doctoral Program in Clinical Psychology
Adjunct Supervising Psychologist, Roosevelt Hospital, New York City

Arnold Wilson, Ph.D.
Assistant Professor, New School for Social Research, Graduate Faculty, Division of Clinical Psychology, New York City

Introduction

In recent years there has been a growing interest in expanding the psychoanalytic base for the study of people by means of projective techniques. From the relatively narrow but solid foundation established by Rapaport and articulated further by Schafer, Holt, and Mayman, recent advances in the psychoanalytic understanding of primitive mental states (including borderline, narcissistic, and psychotic disturbances) have dramatically expanded this base by providing new formulations for significant and exciting theoretical, clinical, and research efforts. Examples include the investigation and systematic assessment of core psychoanalytic concepts such as object representation, defense, thought process, and transitional objects utilizing the Rorschach and TAT as well as the development of new and creative measures including early memories (Mayman, 1968), open-ended descriptions of self and significant others (Blatt, Wein, Chevron, and Quinlan, 1979), and semistructured object relations profiles (Burke, Summers, Selinger, and Polonus, in press). Collectively, these endeavors have sought to operationalize newer, more phenomenological concepts in psychoanalytic theory and have provided methodologies and instruments for systematically assessing and evaluating the validity and clinical utility of constructs generated by this expanded body of knowledge.

The development of psychoanalytic thought over the past century can be viewed in a broad theoretical context as part of a major scientific revolution that began in the middle of the nineteenth century. As Blatt and Lerner (1983b) observe, developments in mathematics involving the realization that the conception of the universe based on Euclidean geometry and rectilinear Cartesian coordinates is only one among a number of ways of conceiving the universe. With the development of non-Euclidean geometry and new concepts of curvilinearity, it became possible to understand the universe in a number of equally valid ways. Similar advances took place in physics, Einstein's theory of relativity replacing Newtonian physics. These advances contributed to the growing realization that the experience and conception of reality is influenced by the relative position and assumptions of the observer. In philosophy there was an increasing awareness that nature was not simply observed, but rather was constructed according to a particular vantage point.

These developments had major epistemological implications in that the conceptualization of multiple and relative perspectives carried with it the implication that manifest phenomena could no longer be accepted at face value, as the only valid way of comprehending reality. There was an important recognition that to understand phenomena one has to identify the structure and organizing principles underlying surface appearances. The emphasis on internal structure became, according to Michel Foucault, a major cultural episteme of the twentieth century. The concept of internal, underlying structure and with it the search for an identification of the inherent principles of organization which define the relationships among elements and their potential transformations in hierarchical organized systems has had a significant influence on the physical and biological sciences as well as in the humanities.

> Despite this emphasis on internal structure in numerous fields throughout the twentieth century, a large segment of American psychology and psychiatry still maintains an exclusive interest in manifest behavior and overt symptomatology. There have been notable exceptions . . . and these exceptions have made major contributions to the understanding of some of the structural principles inherent in human behavior. These notable exceptions include the Gestalt analyses of perception, contemporary approaches to cognitive processes including the work of Piaget and Werner, and psychoanalytic theory [Blatt, 1978, pp. 87–88].

Blatt and Lerner (1983b) note further that efforts in the human sciences to investigate principles of structural organization underlying manifest behavior must consider two dimensions fundamental to the human condition: (1) the person's capacity for complex symbolic activity; and

(2) the complex interpersonal matrix within which we evolve and exist. These factors are unique to the human condition and must be accounted for in understanding the underlying structural principles and factors that integrate the multiple perspectives from which manifest behavior may be observed.

Psychoanalytic theory as well as psychodiagnostic test theory are not static bodies of knowledge but rather are in a state of constant evolution. Historically, psychoanalytic theory has evolved from an early concentration on the identification of the instincts and their development, through a focus on the characteristics, synthesis, and functions of the ego, to the current interest in the early mother-child dyad and its decisive impact on ego development and object relations. The comparatively recent integration of a systematic psychology of the self, a broadened psychodynamic developmental theory, and a modern object relations theory into the mainstream of classical psychoanalytic thought is now providing a conceptual basis for a more comprehensive and phenomenological clinical and test theory. This evolution is in concert with a theoretical movement away from an "experience-distant" metapsychology couched in a mechanistic natural science framework of impersonal structure, forces, and energies to a more "experience-near" clinical theory concerned primarily with the representational world and subjective meanings as core elements (Atwood and Stolorow, 1984). Changes in diagnostic psychological testing have in no small way paralleled these changes in personality theory. From a virtually exclusive adherence to the structural and energy models of psychoanalysis, psychodiagnostic test theory and usage currently reflect a strong interest in more experiential aspects of the person.

Recently, many of what were once regarded as quintessential tenets of psychoanalytic theory have been drastically reformulated. While instinct theory and, later, ego psychology were once the conceptual centerpieces of psychoanalytic theory, psychoanalysis has increasingly become a developmental psychology of self and object relations. The shift from classical psychoanalytic drive psychology to the emergence of developmental theory, self psychology, and object relations theory is part and parcel of the "widening scope of psychoanalysis" (Stone, 1954)—the theoretical, clinical, and research interest in more disturbed patients extending beyond an exclusive focus on the intricacies of neurotic conditions so lucidly articulated by Freud. This shift stems in part from the observation that the complaints of patients seeking help today differ from those described in the literature twenty-five or fifty years ago. In the classical neurosis an integrated personality was suddenly disrupted by alien actions, impulses, affects, and thoughts, often of a sexual and aggressive nature. Today it is less a question of dealing with a conflicted, infringed-upon, structuralized, and cohesive personality, but rather of confronting a personality that is itself split, malformed, and arrested, one in which there is a blurring of personality and symptom.

The current volume is an extension of our earlier compendium, *Borderline Phenomena and the Rorschach Test* (Kwawer, Lerner, Lerner, and Sugarman, 1980). As did the earlier work, this volume brings together original articles by leading psychoanalytically oriented psychologists. Writing specifically for this book, they detail their most recent work regarding clinical, theoretical, and research applications of the Rorschach to an understanding of primitive, archaic, or preoedipal phenomena and psychopathology. The present collection, again like the previous book, grew out of a number of annual meetings of the Society of Personality Assessment, which has provided a lively forum for the exchange of ideas. This compendium reaches beyond "borderline phenomena" to include what many clinicians and researchers refer to as "primitive mental states"—that is, borderline, narcissistic, and psychotic disturbances. Included under the rubric are patients exhibiting major affective disorders as well as the specific syndromes of eating disorders and alcoholism. "Primitive mental states" also includes such diverse and vexing clinical phenomena as masochism, suicide, incest, and perversion. These conditions seem to share archaic personality elements that become manifest in profound regressions, particularly within the transference. They exhibit a variety of etiologies, spanning biological and experiential dimensions, which in one way or another have led to frustrating rather than satisfying early object relations. Almost by definition, treatment of these patients is characterized by such adverse clinical occurrences as premature terminations, turbulent transference/countertransference struggles, chaotic acting out, negative therapeutic reactions, and treatment stalemates.

Techniques currently used by diagnostic clinicians and researchers to assess "primitive mental states" include checklists and questionnaires, patient interviews, and psychological testing. Kernberg-Bardenstein (1985) has outlined the strengths and limitations of each approach. A major limitation of questionnaires and inventories is the loss of individual details of the patient's behavior, as the patient is pigeonholed into predetermined descriptive categories. As Kernberg-

Bardenstein notes, "The richness of an idiographic report may be sacrificed for a more research-convenient nomothetic instrument" (p. 12). A second limitation is the absence of cross-verification of the subject's self-report. Third, these measures tap only conscious phenomena and manifest features.

Interviews have been developed using a variety of theoretical orientations and different degrees of structure and focus. Nevertheless, they all share several features in common. Questions are targeted to the patient's conscious rather than unconscious process. As Kernberg-Bardenstein notes, "These interviews are not geared to those 'forgotten' aspects of experience which remain unintegrated, such as partly formed thoughts or feelings, which are uninfluenced by everyday logic or reality" (p. 13). Depending on the patient's self-report, problems arise if the individual remains aloof, unresponsive, or grossly distorts or denies significant material. Again, one may question the validity of data obtained without external criteria or built-in mechanisms to check the accuracy of the patient's report.

Psychological testing offers a more consistent form of administration than interviews, richer and more meaningful content than checklists and questionnaires, and a means of coding and evaluating data consistently. Psychological testing also limits the stimuli to which the patient is asked to respond, permitting the development of norms with which to compare the results of test analyses. Further, psychological testing in general, and the Rorschach in particular, provides a less familiar, less structured setting than do interviews; consequently, the test situation itself facilitates the expression of underlying personality structures and dynamics.

Rapaport (1954) has outlined three basic theoretical assumptions of psychodiagnostic testing: (1) every segment of behavior bears the imprint of the organization of the personality and permits, "if felicitously chosen," the reconstruction of the specific organizing principles of that personality; (2) pathology is an exacerbation or decompensation of trends existing in the premorbid personality, and "hence fundamentally diagnosis is always personality diagnosis"; and (3) diagnostic psychological testing can show how, by what processes, the organizing principles of the personality and their pathological alterations are carried over into test performance.

In recent years two somewhat divergent approaches to the Rorschach may be discerned. On the one hand, an atheoretical and highly empirical "sign" approach focuses on a myriad of traditional

Rorschach scores and ratios. This approach approximates an application of psychometric principles and values to projective data. On the other hand, Weiner (1977), Blatt and Lerner (1983b), and Blatt and Berman (1984) have advocated a "conceptual" approach geared toward integrating the plethora of isolated Rorschach scores into a smaller number of discrete and theoretically relevant variables. As Blatt and Berman (1984) note,

> It is important to stress that often these [conceptual] approaches to the Rorschach are not based on a theory of the test procedure alone but rather, they utilize implicit or explicit personality theories as broad conceptual models for integrating traditional Rorschach scores into more molar variables which express important personality dimensions. Some of these new approaches to the Rorschach have demonstrated that these more molar variables can be scored with acceptable levels of reliability and they are related to important personality dimensions [p. 227].

Examples of these newer, more conceptually based approaches to the Rorschach include the contributions of Mayman and his colleagues at the University of Michigan and Blatt and his colleagues at Yale on the object representation construct (Blatt and Lerner, 1983a), as well as the work of Lerner and Lerner (1982) on defenses. Several studies presented in this volume demonstrate how Rorschach scales representing composite variables in addition to traditional Rorschach scores can offer a superordinate organization of projective test data that is rooted in a conceptual model. This higher order organization provides a framework for integrating multiple dimensions of Rorschach responses in a way that is clinically relevant, reliable, and the focus of extensive validation and research. The selections offered in this volume demonstrate the wide range of diagnostic, developmental, clinical, and research distinctions and formulations that can be made on the basis of variables derived from contemporary psychoanalytic theory.

The volume is organized in the following way. The first part (Theoretical Contributions) contains articles applying two distinct theoretical systems to Rorschach data. In Chapter 1 Fried and his colleagues consider a discrete phenomenon, described by Isakower, that consists of unusual bodily sensations, bewildering perceptions, fears of losing control over bodily contents, a subjective sense of floating or flying, overwhelming feelings of anxiety, and cognitive disorientation. Isakower related these experiences to early disturbances in the mother-child relationship. Convinced that the Isakower phenomenon is related also to early narcissistic injuries, the authors outline ways in which the Rorschach can be used to identify the phenomenon and then delineate the variety of ways individuals have attempted to escape it.

Arnow and Cooper (Chapter 2) broaden the conceptual basis of the Rorschach by systematically applying to Rorschach material insights derived from self psychology. Using concepts and formulations developed by Kohut and his colleagues, they draw attention to aspects of the patient-examiner relationship which previously had been neglected (i.e., the effects of empathic failures), identify Rorschach indices predictive of atypical transference paradigms (mirroring transference, idealizing transference) and discuss Rorschach manifestations of specific forms of self-pathology (understimulated self, overstimulated self).

As Paul Lerner (Chapter 3) points out, "The increasing penetration of object relations theory and self psychology into classical psychoanalysis has opened a veritable gold mine of immensely rich clinical concepts whose translation into empirical, test-related terms is a challenge to the psychological examiner." Articles in the second part, Clinical Concepts, represent varied attempts to operationalize more specific concepts and formulations emerging from the newer models within psychoanalysis.

Based on the observation that the depressive affect experienced by certain narcissistic patients is distinctive and that such patients employ common defenses to ward off the affect, Lerner in Chapter 3 outlines Rorschach indices reflective of depletion depression, defensive grandiosity, the false self, and projective identification.

Levine (Chapter 4) also discusses Rorschach manifestations of projective identification. Based on more recent contributions to object relations theory and Racker's comprehensive discussion of transference and countertransference, she reexamines the patient-examiner relationship as a rich source of countertransference data and then demonstrates how such data can be used to infer more primitive defenses and primitive modes of object relating.

A concept which has gained increased currency in the psychoanalytic literature is internalization. The concept has been viewed from four perspectives: as a process implicated in structure building and therefore growth and development; as a process that when gone awry results in specific forms of psychopathology; as a core element in psychoanalytic treatment; and as a defense. Conceiving of internalization as a defense, especially in depressed patients, Lovett (Chapter 5) has developed scales for assessing submechanisms of internalization and has applied them to the Rorschach protocols of a group of acutely depressed patients, a group of remitted depressed patients, and a normal control group.

With the broadening of the scope of psychoanalytic theory has come a reappraisal of the concept of suicide. Based on the renewed interest in the relation between cognitive processes and psychopathology, especially depression, Fibel (Chapter 6) outlines and presents clinical material related to the cognitive aspect of suicidality and its manifestation on the Rorschach. Using the concept "ego vulnerabilities" (i.e., certain patterns of ego functions and self-other representations which predispose an individual toward dealing with frustration or disappointment with suicidal behavior), Smith and Eyman (Chapter 7) identify six variables (presence of conflicted passive oral yearnings, sober but ambivalent attitude about death, high self-expectations, tendency to overcontrol aggression, nature of patient-examiner relationship, coping in isolation) which distinguished mild from serious suicide attempters. Scales were developed to assess each of these variables and applied to the Rorschach and TAT protocols of twenty-six serious suicide attempters and twenty-six mild suicide attempters.

Although sexual abuse has of late been receiving greater social and psychiatric attention, to date there has been no systematic research using the Rorschach to assess sexually abused families. Meyers (Chapter 8) examines the effects of sexual molestation by critically reviewing the Rorschach protocols of ten adult women who as children or adolescents were incest victims. Each record was studied to assess ego state, level of defense, modulation of anxiety and other affects, quality of object relations, and body image. A relatively neglected concept in the contemporary Rorschach literature is body representation. Because body representation is a core aspect of self-representation, it is crucial in facilitating the integration and regulation of disparate aspects of the personality that contribute to the eventual attainment of ego identity. Sugarman and Jaffe (Chapter 9) present the Rorschach protocols of two patients who differ markedly with respect to their body representations and then use the Rorschach data as a basis for clarifying the relationship between body representation and self-representation.

With advancements in psychoanalytic theory have come new models of personality formation and psychopathology. Whereas earlier models were derived from theories of drive and impulse/defense interplay, these newer models issue from theories of structure and structure formation in psychic development. These views start from the notion that development involves the growth and differentiation of psychological functions that crystallize into more stable psychic structures. Psychic conflict can occur among these various structures and can lead to psychopathology, as the earlier views maintained, but in addition the structures themselves can be pathological, as a result of incomplete or arrested development. This view of psychopathology as representing an impairment in psychic structure formation has given rise to diagnostic efforts aimed at evaluating the quality of the structures themselves (self system, internalized object relations, etc.), the degree to which they have been internalized and hence become stable and autonomous, and their genetic roots. Chapters in the third part, Clinical Syndromes, reflect this changing emphasis in views of psychopathology.

Despite descriptive and definitional disagreements, great interest is being shown in the narcissistic patient. Howard Lerner (Chapter 10) traces the history of the concept of narcissism, describes the narcissistic patient, and using a conceptual model developed by Kernberg details Rorschach indices reflective of narcissistic pathology. That is, he presents Rorschach indicators of specific and nonspecific manifestations of ego weaknesses, affect organization including anxiety and depression, difficulties with aggression, pathological internalized object relations, and primitive defenses.

Farris (Chapter 11) addresses the relationship between narcissistic personality disorders and borderline personality disorders. Using several scoring scales applied to Rorschach data, he examines differences in the nature and level of severity of disturbance between these disorders.

As Bram (Chapter 12) points out, "Given the rich and extensive literature on diagnosis, personality, and dynamics of patients with eating disorders, it is remarkable that so little attention has been paid to the contribution of psychological testing." Both Bram and Piran (Chapter 13) attempt to rectify this state of affairs. Based on a careful review of test reports, Rorschach protocols, and notes made during the testing process, Bram reports on a sample of eating-disordered patients in terms of sociobehavioral context, setting, physical appearance of the patient, the patient's mood, affect, and attitude, and the nature of the patient-tester interaction. Piran studied borderline phenomena in two subtypes of eating-disordered patients. The Rorschach protocols of 31 anorexics and 34 bulimics were compared on scales reflecting reality testing, integrity of thought processes, primitive defenses, level of object representation, primitive modes of interpersonal relationship, quality of aggression, and test references to fatness.

Comparatively little has been reported in the Rorschach literature regarding perverseness in general and transsexualism in particular. With renewed interest in narcissism and the development of gender identity, however, both syndromes are being accorded greater study. Based on the assumption that the perverse character organization is a stable organization and lies within the borderline range of character pathology, Merceron, Husain, and Rossel (Chapter 14) report on their attempts to identify Rorschach manifestations of perverse character organization. In addition to traditional content and formal elements, they creatively demonstrate the usefulness of a systematic appraisal of the patient's verbatim verbalizations.

Karmel (Chapter 15) discusses his work with a population of male transsexuals. Theoretically rooted in a theory of symbolization begun by Klein and extended by Segal, he reviews the Rorschach protocols of a group of male transsexuals in terms of a genital symbolization defect hypothesis.

Milden, Ludolph, and Lerner (Chapter 16) address some of the challenges facing psychoanalytic psychologists working with seriously disturbed patients in settings in which assessment is increasingly defined according to biological psychiatric parameters. It is their position that psychoanalytically oriented psychological assessment, in particular the Rorschach, can have a significant role in these settings. The approach described in this chapter involves using the Rorschach to explore the impact of recurrent affective episodes on self-representation. The authors describe the unique response of affective patients to the testing situation and a number of themes characteristic of their test protocols, suggesting that these features may be not only primary to the endogenous affective illness but also secondary, both to the illness and to psychobiological treatment.

Several lines of investigation have resulted in a growing consensus that there are two distinct forms of depression: a developmentally later, guilt-ridden form characterized by the sense that something bad has occurred, and an earlier, empty form characterized by feelings of depletion and helplessness, intense object seeking, and difficulties in self-regulation. Wilson (Chapter 17) demonstrates that each form is manifested differently on the Rorschach and that to assess depressive affect the tester must be aware of this.

Ludolph, Milden, and Lerner (Chapter 18) report data from an extensive study in which the Rorschach was employed to investigate the premorbid and interepisode personality of patients suffering from unipolar and bipolar depressive illness. Rorschach protocols of two patients obtained during the acute depressive period, at time of discharge, and several months after discharge are presented.

Based on the proposition that alcoholism may profitably be viewed as an example of the generational transmission of psychopathology, especially psychopathology of a pregenital nature, Gallagher and Slater (Chapter 19) present Rorschach protocols of mother-son-wife triads to illustrate and detail the transactional aspect of alcoholism.

Basic to the diagnosis and understanding of schizophrenia has been a consideration of the issue of thought disorder. Traditionally, the Rorschach has been viewed as an especially sensitive and useful means for assessing this variable. Cerney (Chapter 20) presents and discusses changes in thought disorder as reflected on the Rorschach among four schizophrenic patients involved in different types of treatment.

As Leichtman (Chapter 21) cogently notes, "Insofar as the psychological concept of 'primitivity' is associated with early periods of normal development or severe forms of psychopathology, studies of young or profoundly disturbed children should provide bases for significant contributions to an understanding of the relationship between the Rorschach test and primitive mental states." In keeping with this observation, chapters in the book's final section, Primitive Mental States in Children and Adolescents, deal with severe disturbances in children and adolescents or describe normal development processes which have implications for understanding such disturbances.

Leichtman raises the penetrating question of how children become capable of taking the Rorschach test and then suggests an answer by outlining a developmental model involving stages in the mastery of the test. His description of the various stages—perseverative approach, partial perseveration, confabulatory Rorschach, the Rorschach as a test—has important implications for developmentally ordering various modes of thinking as manifest in adult forms of severe psychopathology.

Russ (Chapter 22) studies a normal developmental process which has important implications for diagnosing and understanding primitive mental conditions. She reviews theoretical perspectives and definitions of primary process thinking in normal development, discusses the role of children's play as a vehicle for expressing primary process thinking, and delineates the role of such thinking in children with borderline and narcissistic features.

The relation between the precocious presence of M and severe character disturbances in latency age children is discussed by Campo (Chapter 23). From an intensive study of individual Rorschach records as well as a more extensive research project, she reports on a group of children whose high M production reflects cognitive and attitudinal rigidity, pseudomaturity, emotional isolation, and an excessive need for affective and behavioral control.

Replete throughout the gender identity literature is controversy as to whether disturbances in gender identity are isolated phenomena occurring within a relatively intact personality structure or whether such disturbances are part of a more general and pervasive psychopathology. Speaking to this controversy, Coates and Tuber (Chapter 24) review their study which examined the level and quality of self- and object representations in a group of extremely feminine boys.

Convinced that sense of self and self-experience are central to an understanding of individual development during adolescence, Rubenstein (Chapter 25) discusses Rorschach manifestations of self-organization in adolescents. In addition to exploring and identifying Rorschach indicators of self-experience, the author also describes a creative method of test administration designed to actively involve the adolescent in the consultation process.

Finally, the editors would like to extend their warm thanks and deep appreciation to Paulette Lockwood and the rest of the staff of the University of Michigan Department of Psychiatry Word Processing Center. Without this group's dedication, patience, and exceptionally high level of professional competence, this volume would not have been possible.

REFERENCES

Atwood, G., & Stolorow, R. (1984), *Structure of Subjectivity: Explorations in Psychoanalytic Phenomenology*. Hillsdale, NJ: Analytic Press.

Blatt, S. (1978), Paradoxical representations and their implications for the treatment of psychosis and borderline states. Paper presented to the institute for Psychoanalytic Research and Training, New York City, May 18.

_____ Berman, W. (1984), A methodology for the use of the Rorschach in clinical research. *J. Personal. Assess.*, 48:226–239.

_____ Lerner, H. (1983a), Investigations in the psychoanalytic theory of object relations and object representations. In: *Empirical Studies of Psychoanalytic Theories: Vol. 1*, ed. J. Masling. Hillsdale, NJ: Analytic Press, pp. 189–249.

_____ _____ (1983b), Psychodynamic perspectives on personality theory. In:

The Clinical Psychology Handbook, ed. M. Hersen, A. Kazdin, & A. Bellack. New York: Pergamon Press, pp. 87–106.

———— Wein, S., Chevron, E., & Quinlan, D. (1979), Parental representations and depression in normal young adults. *J. Abnorm. Psychol.*, 78:388–397.

Burke, W., Summers, F., Selinger, D., & Polonus, T. (in press), The comprehensive object relations profile: A validity and reliability study. *J. Personal. Assess.*

Kernberg-Bardenstein, K. (1985), *A Rorschach Analysis of the Anorexic Personality*. Unpublished doctoral dissertation. University of Michigan, Ann Arbor, Mich.

Kwawer, J., Lerner, H., Lerner, P., & Sugarman, A., Eds. (1980), *Borderline Phenomena and the Rorschach Test*. New York: International Universities Press.

Lerner, H., & Lerner, P. (1982), A comparative analysis of defensive structure in neurotic, borderline, and schizophrenic patients. *Psychoanal. & Contemp. Thought*, 5:77–115.

Mayman, M. (1968), Early memories and character structure. *J. Proj. Tech. & Personal. Assess.*, 32:303–316.

Rapaport, D. (1954), The theoretical implications of diagnostic testing procedures. In: *Psychoanalytic Psychiatry and Psychology: Clinical and Theoretical Papers*, ed. R. Knight & C. Friedman. New York: International Universities Press, pp. 575–608.

Stone, L. (1954), The widening scope of implications for psychoanalysis. *J. Amer. Psychoanal. Assn.*, 2:567–594.

Weiner, I. (1977), Approaches to Rorschach validation. In: *Rorschach Psychology*, ed. M. Rickers-Ovsiankina. Huntington, NY: Krieger.

Part I
Theoretical Contributions

Chapter 1

The Paradox of Pregenitality:
Longing for Contact, Fear of Intimacy

Risto Fried
Eero Rantasila
Matti Reinikainen
Elina Malkavaara-Kallinen
Marja-Helena Huttunen

THE UNOPENED LETTER

A thirty-year-old man carried about with him an unopened letter from his girlfriend. Had she written him that she loved him and wanted to continue their relationship, or that she wanted to break it off? Whenever he came to see his therapist he brought the letter with him. He discussed his hopes, his fears. And left the session with the envelope still sealed.

He lived with his mother and father, and could not imagine another arrangement, though he dreamed of going to sea. He had left school because of anxious tension and was on leave from his job for the same reason. Attractive in appearance and fluent in his speech, he told his therapist he would commit suicide if he had the guts. Actually, he conceded, the situation at home was no longer as difficult as it had been when he was a boy. Once he and his mother had to take refuge in the toilet while his father tried to break down the door with an axe.

The young man's Rorschach responses revealed the extent of his preoccupation with being a victim of violence. Card II was seen as the bloody remains of some small animal, a mole perhaps, that had been

FIGURE 1: The case of the unopened letter: Wartegg test drawings.

run over by a car. There were people fighting and "something violent about" Card III. Card VI was the skin of an animal that had been killed, and reminded him of death. On Card IX he saw the remains of an accident victim, his innards spilled onto the pavement. He was unable to evolve a response to Card IV, the "Father" card: "What could one say about that? Nothing, really."

Card VII, so light and graceful compared to its predecessors, seemed at first to offer relief from anxiety. "That seems like a place of security," he pondered, pointing to the central white space, "and this"—indicating the top of the card, the narrow entrance to the safe harbor—"attracts, entices, but one could get caught here. It could be a trap. Getting in is easy, but then it could close on one." On the Post-Rorschach (Fried, 1973, 1980) he chose this card twice as "most frightening," but also as best picturing his own self. "It could represent a shipwreck," said this man who lived at home and dreamed of going to sea.

The whole Rorschach, he said, had a nightmare quality for him. On the Wartegg Drawing Test, he even drew a picture of his recurrent nightmare (Figure 1: square 2, drawn last): a wavy spiral line with a black cross at its center, concerning which he said that "everything begins to whirl toward the center, where death is."

When this case was presented by the patient's therapist before a group of psychologists, we asked those present to react to the patient's dream as if it were their own (Ullman, 1984) and then to tell the group of the feelings it aroused. One psychologist told of being sucked into the vortex of a whirlpool, another of becoming dizzy and faintly nauseous. Several told of the intense anxiety they had begun to feel. Another said that although he too felt anxious, it seemed as if part of himself split off from the one who was frightened and stood by, a dispassionate bystander who tried to observe the experiences of his other half. Yet another told of the circular movement coming closer and closer until it seemed like a huge sphere that would obliterate her. Another experienced movement in the opposite direction, away from herself, with the sphere becoming a tiny point that vanished in the distance. In either case, the growth or diminution seemed to be not only that of an object, but of one's own body. The end stage of the process was an agonizing sensation that one would cease to exist. Still another sensation, simultaneously tactile and visual, was of an excruciating simultaneity of irreconcilable opposites, as of something excessively thin, sharp, and pointed, yet thick, dull, and turgid.

With other dreams, the group had been surprised at finding how similar their feelings were. An emotion barely hinted at in the dream's content would be sensed by most or all of those present and, despite individual variations, was recognized by all as essentially the same feeling. These experiences made members of the group feel increasingly confident of the validity of their empathic intuitions. Now, however, it seemed as if the dreamer's nightmare had stimulated bewilderingly divergent experiences.

There was evidence from the tests, however, that the group members' experiences, if summated, resonated with those of the patient. Some of his other Wartegg drawings, while not explicitly connected by him with the nightmare spiral, seemed to illustrate some of the group's associations to his dream. His first drawing, an elaboration of the arc depicted in the last of the eight squares, was a large sun setting into the sea. The first square on the test, which has a tiny black point at its center, had been left unelaborated by him. Instead of drawing any additions to the point, he had contented himself with interpreting it as "the globe of the earth in the All of the world." In sum, his Wartegg test began with a depiction of Earth, so huge from our own perspective but tiny almost to the point of nonexistence in relation to the cosmos, and ended with a depiction of the sun, so many times the size of the earth, but about to disappear from view. The theme of the huge sphere that becomes small as a pinpoint, or completely invisible, was hence twice repeated on the Wartegg before the patient drew his concluding picture of the nightmare vortex with death at its center. A related symbol had been central to his apperception of the Rorschach blots. Here Card VII, which he had seen first as a haven of safety, had then been identified as a shipwreck, as himself, and yet also as the end of his own existence. The setting sun of the Wartegg becomes, on the Rorschach, his own ship, his own self, that disappears into the ocean depths. The response takes on added significance if one considers VII as the "Mother" card and the ocean as a maternal symbol. Whether one tries to individuate by shipping out from home or to find security by remaining in a symbiotic relationship, the result is annihilation.

THE ISAKOWER PHENOMENON AS A PARADIGM OF PREGENITALITY

A coherent theory accounting for the bewildering multiplicity of experiences evoked in our group of psychologists by the picture of the spiral nightmare was first proposed by Otto Isakower (1938). The phenomenon named in his honor includes even more components than the ones already enumerated: auditory sensations including humming, murmuring, or insistent throbbing rhythm; temperature disturbances including a feeling of body heat or perception of a fire; tactile sensations of something crumpled, sandy, or dry within the mouth, on the skin, or exterior to oneself; equilibrium disturbances, including sensations of flying or floating; fear of loss of control over body contents; the sensation of a large mass in or just outside the mouth or hand; and uncanny sensations like déjà vu or return to the womb. These experiences are likely to be connected with disturbances of the sense of self: simultaneity of sensations inside and outside oneself; confusion concerning one's body boundaries; splitting of the self; and impending cessation of the self. These experiences are typically difficult to verbalize, associated with early childhood and particularly fever during illness, and most likely to occur during transition between sleep and waking.

Beyond noting the underlying connectedness of these experiences, Isakower advanced bold interpretive hypotheses. He postulated that the phenomenon was based on regressive alterations in the structure of the ego, with decathexis of the real external world, disintegration of capacity for differentiated critical thinking and reality testing, and hypercathexis of the body ego. In this state, physical sensations are intensified, but the boundary between self and environment is blurred, so that it is difficult to distinguish inner from outer, or to localize the source of sensations. From this structural hypothesis, Isakower made the leap to an etiological hypothesis: the phenomenon represents an attempt to return to the situation of the infant falling asleep at the mother's breast. "The large object which approaches probably represents the breast, with its promise of food. When satisfied, the infant loses interest in the breast, which appears smaller and smaller and finally vanishes away" (Isakower, 1938, p. 341). Then, to explain why his phenomenon is indicative of disturbance and does not normally accompany the process of falling asleep, Isakower postulated that it occurs at moments of conflict between progressive and regressive tendencies. A child masturbating prior to falling asleep may find that incestuous fantasies are countered by prohibitions from the superego. Regression to the situation at the breast, which is "innocent and not subject to any prohibition" (p. 344) resolves the conflict and prevents anxiety from arising, since both the superego prohibition and the wish for fantasied sensual gratification are satisfied. But while the regressive part of the ego indulges in renunciation of reality testing so that it may "conjure up lost objects and

submerged worlds" (p. 345), the reality ego engages in intensive observation of the process so as to maintain control and prevent too deep a regression.

The magnitude of Isakower's contribution, which despite its brevity and the paucity of his other publications make him one of the outstanding figures in psychoanalysis (Fisher, 1976), can be appreciated only if one considers how many others tried, and failed, to make sense of the phenomena he so lucidly conceptualized. Thinkers of the prescientific period had for centuries tried to explain or achieve control over the terrifying vortex through myth, meditation, art, and dance (Dechend and Santillana, 1969; Purce, 1974). In the early period of scientific psychology, Müller (Purkyne, 1827a; Isakower, 1974) tried systematically to analyze the full compass of subjective and objective visual phenomena but came so close—coincidentally with his venture into marriage—to being overwhelmed by psychosis that he abandoned the attempt and shifted over to biology. Purkyne (1821, 1823, 1827b, 1846),[1] who as a child dreamed of being at the vortex of a sea of flame (1820), became a pioneer in areas extending from sensory physiology to preventive health care (Fried, 1983; John, 1959). Though he drove himself to the limits of physical injury and experimented with drugs in his self-observations, he maintained his mental balance. He did not, however, venture far into investigation of the psychological significance of the experiences he explored. The celebrated Purkyne Phenomenon, dealing with changes in the perceived relative brightness of colors as illumination is diminished, attests the sensitivity of his powers as an observer, but is strictly neuropsychological, unrelated to personality factors. Guthrie (1899), who gave Ellis (1911) and Federn (1914) the idea of "Icarian" dreams (Fried, 1984b), cites more examples of the Isakower phenomenon in his brief paper on nightmares than have more recent writers in entire books on the subject. He did not hesitate to describe his own nightmares alongside those of patients, but lacked the psychoanalytic theoretical framework that might have enabled him to develop his ideas further. Mourly Vold (1912, pp. 869–871) described a hypnagogic experience in which the dreamer felt himself to be a sphere that collided explosively with another sphere and coalesced with it. Interpretation was in terms of fever, eczema, overexertion, and

---

[1]My thanks to Professor T. Radil of the Institute of Physiology of the Czechoslovak Academy of Sciences for letting me have these papers in the beautiful Prague edition of the Collected Works.

increased flow of blood to the brain, without any attempt at psychological explanation. Rorschach (1912a, 1927) described the fantasy of being within a transparent sphere (Volkan, 1979; Fried, 1980), but while appreciating its regressive connotations gave it an essentially genital rather than pregenital interpretation. Christoffel (1923), in one of the first published comments on the Rorschach method, gave striking examples of Isakower nightmares. One of his patients was plagued during periods of insomnia by the recurrent vision of a bright disc with a black point at its center. Disc and point increased in size, but at differential rates, until the point swallowed the disc and both vanished. If the anxiety state occurs during sleep rather than in the twilight state between sleep and waking, Christoffel observed, the elementary geometric forms may become elaborated into more complex ones as in the experience of another patient, who saw brilliant desert sands and a caravan of camels that came straight at him, increasing in size until they became monstrous, blotted out the bright background, and seemed about to crush the dreamer. This dream is strikingly similar to one analyzed by Lewin (1953), who, well acquainted with the Isakower phenomenon, interpreted the dreamer's vision of a "slightly rolling, sandy desert" as an image of the breast onto which was projected the "thirst implicit in the dry, sandy, desert wastes" and the "sandy, granular, tactile quality" of the interior of the frustrated baby's mouth (pp. 186–187). Christoffel's patient, by adding camels to his desert, added yet another dimension of breast symbolism. What could make a better breast symbol than a camel's hump, full of nourishment for long journeys through arid wastes? The implication is that if one were a camel one could take the mother's breast with one as a "transitional object" that gradually diminished in size as its stores were exhausted, but which one never had to give up. In Christoffel's patient's dream, of course, this stratagem does not work: the dreamer loses his desert thirst only to be overwhelmed and suffocated by a breast that has come entirely too close. One would have thought that, having equated this dream with that of the other patient, in which fear related not to being crushed but to being swallowed, and in which the imagery was that of a circle with a point at its center, Christoffel certainly would have had the insight that both dreams involved breast symbolism and conflict related to early oral trauma. Yet this insight escaped him. In explaining the dreams, he limited himself to a discussion of dark-light and chromatic sensations, with conclusions erroneous because of his lack of knowledge about color symbolism in different cultures. Leonard (1927), whose experience of a particularly terrifying hallucinatory form of the Isakower phenomenon became the starting point of agoraphobia that made him a virtual social isolate, devoted the remainder of his life to an attempt at cure through self-analysis. He traced his vision to early childhood incidents, particularly that of having been terrified by an oncoming locomotive, but failed to connect his screen memories to earlier oral trauma. In sum, Isakower's predecessors lacked the prerequisite theoretical knowledge, or the courage and inner stability to use such knowledge in exploring their own earliest anxieties, that enabled Isakower to arrive at his unique insight.

Following Isakower's lead, many other analysts wrote on his phenomenon, some providing important modifications, extensions, or confirmation (Lewin, 1946, 1948, 1953; Spitz, 1955, 1965; Almansi, 1960; Fink, 1967). A pointedly critical reinterpretation was proposed by M. M. Stern (1961). Where Isakower postulated the infant's blissful experience at the mother's breast as the phenomenon's source, Stern postulated an intensely traumatic nursing experience. Where Isakower interpreted the approaching or receding spheres as direct reminiscences of the breast, Stern postulated that early oral trauma can result in agitation, stupor, or shocklike states associated with vestibular disturbance that results in fargoing disruption of the body image and of sensory perception (Schilder, 1935, 1939). The imposition of a "good Gestalt," such as a sphere, on this cognitive chaos may to some extent reduce anxiety and reestablish ego control, but its connection with the mother's face or breast is a subsequent elaboration. Where Isakower saw regression to the oral stage, in the face of the threat of prohibited genital intimacy, as restoring a sense of security, Stern saw advance to genitality as threatening because reminiscent of the prior trauma suffered in oral relationships. Isakower, in short, saw his phenomenon as regressive, unrealistic, and occurring at times of stress, but essentially as a positive experience that provides the illusion of long lost bliss having been restored. His model, essentially, is Freud's hedonistic model of the dream as wish-fulfillment (1900). Stern, by contrast, saw the Isakower phenomenon as a reparative repetition of infantile night terror attacks, his model being Freud's post-hedonistic theory of the repetition compulsion as a coping mechanism in the face of unbearable anxiety (1920). Stern describes two avenues to mastery: experimentation, as in purposeful induction of the phenomenon and attempts to investigate it, and negation or denial, either of the phenomenon itself or of the dysphoric affect connected with it. Stern agrees that some observers report the phenomenon to be associated with neutral or even highly pleasant emotions. But where Isakower would see these as derived directly from memories of oral gratification, Stern would see them as based on denial of oral deprivation.

On the whole, Stern's formulation seems better to accord with clinical observations than does Isakower's. His point that the agreeable components of the nursing situation, like a warm flow of milk into the mouth, are absent from the Isakower phenomenon, is well taken. The culmination of the phenomenon, moreover, is the imminent threat to existence itself. Dread is the emotion most appropriate to this threat, and any other feeling is likely to be defensive. It should be emphasized, furthermore, that for a helpless infant entirely dependent on its parents, the fear of the cessation of existence is no mere fantasy. In Western culture, infant mortality is no longer the commonplace that it was in the past, and that it still is in developing countries. Effective contraception has helped us forget how common infanticide was, even in the most civilized countries, as late as the last century. But abortion is still a problematic issue and the prevalence of child battering is only now coming to be acknowledged (Kruell, 1983-1984). The infant's fear of abandonment or hurt is based not merely on its inability to tolerate delay or to control its emotions, but quite possibly on a realistic sensitivity to the fact that it was unwanted, that its existence lay in the balance for a long time after its conception, that the parents' willingness to give it care is highly ambivalent, that its death sometimes continues to be wished for by the very people on whom its life depends.

But adults who experience the Isakower phenomenon are, of course, survivors. Their fear of death during childhood did not come true. Even if starved, abandoned, ignored, frightened, or beaten, the child must have received the occasional smile, caress, admiring glance, sweet mouthful, or loving word that made mother or father objects of intense attachment. The regressive pull toward the past could not be so powerful if there had never been anything positive there. That is why Isakower's formulation continues to be a necessary adjunct to Stern's.

Contact has been experienced as pleasurable in the past, and is longed for in future. One essential difference between pregenitality and genitality, however, is that genitality involves more than contact; it involves commitment. The oral and anal periods pass rapidly, and involve no troublesome fixations if weaning and toileting have been smoothly achieved. But mature genitality signifies, beyond the moment of pleasure in togetherness, the willingness to bring into being a new person who will be jointly cared for over a great part of one's lifespan. It signifies attachment both to the marital partner and to the offspring. It is this readiness for prolonged commitment that is frightening to the individual whose experience of close human relationships has been insecure and frustrating. Genitality would involve a break with the past and a commitment to the future, and either or both may rouse anxiety.

The adult in whose personality constellation the Isakower phenomenon prominently figures is likely to be caught up in just such a dilemma, in which continuation of a dependent relationship is intolerable, loneliness dreaded, and advance to a new relationship, which might prove as bad as previous ones, frightening. These realistic considerations, however, are not likely to be present in the mind of the child when first experiencing the phenomenon, and cannot be essentially related to its etiology. It should be noted that the phenomenon is preoedipal rather than oedipal, concerned not with triangular relationships, rivalry with a stronger competitor, or the threat of castration, but with the dyadic relationship, being overwhelmed or abandoned by the loved one, and the threat of annihilation. One reason for the recurrence of the Isakower nightmare in adult situations where there is a threat that an ongoing relationship will be terminated, or a new one initiated, is the conception of genital relationships in pregenital terms: sucking with the danger of being drained (Karon and Vandenbos, 1981); biting, with the danger of being devoured; nausea and excretion, with the gift not of a life-producing substance but of dirty wastes. Even this formulation, however, accounts for only part of the anxiety-rousing character of the Isakower phenomenon. Prior even to these pregenital fantasies is the multiplicity of bodily sensations along all sensory modalities, without hierarchic organization or homeostatic control, without capacity for location in a specific part of the body, without the reassuring presence of a trusted parent who would help in the establishment of a cohesive self (Kohut, 1971). Even in the adult who basically has achieved a self adequate for function under ordinary circumstances, intense conflict involving the arousal of multitudinous irreconcilable emotions may rearouse this type of infantile experience and dread of fragmentation.

Yet another important component of the Isakower phenomenon is the insistent rhythmic throbbing that intensifies to the point of being intolerable and threatens to culminate in a climactic cessation of being. For the adult this evokes associations of orgasm, but before puberty the pregenital modes of erotic gratification offer nothing comparable. It can probably best be understood as an expression of rage, the throbbing, pulsing increase of aggressive feeling that even in an infant may lead to explosive outbursts followed by exhaustion. Rage characterizes all relationships in which the child's needs for security and affection have not been met, or the need for individuation and independence not acknowledged. It is the fusion and confusion of rage with affection and dependence, the experience of genital sexuality as explosive anger that may destroy both lover and loved one, that makes pregenitality seem safer than genitality, and that leads to the existence-threatening character of the Isakower phenomenon.

Isakower (1938, p. 343) was of the opinion that his phenomenon is experienced "only be certain people." Stern (1961, p. 214), recalling Glauber's description of one such patient as a "museum of oralities" (Lewin, 1953, p. 182), refrains from discussing the specific character involved except to comment on "astonishingly good adjustment to reality in view of the deep-rooted pathology." In the absence of systematic research on appropriately large samples, we will refrain from committing ourselves as to the precise characterological significance of the Isakower phenomenon. Since, in lectures in which it has been described and discussed, all or most participants have been able to recall it, we doubt that it is restricted to individuals with deep-rooted pathology. We have found, however, that where a person has a proneness to primitive reactions or performance of grandiose and unrealistic actions, the phenomenon may be particularly salient. In interviews we try to see whether it can be elicited with minimal suggestion, in response to such questions as "Have you had recurrent dreams?" "What are your nightmares about?" or "Did you have many illnesses with high fever as a child?" These questions are normally answered without reference to Isakower-like experiences. If the phenomenon, however, is readily reported, with signs of intense involvement, it may be a key to a lack of commitment to the reality principle, fundamental splits in the self, and preference for pregenitality in interpersonal relations. Where there is evidence for the phenomenon's denial or its concealment by defensive elaborations, it may be worthwhile to work at uncovering it, because of its relation to the patient's deepest fears.

The Rorschach is not particularly suited to direct elicitation of the Isakower phenomenon. Its symmetric but irregular figures are not reminiscent of the Isakower spheres, nor does the Rorschach provide spirals or granular gritty surfaces. The blot most productive of a "looming response" (Schiff, 1965), and also, interestingly enough, capable of being perceived as a receding figure by those more concerned with loss than with confrontation, is Card IV. This card is so highly masculine that it tends to elicit information about the father rather than the mother relationship. Moreover, its perception as an approaching or departing human figure requires considerable maturity and conceptual ability, so that those most traumatized in their relationship to the father, or to a dominant and threatening mother, are often incapable of producing this response (Mohr, 1944). As has been seen, however, where the importance of the Isakower phenomenon has come to light through dreams or drawings, the Rorschach is likely to give supplementary information highly relevant to its diagnostic understanding.

THE UNDREAMT DREAM

Twenty-year-old Antti (this is his Finnish code name, in English we could have called him Andy) came to the Cape Matthias Dream Laboratory two months after entering therapy for a depression that had culminated in attempted suicide. His therapist had suggested him for participation in our dream study (Fried, Lyytinen, Hanikka, Peltola, Puhakka, and Rantasila, 1983) because his progress in therapy was so laborious. Our research team had been impressed by Cartwright, Tipton, and Wicklund's finding (1980) that an opportunity to explore the relationships between dreams and real-life experiences reduced the tendency for patients with a guarded prognosis to drop out of therapy prematurely. Our plan was to adapt their method from use with patients about to start therapy to patients already involved in therapy. Volunteer patients were awakened during REM episodes and their dreams recorded. In the morning the laboratory observer asked the patient whether dreams seemed to connect up with one another or with actual life events, but left interpretation to the therapist.

Most of Antti's dreams were mere fragments, plotless, sometimes even imageless, stray sense impressions and thoughts. At his first awakening he reported: "I awoke and felt cold. Then it occurred to me to wonder about what I might have seen and where the cold feeling had come from." At the second awakening he emphasized that whatever it was he had experienced, at least it wasn't a nightmare, "so there ought to be no anguished sweat, anyway."

According to some investigators, experiences like these do not even qualify as dreams. Our experience has been, however, that even the briefest reports deserve analysis, and can be as revealing as dreams rich in symbolism and drama. Pondering Antti's nondreams, our research group was reminded of Kohut's observation (1971) that "the ability, within certain limits, to regulate skin temperature and to maintain a feeling of warmth appears to be acquired" by internalization of the mother's caring activities. "Narcissistically disturbed individuals tend to be unable to feel warm or to keep warm. They rely on others to provide them not only with emotional but also with physical warmth. Their skin tends to be poorly vascularized and they are unusually sensitive to lowered temperatures ('drafts')" (p. 64).

Antti cannot recall the visual imagery of his first dream in the lab, but he feels cold, abandoned, and unable to sustain homeostatic temperature control unaided. After his next dream, which again has vanished beyond recall, he still seems preoccupied with body temperature control. Now it is the other extreme, excessive heat, that has come to mind, for he talks of perspiration. His statement, however, comes in the form of a denial: he did not sweat, and the reason he didn't was that he had seen no nightmare. Is it the fear of producing a nightmare that makes Antti jam on the brakes of his mental apparatus so hard as to be unable to come up with a proper dream at all? The theme recurs at Antti's third awakening, when he reports "such a peaceful and balanced feeling, let's say that there was nothing horrible. I can't say exactly what it was. Whatever it was, it was peaceful and soft, not at all like a nightmare." If Antti had such pleasant dreams, why can't he recall them, and why must their nightmare quality be repeatedly denied? Freud (1925) emphasized the usefulness of a patient's denials in putting the analyst on the track of what the patient fears, and R. M. Jones (1965) even worked this principle into projective test administration. The elements whose nightmare quality Antti denies—body temperature, equilibrium, and softness—bring to mind the Isakower phenomenon. Too bold a conclusion? In the morning, relieved at having had no nightmares, Antti tells about the ones that most terrified him in childhood: "Someone came toward me and got bigger and bigger. Then I'd wake up and get in bed next to Mother. . . . There was a sound connected with it, like whining or something dark and like a hand or something. I'd run from it—no, I couldn't run. I tried somehow to escape it. It just came at me and grew and grew."

Awake, in full control of the situation, at a safe distance of many years from the events he is describing, Antti is able to tell about the essential experience of the Isakower phenomenon. His Rorschach provided still more detail. On Card VIII he saw rats climbing up a slope and trying to hold on, after which a hand took shape and was seen as holding on to the rats. On IX there was fire and smoke, and a kettle with something—poison—boiling over. On X he saw the gray figures at the top (D_{11})—using the location system of Beck (1950) and Exner (1974)—leaning against something and sucking it. Finally, the small green central figure (D_{10}) was a man "in a state of flight—but without a parachute," and the extensions usually described as either wings or a parachute were "smoke coming from under his armpits."

The themes of helpless dependence on VIII (rats) and X (gray creatures) is connected with images of a hand and of sucking: the core situation of the Isakower phenomenon. It is significant, as a synthesis of the temperature and oral themes, that the substance depicted as boiling over from the kettle is poisonous. Not only is the mother incapable of providing a secure, warm relationship, but the nourishment she offers is bad, deadly, rather than life-sustaining. Connected with the theme of lack of control over temperature is that of equilibrium disturbance: the very last item on the test is the figure of the man, first bravely described as flying, who turns out to be falling with no hope of being saved. And as he falls he burns—like Icarus or Phaëthon—with the smoke that billows from under his armpits belying Antti's assurance, concerning his dreams, that they were free of "anguished sweat."

The wish to flee, and the hopelessness of flight, were expressed in yet another response relevant to the symbiosis-individuation conflict (Kwawer, 1980) in Antti's current family situation. Card VII, selected as Mother card on the Post-Rorschach, was interpreted as two witches dragging a butterfly. The fragility of the insect, its inability to use its wings, its helplessness in the grasp of the women, convey a feeling of despair.

Antti had in fact returned home to live with his parents after discharge from military service. His suicide attempt was made after the girl with whom he was going steady had an abortion. To Antti, this event was immensely depressing for reasons that he had not quite clearly formulated to himself. One was that the abortion meant his not being completely accepted by his girl, her not being ready for a shared life with him. Her having the baby would have compelled him to marry, providing him in effect with a passport away from the parental home that he was unable to leave simply of his own volition. But the girl's willingness to kill their infant signified that she might be even more malevolent than his mother.

The Isakower phenomenon had made its appearance in Antti's nightmares at the time he started school, and again when he reached puberty. Major moves ahead toward maturity brought on overwhelming anxiety. It is understandable that in the current critical phase of his life, invited in the laboratory to allow himself to relax his controls, fall asleep and dream, Antti feared a recurrence of the Isakower nightmare, and tried through overcontrol to protect himself against it.

Why was Antti's Rorschach so much more revealing than his dreams? Hermann Rorschach (1921, p. 123) had anticipated just the opposite: "The test . . . is far inferior to the other more profound psychological methods such as dream interpretation . . . [It] does not induce a 'free flow from the subconscious' but requires adaptation to external stimuli. . . ." Rorschach thought his blots were too structured, too close to reality, to rival the symbols achieved by the unconscious mind when given free play during sleep. Paradoxically, however, Antti was sufficiently self-confident and trusting to let go and give the psychologists access to his fantasies so long as he was awake and confronted with stimuli he thought he could control. But asleep, wired to an apparatus under the control of someone else, he brought his dream production to a virtual halt. Only in his penultimate dream, the fifteenth, having discovered that he was after all negotiating the dream laboratory experience, did Antti tell a dream that touched on sex and betokened a victory, of sorts, over the Isakower phenomenon.

"That's terrifically *handy*! I mean like, for closing a bra, like what women have. Terrifically *handy,* like for those electrodes. Is that how they're fixed to the head, and but, they've stayed fixed real nice."

The confused speech indicates that Antti had not completely awakened from his dream. He was simultaneously talking about two things: the EEG electrodes taped to his face, and the hooks for opening and closing his girlfriend's bra. We had had difficulty with the electrodes, which sometimes required considerable adjustment. Antti in turn had had difficulty with his girl's bra, and was relieved when she bought a new model with a superior catch. In the dream he exults in the control he now has over emergence and concealment of his girlfriend's breasts. Or is he a little confused as to the identity of the spherical object to which something is attached, as to its being his girl's breast or his own head? If so, at least he is sure that he would rather be in an active than in a passive role. He seems to be rejecting his actual role as sleeping subject and identifying with the viewpoint of the experimenter. His dreamwork has ingeniously created a gadget that enables the laboratory observer to master the troublesome electrodes. And so, with hand controlling breast and head, and wishfully in charge of the laboratory situation, Antti was prepared to take leave of the experiment in which he had succeeded in having no nightmares.

The prominence of the Isakower phenomenon in the mental imagery of Antti and the man with the unopened letter appeared to be related to highly similar life situations. Both were young adults confronted with the dilemma of feeling that to continue living with their parents was intolerable, but that the prospect of founding a new home afforded no simple solution. They feared that whether in a parent-child relationship or an intimate relationship between adults, they were threatened by loss of identity either through absorption into the stronger personality of the partner on whom they were dependent, or through breakthrough of ego-dystonic emotions and disintegration into madness. Immobilized, able to move neither backward nor forward, both considered suicide as a way out. Still they persisted in seeking, with the help of a therapist, a more constructive solution. (Antti, finally, was unable to persist in his search. Some two and a half years after our contact in the dream lab, we heard that he had dropped out of therapy and had taken his life with an overdose of sedatives.)

In our first two case examples, the subjects had not been able to make the step from dependence on their parents to formation of an intimate adult relationship. There are many instances in which the pressure of inner needs, supported by social pressure, propels the individual into ostensibly taking this step, without this necessarily meaning that the pregenitality-genitality dilemma has actually been resolved. The individual's primary ties may continue to be to the parents rather than the marital partner, or the partner may be reacted to as a parental figure in relation to whom the conflicts of childhood continue to be lived out. The following cases are of this latter type. In this context we want to illustrate, since the depressive mode has already been considered, three more types of attempted conflict resolution: violent, creative, and transcendental.

A Violent Solution

The so-called "sudden murderer" (Blackman, Weiss, and Lambert, 1963) is an overcontrolled individual, with no previous record of crime or antisocial activity, who commits a single, unexpected violent act on what seems like insufficient provocation. In cases of this type, the venting of long pent-up rage onto an external target may be the only alternative to personality disintegration, and hence a way of forestalling psychosis (Menninger and Mayman, 1956; Tuovinen, 1973). But the hypothesis that there may have been danger of psychosis before the crime, and that this danger has subsequently been lessened, is difficult to confirm in the absence of comparative diagnostic data from periods before and after the outburst. One item of interest in this case is the availability of such data.

Lasse (the English form of this Finnish pseudonym would be Larry), a skilled workman with an excellent employment record, reported to a clinic with a complaint of severe chest pain that made it difficult for him to speak. When a thorough medical check of this athletic twenty-six-year-old bachelor, who lived with his ailing mother, discovered no organic basis for his complaint, he was referred to a clinical psychologist.[2] The psychologist intuited that the pain might be an internalization of the mother's lost breast, a breast that caused suffering instead of giving satisfaction. The associated speechlessness was a blockage of the patient's impulse to cry out and a way of concretizing his inability to speak about what troubled him. But there was to be no opportunity, at that time, for verifying these hypotheses.

The responses to the first six Rorschach cards were conventional and unrevealing, consistent with the alexithymia typical of so many patients with psychosomatic complaints. Then the record began to show signs of more severe pathology. Card VII was rejected. Card VIII was interpreted in a highly confused manner that suggested turmoil in relation to the symbiosis-individuation dilemma: There was a lizardlike animal either attached to, or being held by, a bat, or perhaps the bat (D_5) was carrying the lizard (D_4) and being held by the two animals at the sides, which he identified as "gluttons" (we use the British term rather than the American "wolverine" because the animal's Finnish name, *ahma*, connotes devouring, ravenous eating).

On Card IX he saw a trophy cup (DS_8) and, standing at its edge, two men (D_3) eating ice cream. This seems a peculiarly awkward attempt to combine childlike oral dependency with masculine athletic ambition. On the Post-Rorschach, Lasse picked this card as portraying Himself, and as Best Liked.

His response to Card X was a Fabulized Combination: Two men (D_{9+6}) shaking hands, while each held a crab (D_1) in his other hand. He

[2] This patient was first seen by Marja-Leena Huttunen.

explained that despite their exchange of greetings, the men were angry at one another, the crabs being manifestations of their anger. This response, to a card chosen as Least Liked, is an example of primary process thinking. It is suggestive of the strain Lasse experienced when trying appropriately to express hostile feelings at variance with his customary overcontrolled and polite behavior.

On the basis of these responses, the psychologist feared that decompensation from psychosomatic symptoms to psychosis might be imminent. She urged psychotherapy. But Lasse was resistant to this idea. Their contact was limited to three sessions.

When I[3] retested Lasse four years later, after he had shot another person and had himself been wounded by the police, there was no more card rejection nor disordered thinking on his Rorschach. It was a record with a limited content range, prominent anatomy responses, and some falling off of quality at the end, but free of psychotic flavor or signs of imminent crisis.

Asked about events leading up to the shooting, Lasse tried to be cooperative but recalled very little. He had quarreled with his wife because she wanted to go out dancing while he felt her place was at home with him, looking after their baby. She had defied him, and he had begun to drink. Then he had gone out to settle an old grudge, taking a gun to lend force to his arguments. He had not intended to use the gun, and the person who got in his line of fire was not the one he had wanted to threaten. It seemed evident, though he himself displayed no such insight, that he had displaced onto his inconsequential victim aggression essentially intended for his wife.

Lasse's male figure on the Draw-a-Person test (Figure 2) had the small head and broad shoulders of a husky male, but was dressed in what looked like one-piece coverall pajamas tidily buttoned from crotch to neckline. The psychologist who had given Lasse his first tests exclaimed, when I showed her the drawing, that it looked as if Lasse wanted to be a baby with a mother who would lovingly open or do up all those little buttons for him. This immediate interpretation startled me because, unlike her, I already had access to information that so pointedly supported it. On the Shneidman Make-a-Picture-Story test (MAPS), Figure 3, Lasse had selected the nursery as his free-choice background. For this he had chosen two figures from my Finnish revision (approved by E. S. Shneidman) of the test: a baby and a young woman. The story was simply of a mother putting her child to sleep.

[3]Here and in subsequent sections, first person singular pronouns refer to the senior author.

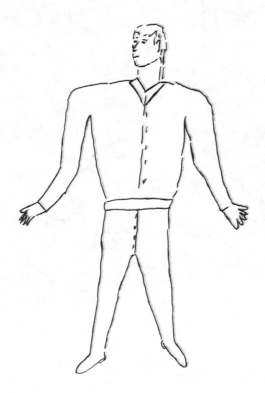

FIGURE 2: Draw-a-person Test: Lasse's drawing of a man.

When the patient's mother had been interviewed, she had put the blame for the shooting on her son's wife: "She just didn't know how to handle him. When he drank and made jealous scenes, she shouldn't have fought back. She should have lifted him into bed, taken off his shoes, cared for him." As she said this, she smiled as if looking down at a baby, and with gestures acted out the whole process of putting him to bed.

I couldn't resist asking how it was, if she knew so well how a drunken husband should be handled, that hers had so often beaten her? Lasse's earliest memories, he had told me, were of his father brutally strapping and kicking his mother. "Oh," she said, a coquettish smile suddenly lighting up her wrinkled features, "but I gave him plenty of reason to! I was young and lively then, I flirted with all the men in the village."

It was notable that on the MAPS the same woman selected by Lasse as mother for the nursery had earlier been picked by him for the

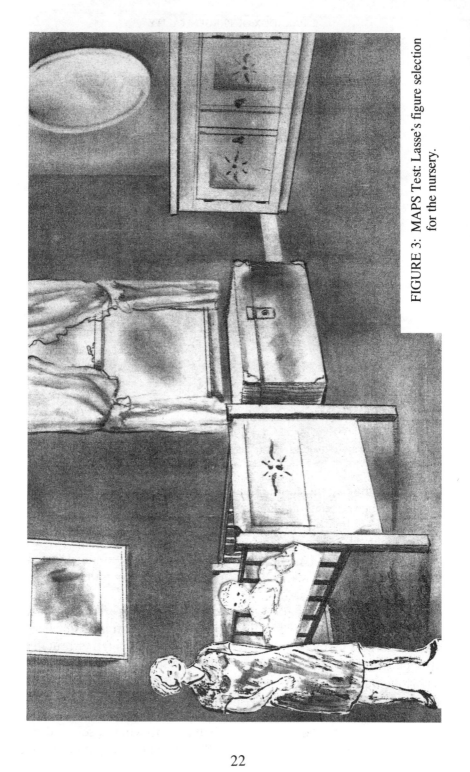

FIGURE 3: MAPS Test: Lasse's figure selection for the nursery.

FIGURE 4: MAPS Test: Lasse's figure selection for the bridge.

Bridge background, where she was depicted going for an evening walk with the most handsome and virile (M-15) of the male figures (Figure 4). Lasse had criticized the woman's dress. She had indoor clothes on, the sleeves should be long, the color (all the figures are gray!) was wrong. The latent message seemed to be that women should be "barefoot in winter and pregnant in summer," never leaving home and hearth. Lasse didn't want a wife but a mother, and he wanted her to be the ideal ever-present mother who completely devotes herself to her baby.

I asked Lasse about the physical complaints that had first brought him to the clinic. He told about the chest pain and said that otherwise he had always been healthy, except that sometimes he'd have a fever that lasted just one day. Did he recall ever having any peculiar experiences in conjunction with his fevers? "Yes," he responded, "like a rolled-up bundle that turned round and round, went far off or came closer." (Any feeling connected with it?) "It was disgusting, abominable." This recurrent nightmare was the only dream he could remember ever having, except for an almost equally frightening dream of falling.

As far as he knew, he had been breast fed. His mother, corroborating this, told proudly of her ample milk supply. Lasse had never needed a bottle or any solid food. Not until he was nine months old, at which time he was abruptly weaned because a little brother was on the way.

Before I had gotten around to asking about his infancy, Lasse had begun his account of his childhood by telling of his father's departure from their home. Lasse, then eight years old, didn't see him again until himself a man. For years he had thought he would take vengeance on him if he ever met him. But when the meeting finally took place they just had a casual talk.

Just a little prior to the father's departure, a sister of Lasse's had died. He himself had also been hospitalized. This was on account of some "substance" they had "got inside" them.

It was only when I interviewed the mother that I discovered how these consecutive, yet seemingly unrelated items from Lasse's interview hung together. When the mother had requested an autopsy after her daughter's death, it was found that the children had ingested a toxic medication their mother took for a heart ailment. The mother believed that her husband had mixed the medication with the milk she habitually used with her coffee, intending to murder her, but that he had inadvertently poisoned the children, who helped themselves to the milk while their mother was out. That was why she had divorced the man.

I asked if Lasse knew this. She said she was sure she had never told him. But family secrets have strange ways of permeating fantasy and of motivating symptoms or compulsive reenactments of the traumatic events that could not openly be talked about and worked through. Putting together Lasse's and his mother's interviews, these stories each had carried along for years without ever discussing them, we arrive at what amounts to a family myth. Lasse, as an infant, was given all the love he needed and all the milk he wanted from his mother's abundant breast. But then she abandoned both Lasse and his father, teasing the one by giving the breast that was formerly his to his brother, the other by flirting ostentatiously with other men. When the father chastised his wife, frightening though it was to witness, was he not also expressing Lasse's rage at being abandoned? On one occasion when their mother was out, the children tried to reestablish contact with her by drinking her milk, the milk set aside for her coffee. But this milk was poisoned: even more terrible than lack of milk was this milk that could kill. It was, however, Father and not Mother who had made the milk bad, and therefore he had to leave. Father's bad deeds—hurting Mother, and leaving her—must never be repeated: Lasse must be a good boy who would never be aggressive and would never leave his mother.

The mother's pride in Lasse's having been a model child, and her resistance to his marrying, were explicit in her interview. She said she wouldn't have been surprised if his brother had committed a crime—but Lasse! She could not recall the persistent enuresis, nor his brother's encopresis, which Lasse told about and which seem to have been their channels for surreptitious expression of craving for care and of angry protest.

The extent to which his mother had succeeded in getting Lasse to disown his aggressiveness was evident in his TAT responses. He invariably spoke of adult male protagonists as "the boy." The pistol in Card 3BM was apperceived as a slingshot, broken by the boy's mother because he had shot little birds. The boy on 8BM was not described in accordance with any of the standard plots for the picture (dreaming of becoming a doctor; accidentally or intentionally having shot someone) but as a nurse who helps the doctors. His choice of a typically female profession for the boy is suggestive of the extent to which his mother, in blocking the normal expression of aggressiveness, interfered with Lasse's masculine identity development. His sexual inadequacy was given expression on 13MF, the picture of a nude woman in bed, and of a man who stands with his back turned to her. His story was of an inexperienced man who failed in his attempt at lovemaking because the woman had not helped him. This story of a man in need of a woman's care and guidance complements the MAPS sequence of the man who, having walked his errant wife home, seems to turn into a baby who is given milk and put to bed. It is a conception in oral terms of what ought to be a genital relationship.

On the blank card of the TAT, Lasse pictured a winter scene with a hunter on skis, waiting for his dog to chase a hare into his field of fire. As the climax approached, with the hunter holding his fire for fear of hitting the dog rather than the hare, Lasse made a slip of the tongue, and had the hunter doing exactly what he wanted to avoid. He noticed and hurriedly corrected his slip. This story may be seen as a summation of all his other gun and sex stories. Boys shouldn't be given slingshots or guns, they shouldn't grow up into soldiers but into nurses, they should be looked after by women who teach them how to use their male equipment nicely—for if they do grow up into men and acquire guns, no matter how careful they may try to be, they will wind up doing something violent. Actually this is quite a realistic account of Lasse's life, with his many years of self-control eventuating in his sudden violent crime. Unpremeditated and accidental though Lasse's crime was, it would seem that his entire life history inexorably led up to it. If all his mother's efforts were aimed at making Lasse unlike his father, his only way of achieving a real male identity to replace the vacuum left by his nonidentity was to become like his father after all. In this unconscious endeavor Lasse succeeded, not merely in the general way of doing something violent, but right down to the detail of making an innocent person the victim of deadly feelings intended for his wife.

Shortly after administration of the first Rorschach, Lasse had succeeded in breaking away from his mother. He had set up an independent household, married, and fathered a child. Perhaps all would have gone well had not his wife so strenuously resisted his attempts to turn her into the lost ideal mother of his infancy. When she began, instead, to behave just as his mother had done before the separation from his father, provocatively going out dancing and flirting with other men, the rages and nightmare fears of his childhood were revived. He was about to lose the breast, about to be let fall. His chaotic confusion of rage and longing could have precipitated loss of contact with reality, or he could, as his mother believed his father had tried to do, have murdered his wife. The second alternative was the one he came closer to, though he was able to avoid its literal realization. Is it justifiable to conclude that the shooting was a factor in reducing Lasse's potential for psychosis? He had finally expressed the murderous rage that he had tried to control most of his life. This must have brought about relief from tension. He had in a sense made contact with his lost father, and proved that he too could be a potent, dangerous man rather than a goody-goody, castrated sissy. He had been able to avoid hurting any of the people he was angriest at, but whom he also loved, so that injuring them would have provoked intolerable guilt: wife, child, brother, father, mother. But he also had inflicted irreparable harm on a human being, and himself sustained severe injury. So he had run up against the irrevocability of a reality in which one cannot act out fantasies without bearing the consequences. He discovered that he had after all been right in controlling himself and conforming to social rules. He had achieved independence from his mother, he was now surviving loss of his wife through divorce, and he was perhaps ready to start in again, with less impossible demands on life.

Lasse recovered from his wounds, though, initially it was feared they would make him a lifelong invalid. Five years after our diagnostic study, he was keeping company with a young woman, was steadily employed, and reported no complaints.

Postscript. After this account of Lasse's case was written, we were informed of his suicide. In the note found beside his body, he stated that he was in full command of his senses but could not go on after learning that the woman he loved had been deceiving him. He drove into the woods, attached one leg of his rubberized hunter's coveralls to the exhaust pipe of his car, passed the other leg to the interior through the trunk, and so put himself to sleep.

A Creative Solution

"A sewer. Here's the pipe in the center, and the current, flowing. There's sewage flowing in it, into a lake. You get a sense of depth here, the pipe is down in a ditch. And here's the opening from which the sewage comes. The sewage has spread to the sides of the ditch too. . . ."

The response was to Card VI of the Rorschach, by a middle-aged woman artist, successful in her work, unsuccessful in her marriage, in treatment for agoraphobia. Though her test record also included people and colorful flowers, this was the card she chose as most like Herself:

"Of course I wouldn't want to be a drainage ditch for sewage, but there's something about that flow . . . something is being spread all around—but I wouldn't want it to be filth, after all." (What would you like it to be?) "Something good—something that influences the environ-ment, positively." (Like what, for instance?) "Of course I think of my art."

Few present-day psychoanalysts, explaining an artist's work as a sublimation of infantile pregenital strivings, would venture quite so crudely to postulate an equation between creativeness and the spreading of manure. But this woman, without higher education and innocent of Freudian theory, was as outspoken as Mozart (1778) in a letter in which he promised his mother that he would not "write" but "smear" and "piss" a new concerto.

The Rorschach record also contained oral and genital responses. Forthright, impulsive expression of appetites could be inferred from the "pink hams" (D_6) on VIII, determined solely by the color. On III, however, many protests and circumlocutions interfered with admission that she had seen a woman's open, bleeding genitals in a manner suggestive of utter helplessness, exposedness, and vulnerability. Taken together, the responses evoke the agoraphobic's dilemma of being doubly helpless: because of excessive dependence on others, be they trustworthy or dangerous, and because of lack of confidence in control over one's own powerful lusts. Somehow this woman's defenses did not seem synchronized with the impulses she was trying to inhibit and the dangers she was trying to fend off. Her human figures all had animal traits and struck her as strange or uncanny, as if she were on good terms neither with other people nor with her own feelings. Her initial response to the test was "bird," and birds reappeared during her therapy as symbols of freedom and joyous, soaring flight. But her Rorschach bird was a "specter bird" that made her feel uneasy, and her first response to the Post-Rorschach question about a card that reminded her of herself was a denial of its being this bird. Evidently she could not accept her own strivings for greater independence. They seemed connected with forebodings of death.

Her first crisis had come over twenty years earlier, as a young adult about to leave home. At that time, her mother coming into bed with her had helped her over her worst anxiety attacks. The current crisis erupted when, after years of modest success, she had begun to acquire a widespread reputation, which required her to make increasingly long and frequent trips. At the same time her husband, evidently envious, tried to exert greater control over her, advise her, and interfere with her work. The marriage had never been a really good one. Like her father, her husband drank. There was virtually no sexual contact. But he was, as she said, a better housewife than she, and a better parent. Their relationship had been a secure one. This security was now threatened from two directions, the lesser freedom her husband allowed her at home, and the greater freedom afforded by travel. At this point she began to have panic reactions that forced her first to curtail, then to cancel her trips. Not only was she overpowered by anxiety, she had strange experiences of bodily disintegration, apprehensions that her legs would be severed or her head go flying off into space. These made her fear she was losing her mind. She asked her aged mother to come stay with them and again share her bed, but this time there was no comfort in this. She came into therapy.

It soon became transparently evident that every trip represented to the patient an opportunity to meet men, perhaps a new partner who would offer her a marriage better than her present one. She could not, however, admit into consciousness her craving for extramarital gratification. Eventually, a dream brought her conflicts into the transference situation.

She had by this time been in therapy for a year, and was improved to the point where she had ventured to make a trip, important to her progress as an artist, without being accompanied by her husband. At the hotel where she spent the night, however, she had had a nightmare, followed by a panic attack on the trip home. After these reverses, she wondered whether she was after all well enough to dare accept future invitations to travel.

The dream had been of being in the street, in the city she was actually visiting, and seeing elephants, of which she was terrified. She ran into a church for refuge. The elephants did not follow her into the church, but three dogs did, and she feared that they would bite her.

It seemed like a classic example of street phobia due to fear of encounter with male genitals. The therapist could envision the elephants coming head-on, their sheer bulk like that of the Isakower sphere, but with their upraised trunks like erect penises, and the big ears on either side like testicles (Figure 5). When the dream was discussed with a class of psychology students, mostly women, many pictured the elephants in just this way, making the same connection with the erect phallus. Still, the therapist could not be sure that this picture of the dream accurately reproduced the patient's. There was a puzzling element: she said the elephants had been "flat." It can be illuminating, in cases like this, to ask the patient to draw the dream image (Marcinowski, 1912; Freud, 1917; Fried, 1985). Incidentally, Freud's only reference to Rorschach, added in 1914 to *The Interpretation of Dreams* (1900), is to a note in which Rorschach (1912b) had interpreted the drawing of a nineteen-year-old girl as clearly showing that a man's necktie, pictured as turning into a snake, can be a phallic symbol.

The patient's drawing of her dream elephant (Figure 6) was not a head-on view, but a profile. Its trunk hung down. It looked rather toylike and not terribly phallic—certainly not erect. She said she had

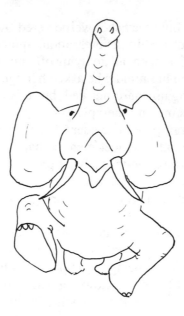

FIGURE 5: Elephant Dream: the therapist's association.

FIGURE 6: Elephant Dream: the patient's drawing.

seen the elephants in her dream just like that, from the side, not coming at her. Why then was the dream so frightening?

Free association was difficult for the patient. Her ineptness, I suspected, was due to resistance motivated by profound anxiety.

Eventually associations led to a painting, the work of another artist, a young man with whom she had been secretly infatuated. Visiting at their home, he had offered to give her and her husband the painting, suggesting that their bedroom would be a good place for it. But her husband had become unaccountably angry and rejected the gift. She had decided that with her husband so absurdly jealous, she must stifle her infatuation.

This account was a breakthrough; it was her first open acknowledgement of attraction to another man. Even so, the admission was hedged about by defenses. On the crude sexual level, after years of frustration by her indifferent and impotent husband, she craved an encounter with a vigorous man who she hoped would be, as the saying goes, "hung like an elephant." But her dream image, like her account of the infatuation which had been prevented by her discretion from evolving into an affair, emphasized esthetics: The elephant was two-dimensional, like a painting, and it was only the painter's art, not him, that she would have admitted to her bedroom.

At the next session, the patient said she was too anxious for therapy. It had been almost impossible for her to come to see me. She sat on the very edge of the couch. She then said she felt so bad that she would need to lie down with the lights out. I told her she was welcome to stretch out on the couch if that would make her feel better. Instead, she continued to sit tensely on its edge.

What did sitting on the edge of the couch mean to her? To this question she replied that it meant readiness to leave at a moment's notice. She was unable to say, however, why she should want to leave.

The following week the patient said she had taken a tranquilizer to enable her to come to her session. She had had a fantasy of collapsing and dying at my doorstep. Before awakening that morning, she had dreamt that a fuel truck parked outside her door had caught fire. She was afraid it would explode and destroy her home.

I said we must try, jointly, to figure out why it had now become frightening for her to come to the very place she was supposed to get help with her fears. Her fantasy of dying at my doorstep suggested fear of something terrible happening if she came in. At our last session, her sitting on the edge of the couch had indicated that she wanted to be sure she could leave in a hurry if necessary. This was similar to her dream situation of having to run out in a hurry because her home might be destroyed.

But why act as if she had to make a sudden dash for freedom? Rationally she knew that she was free to leave whenever she wanted to. The position she had spoken of while actually sitting on the edge of the couch had been antithetical: lying on her back, with the lights out. What is implied by a woman, in a room with a man, lying down and putting out the light? Lovemaking, of course.

The patient denied any such thought having entered her mind.

The therapist said he was perfectly willing to believe that consciously she had had no such thought.

She protested that at home she also lies down with the lights out.

The therapist answered that an action that is perfectly innocent in the privacy of one's home takes on a different connotation when in the same room with a man. Her continuing to sit on the edge of the couch even after being told she could stretch out meant that she did not trust the therapist. If in response to her unconscious message he had made an improper approach, she wanted to be ready to run out the door—to avoid a sudden flaring up of emotion, an "explosion" that could cause her "death" and destroy her home.

She was now listening intently, no longer protesting. The therapist pointed out to her the resemblance between the situation here in the treatment and the occasions when she canceled a trip. Her panic reactions at airports and railway stations were like the panic that had overcome her before the session. Consciously she had only innocent aims, but the unconscious infidelity fantasies that she feared would wreck her family life if acted on roused her anxiety and made her want to return home.

It was now possible for us to work through, concretely and in detail, her powerful appetites, as symbolized by the pink ham; her feeling of helplessness when confronted by her own desires, as symbolized by the woman exhibiting her genitals; her projection of these needs onto others, as symbolized by the terrifying elephants; and the inadequacy of her defenses, so that panic broke through and necessitated physical flight from conflict situations. In the city, the therapist said, you see the streets as being full of elephants, of men who are all penis, ready to overwhelm and enter you. Your only refuge is the church, your moral standards. Or is the dream church also your mother, whom you would like to take you into her bed, into her lap, back inside her, into her womb? Even this would not be a safe place. Even if your mother could protect you from strange men, she herself never satisfied your need for love, and therefore could not protect you from the vicious dogs, the hungry rage that is meant also for her. Now you are afraid that if you seek safety with me, you might become attached to me and that I would take advantage of this—or that if I succeeded in curing you of your fears, that might mean the end of your marriage.

The patient was now able not only to accept this interpretation but to make the connection herself between the current situation and that of her late adolescence, when she had invested all her feelings in dreams of romance, but dreaded leaving her mother and feared that her physical unattractiveness would make it impossible for any man to love her. Her body was, she felt, unshapely, her features repellent, her complexion bad, her eyes, if looked into, revelatory of guilty secrets. Her genitals, in her depressive and condemnatory view of herself, were a filthy cloaca. She did not believe she could transform herself, but she could create art works that would express the beauty absent from her physical body and its raw, crude feelings. The eventual outcome of therapy was a reaffirmation of this resolution of her conflict. With her unconscious conflicts made conscious, she was able to make a firm decision to maintain her marriage, frustrating though it was, for the sake of the security it gave her. She would embark on no affairs, and this resolution freed her to travel. Her sensual desires and romantic dreams found expression in harmonious abstract patterns that revealed no inner conflict, and in delicately lyrical designs that disclosed none of the greedy orality or polluting anality that she feared would contaminate any actual, intimate human relationship. She resigned herself to a life devoid of love and sexuality whether in marriage or outside it.

In this case the Isakower phenomenon was barely recognizable, because the dreamer had elaborated it into the form of a stylized elephant. She had eliminated its third dimension and with it the ominous looming quality. She had, as it were, stepped out of its way to see it in profile. In another case of far-reaching modification of the Isakower phenomenon, the dreamwork progressed in the opposite direction, restoring a third dimension to a flattened sphere. The patient was a man who suffered a recurrence of depression when loss of his girlfriend coincided with impending interruption of therapy for a long summer vacation. He then came to a session in an elated state (Lewin, 1951; Harrison, 1960), to tell a dream of having received a gift of valuable coins. The coins were unusual in that they were not flat, but had at one edge a triangular projection at right angles to the surface of the coin. This triangle was not jagged, but flowed from the rim of the coin in a sweeping line, while its edge was tooled to be gently rounded and softened. The coins seemed intensely real and their possession made the dreamer very happy. When he awakened, however, he found that one of his limbs had "gone to sleep," and that he could not get up until its paralyzing numbness had worn off. As he told this, he suddenly saw the connection between the circle-plus-triangle motif of the coin, and the numb-plus-stinging sensation of the limb, with his terrifying experiences of the Isakower phenomenon, in which the paradox of dull, doughy, and sharp-pointed sensations had been pronounced.

When I asked him to draw a picture of his dream coin, its source became apparent. Displayed on my office wall is a large photographic reproduction (Lengyel, 1952, plate 22) of an ancient Greek coin with the Arethusa motif, a beautiful girl's head surrounded by cavorting dolphins. Next to its enlargement, the coin is reproduced in natural size, so that both the huge and the tiny circles of the Isakower phenomenon could be said to be included in a single picture. When the patient had finished his drawing, it became obvious that the raised flange on the dream coin looked like a dolphin fin, so that the fin, which in fact was only a small element of the Arethusa coin's design, had been magnified and made to protrude three-dimensionally.

Analysis revealed three important motives for this change. One was an association to Country Joe McDonald's song "Happiness is a Porpoise Mouth" (1967), with its erotic reference to a man's hunger for the lips of his loved one's vulva. The second association was to a shark's fin cleaving the surface of the water before its attack on a swimming girl, so that the dependent oral longing for the woman who had rejected him was seen to be accompanied by a vengeful urge for sadistic incorporation. The third wish, on the transference level, was to receive a precious gift from the analyst instead of being rejected by him, and to own an art treasure superior to his in that it was no mere picture of a valuable coin, but more three-dimensional than even the real coin would be.

This improvement on reality was consistent with the patient's elated state, also an improvement on a reality that was in fact depressing. Having worked through this analysis of his dream, the patient lost his elation, but also overcame the worst part of his depression, in which guilt over unacceptable rage complicated what would otherwise have been appropriate mourning over a loss.

The attentive reader may have noted that the dolphin coin dream, in which the breast is rendered in highly abstracted form, is in this sense analogous to the disc dream reported by Christoffel (1923), while the elephant dream, in which the breast is elaborated into an exotic animal, is analogous to the camel dream he described in the same paper.

Comparing the dolphin with the elephant dream, it is interesting to contrast the attempt to alleviate anxiety by robbing the threatening, overwhelming Isakowerian sphere of its third dimension with the attempt to alleviate depression by adding a third, highly tangible dimension to the receding, lost sphere. The dolphin coin dream was also interesting to me because it provided a specific physiological explanation for the sharp-dull or "trylon-and-perisphere" aspect of the Isakower phenomenon, the origins of which have never previously, to my knowledge, been adequately elucidated (see Sperling, 1957). "Pins and needles" in an arm or leg that has "gone to sleep" may be a mere nuisance for an adult or older child, but it is understandable that on its first occurrences, when it is unfamiliar and inexplicable, it can be a highly anxiety-rousing experience linked to immobilization and to loss of body cohesiveness and control. That the pertinence of this interpretation is not unique to this particular case will become evident in the next presentation.

A TRANSCENDENTAL SOLUTION

On Prince of Wales Island in Alaska, in 1952, on the narrow coastal road between the Tlingit village of Klawock and the mixed white and native village of Craig, three young Haidas told me of a recent appearance of the dreaded Koosh-ta-kah. A Koosh-ta-kah is the spirit of a man drowned at sea, whose body has not been found, and who has taken on the form of a giant otter. The Koosh-ta-kah had been seen by two telephone line repairmen near the home of a fisherman's widow. The widow, fearing it to be the spirit of her husband returning to visit her, asked her relatives for protection. They came to her house that evening, armed with guns and flashlights, and waited in the dark. Late at night they heard footsteps just outside the house. They opened the windows and tried to turn on their flashlights, but not a light went on. Then they tried to shoot, but not a gun went off. Moments later, when the steps could no longer be heard, the flashlights went on. When the men now again tried to fire their guns, they functioned perfectly. In the morning they found the clear footprints of a gigantic otter circling the house.

My informants had initially denied any knowledge of native folk-lore or belief in the supernatural. After I had sung them a folksong from my native country, they admitted that they too were acquainted with something other than the popular songs that came over the radio, and taught me a Haida song. They asserted that only the Tlingits, ancient rivals and less acculturated to white civilization than themselves, still believed in spirits, and the Koosh-ta-kah incident had occurred not in their village, but in Klawock. As they warmed to the story, however, it seemed to me that their skepticism diminished and that they ended by trying to convince me of its truth. My main informant, seventeen years old and already a skilled commercial fisherman, later let me give him a Rorschach during an idle stretch of time aboard a seine boat at sea. His record included six Popular responses, content pertaining to the local environment (kelp, sea cucumber, red jellyfish, old-time spearhead), and percepts that revealed interest in a world with which he had no direct experience (circus elephants, coral). The totem pole he saw on VI referred to a very familiar sight—but is of course a response also given, internationally, by many who have never been near a totem pole. There were responses suggestive of anxiety in particular interpersonal rela-tions, but none pointing to disturbed reality contact. At least one anthropological study (Billig, Gillin, and Davidson, 1947–1948) has suggested that the medicine men who actively propagate belief in the supernatural have Rorschach records more indicative of severe distur-bance than do ordinary people whose belief in spirits is based on acquiescence in their group's cultural traditions rather than on personal experience. Psychologists and anthropologists tend to be appropriately cautious, however, in assessing the possible psychopathology of indi-viduals from other cultures in accord with diagnostic criteria developed in our culture. It was therefore a unique opportunity, over thirty years after my Koosh-ta-kah experience, to meet and test, within Western urban culture, practitioners of distance-healing who believed them-selves to be in direct contact with an Other Reality.

My visit to the Haidas and Tlingits had taken me from Harvard Square to America's Last Frontier. My colleague Matti Reinikainen and I now felt it peculiar to be proceeding, in our quest for folk healers, from our home in Finland's forest and lake country to Helsinki, the nation's capital. The newly constructed metro with its vandal-proof orange plastic seats sped us from the railway station to our destination, a high-rise suburban development. Our subjects had already been interviewed in conjunction with a study of alternative medicine, and we had been called in to assess the personalities (Fried and Reinikainen,

1983) of some of the most prominent healers. Our principal subject on this assignment was to be a woman, typical of healers in that she had no higher education, practiced healing outside working hours and without accepting direct payment, and had built up a widespread practice. Her husband, a skilled technician, had recently found that he too possessed healing powers. Because we were interested in their patterns of interaction as well as in the personality of each, we had planned to give them a Consensus Rorschach (Blanchard, 1968; Willi, 1973; Fried, Halme, Jalonen, Keskitalo, and Suokas, 1983; Klopfer, 1984) after testing each separately.

This plan had to be abandoned when we were met not by two healers, but three. The Wife told us that she had invited a friend, the Spiritual Leader of their circle, to meet us. While the initial atmosphere was tense, we felt that our hosts entertained some hopefulness about our encounter: establishment scientists though we were from their point of view, perhaps we would find evidence for the validity of their beliefs, and contribute to their credibility in the scientific community. Since our initial assurances of open-mindedness did not seem sufficient to achieve a working relationship, we told of studies of medicine men who exhibited social understanding and therapeutic skills in some cases superior to those of physicians. Our hosts were now ready to believe that if not committed to their approach, at least we were not sharply biased against it.

Surprisingly, the first item spontaneously brought up by them was the harm that could be done by healers. I had thought this would be a touchy subject, to be approached only after good rapport had been achieved. The Leader told us of a person who, instead of transmitting positive forces, was sucking goodness and health out of the people close to him. He read us a letter, a much folded piece of paper he took from his pocket, written in an effort to intervene. Neither Matti nor I were able to understand this oddly worded text, but Husband and Wife nodded assent. It was part of their effort to combat evil. The Husband said he was fasting to rid his body of poisons. The Leader told of his need to get away from the pollution of the city. He told of hikes in Lapland, and of his talks with the spirits of trees and brooks, each of which has its own music. Even people who can't hear the music of a brook as he can, he said, will be more likely to camp by a stream with a particularly beautiful melody. Once he had picked something from a tree, whereupon another tree asked him to take something from it as well. On a trip abroad, he once heard fascinating music in the mountains. Later, he heard the same piece in the dining room of his hotel.

When he told the waiter of having heard this music on a hike miles away, the waiter explained that when played over their outdoor speaker system, it could indeed be heard for miles. This interlacing of realistic accounts with supernatural ones, as if they were entirely equivalent, was typical of the conversation.

They talked of their past existences. The Wife said that, still a novice at spiritual development, she could recall only a few details of previous lives. The Leader could trace his lives back four thousand years. He and the Wife had been brother and sister in the past. A relationship that has endured over many lives is of course more meaningful, he continued, than one which may by ordinary standards be closer, like that of husband and wife, but which has been limited to a single lifetime. As Wife and Leader beamed at each other and touched hands, the Husband sat immobile, eyes closed, as if totally left out.

The Leader then told about his most recent life. On leave from the front, he had come to an open-air market. He noticed a lovely young flower vendor who looked gravely ill. He bought all her flowers so as to enable her to leave, walked her home, and gave her the flowers at her threshold. On his next leave, he made straight for that town and its market square. Inquiring after the girl, he was told she had died. He returned into combat with no further desire to live, and indeed "remained at the front."

In the Other Reality they met and decided to return to our world as quickly as possible so as to be able to live together. "Now she has been my wife for twenty-six years," the story concluded.

Matti asked at what age they had become aware of their spiritual gifts. The Husband, least confident, did not reply. The Wife said she had begun to develop hers only recently, while the Leader dated his back to early childhood. He had gone to sleep in a room in which others were present. He had then separated from his body and seen his own form on the bed, but had mistaken it for that of his brother. When he awoke he asked where his brother had gone, and was told that only he had lain on that bed. He connected this experience with other instances of separation from his self, which also included sensations of objects and people approaching and growing in size, or receding and shrinking. The latter experience gave him a feeling of power, especially in school if he could make teacher and blackboard become tiny as he moved them off to a great distance. Matti and I exchanged glances. We had planned to lead up to a question on the Isakower phenomenon, and now it had emerged without prompting. To confirm that the experience of splitting and that of approach or recession with macropsia or micropsia really were components of the Isakower phenomenon, I asked if there were any other accompanying feelings. Yes, the Leader answered, a persistent humming sound, and a nearly intolerable feeling of something excruciatingly sharp in conjunction with something indefinite and soft. This latter feeling sometimes occurred in isolation, without the other components. He was very sensitive to sharpness. Even in talking on the phone to a friend as close as his spiritual sister, he might have to request: "Your voice has become too sharp, please transfer it to another register."

In an awed voice, with dramatic gestures, he went on to tell of his most important visionary experience. He had seen legs, dark legs, tied with a rope. Then another pair of dark legs, similarly tied. Then white feet with a nail driven through them, bleeding. And then a voice had commanded him to carry on with the work of suffering for others, saving and healing.

From this he went on to tell of his exhilarating dreams of flying. As a schoolboy he had nightmares of being followed and threatened. If he succeeded in taking off and flying over his pursuers' heads, he could look down and laugh instead of being afraid. Husband and Wife now joined in to say that they too had dreams of flying. Each enthusiastically gestured to illustrate their style of flight, one flapping his arms like a bird's wings, one gliding, one soaring like a delta jet. For a moment it looked as if the couch on which all three sat side by side were about to take off.

This may be an appropriate point at which to interrupt the narrative for an interpretive comment. The Leader had told us of two significant experiences in his life—the childhood event that made him aware of his supernatural powers, and the vision that confirmed him in his vocation as a healer. In the former, the visual, auditory and tactile modalities were involved as changes in perceived size, a humming sound, and a paradoxical sharp-soft sensation, without these being interconnected or endowed with meaning. The observing self, split off from the sleeping self, did not even recognize these sensations as pertaining to itself, but tried to distance them by seeing the sleeper as if from without, and identifying him with another person. In the adult visionary experience, the multisensory perceptions recur in a highly structured and elaborated form. The sound is now not a mere hum but a portentous voice (Isakower, 1939, 1954; Fisher, 1976) with an important message. The sharp sensation has been incorporated in the visual imagery to become a nail driven through the feet. The entire experience has evidently been given meaning by being assimilated to memories of paintings of Christ on Golgotha, crucified between the two thieves, who often are represented as tied rather than nailed to their crosses. The dream has succeeded in making not only understandable, but highly valuable, all that was diffuse, chaotic, and anxiety-provoking in the nightmares of his childhood. He is in effect told that his suffering is Christlike, that he is the chosen of God, and that he has been given godlike power to heal and save.

Two details of his vision deserve particular emphasis. One is the strange circumstance that only legs were seen, rather than the entire spectacle of the crucifixion. These disembodied legs suggest an experience of body fragmentation, a lack of capacity for achievement of the cohesive self. The flight fantasies about which the Leader told in direct association to his account of the vision may hence serve, much like the symbol of the crucified and resurrected Savior, as compensations against fears of dismemberment. A similar mechanism has been noted (Fried, 1980) in artistic depictions of the fallen Icarus as dismembered.

The other detail is the juxtaposition of fettered and nailed feet. Immobilization is here a common factor and, like dismemberment, this is a state of being antithetical to flight (Federn, 1914; Hubbard, 1971). As for the distinction between the two ways in which immobilization is depicted, being tied may refer specifically to numbness and congestion, while the nail refers to the simultaneous sharp and stinging sensations. This paradoxical combination of sharp and dull sensations with impeded motility would seem to support the interpretation, made in conjunction with the dolphin coin dream, of anxiety provoked by a limb paralyzed during sleep as the basis for one hitherto baffling component of the Isakower phenomenon.

As we continued with the interview, the trio's accounts of their activity as healers made clearer to us their fear of harming their patients. They told us that a term like "mediator" would be preferable to "healer." What they did involved no active application of knowledge or skills. Rather, they functioned as channels between sufferers in this world and healing spirits in the Other Reality, transferring forces from the ones to the others. Their essential passivity signified that it would be possible, however little they would want it to happen, for them to be used as conduits for evil forces rather than for good ones. They were certain that a few centuries ago, they would have been persecuted as witches. A little inconsistently, perhaps, they described the witches of the past as innocent victims of malevolence, yet acknowledged that witches would have been capable of doing great harm. Their own desire to do good was exemplified in their weekly sending of extrasensory messages to Reagan and Brezhnev, exhorting them to avoid resort to war. Neither of us had the impertinence, in the face of our hosts' utterly sincere conviction of their effectiveness, to observe to them that Brezhnev was dead. Had such a comment been made, however, I suspect that it would not have disconcerted them. It would have been in keeping with the tenor of our conversation for them to have explained that their rapport with the late Soviet leader was so good that, after his death, they preferred to go right on communicating with him, trusting him to pass on their messages to his successors.

Though the individual testing phase had to be abandoned, we now asked the healers whether all three would be willing to participate in a Consensus Rorschach. They were. The Wife sat between the two men.

The Husband took the initiative. Picking up Card I, he said it looked like a person's anatomy, a pelvic bone. The Wife saw "something from the unpleasant side of mental images," something that artists draw but that decent people do not talk about. She made up for this defensive skirting of her sexual apperceptions by giving a flood of innocuous responses: bat, hourglass, butterflies, hands, "various animals." Very much involved though last to speak, the Leader interrupted the Wife, exclaiming, "Now, now you have already received my thoughts." Moments later, he complained that interference from the others' thoughts kept him from formulating his own. "I see your thoughts as if in my thoughts," he explained. Later, convinced that he and the Husband shared a perception, he asked which of them should say it first. The boundary between the Leader's self and those of the others was, it appeared, highly permeable. When excited by a percept, he was sure that he shared it with, or could transmit it to, one of the others. If a disagreeable thought came to mind, he attributed its origin to someone else. As we followed his way of handling the simple instruction to tell about what the Rorschach inkblots brought to mind, we gained a better appreciation of his intense fear of being penetrated, the sense of vulnerability this engendered, and the need to maintain a balance by being in turn the wielder of power, the one who exerted influence on the others and was capable of penetrating them.

The Leader began to speak of vertebrae of the neck, wings, and "headless hands." "There's a red thread connecting it all," he continued, "it connects these things right down to the pelvis." No sooner had he used the figure of speech, "red thread," than he saw it concretely represented by the blot's center line, and interpreted it as physically tying together the various parts of the blot. But the others were not on the same wavelength.

Husband: This remains unclear to me from the standpoint of information flow.

Wife: But there's something animal-like in all this.

Leader: No, human.

The discussion had progressed to a critical point. Not only was the trio far from a consensus, but the Leader had flatly contradicted the Wife.

Philosophical and conciliatory, the Husband observed that perhaps one wouldn't get the same picture from any two people even if one were to ask a thousand. But the Leader began to speak as if inspired. He said that the "colors" were coming to life, that they were moving, changing direction. The Wife immediately followed his lead: "It's becoming lighter and then again darker," she exclaimed. The threatened breach had been averted, the Leader had asserted his spiritual powers, and the Wife was sharing his experience. He asserted that he was now penetrating to the depths of the matter and seeing more than before. He started to make sense of the fragmented body parts he had seen earlier, combining them into a winged but headless creature that was trying with its hands to reach out for its missing head. In this one response he was combining the anxious concern over a dismembered body image and the grandiose flight fantasies already familiar to us from his dreams.

"Because it is only a shadow, one can only see its hands," the Leader observed somewhat illogically about the winged figure.

"And darkness spreads from it," the Wife took him up, "from its thoughts, from its being, from its thoughtlessness." "Yes," from the Leader, "yes." "It could be whosoever," she continued, "an undeveloped soul."

"Shall I tell you one more thing?" put in the Leader. "The pelvis, that's clearly visible." With this remark, the Leader suddenly switched away from the visionary speculations he had initiated and returned to the one response that, at the very outset, had been given by the Husband. His trancelike vision had averted the threat of a break between him and the Wife. Was their harmony, to the exclusion of the Husband, now in turn becoming too threatening? Or was the threat in the Wife having taken the lead from him?

The Husband responded emphatically to the approval that had been given his percept. He now began for the first time to join in becoming visionary: "It is indeed the pelvis, and from the pelvis, through the spine, there are connections to the starting point of the earth." Then, studying the blot, all three began to find spots, central points, currents, channels, a central channel. The connections between the human body and the universe had been established, and the three were satisfied they had reached a consensus.

From the standpoint of formal response quality, their achievement was not impressive. But from the standpoint of both individual and group dynamics, it was considerable. The sex-linked anxiety and dysphoria that troubled the Wife, and the Leader's fear of disintegration, had been dispelled and projected onto an external character, the darkness-spreading "undeveloped soul," the kind of person whom they, as healers, could free of suffering, or counteract if dangerous to others. Simultaneously with individual cohesiveness, group cohesiveness had been achieved. The competition between the Wife (seven responses) and the Leader (six responses) had been resolved in favor of the Husband, who had been least involved in the discussion, but who was brought back in at the end by having his initial response jointly approved. The Husband's inclusion had also prevented too close a couple relationship from developing between Leader and Wife, while sexual concerns had been safely translated onto a spiritual plane. Unrealistic as the solution might seem to an outsider, it served the purpose of resolving intra- and interpersonal conflicts for those directly concerned.

The Leader was clearly the most bizarre of the trio. The Wife, equally productive and usually more realistic, at times competed with him, at times refused to go along on his most venturesome excursions. Her influence as an anchor to reality was not, however, very potent. His visionary inspiration was too attractive. If she led off with a good response, like "Bears exchanging greetings" on Card II, the Leader might reply with highly anxious and hostile percepts: "Bloody teeth" (D_3), "a bird with its wings cut off" (DS_5). Unable to influence the Leader, the Wife might notice that her Husband, eyes closed, was motionless and out of contact. She would turn to him with sudden affection: "Poor little baby! How cold your hands are!" The Husband passively allowed himself to be mothered. But he might suddenly emerge from his encapsulation to support not his Wife but the Leader with his talk of power. The Wife, finding herself alone, would give in and join the men's alliance. This pattern of group dynamics was repeated, with variations, on subsequent cards. The wife, between the Husband's schizoid withdrawals and the Leader's delusional flights, came closest to representing reality, but was easily induced to abandon it. In their unstable triangular relationship, each took turns at being odd man out when the other two formed a mutually supportive dyad, but the dyad would dissolve to readmit the outsider if its accord became too intense.

The shifting interplay of projection and introjection evident in the Leader's relation to the test material was seen also in his relation to the people with whom he discussed it. He saw our faces undergoing dramatic color changes, indicative of our emotional states as perceived by him, and similarly he saw the inkblots as fluid, in motion, changing shape and color. He saw lines of flow, currents, waves, a heart that sucked power into itself through its roots, the pressure in an erupting volcano that changed into a vomiting throat. His projection of feelings into the external environment made it unstable and subject to unpredictable alterations, while his inability to choose between good and bad introjections seemed at times to make him acutely uncomfortable, forced to spew out what he had inadvertently taken in.

On Card IV the Wife led off with a description of a powerful figure standing on mighty feet. Moments later the Leader saw "the chin of a nice person, he is spitting out something bad caused him by someone else." Not long after this he told me that my face was changing, my features becoming sharp. This was, he explained, because I was approaching "the matter" on which I was expert, and "getting inside it." He for his part was quick to notice changes in the structure of another's face, he said, and these revealed everything to him. I gave no verbal reply, but sat back in my chair, increasing the distance between us, and when I spoke again, it was in a lower and softer voice. I had understood him to say he felt threatened by my physical closeness and by the possibility that I was understanding him too well. Instead of being able to say that he felt uncomfortable, he had translated his feelings into physical perceptions, believed my face to be undergoing structural transformations, and then regained his sense of power by asserting his ability to read my mind.

A surprising development occurred on the "Sex Card," Card VI. This blot immediately made the Husband feel uncomfortable. When the Leader began to talk of part (D_2) of the blot as the "life-fluid's flow-pipe," the Husband excused himself, saying he had to make a phone call. Moments later, the sound of a flushing toilet could be heard from the room into which he had retired. Meantime, however, the Leader had discovered a bearded profile (D_4), chuckled with excitement, grasped the blushing Wife by the chin, and teased her: "You don't have a beard—ha-ha—or do you?" They acted like teenage lovers, oblivious of the psychologists' presence. Then the Leader, regaining his composure, put a question to the Husband, and affected surprise at noticing his absence. Later, as the Wife and Leader walked Matti and me to the subway station, they talked with concern of the Husband's sometime jealousy, his failure to appreciate the spiritual, brother-sister character of their relationship.

For one brief moment during the test, the simple human need for physical contact had broken through all the transcendental talk and enabled the Leader to touch the woman he so clearly felt attracted to. But was the need for contact so simple? Why had he taken her precisely by the chin, and playfully asked her whether she had a beard? He had seen a bearded man on the Rorschach; the only bearded man actually present was myself. The Leader's and the Husband's interchanges about the Rorschach blots had centered about exchanges of power through sucking and flowing. Had he needed to reassure himself that he wanted to touch a woman, not engage in a sexually colored power struggle with a rival male authority?

Just as sexual intimacy was threatening to the members of the trio because their selves were so frail, so endangered by fears of fragmentation, penetration, being sucked empty, or destroying other persons, so their profession of healing contained the same threatening elements. This seemed to be why, despite their talk of heat- and health-transmitting hands, they preferred to heal at a distance, by telephone. The one incident of healing the Wife told about in detail concerned a man whose pain was so great that she saw she would have to hold his head. When she asked whether she might do this, he protested. She said that all right, she would ask his wife into the room. With his wife present, and despite his protests, she now touched the right places, and all pain disappeared. "What did you do to me?" the patient asked repeatedly, and the healer replied that he knew exactly what she had done, "and your wife was here and saw it too. I only held your head." The whole story centered not so much on suffering and healing, as on her having to defend herself against the married couple's suspicions that she was trying to seduce the patient. The Leader told of curing entire trainloads of fellow passengers of their ills, assisted by the rhythmic motion of the train in which all of them participated. It was evident that in these contactless mass cures, there was no evidence beyond the healer's subjective conviction that anyone had been suffering, or had been helped.

The healers were highly critical of medical doctors, who give patients so little time and show so little interest in them as people. Their own long-distance methods, however, tended to give the patient even less time in direct communication, and no physical contact at all. The

Rorschach responses suggested that all three healers, like others we have tested, have very little capacity for empathy as reflected in human movement responses of good form quality. They produce either fragmented body parts which they then try to connect and bring to life through fabulization, or human movement responses that have been distorted or endowed with bizarre features. Their own sense of identity is far too uncertain for them to be capable of genuine empathy, of a relation in which the other is listened to and understood. But if these healers lack empathy they certainly do not lack charisma, an ability to talk of their experiences in a convincing and moving manner, to impress with their knowledge and power, and to arouse in sufferers a confident belief in their capacity to help.

The healers' own sense of emptiness is alleviated by an inflow of goodness from helpers in the Other Reality, idealized substitutes for their inadequate parents. This constant inflow is balanced by a reciprocal outflow, which enables them to see themselves as transmitters of goodness, not just dependent receptacles. The most precarious part of the system relates to the problem of being certain that this in- and outflow is good, not bad; spiritual, not sexual. To the extent that they succeed in maintaining this certainty they succeed in being healers, not witches in danger of persecution or paranoiacs in need of hospitalization.

CONCLUSION

In the *Ion* of Euripides a mother abandons her baby, refusing him her breast despite his piteously outstretched arms. No sooner has she been reunited with him, years later, than she tries to poison him. On both occasions, only the interference of the gods rescues Ion. This study has dealt with eight individuals—the man with the unopened letter, the man with the undreamt dream, the "sudden murderer" who ended as a suicide, the elephant dream woman, the dolphin dream man, and the three healers—who tried in their different ways to deal with Ion's (or Isakower's) dilemma, seeking security and love despite early experiences with maternal breasts that threatened life, either by giving nothing or by giving something noxious. Each of these people longed for contact, for the reassuring touch that signifies that one is not alone, not insensate and dead, but close to someone else. In the course of normal development, contact is preliminary to mutual arousal, to a sequence of reciprocal touches that become ever more gratifying, and that may lead to a relationship in which both partners can count on a continuation of these contacts over time. Pregenitality develops into genitality, its pleasures coaxing one into a willingness to take on responsibility, into a confidence that one can care not only for another but for a new being who will embody the living fusion, the no longer sunderable togetherness of the partners. The difference between pregenitality and genitality, in this sense, is not merely anatomical but temporal and interpersonal. A relationship is pregenital not because the partners enjoy their oral and anal zones, their eyes and hands and hair and skin, but because their contact is of a type that antecedes that stage of maturity at which one will be ready to engage in enduring mutuality and to create progeny. The genital organs can be used for coitus that is pre- or pseudo- rather than truly genital, while other body parts, sense modalities, and activities can be used for contacts that serve as a prelude to, or context for, true genitality. The focus here has been on situations in which progressive development toward genitality has failed to occur because contact in the normally pregenital phases of childhood development had been experienced not as dependably gratifying and reassuring, but as arousing, alongside pleasurable feelings, anticipation of discontinuity and loss, or of being misunderstood, hurt, overwhelmed, fettered, sucked dry, devoured, annihilated. Though each new attempt at contact may involve at least the seed of a potential development into the intimacy of true genitality, those who have too often been disappointed feel in danger of being overcome, whenever about to terminate an old relationship or commit themselves to a new one, by a renewal of the terror they felt as children when their imperfectly formed selves had seemed about to go to pieces, shrink into nothingness, polarize into an anguish of irreconcilable sensations, or coalesce with a mass that signified the cessation of their own existence. As frightening as the fear of one's own destruction may be the fear that one will destroy the other, that one's tentative love will turn into rage, and the loved one into something hateful, disgusting, dead.

In this chapter we have tried to present a sampling of the variety of ways in which people under these circumstances can try to cope with their problematic life situations, and with the anxiety-rousing, bewildering nature of the particular kind of cognitive disorganization known as the Isakower phenomenon. Isakower originally described his phenomenon as associated with the process of falling asleep, that is to say, with the experience of loss of contact both with external reality and with a sense of the cohesive intactness of one's own body and self. This phenomenon is seen as significant because it makes explicit, on a dream level of experience, the unverbalized primitive turmoil inherent in pathologically pregenital relationships. It brings to the threshold of awareness, in however opaque and protean a form, the prototypal conflicts that render impossible a realistic assessment and gratifying utilization of present opportunities for the enjoyment of intimacy.

After describing the phenomenon in some of its classical forms, we have provided examples of some of the extreme transformations it can undergo. It can be reduced to mere fragments of its multisensory totality under the impact of negation, the attempt to avoid altogether having to experience it. Alternatively, it can be highly elaborated through assimilation to images and experiences from later periods of life, and thereby made seemingly more understandable, less frightening, perhaps even enjoyable. For the practicing clinician, the Isakower phenomenon is a challenge in much the same way as for the patient. It is difficult to master, both from the standpoint of intellectual comprehension and from that of working through of the emotions involved. To the extent that mastery has been achieved, the therapist will be sensitized to recognition of the phenomenon when it occurs in a patient, and capable of offering the insight and support needed in such a period of regressive crisis.

REFERENCES

Almansi, R. J. (1960), The face-breast equation. *J. Amer. Psychoanal. Assn.*, 8:43–70.

Beck, S. J. (1950), *Rorschach's Test: I. Basic Processes.* New York: Grune & Stratton.

Billig, O., Gillin, J., & Davidson, W. (1947–1948), Aspects of personality and culture in a Guatemalan community: Ethnological and Rorschach approaches. Parts I & II. *J. Personal.*, 16:153–187; 326–368.

Blackman, N., Weiss, J. M. A., & Lambert, J. W. (1963), The sudden murderer. *Arch. Gen. Psychiat.*, 8:289–294.

Blanchard, W. H. (1968), The consensus Rorschach: Background and development. *J. Proj. Tech. & Personal. Assess.*, 32:327–330.

Cartwright, R. D., Tipton, L. W., & Wicklund, J. (1980), Focusing on dreams: A preparation program for psychotherapy. *Arch. Gen. Psychiat.*, 37:275–277.

Christoffel, H. (1923), Affektivität und Farben, speziell Angst und Helldunkelerscheinungen. *Zeitschrift für die gesamte Neurologie und Psychiatrie*, 82:46–52.

Dechend, H. von, & Santillana, G. de (1969), *Hamlet's Mill: An Essay on Myth and the Frame of Time.* Boston: Godine.

Ellis, H. (1911), *The World of Dreams.* Boston: Houghton Mifflin, 1922.

Exner, J. E. (1974), *The Rorschach: A Comprehensive System.* New York: Wiley.

Federn, P. (1914), Über zwei typische Traumsensationen. *Jahrbuch der Psychoanalyse*, 6:89–134.

Fink, G. (1967), Analysis of the Isakower phenomenon. *J. Amer. Psychoanal. Assn.*, 15:281–293.

Fisher, C. (1976), Spoken words in dreams: A critique of the views of Otto Isakower. *Psychoanal. Quart.*, 45:100–109.

Freud, S. (1900), The Interpretation of Dreams. *Standard Edition*, 4–5. London: Hogarth Press, 1953.

_____ (1917), Introductory Lectures on Psycho-Analysis. *Standard Edition*, 16. London: Hogarth Press, 1963.

_____ (1920), Beyond the pleasure principle. *Standard Edition*, 18:3–64. London: Hogarth Press, 1955.

_____ (1925), Negation. *Standard Edition*, 19:235–239. London: Hogarth Press, 1961.

Fried, R. (1973), Mother and father images as related to the Rorschach by 1025 Americans and Finns. *Reports from the Department of Psychology*, 148, University of Jyväskylä, Finland.

_____ (1980), Rorschach and Icarus. In: *Borderline Phenomena and the Rorschach Test*, ed. J. Kwawer, H. Lerner, P. Lerner, & A. Sugarman. New York: International Universities Press, pp. 107–132.

_____ (1983), Therapy for the people: The gold of psychoanalysis for the benefit of all. *Reports of Psychiatria Fennica*, 48:5–29.

_____ (1984), Icarian personality in psychology and the arts. In: *Personality Psychology in Europe*, ed. H. Bonarius, G. Van Heck, & N. Smid. Lisse, Holland: Swets & Zeitlinger, pp. 349–367.

_____ (1985), Freud's dream theory: Outdated or underrated? In: *Symposium on Psychopathology of Dream and Sleeping*, ed. K. Achte & T. Tamminen. Helsinki: Psychiatria Fennica Supplementum.

_____ Halme, S., Jalonen, L., Keskitalo, P., & Suokas, A. (1983), The diagnostic team and the alcoholic family. In: *Research on Psychotherapeutic Approaches*, ed. W.-R. Minsel & W. Herff. New York: Peter Lang, pp. 284–290.

_____ Lyytinen, H., Hanikka, E., Peltola, M., Puhakka, P., & Rantasila, E. (1983), The dream laboratory as an aid to psychotherapy in difficult cases. Paper presented at the Symposium on Psychopathology of Dream and Sleeping, Helsinki, September 1983.

_____ Reinikainen, M. (1983), Witchcraft in a modern urban community: Rorschach-MMPI analysis of a "good witch." Presented at the Eighth International Conference on Personality Assessment, Copenhagen, August 4–6.

Guthrie, L. (1899), On night terrors, symptomatic and idiopathic, with associated disorders in children. *Clin. J.*, 14:97–109.

Harrison, I. B. (1960), A clinical note on a dream followed by elation. *J. Amer. Psychoanal. Assn.*, 8:270–280.

Hubbard, D. G. (1971), *The Skyjacker: His Flights of Fantasy*. Rev. ed. New York: Collier, 1973.

Isakower, O. (1938), A contribution to the patho-psychology of phenomena associated with falling asleep. *Internat. J. Psycho-Anal.*, 19:331–345.

_____ (1939), On the exceptional position of the auditory sphere. *Internat. J. Psycho-Anal.*, 20:340–348.

_____ (1954), Spoken words in dreams. *Psychoanal. Quart.*, 23:1–6.

_____ (1974), Self-observation, self-experimentation, and creative vision. *Psychoanalytic Study of the Child*, 29:451–472. New Haven, CT: Yale University Press.

John, H. J. (1959), *Jan Evangelista Purkyně: Czech Scientist and Patriot*. Philadelphia: American Philosophical Society.

Jones, R. M. (1965), The negation TAT. In: *Psychological Test Modifications*, ed. M. Kornrich. Springfield, IL: Charles C Thomas, pp. 152–163.

Karon, B. P., & Vandenbos, G. R. (1981), *Psychotherapy of Schizophrenia: The Treatment of Choice*. New York: Aronson.

Klopfer, W. G. (1984), Application of the consensus Rorschach to couples. *J. Personal. Assess.*, 48:422–440.

Kohut, H. (1971), *The Analysts of the Self*. New York: International Universities Press.

Kruell, M. (1983-1984), On abuse, harassment and disasters. *Rev. Psychoanal. Books*, 3/4:383-388.

Kwawer, J. (1980), Primitive interpersonal modes, borderline phenomena, and Rorschach content. In: *Borderline phenomena and the Rorschach test*, ed. J. Kwawer, H. Lerner, P. Lerner, & A. Sugarman. New York: International Universities Press, pp. 89-105.

Lengyel, L. (1952), *Chefs-d'oeuvre des monnaies grecques*. Montrouge/Seine: Editions Corvina.

Leonard, W. E. (1927), *The Locomotive-God*. New York: Century.

Lewin, B. D. (1946), Sleep, the mouth, and the dream screen. *Psychoanal. Quart.*, 15:419-434.

———— (1948), Inferences from the dream screen. *Internat. J. Psycho-Anal.*, 29:224-231.

———— (1951), *The Psychoanalysis of Elation*. London: Hogarth Press.

———— (1953), Reconsideration of the dream screen. *Psychoanal. Quart.*, 22:174-199.

Marcinowski, J. (1912), Gezeichnete Träume. *Zentralblatt für Psychoanalyse*. 2:490-518.

McDonald, J. (1967), Happiness is a porpoise mouth. Tradition Music, BMI. Phonograph recording: *Country Joe and the Fish*. Vanguard VSD 79244.

Menninger, K., & Mayman, M. (1956), Episodic dyscontrol: A third order of stress adaptation. *Bull. Menn. Clin.*, 20:153-165.

Mohr, P. (1944), Die schwarze und sehr dunkle Tönung der Rorschach'schen Tafeln und ihre Bedeutung für den Versuch. *Schweizer Archiv für Neurologie und Neurochirurgie*, 53:122-133.

Mourly Vold, J. (1912), *Über den Traum*. Vol 2. Leipzig: Johann Ambrosius Barth.

Mozart, W. A. (1778), Letter to his mother, 31 January. *Mozart: Briefe und Aufzeichnungen*. Vol. 2. New York: Bärenreiter, 1962, p. 246.

Purce, J. (1974), *The Mystic Spiral*. London: Thames & Hudson.

Purkyně, J. E. (1820), Beyträge zur näheren Kenntniss des Schwindels aus heautognostischen Daten. *Opera Omnia*, 2:15-37. Prague, 1937.

———— (1821), Auch etwas über die Traumwelt. *Opera Omnia*, 2:5-6. Prague, 1937.

———— (1823), Beiträge zur Kenntniss des Sehens in subjektiver Hinsicht. *Opera Omnia*, 1:3-59. Prague, 1918.

———— (1827a), Ioannis Müller de sensibus libri duo. *Jahrbuch für wissenschaftliche Kritik*, 1:190-228.

———— (1827b), Über die physiologische Bedeutung des Schwindels und die Beziehung desselben zu den neuesten Versuchen über die Hirnfunktionen. *Magazin für die gesamte Heilkunde*, 23:284-310.

———— (1846), Sinne im Allgemeinen. *Übersicht der Arbeiten*. Vol 3. Braunschweig, pp. 352-359.

Rorschach, H. (1912a), Über "Reflexhalluzinationen" und verwandte Erscheinungen. *Gesammelte Aufsätze*. Bern: Hans Huber, 1965, pp. 105-152.

———— (1912b), Zur Symbolik der Schlange und der Krawatte. *Gesammelte Aufsätze*. Bern: Hans Huber, 1965, p. 161.

———— (1921), *Psychodiagnostics*. 4th ed. New York: Grune & Stratton, 1949.

———— (1927), Zwei schweizerische Sektenstifcer. *Gesammelte Aufsätze*. Bern: Hans Huber, 1965, pp. 256-299.

Schiff, W. (1965), Perception of impending collision: A study of visually directed avoidant behavior. *Psychological Monographs: General and Applied*, 79(11):1-26.

Schilder, P. (1935), *The Image and Appearance of the Human Body*. New York: Wiley, 1964.

———— (1939), The relations between clinging and equilibrium. *Internat. J. Psycho-Anal.*, 20:58-63.

Sperling, O. E. (1957), A psychoanalytic study of hypnagogic hallucinations. *J. Amer. Psychoanal. Assn.*, 5:115–123.

Spitz, R. A. (1955), The primal cavity. *Psychoanalytic Study of the Child*, 10:215–240.

——— (1965), *The First Year of Life*. New York: International Universities Press.

Stern, M. M. (1961), Blank hallucinations: Remarks about trauma and perceptual disturbances. *Internat. J. Psycho-Anal.*, 42:205–215.

Tuovinen, M. (1973), Crime as an attempt at intrapsychic adaptation. *Acta Universitatis Ouluensis*, Series D. Oulu, Finland: University of Oulu.

Ullman, M. (1984), Group dream work and healing. *Contemp. Psychoanal.*, 20:120–130.

Volkan, V. D. (1979), The "glass bubble" of the narcissistic patient. In: *Advances in Psychotherapy of the Borderline Patient*, ed. J. LeBoit & A. Capponi. New York: Aronson, pp. 405–431.

Willi, J. (1973), *Der gemeinsame Rorschach-Versuch*. Berne: Hans Huber.

Chapter 2

Toward a Rorschach Psychology of the Self

David Arnow, Ph.D.
Steven Cooper, Ph.D.

Psychoanalytically oriented psychologists have long endeavored to bring advances in psychoanalytic theory to the interpretation of psychological testing. Due to the historical affinities and formal parallels between the Rorschach and psychoanalysis, Rorschach interpretation in particular has continually integrated (and has often contributed to) new theoretical developments. It is in this tradition that we seek to apply the insights of self psychology to the Rorschach. In exploring a Rorschach psychology of the self, it is our task to provide an initial survey of the interpretive domain which loosely parallels Kohut and Wolf's outline (1978). We discuss a self psychological view of the testing situation and our general interpretive stance toward the response and its referents. We then take up the interpretive significance of drives, defenses, and character style. Finally, we review the various syndromes of self pathology and their Rorschach manifestations. Clinical material is presented throughout. Though this interpretive approach is particularly relevant to patients with narcissistic personality and behavior disturbances it is not limited to these individuals. Rather, we seek to provide a more general interpretive stance that we feel yields additional insight into the problems of patients with a wide range of diagnoses.

THE TESTING SITUATION AND THE RESPONSE PROCESS

In addition to presenting an individual with a series of inkblots, the Rorschach test includes an interpersonal dimension, the importance of which was first stressed by Schafer (1954). More recently, we ourselves have explored the impact of the Rorschach situation on borderline patients (Arnow and Cooper, 1984). In our view, the testing situation has many dynamic implications which actively contribute to the response process for all but the healthiest individuals. At the most general level, during the Rorschach a patient is asked to express him or herself. If there have been major empathic failures on the part of early selfobjects, it should be plain that asking for self-expression is no simple request and is colored by a long and painful history. Minimally, the self wants to be recognized by a respected object.

From the perspective of the psychology of the self, the interpersonal aspects of the testing situation represent an opportunity for expressing a patient's primary needs from selfobjects and the feelings aroused when these needs are not met. Here, as in the selfobject transferences, the testing situation provides an environment which mobilizes the unmet needs for mirroring of the self, or for merger with an idealized selfobject. It is important to note that the Rorschach situation, in contrast to an optimally empathic therapeutic milieu, does not permit the development of a well-articulated narcissistic transference. It can, however, illuminate some of the early, tentative, and sometimes subtle manifestations of such a transference, and this can help the therapist remain well enough in tune with the patient to allow the full emergence of a selfobject transference. At the same time, since the testing situation is not usually experienced by patients as optimally empathic it becomes an excellent opportunity to study how a patient responds to less than optimal empathy. This understanding can sharpen the therapist's awareness of a patient's response to the inevitable empathic failures of the therapist. Data of this sort are also useful in helping a therapist understand a patient's reactions to the many settings and relationships (work, school, and other everyday encounters) which are inherently not well suited to function as selfobjects.

We now turn to a more detailed analysis of what can be learned from a patient's reactions to the testing situation about underlying needs for mirroring or idealized selfobjects. The need for mirroring from the examiner (and from other potential selfobjects) takes many forms involving attempts to be impressive either in the quality or quantity of speech or perception. Many instances of intellectualization, including the use of technical jargon, copiously detailed description, and so forth (see Schafer, 1954), can be seen as efforts to obtain the examiner's recognition and admiration. Likewise, attempts at wit or humor through "off the record remarks" or humorous images often contain the wish to be more impressive and the underlying need for a mirroring selfobject. When an examiner experiences the Rorschach as a performance and feels either lectured to or entertained, it is likely that the patient has assumed a role in order to maximize the supply of mirroring.

These expressions of the grandiose self's needs for mirroring having been noted, it must be said that often the Rorschach situation does not accommodate these needs. It is true, however, that the examiner is extremely interested in what the patient sees and in obtaining the patient's words verbatim. For some individuals this constitutes adequate mirroring, though for most it is insufficient. The testing situation therefore provides a good opportunity to assess a patient's capacity to cope with relatively deficient mirroring. Incidentally, comments about the examiner's need for verbatim recording, including comments about the need for tapes or shorthand, not only reflect the devaluation of objects, but also convey the wish for perfectly responsive selfobjects.

With respect to deficient mirroring, one may note a range of reactions, from mild frustration or irritation to boredom and finally suspiciousness or despair. Often during inquiry one senses withdrawal of interest and sullen fury as it becomes even more clear that the examiner fails to offer even a hint of acclaim for the patient's performance. These reactions to the examiner's unresponsiveness show the nature, if not always the intensity, of an individual's response to an empathically out of tune mirroring selfobject.

The need for an idealized selfobject may also be apparent in the brief relationship that develops between patient and examiner. This type of selfobject relationship takes two forms. The first involves archaic needs for soothing (Buie and Adler, 1982) and calming when stimulation becomes excessive. These are individuals who feel overwhelmed by the examiner's attention, but who lack the capacity to prevent a painful intensification or spreading of affect from one situation (or one response) to the next. For such people the Rorschach transaction becomes painful, not so much because of what they imagine the blots look like but because of the overstimulation of being closely looked at by another human being. Reactions of acute panic and embarrassment are common in this context. When testing these seemingly histrionic patients, one will often need to provide calming in the face of excessive affective involvement, if only by offering a reminder to describe what the blot looks like, rather than what it feels like. Here the countertransference involves fantasies of soothing, rocking, or simply holding a child who is not angry but rather is overwhelmed and near disintegration at the end of a long and too exciting day. Overstimulation of this sort, without the necessary calming, may be compounded by the input from the blots and is certainly expressed in confabulatory responses.

Easier to appreciate, but less frequent, are indications of the need for a powerful idealized object which focuses on the examiner. Blatant flattery of the examiner (Cooper and Arnow, 1986), often echoed in idealized imagery (Lerner and Lerner, 1980; Cooper and Arnow, 1986), betokens the search for the idealized selfobject, merger with whom allows one to share in this object's power and grandeur. Consistent devaluation of the examiner may likewise indicate such needs; here, however, their disappointment has led to a strategy of pushing away objects before they prove too disappointing, unable, as it were, to sustain the mantle of idealization.

THE RESPONSE AND ITS REFERENTS

The meaning attributed to the Rorschach responses depends on what one takes as the referent for Rorschach imagery, and this choice hinges on one's theoretical orientation. Our approach to this question grows out of a theory stressing the etiological role of the selfobject's empathic failures in the development of self-pathology. At the risk of oversimplification, it can be said that the self reflects the relative adequacy of its early selfobjects and that new objects will be experienced in the light of predominant yearnings and frustrations regarding those selfobjects. New relationships are dynamically shaped on the one hand by the chronic empathic failure of selfobjects, which leads to a poorly structured self and a resulting search for objects to function as primitive selfobjects, and, on the other, by efforts to protect the self from the pain and peril of reexperiencing empathic failure.

In this light each response can be viewed as having three interpretive dimensions. These include the response (1) as a reflection of the state of the self (a self-representation), (2) as a perception of an archaic selfobject, and (3) as an indication of how new objects will be experienced.

The first dimension, focusing on the self-representational or self-state aspects of the response, is analogous to Kohut's concept of self-state dreams (1977). Here one assesses the structural properties of the self in terms of cohesiveness and vitality versus fragmentation or enfeeblement. This dimension also examines the predominant needs (i.e., mirroring or idealizing) expressed in regard to selfobjects. As a representation of selfobjects the response provides insight into how the self perceived its selfobjects vis-à-vis their capacity to provide to provide mirroring or to serve as suitably idealizable sources of calming or of images of power and omnipotence. The interaction of these two dimensions (self-representation with selfobject representation) provides a glimpse into how new objects will be perceived and experienced. It should be stated that these three interpretive approaches should not always be given equal weight, as a particular dimension will occasionally be more or less salient. Gathering a patient's associations to responses, as suggested by Aronow and Reznikoff (1976), or conducting an affect inquiry (Holt, 1977) can often help clarify this issue. Our approach is most valuable when applied to idiosyncratic features of the percept, the resulting interpretation becoming more compelling with an accumulation of supporting evidence drawn from the Rorschach or other testing data. The following examples illustrate our general approach to interpretation.

Card IV. A giant but the arms are too small and sickly, like they don't belong with the rest of it.

As a self-representation the response conveys a sense of being flawed or inadequate with feelings of impotence. The focus on a part of the body points to feelings of fragmentation perhaps expressed in hypochondriacal concerns. Analyzing the percept as reflecting a subjective experience with a selfobject, we have an idealized image of a father who proved disappointing, i.e., incapable of meeting phase-appropriate needs for an idealizable object. Taken together, these two interpretive dimensions point to a specific way in which new objects are likely to be experienced. Kohut and Wolf's description of the ideal hungry personality (1978) is pertinent: "The ideal-hungry feels the persistence of the structural defect and, as a consequence of this awareness, he begins to look for—and, of course, he inevitably finds—some realistic defects in his God. The search for new idealizable self-objects is then continued, always with the hope that the next great figure to whom the ideal-hungry attaches himself will not disappoint him" (p. 421).

Card VII. Two statues facing each other but without much expression on their faces.

The self-representation contains an image of formality and coldness, an overall discomfort with self-expression. Here the maternal selfobject (responses to Card VII often reflect feelings about one's mother) was likely to have been perceived similarly, i.e., as lacking in spontaneity and therefore having difficulty providing sufficiently enthusiastic mirroring. In new relationships this person is likely to avoid intimacy based on his feeling that women do not adequately respond to him. Rather than overtly expressing his needs for mirroring he is likely to hide behind a cool and controlled exterior. These dynamics are common in people described by Kohut and Wolf (1978) as "contact-shunning personalities."

THE INTERPRETIVE SIGNIFICANCE OF DRIVES, DEFENSES, AND CHARACTER STYLES

The psychoanalytic interpretation of Rorschach data has long been concerned with describing the complex interactions between drives, the specific defenses they mobilize, and the overall character style spawned by the dynamic interplay between drive and defense. Though continuing to descriptively recognize their presence, a self psychological approach to the Rorschach yields a different interpretation of material revealing drives, defenses, and character style. For example, rather than exclusively forming a basis for nuclear conflicts, drives are seen as disintegration products secondary to a rupture in the self-selfobject milieu. Aggression points to the frustration of the needs for mirroring or for idealized selfobjects. Excessive libidinal drive material suggests a tendency for fragmentation engendering the need to seek a high degree of stimulation through which to ward off feelings of emptiness or deadness. In the context of excessive libidinal drive material (oral, anal, or phallic), the predominant psychosexual level points to the developmental period as prototypical of the kinds of selfobject functions with which parents had difficulty. (For discussion of the relationship between drives, character structure, and the psychology of the self, see Kohut, 1977, pp. 69–83.)

Likewise, defenses are seen not primarily as specific modes of coping with structural conflict but as ways in which an endangered self learns to protect itself from a response from a selfobject which constitutes a threat to the self's cohesion and vitality. For example, affect is isolated when its intense expression has not been welcome and when the self has felt alone with and unable to share joy or pain with a suitably responding selfobject. Anger is projected and denied when the narcissistic needs of parents require its banishment. Typically, such parents conditionally serve as selfobjects to the child only when he is not angry, a situation stimulating lack of trust and the subsequent development of other paranoid features.

Character structure has similar roots. The obsessive-compulsive's preoccupation with the affectless side of life, striving for perfection, and struggles for control all represent complex characterological structures to protect the self from a shattering response to relaxed emotionality. At the same time these character traits also seek to guarantee mirroring for at least a part of the self. The paranoid character style is also seen as an adaptation to a pathologically unempathic environment rather than as deriving exclusively from a pathological attempt to deal with one's inherent aggressive or sexual impulses. For example, the paranoid's suspiciousness, searching for clues, and need to conceal himself can develop in a selfobject milieu that has been fraught with the inconsistency of receiving recognition one moment and losing it the next, in conjunction with repeated disappointments in idealized selfobjects. So, too, the hysterical patient's intensity of experience, craving for attention, and difficulty modulating affect can represent characterological ways of avoiding the anxiety of fragmentation as well as seeking to obtain recognition from a less than optimally responsive selfobject. These individuals may have felt they went unheard or were not taken seriously when they spoke about ideas and so resorted to theatrics for better effect.

In light of what has been discussed, we present an extended clinical example. Two Rorschach responses have been chosen to demonstrate the kinds of hypotheses stimulated by a self psychological approach. The first response is not dramatically revealing and generates some tentative hypotheses that are supported by the second example. Both responses were given by a young man who was referred for testing by the court on a charge of petty theft, following a breakup with his girlfriend. At this point his parents threw him out of the home. The patient had been elected to a high office by his senior class in high school.

Card II. Free Association: The center figment looks like a chandelier. I mean the inside. Looks like some sort of art deco chandelier. Inquiry: shape. Feeling inquiry: Very, very warm, of the past. Grandmother's house. You told me to imagine and only by imagining could I see that.

Viewed as a self-state percept, the image hints at exhibitionistic strivings with the wish to be admired and looked up to, as it were. This is supported by the patient's improper use of the word *figment*, which may in part reflect his tendency to use impressive-sounding words. At the same time, this "slip" may also be evidence of the kind of fragmentation described by Kohut and Wolf (1978): "even our mental functions will show signs of discoordination" (p. 419). It is possible that the examiner's predominant focus on one aspect of the patient's behavior, namely, his Rorschach performance, was experienced as disintegrative, as inducing a mild form of fragmentation. The presence of this vulnerability raises etiological questions which we will discuss later. The preceding issues seem to be embedded in an obsessive character style, inferred from the presence of reaction formation against hostility [space location combined with benign imagery (Schafer, 1954) and the concern with art-historical detail]. A later comment ("You told me to imagine . . .") raises a question of protectiveness or suspiciousness in reaction to the feeling inquiry in which the patient is asked to reveal himself more deeply. Looking at the response in terms of what it conveys about the patient's selfobject experiences, we can hypothesize that this degree of guarded exhibitionism may have grown out of difficulty with a mirroring selfobject. (It must be mentioned that the patients' failure to perceive the near-popular response of two interacting figures highlights the exhibitionistic quality of his response.) The percept may express a wish to bask in the warm light of a radiant smile. Significantly, that the image is associated with grandmother raises the possibility that she was an important source of mirroring. Here the word *figment* suggests an illusory quality to his experience of mirroring. Perhaps an obsessive and guarded character style developed to protect the young child from experiencing an unempathic response to the spontaneous expression of his feelings. This man is likely to bring his unmet needs for mirroring into new relationships and, in treatment, to establish a mirroring transference. He may use his obsessive style and guardedness to avoid being hurt by the therapist, whom he will expect to provide yet another dull smile.

Card VII. Free Association: Don't know. I can see the shape of—a cartoonish figure of an alien being, what do you call them? From outer space. Looks like he's in a suit. A protective suit. Don't mean the outside, the inside if you look at it a certain way. (A protective suit?) I think an alien being landing in new territory would want a suit for protection. (Suit?) The high shoulder. Feeling inquiry: Unknown. You see them on TV. An unanswered feeling.

Here the patient is more overtly describing his feelings of being so different and so apart from others that there seems to be little basis for mutual acceptance or understanding. The patient feels alone in an inimical environment from which he must remain protected. As with the previous response, the location again utilizes space, indicative of significant negativity or hostility associated with these issues. We would speculate that the patient's painful view of himself as different or alien stems from a serious maternal empathic failure leaving him perpetually angry and fearful of letting others really know him. In new relationships (new territory) he would certainly wear his protective suit. In conjunction with his response to Card II we can begin to see this patient as an individual who may have felt chronically unresponded to and has developed a variety of ways of avoiding that painful kind of experience. He avoids mutual interaction, is suspicious, and puts on a front, both to mislead others and to protect his vulnerable and genuine self. The tendency of adopting an angry oppositional stance reflects pain from the old hurt and the attempt to keep others at a safe distance.

PSYCHOPATHOLOGY AND SYMPTOMATOLOGY

Following Kohut and Wolf (1978), we will now describe some of the Rorschach manifestations associated with certain syndromes of self-pathology. As noted by Kohut and Wolf, these are not to be regarded as truly discreet syndromes but as overlapping clusters of experience.

The Understimulated Self

On the Rorschach, as in other clinical settings, expression of the understimulated self takes two major forms: (1) massive attempts to seek stimulation and (2) an empty depression that lies beneath this frantic search and comes to the fore when it fails. The sought-for stimulation may be directly expressed in imagery depicting a high level of sensory input—carnivals, brilliantly vivid landscapes, performances, etc.—but the imagery may also deal with the search itself: "A rocket getting refueled so it can blast off" or "A top that's tilting forward and needs rewinding." These concerns can be even more directly expressed, as in the following: "Here's a person in the middle and these two figures on the sides are looking away from it like they don't even notice that guy in the middle." The same problem can be inferred when libidinal drive material is overtly expressed in the activity of figures or when content focuses on isolated body parts or functions involving the drives.

The understimulated self may be reflected by the presence of various formal scores as well as by imagery. In the use of color, weaker form dominance (CF) is often present (as are comments about color) and in this context indicates a perceptual approach geared to intensify sensory input. Likewise, responses with multiple determinants, whether or not they are form dominant, also point to a perceptual-cognitive strategy seeking to maximize input. In the same way, though to a more pathological extent, responses that are elaborated with inappropriate affect or detail highlight the need to see the world as vivid and stimulating.

More familiar are instances in which the understimulated self has been unable to mask its core of empty depression. Depressive imagery may be predominant or may be interspersed with attempts to ward off depression. [For an ego psychological view of similar material see Schafer's (1954) description of unstable hypomanic denial.] Significantly, the type of depression under consideration is often depicted through imagery dealing with barrenness and desolation rather than with the themes of guilt or punishment.

Many patients of this sort reveal significant depressive and paranoid pathology in their responses to achromatic cards, which provide less sensory input. By contrast, the stimulation of color helps these individuals to feel more alive and to cope with the Rorschach more effectively. Where understimulation is the issue, one will regularly observe extreme sensitivity to fluctuations in the degree of external stimulation, with increases associated with less dysphoria. This contrasts with the overstimulated self, who is equally sensitive to stimulation but who reacts oppositely, revealing more pathology when stimulation becomes excessive.

Given the limits of standard administration, the examiner testing individuals with core issues of understimulation is likely to feel particularly withholding, embarrassed, or awkward, similar to an adult who feels uncomfortable playing with a child and so insists on a "more mature" way of relating. In their interactions with the examiner these individuals may initially seem naive or childlike in their readily apparent expectation of greater responsiveness from the examiner and their evident appeals when this is not forthcoming. Here the underlying aim is to ward off feelings of inner deadness associated with an unresponsive selfobject. The same aim often prompts the subject to sexualize the testing situation through seductiveness or by playing on the examiner's voyeuristic impulses.

In contrast to some of the following syndromes, in which the examiner will feel a pull for a more differentiated type of response (e.g., archaic mirroring or calming), these patients crave stimulation of any sort and tend to provoke particularly strong and varied affects. That one senses these needs to be insatiable (the emptiness is like a bottomless pit) helps explain why testing such patients can be so unusually draining.

The Overstimulated Self

The overstimulated self reflects two kinds of difficulties with selfobjects, in both of which the self feels inappropriately required to function as a selfobject to others. In distinct but often concurrent ways, the self feels drawn into the task of maintaining the delicate narcissistic equilibrium of its selfobjects. One set of difficulties involves the experience of feeling that a selfobject has selectively responded to the self's exhibitionistic behavior, focusing excessively on accomplishments or achievements in isolation from the larger self. The second revolves around the selfobject's excessive needs for self-display and admiration. As children, patients experiencing this sort of difficulty had often felt that they were viewed as extensions of their parents; to these children fell the job of maintaining their parents' shaky self-esteem.

In the object relations of overstimulated individuals several general themes are often expressed throughout the Rorschach. These patients tend to feel perpetually disappointed; even the most enthusiastic reactions of others are experienced as faint praise in comparison with their archaic grandiose fantasies. The considerable tensions between these fantasies and reality leads to shyness, inhibition, and depression. In addition, because the achievements of the self were responded to in isolation, accomplishments tend to remain unintegrated with developing self-representations. These themes are highlighted in the following kinds of responses: *Card V.* It looks like a dancer in a fantastic costume. It's almost like she's hidden behind the costume. *Card VIII.* A sad-looking circus clown. (Feeling inquiry.) I bet the audience thinks he's great, but that isn't enough.

Overstimulation by an overly exhibitionistic selfobject leaves the self feeling extreme ambivalence about its own needs to merge with an archaic idealized object. Because ideals tend to remain external such a merger is sought; it is feared and avoided because of the discomfort aroused when the self feels used by a demanding selfobject. On the Rorschach this dilemma can be directly expressed, as on Card VI ("It looks like a Sun God, but the blackness gives it a demonic feeling, too"). The same problem may also be inferred when an idealized percept is followed by one suggesting the need for distance. For example, on Card

VII a patient responded "Two beautiful statues," only to follow this with "An aerial photograph of a lake."

Both aspects of the overstimulated self contribute to the fact that objects and selfobjects on the Rorschach are often described as having part-functions revolving around either the object's capacity to achieve greatness or to respond to the patient's sense of greatness. Objects tend to be articulated with regard to function and role (e.g., dancer or gladiator), but with relatively spare articulation of such dimensions as appearance and motive. Often objects are of a sort that is admired or that actively displays a talent, as in the dancer and gladiator examples.

Grandiose statements as to the individual's ability to provide original Rorschach responses are common, as is the unconscious expectation of approbation from the examiner. Sometimes patients struggling with conflicts related to the overstimulated self feel disappointed in the examiner's lack of manifest approval of their responses and become reactively deprecating in remarks toward the examiner.

Formal scores often reflect high levels of ambition and implicitly grandiose expectations of the self, and selfobjects with little capacity for the delay of impulses necessary for the achievement of long-term goals. The number of wholes (W) is often quite high relative to the number of human movement (M) responses, suggesting that ambition may outstrip intellectual capacities to achieve goals. The number of Rorschach responses is high but the quality and originality of these responses may be quite suspect (often repetition is evident), again reflecting the need for self-display rather than enjoyment in thinking, problem solving, and creative efforts per se. The dysphoria associated with grandiose strivings may be expressed through the use of achromatic color (used simply as a determinant and not necessarily as a stimulus for excessive affective embellishment) in conjunction with idealized objects.

The Fragmenting Self

The fragmenting self reflects conditions of narcissistic disequilibrium secondary to the failure of selfobjects to provide integrating responses or responses to the whole self rather than to the selective parts that gratify the narcissistic needs of the selfobject. Within the clinical context, as well as on the Rorschach, this may be a chronic or an intermittently appearing self state. Rorschach imagery provided by patients with these concerns is often laden with themes of uncertainty about the integrity of objects, concealment of parts of objects, and hypochondriacal preoccupations. Experiences of the self as fragmenting are reflected in images that are broken, coming apart, or disintegrating—"a broken vase" or "pieces of a puzzle, all scattered and in disarray." Sometimes such images reveal experiences of imminent fragmentation immediately reactive to fluctuations in self-esteem incurred by the nature of the examiner-selfobject's responsiveness. Use of verb tenses is often telling with regard to how imminent this fragmentation is felt to be. For example, in contrast with "A melted candle," the Rorschach response "A candle melting" reveals a more acute and current sense of an object (possibly phallic in nature) dwindling or disappearing; the former response may be more indicative of a past experience of such loss.

It is important here to examine to what extent thought disorder is present in Rorschach imagery that reflects an experience of fragmentation. For example, confabulatory responses such as "It's a person blowing into pieces before my eyes" suggests a more primary form of fragmentation associated with ongoing thought disorder and psychotic process. Imagery indicative of the propensity for fragmentation is also expressed through somatic preoccupations. Percepts are often of the human-part rather than the human-whole, reflecting integrative failure. Here one frequently finds percepts overtly laden with concerns about the intactness or strength of the skeletal anatomy.

The fragmenting self is manifest in both the location and the determinant categories of formal scoring. Integrative efforts involving location are often minimal and passively sought. Whole responses occur less often with patients struggling with a fragmenting self, and these whole responses frequently involve vague wholes such as "clouds" and "pillows." Responses involving the integration of several details into a complex interrelated aggregate are extremely rare. Such patients often express whole responses which selectively omit details that would require greater cognitive ambition and combinatory efforts. Their responses, in contrast to those of the understimulated self, often involve single determinants, with multiple determinants rather rare. Color dominance (CF) is often present, but in contrast to the understimulated self, which seeks to actively intensify sensory input through the CF response, the fragmenting self more passively experiences emotion and environmental stimulation.

A major caveat regarding manifestations of the fragmenting self is that the extent to which these "signs" occur in the context of thought disorder and extensive associative or affective elaboration must always be determined. Rorschach protocols reflective of difficulty related to the fragmenting self may appear in the context of disturbances in thought that are only minimal.

The Overburdened Self

As described by Kohut and Wolf (1978), the overburdened self reflects an insufficient opportunity to merge with an omnipotent, soothing selfobject. Rather than providing calming, the experience of turning to their selfobjects subjectively resulted in the intensification of dysphoric affect: "The result of this specific empathic failure from the side of the self-object is the absence of the self-soothing capacity that protects the normal individual from being traumatized by the spreading of his emotions, especially by the spreading of anxiety" (p. 420).

The object relations of such individuals include schizoid and paranoid trends pointing to the danger of exposing the self to situations that will threaten its capacity to modulate affect. The fear of losing emotional control colors how the overburdened self perceives involvement and underlies characteristics of guarded aloofness and obsessional preoccupations with control. When these character defenses falter, one sees increasing paranoid trends, struggles for control, and mounting anxiety and depression together with the angry search for calming.

Schafer (1954) offers an excellent description of how suspiciousness and guardedness as well as control issues are manifested on the Rorschach. In addition to evidence of obsessional defenses (isolation, rationalization, intellectualization, etc.) and projection, one also sees imagery more directly expressive of the overburdened self and the theme of "unshared emotionality": *Card VIII.* A volcano on the inside but it's frozen over on the top where no one could guess what's inside. *Card IX.* These two are trying to keep this fire from spreading through this forest. Looks as if it's too big for both of them. *Card VII.* It's a face—childlike—but that hairdo is trying to make it look older than it is.

The configuration of formal scores associated with the overburdened self again parallels some of Schafer's observations about paranoid and obsessional symptomatology. Complex whole responses are frequent, indicating the striving for control. Small detail locations may also be present and point both to guardedness and to the fear of excessive involvement. The percentage of exclusively form responses (F%) tends to be high, as does the frequency of form dominant determinants. Color responses are few. Human movement responses are generally present, in this context attesting to the need to turn inward and to live in fantasy in lieu of relating to others.

In relating to the examiner the overburdened self tries to maintain a quiet detachment, as if to say, "You can't help me so who needs you?" When character defenses are less extreme (or acutely unstable), involvement with the examiner increases. It becomes important to the patient if the examiner can see various responses. Likewise the patient may wonder how the examiner remains so calm and may actually try to test the examiner's capacity to modulate affect by occasionally presenting a "shocking" response. The examiner's countertransference with patients of this sort is telling. Despite revealing imagery, the testing will feel dry, mechanical, and more businesslike than usual. At the same time, one will have a strong feeling that such patients have seen and felt a good deal more than they are willing to share.

We have explored some of the applications of self psychology to clinical analysis of the Rorschach. It has not been our intention to be definitive but rather to offer an attempt at integrating an important new theoretical development with projective testing. Many issues remain unexplored, including a more precise articulation of the relationship between self pathology and more traditional diagnosis, the need for a more differentiated approach to the question of levels of self pathology, and the psychodiagnostic utility of the concept of a bipolar self. Also intriguing is the possibility of bringing a self psychological perspective to the interpretation of other widely used psychological tests, such as the Wechsler Adult Intelligence Scale and the Thematic Apperception Test. At this juncture, however, our hope is to stimulate interest in what we consider an enriching and clinically useful dimension of Rorschach interpretation.

REFERENCES

Arnow, D., & Cooper, S. (1984), The borderline patient's regression on the Rorschach test: An object relations interpretation. *Bull. Menn. Clin.*, 48:25–36.
Aronow, E., & Reznikoff, M. (1976), *Rorschach Content Interpretation.* New York: Grune & Stratton.
Buie, D. H., Jr., & Adler, G. (1982), Definitive treatment of the borderline personality. *Internat. J. Psychoanal. Psychother.*, 10:40–79.
Cooper, S., & Arnow, D. (1986), An object relations view of the borderline defenses. In: *Assessing Object Relations Phenomena*, ed. M. Kissen. New York: International Universities Press, pp. 143–171.

Holt, R. R. (1977), Method for assessing primary process manifestations and their control on the Rorschach. In: *Rorschach Psychology*, ed. M. Rickers-Ovsiankina. New York: Krieger, pp.375–420.

Kohut, H. (1977), *The Restoration of the Self.* New York: International Universities Press.

——— Wolf, E. S. (1978), The disorders of the self and their treatment: An outline. *Internat. J. Psycho-Anal.*, 59:413–425.

Lerner, P., & Lerner, H. (1980), Rorschach assessment of primitive defenses in borderline personality structure. In: *Borderline Phenomena and the Rorschach Test*, ed. J. Kwawer, H. Lerner, P. Lerner, & A. Sugarman. New York: International Universities Press. pp. 257–274.

Schafer, R. (1954), *Psychoanalytic Interpretation in Rorschach Testing.* New York: Grune & Stratton.

Part II
Clinical Concepts

Chapter 3

Rorschach Measures of Depression, the False Self, and Projective Identification in Patients with Narcissistic Personality Disorders

Paul M. Lerner, Ed.D.

Psychoanalytic theory, as Easer (1974) has noted, has never been a static body of knowledge. From an early concern with identifying the instincts and their vicissitudes during development, and a later focus on delineating the characteristics, functions, and synthesis of the ego, emphasis is now shifting to an interest in early object relations and their impact on the nature and cohesion of the self and the quality of later object relations. With this shift in emphasis new models of personality formation and psychopathology have emerged. Whereas earlier models were derived from theories of drive and the interplay of impulse and defense, these newer models issue from theories of structure and structure formation in psychic development. These theories start from the notion that development involves the growth and differentiation of psychological functions that crystallize into more stable structures. Although psychic conflict can occur among the various structures and can lead to psychopathology, as the earlier views maintained, the structures can themselves be pathological as a result of incomplete or arrested development.

With the emergence of these newer conceptual models has come a renewed and informed interest in more primitive (i.e., developmentally earlier), preoedipal conditions, including narcissistic disturbances.

In "On Narcissism" Freud (1914) laid the conceptual foundation for further explorations of the concept of narcissism. There he defined secondary narcissism as a withdrawal of libido from the outer world and its redirection onto the ego,[1] designated the ego ideal as the "heir" or adult version of infantile narcissism, recognized the intimate relationship between self-esteem and narcissistic libido, and identified a particular type of object choice and object relation to be referred to as narcissistic on the basis of the quality of need for the object and the psychic function served by the object. Authors subsequent to Freud have replaced "ego" with "self" and elaborated and refined the concept of self (Hartmann, 1950; Jacobson, 1964; Kohut, 1971; Lichtenberg, 1975); dispensed with the concept of libido (Stolorow, 1975); attempted to explicate the relation among narcissism, ego ideal, and self-esteem (Jacobson, 1964; Kohut, 1971); and sought to detail the complex connection between narcissism and object relations (Jacobson, 1964; Modell, 1968; Schafer, 1968; Kohut, 1971; Kernberg, 1975).

Despite recent major breakthroughs in the understanding and treatment of narcissistic patients, historically the field has been beset by a lack of agreement as to what constitutes a "narcissistic patient."

Kernberg (1975), for example, is explicit in reserving the designation for those patients "in whom the main problem appears to be the disturbance of their self-regard in connection with specific disturbances in their object relationships . . ." (p. 227). Viewing most narcissistic patients as a subvariant of the borderline level of personality organization, he characterizes such patients as manifesting a heightened degree of self-absorption, an inordinate need to be loved and admired, and an overinflated sense of themselves amid a desperate desire for adoration. He further notes that their emotional life is shallow, they exhibit little empathy for the needs and feelings of others, and unless their self-regard is being nourished they feel restless and bored. Beneath a veneer of charm and a tendency to either idealize or depreciate the other, Kernberg sees such individuals as cold, arrogant, ruthless, and exploitive.

Kohut (1971) has identified a certain symptom complex as characteristic of the narcissistic patient (i.e., lack of enthusiasm and zest, perverse activity, subjective feelings of deadness). However, he views this cluster of symptoms as insufficient for establishing a differential diagnosis; instead he uses the concept of the "cohesive self." For Kohut

---

[1]This formulation served as the basis for the later distinction he was to make between mourning and melancholia (Freud, 1917).

the instability or regressive potential of this psychic structure constitutes the crucial diagnostic sign of a narcissistic personality disorder. He points out that in treating a neurotic patient the undermining of the defensive narcissistic position will result in the emergence of oedipal conflicts. By contrast, the same type of intervention with a narcissistic patient will prompt a massive regression involving the breakup of the cohesive self. In addition Kohut has identified and described several atypical transference patterns which unfold in the treatment of patients with narcissistic disturbances. Referred to in general as "selfobject" transferences, specific subtypes include the mirroring transference and the idealizing transference.

Because Kernberg builds his theories around the idea of a disturbance in object relations and Kohut builds his around that of a disturbance in the cohesive self, the narcissistic patients they describe seem significantly different. (That Kernberg observed hospitalized patients while Kohut observed outpatients is a factor also contributing to this impression.) Kernberg, as noted previously, sees the narcissistic patient as organized at a borderline level. Kohut, by contrast, places the narcissistic patient closer to the neurotic end of the psychopathological continuum and clearly distinguishes between narcissistic patients and borderlines; he conceives of the borderline as having a basically psychotic makeup. The patients to be described in this chapter approximate more closely to Kohut's characterization of narcissistic disturbances.

Another vexing question involves the narcissistic patient's capacity to experience genuine feelings of loss for another. Kernberg (1975) unequivocally posits that such patients are not capable of mourning the loss of others: narcissistic patients "are especially deficient in genuine feelings of sadness and mournful longing. . . . When abandoned or disappointed by other people they may show what on the surface looks like depression, but which on further examination emerges as anger and resentment, loaded with revengeful wishes, rather than real sadness for the loss of a person whom they appreciated" (p. 229). Based on a broader conceptualization of depression, Kohut (1977) has described a distinct depressive affect which he believes is particular to narcissistic patients. This "depletion depression" he characterizes as involving unbearable feelings of emptiness, deadness, and nonexistence, as well as a self-perception of weakness, helplessness, and vulnerability.

Kohut's description of depletion depression is reminiscent in several respects of Freud's discussion of melancholia (1917). Freud noted that although melancholia, like mourning, may occur in reaction to the loss of a loved object, at the same time it differed from mourning in that "one cannot see clearly what it is that has been lost. . . . That he knows *whom* he has lost but not *what* he has lost in him" (p. 245). In a similar vein Freud observed that "in mourning it is the world which has become poor and empty; in melancholia it is the ego itself" (p. 241).[2]

Apart from disagreements regarding the narcissistic patient's capacity for experiencing depressive affect, there is consensus that such patients are especially vulnerable to lowered feelings of self-esteem. Reich (1960) has pointed out that because of the archaic nature of their ego ideal, narcissistic patients tend to rapidly vacillate between a grandiose self-image and bouts of low self-esteem. Similar observations have been reported by Kohut (1971), Easer (1974), and Kernberg (1975).

Using Freud's distinction between mourning and melancholia, Reich's contributions regarding self-esteem, and Kohut's description of "depletion depression" and conceptualizations regarding the role of grandiosity, in the next section I will specify ways in which the depressive affect of narcissistic patients is manifest in the Rorschach testing situation. In later sections I will discuss Rorschach indices reflective of two particular defensive operations—the false self and projective identification.

DEPRESSION

In assessing depressive affect in narcissistic patients the examiner is confronted with several challenges. Not only must it be established that the individual being assessed falls within the narcissistic range of character pathology; in addition the tester must be alert to the distinctive defenses of the narcissistic patient.

Tyson (1983) has identified three dimensions of narcissism—self-constancy, omnipotence, and self-esteem. These dimensions will serve as a framework for presenting clinical considerations regarding the assessment of depression and attendant defensive maneuvers.

Self-constancy. This is a complicated concept that concerns the continuity of the sense of identity over time. It requires the ability to maintain self-intactness in interaction with one's objects as well as the capacity to sustain an image of one's self that integrates different affectively toned "good" and "bad" self-representations. The attainment of self-constancy serves as an inner support nourishing the child's

---

[2]Freud attempted, unsuccessfully, to apply the concept of narcissistic object choice to melancholia; however, more recent findings confirm such a relationship (Lerner, 1984).

safety, autonomy, and mastery, just as does the constant representation of the mother and others.

Mayman (1967, 1977) has identified aspects of the human movement response that distinguish individuals who are able to maintain self-other differentiation in interpersonal interactions from those who are not. According to Mayman, individuals who are able to enter into object relations without a dissolving of self-other boundaries offer M responses in which (1) there is a broad and complex array of images of others; (2) the response takes into account realistic aspects of the blots themselves—that is, there is objectivity; and (3) from the description of the percept it is clear that the subject is talking about someone else. By contrast, individuals who are unable to maintain self-other differences, who tend to blur and obliterate boundaries, offer M responses in which (1) the response is reported with undue vividness and conviction; (2) the action ascribed and the attributes provided are largely fabulized rather than inherent to the percept itself; (3) there is intense absorption and involvement in the behavior of the perceived figures; and (4) the subject seems to infuse himself into the figure he is describing, vicariously sharing in the other's experience. In essence, implicit in Mayman's indices is the assumption that the nature of the relationship between subjects and their M responses, in terms of such dimensions as range, objectivity, and distance, reflects the quality of relationship they establish with their objects.

Patients who are unable to maintain self-intactness in their interactions with others, whose self/other boundaries are precarious, and whose sense of continuity is easily disrupted, are especially vulnerable to feelings of emptiness. For Freud (1917), according to Levy (1984), "the path from object loss to ego disturbance is facilitated by the initial narcissistic nature of the object choice. In this regard, to the extent the lost object represents a part of the self or enhances certain self-representations, loss of such an object results psychologically in loss of part of the self, leading to feelings of emptiness" (p. 392).

For other authors, self-intactness or sense of continuity is viewed as background self-feelings, which, when disturbed, result in the subjective sense of emptiness. Kohut (1977), for example, relates emptiness to disturbances of the self, especially the failure of selfobjects to nourish and sustain primitive self structures including the archaic grandiose self and ideal parental images. Such failures, Kohut insists, lead to fragmentation of the self together with feelings of "empty depression, i.e., the world of unmirrored ambitions, the world devoid of ideals" (Kohut, 1977, p. 243).

Emptiness, as Levy (1984) noted, involves a painful sense of an inner impoverishment of feelings. "There is a sense of deadness or absence of inner feelings, fantasies, and wishes, as well as a lack of responsiveness to external stimuli or the experience of only mechanical responsiveness. Convictions, enthusiasms, and relatedness to others all seem lost and replaced by feelings of deadness, boredom and superficiality" (p. 388).

The loss of enthusiasm, relatedness, and interest described by Levy has also been observed by Schachtel (1966), who has attempted to translate such characteristics into test-related concepts. Schachtel has noted that emptiness, like boredom, can interfere with one's firmness of perceptual hold in the Rorschach testing situation. Specifically, he points out that emptiness, with its accompanying loss of interest, prevents "the type of perceptual hold which derives from turning to the object fully and with receptive openness... the richness, vividness and full presence of the object are lost" (p. 107).

The weak perceptual hold noted by Schachtel finds expression in formal as well as content aspects of a Rorschach record. In general, patients experiencing feelings of emptiness provide enfeebled records in which there is a sparseness of responses. A few dimensions (i.e., color, shading, movement, etc.) are used in fashioning a response, but even when such properties are employed they are typically devoid of vividness and impact. Indeed, one's overall sense of the protocol is of its muteness, drabness, lack of vitality, and meaninglessness. Most responses are form-determined and the quality of form level is typically ordinary or vague (Mayman, 1967). Such patients seem lacking in energy and availability of inner resources to go beyond the commonplace or to enrich a percept to the point that it comes alive and makes an impression on the examiner. An attunement to striking white areas (space response) is commonly found in these protocols. When these space areas are perceived it points to the subject's sensitivity to the theme of hollowness. The empty patient is reality-bound, yet the contents that are perceived typically have a quality of emptiness and deadness. Thus, throughout the test record are found such percepts as skeletons, deserts, faceless creatures, and dead trees.

Omnipotence and self-esteem. These are the second and third dimensions of narcissism specified by Tyson. Patients who present with omnipotence or grandiosity, and use this grandiosity to both maintain self-coherence and to ward off chronic feelings of low self-esteem and low self-regard, typically enter testing with a compelling need to be treated as special, a craving to be admired, and an alienating sense of entitlement. As a consequence of these needs, such patients continuously assault the structure of the testing procedure. Such routine mechanics as the setting up of appointments, adherence to session times, and ways of administering the tests quickly become complicated issues of contention. In reaction, the examiner feels tempted, even pressured, to depart from standard testing method and to accord the patient "special" treatment. In addition to this unrelenting pressure on the examiner, the grandiosity of such patients becomes evident also in Rorschach responses. Overall, their test responses are not offered with the intent of conveying meaning or sharing an experience. Rather, their responses are prompted by the desire to impress the examiner as well as to create a product they feel will do justice to their inflated sense of self. Their Rorschach protocols, therefore, are often filled with over-elaborate, fantasy-drenched, pretentious productions, which, when the embellishments are stripped away, prove to be quite conventional responses. For example, when a patient on Card V created an elaborate Count Dracula scene and then was asked what precisely it was she saw, she responded, "A black bat." One also sees in their protocols such self-aggrandizing percepts as kings, goddesses, supermen, temples, insignias, crests, and crowns. By contrast, patients with undefended low self-esteem and low self-regard view the Rorschach as a laborious, onerous task in which nothing they produce will be good enough. Pervading their responses are themes of deficiency, damage, and inadequacy. Rotted tree stumps, withered plants, spoiled food, diseased lungs, flimsy wings, and broken pieces of glass are characteristic responses, reflective of their inner experience of some vital lack.

FALSE SELF

Patients whose sense of self lacks coherence, stability, and harmony typically defend against this vulnerability and its accompanying affects by constructing a false self. Winnicott (1961) conceived of the false self as serving defensive needs to hide and protect the true self by means of compliance with external demands. The origins of the false self are found in the infant's seduction into a compliant relationship with a nonempathic mother. When a mother substitutes something of herself for the infant's spontaneous gestures (i.e., her anxieties over separation in response to the infant's need to search and explore), the infant experiences traumatic disruptions of his developing sense of self. When such impingements are a core feature of the mother-child relationship, the infant will attempt to defend himself by developing a second, reactive personality organization—the false self. The false self vigilantly monitors and adapts to the conscious and unconscious needs of the mother and in so doing provides a protective exterior behind which the true self is afforded the privacy it requires to maintain its integrity. The false self, as such, thus becomes a core feature of the personality organization and functions as a caretaker, managing life so that an inner self might not experience the threat of annihilation resulting from excessive pressure on it to develop according to another's needs.

Basic to the false self, then, is hyperalertness and heightened sensitivity to the expectations and anticipations of others, with a concomitant tendency to mold one's own feelings, behaviors, and attitudes accordingly. I have found a specific test-taking attitude; two formal Rorschach scores—the (c) score and the color-arbitrary score (Carb); and specific contents (i.e., masks, costumes, etc.), especially sensitive to these aspects.

Patients who present with a false self often begin testing under a cloak of great vigilance, with a subtle readiness to be distrustful. They are, as it were, there, but with one foot out the door. Quickly, all aspects of the examiner, including attire, office furnishings, tone of voice, and testing directions, come under careful scrutiny. For example, if on the Rorschach one inquires after each card, then after the first such series of inquiries such patients often attune to what is being asked for, supply such information during free association, and render the examiner's role unnecessary. They move toward self-sufficiency and virtually begin testing themselves. If the examiner recalls a response or incident mentioned in a previous session or responds in a particularly empathic manner, then the patient feels together and regards the examiner as an ally. By contrast, let the examiner cancel a session or respond with a trace of irritation, then the patient reacts with hurt or pain, emotionally withdraws, and experiences the examiner as hostile, distant, and uncaring. The examiner's experience, paradoxically, is that of being viewed under a microscope. Not only is every movement closely monitored, but comments are carefully scrutinized and regarded as evidence to be judged and weighed before the relationship is allowed to deepen and possibly move toward mutuality. This stance quite understandably evokes a marked countervigilance and hypercaution on the part of the examiner. Realizing that certain comments, intended to be helpful or informative, might be met with an overreaction and taken as an attack, the examiner becomes less spontaneous, less relaxed, and more inhibited.

As noted above, I have found two formal Rorschach scores especially sensitive to false self features. One, the (c) score, is applied to responses that are delineated and determined by variations in shading. Because these variations are subtle and not striking, to achieve a (c) response subjects must seek out, discover, and attune to finer nuances as well as feel their way into something that is not readily apparent. To do this requires perceptual sensitivity in addition to a searching, articulating, and penetrating type of activity. Schachtel (1966) has described this mode in terms of a perceptual attitude "of a stretching out of feelers in order to explore nuances" (p. 251). While such an attitude of heightened sensitivity and penetrating activity can reflect and underlie an adaptive capacity for achieving highly differentiated responses, attuning to subtleties of feelings, and empathizing with the nuances of another's experience, it can also go awry. We are all familiar with the person who has his antennae out, as it were, to feel out an anticipated unfriendly environment, hostile and cold. In such an individual I have observed a constant state of hypervigilance, heightened sensitivity, excessive vulnerability, and painful thin-skinnedness, and each of these characteristics is consistent with aspects of the false self.

A second formal score reflective of false self is the color arbitrary score (Carb). This score is reserved for responses in which the use of color is obviously incompatible with the content (blue monkeys, pink beavers, etc.), but the subject nonetheless clings to its arbitrary inclusion. While several authors (Rapaport, Gill, and Schafer, 1945; Schachtel, 1966) have discussed the response as indicative of difficulties in integrating affects into one's mental life, Schachtel has also highlighted the role of compliance. He notes that one gets "the impression that the testee had felt it incumbent on him to include the color in his response even though no natural combination occurred. . . . The color is not experienced as particularly striking or stimulating but it is noticed and then endowed by the testee with the same exaggerated demand quality that he attributes to the whole test situation" (p. 181). While I agree with Schachtel's view regarding the color arbitrary score as reflective of compliance, there is yet another connection between this score and the false self, and this relates directly to Winnicott's notions regarding thinking.

For Winnicott, self-development and symbol formation are inextricably related. According to Winnicott, with the mother's repeated success in greeting the infant's spontaneous gestures, experience becomes imbued with realness and an inchoate capacity to use symbols begins. Here Winnicott envisions two possible lines of development. In the first, with good enough mothering and empathic responsiveness to spontaneous gestures, reality is introduced almost magically and does not clash with the infant's omnipotence. With a belief in reality, omnipotence can be gradually relinquished—"The true self has a spontaneity, and this has been joined up with the world's events" (Winnicott, 1960, p. 146). An illusion of omnipotent creating and controlling can be enjoyed and the illusory element can be gradually recognized through play and imagination. For Winnicott, then, the basis for the symbol is both the infant's spontaneity and the created and cathected external object. That is, symbol formation evolves from actions and sensations joining the infant and the mother. Conversely, when the infant's actions and sensations serve to separate rather than join subject and object, symbol formation is inhibited. In this second instance, which involves mothering that is *not* good enough, the mother's adaption to the infant's spontaneous gestures is deficient and symbol formation either fails to develop or, in Winnicott's terms, "becomes broken up." The infant not only is seduced into a false self compliance but in addition reacts to environmental demands passively, through imitation and with accompanying feelings of unreality. The passivity and the feelings of unreality observed by Winnicott are quite similar to what Rapaport has conceptualized as a loss of ego autonomy with a resultant enslavement to environmental stimuli. That is, for Rapaport, a maximizing distance from drive forces results in a corresponding dependence upon environmental forces. While Rapaport would conceive of this condition in terms of the ego and drive forces and Winnicott in terms of the self and inner experience, what both theorists appear to be describing is a state of affairs in which the development of selfhood has been critically interfered with and in which the individual is therefore unable to maintain distance from the environment and becomes excessively dependent upon it.

It is my belief that involved in the color arbitrary score is a loss of detachment and perspective. It is as if the subject, in fashioning such a response, has abandoned or suspended a more objective, critical, judgmental attitude. For individuals in which there is a loss of optimal perspective, life events are not critically examined or placed in context, but rather are seen and experienced only in terms of their most obvious and immediate qualities. The present dominates, and the significance of the past and of the future vanishes. In summary, involved in the color arbitrary score is compliance, cognitive passivity marked by a loss of detachment and perspective, and nagging feelings of unreality.

In addition to being evident in a test-taking attitude of hypervigilance, heightened sensitivity, and defensive self-sufficiency, as well as in two formal Rorschach scores, indications of false self formation appear also in the content of Rorschach responses. On a rational basis one would expect that individuals who are constantly alert to danger and peril, who are concerned with protection and privacy, who relate themselves to others in a compliant way, and who experience fleeting feelings of unreality and inauthenticity, would offer Rorschach imagery reflective of these experiential themes. Indeed, such themes do appear in the protocols of patients who present with a false self. In test records one finds content—masks, costumes, chameleons—emphasizing hiding, protection, and accommodation. Human or animal figures are also typically seen as performing or serving (clowns, trained seals, circus bears, waiters, etc.).

A single, thirty-two-year-old physician offered the following sequence of responses to Card V: "A bat . . . beautiful, billowing, and showing its splendor. Head looks erect and extended. Yet there is pain in the wings, they look racked and crumbled." This was immediately followed by: "It also reminds me of those dancing girls you see in Las Vegas with costumes on, head gear and little feet." While there are several meanings to be inferred from these responses, in keeping with the focus on the false self, I believe one can see the initial emphases on exhibitionism (showing its splendor, head looks erect) with an implicit request for mirroring and self-enhancement, the anticipation of not being responded to and this resulting in a loss of self-esteem and depressive affect (wings racked and crumbled), and then the appearance, for defense, of the false self (dancing girls with costumes). This same patient saw on Card VII "an ornate Chinese bowl with a couple of performing figurines." In this response one sees a kinesthesia related to performance in addition to the creation of an inanimate, lifeless, decorative figure.

PROJECTIVE IDENTIFICATION

Another defense I have commonly found in narcissistic patients who present with depressive affect and false self features is projective identification. The term was originally developed by Melanie Klein to describe a developmental and defensive process in which "parts of the self and internal objects are split off and projected into the external object, which then becomes possessed by, controlled and identified with the projected parts" (Segal, 1974, p. 27). Projective identification, according to Klein, has several aims. When directed toward an idealized object it wards off the danger of separation, whereas when directed toward a bad object it serves to gain control over the source of danger. Various aspects of the self may also be projected, again for any of several aims. For example, bad parts of the self may be projected to get rid of them as well as to attack and destroy the object. In like fashion, good parts of the self may be projected in order to prevent separation or to improve the external object; the latter Segal refers to as "a kind of primitive projective reparation" (pp. 27–28). Although projective identification is thought to originate in the paranoid-schizoid position and in relation to the mother's breast (a part object), it often persists and becomes intensified in the depressive position when the mother is perceived as a whole object.

While the concept has been discussed and enlarged upon by several authors (Fairbairn, 1944; Grotstein, 1981; Ogden, 1983), Bion (1956) extended the notion of projective identification in terms of the metaphor of container and contained. Underlying this metaphor is the image of an infant emptying its bad contents into the mother, who accepts the unwanted projection, contains it, and alters it in such a way as to permit its reintrojection by the infant. For Bion, "projective identification is an interpersonal process in which one finds oneself being manipulated so as to be playing a part, no matter how difficult to recognize, in somebody else's phantasy. In the interpersonal setting, the person projectively identifying engages in an unconscious fantasy of ejecting an unwanted or endangered aspect of himself and of depositing that part of himself in a controlled way" (Ogden, 1983, p. 232). Implicit in this description are several subprocesses including the presence of an unconscious fantasy, pressure on the other to experience himself and behave in a way congruent with the unconscious fantasy, the defensive aspect of ridding oneself of unwanted parts, and the unrelenting attempt to control the external object. Although not explicitly stated by Bion, it is my experience that also involved in projective identification is a particular nonverbal type of communication in which the projector is expressing parts of the self and of self-experience which cannot be communicated in any other way.

Concerned with the multiple meanings ascribed to the concept, and with the extent to which it has been confused with the more classical notion of projection, Meissner (1980) has argued for a more restrictive definition of projective identification. He would reserve the term to describe a psychotic mechanism through which parts of the self are projected into the object, to be experienced there as belonging to the object. Diffusion of ego boundaries and loss of self-object differentiation are stressed in Meissner's conceptualization. While I agree with Meissner's emphasis on self-object differentiation, I do not believe that projective identification is necessarily a psychotic process. Also, his restriction of the concept's meaning is purchased at the cost of its clinical richness and utility. I would suggest instead that there are various levels of projective identification, depending on the aim (defense, control, communication) and the degree to which self boundaries are blurred and diffused.

Building on Fairbairn's conceptualization of internal object relations (1944), Bion's notion of projective identification (1956), and Racker's discussion of transference and countertransference (1957), Ogden (1983) has attempted to apply the concept of projective identification to the issues of transference and countertransference. His discussion has important implications for the assessment of projective identification in the Rorschach situation. In line with Fairbairn's observations, Ogden suggests that transference and countertransference can be viewed from the perspective of the interpersonal externalization of an internal object relation. Transference, he points out, can take one of two forms, depending on which role in the internal object relation—self or self identified with the internal object—is assigned the other person in the externalizing process. In one instance, when the role assigned is that of the internal object (i.e., the self identified with the internal object), the patient experiences the other person as he had unconsciously experienced the internal object. Here countertransference involves the therapist's unconscious identification with that part of the patient identified with the internal object. Projective identification comes into play in terms of the interpersonal pressure on the therapist to engage in the identification and to experience self in a way congruent with the representation of the object in the internal object relation. Also involved in the projective identification, according to Ogden, is the unconscious fantasy of expelling part of oneself and entering the object in a controlling way. A twenty-eight-year-old female patient sought treatment precisely four years after her father's death. Most striking in treatment was her hypervigilance, heightened sensitivity, and excessive vulnerability. Aware and respectful of her thin-skinnedness, I found myself treating her from a distance in an overly cautious, at times inhibited way. Fearing a strong defensive reaction, I made few interpretations and rarely confronted her occasional lateness. Increasingly, the patient complained of my distance and cautiousness and began to experience me consciously much as she had experienced her father unconsciously—that is, as distant, remote, overcontrolled, and uninterested in her. Here the object component of her internal relation with her father was projected into me as her therapist, and I felt controlled by it.

The second form of transference is seen when the patient projects the self component of the internal object relation into the therapist, who is then experienced as the internal object once experienced the self. The countertransference in this instance consists of the therapist's identification with the self component of the patient's internal object relation. Here projective identification involves interpersonal pressure on the therapist to identify with the projected self and to comply with the fantasy by experiencing self just as the patient's self had experienced the internal object. A thirty-eight-year-old single female patient entered analysis following the termination of an intense, conflict-laden two-year relationship with a married man five years her junior. She progressively entered into an idealizing relationship with her analyst in which she regarded his interest in her, and his observations about her, as precious gifts that were to be rewarded with offerings of adoration and flattery. By contrast, when her analyst was silent or nonresponsive, she withdrew, became depressed, and contemplated terminating treatment. Tantalized by the patient's adoration, pained by her withdrawal, and frightened by her threats to leave, the analyst found himself becoming more active, more giving, and more dependent on the patient's praise. In time, both analyst and patient were able to understand this transaction in terms of the patient's early relationship with a depressed mother. More specifically, the patient was actively doing to her therapist what she had unconsciously experienced her mother as having done to her. That is, in excessively rewarding closeness and depressively withdrawing in reaction to separateness and autonomy, the patient's mother had created within the patient an addiction to adoration and praise.

Ogden concludes, and I agree, that projective identification is an inevitable aspect of the externalization of an internal object relation. Further, in the treatment relationship there is always a component in the therapist's countertransference that represents an induced identification with a part of the patient's ego that is enmeshed in a particular unconscious internal object relation. As such, involved in projective identification are the following subprocesses: the presence of an unconscious fantasy embedded in a significant internal object relation; interpersonal pressure on the other to identify with either the self component or the internal object component of the internal object relation and to experience self accordingly; the defensive aspect of expelling unwanted parts; the need to control the other; and a special form of nonverbal communication.

Attempts to assess projective identification by means of the Rorschach have appeared sparingly in the literature. Lerner and Lerner (1980), based on Kernberg's somewhat narrow definition of the mechanism as a process in which parts of the self are split off and projected into an external object so as to control it, used the following indices as reflective of projective identification: confabulatory responses involving human figures in which the form level is Fw— or F—, and human or human detail responses in which the location is Dr, the determinant is F(c), and the figure is described as either aggressive or as the object of aggression. These two scores were assumed to assess three subprocesses involved in projective identification: an externalization of parts of the self with a disregard to real characteristics of the external object; a capacity to blur boundaries between self and object; and a compelling need to control the object. Lerner and Lerner (1980) found that these Rorschach indices of projective identification appeared significantly more frequently in the test records of borderline patients as compared with those of neurotic and schizophrenic patients.

Cooper (1983) extended the work of Lerner and Lerner both conceptually and methodologically. Based on Kernberg (1975) as well as Klein's earlier writings (1949), he conceived of projective identification as involving the following three subprocesses: (1) fantasies of concretely putting a dangerous or endangered part of the self into another for the purpose of controlling or destroying the other; (2) fearful empathy with objects into whom aggressive aspects of the self have been projected; and (3) hyperalertness to external threat accompanied by expressions of primitive rage. Although Cooper adopted several of the Rorschach indices used by Lerner and Lerner, he did not restrict himself to exclusively human or quasi-human responses. Rather, he broadened his data base to include percepts such as animals, objects, and natural phenomena. In consequence, Cooper's scale includes a greater variety of test indices and tends to rely more heavily on content analysis. For example, animals or objects capable of putting dangerous substances into others (spiders, poisonous snakes, poisonous plants, etc.) are taken as indicators of the fantasy of placing an endangered part of the self into another for purposes of control and destruction. Similarly, responses that include a direct statement of identification with an aggressive figure (e.g., "An angry man—I'm angry too") are considered to indicate fearful empathy.

To assess concurrent validity, including the relative discriminatory power of particular defenses within each scale to differentiate various diagnostic groups, Lerner, Albert, and Walsh (1984) applied both the Lerner Defense Scale and Cooper's Rorschach Defense Scale to independently selected and diagnosed groups of neurotic, outpatient borderline, inpatient borderline, and schizophrenic patients. Overall, the Rorschach Defense Scale was found to be slightly more effective in distinguishing among diagnostic groups; however, the indices of projective identification failed to differentiate the groups to any statistically significant degree. By contrast, measures of projective identification on the Lerner scale occurred exclusively within the borderline groups and significantly distinguished them from both neurotics and schizophrenics but not from each other.

Levine (Chapter 4), employing a definition of projective identification more in keeping with the broadened one used here, has drawn attention to the examiner's countertransference reaction during the testing as a potential basis for inferring the presence of this defense. Mindful that more disturbed patients often provoke in the examiner intense feelings and fantasies, both aggressive and sexual, Levine has found it helpful to note her own thoughts, fantasies, and feelings as they arise during administration of the Rorschach. She observed that at times her own subjective reactions paralleled the nature of object relationships as expressed in the content of responses, whereas at other times it did not. With regard to the latter she notes, "Sometimes an emotional response which seemed discordant and contradictory to the patient's presentation and Rorschach responses has alerted me to an underlying emotional state of the patient." Levine contends, and I agree, that such countertransference reactions are especially helpful in enabling the examiner to understand and grasp preverbal communications.

A particular technique of Rorschach administration that Levine found useful in facilitating projective identificatory processes (thus allowing their closer observation) was the inquiry:

With some preoedipal patients the examiner's adherence to the objective, neutral questioning of responses, despite the patient's disparagement and sadistic criticism of both the test and the examiner, appears to provide a structured, safe, and containing environment for the patient's expression of destructive and poorly organized and controlled affects and impulses. . . . For these patients, the inquiry may facilitate a useful process of projective identification by which the patient is enabled to externalize unwanted and destructive aspects of the self into the examiner and the blot. . . .

As with other psychological processes, indications of projective identification on the Rorschach are to be found in the patient-examiner relationship, select formal scores, and specific thematic content.

Like Levine, I have found countertransference data to be an especially important source of information for inferring this defense. As an unsuspecting and at times unwilling partner in the projective identificatory process, the examiner may end up not only experiencing intense feelings and fantasies about the patient, but also being coerced or pressured into a role which seems to have little to do with the realistic aspects of the testing. For example, rapidly aroused and intense feelings of anger and confusion may provoke in the examiner a dread of testing the patient, whereas equally intense erotic feelings may stir highly charged sexual fantasies as well as a compelling desire to spend extra time with the patient. While such reactions may at times be consonant with the types of human interaction manifest in the content of responses, at other times they are not. What such subjective reactions tend to be consistent with are the patient's more spontaneous comments, actions, and gestures throughout the testing.

A fifty-two-year-old hospitalized patient, unmarried, was referred for testing to assist in determining her suitability for long-term individual treatment. A high school teacher, she was hospitalized following a highly serious suicide attempt. Although it was standard practice for all newly admitted patients to be tested, the staff seemed especially interested in her results, as she had evoked in them strong feelings of concern, sympathy, and compassion. Somewhat uncharacteristically, they seemed to overempathize with her sense of herself as a tragic victim of life's harshness. Quite rapidly, and in marked contrast with other staff, the psychological examiner found himself enraged with the patient. The patient missed the first testing session, claiming she was too upset and distraught to "face being tested." The staff colluded with the patient in her decision and in her feeling that the psychologist and his test were a source of danger and fear. The patient attended the next session and complied with the testing instructions in body, but with little spirit. Interspersed with her overly terse answers were snide, caustic remarks about the examiner's office, his attire, and the "juvenile" quality of his tests. Putting "blocks" and "puzzles" together made her feel like a first-grade schoolchild, and this she found humiliating. The second session involved administration of the TAT. After telling the barest of stories and complaining of the ambiguity of the pictures, the patient noticed a picture on the wall as she was leaving. She commented on its evocativeness, and proceeded to offer a detailed story about it that included various aspects asked for but not given with the TAT cards. Sensing the examiner's mounting fury, the patient, during the final session, provided a highly inhibited, constricted Rorschach in which the few responses offered were vague and banal. Following the evaluation, based on a sense of himself as impotent, helpless, and incompetent, the examiner felt murderous rage toward the patient. At a subsequent case conference it became clear that the patient had projected into the examiner a disowned part of her self, namely, that part of her that felt helpless, ineffective, and consequently enraged at her cold, distant, unfeeling, and impenetrable father.

With other patients, countertransference manifestations of projective identification are often more subtle and less dramatic. For instance, in the course of Rorschach administration the examiner might experience a sudden, intense, and unexpected emotional reaction to one particular percept. Levine offers the example of her own subjective reaction to a patient who on the first card saw a "crab": "During the inquiry, when I asked the patient what it was about the blot that made it look like a crab, I had the silent thought 'I would like to kill her.' No sooner did I have that thought than the patient blurted, 'Did I kill you?'"

Another subtle countertransference manifestation involves the examiner experiencing a particular affective state (depression, anger, elation, etc.) following a testing session and then, after retrospectively reviewing the session, being unable to locate the source of the feeling. In such instances one is led to conclude that the patient undetectably projected the feeling into the examiner, perhaps for the purposes of containment and communication. When I have discussed such emotional reactions with patients in later sessions, they inevitably verify the feeling; such interchanges often lead to a deepening of the testing relationship.

In addition to countertransference reactions evoked in the patient-examiner relationship, select formal scores may be used to assess several of the subprocesses involved in projective identification (Mayman, 1962).

Confabulatory responses involving human figures in which the form level is Fw— or F—. A confabulatory response is one in which a percept is overembellished with associative elaboration to the point that real properties of the blot are disregarded and replaced by fantasies and affects. Although the score has traditionally been regarded as a cardinal index of disturbed thinking (Rapaport, Gill, and Schafer, 1945), more recent authors (Athey, 1974; Blatt and Ritzler, 1974) have found the response to be indicative of regressed modes of object relations. More specifically, these authors have demonstrated that the quality of an individual's thoughts as organized on the Rorschach parallels the ways in which that person experiences and organizes object relations. For example, the tendency to lose the conceptual boundary between one idea and another is paralleled by a proclivity for losing the experiential boundary between self and other. Based on these latter conceptualizations, Lerner and Lerner (1980) used the confabulatory response involving figures to indicate the tendency to blur boundaries between self and other, and thus to permit placing disowned parts of the self into the other. In line with the theoretical stance being taken in this chapter, this score is considered as indicating more severe instances of projective identification, in which there is self-other blurring and the aim of the process is to control the other.

Human or human detail response in which the location is Dr, the determinant is F(c), and the figure is described as either aggressive or as the object of aggression. Involved in the (c) response is perceptual sensitivity coupled with a searching, penetrating, and articulating type of activity. Patients whose Rorschach records include this score present as hyperalert, heightenedly sensitive, thin-skinned, and excessively vulnerable. Lerner and Lerner (1980), cognizant of the defensive aspects of the hyperalertness and heightened sensitivity, included this score as an indicator of projective identification based on the assumption that the high level of control implicit in the response reflects an insistent need to control the perceived dangerous other. Cooper (1983) included this index in his manual as well; however, he conceived of the score as reflecting fearful empathy as well as a hypersensitivity to aggression in others. While I agree with both of these views, it is my experience that this response also reflects a tendency to rely heavily on preverbal communication. Patients who offer this response are especially attuned to the visual, gestural, and emotional aspects of others. Their relationships, in this respect, may be likened to the infant's early experience with the mother. Genetically, the perception of emotional tones and of tension by the young child precedes the learning of language and the understanding of spoken content (Schachtel, 1966). It develops from the infant's perception of comfort or discomfort with the mothering one, including an awareness of her moods and tensions. As development progresses, and with "good enough" mothering (Winnicott, 1960), attention to the obvious and to verbal content supersedes the need for perceiving finer visual and emotional nuances. In the absence of "good enough" mothering this transition is tenuous and incomplete.

In my clinical experience I have found that patients who offer the Dr, F(c), aggressive content score but do not offer confabulatory responses often engage in higher level forms of projective identification. While they do not blur self-other boundaries, they do see the environment as dangerous, defensively empathize with potential sources of danger, and rely heavily on preverbal modalities, such as putting parts of themselves (affects, fantasies, etc.) into others, as a way of communicating. For such patients, projecting parts of the self into another is also controlling, in that it serves to ward off threats of separation and abandonment.

A third dimension of the Rorschach from which one can infer projective identification is thematic content, specifically content involving human figures and their interaction.

Responses in which a human figure puts a substance or feeling into another human figure for the purpose of controlling, destroying, safeguarding, or repairing that figure. This score is an application of Klein's initial formulations regarding projective identification. As such it reflects the subprocesses of placing a disowned part of the self into another for the purpose of control, destruction, or reparation (i.e., warding off threats of separation). In his manual Cooper (1983) devised a similar index; however, he broadened it to include not just human figures but animals and objects as well. For Cooper, the response "These tarantulas are injecting their poison into the grass-hoppers" would exemplify this category.[3]

Human responses in which the subject is intensely absorbed in the behavior of the perceived figure, ascribes attributes and actions that are largely fabulized rather than inherent in the percept itself, and depicts with insistent regularity a narrow range of human interactions. Mayman (1967), using the assumption that such responses reflect a loss of objectivity, detachment, and perspective, suggested that patients who offer these responses have difficulty maintaining self-other differences in interpersonal interactions. While I agree with Mayman that these responses can reflect a tendency to blur self-other boundaries, I believe that such responses, with their insistent depiction of "a narrow range of interactions," also reflect the presence of select, highly charged, preemptory internal object relations which, when activated, as in treatment, result in a compelling need to pressure or coerce the other into experiencing and playing out a particular projected role.

SUMMARY

The increasing penetration of object relations theory and self psychology into classical psychoanalysis has opened a veritable goldmine of immensely rich clinical concepts whose translation into empirical, test-related terms is a challenge for the psychological examiner. In a series of papers (Lerner, 1983, 1984) I have described a subgroup of narcissistic patients who present with hypervigilance, heightened sensitivity, thin-skinnedness, and excessive vulnerability. In examining these patients more closely I have also found a particular type of depression marked by feelings of emptiness, a pervasive defensive structure built around a false self, and a strong tendency to rely on projective identification for defensive purposes as well as for communicating. Using the theoretical formulations of Kohut (1971), Winnicott (1961), and Ogden (1983) and the clinical test work of Mayman (1967), Lerner and

---

[3]In keeping with the theoretical and empirical work of Lerner and Lerner (1980) and in contrast with Cooper (1983), in this chapter I restrict indices to responses involving human figures. Lerner and Lerner found that defensive processes and object representational capacities were inextricably related. Hence, to equate patients who use such defenses and are able to internally represent objects with patients who are not is to make, in my view, unwarranted assumptions.

Lerner (1980), Cooper (1983), and Levine (Chapter 4), I have in this chapter attempted to identify Rorschach indices that allow one to assess the concepts of empty depression, false self, and projective identification.

REFERENCES

Athey, G. (1974), Schizophrenic thought organization, object relations and the Rorschach test. *Bull. Menn. Clin.*, 38:406–429.

Bion, W. (1956), Development of schizophrenic thought. In: *Second Thoughts*. New York: Aronson, 1967, pp. 36–42.

Blatt, S., & Ritzler, B. (1974), Thought disorder and boundary disturbances in psychosis. *J. Consult. & Clin. Psychol.*, 42:370–381.

Cooper, S. (1983), An object relations view of the borderline defenses: A Rorschach analysis. Unpublished manuscript.

Easer, R. (1974), Empathic inhibition and psychoanalytic technique. *Psychoanal. Quart.*, 43:557–580.

Fairbairn, W. (1944), Endopsychic structure considered in terms of object relationships. In: *An Object Relations Theory of the Personality*. New York: Basic Books, 1952, pp. 82–136.

Freud, S. (1914), On narcissism: An introduction. *Standard Edition*, 14:69–102. London: Hogarth Press, 1957.

————— (1917), Mourning and melancholia. *Standard Edition*, 14:243–258. London: Hogarth Press, 1957.

Grotstein, J. (1981), *Splitting and Projective Identification*. New York: Aronson.

Hartmann, H. (1950), Comments on the psychoanalytic theory of the ego. In: *Essays on Ego Psychology*. New York: International Universities Press, 1964, pp. 115–141.

Jacobson, E. (1964), *The Self and the Object World*. New York: International Universities Press.

Kernberg, O. (1975), *Borderline Conditions and Pathological Narcissism*. New York: Aronson.

Klein, M. (1949), *Contributions to Psychoanalysis*. London: Hogarth Press.

Kohut, H. (1971), *The Analysis of the Self*. New York: International Universities Press.

————— (1977), *The Restoration of the Self*. New York: International Universities Press.

Lerner, H., Albert, C., & Walsh, M. (1984), The Rorschach assessment of borderline defenses: A concurrent validity study. Unpublished manuscript.

————— Lerner, P. (1982), A comparative study of defensive structure in neurotic, borderline, and schizophrenic patients. *Psychoanal. & Contemp. Thought*, 5:77–115.

Lerner, P. (1983), Rorschach contributions to the psychoanalytic treatment of the vulnerable patient. Paper presented to the Society for Personality Assessment, San Diego, March 1983.

————— (1984), Rorschach indices of the false self concept. Paper presented to the Society for Personality Assessment, Tampa, Florida, March 1984.

————— Lerner, H. (1980), Rorschach assessment of primitive defenses in borderline personality structure. In: *Borderline Phenomena and the Rorschach Test*, ed. J. Kwawer, H. Lerner, P. Lerner, & A. Sugarman. New York: International Universities Press, pp. 257–274.

Levy, S. (1984), Psychoanalytic perspectives on emptiness. *J. Amer. Psychoanal. Assn.*, 32:387–404.

Lichtenberg, J. (1975), The development of the sense of self. *J. Amer. Psychoanal. Assn.*, 23:453–484.

Mayman, M. (1962), Rorschach Form Level Manual. Unpublished manuscript, Menninger Foundation.

———— (1967), Object representations and object relationships in Rorschach responses. *J. Proj. Tech. & Personal. Assess.*, 31:17–24.

———— (1977), A multi-dimensional view of the Rorschach movement response. In: *Rorschach Psychology*, ed. M. Rickers-Ovsiankina. Huntington, N.Y.: Krieger, pp. 229–250.

Meissner, W. (1980), A note on projective identification. *J. Amer. Psychoanal. Assn.*, 20:43–68.

Modell, A. (1968), *Object Love and Reality*. New York: International Universities Press.

Ogden, T. (1983), The concept of internal object relations. *Internat. J. Psycho-Anal.*, 64:227–243.

Racker, H. (1957), The meanings and uses of countertransference. *Psychoanal. Quart.*, 26:303–357.

Rapaport, D., Gill, M., & Schafer, R. (1945), *Diagnostic Psychological Testing*. Rev. ed. New York: International Universities Press, 1968.

Reich, A. (1960), Pathologic forms of self-esteem regulation. *Psychoanal. Study of the Child*, 15:215–232.

Schachtel, E. (1966), *Experimental Foundations of Rorschach's Test*. New York: Basic Books.

Schafer, R. (1968), *Aspects of Internalization*. New York: International Universities Press.

Segal, H. (1974), *Introduction to the Work of Melanie Klein*. 2nd ed. New York: Basic Books.

Stolorow, R. (1975), Toward a functional definition of narcissism. *Internat. J. Psycho-Anal.*, 56:179–185.

Tyson, R. (1983), Some narcissistic consequences of object loss: A developmental view. *Psychoanal. Quart.*, 52:205–224.

Winnicott, D. (1960), The theory of the parent-infant relationship. *Internat. J. Psycho-Anal.*, 41:385–395.

———— (1961), Ego distortion in terms of true and false self. In: *The Maturational Processes and the Facilitating Environment*. New York: International Universities Press, pp. 140–152.

Chapter 4

Contributions of Countertransference Data from the Analysis of the Rorschach: An Object Relations Approach

Ronnie Levine, Ph.D.

The continued interest in treating borderline, narcissistic, and preoedipal patients has generted interest in applying psychological tests in new ways. Patients evincing such pathology are difficult to treat and are often referred for psychological testing. Testing these patients provides examiners the opportunity to investigate primitive emotional communication and to explore internal object relations as they are played out within the context of the testing session. Such explorations are increasingly valued, in both inpatient and outpatient settings. Seriously disturbed patients frequently develop confusing, emotionally intense, and destructive interactions with their therapists and other treatment staff. These often create confusion in the therapist and may evoke disturbing reactions in all the treating staff, which can in turn produce interventions and diagnoses that are not always in the best interest of these patients. Faced with emotional, dramatic interchanges, therapists or treatment teams may lose their objectivity, which may cause them unwittingly to devise interventions or rediagnose as a way of discharging frustrating experiences; at other times it may cause therapists to accept their patients' devaluing judgments and become demoralized and confused.

   In my experience as a psychological examiner and supervisor, I have found that confused, vague, poorly articulated referrals for testing, including puzzling questions regarding diagnosis, are more often the result of a therapist's being overwhelmed by intense and confusing experience with a patient, rather than of any particular lack of knowledge regarding personality dynamics. These vague requests for diagnostic clarity or assessment of ongoing treatment are frequently a plea for help by therapists who hope to use the understanding afforded by psychological testing for insights into treatment dilemmas and for help in developing a treatment strategy. In such situations testing is requested not just for personality and cognitive assessments, but to provide a framework in which to understand and unravel the complex interactional patterns occurring in the therapeutic process. When psychological consultations address these underlying concerns, the referring therapist or staff often respond with relief at having had their chaotic experience comprehended and articulated. This usually allows therapists to resume their objective investigation of the therapeutic interaction.

Psychological testing offers a unique opportunity to investigate communication and interactional process. The Rorschach, particularly, provides a context analogous to that of psychoanalytic psychotherapy. Like that modality, the Rorschach offers an unstructured and ambiguous experience with defined limits. It invites and investigates the expression of a range of conscious and unconscious material and allows transference and countertransference reactions to occur. In the testing experience, the inkblot and the examiner can be understood as functioning as a container (Bion, 1967) or holding environment (Winnicott, 1960) for the patient's pathological contents and defensive transactions (Epstein, 1979a). Further, the cards themselves may take on qualities of transitional phenomena (Winnicott, 1951). Thus, a study of the testing experience may reveal pertinent information concerning a patient's object world and defensive operations. Because of this, the Rorschach investigator has an opportunity to study personality issues and the psychoanalytic process using a variety of approaches and theoretical orientations.

Traditional analysis of the Rorschach, which has been derived from ego psychology, is concerned with ego structure and cognitive organization. In this vein, Rapaport, Gill, and Schafer (1945) and Schafer (1948) developed a brilliant analysis of content, structure, and organization of testing responses to make personality and cognitive inferences. In this tradition, testing was conducted to provide an articulation of impulses and defenses, ego functions and ego deficits.

The recent study of borderline and preoedipal phenomena, however, has generated a shift to object-relational models. Psychological examiners are now attempting to clarify concepts of internal self, object representation, interactional paradigms, primitive communications, and defensive operations and to translate this understanding of psychological processes into meaningful contributions to the therapeutic process.

More recent investigations of the Rorschach using Mayman's thematic analysis (1963, 1967) and Blatt's structural analysis (Blatt, Brenneis, Schimek, and Glick, 1976; Blatt and Lerner, 1983) have been applied to gain information concerning interpersonal paradigms and internal object relations. However, the impact that patient and examiner have on each other, details of their interactional process, and what these data may suggest about internal relations have as yet received only limited attention in psychological testing (Sugarman, 1981).

For object relations theorists, the interactional process provides important data for analyzing primitive defenses. This is a qualitatively different approach than an ego psychological analysis of defenses. Traditional analysis of defenses on psychological tests has been based on drive theory and ego psychology, which focus on control and tolerance of impulse and affect, and the effect of this on the organization of thought processes. This analysis of defense based on a drive-structure model studies defensive operations as part of an individual's intrapsychic structure; thus, when attempts are made to analyze primitive defenses involving interactional and interpersonal properties, test analysis becomes difficult. What is needed is an object relations structural model that can incorporate the external object as part of the structure of these primitive defensive operations. This lack has hampered the development of a concept of projective identification on the Rorschach and its differentiation from the classical concept of projection.

COUNTERTRANSFERENCE

The investigation of the interactional process between the patient and the examiner on the Rorschach demands a sensitivity to understanding the patient's communications. Communications vary in function and may not be exclusively or even at all vehicles of symbolic meaning. Preoedipal patients may use communication to discharge affect or to form an affective relationship with the examiner. For such patients verbal expression is often charged with an immediacy and intensity that conveys emotional rather than intellectual meaning. Affective verbal productions of this sort can be experienced by the examiner as confusing when understood solely on the basis of content.

Countertransference theory has made major advances in clarifying the nature of communication in the interactional process. Countertransference data has received increased respect despite a previous reluctance to make use of clinical material that seems so dependent on the examiner's subjective experience. The classical position, as articulated by Freud and Annie Reich, viewed countertransference as a pathological interference, resistance to the analytic process (Epstein, 1979a). However, other theorists, many of them influenced by object relations theory, have seen it as an effective and often crucial means of studying primitive interaction (Heimann, 1950; Little, 1951; Winnicott, 1960; Racker, 1968; Kernberg, 1976; Langs, 1976; Epstein, 1979b; McDougall, 1979; Searles, 1979). These analysts vary in their understanding of the data, and there is controversy as to how it may be used to benefit the patient. Nevertheless, there is a general consensus among these theorists that countertransference can be an important tool in understanding a patient's conflicts, defenses, and internal object world, and that these reactions can be an inevitable and nonpathological part of the therapeutic process with preoedipal patients.

Winnicott (1947) helped change the prevailing view of countertransference as a hindrance to treatment by distinguishing two types of countertransference reaction—objective and subjective. Subjective reactions are the unique, idiosyncratic reactions of the therapist that might reflect aspects of the therapist's personality. These reactions have been viewed by many as interferences to treatment. By contrast, objective (or induced) countertransference reactions are evoked by the patient and can provide useful information concerning the patient's emotional life and internal object relations. By making this distinction, Winnicott sanctioned and facilitated an exploration of the analyst's emotional reactions. He also directed attention to the analytic interaction.

Racker (1968), in systematically elaborating the communication process between patient and analyst, distinguishes concordant and complementary identification. Concordant identification arises when the therapist has an empathic response to the patient; attention to this response will help him understand what the patient is feeling. Complementary identification develops when the patient projects into the analyst unwanted aspects of himself. Attention to the emotional experience this evokes may provide the analyst an understanding of functional aspects of the patient's communication and the quality of the internal object relationship. The process by which the patient expels aspects of the self and places them into the therapist is the process of *projective identification*. Influenced by Klein (1932), Racker makes use of this concept in his understanding of complementary identifications. For Racker this process is a rich and essential source of data to be utilized by clinicians in understanding patients.

In this discussion, the definition of projective identification formulated by Malin and Grotstein (1966) has been utilized. This definition includes and underscores the effect of the process on the therapist and thus highlights the importance of countertransference and investigation of the interaction. Malin and Grotstein define projective identification as a threefold process: (1) there is an unconscious fantasy of projecting a part of oneself into another person and of that part taking over from within; (2) there is pressure exerted through the interpersonal interaction such that the recipient of the projection experiences pressure to think, feel, and behave congruently with the projection; and (3) after the projection is psychologically metabolized and processed by the recipient, the projected feelings are reinternalized by the projector. Projective identification is thus distinguished from projection in its reliance on the other person's active participation in the defensive operation. An awareness of projective identification can be of value in understanding the treatment process; it provides information concerning the patient's ego state, emotional communication, use of primitive defensive operations, all of which may be used in formulating effective therapeutic strategies.

Objective countertransference reactions are an important means of clarifying projective identification processes. Through self-observation the well-trained and well-analyzed psychological examiner can understand induced reactions in terms of the patient's communicational style and object relations.

COUNTERTRANSFERENCE AND THE RORSCHACH

I have attempted to apply these concepts to Rorschach analysis. Whenever possible I have noted my thoughts, feelings, and fantasies during administration of the Rorschach and during the inquiry which follows each card. When investigating countertransference data it is important to keep in mind that borderline and psychotic patients can evoke intense primitive fantasies or feelings, both aggressive and sexual. In order that acquisition of this data not be inhibited, a nonjudgmental, receptive approach is necessary initially.

Countertransference data may be used to explore primitive defensive communications. For example, an ordinary and popular response such as a bat on Card I may require additional formulation when the examiner suddenly experiences what seems to be induced sexual or aggressive feelings. A general exploration of the countertransferential experience of the whole test may reveal the kind of internal relations that become established in the patient's interpersonal and therapeutic relationship. Countertransference may involve either complementary or concordant processes. There are times when my experience of the interactional process appears to be an empathic concordant process paralleling the object relations expressed in the content of responses. Thus, in one instance, I found my experience of oscillation from closeness to remoteness to be parallel and concordant to the themes of detachment/disengagement and dependency/merger of the Rorschach responses, a core issue for this particular patient.

In many cases which activate complementary reactions, I have found that the patient creates a drama in which the examiner is an unwitting actor. This drama, propelled by the powerful unconscious forces of projective identification, can yield information concerning the kind of transactions the patient typically engages in. Thus, in testing many preoedipal and borderline patients, in whom paranoid sadistic issues arise and exploitative concerns are prominent, the examiner is often cast as the torturer and the patient as the victim. Such interchanges may vary in intensity. Some are easily dispelled; in some the examiner feels trapped as the torturer; in some the examiner is pressured into torturing; and in some, as more frequently occurs, the examiner feels victimized both by the coercive power of the defense and by the victim's accusations. With these rich dramatic interchanges the examiner can elucidate, for therapists or treatment staff, the dilemmas of the patient's internal object relations as well as the kind, quality, and intensity of interactions that typically occur with a given patient.

Sometimes an emotional response which seemed discordant and contradictory to the patient's presentation and Rorschach responses has alerted me to an underlying emotional state of the patient. This was particularly significant in a case in which I became aware of feeling frightened by a patient who appeared composed and initially gave organized responses. My frightened reaction led me to wonder how menacing this patient could be; later I discovered that the patient had an overlooked history of episodic violent behavior and that the inpatient staff's underlying motive for their request for a personality assessment was an unexplained, unexpressed fear of the patient. In this case, together with other testing data, my countertransference data was helpful in directing me to the patient's preverbal communication, its defensive and threatening properties, and the powerfully controlling effect it had on the staff. I was thereby able to provide the staff a reassuring validation and to alert them to this patient's potential for destructive behavior.

Finally, I try to attend to my countertransferential responses during the inquiry, and to study the effect of the inquiry on the patient, as such information can provide additional diagnostic information and treatment suggestions.

Following is a case that illustrates the use of countertransference in understanding a psychotic patient's primitive communication.

CASE STUDY

The powerful interplay between aggressive forces in the processes involved in projective identification can be explored in the investigation of the responses and counterresponses of a hospitalized psychiatric patient who was referred for a personality evaluation. The patient, Carol, is an overweight woman in her early thirties. She had been admitted following the disclosure of her mother's prediction that she would spend the rest of her life in a mental hospital as soon as her parents died. The patient soon after decompensated and appeared in a frenzy, presenting a racing array of frightened and desperate words, thoughts, and images that barraged all who came in contact with her. The experience was too exhausting for most staff members, and only abbreviated contact was maintained. The need to evaluate was apparent, but the difficulty in maintaining sustained contact seemed to be the cause for the psychological testing request.

On the first card of the Rorschach, the patient's initial response was a crab, and then a bat or a butterfly. During the inquiry, when I asked the patient what it was about the blot that made it look like a crab, I thought silently "I would like to kill her." No sooner did I have that thought when the patient blurted, "Did I kill you? I didn't kill someone." When I proceeded with the inquiry, the patient responded that it looked like a crab because the tentacles are coming out. The next question, about the bat or butterfly, brought this response: "No butterfly, no bat, it's a crab, a bat, it looks like a butterfly a little, it looks pretty." Then in a panicked tone she said, "I have to get out of here."

One sees in this response fluidity, instability, and a loss of distance. As such the response reflects the patient's passivity and fear of being overwhelmed by her own thoughts. Her image of the crab, a devouring image of self, with a phobic concern regarding harm, allows us to infer an instability of defenses, difficulty in maintaining repression, and a weakened hold on a stable reality.

What interested me here was my thought of killing her and the patient's almost immediate response: "Did I kill you? I didn't kill someone." It is true that the barrage of unstable thoughts and images may have evoked my anger and frustration, or that her urgent, demanding dependency and wish for merger may have triggered in me a *subjective* countertransferential reaction. I may well have wanted to put both myself and her out of our misery, and in fact the hospital staff may have avoided this patient for a similar reason.

However, I would like to consider another possibility—that the processes of projective identification (projection and introjection) were operating so as to communicate the patient's emotional experience to me through a process of introjection. Content analysis of the response might suggest that the patient in fact was attempting to devour and destroy my ego integrity, taking as much as she could. In addition to devouring, the patient seemed to respond reactively. Her verbalizations seemed to reflect a paranoid anxiety that may be understood as a fear of retaliation; she may in that moment have had an unconscious understanding that she in some way may have been causing harm to me by ejecting her overpowering, devouring aggressive impulses and injecting them into me in an attempt to destroy my boundaries and fuse with me. Thus, the rise of paranoid concern and the wish to leave may have expressed a fear that I might launch a counterassault. A later response ("little sheep, little doggies") produced additional verbalizations: "I'm not trying to bother no doctors no more, Hickory killed the President." Her vulnerability, the instability of her defenses and boundaries, was extreme. An analysis of the countertransference provided a vivid portrayal of the interplay of primitive defenses, her desperate and destructive attempts to maintain unstable object representations, and the terrifying paranoid concern that so affected the treatment staff.

NOTES ON INQUIRY

It is important for the examiner to understand the nature of the relationship being established during the Rorschach test, as interaction between the subject and the examiner determines the quality and style of administration. Such interactions effect and transform the testing experience, so that with certain patients the inquiry and the ensuing interaction acquire different meanings. The Rorschach inquiry is an attempt at objective investigation of the patient's organization, and is typically the essential vehicle of expression and intervention by the examiner. The inquiry, however, is itself a process—a process which for disturbed patients may stimulate primitive affects, facilitate projective identification, and create a medium for the externalization of the patient's deficiencies. It is important for examiners to attend to their internal responses in order to understand the quality of interaction. Using these countertransference data, well-trained and experienced examiners can become aware of the effect that inquiry is having on the patient and can use this understanding for diagnostic purposes and in adjusting and monitoring their questioning techniques.

Some borderline and preoedipal patients may not take the inquiry in good faith. The inquiry demands a capacity for observation and rational articulation that may not be available to them. Patients who lack a separate experience of self may not be able to share in a cooperative process of mutual investigation. In short, the inquiry may be experienced in a variety of ways.

With some preoedipal patients, the examiner's adherence to the objective, neutral questioning of responses, despite the patient's disparagement and sadistic criticism of both the test and the examiner, appears to provide a structured, safe, and containing environment for the patient's expression of destructive and poorly organized and controlled affects and impulses. These patients appear to regard the neutrality of questions as a sign of acceptance, as an indication of being taken seriously or at least an indication of not being dismissed. Because such questions are unaffected by the patient's ongoing hostility, the questions themselves imply that the hostility has not harmed the examiner. For these patients, the inquiry may facilitate a useful process of projective identification by which the patient is enabled to externalize unwanted and destructive aspects of the self onto the examiner and the blot, and in consequence is able to participate and be sustained in the testing situation. These patients often find the testing experience a therapeutic encounter, a containing or holding environment in which they experience a sense of being understood emotionally.

For other patients, paranoid and persecutory anxiety is so great that they experience the questioning of their responses as an overwhelming challenge, and attack on themselves, and as a disruptive reminder of their aloneness. The inquiry in such cases does not provide containment, is experienced as a threat to the patient's omnipotent control, and activates an intolerable degree of anxiety, a danger of loss, that can bring the testing to an abrupt termination. It would seem that these patients are unable to use the testing for the expression of destructive or disavowed contents relatively free of the fear of potential disorganization or loss of control. With such patients the examiner may have to adjust his technique and allow for some flexibility in his style of questioning and in responding to the patient's questions. Maintenance of the testing situation may depend on management of the frustration engendered by the testing situation and the inquiry. If the testing is maintained, both of these groups can eventually find the testing experience a therapeutic encounter, and at times may seek out the examiner for a continuation of the relationship.

There is another group of patients whose communications are charged with hateful and malevolent contents and seem bent on destroying both the examiner and the testing situation. Here the testing would appear to stimulate an excessive degree of regression, aggression, and envy, which cannot be suitably contained by the examiner or the situation. With such patients the examiner often experiences the testing as something simply to survive. While maintenance of boundaries and the neutral inquiry may be of some help in sustaining and insulating the examiner, the onslaught can lead to the tester's withdrawal, to testing disruptions, or to a breakdown of the testing experience.

When psychological examiners ignore, dismiss, or negate the dramatic interplay between patient and examiner, they are likely to discharge these intolerable experiences in unacknowledged ways that may further stress and deteriorate the testing situation. A frustrated examiner experiencing difficulty containing assaultive and regressive communicators may seek relief by using the inquiry to attack the patient. The examiner may ask poorly timed, overly exacting, or challenging questions; may not ask enough questions; or may conduct the inquiry in a denigrating manner in an attempt to be rid of unwanted projections and to punish the patient for causing the distress.

In other situations, difficulty in containing induced distressing affects may lead to the examiner's despairing retreat and submission to the patient's productions. In some instances, narcissistic dismissal by the patient may lead to the examiner's becoming bored, self-preoccupied, and uninterested in picking up cues in the patient's responses or behavior. The examiner may disqualify the effect of the patient by developing a negative and aversive attitude toward psychological testing.

When understood as data, these countertransference reactions can reveal information about the patient's narcissistic object relations, and can contribute to significant diagnostic and therapeutic formulations.

REFERENCES

Bion, W. (1967), *Second Thoughts*. New York: Aronson.

Blatt, S., Brenneis, C., Schimek, J., & Glick, M. (1976), Normal development and psychopathological impairment of the concept of the object on the Rorschach. *J. Abnorm. Psychol.*, 85:364–373.

———— Lerner, H. (1983), The psychological assessment of object representation. *J. Personal. Assess.*, 47:7–28

Epstein, L. (1979a), The therapeutic function of hate in the countertransference. In: *Countertransference: The Therapist's Contribution to Treatment*, ed. L. Epstein & A. H. Feiner. New York: Aronson, pp. 213–234.

———— (1979b), The therapeutic use of countertransference data with borderline patients. In: *Countertransference: The Therapist's Contribution to Treatment*, ed. L. Epstein & A. H. Feiner. New York: Aronson, pp. 375–405.

Grotstein, J. (1981), *Splitting and Projective Identification*. New York: Aronson.

Heimann, P. (1950), On countertransference. *Internat. J. Psycho-Anal.*, 31:81–84.

Kernberg, O. (1976), *Object Relations Theory and Clinical Psychoanalysis*. New York: Aronson.

Klein, M. (1932), *The Psycho-analysis of Children*. London: Hogarth Press.

Langs, R. (1976), *The Therapeutic Interaction*. Vol. II. New York: Aronson.

Little, M. (1951), Countertransference and the patient's response to it. *Internat. J. Psycho-Anal.*, 32:32–40.

Malin, A., & Grotstein, J. (1966), Projective identification in the therapeutic process. *Internat. J. Psycho-Anal.*, 47:26–31.

Mayman, M. (1963), Psychoanalytic study of the self-organization with psychological tests. In: *Recent Advances in the Study of Behavior Change: Proceedings of the Academic Assembly on Clinical Psychology*, ed. B. T. Wigdor. Montreal: McGill University Press, pp. 97–117.

———— (1967), Object representations and object relationships in Rorschach responses. *J. Proj. Tech. & Personal. Assess.*, 31:17–24.

McDougall, J. (1979), Primitive communication and the use of countertransference. In: *Countertransference: The Therapist's Contribution to Treatment*, ed. L. Epstein & A. H. Feiner. New York: Aronson, pp. 264–304.

Racker, H. (1968), *Transference and Countertransference*. New York: International Universities Press.

Rapaport, D., Gill, M., & Schafer, R. (1945), *Diagnostic Psychological Testing*. Rev. ed. New York: International Universities Press, 1968.

Schafer, R. (1948), *The Clinical Application of Psychological Tests*. New York: International Universities Press.

Searles, H. (1979), *Countertransference and Related Subjects.* New York: International Universities Press.

Sugarman, A. (1981), The diagnostic use of countertransference reactions in psychological testing. *Bull. Menn. Clin.*, 45:473–489.

Winnicott, D. W. (1947), Hate in the countertransference. In: *Collected Papers.* New York: Basic Books, 1958, pp. 194–203.

———— (1951), Transitional objects and transitional phenomena. In: *Collected Papers.* New York: Basic Books, 1958, pp. 229–242.

———— (1960), The theory of the parent-infant relationship. In: *The Maturational Processes and the Facilitating Environment.* New York: International Universities Press, 1965, pp. 24–26.

Chapter 5

The Rorschach Assessment of
Internalization Mechanisms in Depression

Christopher G. Lovett, Ph.D.

Although often used in an ambiguous and confusing fashion, the term *internalization* is usually employed in psychoanalytic theory to refer to psychological events and processes through which characteristics of others and interactions with one's environment are transformed into intrapsychic characteristics and structures (Schafer, 1968a). Identification and introjection are the specific mechanisms that bring about such transformations.

The central problem here with regard to internalization concerns the nature of the psychological process that transforms object representations into self-representations, internal objects or introjects, and inner modifications of ego structure. It is important at the outset to distinguish internalization from the ego function of representation-formation, through which objects in the external world acquire mental representation (Heimann, 1952). Representation-formation is antecedent to internalization, as one can neither identify with another person nor introject aspects of that person unless the ego has first composed a mental model, however primitive, of that person (Sandler, 1960). As pointed out by Schafer (1968a), "identification takes place not with a person, but with one or more representations of that person" (p. 142). Specific representations reflect the person's level of self-object differentiation, the quality of the object that can be cathected, and, therefore, the quality of the object representation that can be employed as a model for identification.

107

The concept of internalization has been discussed in the psychoanalytic literature from four main perspectives: first, the relationship between internalization and processes of growth and development; second, the importance of inadequate or distorted internalizations to any comprehensive assessment of psychopathology; third, the role of internalization as a crucial variable in the therapeutic process; and fourth, the function of internalization mechanisms as defenses. The defensive aspects of internalization processes provide the essential focus for this study, although their roles in normal development and psychopathology are employed as a conceptual basis for distinguishing different types of internalization.

The analysis of defensive operations was introduced into psychological testing theory and practice by Schafer (1954), and since that time psychological testing has provided a research method for systematically evaluating psychoanalytic concepts of defense. In Schafer's view, specific defenses may be expressed through formal response properties, thematic content, or some combination of scores and content. Schafer used this approach to delineate the operation of several defenses in Rorschach protocols, including repression, projection, denial, regression, isolation, reaction-formation, and undoing. More recent studies have attempted to assess specific primitive defenses such as splitting and projective identification through the analysis of Rorschach records (Grala, 1980; Lerner and Lerner, 1980, 1982; Lerner, Sugarman, and Gaughran, 1981; Cooper and Arnow, 1984). The one major defensive strategy that has been largely neglected in the literature concerning the Rorschach assessment of defenses is that involving the internalization mechanisms of identification and introjection.

For this study a scale was designed that would allow the systematic assessment and scoring of the defenses of introjection and three different levels of identification: psychotic, narcissistic, and selective. These four categories of internalization were distinguished on the basis of the degree of self-object differentiation depicted and the type and relative maturity of the object relationship implied in Rorschach responses.

Beginning with Freud's classic paper, "Mourning and Melancholia" (1917), clinical observation has confirmed many times the close relation between depression and the processes of introjection and identification (Abraham, 1924; Rado, 1928; Jacobson, 1953). Not surprisingly, then, the conceptual understanding of internalization mechanisms has evolved in a reciprocal fashion with developments in the psychoanalytic theory of depression (Blatt, 1974). In view of this intimate connection, depressed and depression-prone individuals were the groups selected to be examined in this study.

In what follows, four different mechanisms of internalization are defined: psychotic identification, narcissistic identification, selective identification, and introjection. These terms are then operationalized in order to explore whether their manifestations can be located on the Rorschach test, and studied in relation to depressive psychopathology. A developmental model of internalization is also presented which employs, as a basic framework, Mahler's stages of symbiosis and separation-individuation (Mahler, Pine, and Bergman, 1975). The gradual maturation of incorporative fantasies and aims is described in relation to these developmental stages and the evolution of self- and object representations. Each internalization mechanism is viewed as appropriate to a particular phase of development, and their usage in early childhood as establishing particular schemas of experience that lay the foundation for their emergence in adulthood as defense mechanisms. The specific relation between particular mechanisms and pathology is also described.

FREUD ON INTERNALIZATION

Freud's contributions to the subject of internalization were scattered throughout his writings but included several essential points. First, he suggested that the process of internalization evolves from the instinctual mode of oral incorporation (Freud, 1905). Second, internalization mechanisms are viewed as impelled by ambivalence conflicts, and they represent a special form of defense against the dangers posed by ambivalence (Freud, 1921). Third, an experience of loss is considered the usual precipitant to internalization, whether the actual loss of a love object, the relinquishment of an object as an infantile source of gratification, or a narcissistic injury which exacerbates an underlying ambivalence and brings about a decathexis of the object. Fourth, Freud (1923) also employed identification and introjection to account for the process of character development. Fifth, internalization mechanisms were viewed as the vehicles for the building up and protection of a person's store of narcissism and self-esteem (Freud, 1914).

Freud's (1923) claim that development involved the transformation of the ego so as to resemble its past objects placed internalization at the center of issues concerning character, internal conflict, and integration of the ego. It implied that the self is made up of a synthesis of internalizations, which allowed the conclusion that certain affects, character attitudes, or symptomatic acts may derive from an internalization that is not fully integrated within the personality (Brierley, 1944). It also led to the observation that certain identifications or introjects could be defended against or denied altogether (Greenson, 1954).

In Freud's (1923) view all processes of internalization involve the conversion of object cathexis into narcissistic cathexis. Hartmann (1950) suggested that a narcissistic shift of cathexis involves an inner redirection of libidinal or aggressive affects onto certain self-representations. This implied that the self-representations are the principal units of change in the process of internalization. The least that can change in any internalization are the self-representations (Schafer, 1968a), although such changes may also result in far-reaching modifications in the ego and its functions (Sandler and Rosenblatt, 1962). The self-representations transformed through internalization are invested with an altered emotional value and then exert an influence that reflects their new emotional coloring onto the remaining self-representations and the ego's regulation of behavior (Eisnitz, 1980).

Narcissistic Phenomena and Internalization

Freud (1917) distinguished between the state of mourning and the pathological process of melancholia on the basis of differences in self-esteem and internalization, indicating a direct relation between the two. Self-esteem has been defined as the ideational and emotional expression of a person's conscious and unconscious self-evaluation, reflecting the balance of libidinal and aggressive cathexis of the self-representations. Wishes for narcissistic gratification, often referred to as narcissistic supplies, are aimed at raising the libidinal cathexis of the self-representations (Jacobson, 1975).

Within the psychic economy it is the gratification of narcissistic needs which maintains the person's sense of well-being and self-esteem (Dare and Holder, 1981). Narcissistic needs are comparable to instinctual drive needs in their potential for creating mental conflict and mobilizing defenses to maintain or restore self-esteem and fend off narcissistic injuries (Dare and Holder, 1981). Narcissistic needs become a principal motive for defense in the form of superego anxiety (Freud, 1926), which confronts the ego with danger on two fronts: it may be deprived of libidinal investment by the ego ideal, resulting in a fall of self-esteem and feelings of inferiority; or the ego may be the object of the superego's hatred, giving rise to feelings of guilt and worthlessness (Rinsley, 1979). A principal defensive aim of internalization mechanisms thus entails the reduction of mental conflict created by the frustration of narcissistic needs.

The Defensive Function of Internalization

Freud (1926) suggested an intimate connection between specific defense mechanisms and particular forms of psychopathology, including internalization mechanisms and depression. Each defense mechanism is said to represent the adaptation of a primary process mode and its repudiated wish to the purposes of the ego (A. Freud, 1936). The functioning of defenses is usually described in terms of unconscious, automatic mechanisms that operate in keeping with certain unconscious fantasies (Isaacs, 1952; Schafer, 1968b). The referents for the term *defense mechanism* are thus unconscious wishful fantasies and motivated changes in the organization, content, and emphasis placed on particular internal representations (Schafer, 1968c).

Freud (1926) attempted to differentiate pathological from successful forms of defense in terms of the degree to which the operation of the defense is infiltrated by primary process modes of functioning. Within this framework defenses may be placed along a continuum from primary to secondary process modes of operation. Primitive defenses are themselves a source of anxiety as a result of their primary process nature, and secondary defenses are developed to avoid a crippling of the ego by the more regressed defenses (Frosch, 1983). During development a hierarchy for each defense evolves, which is unified by a common unconscious fantasy but extends across a range of structuralization (Schafer, 1968b). The different levels of the hierarchy may therefore be defined by the degree of differentiation of self- and object representations and the amount of primary process apparent in the operation of the defense.

The different internalization mechanisms may be viewed as a layered series of defenses differing in their specific unconscious aims, subjective experiences, and representational-structural alterations. At each level of organization, however, internalization mechanisms are instigated by anxiety over losing an object that serves as a source of narcissistic support, and the fundamental aim of each is to preserve the object as a source of gratification through its internalization (Balint,

1943; Fenichel, 1945; Jacobson, 1964). In addition, each mechanism of internalization is unconsciously experienced as a concrete act of oral incorporation (Isaacs, 1952).

INCORPORATION

Although the term *incorporation* has at times been used to refer to a process, recent usage tends to restrict it to the primary process aspect of internalization expressed through oral fantasy material (Loewald, 1962; Schafer, 1968a). Fantasies of oral incorporation are closely related to but distinct from the psychological mechanisms of introjection and identification. Oral fantasies, however, appear to represent a necessary component to the changes in the organization and shape of the self-representations brought about by internalization mechanisms (Jacobson, 1964).

The ego's construction of an inner world of self- and object representations provides the contents of experience for all of the ego's functions, including defense (Sandler and Rosenblatt, 1962). The operation of every defense mechanism thus involves self- and object representations that reflect a certain internalized object relation (Kernberg, 1980). Incorporative fantasies provide the contents of internalization mechanisms, and they are made up of self- and object representations experienced as interacting under the influence of oral wishes and anxieties over such wishes (Kernberg, 1980; Sandler, 1981). Through development internal representations become increasingly differentiated, complex, and accurate (Blatt, 1974; Kernberg, 1975). Different levels of defensive organization may therefore be distinguished on the basis of the degree of integration and differentiation of the relevant object representations. The level of organization present in a person's internalizations can thus be examined through the form in which oral incorporative fantasies are expressed.

IDENTIFICATION

As a general psychological term *identification* refers to a mostly unconscious process in which a person modifies motives, behavior patterns, interests, or attitudes in order to experience being like, the same as, or merged with one or more representations of a person, creature, or thing (Schafer, 1968a). An increase in the subject's resemblance to an object is brought about at all levels of identification, but this change may be either progressive or regressive depending upon the nature of the alterations brought about in the quality of the self-representations and the organization of the ego (Friedman, 1980).

INTROJECTION

Freud (1923) proposed that it is a process of introjection that brings about the "precipitate in the ego" referred to as the superego. Freud's earlier description of depressive introjects (1917) was consistent with this depiction of the superego and his suggestion that it is formed through introjection. Such internal objects seemed able to function as apparently independent centers of psychic activity and to substitute for external objects as sources of gratification or frustration. An introject has been defined as an inner presence to which the self feels dynamically related (Schafer, 1968a). The introject is sometimes experienced as though it had actual concrete substance and existence as a person or creature within the self, referred to by Schafer (1968a) as a "primary process presence" (p. 84). The self may feel passive and at times helpless or masochistic in relation to introjects (Maltsberger and Buie, 1980), but may also feel protected and loved by these internal objects (Klein, 1935).

FOUR INTERNALIZATION MECHANISMS

The four internalization mechanisms that comprise the focus of this study are defined next in increasing order of organization and adaptiveness. Their origins in development and their role in depressive illness is then described.

Psychotic Identifications: The Wish for Merger

This "psychotic" defense mechanism is aimed at merger and involves total and often delusional fusions between self- and object representations. This brings about a pathological reorganization experienced as the total incorporation of an object and a regressive, global transformation of the self into the object (Jacobson, 1954b). These "merging identifications" often give rise to a loss of reality testing and psychotic symptoms.

Freud's description of primary identification (1923) was later described by Jacobson (1964) as involving a fusion of early self- and object representations. Research on early development, however, indicates that it is unlikely that there is ever a completely undifferentiated stage of development during which the child consistently confuses self and other (Stern, 1983). A symbiotic phase of development as proposed by Mahler (Mahler, Pine, and Bergman, 1975), therefore, may be most meaningfully considered in terms of affectively significant but discrete moments of nondifferentiated oneness. These "symbiotic moments" (Pine, 1981, p. 23) are repeated again and again in the infant's experience, and through this repetition they are integrated with one another as a schema of experience that assumes multiple functions.

Repeated early episodes of frustration give rise to the first experiences of loss and to the earliest compensatory fantasies of total incorporation of the object. The re-fusion of self- and object representations for the purpose of defense thus acts as one of the earliest magical defensive maneuvers against such painful experiences (Jacobson, 1964). Based on memories of symbiotic moments, these re-fusions are gradually organized into a repeatable, unconscious defense mechanism motivated by archaic incorporative wishes for merger. When this process is excessively maintained it may give rise later in development to what Jacobson (1954a) referred to as "psychotic identifications" (p. 244) based on the delusional re-fusion of self- and object representations.

Introjection: The Wish to Possess the Object

This is a process involving a partial fusion between self- and object representations, based on an unconscious wish to incorporate the object orally in order to forestall loss of the object and then possess it internally as a substitute for the real object (Schafer, 1968b). The self-representations assume characteristics of object representations, bringing about a change in ego organization in which the resulting introject is experienced as a separate suborganization or entity residing within the self. An introject seems capable of exerting an influence on self-representations and the functioning of the ego on the strength of its own motivations, independent of conscious efforts to control it (Schafer, 1968a). "Good" introjects promote the integration of the ego and mature independence, such as the superego–ego ideal system, which provides a stable, internalized source of self-esteem. Pathological introjects, often laden with intense hostility, forestall integration and disrupt the ego's stable functioning and the maintenance of narcissistic equilibrium.

Introjection first appears during the rapprochement subphase of separation-individuation, from fifteen to twenty-four months, during which a vast increase in the realization of separateness occurs (Mahler, 1972). The child now possesses the capacity to retain narcissistic injuries and harbor a sustained sense of failure, hopelessness, and aloneness (Pine, 1980). It is also during this period that the child begins to consider space as a conceptual entity (Piaget and Inhelder, 1948). Early representations of the self are thus strongly influenced by archaic, concretistic notions of places, spaces, and the passage in and out of substances (Schafer, 1972). Introjection, a defense against abandonment and aloneness, emerges in its most primitive form, consisting of the setting up of an internal object felt to be located in space in a concrete way (Schafer, 1968a). The crystallization of self-awareness during this time (Pine, 1982) features certain "introjective" moments, in which the child is both an agent and a recipient object within an internalized interaction.

Early introjects, such as various superego precursors, provide the foundation for the self-critical functions of the mature superego, which synthesizes the various pressures exerted by early introjects into an autonomous internal system (Jacobson, 1964). Continued pressure from archaic introjects is thus indicative of states of incomplete integration (Tyson and Tyson, 1984). The formation of introjects too infused with aggression to allow their gradual assimilation contributes to the negative outcome of the rapprochement subphase described as the establishment of a "basic depressive mood" (Mahler, 1966, p. 161). This stems from the restitutive effort to repair a narcissistic injury through splitting and replacement of the deflated love object with an omnipotent introject. Overreliance on splitting leads to a predominance of pathological introjections and a precocity of superego formation (Mahler, 1966). A chronic instability of self-esteem and a vulnerability to depressive episodes result, due in large part to the intense sadistic hostility available to this archaic superego.

Narcissistic Identification: The Wish for Sameness

The term *narcissistic identification* refers to a process based on the partial fusion of self- and object representations, which results in the perception of the object and the self as the same, or as twinlike replicas. These "sameness identifications" may not necessarily be aimed at achieving sameness of overt behavior, but may emphasize ways of thinking or feeling intended to enhance an inner experience of sameness (Schafer, 1968a).

Freud (1910) likened narcissistic identification to unconscious imitation, and later concluded that this sort of identification could take place only when a person's object-choice was established on a narcissistic basis (Freud, 1917). The narcissistically experienced object employed as a model for identification is only partially recognized as separate. This gives rise to object relationships involving "the relation to an object that represents the self while the self is identified with that object" (Kernberg, 1975, p. 325). The object functions as an extension of the self, a "mirror" sought to compensate for narcissistic defects, e.g., in the maintenance of self-esteem (Kohut, 1971).

Deutsch (1942) traced the narcissistic identifications of the "as if" character to a developmental stage of imitative identifications. Imitation is intensely valued by the child during the period of development from approximately ten to fifteen months of age, which corresponds to the practicing phase of separation-individuation (Mahler, Pine, and Bergman, 1975). During this time earlier wishes for merger gradually recede and give way to more differentiated wishes to be the same as one's love objects. The role of the mother during this phase has been likened to acting like a mirror, reflecting qualities of the child's developing self back and confirming the child's expanding self-esteem (Kohut, 1971). Narcissistic identifications based on imitation have been referred to as "mirroring identifications" (Mahler, 1968, p. 158). According to Mahler (1968), a "mirroring frame of reference" (p. 19) is established between mother and child which may derive from certain "reciprocal imitative exchanges" (Meltzoff and Moore, 1983, p. 298), such as simultaneous vocalizing and mimicking. These developmental moments of sameness are repeated, integrated with one another as a schema of experience, and may be further organized into an unconscious mechanism of defense founded on magical incorporative fantasies of being the same as certain important objects.

Most of the time early imitative identifications gradually mature into selective identifications as the self- and object representations become more complexly realistic (Hendrick, 1951). In some cases, however, they remain prominent or reappear later in development as narcissistic identifications, and their prevalence reflects difficulty in fully elaborating the mental representation of the object (Ritvo and Solnit, 1958).

Selective Identifications: The Wish for Likeness

This process involves attempts to develop a realistic likeness to an object through the development of capacities and attitudes pertinent to the model object. These "likeness identifications" play a major role in the achievement of object constancy and self-constancy in normal development. They may also be employed as a neurotic-level defense mechanism, at which times they are carried out with separate objects to deflect ambivalent hostility away from the object.

Selective ego and superego identifications, also referred to as partial or secondary identifications by Freud (1921, 1933), are carried out with respect to one or a few characteristics of an object whose complexity and separateness is appreciated (Loewald, 1962; Schafer, 1968a). Their partial quality presupposes a relatively secure differentiation of self and object and the consolidation of self- and object representations into stable, realistic representations (Milrod, 1982). This development promotes the capacity to evaluate various aspects of an object in order to compare it with others and the self for similarities and differences (Blatt, 1974). Selective identifications also both depend upon and enhance the strengthening of libidinal object ties and the consequent integration of "good" and "bad" part-object representations that marks the beginning of libidinal object constancy (Mahler, Pine, and Bergman, 1975).

Selective identification is the process common to the completion of the process of separation-individuation and the successful resolution of the oedipus complex (Horner, 1983). Such identifications foster successful self-assertion in the world of reality and thereby contribute to the development of realistic self-esteem (McDevitt and Mahler, 1980). The final subphase of separation-individuation, from twenty-four to thirty-six months, has as its main task the consolidation of the self and the stabilization of libidinal object constancy (Mahler, Pine, and Bergman, 1975). Only those identifications which originate in enduring libidinal investments and are selective in quality can be integrated in a way that fortifies self-cohesion (Jacobson, 1964). Partial identifications that are incompletely integrated can, however, also give rise to neurotic symptoms and behavior. When the ambivalence underlying the identification is not fully resolved, the "incomplete identification" (Schafer, 1983, p. 221) may express itself through any symptomatic behavior or neurotic character feature.

DEPRESSION AND INTERNALIZATION

The etiology of depressive states has traditionally been traced to a "pathognomonic introjection" (Fenichel, 1945, p. 396). Jacobson (1953), however, viewed the onset of simple depression, featuring a loss of self-esteem, as the result of a narcissistic identification. Disappointment at the hands of an object leads to its devaluation, followed by a narcissistic identification with the deflated object representation. This causes the person's total self to feel inadequate and impoverished. Jacobson explained the evolution from simple depression to melancholic depression, involving the emergence of excessive guilt and profound despair, as the result of an attempt at restitution of the love object through the use of introjective mechanisms.

Freud and others based their formulations of melancholia upon a single internalization, but Rado (1928) viewed depression as the result of a double introjection of the lost object. Rado's twin introjects derived from a single disappointing object, and they are described as idealized and devalued part-objects. Rado's contribution is thus valuable for his recognition of the close connection between introjective and splitting mechanisms.

At the onset of a melancholic regression the extreme ambivalence of the depressive gives way to melancholic splitting operations, and representations of self and object are stripped of their realistic complexity. The quantum of aggressive impulses attached to the part-object introjected into the superego brings about a regressive transformation of that agency's structure and a rise in its sadism. The specificity of higher-level superego functioning, based on selective identifications, breaks down, and superego approval and disapproval comes to refer to polarized, black-and-white representations of the total self rather than special, unacceptable impulses and wishes (Jacobson, 1957). A widening defusion of the ego ideal and the superego may also be provoked if the splitting of the object is particularly severe (Parkin, 1976). This result induces a regressive repersonification of the superego as an omnipotent and sadistic introject (Jacobson, 1953). The idealized part-object is introjected into the ego ideal and fuses with the archaic ideal self-representations. As a result the ego ideal grows so overinflated and unattainable that it loses its function as a source of positive self-esteem, and the self feels abandoned and depleted (Parkin, 1976).

RORSCHACH PHENOMENA AND INTERNALIZATION

There has been little attention to the study of internalization through the Rorschach, and no study has been reported which employed a formal scoring system for the qualities of Rorschach percepts relevant to internalization. Information pertinent to the study of identification and introjection, however, has been explored in Rorschach research on object representations, defenses, and depression. Schafer (1954), for instance, did not study internalizing defenses explicitly, but he did emphasize that such oral-incorporative modes of defense should be reflected in oral content within Rorschach responses. Schafer described a series of oral content categories including responses emphasizing food, food sources (breasts, udders), food-related objects (frying pan), food providers (waiters), passive food receivers (nursing lamb), food organs (stomach), nurturers (cow), oral erotism (figures kissing), devouring people or animals (cannibals, shark), engulfing figures and objects (octopus, pit), and oral assault (persons yelling or spitting).

Mayman (1967) and Krohn and Mayman (1974) used Rorschach responses to study the thematic elements of object representations. Oral content was employed as representative of an incorporative relationship paradigm. This category included percepts emphasizing themes of being swallowed, engulfed, suffocated, or bitten. Sugarman, Bloom-Feshbach, and Bloom-Feshbach (1980) drew attention to the perception of solitary body organs, such as a mouth, with no mention of the person possessing that organ. They conceptualized such responses as reflecting an inability to integrate primitive aims into a whole object relation, indicative of part-object representations.

Kwawer (1979, 1980) described categories of response indicative of modes of primitive object relatedness, including themes of primitive incorporation, narcissistic mirroring, and womb imagery. The categories included (a) malignant internal processes, including incorporation (views of internal organs, transparencies affording views of body contents, or perspectives highlighting the experience of the body's interior as a container); (b) engulfment (often scored as "vague" or "+/—" form level due to their lack of explicit formal differentiation); (c) boundary disturbance (often reflecting internal-external confusion and implying incorporative engulfment, e.g., Jellyfish—you can see through to the blood vessels); (d) womb imagery. Schafer (1954) and Silverman and Silverman (1960) also related womb imagery on the Rorschach to oral incorporative fantasies.

Harty (1986) studied internalization phenomena by means of the Rorschach through an analysis of two protocols of a single depressed patient. In Harty's view internalization is reflected in certain qualities of percepts which suggest inferences about transactions between inside and outside as experienced by the individual. These include (a) percepts that implicitly or explicitly refer to the passage of some object or substance from outside to inside; (b) percepts that involve bodily orifices or sensory organs readily experienced as the site of transactions between inside and outside the body; (c) percepts with an actual or potential containing function.

Roth and Blatt (1974a, 1974b) also studied phenomena related to percepts with a containing function. They found that preoccupations with volume or depth in Rorschach percepts were associated with oral aggression, depression, and the use of introjection in clinical settings. Blatt and Ritzler (1974a) found that representation of transparency and translucence, referred to as a three-dimensional percept without the representation of volume, occurs primarily in suicidal patients as opposed to controls. Blatt and Ritzler related this type of response to the dissolution of boundaries in psychotic depression.

Relevant to the study of internalization is Exner's work regarding "reflection responses" (1969, p. 325), described as an indicator of narcissism. Reflection responses are defined as percepts based on the symmetry of the blots which use the concept of reflection, either directly through use of the word "reflection" or by wording such as "mirror-image." Such reflection responses would appear to represent a Rorschach manifestation of narcissistic identifications, based on wishes for sameness. Harty (1986) characterizes reflection responses as the depiction of a shared boundary with an identical object, indicative of a defensive shift to narcissistic mirroring.

Exner (1969) found that subjects described as highly narcissistic, such as psychopathic characters, gave significantly more reflection responses than recently suicidal depressed patients. Urist's Rorschach scale to measure the level of object relations (1976) also included a category, "reflection-mirroring," in which one figure is seen as a reflection of another. Records notable for reflections were significantly correlated with clinical descriptions of narcissism. Exner (1974) also found that reflection responses were relatively rare in the records of acutely depressed patients, and that as depressed patients improved in their mood they used significantly more reflection responses.

Exner's research on narcissistic manifestations on the Rorschach (1969) also indicated that depressives gave a significantly greater number of vista responses than either controls or groups considered highly narcissistic. Rorschach (1923) and Beck (1944) perceived the vista response as indicative of a morose feeling tone involving depressed affect and inferiority feelings. Beck included within this category percepts of valleys, abysses, pits, cave entrances, or other depths. It would appear that many vista responses emphasize depths or objects with a containing function in a manner similar to the responses highlighted by Roth and Blatt.

Klopfer, Ainsworth, Klopfer, and Holt (1954) described the vista response as reflecting an attempt to cope with the frustration of affectional needs by turning inward. Phillips and Smith (1953) saw the vista response as indicative of an acute awareness of a judgmental "I" and an acting and behaving "I," which implied excessive self-judgment and criticism, feelings of helplessness and inadequacy, and low self-esteem. Exner (1974) suggests that vista responses represent a painful kind of narcissistic cathexis and introspection, and Harty (1986) points out that some vista responses have overt incorporative connotations (e.g., a whirlpool). Vista responses depicting depths and containers, like the container responses described by Roth and Blatt, seem to denote introjective experiences in many aspects, including their relation with superego qualities such as self-criticism and fluctuations in self-esteem.

Rorschach research focusing on the structural dimensions of object representations has added to the number of formal response features relevant to differentiating levels of defensive operation. Blatt and Ritzler (1974b) and Blatt and Wild (1976) conceptualized various levels of thought disorder on the Rorschach as reflecting the level of self-object differentiation. The contamination response, considered the most serious thought disorder score, was regarded as indicative of a breakdown of the self-other boundary. Schwartz and Lazar (1984) view the contamination response as reflecting a wish for merger and a tendency toward the fusion of self- and object representations. They also point out that incorporative fantasies are often evident in the content of contaminated responses, indicating that fusions would come about as the result of primitive internalization mechanisms.

Blatt, Brenneis, Schimek, and Glick (1976) developed a scale for assessing the developmental level of human object representations on the Rorschach. Blatt and his colleagues have assessed the developmental level and content of human responses in Rorschach records of depressed patients. The patients in these studies are divided into two categories, in keeping with Blatt's (1974) distinction between anaclitic and introjective syndromes. Anaclitic depression is described as a simple, primary form of depression featuring feelings of helplessness and abandonment. Introjective depression is described as a self-critical, guilty type of depression that involves the use of introjection and identification with the aggressor as defenses. Blatt and Shichman (1981) noted that the Rorschach records of introjective depression featured an array of vampires and biting, predatory animals. Blatt and Lerner (1983) found that states of introjective depression were reflected by inaccurately perceived, quasi-human details (part-objects), which were inappropriately elaborated and included destructive, malevolent content. The frequency of this type of response in any record was related to the severity of the depression. The authors suggest that such responses (e.g., vampires, ugly troll) reflect the experience of negative, hostile introjects.

Lerner and St. Peter (1984) examined differences in the developmental level of object representations among neurotic, outpatient borderline, inpatient borderline, and schizophrenic patients. They found that the hospitalized borderline patients were the only patients, with the exception of one outpatient borderline subject, to offer the inaccurately perceived responses with malevolent content described by Blatt and Lerner (1983) as indicative of hostile introjects. Viewing such responses as reflective of hostile introjects is consistent with Kernberg's emphasis (1975) on a predominance of negative introjections as a principal contributing factor in the etiology of borderline pathology. The significant presence of these responses in introjective depressive and borderline protocols may be viewed as consistent with studies of comparative symptomatology, course of illness, genetic family history, and biological markers that support the conclusion that a sizable portion of borderline psychopathology represents a subclinical manifestation of affective disorder (Stone, 1979; Akiskal, 1981).

STATEMENT OF THE PROBLEM

The preceding review of the literature on internalization mechanisms provides a basis for defining the important elements of these defensive operations. With these elements a scale has been constructed that permits the assessment of Rorschach response qualities presumed most likely to reflect an individual's use of introjection and the three types of identification. The principal purpose of this study was to evaluate both the reliability and the validity of the Internalization Assessment Scale. The experimental questions addressed whether acutely depressed subjects would use Rorschach indices of internalization mechanisms in ways differing from a group of normal and a group of remitted depressives. In addition, it was hypothesized that remitted depressives would show some aspect of their predisposition to depressive episodes by using indices of internalization in ways distinct from those normals.

Questions pertaining to the scale's construct validity were thus approached by investigating differences in the expression of content deemed indicative of internalization among groups differentiated on the basis of clinical diagnosis. Support for the Internalization Assessment Scale as a valid measure of internalization mechanisms would be obtained if the groups distinguished on the basis of diagnosis were found to differ in the various scores on the scale and if these differences were in the expected direction. A group of acute major depressives was chosen as the group which psychoanalytic writings on the subject of internalization indicated would be most likely to use internalizing defenses as a characteristic psychological operation. Formerly depressed patients now in remission were chosen as a group that would provide information about the role of internalization in the transition between states of depression and relative health.

SCORING SYSTEM

General Scoring Considerations

Scoring for the Rorschach Manual for the Assessment of Internalization Mechanisms[1] is directed toward locating responses containing some reference to oral incorporative wishes, either through explicit reference to oral content or implicit reference to incorporative wishes through images of containment or potential containment, passage of substances from outside to inside, or a state of identification in which two objects are noted to be the same or like one another. Each response is assigned to one of five main categories and is assigned a weighted score corresponding to its category. Certain responses may combine elements of two categories in their content and structure, and these are given a weighted score that represents the midpoint between the two categories. A score of NA (Not Applicable) is employed for all responses that have no apparent internalization qualities. Certain oral perceptual features, such as a mouth or breasts, should not be scored unless seen alone or emphasized when included as part of a larger response.

The Specific Mechanisms of Internalization

No Internalization (NA). There is no incorporative content in the response, either explicitly in references to oral themes or implicitly

---

[1]Copies of the complete Rorschach Manual for the Assessment of Internalization Mechanisms are available upon request from Dr. Christopher Lovett.

through reference to derivative oral themes such as engulfment, containment, greed, volume or depth, or states of sameness or likeness.

Selective Identification (SLI). Weighted Score = 2. Refers to a neurotic-level defensive operation carried out in the context of relationships with clearly separate objects. These partial identifications have a realistic quality and are carried out with respect to one or a few aspects of an object whose complexity is recognized. Score SLI for the following:

A. A well-seen percept involving two clearly separate figures involved in a mutual activity with oral connotations. Indications of hostility or ambivalence, if present, are mild, and the oral incorporative content is modulated. Examples: (1) "Maybe men in tuxedos serving. I suppose they could be waiters serving" (Card III); (2) "Two figures, kissing and nuzzling" (Card II).

B. A well-seen percept in which a single figure is involved in an orally related activity described in a modulated and controlled fashion. Includes figures with an oral identity or oral social role. Examples: (1) Food providers: "waiter," "baker," "cook," "butler serving food" (Card III); (2) "large motherly figure because of the large bosom" (Card I).

C. Any response in which reference is made to two figures being "like" one another but not identical. Examples: (1) "A person sleeping, there's another one like him over here" (Card V); (2) "Two sisters fighting" (Card VII).

Narcissistic Identification (NRI). Weighted Score = 4. Refers to a defensive operation manifested in a perception of the object and the self as identical in some way or as twinlike replicas, although the separateness of the object is moderately well preserved. Score NRI for the following:

A. Reflection responses. Defined by the symmetry of the blots, two objects are perceived as identical with one another, or as a "mirror image" or reflection. Examples: (1) "A little girl looking in the mirror" (Card VII); (2) "Two people working on something. The red shows that they're thinking exactly the same thing" (Card III).

B. Images depicting figures known for using imitation. Examples: (1) "A parrot" (Card III); (2) "Something made up like a mime" (Card II).

Introjection (INT). Weighted Score = 6. Refers to a defensive operation in which the subject modifies certain self-representations in order to experience possessing the object internally as a substitute for the real object. In its more pathological form, introjection is often closely related to the defense of splitting, and such introjects may be manifest in bodily symptoms or fantasies of containing primitive, distorted figures who are hostile and powerful. Score INT for the following:

A. Images of containment or enclosure. The response refers to situations involving things in enclosures or objects with a potential containing function. Examples: (1) "The center area looks like a cave or an entrance to a cave. The black part gives you a sense of depth" (Card II); (2) "Two babies—like inside a womb" (Card X); (3) "Looks like internal organs" (Card VII).

B. Oral-sadistic images of parasitical creatures or entrapping oral creatures. Examples: (1) "Tapeworm" (Card X); "Cannibals" (Card III); (2) "Spider with its web" (Card VIII); (3) "A Dracula bat—a vampire bat" (Card V).

C. Part-object representations of oral body parts in isolation. Examples: (1) "Grasping mouth—it's going to bite off this part" (Card I); (2) "Tongue," "Lips," "Throat," "Teeth," "Beak," "A stomach," "Intestines."

D. Food responses indicating object relationships based on need-satisfaction, with no indications of more primitive boundary diffusion (see under Psychotic Identification). Examples: (1) "Plate of spaghetti" (Card X); (2) "Two hunks of raw meat" (Card II).

E. Carnivorous animals or any image of animals engaged in an oral activity that seems relatively unmodulated, pervaded by hostile urges, and in which there is a sadomasochistic imbalance in the relationship. Examples: (1) "An alligator" (Card V); (2) "Frightened figure, going to be eaten by these four figures" (Card X).

F. Figures depicted in ways which exaggerate oral perceptual or functional features. Examples: (1) "The head of a giant ant. It had eyes that looked like it was mean, like it was trying to eat you, and a big nose to suck your blood" (Card IX); (2) "A very gaunt person" (Card V).

Psychotic Identification (PSI). Weighted Score = 8. Refers to a primitive defense which involves total and often delusional fusions between self- and object representations and often leads to a loss of reality testing and the formation of psychotic symptoms. Score PSI for the following:

A. Contaminated responses that show evidence of incorporative content. Contamination is indicated when the boundaries between two concepts are so fluid that they fuse into a single percept or idea. Examples: (1) "Woman eating shrimp" (Card VII)—the two halves of the blot are seen as three separate shrimp and the figure of a woman; (2)

"This reminds me of a wolf and he swallowed the sheep and this is the sheepskin. The sheep came out in the shape of the wolf's body, like a sheepskin" (Card VI).

B. Clearly oral responses that involve an aspect of diffuse or dissolving boundaries between different parts or between outside and inside, such as in transparency responses. Examples: (1) "Flavors of ice cream, all flowing into one another" (Card IX); (2) "Piece of cheese— the light parts are semitranslucent, that's the texture of the cheese" (Card VII).

SUBJECTS

Subjects in this study were drawn from a large group of psychiatric inpatients and outpatients treated at the New York Hospital–Cornell Medical Center, Westchester Division. The patient samples for both the acutely depressed and remitted groups were diagnosed independently by hospital treatment staff, and were selected for inclusion in the research according to the following basic criteria: (1) a history of at least one episode of major depressive illness, either acutely present or considered to be in remission, diagnosed according to criteria in DSM–III; (2) absence of a diagnosable nonaffective psychiatric disorder such as schizophrenia, chronic brain syndrome, or anorexia nervosa; (3) absence of any evidence of past episodes of mania.

The acutely depressed sample, consisting of twenty-five inpatients, was selected through chart review of inpatient records. The sample consists of twenty-five patients with a confirmed clinical diagnosis of a major depressive episode who received psychological testing, including a Rorschach, within approximately one month following admission to the hospital. The sample of major depressives in remission was selected from a population of hospital clinic outpatients. Major depressives in remission were chosen as an intermediate group of subjects for three principal reasons: first, the clinical observation that patients are predisposed to depressive episodes through overreliance on internalization mechanisms (Jacobson, 1971); second, the unavailability of a group of patients at risk for major depression who could be studied before onset; and third, evidence that major depressives tend to have episodic courses of illness (Winokur, 1981).

The remitted patient sample consists of only twenty-one subjects, because that was the number of patients contacted who agreed to take part in the study. They were chosen on the basis of chart review and a subsequent discussion with the patient's therapist to confirm the state of remission. Normal control subjects were volunteers obtained by hospital advertisements for participation in a research study of highs and lows in mood. The twenty-five control subjects were chosen according to two criteria: (1) absence of any psychiatric history; (2) a score of less than 10 on the Hamilton Rating Scale for Depression (Hamilton, 1967), an interview scale designed to measure the presence and severity of depressive symptoms. The correlation between the scale and global clinical judgment has been found to be 0.84 and upward while interrater reliability is of the order of 0.9 (Hamilton, 1982). The scale was administered to the remitted and control subjects and completed in the course of a brief interview structured according to the items on the scale.

PROCEDURE

Each subject in the acutely depressed group had already received psychological testing while an inpatient at New York Hospital. Verbatim Rorschach transcripts and the WAIS Full Scale IQ scores were obtained from a file of raw data maintained on all patients tested at the hospital. Each subject in the remitted depressive group and in the control group was seen individually by a member of the larger research project on personality characteristics of patients with affective disorders in remission. Testing in all of these cases was carried out by psychology interns, fellows, or staff trained in the Rapaport, Gill, and Schafer (1945) method of test administration and scoring. After collection, all Rorschach protocols were uniformly typed by the psychology department secretarial staff at New York Hospital, and a code number was assigned to each case by random number methods.

Twenty-one Rorschach records were scored independently and blindly according to the Rorschach Manual for the Assessment of Internalization Mechanisms by the investigator and an advanced graduate student in clinical psychology with extensive testing experience. This stage in the scoring of the data followed a period of training of the other rater by the investigator, the practice rating of five Rorschach protocols randomly selected from the hospital testing files, and the discussion of scoring problems and differences. Once reliability was established, discussions between the two raters were held in order to achieve agreement for the twenty-one records. The remaining fifty records were then scored by the advanced graduate student. In order to avoid any halo effect distorting the data, all scoring was done on a card-by-card basis across all records rather than scoring each record as a whole at one time.

RESULTS

Reliability

The reliability of the Internalization Assessment Scale was examined by two methods: (1) percentage of agreements between the raters, and (2) interrater reliability (Pearson product-moment) coefficient. The percentage of agreements between raters and the reliability coefficients are presented in Table 1. Percentage of agreement between raters was calculated both in terms of the total number of Rorschach responses across all records (93 percent agreement) and for all those responses which at least one of the raters scored as representing an instance of internalization (75 percent agreement). For the latter percentage, cases in which both raters scored a response as representative of internalization but disagreed in terms of its category code were counted as disagreements. Interrater reliability was calculated for the total weighted score given to each Rorschach record ($r = 0.96$), and for each of the categories of internalization included as part of the scale:

TABLE 1

Reliability of the Internalization Assessment Scale in Terms of Percentage Agreements and Reliability Coefficients ($N = 21$)

	Number of Responses	Percentage Agreements
Total Number of Responses	498	93
Internalization Responses	127	75

	Frequency of Rating[a]	Reliability Coefficient
Total Weighted Score	21	.96
Selective Identification	13[a]	.64
Narcissistic Identification	14[a]	.93
Introjection	96[a]	.91
Psychotic Identification	4[a]	.89

[a]Indicates the number of responses rated for this category by either rater, with responses rated by both raters for the same category counted only once.

Selective Identification ($r = 0.64$), Narcissistic Identification ($r = 0.93$), Introjection ($r = 0.91$), and Psychotic Identification ($r = 0.89$). The percentage of agreements and nearly all obtained reliabilities were satisfactory, and in several cases may be considered fairly high for Rorschach scales.

Validity

The question of the validity of the Internalization Assessment Scale was first approached by determining to what extent the categories of internalization mechanisms included in the scale can be seen as conforming to the hierarchy represented by the differences in weighted scores. If this was the case then one would expect little coincidence of the mechanisms at either end of the scale and a more significant correlation between those mechanisms described as adjacent to one another along the continuum. Table 2 presents the intercorrelation between the four categories of internalization mechanisms in the total sample and within each group. All notable correlations occurred between categories adjacent to one another in the scale's hierarchy, indicating that the arrangement of operations on the scale is valid in terms of the order described. The category of psychotic identification was the only mechanism that did not show any sizable correlation with any other category, but this is most likely due to the rarity with which it was used (ten times in the total sample).

The principal tests of validity consisted of assessments of the expected relationships between the clinical diagnosis of depression and the number, quality, and type of internalization mechanisms employed. In light of the clinical and research literature indicating sex differences in the epidemiology of depression (Weissman and Klerman, 1977), typical experiences of depression (Blatt, Quinlan, Chevron, McDonald, and Zuroff, 1982), and internalization (Reich, 1954; Blum, 1976), t tests were performed to determine if there was a tendency across groups for males or females to score higher on the two basic measures of average level of internalization (IL) and the total number of internalizations employed (TI). The results of the t tests indicate that there are significant differences between males and females with regard to TI ($t = -2.93, p < .01$) but not for IL ($t = -1.10$, n.s.). Specifically, males showed a greater tendency to use Rorschach indices of internalization mechanisms. All tests of significance on the dependent measures were therefore carried out as two-way analyses of variance classified by sex

TABLE 2

Pearson R Intercorrelation Between All Indices of
Internalization Mechanisms in the Total Sample and as a
Function of Diagnostic Groups

	Selec-tive Identi-fication	Narcis-sistic Identi-fication	Intro-jection	Psy-chotic Identi-fication
(1) All Subjects (N=71)				
Selective Identification	1.00	.19*	.10	.02
Narcissistic Identification		1.00	.37**	.00
Introjection			1.00	.03
Psychotic Identification				1.00
(2) Normals (N=25)				
Selective Identification	1.00	.32*	.06	.15
Narcissistic Identification		1.00	.30***	.04
Introjection			1.00	.15
Psychotic Identification				1.00
(3) Remitteds (N=21)				
Selective Identification	1.00	− .16	.26	− .13
Narcissistic Identification		1.00	.37****	− .10
Introjection			1.00	− .16
Psychotic Identification				1.00
(4) Acutes (N=25)				
Selective Identification	1.00	− .15	− .01	− .09
Narcissistic Identification		1.00	.45****	− .01
Introjection			1.00	− .01
Psychotic Identification				1.00

$*p < .06.$ $**p < .01.$ $***p < .07.$ $****p < .05.$

and sample group. Differences between subjects in overall response productivity (R) were controlled for by an analysis of covariance procedure in analyses in which the quantity of specific responses represented the dependent variable. By employing R as a covariate in an analysis of variance, differences between groups may be attributed to diagnostic or sex distinctions.

Table 3 presents the means, standard deviations, and two-way analyses of covariance for internalization measures concerning quantity of particular responses. The comparison among groups was done

TABLE 3

Means, Standard Deviations and Two-Way Analyses of Covariance by Sample Group and Sex for Quantity of Internalization Measures

Part A: Sample Group

Variable	Acute Depressives (n=25)		Remitted Depressives (n=21)		Normal Controls (n=25)		Total (n=71)	
	M	SD	M	SD	M	SD	M	SD
Total Internalizations	5.28	4.43	4.71	3.26	6.68	3.79	5.61	3.92
$F(2, 64) = 1.60$, ns								
Psychotic Identification	0.16	0.62	0.10	0.44	0.16	0.47	0.14	0.52
$F(2, 64) = 0.10$, ns								
Introjection	4.12	3.89	3.95	2.80	4.56	2.83	4.23	3.20
$F(2, 64) = 2.80$, ns								
Narcissistic Identification	0.52	0.87	0.33	0.73	0.88	1.20	0.59	0.98
$F(2, 64) = 0.98$, ns								
Selective Identification	0.48	0.71	0.33	0.58	1.08	1.00	0.65	0.85
$F(2, 64) = 5.94**$								

(Continued)

TABLE 3 (Continued)

Part B: Sex

Variable	Acute Depressives		Remitted Depressives		Normal Controls		Total	
	Males (n=10)	Females (n=15)	Males (n=09)	Females (n=12)	Males (n=12)	Females (n=13)	Males (n=31)	Females (n=40)
Total Internalizations $F(1, 64) = 5.99*$	7.70	3.67	6.67	3.25	7.00	6.38	7.13	4.43
Psychotic Identification $F(1, 64) = 0.32$, ns	0.10	0.20	0.22	0.00	0.25	0.08	0.19	0.10
Introjection $F(1, 64) = 13.58**$	6.50	2.53	5.67	2.67	5.25	3.92	5.77	3.03
Narcissistic Identification $F(1, 64) = 0.34$, ns	0.80	0.33	0.56	0.17	0.75	1.00	0.71	0.50
Selective Identification $F(1, 64) = 8.71**$	0.30	0.60	0.22	0.42	0.75	1.38	0.45	0.80

$*p < .05.$ $**p < .01.$

by separate ANCOVAs covaried for response productivity. Table 3 is divided into two sections to reflect the separate sets of results for group effects and sex effects on the variables of interest. An inspection of Table 3, Part A, indicates that significant differences between the groups were found only for the category of Selective Identification ($F[2, 64] = 5.94, p < .01$). Normals, in comparison to both depressive groups, gave more Selective Identification responses. Since this category represents the highest level of internalization according to the scale used, this result was anticipated. No significant differences, however, were found among the groups regarding Rorschach indices of Total Internalizations ($F[2, 64] = 1.60$, n.s.), Psychotic Identification ($F[2, 64] = 0.10$, n.s.), Introjection ($F[2, 64] = 2.80$, n.s.), and Narcissistic Identification ($F[2, 64] = 0.98$, n.s.). Examination of Table 3, Part B, reveals significant differences between males and females in their use of Introjection ($F[1, 64] = 13.58, p < .01$) and Selective Identification ($F[1,64] = 8.71, p < .01$), as well as for the category of Total Internalizations ($F[1, 64] = 5.99, p < .05$). Specifically, men showed a significant tendency to use Introjection, as well as internalization mechanisms in general, more often than women. In contrast, women employed Selective Identification more often than men. No significant differences were found between males and females in their use of Psychotic Identification ($F[1, 64] = 0.32$, n.s.) or Narcissistic Identification ($F[1, 64] = 0.34$, n.s.). As indicated in Table 3, Introjection was the category most often used by all three sample groups and both sexes, making up approximately 75 percent of all the internalization responses given (300 of 398).

Table 4 presents the means, standard deviations, and two-way analyses of variance for measures concerning the quality of internalization responses. Internalization Level (IL) represents the average weighted internalization score per subject, and was intended to reflect the overall level of organization and differentiation of a subject's internalization responses. The values for the variable INT/TI represent the degree to which any one subject's total internalizations were made up of introjective responses. NRI/TI and SLI/TI represent similar ratios for Narcissistic Identification and Selective Identification, and all three variables were designed to provide measures of the predominant character or quality of an individual's internalizing defenses. No analogous analysis for Psychotic Identifications was carried out, in light of their rarity in the total sample. As Table 4, Part A, indicates, significant differences among the groups were found for Internalization Level (F

TABLE 4
Means, Standard Deviations and Two-Way Analyses of Covariance by Sample Group and Sex for Quality of Internalization Measures

Part A: Sample Group

Variable	Acute Depressives (n=24)		Remitted Depressives (n=20)		Normal Controls (n=25)		Total (n=69)	
	M	SD	M	SD	M	SD	M	SD
Internalization Level	5.40	1.03	5.67	0.69	5.02	0.86	5.34	0.91
$F_{(2, 63)} = 3.13$*								
INT/TI	74.7	30.0	86.6	17.0	68.7	23.0	76.0	24.0
$F_{(2, 63)} = 3.27$*								
NRI/TI	9.2	15.9	5.1	9.9	12.1	16.5	9.0	14.7
$F_{(2, 63)} = 1.26$, ns								
SLI/TI	12.8	23.7	5.9	10.9	17.2	16.3	12.4	18.4
$F_{(2, 63)} = 2.4$, ns								

Part B: Sex

Variable	Acute Depressives		Remitted Depressives		Normal Controls		Total	
	Males (n=9)	Females (n=15)	Males (n=9)	Females (n=11)	Males (n=12)	Females (n=13)	Males (n=30)	Females (n=39)
Internalization Level	5.63	5.26	5.73	5.26	5.17	4.89	5.47	5.24
$F(1, 63) = 1.42$, ns								
INT/TI	84.4	68.9	86.4	86.7	77.7	60.5	82.3	71.2
$F(1, 63) = 3.90^{**}$								
NRI/TI	10.37	8.41	5.68	4.55	8.46	15.38	8.20	9.64
$F(1, 63) = 0.19$								
SLT/TI	4.67	17.7	2.34	8.73	11.74	22.22	6.80	16.67
$F(1, 63) = 5.53^{*}$								

$^{*}p < .05.$ $^{**}p < .06.$

[2, 63] $= 3.13, p < .05$) and INT/TI (F[2,63] $= 3.27, p < .05$), while NRI/TI (F[2,63] $= 1.26$, n.s.) and SLI/TI (F[2, 63] $= 2.40$, n.s.) failed to distinguish the groups significantly. Specifically, normal subjects obtained a lower mean IL score than either depressive group, indicating a more differentiated and organized quality of internalization. In addition, the remitted group showed the greatest tendency to rely upon introjective mechanisms when internalizing, followed by acute depressives, and then normals. Table 4, Part 8, reveals significant differences between males and females in the extent to which they relied upon Selective Identification (F[1, 63] $= 5.53, p < .05$) as a defense, along with a strong trend for the variable INT/TI (F[1, 63] $= 3.90, p < .06$). Female subjects in each sample group tended to rely upon selective identification more often than males in that group, while men in the normal and acute groups differed from women in those groups in the degree to which introjection accounted for subjects' use of internalization. No significant differences were found between males and females for Internalization Level (F[1, 63] $= 1.42$, n.s.) or NRI/TI (F[1, 63] $= 0.19$, n.s.).

In light of the finding that acute and remitted depressives used the more primitive internalization mechanisms no more often than did normals, it seemed important to determine if some other quality of internalization responses on the Rorschach differentiated depressives and depression-prone individuals from people with no psychiatric history. The distinction between libidinal and aggressive impulses and affects as the principal motives behind internalization mechanisms is one qualitative means by which internalizations have been categorized (Klein, 1935, 1940; Jacobson, 1964). In keeping with this distinction, each response previously scored as an instance of internalization was again rated, by an advanced clinical graduate student, as benign or aggressive in accordance with Holt's guidelines (1970) for scoring Rorschach responses as oral receptive or oral aggressive.

Using the group totals of internalization responses rated as benign and as aggressive, it was found that the benign-aggressive ratio was greater in control subjects ($106/61 = 1.74$) than in either the remitted ($54/45 = 1.20$) or acute ($74/58 = 1.28$) groups. One way to view such a ratio is that for every Aggressive Internalization they employ, normals will employ 1.74 Benign Internalizations, whereas the two depressive groups show a lesser capacity to counteract Aggressive Internalizations with those derived from more benign motives. In addition, scores for the Hamilton Rating Scale for Depression in the remitted group obtained significant correlations with scores for Aggressive Internalizations ($r =$

.46, $p < .05$), but no significant correlation with Benign Internalizations ($r = .21$, n.s.). This was not the case in the group of normals, who as a group showed no consistent relationship between a rating of their mood and measures of either Aggressive ($r = -.04$, n.s.) or Benign Internalizations ($r = .12$, n.s.).

Table 5 presents the means, standard deviations, and two-way analyses of covariance for Benign Internalizations and Aggressive Internalizations and two-way analyses of variance for the variable Benign-Aggressive Internalization Balance (BAIB). BAIB represents a measure of the relative balance of internalization responses rated as benign or aggressive in a subject's record, and each BAIB value was derived by the following formula: (# Benign Internalizations —# Aggressive Internalizations / # Benign Internalizations + # Aggressive Internalizations) $\times$ 100. As indicated in Table 5, Part A, no significant differences between the groups were found for Benign ($F[2, 62] = 2.82$) or Aggressive Internalization ($F[2, 62] = 0.50$) or in BAIB ($F[2, 63] = 0.81$), although the normal controls showed a trend toward using more Benign Internalization responses than either depressive group. Table 5, Part B, reveals that males employed significantly more internalization responses rated as aggressive than female subjects ($F[2, 62] = 10.56$, $p < .01$).

In summary, although the three sample groups generated statistically equivalent amounts of Rorschach responses ($F[2, 69] = 0.88$, n.s.), the normal subjects offered a significantly greater number of Selective Identification responses, obtained significantly lower internalization level scores (indicating more differentiated and organized internalization processes), and showed a nonsignificant tendency to employ more benign internalizations. In comparison, remitted subjects showed a significant tendency to rely more on introjective mechanisms when internalizing, and, in contrast to normals, demonstrated a significant correlation between a rating of depressive symptoms and the use of internalizations rated as deriving from aggressive motives. Across all sample groups, males showed a significant tendency to use introjection more often and more exclusively than females, and to use Aggressive Internalizations more often. Women, on the other hand, used Selective Identification more often and more exclusively than men.

Discussion

The findings of this study indicate that the four categories of internalization included in the scale can be scored reliably. In addition, the

TABLE 5

Means, Standard Deviations and Two-Way Analyses of Covariance and Variance by Sex and Sample Group for Benign and Sadistic Internalizations

Part A: Sample Group

Variable	Acute Depressives ($n=24$)		Remitted Depressives ($n=20$)		Normal Controls ($n=25$)		Total ($n=69$)	
	M	SD	M	SD	M	SD	M	SD
Benign Internalizations								
$F_{(2, 62)} = 2.82$, ns	3.08	2.48	2.70	1.81	4.24	2.57	3.39	2.40
Aggressive Internalizations								
$F_{(2, 62)} = 0.50$, ns	2.09	2.11	2.25	2.02	2.44	2.08	2.26	2.05
Benign-Aggressive Internalizations Balance								
$F_{(2, 63)} = 0.81$, ns	18.34	79.1	17.49	56.6	34.21	45.7	23.93	57.4

Part B: Sex

Variables	Acute Depressives		Remitted Depressives		Normal Controls		Total	
	Males ($n=9$)	Females ($n=15$)	Males ($n=9$)	Females ($n=11$)	Males ($n=12$)	Females ($n=13$)	Males ($n=30$)	Females ($n=39$)
Benign Internalizations $F(2, 62) = 0.05$, ns	4.44	2.27	3.44	2.09	3.83	4.62	3.90	3.00
Aggressive Internalizations $F(2, 62) = 10.56**$	3.38	1.40	3.22	1.45	3.17	1.77	3.24	1.54
Benign-Aggressive Internalizations Balance $F(1, 63) = 3.17$, ns	9.80	22.90	5.80	27.06	14.21	52.68	10.38	34.00

*$p < .01$.

pattern of intercorrelations among the four categories was consistent with the developmental and structural hierarchy in which they were ordered on the scale, indicating some support for the validity of this order. The results pertaining to the use of the various internalization mechanisms provide some partial support for the validity of the scale, although the number of variables which did not significantly distinguish the sample groups indicate possible problems in the construction of the scale and perhaps in the nature of the sample groups as well.

No statistically significant differences were found among normals, remitted depressives, and acute depressives with respect to their overall tendencies to employ internalization mechanisms, or in the amount in which they employed indices of psychotic identification, introjection, and narcissistic identification. Significant differences among the groups were found on the variable Internalization Level, a single, average weighted score intended to summarize the overall level of organization and maturity of a person's repertoire of internalization mechanisms. The level of differentiation and organization in the internalization responses of both depressive groups were much below that obtained by normals, indicating a more regressive level of internalization for depressives. Significant group differences were also found with respect to the tendency to employ indices of selective identification, which was employed most often by normals. Differences among the three groups were also significant for INT/TI, indicating that remitted depressives rely much more exclusively on the mechanism or introjection than normals, even though they use it less often in an absolute sense. These findings provide some support for the prediction that depressives would demonstrate a more primitive defensive organization than normals, as well as having implications for the lack of flexibility in defensive functioning in the remitted depressive group as compared to normals. These latter findings would seem to indicate that the groups differ in ways relevant to internalization, and this implies that the scale possesses a certain degree of validity.

Significant differences were also found between males and females in their use of Rorschach indices of internalization. Men showed significant tendencies to employ introjection and aggressive internalizations more often than women, and males showed a very strong trend toward employing internalization mechanisms in general more often than women. In contrast, women demonstrated a significantly greater propensity to use selective identification more often than men and to rely upon it for a larger share of their internalizing responses.

Sex differences in the etiology (Lewis, 1976), subjective phe-nomenology (Chevron, Quinlan, and Blatt, 1978), and epidemiology (Weissman and Klerman, 1977) of depression have been described and documented by others. Blatt and his colleagues have carried out research on the subjective experience of depression which suggests that there are two primary dimensions of depressive experiences that differ-entiate types of depression: an "anaclitic" or dependent dimension and an "introjective" or self-critical dimension (Blatt et al., 1982). These two types have been found to be connected with gender differences and differences in the sense of sex role congruence (Chevron, Quinlan, and Blatt, 1978). Depressive experiences of the introjective type tend to occur with greater frequency in men, while anaclitic depressive expe-riences occur with greater frequency in women. An important distin-guishing aspect between the two depressive types is the prominent use of the defense of introjection in the introjective type. Thus, the finding in this study of sex differences in the use of internalization, particularly the greater use of introjection by males, is consistent with the findings of Blatt and his colleagues. The results with respect to the differences between males and females may in this context be seen as additional support for the validity of the Internalization Assessment Scale.

The internalizations of the three groups were also examined by dividing responses into those rated as aggressive and those rated as benign. This approach to the data was based in large part on the view articulated by object relations theorists that a predominance of "good" internal objects established through internalization over "bad" internal objects established through internalization is a necessary precondition for healthy psychological functioning (Segal, 1973). Evidence that correlations between scores on the Hamilton Rating Scale for Depres-sion correlated significantly with a measure of aggressive internaliza-tions in the remitted group but not in the normal sample implied that the effects on mood of aggressivized internalizations differed in people prone to depression as opposed to people with no such vulnerability. Since the control group as a whole employed more benign internaliza-tions than either depressive group, it was hypothesized that this effect might be due to the differences among the groups in their use of benign internalizations that might serve to counterbalance the depressing effects of the aggressive internalizations. Analyses of variance found no significant differences between the groups in their use of benign inter-nalizations or in the individual balance of benign and aggressive inter-nalizations, but this approach to the problem of internalization and depression may represent a promising avenue of approach for future research. The implications of this for the clinical theory of depression include the possibility that regressions into states of depression may involve not only an increase in sadistically motivated introjections, but also a falling away of the capacity to call upon more benign or loving internalizations to counteract the disruptive effects of internalized aggression.

LIMITATIONS OF THE STUDY

Since several experimental hypotheses derived from the clinical and theoretical literature on internalization and depression were not supported by the data from this study, the validity of the internalization measures is the first aspect of the study that must be questioned. Introjection accounted for a little over 75 percent of the total number of responses scored as instances of internalization, indicating that the conceptual boundaries of the introjection category are overinclusive. It is likely that this contributed to the failure to find significant differences among the groups for the introjection category. In general, the scale seems to provide too little differentiation among pathological introjection, constructive introjection, and selective identification.

Responses from the category of introjection made up the majority of internalization responses for both sexes, but the greater propensity on the part of women to also employ selective identification may reflect a different overall style of internalization. The subcategory of selective identification most often used by subjects (37/46 or 80 percent of SLI responses) is labeled on the scoring sheet as "Oral mutuality." Such content is consistent with the emphasis placed on the capacity for relatedness and warmth in the feminine sex-role stereotype (Bem, 1974). In fact, females used this subcategory more than twice as often as males (25–12 overall; 16–8 among normals, who used it more often than did the depressives). In contrast, the subcategories for introjection emphasize aggression, competition, and for the most part, solitary or independent figures or objects. The differences found between males and females in the use of selective identification may imply that the contents of the selective identification category reflect higher level forms of identification for women but do not include contents likely to be emphasized in male selective identifications. Higher level male identifications emphasizing independence, assertiveness, and modulated aggressive tendencies are, in a sense, buried within the introjection category.

The second major difficulty in the methodology concerns whether acute and remitted depressives were adequately differentiated as groups. An ANOVA for Developmental Level scores (H. Friedman, 1953) failed to obtain significance, although the group DL scores differed in the expected direction. A certain portion of the remitted sample may have been moving toward acute clinical status, while some percentage of acute cases may have been closer to remission at the time of testing than would be optimal for the purposes of this study. For instance, the two patients who ranked first and fourth in the remitted group in total internalizations obtained Hamilton scores of 15 and 14. All other subjects in the remitted group had Hamilton scores of under 10, indicative of a clinical state of euthymia. In the acute group some patients underwent psychological testing a full five or six weeks after the date of their admission to the hospital. During that time most were under active treatment with antidepressant medication, and thus their clinical status at the time of testing may have been approaching a remission of acute symptoms.

An additional point with regard to the acute depressive sample concerns possible bias in the data due to an inadvertent use of different subtypes of depression. For instance, it has been shown that 20–25 percent of patients treated for major depression will eventually develop an episode of mania, indicating an actual underlying diagnosis of bipolar affective disorder, or manic-depressive illness (Perris, 1968; Strober and Carlson, 1982). In this study two patients in the acute sample gave over fifty responses to the Rorschach. This sort of productivity is atypical in the Rorschachs of depressives, which are usually characterized by constriction (Rapaport, Gill, and Schafer, 1945), and raises the question of whether the composition of the acute sample consists of some patients developing bipolar illness.

The question of sex differences in depression represents one aspect of the larger issue concerning locating subtypes of depression. In this study significant differences were found between males and females in the use of several Rorschach indices of internalization. In addition, some consistent but statistically nonsignificant findings regarding sex differences indicated that men and women demonstrated different patterns of internalization between the three sample groups. It appears possible that women may actually internalize less as they enter an episode of depression, and internalize even less again as they enter a state of remission. By contrast, men may internalize more as they regress, and then, as they begin to recover, decrease the amount in which they use internalization to a point even less frequent than normal. For both sexes the mechanism of introjection increasingly dominates their internalizing processes as they move through an episode of acute depression into a phase of remission. In the course of this process both sexes seem to lose touch with their capacity to rely upon selective identifications to reinforce their sense of being loved and competent. In response to this inner loss, described by Jacobson (1954a) as a breakdown of higher level identifications, men may intensify their efforts to control the object through introjection. Women, on the other hand, may reduce their introjective efforts, but these more primitive operations nevertheless become their primary mode of internalization.

Blatt (1974) has emphasized that the syndromes of anaclitic and introjective depression are associated with the use of different defenses. In his view introjective depression is associated with the use of introjection and identification with the aggressor, while anaclitic depression features the defenses of denial and repression. If the sex differences found in this study are viewed as possible correlates to previous sex differences found for anaclitic and introjective depression, then, contrary to Blatt's views, these results would indicate that the vicissitudes of internalization are important aspects of both syndromes. Women (i.e., anaclitic depressives) may deemphasize internalization mechanisms, while men (i.e., introjective depressives) may intensify their efforts at internalization. Women, however, do not emphasize dependent modes of relating to the exclusion of internalization, as Blatt implies, but instead employ internalizations which emphasize gratifying dependence and relatedness in their content. Depressed men are not without such internalizations, but, as Blatt's group point out, they are not as prominent as for women. The possible intensification of introjection processes in men in acute depression is consistent with the higher rate of suicide in depressed men as opposed to women, as suicide has been specifically linked to sadistic introjections (Maltsberger and Buie, 1980).

THE STATE OF REMISSION IN DEPRESSIVE ILLNESS

In this study the concept of depression-proneness was approached by including a sample of formerly depressed patients in a state of clinical remission. It is difficult to assert, however, that the characteristics of this remitted sample are representative of personality features which may predispose someone to depressive episodes, because its characteristic features may actually represent sequelae of the depressive syndrome rather than predisposing attributes. It does seem feasible, however, to make more straightforward generalizations from the remitted sample's characteristics to the state of remission from a depressive episode.

One of the major findings of this study is that for both men and women the state of remission from an episode of major depression is characterized by comparatively few efforts at internalization of any kind. In comparison to normals, the internalizing style of remitted depressives is dominated by introjective processes emphasizing oral aggression, sadistic control, and removal of conflicts from the interpersonal sphere of external reality to the inner world of psychic reality. This overreliance on introjection may represent one aspect of the remitted depressive's vulnerability to further depressive episodes. Introjection assumes a nearly exclusive dominance over the remitted depressive's internalizing function, but the overall use and quality of internalization is reduced in the state of remission. The presence of internalization mechanisms, like any defense, is a sign of active coping with one's situation or difficulties. Internalization mechanisms in particular can be viewed as indicators of efforts to seek new methods of reacting and coping. Their decline in the process of remission may indicate an avoidance of the internal changes such defenses might precipitate.

These findings regarding depressives in remission may be seen as analogous to Weiner's formulation of remitting schizophrenia (1966). Weiner describes the remitting schizophrenic as in a tenuous state marked by constriction and a censoring of any distressing thoughts or feelings out of a sense of dread of the return of psychosis. Weiner's description of the remitting process in schizophrenia bears great similarity to McGlashan, Levy, and Carpenter's notion of "sealing over" (1975, p. 1269), which they describe as a distinct style employed by people in coping with the process of recovery from a serious decompensation. Sealing over is based on the mechanisms of denial and withdrawal and is contrasted with a style of "integration" (p. 1269) characterized by curiosity and efforts to learn new methods of adjustment. Although the fact that a similar process may characterize the recovery process in depressive illness has not been stressed in the literature, the results in this study can be viewed as preliminary evidence that remitting depression features constriction and withdrawal in a manner similar to remitting schizophrenia.

Further understanding of the reduction of internalizing processes in remitted depression may be gained through reference to clinical writings on efforts to avoid internalization. Greenson (1954) described a syndrome characterized by a "struggle against identifications" (p. 200), while more recently Horner (1983) has discussed a phenomenon she refers to as the "refusal to identify" (p. 113). Greenson's patients are described as people prone to disturbances in mood who had introjected an ambivalently hated object. Through the use of denial and negation they attempted to remain unaware of such introjects, which they unconsciously experienced as ominous and frightening. These patients experienced their moods as something akin to being consumed by their introjects, and the struggle against dysphoric moods was subjectively felt to be synonymous with the struggle against identification with certain introjects. Greenson points out that his patients tended to feel devoured by the introject, and Horner points out that such a refusal to identify is carried out in order to protect a particular self-image or sense of identity.

In general, the state of remitted depression can perhaps be best understood as a defense against further injury to the self. The retreat from a previously disappointing and unpredictable reality that characterizes acute depression is reversed to a certain extent, but the patient continues to cling to a sadomasochistic inner world of critical, punitive figures which, although painful, is unconsciously felt to be more controllable (Mollon and Parry, 1984). A residual depressive structure of internal object relations remains, although the overt symptoms of depression have dissipated, and is expressed in the form of introversion, passivity, social withdrawal, and a sense of fragile vulnerability. The person is dogged by constant anxiety of the loss of good objects, feels impoverished and weakened, and experiences a perpetual dread of regression into acute depression. The process of working through this period may have a great deal to do with the process described by Sandler (1960) as identification with an introject, which involves the gradual integration of the impulses and affects so strenuously defended against through confining them to an introject form. In Rorschach internalization terms, this might be expected to be manifested in the form of a reemergence of selective identification responses.

CONCLUDING REMARKS

One major conclusion that may be drawn from this study involves the degree to which normals utilize internalization. Normals employed every category of internalization as much as or more often than either depressive group. This was even more pronounced for female subjects, whereas men showed a nonsignificant tendency to internalize more in states of acute depression. In either case, however, the pervasiveness of internalization in everyday functioning is apparent, and thus it seems clear that the changes which internalization processes undergo during times of stress or psychological disturbances have as much to do with their quality as with their quantity. This omnipresence of internalization in everyday life would seem to support object relations views of development and normal functioning, which, following Freud's (1923) original formulations, removed internalization mechanisms from the realm of pathological defense mechanisms and placed them at the center of the notions of character development and ego growth (Heimann, 1952).

The psychoanalytic theory of depression has, with certain variations, consistently rested on the concept of certain pathognomonic internalizations which bring about decreases in self-esteem, turbulent internal conflict between ego and superego, and the emergence of a pathological mood state. Although some reference has been made to sex differences in the etiology of depression in terms of differences in superego structure, little distinction has been made between men and women concerning these pathognomonic internalizations considered crucial to the dynamic etiology of the depressive syndrome. The results of this study, however, indicate that men and women use internalization differently as they enter states of depression. Specifically, men may function in a manner that is essentially in accordance with psychoanalytic theory, as they appear to intensify their efforts at internalization as they enter depressive states. Women, by contrast, may actually decrease the amount of internalization they engage in, although the overall quality of the internalizations they do carry out changes in a way that bears some resemblance to that described in the clinical psychoanalytic literature. It may be, however, that the psychoanalytic theory of depression may have to be altered to account for sex differences if further research substantiates these preliminary findings.

Future studies using the scale presented here to explore the nature of depression should await the revisions in the scale suggested above, and may also profit by approaching the problem differently in certain respects. First, clinical diagnosis alone may not be a reliable method to establish criterion groups, especially those under active treatment and prone to undergo fairly rapid changes in their clinical status. Use of a measure more sensitive to current state, such as the Hamilton Rating Scale for Depression, may provide a more valid estimate of the state of depression. In addition, the use of other defense scales, such as the Rorschach Defense Scale (Lerner and Lerner, 1980), in combination with the Internalization Assessment Scale may provide a more comprehensive picture of the relation among various defenses in different stages of depression. Finally, the relation between depression and borderline personality disorders might be studied using the Internalization Assessment Scale, with attention to the nature of depression in borderline disorders (Perry, 1985) and the possible role of internalization mechanisms in borderline psychopathology as a means of exploring the hypothesis that borderline disorders represent a subclinical manifestation of affective disorder (Gunderson and Elliott, 1985).

REFERENCES

Abraham, K. (1924), A short study of the development of the libido, viewed in the light of mental disorders. In: *Selected Papers of Karl Abraham*, ed. D. Bryan & A. Strachey. New York: Brunner/Mazel, 1979, pp. 418-501.

Akiskal, H. S. (1981), Subaffective disorders: Dysthymic, cyclothymic and bipolar II disorders in the "borderline" realm. *Psychiatric Clinics of North America.* 4:25-46.

Balint, A. (1943), Identification. *Internat. J. Psycho-Anal.*, 24:97-107.

Beck, S. J. (1944), *Rorschach's Test: Vol. I. Basic Processes.* New York: Grune & Stratton.

Bem, S. L. (1974), The measurement of psychological androgyny. *J. Consult. & Clin. Psychol.*, 42:155-162.

Blatt, S. J. (1974), Levels of object representation in anaclitic and introjective depression. *Psychoanalytic Study of the Child*, 29:107-157.

_____ Brenneis, C. B., Schimek, J. G., & Glick, M. (1976), Normal development and psychopathological impairment of the concept of the object on the Rorschach. *J. Abnorm. Psychol.*, 85:264-273.

_____ Lerner, H. D. (1983), The psychological assessment of object representation. *J. Personal. Assess.*, 47:7-28.

_____ Quinlan, D. M., Chevron, E., McDonald, C., & Zuroff, D. (1982), Dependency and self-criticism: Psychological dimensions of depression. *J. Consult. & Clin. Psychol.*, 50:113-124.

_____ Ritzler, B. A. (1974a), Suicide and the representation of transparency and cross-sections on the Rorschach. *J. Consult. & Clin. Psychol.*, 42:280-287.

_____ _____ (1974b), Thought disorder and boundary disturbances in psychosis. *J. Consult. & Clin. Psychol.*, 42:370-381.

_____ Shichman, S. (1981), Antisocial behavior and personality organization. In: *Object and Self: A Developmental Approach*, ed. S. Tuttman, C. Kaye, & M. Zimmerman. New York: International Universities Press, pp. 325-367.

_____ Wild, C. M. (1976), *Schizophrenia: A Developmental Analysis.* New York: Academic Press.

Blum, H. P. (1976), Masochism, the ego ideal, and the psychology of women. *J. Amer. Psychoanal. Assn.*, 24:157-191.

Brierley, M. (1944), Notes on metapsychology as process theory. *Internat. J. Psycho-Anal.*, 25:97-107.

Chevron, E., Quinlan, D. M., & Blatt, S. J. (1978), Sex roles and gender differences in the experience of depression. *J. Abnormal Psychol.* 87:680-683.

Cooper, S. H., & Arnow, D. (1984), Prestage versus defensive splitting and the borderline personality: A Rorschach analysis. *Psychoanal. Psychol.*, 1:235-248.

Dare, C., & Holder, A. (1981), Developmental aspects of the interaction between narcissism, self-esteem and object relations. *Internat. J. Psycho-Anal.*, 62:323-337.

Deutsch, H. (1942), Some forms of emotional disturbance and their relationship to schizophrenia. *Psychoanal. Quart.*, 11:301-321.

Eisnitz, A. J. (1980), The organization of the self-representation and its influence on pathology. *Psychoanal. Quart.*, 49:361–392.

Exner, J. E. (1969), Rorschach responses as an index of narcissism. *J. Proj. Tech. & Personal. Assess.*, 33:324–330.

——— (1974), *The Rorschach: A Comprehensive System.* New York: Wiley.

Fenichel, O. (1945), *The Psychoanalytic Theory of Neurosis.* New York: Norton.

Freud, A. (1936), *The Ego and the Mechanisms of Defense.* Rev. ed. New York: International Universities Press, 1966.

Freud, S. (1905), Three essays on the theory of sexuality. *Standard Edition*, 7:130–243. London: Hogarth Press, 1953.

——— (1914), On narcissism. *Standard Edition*, 14:73–102. London: Hogarth Press, 1957.

——— (1910), Leonardo da Vinci and a memory of his childhood. *Standard Edition*, 11:63–137. London: Hogarth Press, 1957.

——— (1917), Mourning and melancholia. *Standard Edition*, 14:243–258. London: Hogarth Press, 1957.

——— (1921), Group psychology and the analysis of the ego. *Standard Edition*, 18:69–143. London: Hogarth Press, 1955.

——— (1923), The ego and the id. *Standard Edition*, 19:12–66. London: Hogarth Press, 1961.

——— (1926), Inhibitions, symptoms and anxiety. *Standard Edition*, 20:87–174. London: Hogarth Press, 1961.

——— (1933), New introductory lectures on psycho-analysis. *Standard Edition*, 22:5–182. London: Hogarth Press, 1964.

Friedman, H. (1953), Perceptual regression in schizophrenia: An hypothesis suggested by the use of the Rorschach test. *J. Proj. Tech.*, 17:171–185.

Friedman, L. (1980), The barren prospect of a representational world. *Psychoanal. Quart.*, 49:215–233.

Frosch, J. (1983), *The Psychotic Process.* New York: International Universities Press.

Goldfried, M. R., Stricker, G. S., & Weiner, I. B. (1971), Friedman's developmental level scoring. In: *Rorschach Handbook of Clinical and Research Applications*, ed. M. R. Goldfried, G. S. Stricker, & I. B. Weiner. Englewood Cliffs, N.J.: Prentice-Hall.

Grala, C. (1980), The concept of splitting and its manifestation on the Rorschach test. *Bull. Menn. Clin.*, 44:253–271.

Greenson, R. (1954), The struggle against identification. *J. Amer. Psychoanal. Assn.*, 2:200–217.

Gunderson, J. G., & Elliott, G. R. (1985), The interface between borderline personality disorder and affective disorder. *Amer. J. Psychiat.*, 142:277–288.

Hamilton, M. (1967), Development of a rating scale for primary depressive illness. *Brit. J. Soc. & Clin. Psychol.*, 6:278–296.

——— (1982), Symptoms and assessment of depression. In: *Handbook of Affective Disorders*, ed. E. S. Paykel. New York: Guilford Press.

Hartmann, H. (1950), Comments on the psychoanalytic theory of the ego. *Psychoanalytic Study of the Child*, 5:74–96.

Harty, M. K. (1986), Preconditions for internalization: Introjective, projective, and boundary phenomena in the Rorschach. In: *Exploring Object Relations Phenomena Through Psychological Tests*, ed. M. Kissen. New York: International Universities Press, pp. 89–126.

Heimann, P. (1952), Certain functions of introjection and projection in early infancy. In: *Developments in Psycho-Analysis*, ed. M. Klein, P. Heimann, S. Issacs, & J. Riviere. London: Hogarth Press, pp. 122–168.

Hendrick, I. (1951), Early development of the ego. Identification in infancy. *Psychoanal. Quart.*, 20:44–61.

Holt, R. R. (1970), Manual for the Scoring of Primary Process Manifestations in Rorschach Responses. Unpublished manuscript, New York University Research Center for Mental Health.

Horner, A. J. (1983), Refusal to identify: Developmental impasse. *Dynam. Psychother.*, 1:111–121.

Isaacs, S. (1952), The nature and function of phantasy. In: *Developments in Psycho-Analysis*, ed. M. Klein, P. Heimann, S. Isaacs, & J. Riviere. London: Hogarth Press, pp. 67–122.

Jacobson, E. (1953), Contribution to the metapsychology of cyclothymic depression. In: *Affective Disorders*, ed. P. Greenacre. New York: International Universities Press, pp. 49–83.

———— (1954a), Contribution to the metapsychology of psychotic identifications. *J. Amer. Psychoanal. Assn.*, 2:49–83.

———— (1954b), On psychotic identifications. *Internat. J. Psycho-Anal.*, 35:102–108.

———— (1957), On normal and pathological moods: Their nature and functions. *Psychoanalytic Study of the Child*, 12:73–113.

———— (1964), *The Self and the Object World*. New York: International Universities Press.

———— (1971), *Depression: Comparative Studies of Normal, Neurotic, and Psychotic Conditions*. New York: International Universities Press.

———— (1975), The regulation of self-esteem. In: *Depression and Human Existence*, ed. E. J. Anthony & T. Benedek. Boston: Little, Brown, pp. 169–181.

Kernberg, O. F. (1975), *Borderline Conditions and Pathological Narcissism*. New York: Aronson.

———— (1980), *Internal World and External Reality*. New York: Aronson.

Klein, M. (1935), A contribution to the psychogenesis of manic-depressive states. *Internat. J. Psycho-Anal.*, 16:145–174.

———— (1940), Mourning and its relation to manic-depressive states. *Internat. J. Psycho-Anal.*, 21:125–153.

Klopfer, B., Ainsworth, M., Klopfer, W., & Holt, R. (1954), *Developments in the Rorschach Technique: Vol. 1*. New York: Harcourt Brace.

Kohut, H. (1971), *The Analysis of the Self*. New York: International Universities Press.

Krohn, A., & Mayman, M. (1974), Object representations in dreams and projective tests: A construct validational study. *Bull. Menn. Clin.*, 38:445–466.

Kwawer, J. S. (1979), Borderline phenomena, interpersonal relations, and the Rorschach test. *Bull. Menn. Clin.*, 43:515–524.

———— (1980), Primitive interpersonal modes, borderline phenomena, and Rorschach content. In: *Borderline Phenomena and the Rorschach Test*, ed. J. Kwawer, H. Lerner, P. Lerner, & A. Sugarman. New York: International Universities Press, pp. 89–105.

Lerner, H. D., & Lerner, P. M. (1982), A comparative study of defensive structure in neurotic, borderline, and schizophrenic patients. *Psychoanal. & Contemp. Thought*, 5:77–115.

———— St. Peter, S. (1984), Patterns of object relations in neurotic, borderline and schizophrenic patients. *Psychiat.*, 47:77–92.

———— Sugarman, A., & Gaughran, J. (1981), Borderline and schizophrenic patients: A comparative study of defensive structure. *J. Nerv. & Ment. Dis.*, 169:705–711.

Lerner, P. M., & Lerner, H. D. (1980), Rorschach assessment of primitive defenses in borderline personality structure. In: *Borderline Phenomena and the Rorschach Test*, ed. J. Kwawer, H. Lerner, P. Lerner, & A. Sugarman. New York: International Universities Press, pp. 257–274.

Lewis, H. B. (1976), *Psychic War in Men and Women*. New York: New York University Press.

Loewald, H. (1962), Internalization, separation, mourning, and the superego. *Psychoanal. Quart.*, 31:483-504.

Mahler, M. S. (1966), Notes on the development of basic moods: The depressive affect. In: *Psychoanalysis—A General Psychology*, ed. R. Loewenstein, L. Newman, M. Schur, & A. Solnit. New York: International Universities Press, pp. 152-168.

_____ (1968), *On Human Symbiosis and the Vicissitudes of Individuation*. New York: International Universities Press.

_____ (1972), Rapprochement subphase of the separation-individuation process. *Psychoanal. Quart.*, 41:487-506.

_____ Pine, F., & Bergman, A. (1975), *The Psychological Birth of the Human Infant*. New York: Basic Books.

Maltsberger, J. T., & Buie, D. H. (1980), The devices of suicide: Revenge, riddance, and rebirth. *Internat. Rev. Psycho-Anal.*, 7:61-72.

Mayman, M. (1967), Object representations and object relationships in Rorschach responses. *J. Proj. Tech. & Personal. Assess.*, 31:17-24.

McDevitt, J. B., & Mahler, M. S. (1980), Object constancy, individuality, and internalization. In: *The Course of Life: Psychoanalytic Contributions Toward Understanding Personality Development. Vol. 1: Infancy and Early Childhood*, ed. S. I. Greenspan & G. H. Pollock. DHHS Publication No. ADM 80-786). Washington, DC: U. S. Government Printing Office, pp. 407-423.

McGlashan, T. H., Levy, S. T., & Carpenter, W. J. (1975), Integration and sealing over. Clinically distinct recovery styles from schizophrenia. *Arch. Gen. Psychiat*, 32:1269-1272.

Meltzoff, A. N., & Moore, M. K. (1983), The origins of imitation in infancy: Paradigm, phenomena, and theories. In: *Advances in Infancy Research*, ed. L. P. Lipsitt & C. K. Rovee-Collier. Norwood, NJ: Ablex Publishing Corp., pp. 265-301.

Milrod, D. (1982), The wished-for self image. *Psychoanalytic Study of the Child*, 37:95-120. New Haven, CT: Yale University Press.

Mollon, P., & Parry, G. (1984), The fragile self: Narcissistic disturbances and the protective function of depression. *Brit. J. Med. Psychol.*, 57:137-145.

Parkin, A. (1976), Melancholia: A reconsideration. *J. Amer. Psychoanal. Assn.*, 24:123-139.

Perris, C. (1968), The course of depressive psychoses. *Acta Psychiatrica Scandinavica*, 44:238-248.

Perry, J. C. (1985), Depression in borderline personality disorder: Lifetime prevalence at interview and longitudinal course of symptoms. *Amer. J. Psychiat.*, 142:15-21.

Phillips, L., & Smith, J. G. (1953), *Rorschach Interpretation: Advanced Technique*. New York: Grune & Stratton.

Piaget, J., & Inhelder, B. (1948), *The Child's Conception of Space*. New York: Norton, 1967.

Pine, F. (1980), On the expansion of the affect array: A developmental description. In: *Rapprochement: The Critical Subphase of Separation-Individuation*, ed. R. Lax, S. Bach, & J. Burland. New York: Aronson, pp. 217-233.

_____ (1981), In the beginning: Contributions to a psychoanalytic developmental psychology. *Internat. Rev. Psycho-Anal.*, 8:15-33.

_____ (1982), The experience of self: Aspects of its formation, expansion, and vulnerability. *Psychoanalytic Study of the Child*, 37:143-167.

Rado, S. (1928), The problem of melancholia. *Internat. J. Psycho-Anal.*, 9:420-438.

Rapaport, D., Gill, M., & Schafer, R. (1945), *Diagnostic Psychological Testing*. Rev. ed.

New York: International Universities Press, 1968.

Reich, A. (1954), Early identification as archaic elements in the superego. *J. Amer. Psychoanal. Assn.*, 2:218-238.

Rinsley, D. (1979), Fairbairn's object-relations theory: A reconsideration in terms of newer knowledge. *Bull. Menn. Clin.*, 43:489-514.

Ritvo, S., & Solnit, A. (1958), Influence of early mother-child interaction on identification processes. *Psychoanal. Study of the Child*, 13:64-85. New York: International Universities Press.

Rorschach, H. (1923), *Psychodiagnostics.* Berne, Switzerland: Hans Huber, 1942.

Roth, D., & Blatt, S. J. (1974a), Spatial representations and psychopathology. *J. Amer. Psychoanal. Assn.*, 22:854-872.

——————— ——————— (1974b), Spatial representations of transparency and the suicide potential. *Internat. J. Psycho-Anal.*, 55:287-293.

Sandler, J. (1960), The background of safety. *Internat. J. Psycho-Anal.*, 59:215-223.

——————— (1981), Unconscious wishes and human relationships. *Contemp. Psychoanal.*, 17:180-196.

——————— Rosenblatt, B. (1962), The concept of the representational world. *Psychoanalytic Study of the Child*, 17:128-145.

Schafer, R. (1954), *Psychoanalytic Interpretation in Rorschach Testing.* New York: Grune & Stratton.

——————— (1968a), *Aspects of Internalization.* New York: International Universities Press.

——————— (1968b), The mechanisms of defense. *Internat. J. Psycho-Anal.*, 49:49-62.

——————— (1968c), On the theoretical and technical conceptualization of activity and passivity. *Psychoanal. Quart.*, 37:173-198.

——————— (1972), Internalization: Process or fantasy? *Psychoanalytic Study of the Child*, 27:411-436.

——————— (1983), *The Analytic Attitude.* New York: Basic Books.

Schwartz, F., & Lazar, Z. (1984), Contaminated thinking: A specimen of the primary process. *Psychoanal. Psychol.*, 1:319-334.

Segal, H. (1973), *Introduction to the Work of Melanie Klein.* Rev. ed. New York: Basic Books.

Silverman, L., & Silverman, D. (1960), Womb fantasies in heroin addiction: A Rorschach study. *J. Project. Tech.*, 24:52-63.

Stern, D. (1983), Implications of infant research for psychoanalytic theory and practice. In: *Psychiatry Update: Vol. II*, ed. L. Grinspoon. Washington, DC: American Psychiatric Association, pp. 8-21.

Stone, M. H. (1979), Contemporary shift of the borderline concept from a subschizophrenic disorder to a subaffective disorder. *Psychiatric Clinics of North America*, 2:577-594.

Strober, M., & Carlson, G. (1982), Bipolar illness in adolescents with major depression. *Arch. Gen. Psychiat.*, 39:549-555.

Sugarman, A., Bloom-Feshbach, S., & Bloom-Feshbach, J. (1980), The psychological dimensions of borderline adolescents. In: *Borderline Phenomena and the Rorschach Test*, ed. J. S. Kwawer, H. D. Lerner, P. M. Lerner, & A. Sugarman. New York: International Universities Press, pp. 469-494.

Tyson, P., & Tyson, R. L. (1984), Narcissism and superego development. *J. Amer. Psychoanal. Assn.*, 32:75-98.

Urist, J. (1976), The Rorschach test as a multidimensional measure of object relations. Doctoral dissertation, University of Michigan, 1973. *Dissertation Abstracts International*, 34:17-65.

Weiner, I. B. (1966), *Psychodiagnosis in Schizophrenia.* New York: Wiley.
Weissman, M. M., & Klerman, G. L. (1977), Sex differences and the epidemiology of depression. *Arch. Gen. Psychiat.*, 34:98–111.
Winokur, G. (1981), *Depression: The Facts.* New York: Oxford University Press.

Chapter 6

Cognitive Regression and Dynamic Factors in Suicide: An Integrative Approach

Barbara Fibel Marcus, Ph.D.

Psychologists, both as diagnosticians and as therapists, are often faced with the awesome responsibility of assessing an individual's risk for suicidal action and directing the course of therapeutic intervention. With so much riding on our clinical judgment, an extensive understanding of suicidality and its manifestations on psychological tests is clinically and ethically requisite. Yet, as recent reviews have indicated (Neuringer, 1965, 1976; Lester, 1970; Levenson, 1974; Shneidman, 1976), empirical studies of such efforts have thus far yielded equivocal findings. This has led some to question the use of standard psychological tests, particularly the Rorschach, for the prediction of suicide (e.g., Lester, 1970; Farberow and MacKinnon, 1974). Lester observed, for example, that tests using personal data or psychiatric history have demonstrated predictive validity for specific subpopulations and concluded that "concentration on the use of standard psychological tests alone would seem to be of little use in the light of present knowledge" (p. 16). Specific measures of suicidal risk, while improving prediction, cannot place the suicidal inclination within the larger context of personality structure and dynamics and thus fail to provide a basis for understanding its development, phenomenology, relationship to other aspects of the personality, or the formulation of a treatment strategy. These goals require that the assessment of suicide risk occur in the context of comprehensive personality assessment. Thus, while the construction and refinement of specific tests for suicide risk are necessary

155

research and clinical tasks, such tests cannot stand alone; the refinement of standard tests for suicide prediction is equally necessary.

The present chapter focuses on the cognitive aspects of suicidality and their manifestations on the Rorschach test. Several factors have dictated this approach. First, substantial investigation of this area has already been conducted and, though only moderately successful, has revealed some intriguing, relatively consistent results deserving of further attention. In addition, there is renewed and extensive interest in the relation between cognitive processes and psychopathology generally, depression in particular (Weingartner and Silberman, 1982). Careful study of the cognitive factors in suicidality may provide important links in this area. Finally, unlike such possibly better predictors as personal history, past psychiatric or suicidal history, or recent life events, cognitive factors, if systematically specified, may be influenced by psychotherapy. Delineation of these factors may therefore hold unique promise for the formulation of more effective intervention.

Emphasis on the cognitive components of suicidality is not meant to preclude consideration of other intrapsychic factors. Dynamic formulations, though they have received much attention in the literature, bear brief discussion here. Most influential was Freud's postulation (1917) that in the suicidal act the ego, in identification with the ambivalently loved and abandoned object, turns the murderous wishes against itself. Others, drawing on Freud's assumption of the centrality of aggression, have elaborated other motives, for example, retaliatory abandonment or revenge (Haider, 1968). Some, like Litman (1968), argue that there has been a "relative overemphasis on aggression and guilt as components of suicide with underemphasis on the helplessness, dependency, and erotic elements". Along these lines are reformulation of suicide as a manipulative effort to gain attention, love, and affection (Toolan, 1968), identification with a depressed or degraded parent (Erikson, 1968; Margolin and Teicher, 1968), or symbolic reunion with the lost love object (Deutsch, 1930; Hendin, 1963; Seiden, 1969; Erlich, 1978; Miller, 1981). Suicide attempts on the part of schizophrenic patients have been understood as the longing for an otherworldly state, surcease from suffering, or reactions to an inner sense of disintegration (Grinker, 1975). The proliferation of formulations of suicide suggests that dynamic considerations, though offering a differentiated understanding of motives, do not specify an underlying process common to all suicidal action.

The present chapter proposes that disorders of cognition underlie the proclivity for suicide quite independent of dynamics. The limited success of previous efforts may be seen as the consequence of the lack of an adequate model of cognition and cognitive dysfunction that might serve as context for conceptualizing suicidal thinking. Indeed, earlier efforts have dealt largely with such unitary, relatively global cognitive functions as faulty logic (Shneidman, 1959, 1976) or field dependence (Levenson, 1974) in isolation from any comprehensive theory of cognitive development. This led to a potpourri of findings only minimally interpretable and impossible to integrate.

Toward a more systematic formulation, the current attempt draws on the vast body of Piagetian theory and research (Piaget, 1954; Inhelder and Piaget, 1958). The cogency of an integration of Piaget's work with psychoanalytic theory has already been established, primarily by Blatt (1974) and Greenspan (1979). Blatt and his colleagues have demonstrated empirically the explanatory power of Piagetian concepts with respect to schizophrenia (Blatt and Ritzler, 1974; Blatt, Wild, and Ritzler, 1975; Blatt, Brenneis, Schimek, and Glick, 1976), and depression (Blatt, D'Afflitti, and Quinlan, 1976; Fibel, 1979). However, thus far only Erlich (1978) has applied a Piagetian framework to the problem of suicidality. His formulation of adolescent suicide as dually determined by dynamic issues and cognitive structural level serves as a springboard for the broader reconceptualization of suicidal thinking and action to be proposed here.

Erlich argues that the developmental emergence of suicidal ideation and impulse can best be understood as a consequence of the convergence of the adolescent resurgence of preoedipal longings for union with the mother and normative changes in the quality of cognitive functioning. More specifically, the longed-for blissful symbiosis typically finds sublimated expression, via displacement and projection, in preoccupation with such cosmic questions and universal themes as the nature of life and death. At the same time, adolescent thinking, as characterized by Piaget (Inhelder and Piaget, 1958), undergoes a transition from concrete operations toward the attainment of formal operations. Unlike the preceding stage, thought no longer takes as its sole object concrete facts, but rather thought itself becomes available for mental manipulation. The adolescent is no longer tied to what is observable or potentially so, but is free to consider the hypothetical. The real becomes subordinated to the possible as merely an instance of all possibilities. Thus, the achievement of second-order propositional logic makes the hypothetical ascendant over the real and the actually possible. However, formal abstract reasoning is not fully attained until the close of adolescence; until then the adolescent has a special propensity for shifts between concrete and highly abstract thinking. The concept of death may thereby be treated as an abstraction to be handled either mentally or concretely, through experimental action. As summarized by Erlich,

> Suicidal preoccupations and acts may result from the interaction of two necessary but in themselves not sufficient conditions: highly intensified longing for maternal union, and specific proneness to vacillation between and mixing of structural-cognitive levels of formal and concrete operations. This regressive-progressive interplay between the two areas may lead to the concrete and actual treatment of death as the symbolic expression of union with the mother. [p. 268]

Erlich's model of adolescent suicide synthesizes brilliantly the dynamic and cognitive-structural aspects of a developmental era. However, his discussion is restricted to normative vicissitudes of adolescence, though his model has wider implications. Clinically, the recrudescence of regressive dynamic material, including but not limited to symbiotic yearnings, may occur in any developmental phase. Of even greater significance for the present discussion, though less well established, cognitive regression may accompany characterological regression. This notion is most commonly associated with psychotic states in which regression from secondary to primary process thinking has been observed (Rapaport, Gill, and Schafer, 1945). More recently, regressive cognitive features, especially concreteness, have been noted in borderline personality disorder (Rubenstein, 1980; Sugarman, Bloom-Feshbach, and Bloom-Feshbach, 1980). Theoretically, a similar confluence of regressive dynamic and cognitive-structural factors may come into play in suicidal states generally.

Erlich's model may be extended beyond the adolescent case with respect to both dynamic and cognitive-structural considerations. While the present discussion focuses on the latter, a more differentiated perspective on dynamic forces deserves brief comment. Erlich's approach underscores the importance of taking developmental level and normative dynamic conflicts into account. Yet the unconscious genesis of suicidal wishes, even in adolescence, need not be confined to fantasies of merger with the preoedipal mother. Indeed, as noted earlier, motivations for suicide are varied and complex. Blatt's concept (1974; Blatt and Shichman, 1983) of two primary configurations of psychopathology suggest a means of organizing a differentiated, developmentally grounded understanding of suicidal dynamics. In Blatt's framework, psychopathology may be organized around either anaclitic or introjective dimensions. Anaclitic pathology refers to defects in the object relations sphere, whereas introjective pathology reflects defects in the development of the self-concept. Both configurations evolve normatively from the most primitive to the most advanced levels, defects representing arrest or regression along one or the other developmental line. Erlich's formulation of the dynamics of suicide reflects primitive anaclitic concerns. However, primitive introjective concerns (e.g., fantasies of unlimited power and glory through death) may also be associated with suicidal intentions.

Turning now to the cognitive-structural component of suicidality, Erlich's observation of the role of adolescent regressive-progressive interplay may be extended across the developmental spectrum. As mentioned above, there is considerable clinical evidence and some research support for the pervasiveness of inconsistent availability of abstract reasoning among primitively functioning individuals. Suicidal individuals may represent a subset of primitively organized individuals who are, either by fixation or regression, prone to excessive oscillation between concrete and abstract thinking. The interaction of related dynamic issues with this incomplete attainment of formal operational thinking creates a vulnerability to the consideration of death not simply as a symbolic solution, but as an actual concrete solution to dynamic conflicts. The interaction of developmentally indexed dynamic and cognitive-structural variables provides necessary though insufficient conditions for suicide.

Before research and clinical evidence is reviewed the nature of the transition from concrete to formal operations must be examined more closely, in order to specify the nature of the hypothesized deficit. In normal development the beginnings of formal operational thinking are observed at the onset of adolescence. At the close of this era it becomes consolidated. Its cardinal feature is the acquisition of second-order propositional logic or so-called hypothetico-deductive reasoning (Inhelder and Piaget, 1958). The child is freed from the bounds of the actual or potentially actual to consider the entire range of possibilities, however abstract. The hypothetical takes on exaggerated importance initially, as seen in the young adolescent's zealous idealism or unrestrained philosophical forays. Preoccupation with the temporally and spatially remote supersedes and frees one from immediate concerns. Propositions rather than concrete events become the object of thinking, and reflexive thinking emerges. Moreover, propositions are now subject to a combinatory system of operations that permits consideration of isolated variables and the examination of all possible interrelations. Alternative and even contradictory propositions can be entertained probabilistically and tested against reality, and the distinction between the real and the possible can be made.

The latter is crucial in the development of formal operations, for it would appear to form the cognitive underpinnings of the capacity to reality test abstract ideas mentally rather than through trial and error. The inability to perform this function reliably and accurately allows the hypothetical to be mistaken for the real and leads to indiscriminate experimentation through action. Greenspan (1979) makes this point in discussing dynamic considerations of the Piagetian model:

> Whether the capacities for formal operations are used in the service of greater self-awareness or defense depends on the issues raised and the accompanying anxiety. If there is intense anxiety due to the drives or to external stresses in adolescence proper, a regression in internal cognitive ability may occur. . . . When the drive-affect structures become very intense and frightening, the hypothetical quality may no longer be possible, and the ability to look at all the possibilities and to determine the real may be lost. [p. 218]

In psychoanalytic terms, such regression implies breaches of the boundary between internal phenomena and external reality. Tenuousness of the internal-external boundary is frequently observed in borderline states, while complete abrogation of the boundary, and thus of reality orientation, is common to psychosis (Rapaport, Gill, and Schafer, 1945; Sugarman, Bloom-Feshbach, and Bloom-Feshbach, 1980; Urist, 1980). Even intermittent boundary disturbance, however, compromises reality testing and leads to gross errors of judgment and behavioral disruption; such regression favors a shift from verbal, symbolic modalities to a more primitive action mode (Greenacre, 1950).

From this vantage point, then, suicidal behavior can be seen as a subcategory of impulsive action resulting from cognitive regression in the face of drive pressure or external stress which impairs the capacity to maintain the distinction between the real and one's internal fantasy elaborations. In the context of anaclitic yearnings for fusion with the ministering mother or introjective strivings for omnipotence and adulation, death and thus suicide represent a symbolic merger with the infinite and universal that may be acted upon concretely, as an actual solution to dynamic dilemmas.

Research and clinical evidence lends empirical support to these contentions. As several comprehensive reviews of the experimental literature on cognitive variables and suicidality are available elsewhere (Neuringer, 1964, 1976; Lester, 1970; Levenson, 1974; Shneidman, 1976), these findings will be summarized briefly and a selective review of the more relevant research will be presented. Although none of the studies reported provides a direct test of the hypotheses under consideration, the thrust of well-established findings are consistent with significant impairment in formal abstract reasoning among suicidal individuals. Following this review, portions of the Rorschach record of a seriously suicidal young adult male will be used to illustrate test features of fluctuating levels of formal reasoning in relation to introjective suicidal dynamic content.

EMPIRICAL INVESTIGATIONS OF COGNITIVE FACTORS AND SUICIDE

The systematic study of suicidal thinking and its manifestation on psychological tests had its beginnings in the 1940s. In the ensuing quarter century, a number of major approaches were developed. Among them were several that made use of Rorschach data: single sign approaches such as color shading (Appelbaum and Holzman, 1962; Appelbaum and Colson, 1968), response to area D6 of Card VII (Sapolsky, 1963), and transparency responses (Blatt and Ritzler, 1974); multiple sign or configurational approaches (Hertz, 1948, 1949; Daston and Sakheim, 1960; Martin, 1960; Weiner, 1961); and content approaches (Fisher and Hinds, 1951; Broida, 1954; Costello, 1958).

Neuringer's review (1965) found single and multiple sign approaches, especially the Martin Checklist, superior to content approaches. However, he noted that the data for even the best established measures were equivocal. Neuringer attributed these inconclusive results to inconsistent use of the Rorschach and other methodological problems.

Similarly, Lester (1970), reviewing research attempts to predict suicidal risk using psychological tests, concluded that personality tests including the Rorschach TAT, MMPI, Bender-Gestalt, and Semantic Differential had not established their validity and reliability. Although arguing for the development of specific tests for suicidality, he noted that Rorschach sign approaches such as Martin's (1960) showed promise.

An examination of the Martin Checklist reveals that the signs included tap into two dimensions; affective responsivity and minimal controls (Cutter, Jorgensen, and Farberow, 1968). These factors are entirely consistent with the present model, in which the intensity of dynamic issues and variable levels of abstract reasoning contribute to a shift toward enactment.

Blatt and Lerner (1983) have provided the most direct test of the current model. They selected Rorschach records of patients considered prototypical of various clinical disorders and examined independently the quality of object representation. As hypothesized (Blatt, 1974; Blatt, Quinlan, Chevron, McDonald, and Zuroff, 1982), in a seriously suicidal patient with an introjective depression they found object representations at a high developmental level alternating with seriously impaired representations as measured by Blatt's cognitive developmentally derived scoring manual for object representation (Blatt, Brenneis, Schimek, and Glick, 1976).

Other, non-Rorschach measures provide further indication of cognitive regression specific to suicidal patients. Of these, Shneidman's investigations of suicide notes (1959, 1976) and the work of Neuringer and his colleagues on cognitive rigidity are the most systematically studied.

Shneidman (1959) argued that suicide notes, since they are typically written immediately before the event, might provide a special window into the suicidal state. He suggested that suicidal individuals reflect failures of logic of four kinds. Catalogic errors confuse the self as experienced subjectively with the self as seen by others and thus lead to suicidality as a response to feelings of worthlessness or helplessness. Normal or Aristotelian logic leads to suicide as the specious solution to severe physical or emotional pain. Contaminated logic emphasizes the self as experienced by others and is associated with ideas of suicide as a transition to another life. The last type of error identified by Shneidman is the paleologic, in which identifications are made based on predicates rather than subjects, as in delusional psychotic states. Shneidman's work suggests that the logical fallacies of the suicidal person need not reflect failure in the structure of deductive reasoning per se, but rather in the consideration of unrealistic premises related to death or suicide. For example, while the premise "People who kill themselves get attention" may be true, the reality of death, including the end of any awareness of the desired attention, goes unacknowledged. Shneidman's work, then, demonstrates the presence of defects in the ability to critically examine premises so as to eliminate logical but unrealistic conclusions from active consideration. Put differently, the logic of suicide is internally consistent but invalid.

In a review of the literature on suicide notes, Shneidman (1976) found little support for content approaches; contrary to the hopes of many researchers, the notes tended to be banal and constricted. However, as Shneidman points out, this finding is interesting in itself, as it fits well with theoretical suppositions regarding narrowing of consciousness and lack of reflectivity or appreciation of consequences among the suicidal, as well as with considerable research data directed at assessing cognitive-structural variables.

Neuringer and his colleagues provided the first systematic test of a cognitive model of suicidality. He first compared dichotomous thinking in serious attempters, nonsuicidal psychiatric patients, and normal subjects using subjects' ratings on Osgood's Semantic Differential Scale (Neuringer, 1961). On this basis he was able to differentiate the psychiatric groups from the normal controls, psychiatric patients showing significantly more extreme dichotomization on scales involving the evaluative factor. No differences were found between suicidal and nonsuicidal patients. After refining the method to control for lethality of the suicide attempt (Neuringer, 1967), and again using the Semantic Differential Scale, he was able to show a greater degree of dichotomous thinking in suicidal as compared to nonsuicidal patients. Similarly, he found more extreme dichotomization of concepts of life and death among suicidal patients than in psychosomatic and normal patients (Neuringer, 1968). He concluded that, while psychiatric patients are generally more polarized than normal controls in terms of concepts of the power and malignancy of events, extreme polarization was unique to suicidal thinking.

Neuringer and Lettieri (1971) took daily measures of dichotomous thinking from four groups of patients along a continuum from high to no risk of suicide over a three-week period following a suicidal crisis. They reported that the high risk group was distinctly different from medium, low, and no risk groups, showing more extreme dichotomization and perceiving a greater divergence between life and death than did other subjects; this extreme polarization did not diminish over time. They contended that these results supported the dispositional rather than state-dependent nature of cognitive rigidity.

Neuringer reasoned that much extreme dichotomous thinking

must be associated with a lack of flexibility, modulation, or capacity to make fine discriminations or judgments. To demonstrate this, he administered the Rokeach Map Test and the California F Scale to groups of suicidal, psychosomatic, and normal hospitalized patients matched for age, socioeconomic status, education, and IQ (Neuringer, 1964). The California F Scale is a measure of rigidity in social attitudes. The Rokeach Map Test measures the ability to shift a problem-solving mental set from a previously successful but not inappropriate strategy to another plan of attack. Neuringer found suicidal individuals significantly more rigid socially and less able to shift strategies than either of the control groups.

Levenson (1973) studied constriction of thinking among suicidal patients using the Unusual Uses Test and the Word Association Test. Serious suicide attempters were characterized by greater cognitive rigidity on both tests as compared to nonsuicidal psychiatric patients and normal subjects matched for age and IQ.

Several studies have extended the concept of constriction and rigidity beyond verbally mediated skills to include perceptual material. For example, Levenson (1974) showed that suicidal patients were significantly more field dependent than nonsuicidal psychiatric patients and nonpatients as measured by the Rod and Frame Test. Patsiokas, Clum, and Luscomb (1979) compared across dimensions of verbally mediated cognitive rigidity, field dependency, and cognitive impulsivity in samples of suicide attempters and nonsuicidal psychiatric controls, using age and diagnosis as motivating variables. They found that cognitive rigidity discriminated best across all age groups and diagnoses. An interaction between field dependence and age was found, with field dependence discriminating suicidal from nonsuicidal subjects in the youngest (19–34) age group only. No significant differences between groups was found on measures of cognitive impulsivity. This study provides support for the discriminating power of verbally mediated cognitive rigidity and limited support for its application to the perceptual realm.

Neuringer contended that cognitive rigidity interferes with adequate problem solving. He and Levenson (Levenson and Neuringer, 1971) examined the capacity for problem solving in suicidal individuals using the Wechsler Adult Intelligence Scale Arithmetic Subtest and the Rokeach Map Test. Suicidal adolescents revealed diminished problem-solving capacities when compared to their nonsuicidal peers. Schaul (1983) replicated the relatively poorer problem-solving abilities of suicidal patients as compared to those of depressed nonsuicidal psychiatric patients. Others have provided support for the inadequate use of planning and judgment (Osgood and Walker, 1959; Gottschalk and Gleser, 1960), factors which may also contribute to impaired reasoning. Levenson (1974), in his review of research on cognitive variables and suicide, notes consistent support for confused, incorrect logic and rigid, inflexible thinking on the part of suicidal individuals. He concludes that, taken together, these variables lead to defective problem-solving ability and coping:

> It is generally felt that the suicidal individual, because of either temporary or permanent cognitive deficiencies, finds it difficult to generate new or alternative solutions to debilitating emotional problems. Such constricted problem-solving ability may be lethal since the person could well feel that there is no way out of an anxiety laden situation except an escape into death. [p. 160]

Thus, the research on cognitive rigidity consistently points to defects associated with the development or maintenance of abstract reasoning and their impact on emotional problem solving. Levenson speculates that the rigidity is a function of a restricted range of hypotheses, although the data do not provide a direct test of hypothesis generation. Alternatively, or in addition, suicidal individuals, as a result of dynamic issues and faulty reality testing, may generate a multitude of hypotheses but select and cling to those that are self-defeating or self-destructive. Either suggestion—actual constriction of the hypothesis-generating process or deficient ability to discriminate realistic solutions—is consistent with the empirical work of Neuringer and the Piagetian framework of impaired hypothetico-deductive reasoning.

Further corroboration of this model is provided indirectly through studies of thinking disorder among depressives; the research reviewed above has shown that cognitive impairments among suicidal patients appear to differ in degree rather than in kind from those of depressed nonsuicidal patients. Several studies of depressives have shown impaired analytic cognition, that is, difficulties in abstraction, concept formation, and the organization of experience. Koh, Kayton, and Berry (1973) and Russell and Beekhuis (1976) have demonstrated that depressed patients cluster related events less completely than unimpaired controls. Weingartner, Cohen, Martello, and Gerdt (1981) found that depressed patients are less able to process and remember unrelated events, but that they are not significantly different from controls in processing and recalling related information. A number of studies suggest that depressives are deficient in tasks requiring active, sustained cognitive activity (Stromgren, 1977; Reus, Silberman, Post, and Weingartner, 1979; Cohen, Weingartner, Smallberg, and Murphy, 1982).

Evidence of impairment in abstract reasoning is provided by Braff and Beck (1974). They found that hospitalized depressives showed deficits in series completion and proverb interpretation and that the degree of impairment was correlated with the severity of illness. Savard, Rey, and Post (1980) also reported deficient abstract reasoning in depressives on the Halstead Categories Tests. Silberman, Weingartner, and Post (1983) found that depressives performed more poorly on a discrimination learning task than did nondepressed controls. A detailed analysis of the types of errors revealed that depressives were not impaired in their ability to generate hypothetical solutions, but rather were unable to narrow the set of possible solutions and tended to perseverate on disconfirmed hypotheses.

The concrete and perseverative quality of depressives' performance on learning tasks and its relation to severity of illness suggest a convergence between depressive cognition and suicidal thinking. Of particular note, the literature on thinking disturbances in depressives suggests that the data on suicidal patients provided by Neuringer may be better interpreted as revealing a failure of hypothesis *testing* rather than of hypothesis *generation*. This interpretation would substantiate the proposed Piagetian interpretation, in which the incomplete consolidation of formal operations may be manifested by the overvaluation of the hypothetical, inconsistent reality testing of hypothetical solutions, and admixtures of abstract and concrete ideas. The perseverative and urgent qualities of the suicidal idea may then reflect the fact that such solutions rest on dynamically determined internal fantasy elaborations poorly tested against external reality.

The Piagetian framework, then, integrates a variety of findings within a single model. Moreover, the model has important clinical applications. Understanding the nature of suicidal thinking may allow the identification of patients at risk for suicidal action, the recognition of subtle regressive shifts in the direction of suicide among depressed patients, and an empirically and developmentally grounded formulation of therapeutic action.

Viewed within this comprehensive and systematic model, the data of the psychological test protocol allow the simultaneous assessment of cognitive-structural and dynamic factors and their interaction. Restricting the current discussion to the Rorschach, the present formulation would predict a test record revealing oscillations between concrete and formal reasoning, an emphasis on the hypothetical, and an inconsistent capacity to distinguish the hypothetical from the actual (marginal reality testing). The following formal aspects of the Rorschach of seriously suicidal patients would be anticipated: (1) moderately poor reality testing; (2) admixtures of concrete and highly abstract responses; (3) significant presence of thought-disordered responses reflecting disturbance of the internal-external boundary, particularly fabulized combinations and/or highly confabulated responses and/or idiosyncrasy (for example, peculiar ideas, arbitrary use of color, or unusual location). These features would be expected to occur in the context of introjective or anaclitic depressive themes. The case example below illustrates these features.

CASE ILLUSTRATION: COGNITIVE REGRESSION AND INTROJECTIVE SUICIDAL THEMES

Evan, a twenty-one-year-old Caucasian male, was the youngest of four children of an upper middle class family. His parents divorced when he was twelve.

Evan's early development was remarkable to his parents for only one perturbation—a spell of obnoxious, boisterous demandingness in the year surrounding the separation and divorce proceedings. Evan, never having distinguished himself previously in his schoolwork, nevertheless recouped quickly and set out on a brilliant academic career, thereby putting his parents at ease. Seemingly, he had developed many friendships and was active and successful in scholastic and extracurricular endeavors. This culminated in his acceptance at a prestigious West Coast university.

Six months later, with no apparent signs of distress preceding the episode, Evan was discovered barricaded in his dormitory room. The brutality of the attack had many convinced initially of a ritualistic homicide until, through miraculous medical intervention, Evan recovered and shared his sense of shame in having failed to kill himself:

An assessment following admission to the hospital revealed a narcissistic personality organized at a borderline level. Introjective depressive themes were noted, most especially "agonizing strivings for perfection" and the vicious self-hatred with which minor failures were met. Fantasies of unlimited power and admiration through intellectual achievements formed an unconscious substrate.

Evan's Rorschach protocol demonstrates not only introjective depressive concerns and their association with death through fantasied merger with an omniscient deity, but also the progressive-regressive interplay of concrete and formal operational thinking described by Erlich. Such interplay occurs in spite of the patient's overall superior level of intellectual functioning.

Evan approached the Rorschach with feigned bravado which nevertheless failed to conceal his trepidation. As the test proceeded, a guarded, self-critical attitude replaced his cavalier facetiousness. His record was a dilated one consisting of forty responses. Fully half of these responses consisted of rare or space details. Only a quarter of his responses were whole percepts. His Experience Balance was only slightly weighted toward affective dominance. His F percentage of 65 fell within the low normal range but, along with a pure C response and three responses containing highly aggressive content, suggested the potential for impulsive aggressive action. As anticipated, his protocol yielded only marginally adequate reality testing (F+% = 52%, F+ extended % = 59%). A more detailed examination showed an alteration of well-perceived responses and weak, distorted ones much as the sequence of his responses to Card VI:

Scoring	Response	Inquiry
DrSF— A	Two pigs	I saw the snout, mouth
WF₀DH Obj	A bearskin rug	The shape and textural quality
DFw— Ad	Mouth of a cat	Because of the whiskers and nose
DF+M A	Two bears doing a Broadway duet	Their stomach, legs going out, bumping against each other in a kind of a Broadway pose
DrSF— A	Two more pigs. I think I'm going to flunk again	Same reason as the first set—their snouts
DrSF— Hd	A dumb-looking man	His lips protruding made him look dumb

These oscillations are accompanied by derogatory self-reference along the introjective dimension vis-à-vis intellectual achievement and followed by a poorly perceived response reflecting such ideation. His disappointed longings for fame and recognition are amply reflected in the entourage of artistic and intellectual geniuses identified and often depreciated. To Card II he responded: "Beethoven waiting for inspiration. He's putting on a little weight, or Pavrotti looking phenomenally depressed as a result of his inability to hit high C." This was followed by the response "a mushroom cloud explosion" and "an angry Bishop," "a ghost or goblin." His willingness to take leave of reality and the unrestrained aggression in response to dysphoric content in the context of the rather concretized preoccupation with a special relation to divine powers and the limitless talent it confers further illustrates the interrelation of introjective depressive concerns, suicidal ideation, and the tenuousness of formal abstract reasoning.

Juxtapositions of highly abstracted symbolic responses with concrete use of the blot were frequent. To Card VIII he offered: "An infrared photograph of Hebrides reminiscent of the last scene in *2001* and therefore representing wisdom or a pink ape because it *is* an ape and it is pink." Also seen were Evan's arbitrary use of features of the blot and an inability to screen out aspects which though present are irrelevant—defects reminiscent of both Weingartner's findings regarding the impaired deductive reasoning of depressives and the work of Neuringer on the cognitive rigidity and field dependence of suicidal patients.

Arbitrariness was not restricted to Evan's use of color, but extended to conceptual elements of his responses as well. Although devoid of contaminations, his record is replete with fabulized combinations ("Kafka's cockroach with a butterfly on top") and confabulations ("Four ghosts sitting around a campfire singing camp songs. They're white and round on top and they're sitting in a circle either dancing Hava Nagila or campfire songs and there's enough Judaism in the hospital already. The doctors are Jewish, the patients. At camp, I was all alone.") Breaches of the internal-external boundary, as exemplified here, can be understood then as jointly determined by dynamic content associated with self-contempt (cockroach) and death and resurrection (ghosts) and by the incapacity to sustain abstract reasoning on which the ability to accurately integrate external perceptual and inner ideational components within a single response depends.

CONCLUSION

In summary then, Evan's Rorschach displays all the features expected on the basis of a cognitive, developmentally informed psychodynamic model: marginal reality testing, rapid shifts between concrete and symbolic thinking, disruption of the internal-external boundary, and uncritical and overvalued involvement with idiosyncratic perceptual and ideational material. Further, Evan demonstrates that these cognitive-structural features may occur not only in relation to anaclitic issues, as shown by Erlich, but also with respect to introjective themes. Of course, many patients, certainly some suicidal ones, share features in common with such a profile. Indeed some have suggested that some aspects, particularly moderately poor reality testing and tenuousness of the internal-external boundary, are pathognomonic of borderline personality disorder (Lerner and Lerner, 1980; Sugarman, 1980). However, self-destructive and suicidal behavior *is* typical of the borderline. Systematic empirical studies may reveal distinctions not so much on qualitative grounds, then, but rather with respect to the pervasiveness of such factors. Work showing a relationship between degree of cognitive impairment, severity of suicidality, and depression lends credence to this hypothesis. Moreover, some research supports the contention that borderline character organization in concert with depression poses a greater risk of lethality than does depression alone (Friedman, Aronoff, Clarkin, Corn, and Hurt, 1983). These observations suggest an intriguing convergence among suicidal thinking, depression, and borderline personality organization.

In conclusion, a psychoanalytic model informed by Piagetian developmental constructs yields an understanding of suicide that is parsimonious while integrating a variety of empirical findings. It permits elaboration along many lines, links to an empirically grounded developmental model of depression, a broader conceptualization of the role of cognition in psychopathology, and the development of a testable theory of the interrelation of cognition and affect. In the clinical realm, although the model awaits further research verification, it provides a basis for the identification of patients at risk and recognition of signals of decompensation in the direction of suicidal solutions in the course of treatment. Of course, developmental phase, life stresses, and other factors may influence the timing or course of action. While the proposed model does not purport to exhaust the etiological factors or processes that lead to suicide, it may contribute to a more empirically grounded, systematic, and differentiated formulation of suicidal action and its internal mediation, a formulation that may inform more effective treatment strategies.

REFERENCES

Appelbaum, S. A., & Colson, D. B. (1968), A reexamination of the color-shading Rorschach test response and suicide attempts. *J. Proj. Tech. & Personal. Assess.*, 32:160–164.

——— Holzman P. S. (1962), The color shading response and suicide. *J. Proj. Tech.*, 26:155–161.

Blatt, S. J. (1974), Levels of object representation in anaclitic and introjective depression. *Psychoanalytic Study of the Child*, 29:107–157. New Haven, CT: Yale University Press.

——— Brenneis, C. B., Schimek, J. G., & Glick, M. (1976), Normal development and psychopathological impairment of the concept of the object on the Rorschach. *J. Abnorm. Psychol.*, 85:364–373.

——— D'Afflitti, J. P., & Quinlan, D. M. (1976), Experiences of depression in normal young adults. *J. Abnorm. Psychol.*, 95:383–389.

——— Lerner, H. (1983), The psychological assessment of object representation. *J. Personal. Assess.*, 47:7–28.

——— Quinlan, D. M., Chevron, E. S., McDonald, C., & Zuroff, D. (1982), Dependency and self-criticism: Psychological dimensions of depression. *J. Consult. & Clin. Psychol.*, 50:113–124.

——— Ritzler, B. A. (1974), Thought disorder and boundary disturbances in psychosis. *J. Consult. & Clin. Psychol.*, 42:370–381.

——— Shichman, S. (1983), Two primary configurations of psychopathology. *Psychoanal. & Contemp. Thought*, 6:187–255.

——— Wild, C. M., & Ritzler, B. A. (1975), Disturbances of object representation in schizophrenia. *Psychoanal. & Contemp. Sci.*, 4:235–288.

Braff, D. L., & Beck, A. T. (1974), Thinking disorder in depression. *Arch. Gen. Psychiat.*, 31:456–459.

Broida, D. C. (1954), An investigation of certain psychodiagnostic indications of suicidal tendencies and depression in mental hospital patients. *Psychiat. Quart.*, 28:453–464.

Cohen, R. M., Weingartner, H., Smallberg, S. A., & Murphy, D. L. (1982), Effort in cognitive processes in depression. *Arch. Gen. Psychiat.*, 39:593–605.

Costello, C. G. (1958), The Rorschach records of suicidal patients: An application of a comparative matching technique. *J. Proj. Tech.*, 22:272–275.

Cutter, F., Jorgensen, M., & Farberow, N. L. (1968), Replicability of Rorschach signs with known degree of suicidal intent. *J. Proj. Tech. & Personal. Assess.*, 32:428–434.

Daston, P. G., & Sakheim, G. A. (1960), Prediction of successful suicide from the Rorschach test using a sign approach. *J. Proj. Tech.*, 24:355–361.

Deutsch, H. (1930), Hysterical fate neurosis. In: *Neurosis and Character Types.* New York: International Universities Press, pp. 14–28.

Erikson, E. (1968), *Identity: Youth & Crime.* New York: W. W. Norton.

Erlich, H. S. (1978), Adolescent suicide: Maternal longing and cognitive development. *Psychoanalytic Study of the Child*, 33:261–277. New Haven, CT: Yale University Press.

Farberow, N. L., & MacKinnon, D. (1974), Prediction of suicide in neuropsychiatric patients. In: *Psychological Assessment of Suicide Risk*, ed. C. Neuringer. Springfield, IL: Charles C Thomas.

Fibel, B. (1979), Toward a developmental model of depression: Object representation and object loss in adolescent and adult psychiatric patients. Doctoral dissertation, University of Massachusetts, Amherst.

Fisher, S., & Hinds, E. (1951), The organization of hostility controls in various personality structures. *Gen. Psychol. Monographs*, 44:3-68.

Freud, S. (1917), Mourning and melancholia. *Standard Edition*, 14:243-258. London: Hogarth Press.

Friedman, R. C., Aronoff, M., Clarkin, J. F., Corn, R., & Hurt, S. W. (1983), History of suicidal behavior in depressed borderline patients. *Amer. J. Psychiat.*, 140:1023-1026.

Gottschalk, L. A., & Gleser, G. C. (1960), An analysis of the verbal content of suicide notes. *Brit. J. Psychol.*, 33:195-204.

Greenacre, P. (1950), General problems of acting out. *Psychoanal. Quart.*, 19:455.

Greenspan, S. I. (1979), *Intelligence and Adaptation: An Integration of Psychoanalytic and Piagetian Developmental Psychology*. New York: International Universities Press.

Grinker, R. R. (1975), Anhedonia and depression in schizophrenia. In: *Depression and Human Experience*, ed. E. J. Anthony & T. Benedek. Boston: Little, Brown.

Haider, I. (1968), Suicide attempts in children and adolescents. *Brit. J. Psychiat.*, 114:1113-1134.

Hendin, H. (1963), The psychodynamics of suicide. *J. Nerv. & Ment. Dis.*, 136:236-244.

Hertz, M. R. (1948), Suicidal configurations in Rorschach records. *Rorschach Research Exchange & J. Proj. Tech.*, 12:3-58.

———— (1949), Further study of "suicidal" configurations in Rorschach records. *Rorschach Research Exchange & J. Proj. Tech.*, 13:44-73.

Inhelder, B., & Piaget, J. (1958), *The Growth of Logical Thinking: From Childhood to Adolescence*. New York: Basic Books.

Koh, S. D., Kayton, L., & Berry, R. (1973), Mnemonic organization in young nonpsychotic schizophrenics. *J. Abnorm. Psychol.*, 81:299-310.

Lerner, P. M., & Lerner, H. D. (1980), Rorschach assessment of primitive defenses in borderline personality structure. In: *Borderline Phenomena and the Rorschach Test*, ed. J. Kwawer, H. Lerner, P. Lerner, & A. Sugarman. New York: International Universities Press, pp. 257-274.

Lester, D. (1970), Attempts to predict suicidal risk using psychological tests. *Psychol. Bull.*, 74:1-17.

Levenson, M. (1973), Cognitive and perceptual factors on suicidal individuals. Unpublished doctoral dissertation, University of Kansas, 1972. *Dissertation Abstracts International*, 33, 5521B (University Microfilms. No. 73-11, 914).

———— (1974), Cognitive correlates of suicidal risk. In: *Psychological Assessment of Suicidal Risk*, ed. C. Neuringer. Springfield, IL: Charles C Thomas.

———— Neuringer, C. (1971), Problem-solving behavior in suicidal adolescents. *J. Consult. & Clin. Psychol.*, 37:433-436.

Litman, R. E. (1968), Sigmund Freud on suicide. In: *Essays on Self-Destruction*, ed. E. S. Shneidman. New York: Holt, Rinehart, & Winston.

Margolin, N., & Teicher, J. (1968), Thirteen adolescent male suicide attempts: Dynamic considerations. *J. Acad. Child Psychiat.*, 296-315.

Martin, H. A. (1960), A Rorschach study of suicide. Unpublished doctoral dissertation, University of Kentucky, 1951. *Dissertation Abstracts*, 20, 3837.

Miller, D. (1981), Adolescent suicide: Etiology and treatment. *Adoles. Psychiat.*, 9:327-342.

Neuringer, C. (1961), Dichotomous evaluations in suicidal individuals. *J. Consult. & Clin. Psychol.*, 25:445-449.

———— (1964), Rigid thinking in suicidal individuals. *J. Consult. & Clin. Psychol.*, 28:54–58.

———— (1965), The Rorschach test as a research device for the identification, prediction, and understanding of suicidal ideation and behavior: A review. *J. Proj. Tech. & Personal Assess.*, 29:71–82.

———— (1967), The cognitive organization of meaning in suicidal individuals. *J. Gen. Psychol.*, 76:91–100.

———— (1968), Divergences between attitudes toward life and death among suicidal, psychosomatic, and normal hospitalized patients. *J. Consult. & Clin. Psychol.*, 32:59–63.

———— (1976), Current developments in the study of suicidal thinking. In: *Suicidology: Contemporary Developments*, ed. E. S. Shneidman. New York: Grune & Stratton.

———— Lettieri, D. J. (1971), Cognition, attitude, and affect in suicidal individuals. *Life-Threatening Behavior*, 1:106–124.

Osgood, C., & Walker, E. G. (1959), Motivation and language behavior. *J. Abnorm. Psychol.*, 59:58–67.

Patsiokas, A. T., Clum, G. A., & Luscomb, R. L. (1979), Cognitive characteristics of suicide attempters. *J. Consult. & Clin. Psychol.*, 74:478–484.

Piaget, J. (1954), *The Construction of Reality in the Child.* New York: Basic Books.

Rapaport, D., Gill, M., & Schafer, R. (1945), *Diagnostic Psychological Testing.* Rev. ed. New York: International Universites Press, 1968.

Reus, V. I., Silberman, E., Post, R. M., & Weingartner, H. (1979), d-Amphetamine: Effects on memory in a depressed population. *Biolog. Psychiat.*, 14:345–356.

Rubenstein, A. H. (1980), The adolescent with borderline personality organization: Developmental issues, diagnostic considerations, and treatment. In: *Borderline Phenomena and the Rorschach Test*, ed. J. Kwawer, H. Lerner, P. Lerner, & A. Sugarman. New York: International Universities Press, pp. 441–467.

Russell, P. W., & Beekhuis, M. E. (1976), Organization in memory: A comparison of psychotics and normals. *J. Abnorm. Psychol.*, 85:527–534.

Sapolsky, A. (1963), An indicator of suicidal ideation on the Rorschach test. *J. Proj. Tech.*, 27:332–335.

Savard, R. J., Rey, A. C., & Post, R. M. (1980), Halstead-Reitan Category test in bipolar and unipolar affective illness: Relationship to age and place of illness. *J. Nerv. & Ment. Dis.*, 168:297–304.

Schaul, J. F. (1983), Adolescent suicide: An object relations perspective. Unpublished doctoral dissertation, City University of New York.

Seiden, R. (1969), Suicide among youth: A review of the literature, 1900–1967. *Bull. Suicidol.*, Supplement.

Shneidman, E. S. (1959), The logic of suicide. In: *Clues to Suicide*, ed. E. S. Shneidman & N. L. Farberow. New York: McGraw-Hill.

———— (1976), Suicide notes reconsidered. In: *Suicidology: Contemporary Developments*, ed. E. S. Shneidman. New York: Grune & Stratton.

Silberman, E. K., Weingartner, H., & Post, R. M. (1983), Thinking disorder in depression. *Arch. Gen. Psychiat.*, 40:775–780.

Stromgren, L. S. (1977), The influence of depression on memory. *Acta Psychiatrica Scandinavia*, 56:108–128.

Sugarman, A. (1980), The borderline personality organization as manifested on psychological tests. In: *Borderline Phenomena and the Rorschach Test*, ed. J. Kwawer, H. Lerner, P. Lerner, & A. Sugarman. New York: International Universities Press, pp. 39–57.

———— Bloom-Feshbach, S., & Bloom-Feshbach, J. (1980), The psychological dimensions of borderline adolescents. In: *Borderline Phenomena and the Rorschach Test*, ed. J. Kwawer, H. Lerner, P. Lerner, & A. Sugarman. New York: International Universities Press, pp. 469–494.

Toolan, J. M. (1968), Suicide in childhood and adolescence. In: *Suicidal Behavior*, ed. H. L. P. Resnik. Boston: Little, Brown, pp. 220–227.

Urist, J. (1980), The continuum between primary and secondary process thinking: Toward a concept of borderline thought. In: *Borderline Phenomena and the Rorschach Test*, ed. J. Kwawer, H. Lerner, P. Lerner, & A. Sugarman. New York: International Universities Press, pp. 133–154.

Weiner, I. B. (1961), Cross-validation of a Rorschach checklist associated with suicidal tendencies. *J. Consult. Psychol.*, 25:312–315.

Weingartner, H., Cohen, R. M., Martello, J. D. I., & Gerdt, C. (1981), Cognitive processes in depression. *Arch. Gen. Psychiat.*, 38:42–47.

———— Silberman, E. (1982), Models of cognitive impairment: Cognitive changes in depression. *Psychopharmacology Bull.*, 18:27–42.

Chapter 7

Ego Structure and Object Differentiation in Suicidal Patients

Kim Smith, Ph.D.
James Eyman, Ph.D.

Several recent studies (e.g., Klagsbrun, 1976; Mishara, Baker, and Mishara, 1976; Smith and Crawford, 1986) have documented the fact that most people, by late adolescence, have considered killing themselves. In spite of suicidal deaths being a relatively rare event (12 suicides per 100,000 in 1981), Mintz (1970) found that about 4 percent of the U.S. population had made at least one suicide attempt (4,000 per 100,000). The studies cited above suggest that from 8 to 15 percent of all late adolescents have made at least one suicide attempt. As therapists and diagnosticians it behooves us to sharpen our thinking about this rather common but potentially lethal set of behaviors. Most of these attempts, as might be expected, appear to be of a very mild, nonlethal nature (Smith and Crawford, 1984). Those who make only mild, very manipulative attempts have been found repeatedly to differ from those who make all-out efforts to end their lives. In spite of this finding, such differences have not received proper consideration; in fact, many psychological test studies and psychoanalytic theories regarding successful suicide have been based on clinical data derived from patients who only talk about suicide or who make attempts of unspecified seriousness.

Several studies have shown (e.g., Farberow and Shneidman, 1961; Maris, 1981) that those who succeed or make serious attempts at suicide tend to differ in important respects from those who make only mild attempts. Among the most important of these differences is the overall goal of the act. On a continuum of the lethality of various suicidal acts, at one end would be the person who attempts to alter the environment by low-lethality actions that *resemble* efforts to kill one's self—light scratches to the wrist with a plastic spoon, the ingestion of ten to twelve aspirin. As Figure 1 schematically conveys, this "mild attempter" may have very little conscious or unconscious wish to actually die; the goal is rather to alter the way others respond to or feel about the person. At the other end of the continuum are those who wish to end at least their conscious existence, with little emphasis on making

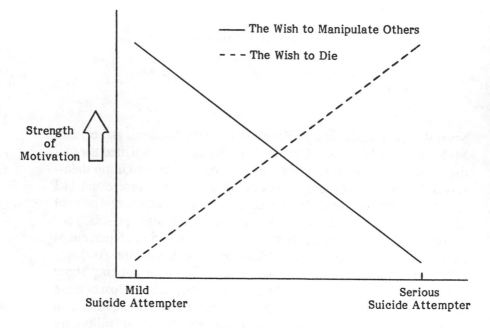

FIGURE 1. The Theoretical Distribution of the Wish to Die and the Wish to Manipulate on the Continuum of Suicide Attempt Lethality.

others more responsive; for these people the goal is to escape or avoid some perceived uncontrollable anguish via real, physical death. Attempts at this level would include a large-caliber gunshot to the head or jumping from an eight-story building. "Suicidal" people, then, can have varying proportions of manipulative and actual death motives. As a general rule, the mild attempter wishes to *live* in better control of the environment, while the more serious attempter wants to stop living.

This is not to deny the fact that many serious attempters act with the hope that a loved one will forever be hurt or will be otherwise affected. It is suggested only that the wish to affect someone and *survive* is not prominent among those who make very serious attempts. There is probably no mild suicide attempter who is without some wish to die, just as there is probably no deadly serious attempter who is without some wish to manipulate others. It is reasonable to speculate that it takes people with different personality characteristics, not just different motivations, to make serious as opposed to mild attempts.

As clinicians, we are typically asked by referral sources to state whether a depressed person is "suicidal." On such occasions some of us may review our patient's psychological test protocols for "signs of suicide." One problem with this approach is that suicidal behavior encompasses a wide range of suicidelike actions and is much too multiply determined for a "suicidal or not" judgment. An additional problem with such an approach is the assumption made about the nature of suicide, namely, that suicide is an action cut off in meaning from the therapeutic process and from the person's psychodynamics. From this perspective, suicide is simply an affect-related action. The practical importance of this type of "suicide" assessment is to ascertain whether a person is close to action and needs immediate additional support, such as hospitalization. The person's psychodynamics and ego structures, which influence the person's progress toward a mild or seriously lethal attempt, may be ignored.

This chapter is based on an "ego vulnerabilities" approach to suicide assessment (Smith, 1985). By ego vulnerabilities we mean that certain patterns of ego functions and self-other representations tend to *predispose* a person toward facing major life frustrations with various but largely predictable types of suicidal behavior. The concept of "ego deficit" is not implied in the concept of "ego vulnerabilities." Smith (1983) has suggested that people who make very serious suicide attempts tend to have ego features that predispose them to such actions. These vulnerabilities have little to do with motivation, but are instead ego structures that make the person prone to experience serious life disappointments, make adjustment to these disappointments difficult, and encourage suicide to be seen as a solution. Four features, which can be identified using a battery of psychological tests, were found to differentiate mild and serious suicide attempters; serious attempters were characterized by the presence of conflicted passive oral yearnings; a sober but ambivalent attitude toward death; high self-expectations; and a characterological tendency to overcontrol aggression. These four ego features were derived using a clinical assessment methodology based on a combined ego analytic and object relations model. One of the goals of the present study was to replicate, using these features as criteria, a valid differentiation between mild and serious suicide attempters.

Conflicted Passive Oral Yearnings. The more "lethal" patients gave test responses suggesting such conflicted yearnings. These patients were unable to relinquish early infantile hopes for nurturance and dependency, but were unable also to allow themselves to be openly dependent. Rorschach responses that conveyed the passive dependent element included percepts such as "fetus," "baby birds being fed," "embryo," "umbilical cord," and "babies sucking on a breast." The seriously suicidal patients erected a variety of defenses against directly experiencing these wishes. Some of these defenses could be seen in such Rorschach content as "a brassiere" or a "torn-up teddy bear." More typically, the suppressive attitude toward these yearnings was seen in the patient's giving only one or two of these responses in a full protocol. These percepts were the small windows through which well-sequestered, treasured hopes could be glimpsed. The high-risk person, then, wants a great deal from others but cannot readily accept it. Patients with many percepts reflecting passive oral yearnings were not considered to fit the construct. They presumably were more openly accepting of their primitive dependency wishes and thus likely made the fulfillment of these wishes a major part of their relationships. In the original study, patients with such tendencies were much more often found among the mild attempters. The clinical picture implicit in guarded passive oral content was thought to be a patient who yearned for a degree of fulfillment in relationships that likely was impossible, frequently leading to major disappointments. Usually such wishes were seen in males with counter-dependent features and women with help-rejecting and complaining personality styles.

Sober but Ambivalent Attitude Toward Death. Seriously suicidal patients manifested a very cautious and ill-at-ease attitude toward themes of death. Though death also seemed to hold an allure, these patients did not relish or revel in themes of death. When Rorschach percepts or TAT stories involved such themes, the patient's communications took on a serious tone. Often TAT stories about death were not so much avoided as told with obvious anxiety, as suggested by their logical awkwardness, the many pauses and reworkings of parts of the story, and the presence of sudden, ill-thought-out endings. It was as if these seriously suicidal patients were experiencing the anxiety involved in considering the possibility of death as a real ending to their life, not just a cessation of their pain.

High Self-Expectations. Lethality was found to increase with the presence of such expectations. These self-expectations ranged from paranoid grandiosity in more psychotic patients to narcissistic self-aggrandizement in borderline patients to what might be termed the oversensitive egocentricity or excessive pride of higher functioning persons. This construct was evident in Rorschach images that conveyed a sense of importance and specialness; they often hinted at the presence of highly romanticized notions about life. Such percepts included "a crown," "King Tut," "a statue on a pedestal," "performing poodles," "champagne glasses," and "the Eiffel Tower."

Characterological Affective Overcontrol. Lethality increased with evidence in higher functioning patients that they actively worked at maintaining rigid and tight control over the expression of aggressive feelings. Evidence for this construct was seen in a patient's reluctance to give aggressive responses on the Rorschach or by efforts to minimize perceived aggression (e.g., "attacking animals; growling and snarling; but they have heads like raccoons"; "missile with outrageous fins for better control"). Also, color responses on the Rorschach tended to be very form-dominated, sometimes to the point of indicating an excessive effort to master all affective experience. The "Experienced Balance" ratio tended to be M-dominated. In the 1983 study it was also suggested that seriously suicidal psychotic patients tended to handle their aggression rather differently. The content of their Rorschach and TAT protocols was very aggressive in nature. Though these patients showed evidence of preferring to control affect experience, the intensity of their aggression would often outstrip their ability to do so. For the present study it was hypothesized that the most blatant and animated type of aggressive ideation would be found primarily in patients in the lower borderline and psychotic range. Rorschach percepts exemplifying this type of ideation were "Two wolves fighting over some meat tissue being pulled apart, there is blood"; "High voltage electric arc, sort of blue with red on the outside, the air is very excited, very high voltage, very high amperage."

To the original four ego features two new variables were added for the present study.

Patient-Evaluator Relationship. On the basis of clinical experience it was hypothesized that seriously suicidal persons would tend to erect barriers to helpful, supportive, and nurturing interaction with others. It was believed that the seriously suicidal patient would tend to distance and reject the evaluator by such maneuvers as provocative devaluing behavior, possibly eliciting angry or withdrawing responses from the examiner. We also tried to be sensitive to passive stances by the patient or power struggles that resulted in an intrusive, overly inquiring reaction on the part of the evaluator.

Coping in Isolation. It was hypothesized that lethality would likely increase to the extent that a person attempted to cope with major problems through social withdrawal or by negating the help of others. Evidence for this construct was found primarily on TAT cards that suggested the person's interpersonal tendencies during major conflict. Stories in which the protagonist struggles alone with a major problem, lacking or rejecting help, were seen as indications of the construct's presence.

The present study had several aims. First, we wished to determine whether the four features found to differentiate mild and serious attempters in the original study would continue to make this differentiation with a new subject group and a different methodology. In the first study a clinical case study process was employed. In the present study, two raters evaluated the constructs using rating scales. It was our intent here to determine whether these individual items, as well as their overall pattern, would again allow us to distinguish mild and serious suicidal patients. We also wished to discover whether this differentiation could be enhanced by the Coping in Isolation and Patient-Evaluator Relationship constructs. In contrast to the first study, we evaluated males and females separately, in order to discover any sex differences that might be present.

We also wished to determine whether serious suicidal behavior was related more to the level of object differentiation or to the various ego structures mentioned above. Upon surveying the literature, we decided to combine three scales developed by Urist (1980). His three scales, intended to measure object relatedness, include the degree of richness and complexity the person perceives in others, the degree of individuality experienced in the self and in others, and the level of object constancy. The scale we initially used combined Urist's three scales into a single seven-point scale. We applied this scale to several Rorschach and TAT protocols and found it lacking in several regards. The scale seemed most appropriate for evaluating object relations tendencies from a patient's description of current or historical interactions with others, a perspective we found difficult to carry over into work with psychological test data. In addition, the scale did not provide a sufficient degree of differentiation in the lower ranges of object development. Finally, it did not reflect the degree of drive intensity, which we considered a significant aspect of object quality.

The level of object differentiation scale actually used in the study was developed by integrating the work of Smith (1983, 1985) and Urist (1980). The scale assesses the convergence of four aspects of image quality: the degree of merging of two objects or the permeability of their boundaries; the degree of drive neutralization; the degree to which object form is spoiled or otherwise distorted by drive or need issues; and the ratio of part animal and human to whole responses. The authors believe that self-object differentiation can be used as an indicator of the overall level of ego development, and is reflected in each of the processes measured.

METHOD

The Rorschach and TAT protocols of 13 males and 13 females who had made very serious suicide attempts and of 13 males and 13 females who had made attempts with little chance of death comprised the data base. These 52 patients were selected from a list of 340 patients who had made suicide attempts of varying degrees of seriousness. The patients selected were the most serious and least serious male and female attempters in that group who had the appropriate test protocols and had not been part of the previous study.

The characteristics of the patients in the four groups can be found in Table 1. These were significant differences ($F = 20.11$, $df = 1/48$, $p < .001$) in the mean ages of these four groups. The average age of the serious attempters was 35.4 years, almost 14 years older than the mild attempters, who averaged 21.5 years. The groups were not matched for age, as to do so would have distorted these natural findings. If age is correlated with the ego qualities and object tendencies examined in this study, then matching would have removed important, naturally occurring differences. It could be argued that the younger mild attempters will eventually become the older serious attempters, but the data do not support this. First of all, the average length of time between the first and last suicide attempts for the serious group was 22.0 months, and for the mild attempters 15.1 months. That the serious attempters were "suicidal" for less than 2 years suggests that, at least in this population, the

TABLE 1

Patient Characteristics among the Four Groups

	Serious Males	Serious Females	Mild Males	Mild Females
Age (mean)	31.9	38.9	19.8	23.1
(range)	18–60	19–62	16–29	19–52
Lethality (mean)	9.1	8.8	1.7	2.0
(range)	8.0–10.0	8.0–10.0	1.0–3.5	1.0–3.5
Number of Attempts				
mean	2.2	2.7	5.5	6.1
Diagnoses (#):				
Depressive Neurosis	2	1	0	1
Affect Disorders	1	7	0	1
(manic-depression)	(0)	(3)	(0)	(0)
(schizoaffective)	(1)	(4)	(0)	(1)
Personality Disorder	2	3	6	2
Schixophrenia	7	2	7	9
Other (acute para- noid disorder)	1	0	0	0

older serious attempters did not begin as young mild attempters. Furthermore, the mild attempters averaged over twice as many suicide attempts as did the serious attempters (see Table 1). If it were likely that the mild attempters really represented only "immature" serious attempters then one would expect the reverse pattern: more attempts with increasing age. Overall, the data indicate that serious attempters tend to be different and older in comparison to mild attempters.

The degree of seriousness of each attempt was rated according to the Lethality of Suicide Attempt Rating Scale (Smith, Conroy, and Ehler, 1984). The most serious attempt made by an individual at any time before or during long-term inpatient treatment, or within two years after leaving it, determined whether the patient was placed in the mild or serious attempters group.

All test protocols were rated blindly by both authors on seven scales: Affective Overcontrol, High Self-Expectations, Conflicted Passive Oral Yearnings, Attitude Toward Death, Coping in Isolation, Patient-Evaluator Relationship, and Degree of Object Differentiation (see Appendix).[1] Each of these constructs, except Degree of Object Differentiation, was rated on a "present," "not present," or "undetermined" basis. Degree of Object Differentiation was rated on a seven-point scale. The scales were rated independently, with all differences between raters discussed until a consensus could be reached. In a conservative move, all "undetermined" ratings were assumed not to be clear examples of the construct and were thus combined with the "not present" data. The data were analyzed by Chi-squares and, where it was possible, by F-tests on a 2 (male-female) $\times$ 2 (serious-mild) factorial design. Because of the nominal nature of much of the data, multivariate procedures such as the discriminate function were not appropriate. Since we had clear hypotheses as to the direction of the findings, one-tailed tests of significance were used to maximize the statistical sensitivity.

RESULTS

Reliability. Interrater reliability ranged from a high of 85 percent for the Patient-Evaluator Relationship to a low of 62 percent for Coping in Isolation. The percentage of agreement for the rest of the scales was 71 percent for Attitude Toward Death, 77 percent for Affective Overcontrol, 79 percent for High Self-Expectations, and 81 percent for Conflicted Passive Oral Yearnings. While the level of agreement ranged from tolerable to substantial, two factors interfered with the attainment of better initial agreement. First, as all the protocols were handwritten, several proved difficult to read. Over half the disagreements occurred because one or the other of us could not clearly decipher the handwriting of our colleagues. When the data were clarified, usually there was ready agreement. A second and more troublesome source of disagreement was the fact that clinical judgment at times clashed with what might be rated using the operational definition of a construct. Although the scales were fairly good approximations of our clinical judgment, there were several cases for which the scales proved inadequate. With one exception, we suspended clinical judgment in favor of rating on the basis of the written scale. The one exception was the Affective Overcontrol scale. After rating several cases, we discovered that the dissonance between clinical judgment and our operational definition was

---

[1]We wish to recognize Dr. Bob Athey of the Menninger Foundation and Dr. David Hayes of Harding Hospital for their extensive contributions to earlier forms of these scales.

great enough to require restructuring of the scale to reflect the more process-oriented nature of this construct. All cases were subsequently rerated using the new scale.

Original Four Features. Tables 2 and 3 contain the summary of ratings for each group. The four features previously found to distinguish serious from mild attempters were found to distinguish serious from mild *male* attempters. In particular, male serious attempters tended to overcontrol or have particularly lively aggressive ideation ($X^2 = 4.89$, $df = 1, p < .02$); to have high expectations of themselves ($X^2 = 2.70, df = 1, p < .05$); to have conflicted passive oral yearnings ($X^2 = 5.85, df = 1, p < .01$); and to have an ambivalent, nonfrivolous attitude toward death ($X^2 = 5.57, df = 1, p < .01$). By contrast, the serious and mild female attempters differed on only one of these constructs: Affective Overcontrol ($X^2 = 13.76, df = 1, p < .001$). When the male and female groups were combined, the serious and mild attempters differed in their handling of aggressive affects ($X^2 = 17.69, df = 1, p < .0001$) and in

TABLE 2

Summary of Ratings for Each of the Four Groups
and for Each of Six Scales

	Affect	Death	Yearning	Hi Exp.	Iso-lation	Rela-tion
Serious Females						
present	13	7	6	10	7	4
not present	0	6	7	3	1	9
undecided	0	0	0	5	0	
Serious Males						
present	12	10	11	10	8	10
not present	1	3	2	3	3	3
undecided	0	0	0	0	2	0
Mild Females						
present	4	8	8	7	10	8
not present	9	5	4	6	2	4
undecided	0	0	1	0	1	1
Mild Males						
present	7	4	5	6	8	7
not present	6	7	8	7	4	6
undecided	0	2	0	0	1	0

TABLE 3

The Mean "Degree of Objective Differentiation Scale"
(DOODS) Ratings for Each of the Four Groups

	Serious	Mild
Males	3.1	2.8
Females	3.9	3.5

self-expectation ($X^2 = 4.06$, $df = 1$, $p < .03$), and tended to differ in their attitudes toward death ($X^2 = 1.95$, $df = 1$, $p < .09$).

Approximately half of the current group of *serious* males (53.8 percent) manifested the more openly excited aggressive imagery. Only 5.4 percent of the combined male and female *mild* attempters conveyed this kind of aggression. Of females who made serious attempts, only 7.7 percent showed this excited attitude toward aggression. This more volatile type of aggressive imagery was seen primarily in both serious and mild male attempters (75 percent). As was found previously, the presence of this intense, vivid, and animated aggressive imagery was associated with lower levels of ego functioning. Among seriously suicidal patients of both sexes, only one person, a male, manifested this type of aggressive content *and* had a Degree of Object Differentiation score above 3.0. When all the patients in the study were combined (see Table 4), there was a clear and significant tendency for developmentally more advanced patients to manifest the "inhibition" (rather than the vividly aggressive ideation) pattern and, conversely, for less developed patients to reverse this pattern ($X^2 = 9.42$, $df = 1$, $p < 0.01$).

Degree of Object Differentiation. There was no tendency for the level of object differentiation to vary with the degree of lethality (see

TABLE 4

Type of Aggressive Ideation According to the
Level of the "Degree of Objective Differentiation
Scale" (DOODS)

DOODS Ratings	Inhibitory	Excited Aggression	Other
$3.1 \geq$	17 (63.0%)	2 (7.4%)	8 (29.6%)
$3.0 \leq$	7 (28.0%)	10 (40.0%)	8 (32.0%)

Table 3). There was, however, a significant tendency for the females in this study to have an overall higher level of ego development ($F = 8.22$, $df = 1, 48$; $p < .01$).

Ego Vulnerabilities Pattern. The pattern of all four ego features was examined to see whether it distinguished serious from mild attempters. Ten of the serious attempters evinced all four features compared to only one of the mild attempters ($X^2 = 9.34$, $df = 1$, $p < .001$). All of the males and 80 percent of the females who had all four features were in the serious groups. Seriously suicidal males had a clear tendency to show all four indicators ($X^2 = 7.80$, $df = 1$, $p < .001$), as approximately half (46.2 percent) did so. Seriously suicidal females showed a weaker tendency in this regard, only 30.8 percent showing all the features (as compared to 7.7 percent of mild female attempters). When the criterion of three or more of these features was employed, more of the serious attempters (69.2 percent of both sexes) were identified ($X^2 = 9.32$, $df = 1$, $p < .01$). Three or more of these features characterized 26.9 percent of the mild attempters. Again, males showed a greater tendency for these features to be associated with serious suicidal behavior than did females. This pattern identified 84.6 percent of serious male attempters and only 30.1 percent of mild male attempters ($X^2 = 7.72$, $df = 1$, $p < .001$). Only slightly more than half of the serious female patients (53.8 percent) and 23.1 percent of the mild females showed three or more features ($X^2 = 2.60$, $df = 1$, $p < .06$).

Additional Two Constructs. There was no difference between serious and mild attempters on the Coping in Isolation variable. The Patient-Evaluator Relationship showed little tendency to distinguish lethality when males and females were examined separately. However, when both sexes were combined, there was a tendency ($X^2 = 2.79$, $df = 1$, $p < .10$) for mild attempters to have more difficulty with the evaluator than did serious patients. As this finding was in the opposite direction from what was expected, only a one-tailed test was used.

DISCUSSION

The results support the notion that certain personality features tend to be found in people who make serious efforts to kill themselves and that these features, especially among males, do not typify those who make less serious attempts. In contrast with the previous study (Smith, 1983), this pattern was not present for all of the serious attempters. When it did occur, however, the pattern was an effective discriminator of seriously suicidal patients. With one exception, the full pattern characterized only the serious attempters. The current study suggests that these features may be more prominent among male serious attempters than among female. Approximately half the male serious attempters and none of the males who made mild attempts showed this pattern. When the criterion was lowered to only three of these features, 85 percent of the seriously suicidal males were identified, along with 30 percent of the mild attempters.

It is apparent from the pattern of ego weaknesses among the women subjects that additional ego tendencies will need to be considered. The present results, however, do suggest that one of the most effectively discriminating attributes among women may be their attitude toward aggression. All of the seriously suicidal females registered this construct while only four of the female mild attempters (30.8 percent) did so. Even more promising is the fact that the inhibitory attitude toward aggressive ideation was found in 92.3 percent of the serious females but in only 15.4 percent of those making mild attempts. Only one seriously suicidal female was not rated as exhibiting an inhibited attitude toward aggressive ideation. She presented aggressive content that was embellished more than was typical of the inhibited group. However, several elements were suggestive of the inhibited style. Her aggressive Rorschach percepts did not have the vivid, blatant, and energized quality often found among the lower functioning male serious attempters. She made consistent efforts to minimize and distance the aggression evident in such Rorschach percepts as "a creature in Star Wars . . . looks evil, scary. He was fastened on a pole so he wouldn't be threatening" and "an airplane looking down on an explosion at Hiroshima . . . different colors coming up." Clearly, among females the tendency to overcontrol and suppress aggressive ideation is one aspect of the ego of women who make serious attempts to end their lives. If the discriminating power of this personality tendency continues to hold up in future evaluations, a relatively discernible marker will have been identified with which to separate serious from mild female attempters.

To conceptualize these personality features as structures within the ego that make a person more prone or vulnerable to suicide is very different from considering them "signs" of suicide. Characterological tendencies to inhibit the expression of aggressive ideas or to expect a great deal of one's self are not in themselves pathogenic to suicide. Instead, these features are personality structures which seem to *orient* the person toward serious suicidal actions. While this perspective may be less dramatic than a sign approach, it does allow the clinician to recognize that a particular patient has a strong latent potential to respond to major frustrations of private hopes with quite serious efforts at suicide. It also allows the therapist to know precisely which ego structures make the patient so vulnerable. When this vulnerability is paired with a knowledge of the types of event which make this individual most depressed or hurt, the therapist can better focus the work around such issues. Ongoing analysis of the patient's private hopes, as well as open discussion of suicide contemplated as a way to avoid relinquishing these hopes, is far more effective than discovering only during a crisis that the patient is suicidal.

One of the important contributions of the present study involves the quality of aggressive ideation. The fact that approximately half of the male serious attempters manifested more lively and embellished aggressive imagery establishes this style as more prominent than had previously been thought. This prevalence and the current evidence for an excited ego investment in such imagery suggest that the description of "overcontrol of aggressive affects" is appropriate only for higher level patients. The more openly aggressive imagery seemed to reflect the use of aggressive fantasy to counter underlying feelings of being powerless, masculinely defective, or vulnerable to assault. It is interesting that of the seriously suicidal patients who relied on the defensive use of aggressive fantasy, all but one were male. These lower functioning male patients had developed embellished aggressive fantasies as a defense to protect their self-esteem and to shore up the bulwarks against pressing underlying aspects of a devalued masculine self. Smith (1985) has argued that suicidal motivations, for all their complexity, have two basic aims: to injure or kill the frustrating object and to protect or actualize a preferred sense of self. In the case of the male patients with embellished aggressive fantasies it is worth noting that their attempts tended to be made by actively violent means (see Table 5). It seems that these violent actions, like the violent fantasies, may have served to counter an emerging sense of impotence that may have precipitated the act. Through the potency of violently aggressive action the sense of being a powerful, active, and competent person may have been actualized.

The type of aggressive imagery manifested by the lower functioning patients could be termed the Defensive Use of Intense and/or Embellished Aggressive Fantasy. The category that embraces the

TABLE 5

Frequency of Methods Used in Suicide
Attempts of the Male Serious Attempters

Males With Aggressive Fantasy		Males With Inhibited Aggression	
Gunshot	3	Suffocation	3
Jumping	3	Gunshot	2
Suffocation	1	Overdose	1

aggressive tendencies of both higher and lower suicidal patients, pre-viously termed Affective Overcontrol, should more accurately be termed Defensive Stance Toward Aggression. Seriously suicidal males in the mid-borderline range or higher are very likely to manifest the inhibited attitude, as are most seriously suicidal females independent of their level of functioning. Lower functioning males who are seriously suicidal appear very prone to the defensive use of aggressive fantasy.

Apparently the level of self-object differentiation has no bearing on whether a person is likely to make a serious attempt at suicide. This is an important finding in that one could argue, as have Blatt and Ritzler (1974), that suicide becomes likely when there is a merging of the self with a hated object. The tendency for such merging to occur would seem to be greatest among those with lower ego organization; one would therefore predict more seriously suicidal behavior among this group. The data, however, do not support this assumption. Seriously suicidal behavior does not appear to be linked with particular separation-individuation conflicts but rather with particular ego struc-tures. While separation struggles and ego growth are parallel and mutually interactive processes, the qualitative aspects of ego structures have more to do with the particular ways the person learns to think about self and others and to cope with conflict. Self- and object representations and the coping and defensive style have more to do with character tendencies than with the level of self-object separation achieved.

What seems most important, then, in causing a person to be vulnerable to seriously suicidal behavior are the quality of self-other representations and the coping and defensive style with which that person handles aggressive ideas. Demanding too much of oneself and expecting unreasonable sensitivity and nurturance from others leaves a person prone to disillusionment regarding identity and the potential for nurturance from the environment. The inhibition of aggressive ideas or actions represents an ego-based collusion with the conscience to avoid directly acting in hurtfully aggressive ways toward the frustrating object. Because of the frightening and vivid aggressive imagery of the lower functioning person, such action appears to be suppressed. With such confinement, the person is compelled to use various internal objects as both instruments and targets of the aggression.

Because we had been clinically impressed with the characteristic social withdrawal of seriously suicidal patients in the face of major conflict, we included the construct of Coping in Isolation in the present study. We hypothesized that the suicidal patient would show a marked tendency not to view others as resources during periods of conflict. While seriously suicidal patients were indeed prone to adopt isolative coping styles, this disposition was equally evident among those making mild attempts. It is quite possible that most patients who consider suicide or suicidelike behaviors tend to shun others' help during periods of conflict more than do other patients. The retreat into self-abusive actions in order to control the uncontrollable pain of living may be a reflection of the suicidal patient's sense of impotence about resolving issues with reflective discussion. At times actions do indeed seem more powerful than words.

Mindful of the angry countertransference responses that many suicidal people can elicit (see Zee, 1972; Maltsberger and Buie, 1974), we had believed that the nature of the patient-evaluator relationship would vary with lethality. We were surprised to find the opposite of the tendency we had anticipated. Mild attempters tended to evoke more angry and distancing responses from the evaluators than did serious attempters. In retrospect, it seems probable that our Patient-Evaluator Relationship scale may have been more attuned to deviations in the relationship arising out of the patient's willingness to act out. The tendency for the mild, more manipulatively suicidal patients to act up and act out is probably being registered more than the tendency for the person to erect barriers in an established relationship. Perhaps a limited focus on the patient's attitude toward helping situations or interactions would have been a more sensitive measure of how the patient would respond within an established treatment relationship.

SUMMARY

Suicide, we believe, is a behavior which occurs because of (1) dynamic motivations, (2) a set of ego structures which raise the potential for the person to act in accordance with those motivations, and (3) an external event which is perceived as crushing or frustrating the achievement of major self-object perspectives. The focus of this paper has been on the second of these elements. Without all three being present, suicide would probably not occur except under very extreme circumstances. As many have noted (e.g., Litman and Tabachnick, 1968), the unconscious motivations for suicide are quite varied. Going a step further, Karl Menninger (1933) has pointed out that simply having a motive for dying is not a sufficient explanation for suicidal action. One problem with psychoanalytic theories of suicide is that they tend to account for suicide primarily in terms of motivations (e.g., the wish to return to the womb) and mechanisms (e.g., retroflexively directed aggression). Studies like the one presented here serve to remind us that while content and structure are related, the types of structure that produce the suicide perspective are seemingly more constant across individuals than are specific motivations. While it is not surprising to find ego structures varying with the general goal of a suicidal act (to manipulate or to die) the value of this observation has not been fully exploited diagnostically.

It is important to emphasize once again that we do not consider the ego features of the seriously suicidal person to "cause" the suicide. They are not even to be considered "suicidogenic." These same "high-risk" structures may also encourage high levels of achievement, high moral standards, the capacity to contain intense emotions during business decisions or arguments with a loved one, and the capacity to expect and draw out the best from associates (even if such expectations are problematic in relations with lovers and friends). But upon the traumatic failure of major, usually unconsciously held life hopes (or, as is often the case, their progressive deterioration), these "strengths" are among the features of an ego which can make a loss seem terribly devastating to the sense of self and to the meaningfulness of relationships. The features of high self-expectations, high expectations of others (passive oral yearnings), a defensive stance toward aggressive fantasy and impulses, and a sober attitude toward death as a potential solution to the pain of life (Maris, 1981) are not, then, signs of suicide but indications of a latent vulnerability within the ego to respond suicidally to major frustration. As noted elsewhere (Smith, 1983, 1985), this "frustration" is not just any frustration, but seems to involve the threatened destruction of unconsciously prized, structuralized, and organizing views of self and others.

There are several clinical implications of our findings. First, we have continued to document the differences between people who make serious efforts to end their lives and those whose most serious efforts tend to be low in lethal potential. Those who make one or more mild attempts and also evince the pattern of features that characterizes serious attempters should be considered at high risk for a more serious attempt.

A second implication is that anytime an evaluator detects the constellation of all four features, the patient should be identified as a person vulnerable to respond to the frustration of major life hopes with a serious attempt at suicide. The half-hearted, manipulative attempt is not to be expected from this person. The same principle tends to hold when three of the four features are present. In these cases the evaluator needs to identify the external circumstances most likely to activate the person's idiosyncratic suicide dynamics. In the test report the evaluator should provide the reader clear information as to what ego structures render the person vulnerable, the principle dynamics involved, and the types of circumstances under which such dynamics would be likely to manifest themselves in a serious attempt at suicide.

The third implication is that seriously suicidal men and women differ in the particular features that make them vulnerable. Seriously suicidal women are prone to take an inhibitory stance toward aggressive ideas, probably more so than are seriously suicidal men. Seriously suicidal men tend to show the pattern of all four features more often than do women; the pattern will therefore be more effective in identifying suicidal men. With women who are assessed to be at high risk for suicide on other bases, the presence of an inhibited attitude toward aggression should further underscore the seriousness of this vulnerability.

APPENDIX

Rater: _____ Case: _____
Present _____
Undetermined _____
Not Present _____

Defensive Stance Toward Aggression
(Previously: Affective Overcontrol)

Construct Statement. The establishment of the construct is dependent on the level of ego organization of the individual. Among individuals with a mid-borderline to neurotic level of organization, lethality increases with evidence of withholding and constricting aggressive ideation. The few aggressive responses that are expressed are quickly defused and minimized. Lethality increases among individuals with a low borderline to psychotic level of ego organization when aggressive ideation is graphic and embellished. There is evidence that the person is ineffectively controlling aggressive fantasies and is captivated by them. These fantasies usually serve to counter feelings of impotence and vulnerability.

Operational Definition of Construct. For individuals within the mid-borderline to neurotic range, the construct is registered when the overall picture is one of rigid overcontrol of aggressive ideation. This includes few aggressive responses, form dominance of C, and M dominance of EB. Impulsive expression, the parading of aggression, and well-modulated aggressive ideation are countraindications. For individuals within the lower borderline to psychotic range the construct is established when the picture is one of vivid and excited aggressive ideation. This is seen by several graphic aggressive responses which the person embellishes as if unable to let loose of the idea. In both cases the context of the response (e.g., a consideration of prior and subsequent responses; use or avoidance of colored blot areas; excessive aggression in the patient's comments to the evaluator) is to be weighed as much as the specific content of the response.

Examples of Construct

A. *Mid-borderline to neurotic range*
   1. Responses in which the aggression is quickly neutralized or minimized. "Demons, looks like they were in a fight or kissing. I can't tell what they are, just blobby things"; "An attacking animal growling, snarling, but it has the head of a raccoon."

   2. Affect-laden responses are not "enjoyed" but may be blandly given, "squeezed-out," or diminished (e.g., "reddish" or "pinkish" instead of "red," color determinant provided only after rather persistent or direct inquiry).

   3. Color used in arbitrary, superficial, and defensive ways.

   4. Imagery symbolizing a defense against outward expression of affects: horns turned inward, fortifications, dams, bluff, a wall with two small windows. Objects with hard shells (e.g., "crab with a hard shell") are more reflective of body boundary rather than impulse modulation issues.

5. Few color responses with particular form-dominated attention to C, suggesting an active struggle to master the experience. The result would be a predominance of FC, and EB is M-dominated.

B. *Lower borderline to psychotic range*

1. Indications of being unable to let go of aggressive fantasy is seen by the process of the person excessively embellishing and elaborating the aggressive responses: "Two wolves fighting over some meat, tissue being pulled apart, there is blood."

2. Vivid aggressive responses such as "Penis with barbs on it," "Dante's inferno, brimstone and fire," "Moses breaking the Ten Commandments, screaming."

3. Highly charged, energized responses such as "High voltage electric arc, sort of blue with red on the outside, the air is very excited, very high voltage, very high amperage"; "A rabbit with projections coming out of its eyes, ultraviolet rays."

Rater: _____ Case: _____
Present _____
Undetermined _____
Not Present _____

High Expectations of Self

Construct Statement. Lethality increases when a person takes himself very seriously. High expectations may be seen throughout the range of ego organization and may include paranoid grandiosity, narcissistic self-aggrandizement, overly sensitive egocentricity, and excessive self pride. However, the accent is on a "striving" sense of self-importance, not on the more infantile sense of unconditional specialness.

Operational Definition of Construct. Rorschach images suggesting a sense of personal importance or romantic notions about life. Only one or two such images are sufficient to register the construct. Images which only weakly reflect the construct (e.g., "poodles" as opposed to "performing poodles") need additional evidence before construct is registered.

1. Imagery suggestive of a sense of personal specialness:

   a. Direct expression of a person as ideal, the best, perfect, or a human in an idealized role such as a king, angel, priest, etc.

b. Grand objects such as a spiral galaxy, the universe, the earth.

c. Grand people such as Napoleon, Washington, Churchill, Cleopatra, etc.

d. "Objects" often the subject of others' attention such as show girls, poodles being shown, performing elephants, etc.

e. Prized or expensive objects such as jewels, diamonds, a crown.

f. "Regal" animals such as a peregrine falcon or eagle.

2. Imagery suggesting highly romanticized notions: Eiffel Tower, knight in armor, Paris, heaven, hat with a plume, champagne glass, an ornate shield, family crest, a special magical lamp, something on a pedestal, etc. (These are particularly potent indicators of the construct; only one such image is enough to register the concept.)

Rater:_____ Case:_____
Present _____
Undetermined _____
Not Present _____

Conflicted Passive Oral Yearnings

Construct Statement. Lethality increases with evidence of an inability to relinquish or psychologically mourn the earliest experiences of nurturing and dependency. Especially with males, there are inhibitions against directly experiencing these wishes.

Operational Definition of Construct. Rorschach images or combinations of images containing oral receptive (passive) or symbiotically nurturing wishes. Oral receptive wishes are seen also in references to typically childhood foods. Only one or two of these images is sufficient to register the construct. The more idiosyncratic or vivid the percept, the more likely it is to reflect the construct. If passive dependent wishes are highly ego-syntonic and plentiful in the protocols, this is a contraindication.

Examples of Construct

1. Imagery directly conveying passive oral issues: unattached breasts, nipples, baby bottle, fetus, embryo, umbilical cord, womb, uterus

(not vagina), esophagus, "baby" animals, birth of an animal, stomach.

2. Imagery suggestive of passive oral actions: sucking, nursing, mouth open as if ready to be fed, parasites all connected, breast with arms reaching out to grab you.

3. Presence of "passive" and "oral" imagery within the same protocol. Examples of passive imagery are figures seen as leaning, supported, being lifted up, helpless, sleeping, resting, lying down; drifting clouds.

4. Foods or other objects closely associated with childhood: candy, ice cream, oatmeal, glass of milk, sugar bowl, teddy bears, puppy dog.

5. Imagery which suggests conflicted yearnings: brassiere, muzzle, torn-up teddy bear, breast bone, armor, breastplate, etc.

Rater:_____ Case:_____
Present _____
Undetermined _____
Not Present _____

Attitude Toward Death

Construct Statement. Lethality is heightened by the presence of anxiety or a sober regard for death, especially one's own. These sober/anxious feelings often appear side by side with positive feelings about death. Seriously suicidal people do not speak about the ending of a life (whether suicide or murder) in playful, manipulative, or effusive ways.

Operational Definition of Construct. Evidence for this construct is best seen on the TAT, in interviews about suicidal tendencies, and to a lesser extent on the Word Association and Rorschach tests. Either the "anxiety" or the "sober regard" will always be present. The suggestion of benefit from death will often be evident but not always. Parading of notions of death or efforts to alarm the evaluator are contraindications. Showing an interest in how others will suffer following death is a contraindication for adults (but very characteristic of the "mild" attempter and "threatener"). However, teens, especially younger teens, are more prone to make serious attempts with motivations such as these.

Examples of Construct

1. On the *Rorschach* (Absence of the construct on the Rorschach is not a sufficient basis for a "Not Present" indication.)

   a. Imagery suggestive that the person is perceiving him/herself as deteriorating, "over the hill," perhaps dying: an old leaf that's falling apart, a worn-out rug, a weathered and rotting animal skin, etc.

   b. Imagery of death and/or dying things that are unusual and that create some degree of personal turmoil. The person might follow such a response with a response suggestive of undoing, may forget where he/she saw it, might be uncomfortable about response during inquiry, etc.

2. On the *TAT*

   a. The evidence would include avoidance of suicide, murder, or dying themes; haltings, reworkings of stories; abrupt changes in the story; long or unusually short stories.

   b. Stories of suicide told by high-risk people usually involve only the suicidal person. When others are mentioned, their suffering is not emphasized. There is no "excitement" covertly expressed in the effects on others.

3. On the *Word Association Test*, the reaction time to "suicide" is often unusually shorter than surrounding words, the association more death-oriented in content (e.g., "hate," "murder," "death"). Mild attempters tend to be self-referential (e.g., "me") or otherwise less death-oriented (e.g., "tempting," "bad-sinister," "happiness").

4. During an *Interview* the person is often reluctant to talk about the details of his/her serious attempt. There is often a wish to minimize past attempts. When the person does talk freely of a past attempt, it is with an attitude of pseudocontrol—"everything is understood." The patient who exaggerates the seriousness, hopes to impress, or talks about prior attempts with a self-pleased smile is at lower risk. If there has been no prior attempt, the reluctance can be observed in a "pulling teeth" countertransference experience of the interviewer when inquiring about possible suicidal feelings, fantasies, or plans.

Rater: _____ Case: _____
Present _____
Undetermined _____
Not Present _____

Coping in Isolation

Construct Statement. Lethality increases with suggestion that the person attempts to cope with major problems alone, that is, without eliciting the help of others. Even in the suicide crisis, the person does not call for help or reach out for assistance in dealing with problems. The person has given up on solving problems by changing the environment or by manipulating others. A state of solitary struggle is most evident. The degree to which the person asks for help and shares problems with others is a contraindication of serious suicidal potential.

Operational Definition of Construct. Evidence for this construct is usually found on the TAT, and to a lesser extent on the Rorschach. The TAT stories convey a sense that the person is coping with serious problems essentially alone without asking for or receiving help from others. If other people are present in the stories, there is a sense that they are uninterested or ineffectual. Rorschach imagery or comments about the imagery convey a sense of aloneness.

Examples of Construct

1. On the *TAT*, focus most on those stories that describe a serious problem that the protagonist is facing *and* that reflects other people's stance toward the protagonist and his problem. Particular emphasis should be given to Cards 15, 3BM, and 14 when other people are brought into the story.

   a. The evidence would include stories involving a major problem in which the person is all alone or lacking comforting, supporting, and interested responses from others.

   b. The story may include people who are stated to be "close" but who in fact offer no help or support to the person. They may, however, be spoken of as people who would be hurt in some way by the suicide and thus offered as reasons to continue an empty existence.

2. On the *Rorschach*

    a. Imagery conveying a sense of aloneness or separateness, such as people back to back or solitary figures where two figures are usually seen.

    b. Poor form on Ms; failure to see humans on Cards III or VII.

    c. Very few actively cooperative human movement responses.

Rater:_____ Case:_____
Present _____
Undetermined _____
Not Present _____

Patient–Evaluator Relationship

Construct Statement. The seriously suicidal patient tends to erect barriers between him/herself and nurturing interactions with others. There is often an air of superseriousness and urgency about the patient. Often the patient is overly angry, but this anger is usually denied. Often the patient, especially the female patient, implies that others cannot understand how much pain he/she is in. Male patients are usually counterdependent.

Operational Definition of Construct. Evidence of an overtly distancing and implicitly rejecting stance by patient. This stance is usually conveyed through a conscious context of the patient "trying" to be compliant.

Examples of Construct

1. With an egocentric, urgent, and demanding air, the patient tends to be "innocently" provocative or otherwise elicits angry responses in the evaluator.

2. Patient may be overcompliant while subtly battling for control. Evaluator may respond by withdrawing or engaging in a power struggle.

3. Patient is overly serious, critical of the tests, quarrelsome and otherwise makes the task longer, more painful, and ungratifying than it need be. Only glimmers (at best) are seen of a "working alliance."

4. Evaluator seems to be acting out a "sadistic" role with patient, as by overinquiry or belittling comments.

Contraindications (Any one of these is strong evidence for "Not Present.")

1. Patient is overtly overdependent upon evaluator in ego-syntonic, clingy manner.

2. Patient is able to enjoy the tests, is effusive, entertained and entertaining, agreeable.

3. Patient is able to form a useful and meaningful working alliance.

Rater: _____ Case:_____

Rating: _____

Degree of Object Differentiation Scale

1. Essentially the whole protocol is characterized by simple, banal, noninteractive percepts. The drive quality tends to be either neutral or heavily aggressivized. Highly libidinal or merging percepts would be rated higher.

2. At least 25 percent of the responses involve highly merged or chaotic and violent percepts. Drive and need states are blatant, primitive, and clearly reflect the nature of the drive or need with little evidence of sublimation. Poor form and spoiling of percepts is frequent.

3. At least 10 percent of the responses involve blurred boundaries and merging or parasitic or overdependent themes or aggressively separated or violently aggressive responses. Mirroring responses begin about here. Most of the drive and need states will show some low-level sublimation; there may be one or two highly charged merging or aggressive percepts. Form is occasionally very poor or spoiled (no more than two such responses in a brief record or four in a highly dilated record).

4. There may be several responses involving touching and grasping without actual merging being present. Mirroring responses are frequently seen here. Human movement percepts often involve opposing interactions. Most (with two or three exceptions) aggressive and

libidinal drives show derivative or sublimation quality. The form level of percepts involving separating/drive components is almost completely of an F_{w-} quality or above. (No more than one F— or two F spoils).

5. Occasional (one or two) mirroring percepts may be noted. M's are usually interactive. Only occasionally will aggressive or libidinal percepts show low levels of sublimation. The form level of percepts involving separation/drive issues is generally F_{w+} or above. No F— and no more than one F spoil at this level.

6. With perhaps only one exception, all imagery is clearly separated and defined. No mirroring or low-level drive derivatives or merging themes (e.g., fetus) occur at this level. Males and females may be caricatured. Form level is generally F_{w+} or above.

7. The total protocol involves varied content given in good form and involving separate, often interactive, imagery. None of the responses reflect low-level drive or need influences.

REFERENCES

Blatt, S. J., & Ritzler, B. A. (1974), Suicide and the representation of transparency and cross-sections on the Rorschach. *J. Consult. & Clin. Psychol.*, 42:280–287.

Farberow, N. L., & Shneidman, E. S., Eds. (1961), *The Cry for Help*. New York: McGraw-Hill.

Klagsbrun, F. (1976), *Too Young to Die*. San Jose, CA: H. M. Technologies.

Litman, R. E., & Tabachnick, N. (1968), Psychoanalytic theories of suicide. In: *Suicidal Behaviors: Diagnosis and Management*, ed. H. L. P. Resnik. Boston: Little, Brown, pp. 73–81.

Maltsberger, J. T., & Buie, D. H. (1974), Countertransference hate in the treatment of suicidal patients. *Arch. Gen. Psychiat.*, 30:625–633.

Maris, R. W. (1981), *Pathways to Suicide*. Baltimore: Johns Hopkins University Press.

Menninger, K. A. (1933), Psychoanalytic aspects of suicide. *Internat. J. Psycho-Anal.*, 14:376–390.

Mintz, R. S. (1970), Prevalence of persons in the city of Los Angeles who have attempted suicide: A pilot study. *Bull. Suicidol.*, 7:8–16.

Mishara, B. L., Baker, A. H., & Mishara, T. T. (1976), The frequency of suicide attempts: A retrospective approach applied to college students. *Amer. J. Psychiat.*, 133:841–844.

Smith, K. (1983), Using a battery of tests to predict suicide in a long term hospital: A clinical analysis. *Omega*, 13:261–275.

———— (1985), An ego vulnerabilities approach to suicide assessment. *Bull. Menn. Clin.*, 49:489–499.

———— Conroy, R. W., & Ehler, B. D. (1984), Lethality of suicide attempt rating scale. *Suicide and Life-Threatening Behavior*, 14(4):215–224.

———— Crawford, S. (1986), Suicidal behavior among "normal" high school students. *Suicide and Life-Threatening Behavior*, 16(4):313–325.

Urist, J. (1980), Object relations. In: *Encyclopedia of Clinical Assessment*, Vol. 2, ed. R. Wood, San Francisco: Josey-Bass, pp. 821–833.

Zee, H. (1972). Blind spots in recognizing serious suicidal intentions. *Bull. Menn. Clin.*, 36:551–555.

Chapter 8

The Rorschach as a Tool in Understanding the Dynamics of Women with Histories of Incest

Judith Meyers, Psy.D.

The long-term effects of childhood sexual abuse, especially incest, have not until recently received sufficient study, due mainly to the severe underestimation of the problem. During the era in which Freud's seduction theory was repudiated and replaced with the incest fantasy theory, the rate of detected incest in the United States was 1.2 cases per million in 1910, 1.9 per million in 1920, and 1.1 per million in 1930 (Weinberg, 1955). Today it is estimated at between 800 and 1000 cases per million (Gelinas, 1981).

Many factors are responsible for this marked shift in public and professional awareness. California has been at the forefront of social programs, instituting stringent reporting laws and innovative treatment models. Extensive media coverage has gone beyond mere sensationalism; it has turned public awareness to outrage, as people have been forced to reexamine child care provisions, recognize the breakdown of family structures, and reaffirm the goal of society to protect its children.

The impact on the professional community has been no less dramatic. The issue, however, was not its willingness to think about the problem. Rather it was an unwillingness to reexamine what had already been thought. The literature in this area, which is both sporadic and repetitive, has over the years addressed three central issues: blame, guilt, and the extent of harm (Herman, 1981). An emphasis on the first two issues, however, seems to have obscured our understanding of the third.

203

The first significant research, conducted by Bender and Blau (1937), suggested that long-term effects on the victim were minimal, though they did concede immediate short-term consequences in some instances. Actually, their case illustrations did not deal with incest per se, but with sexual activity in children, often child-initiated. Their study was flawed by several methodological shortcomings not the least of which involved sample selection and a failure to control for socio-economic status and intelligence. The study, the authors concluded, "seems to indicate that these children do not deserve completely the cloak of innocence with which they have been endowed by moralists, social reformers and legislators" (p. 514). Despite these obvious limitations and biases, this article remained the classic in the field for twenty years.

The second significant wave of research came in the 1950s and 1960s. The literature reflected an awareness of the more pervasive nature of the problem and the interplay of family dynamics (Kaufman, Peck, and Taguiri, 1954; Cormier, Kennedy, and Sangowicz, 1962; Heims and Kaufman, 1963; Luftig, Dresser, Spellman, and Murray, 1966). However, with the introduction of a family model came an equal emphasis on the victim's seductiveness, the mother's knowledge and collusion in the act, and incest as a symptom of family pathology. Thus the intrapsychic dynamics of the victim remained obscure. As late as 1964, Weiner was able to conclude from his survey of the literature that

> Incestuous daughters are typically precocious in learning and reality testing and eager to assume adult roles; they are gratified by their father's attention and often use the incestuous relationship to express hostility toward their mothers; these daughters seldom resist or complain about their father's advances and rarely experience guilt; although girls who begin incest in adolescence frequently become promiscuous following termination of the incest, there is little evidence that incest participation, particularly before puberty, causes later psychological disturbance. [Weiner, 1964, p. 152]

Then, in the 1970s and 1980s, came a marked increase in recognition of the problem as well as a shift in conceptualization. Probably as a result of the women's movement and the reaction against exploitation, the literature focused more on the woman as victim, acted upon by developmental and environmental factors over which she had little or no control. As blame was placed outside the women, exonerating them from guilt, more attention was focused on intrapsychic effects. Incest as a symptom of family pathology was also more accepted. Herman and Hirschman (1977) cite disturbances in the family interaction, the daughter becoming overwhelmed by her power in the family. Impaired heterosexual functioning, feelings of isolation, and self-devaluation were part of the constellation they noted in adult women with histories of incest.

Gelinas (1981) reports that these women generally present themselves clinically when some developmental milestone, such as marriage, childbirth, or divorce, causes the negative and often repressed effects of incest to reemerge. Terming this phenomenon a "developmental trigger," Gelinas notes that the presenting problem is most often chronic depression accompanied by poor relationships, self-injurious behavior, sexual dysfunction, dissociative elements, and impulsivity.

A history of parentification and intergenerational risk has been cited as well (Herman and Hirschman, 1977; Gelinas, 1981). Meyers (1979), in discussing mother-daughter relationships over three generations, describes a dysfunctional repetitive family system that involves enmeshed and undifferentiated relationships among the women. The maternal grandmother is seen as central to the current functioning of the family. Due to splitting and projective identification as the major defenses, the daughters are forced to assume rigid roles that interfere with separation-individuation, promote depression, preclude satisfactory heterosexual object relations, and affect future bonding capacities. A history of sexual trauma pervaded all their histories.

Recognizing this three-generational involvement in incest families, Everstein (1984) describes the contradictory roles of the incest victim within her family as well as the pressure this places on generational boundaries. Coerced into the role of incest victim by a shift in family dynamics, the victim believes she is central to the functioning of the family. It appears that moving the child into the incest role prevents a complete breakdown of family functioning and serves as a defense against loss and separation.

Despite this growing body of literature, no systematic research has been done on the Rorschach protocols of such women. Though two studies used a battery of tests, including the Rorschach, to assess personality functioning in adolescent incest victims (Kaufman, Peck, and Taguiri, 1954), no study to date has used the Rorschach as a measure for assessing the dynamic functioning of adult women with histories of incest.

The present study proposes to examine the long-term effects of sexual molestation by looking at the records of a sample of ten women who had incest experiences as children; to generate specific hypotheses regarding the intrapsychic and personal dynamics of sexual abuse; and to consider the implications for treatment. Test records were assessed for ego strengths and weaknesses, defensive structure, affect organization, object relations, and body image.

METHODS AND PROCEDURES

The adult women were drawn from private practice case loads. All were self-referred and identified themselves as sexually abused at the time of the referral or early in treatment. They were experiencing personal difficulties and felt the abuse was significant to their adjustment problems. All had sustained chronic abuse by their father, usually beginning in latency and lasting until early or late adolescence.

The records were scored using Piotrowski's system of percept-analysis (1957). However, two components of the Rapaport System (Rapaport, Gill, and Shafer, 1945)—(c) and Deviant Verbalizations—were incorporated in the discussion to further clarify the data, as was the concept of Texture from the Exner Comprehensive System (Exner, 1974).

DISCUSSION OF THE DATA

Of the ten women, nine presented as having borderline levels of ego organization as characterized by the defenses of splitting and projective identification, difficulty with self-other boundaries, and loss of distance between inner experiences and outer reality. Impaired object relations were reflected in a tendency to relate to others as part objects, acute sensitivity to object loss, and temporary lapses into psychoticlike thinking around interpersonal themes. However, within this range there was a marked variability as to character type (Sugarman, 1980).

Two subjects would be diagnosed as paranoid characters, given the constriction of their record and their attention to small detail and avoidance of affective-laden content. Another two resembled narcissistic characters in the predominance of mirror and reflection response and emblematic content. The majority of the women, five cases, appeared to be depressive-masochistic characters, as indicated by the high level of morbid content, difficulty with separation, and the degree of aggression directed against the self. The remaining subject was judged to be in the symbiotic range of psychosis due to global thinking, highly primitive and merged content, and highly symbolic use of the blots. Thematically, however, her record resembled those of the other incest victims.

Within these personality constellations, there were five consistent indicators revealed in the structural analysis: difficulty with affect and impulse control; depression and suicide potential; difficulty in object relations; severely impaired body image involving confused sexual identification; and externalization of blame, feelings of helplessness, or dissociative reactions.

AFFECT AND IMPULSE CONTROL

There was clear test evidence of difficulty modulating affective expression. Universally, there were more CF and C responses than FC. Usually the Experience Balance was weighted on the color side. By exception, on more constricted paranoid records there was a marked avoidance of color. However, this avoidance was often accompanied by a tendency toward aggressive or dysphoric content on the color cards or sudden expressions of unmodulated C.

For example, one woman did not respond to the color on Card II. This is highly unusual, as this population is generally quite drawn to and stimulated by the card. However, by contrast, on Cards VIII, IX, and X she was reactive to the color and offered several CF and C responses. For example, to Card IX she responded, "A banana split. Banana right down the center and here is all the toppings—strawberry, butterscotch, and blueberry. Probably 'cause I didn't eat breakfast this morning. They're all running together." This example also illustrates the tendency in this population toward marked regressions under stress, with content reflecting a fusion of genital and pregenital urges. While it would appear that the side comment about breakfast indicates some reflective anxiety, the reference to colors "running together," scored m, suggests a tendency to externalize the source of anxiety as outside of her and beyond her control, and to dissociate herself from it. Further, the response is typical of the complex blends common to these records. Rockets, volcanoes shooting fire, and blood or food spilling are images often in evidence.

DEPRESSION AND SUICIDE POTENTIAL

Severe depressive reactions and suicide potential were indicated by a massing of c' responses. Also observed in these records was morbid content (defined as objects that are identified as dead, destroyed, or damaged or that are depicted as having depressive characteristics; see Exner and Weiner, 1982), more than two color-shading blends (Appelbaum and Holtzman, 1962), and several S responses. These patients also appeared prone to anaclitic depression as described by Blatt (1974). Blatt cites a large oral component in the personality that is related to early childhood reactions to narcissistic injury or loss of nurturance. There is a feeling of depletion about being unloved, and fears of abandonment and loss of the love object. Relationships are seen as all-consuming, draining, and exclusively need-gratifying.

The following response to Card IV is taken from the record of a young woman whose tremendous oral rage was discharged somatically:

> [Grimace] Oh this one! what I liked about this one was the dancing in it. One part I like about it, the part in the dance—the toes are flexed, the back arched [side detail generally seen as arms], the arms laid back touching the ball of the heel [motioned], the rest looks dead. [Inquiry] I see the head—no, not really. It's smashed, smashed against something.

> Two people, their hands—they look tired [motioned head resting on hand], two people tired—they have had it [tip of "monster tail"].

> A cobra's head—the kind that comes out of a basket—dancing.

In this record, one sees conflicting emotions embedded in the father-daughter relationship. As for depressive indicators, there is morbid content, a theme of depletion, and constricted movement, as indicated by a tendency to combine M or FM with Dr.

INTERPERSONAL RELATIONSHIPS AND SELF-OTHER BOUNDARIES

Human responses tended to be of the (H), Hd, and (Hd) variety, as opposed to H. This may be taken as an indication of interpersonal difficulties. Acute sensitivity to interpersonal nuance was indicated throughout the records. In some records a marked tendency toward D and dr responses, often combined with (c), suggested a need to ferret out potential harm in the environment. In other records, an emphasis on sensory apparatus, particularly in response to sexual or interpersonal themes, suggested vigilance. Attention to the textural aspects of an image indicated intense affective searching or scrutiny.

Difficulty with self-other boundaries was typical of all the women. This was indicated by fluidity of thought, as evidenced by a score for Deviant Verbalizations greater than 3. Most responses of this type were fabulized combinations and confabulation responses, reflecting poor organizational structure of self-other representations (Smith, 1980).

The following is an example of a confabulation in response to Card IV (note the big-little paradigm in reaction to the father figure): "A monster. You are really small and he's coming at you, he's coming to get you. He looks like he's blowing a hot air stream—a little person and he's covering the person with his mist or poison."

Protocols also reflected boundary disturbances occurring around interpersonal themes of separation-division, birth-rebirth, and fusion. (Kwawer, 1980). For example, "two little amoebas kissing" to the red detail of Card III reflected metamorphosis and merger themes in a fifty-year-old woman whose protocol reflected an unformed identity still rooted in adolescence. Womb imagery was also common, most often to the center white detail in Card II.

BODY INTEGRITY AND SEXUAL IDENTIFICATION

Feelings of body damage and lack of body integrity were striking. These were indicated by a high number of sexual anatomy responses, commonly more than three. Content was usually derogatory, and frequently primitive and visceral. For example, references to bleeding vaginas were extremely common and usually highly confabulized. On records where sexual anatomy responses were limited ($N < 2$), metaphoric responses for body damage were given. The following is an example:

> *Card I:* Dead leaf—somebody had taken it and crunched it up and different spots are broken. After it's been crushed, all the pieces are breaking away. [Inquiry] Oak leaves are nice and green, but when they get old, kids crush it and they break apart.

> *Card III:* Someone had uterine problems and possibly bleeding in there—possibly bleeding, like when you go to a gyno.

The incest had clearly left its mark, as this woman felt damaged and victimized in interpersonal relationships. Her history revealed she continued to act out the conflict by submitting to intrusive medical procedures, thus the reference to a gynecologist.

Sexual identity problems were often expressed by confusion over male and female anatomy or attributes. The following response was given by a woman whose masculine tendencies were split off and acted out in a separate personality named "Judas," whom she described as an angry, defiant "royal bitch," the betrayer.

> *Card III:* Couple of skinny men holding something, just thin, long necks, long legs, coats on, suit and dress shoes.

> [To the upper red detail] Burning guitars, neck, red, burning away—these are musicians, I guess.

> Bowtie with a vagina in the middle.

Here, an opposite-sex identity is imputed to the human figures, with further confusion suggested by the dress shoes. The next response, scored CFm, suggests projection of and dissociation from highly charged and unacceptable impulses. The emphasis on necks and the reference to musicians suggest that the image is a veiled human response. The bowtie is a serious fabulized combination, indicating that her sexual confusion is rooted in boundary problems, possibly a primitive identification with the aggressor.

The tendency for these women to illustrate M with actual body movement suggests actual use of their bodies as a vehicle of expression. It suggests also that these women are still functioning at a level at which representation of the object is concrete and literal and evocative object constancy has not been achieved (Blatt, 1974).

Body image tended to be represented in two alternating ways. The more common was through images charge with aggression and oral rage; here the body was seen as damaged or devalued. The other was the image of the body as an object, an object rare or special; "a Tiffany lamp," "Taj Mahal," and "Oriental vases" are examples.

DISSOCIATIVE TENDENCIES

The tendency of these women to externalize blame and to dissociate was indicated by a high number of m responses, usually more than 3. Reference to dream states was also common. This was often in combination with blocked or passive M, responses suggesting a tendency to feel helpless and victimized, acted upon by forces out of their control.

The following response embodies several of the indicators mentioned above. The drive-dominated response quality of the percept reflects how easily this woman is overwhelmed by the affective stimulation of Card II. Her initial response suggests a serious loss of inner-outer boundaries, regressive longings, and feelings of body damage. She attempts to regain some ego control by distancing and dissociating herself from the body representations. Her overly personalized response is replaced with an image reflecting rigid body boundaries, scrutinization of affects, and dehumanization.

Card II: Uterus—ovary, uterus, vagina. I'm having my period now. [Inquiry] The opening and red coming out. It's plastic, like in the doctor's office. [Inquiry] Red color, unnatural, color red, almost the color of one in the doctor's office.

A DYNAMIC CASE ILLUSTRATION

The following case is presented to illustrate the common themes and dynamics that appear in these women. Self-esteem is always low, with accompanying feelings of helplessness and a sense of lack of control. They regard themselves as damaged or impaired. Menstruation is often experienced as dirty and a symbol of injury. Polarization of images and splitting as a major defense, particularly in regard to the mother figure, are revealed. Maternal images are often cold, sharp, and conflicting. Men are regarded ambivalently, with strong negative feelings tinged by desires for nurturance and projections of power. Their acute sensitivity in interpersonal relationships revolves around closeness and separation. They are highly sensitive to object loss, yet guard against attack or exploitation. Often there is guilt and self-punishment for their narcissistic wishes. The interaction between the pull of the card and the dynamic themes illustrated makes the Rorschach a highly sensitive tool for this investigation.

W.D. is a thirty-six-year-old woman, twice divorced, living with her two children, a son seventeen and a daughter twelve. She first sought advice from a pediatrician regarding her daughter's fecal soiling, which she herself found disgusting. The pediatrician found a physical problem over which the daughter had no control. It arose from years of withholding her stool, which resulted in an expanded colon.

The mother regarded this explanation with suspicion and was particularly angry at her daughter for poor hygiene and personal habits. Often the daughter would hide her soiled panties, lie about the incidents, and fail to clean her own underwear. There was also difficulty managing her menstrual cycle. These were major issues in the household. There were also questions about whether the daughter stole things—money, jewelry, etc.—from other family members, her stepmother, or close friends. The son, by marked contrast, was described in glowing terms.

Because of the daughter's many problems, the pediatrician referred the mother to a psychologist. The mother appeared open to treatment for her daughter and at the same time was able to express a vague awareness of her own tendency to project negatively onto her daughter. Yet she felt justified. She then revealed that aside from her soiling, lying, and stealing, her daughter had compliantly participated in an ongoing sexual molestation.

The mother's history revealed that she had been sexually abused in an incestuous relationship with her father from latency to early adolescence. She described the incidents with disgust and referred to her father as "sick." Her mother was described as ineffectual, weak, and "no help at all."

In late adolescence her eldest son was conceived out of wedlock, and she was rejected by the prospective father's family. She described her upbringing, including being raised in a small town where there was a marked line between the two families in terms of wealth and power. She was not considered good enough. The boy enlisted in the Army, and she did not communicate with him during his term of service. Upon his discharge, he stood up to his mother and they were married.

In short, this whole period is described by her as one in which her husband's family regarded her as a "black sheep." She was ostracized by the community and regarded herself with contempt. Rejected by her husband's family, she bore the baby by herself with steely determination.

Her early marriage and family life was marred by her husband's drinking, excessive work habits, and violence. She described him as cold and yet unwilling to grant her a divorce. W.D.'s daughter, a product of this marriage, reportedly witnessed much violence. W.D. describes her husband as a "genius-type" who assumed a disrespectful, condescending attitude toward most people. However, despite the beatings, she felt that she was special to her husband, and that he considered her an equal. They finally divorced when she began to fear for her personal safety.

W.D. presented as a beautiful woman, stylishly dressed, and currently maintaining an executive sales position. She is in a relationship with a man who troubles her greatly, as he is not as invested in the relationship as she would like. She resents the time that her daughter demands and would prefer to devote all her free time to maintaining this relationship. However, she dislikes this aspect of herself, viewing it as weak. She had been married briefly following her first marriage, but became disillusioned with the relationship. Contact is still maintained, however, reportedly because of the children.

W.D.'s daughter was involved in an incident of sexual molestation with the school janitor. The girl was singled out as his special favorite, and this disturbed the mother greatly. She felt that her daughter was too compliant in this arrangement. Reportedly, the janitor would take the girls out of class, have them perform special chores around the school, and would hug and fondle them.

Aside from the expressed anger at her daughter, she also felt disappointed and somewhat guilty. She said that her daughter often tried to make up to her by doing special favors, such as preparing dinner. At these times she felt that her daughter wasn't so bad, but that she as a mother was incapable of meeting the girl's needs. She worried that her own incestuous history had seriously affected her. At times she contemplated treatment for herself.

This case history exemplifies the social and family patterns common to many women with histories of incest. In early adolescence such patients often feel isolated and regarded as social outcasts; often they run away. Illegitimate pregnancy or early marriage are frequent additions to this picture.

As W.D. describes her early marriage and family life, one can see how her incest role in her family of origin is replicated. She alternates between feeling victimized and feeling special. There are also a series of "closet problems" that she feels she must hide and deal with by herself. She feels a prisoner of circumstances from which she cannot escape. There is always an undercurrent of shame.

W.D.'s relationship with her daughter is highly significant and hints at the intergenerational dynamics between incest mothers and their daughters. Her ambivalence to her daughter is clear, and the repetition of the sexual molestation striking. Particularly noteworthy is that the incident of molestation parallels the daughter's shift into a parentified role with her mother. Also, the daughter's presenting problems are similar to the conflict areas for the mother, in that for both they revolve around denial, boundary issues, and body concerns. A study of the mother's dynamics on the Rorschach will afford some understanding of the intergenerational aspects of this problem as well.

The following is an analysis of W.D.'s Rorschach record (see Fig. 1). The exploration begins with a general discussion of each card and how it was characteristically handled by the participants in this study. A specific analysis of W.D.'s responses follows.

Card I. Percepts of things being 'smashed," damaged, or "shattered" characterize most records. Human detail and anatomy responses involving female sex organs were common. Response patterns suggested that tremendous rage was being discharged, primarily through the body. Content was often drive-laden, showing a condensation of oedipal and preoedipal material. The women's sense of disorganization was reflected in fragmented body images, confusion over body parts, the part-object quality of their human responses, and confusion between internal feelings and external reality. A more benign expression of being weird or headless was given, but this was usually in combination with either a sexual anatomy response or other themes of damage.

On this card W.D.'s overall feelings of inner tension and body damage were dramatically illustrated. She began with a confabulation suggesting poor modulation of drives and affects, particularly in new situations. This is consistent with her depressive-masochistic character, in that it reflects her need to present herself in the worst possible light.

The self-representation of a small, smashed, shattered bat is graphic. She experiences tension outside of herself, yet discharges it through her body. In consequence she is propelled into many painful and self-destructive interactions with her environment.

Her difficulty with inner-outer boundaries is revealed by her second confabulated response. Though she initially reacts to the female form, she elaborates specifically on the internal organs. Further, her associations reflect symbiotic concerns regarding attachment.

Her regression from an anal to an oral level is halted as she recoups with a bland, form-dominated popular response. Yet her elaboration continues to reflect fluidity of body image.

Her final elaboration of the bell is interesting. She ends on a strong note reflecting good reality testing. Yet she sees the image where most see the female form, suggesting a view of the self as an object. The hanging quality suggests static tension, and the reference to a gong, an initial suggestion of sexual confusion.

Card II. With the first introduction of color, this card seemed to elicit conflicts over the control of emotions and aggression, as well as the women's reaction to menses. Color shock was suggested, with pure C a common determinant. There were also a high number of m responses to this card. The sex responses given were all derogatory. S responses were frequent, the center space often seen as an object or womb. The content often reflected inner feelings of emptiness.

W.D. continued to produce confabulated responses reflecting her poor modulation of drives and affects, discharge of impulses through her body, use of projection, and fluidity of thought. There is fusion of phallic and anal drives, raw expression of anal-sadistic impulses and the emergence of depressive trends. Her difficulty with people is revealed by three Hd responses, all reflecting damage or deprecation. Her feelings of dirt and shame around menstruation parallel the developmental problems of her daughter. In addition, the dissected vagina response is followed by a denigrating remark about the penis, suggesting that menstruation ignites feelings of body damage and rage over a sense of violation.

The predominance of m, the color/shading blend and the morbid content suggest high vulnerability to suicide under stress.

Card III. This was generally seen as humans interacting. However, these percepts were not well articulated and suggested a low level of development (Blatt, Brenneis, Schimek, and Glick, 1976). The interpersonal pull of this card, probably combined with the color, produced a series of confabulations suggestive of self-other boundary difficulties, sexual confusion, and separation concerns (Smith, 1980; Lerner, Sugarman, and Barbour, 1985).

W.D.'s responses continued to illustrate how the press of her drives affect her self-other representations. In interpersonal situations the push-pull tug around issues of intimacy is so disorganizing that she is vulnerable to psychotic lapses, sexual confusion, and feelings of victimization. In her first response, people fight for supremacy to ward off merger and loss of identity. Her second response, a metamorphosis theme (Kwawer, 1980), suggests her inability to ward off this regression and her wish to return to a more protected state. This engenders fear and anger, which she projects outward in the monster response. The last response suggests retaliation for these wishes.

It is interesting how the responses alternate, with the more unacceptable states displaced onto the small upper details. As these are both human movement responses, they suggest attempts at depersonaliza-

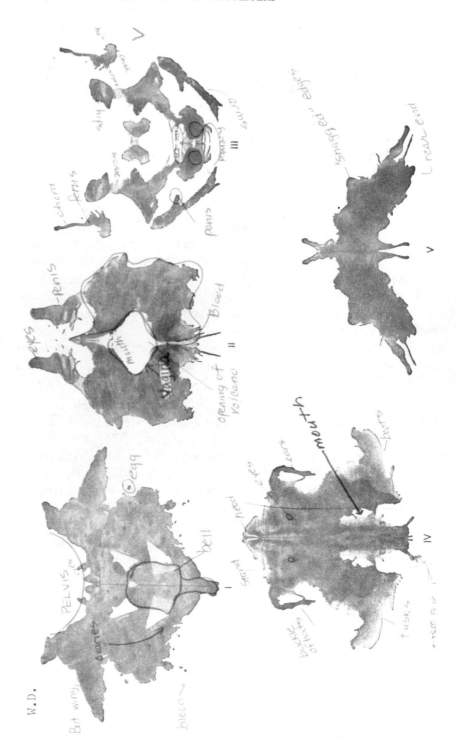

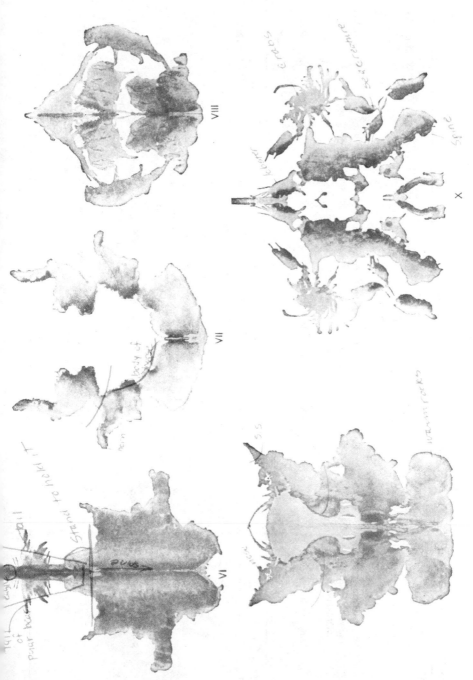

FIGURE 1. Rorschach Diagnostics IX

Card	Free Association	Inquiry	SCORE
10" I	Bat that is smashed into the wall. (Do you want second choices?)	Bat, small, up against the wall. Flew right into it. Blood dripping off it and every-thing else, body, wings — is smashed so it's a lot flatter, with little particles when it hit the wall — just kinda splattered.	WFM-m±A,B1 MOR
	Makes me think of a female — physical shape of a female, female internal organs	Female organs — pelvis, the way it comes down into the shape of female organs. Ovaries come down into uterus, womb, right in there, egg being released. Womb, uterus, coming down into vagina.	WM— Hd Sex
	Little bit like a butterfly	Butterfly — takes so many different shapes. Just looks like butterfly.	WF+ A P
		Bell — hanging in a steeple — has a gong there, down and out.	dF+m+Obj.
8" II	Sad face — like someone is crying	Sad face. I don't see it that much now. Not a normal face, something you dream about—jowls, eyes, eye socket, drawn down. Face looks like it's spitting blood at bottom of mouth, eyes, looks like bleeding, crying blood and spitting blood.	WSM-C Hd MOR
	Volcano erupting	Volcano erupting — like flying over top of volcano and looking down into it. Hole of volcano and spilling out on the edges — red fire, lava, dark volcanic rock, mountain. Red lava pouring out. (Q) Color — dark grey — volcanic rock.	WSm± CF+Fc'± Na
	Female organs when you have your period	Vagina when you are having your period. Pictures show elimination of blood when you have your period. Just a small opening on a messy day. (Q) Shape — obviously dissected. Lips cut in half and you spread it.	DSCF+ Hd Sex MOR
		This looks like two penises to me, sticking straight up. (Q) Shape — definitely small ones, some have 'em and some don't!	DM— Hd Sex
		Two pigs — nose to nose — front hooves meeting.	DFM+ A P

15" III	Two people bending over a glass table. Nothing else.	Two people bending over — this looks like a glass table. Two women — boobs, noses, bottom half looks like man, penis — but they have high heels on — man and woman combined somehow. (Q) Looks like they're fighting for supremacy and each got a part of each other. This looks like each one of their hearts are joined — heart from each one of them is joined.	DM– H Sex (P)
		Unborn fetus — hanging by the umbilical cord. This looks like one of the appendages — of course not fully developed.	DM+ (H)
		Monster man (if turned upside down) — two hearts, bug eyes, forehead, mouth is this part here, arms over his head, waist, hips.	WF+(H)
		Two sacrificial children that he is punishing — bowing their heads with their arms behind their backs. Leg seen from side view, so you don't see second leg, ruffle on bottom of dress. Submissive, head tucked [Subject motions], arms tied up high behind their backs, little short skirt, ruffled. (Q) Weird hair, skirt, long skinny legs.	DM+ H
12" IV	Horror face—monster man	One ugly dude! Really scary monster you'd see in your dreams. Ears on top of his head. Focusing with one right eye.	WSM– (Hd)
		No matter how I turn it, he just keeps looking at me. Real ugly nose that comes all the way down to here. Open cavern is mouth — nose covering part of the mouth. Big shaggy jowls, hanging out — real flaired face — instead of smooth face, flairs out, blubbery-like.	
	Pair of boots in a ski holder — carried ski boots	Ski tote — like a tree stand — base keeps it from falling over. Little handle there and boots hooked on either side. Sitting on snow for awhile. Frozen snow and ice on the boots. (Q) Shape, color, looks real cold (Q) dirty white. Boots are misshapen — dirty white color and jagged edge with snow on it. Side view of ski tote. [Subject motions as if picking up]	WFc'+C$_w$ Obj. P
	Old ancient elephant	Old ancient elephant — furry face with tusk, hairy trunk. (Q) Protruding things on the side, shaggy fur, ears real furry, Ice-age elephant, can't remember name, frozen	WFc'– (Ad)

ice on it. Same eyes as monster. Mean looking elephant, not like elephant we see in the zoo, ice-age survival-type thing.

10″ V			
Butterfly	Butterfly — ugly butterfly, not delicate at all. Head, body, wings, veins showing on wings, bulky, sick-looking thing, not pretty at all.	WF+ A P
Slug that somebody stepped on	Slug — back to when I was a kid, slugs everywhere. Had little antennae poking up, usually thin. This fat worm, green with black dots, he's been stepped on real bad, black and smashed, not sleek and shiny anymore. Still has stupid antennae out, those only go out when he's alive, crawling. Green slug and became black when stepped on, black slime when stepped on it.	WFCp–Fc'±A MOR
Back of a bat	Bat flying — flying, hanging little feet, bat with big ears.	WFM+ A P
Rabbit, someone has filleted in half	Rabbit — someone took and cut down the middle, left skin attached, kept body on either side and laid it flat. Ears, legs, half of face split in half, odd shape is the fur of the rabbit when you cut it. (Q) The line makes it look split.	WF± A MOR
15″ VI			
Piece of fish, ready to cook	Fillet of fish — fish filleted open, tail, spine of fish, ready to throw in a frying pan. Spine is darker color in the middle, fleshy meat on the side. (Q) Hard to get it smooth on edges, chopped up from the knife, jagged edges on the fin of the fish.	WFc'± Fd
Bear rug	Rug split in half — head of bear, lying face down, paws, they kept those, fur from the paws (Q) grain, coloring, makes it look like dirty polar bear, dingy grey, like it got soot on it, used to be white, the white is still showing through, but soiled real bad.	WFc'+ C_w(A) P
Indian totem pole	Indian totem pole — top half has Indian designs, decoration on the side (Q) eagle, two eyes, dark colors.	DFc'+ Obj.

15" VII	Two pretty women looking at each other	Two women looking at each other, hairdo and ponytail sticking straight up. Look pretty, aristocratic look about them. Necks are joined to the head of an ugly man — hair is hanging out or maybe it's a horn, almost looks like he has a horn. Eye, droopy eye, looking down, ugly, fat, pointed nose. Mouth and teeth showing, makes him look real mean. He stops at the neck.	DM+ Hd (P)
	Two ugly monster men looking down at the ground and they are hooked at the necks. Definitely stone faces, all of them.	This doesn't represent anything to me now.	DM— Hd
	Rocking horse	Body of a horse — looks like it would rock — rocking horse.	dF— (A)
8" VIII	Two bears climbing up the mountain. Something very warm — leaving the warmth to climb up to the cold.	Two bears trying to climb an ice mountain. Cold colors to me, blue, white. Like when he touched this part, he started getting cold too. Side view, legs, as he is starting to climb and that's his tail. He's not sure if he wants to leave the warmth, tail still hooked to the warmth. Nose and head going back here. (Q) Warmer in the gold area, comfort and warmth, and he's going away to the colder area, doesn't know if he wants to let go of the warmth.	WFM+CF$_{imp.}$ A,Na P
	Cave with icicles on it	Cave — mountain of ice. Don't really see cave.	
10" IX	Two gods shooting fire at each other	Two gods throwing fire back and forth at each other. Pointed hats on and that's their noses. Throwing fire and spiting fire back and forth. Puffing and blowing. Their mouths are indented. The colors, orange and gold, are glowing.	DM+CF+ (H)
	I hate these ugly colors; seems warm and then the ugliness is the dark greens.	Warm rocks — red just seems warm.	DCF$_{imp.}$ Na

Pink looks like seashells.

Two seashells — all I can see is the top half that is pointed.

10"
X

Looks like the bottom half of the ocean with crabs, lobsters and sea crustaceans. Someone took an axe to the spine and split it. Everything looks like it has pincers — angry pincers — they're after everything.

Bottom of the ocean. Blue crabs with big green pincers. Whoever made this up must be awfully cold — water turned them blue. Two lobster fighting over something in the middle — face, angry, looking at each other. (Q) fighting over a piece of food. Crabs — mean eyes, looking at me too. Something with pincers, sea creatures. The rest looks like rocks and they're climbing around and crawling in and out. Two pink things are the spine, chopped and split in half. Looks like blood — the red — rest of the stuff are pieces of body floating around after it's been chopped.

dF– Na

WFC+FM+CF–
m–A, Ad,Na
MOR P

SUMMARY

Area	Determinants				Content	Ratios
W = 14	M = 4	F+ = 4	Fc = 0	Fc+ = 3	H = 2	Sum C = 5
WS = 3	M– = 6	F± = 1	Fc± = 0	Fc'± = 3	(H) = 3	M:Sum C = 10:5
D = 10	FM = 4	F– = 2	Fc– = 1	Fc'– = 1	Hd = 6	F+% = 60%
DS = 1	FM– = 1	FC+ = 1	cF = 0	c'F = 0	(Hd) = 1	
d = 3		FC– = 0	c = 0	c' = 0	A = 9	
R = 31	m± = 2	CF+ = 3			(A) = 2	
	m– = 1	CF– = 1			Ad = 1	
		C = 1			(Ad) = 1	
		CF_{imp} = 2			Sex = 4	
		FC'_w = 2			Obj. = 3	
		FC–p = 1			Na = 5	
					MOR = 6	
					Fd = 1	
					P = 7	
					(P) = 2	

tion and derealization. The last response is particularly graphic, the self-representation of one who must submit to sacrificial torture. It is as if she can never escape the role of victim.

Card IV. This is traditionally viewed as a father card. Responses appeared to symbolize the father-daughter relationship. For most of the women, the card was fraught with dangerous and frightening imagery. There was usually a loss of boundaries. Common conflicts elicited by this card revolved around active-passive, big-little, and sadistic-masochistic paradigms. Ambivalence toward the male was often noted.

For W.D. as well, there was a serious loss of distance on this card, reflecting her conflicts rooted in the incestuous father-daughter relationship. Her first response again portrayed an interaction which is frightening and inescapable, and suggests her continued use of projection. Her second response suggests the male figure as an object of support, on which she is hooked. The boots are dirty and misshapen, and the affective tone is cold. Here again we see her conflicts about attachment and the sense of degradation this engenders, including a loss of feelings. A third image reflects a beast that is ugly, ancient, but enduring. The attention to texture on this blot suggests an affective searching despite the angry rejection and cold feelings.

Card V. This is a very structured card which elicits bland, readily popular, form-dominated whole responses. However, this card often produced a "spillover" from the intensity of the previous one, producing bizarre drive-laden content, confabulations, symbiotic imagery, and attention to phallic detail.

W.D. reacted similarly. Anal-sadistic rage at being violated continued to be discharged through the body representations and was directed toward the self.

Card VI. This card usually stimulates imagery regarding male-female sexual content. For these incest victims, the imagery was unusually intense, and themes of vulnerability and exploitation were common. Another common feature to all records was either dr or (c), or a combination of the two, often focused on the upper phallic detail, suggesting intense vigilance to phallic stimuli. This, when combined with oral rage, suggested projective identification as a defense.

For W.D. the recurrent themes of sadism and violation continue, as does the fusion of anal and oral drives. The hanging quality noted before is also reintroduced with the "ready to throw into a frying pan." The image of a spongy, pliable consistency alternates with that of a chopped, ragged edge, reflecting conflicting experiences in interpersonal relationships.

There is also ambivalence reflected in the totem response. It is an object of decoration, yet vigilance is also suggested by the imagery. One could speculate that she anticipates either punishment for her narcissism or harm in intimacy. She is on guard for both.

Card VII. On this card, regarded as the mother card, polarization of images suggestive of splitting was common to most records. The top detail was usually seen as a woman positively described and connected in some way to a more negative image on the middle detail. This suggests good/bad maternal representations.

With W.D. we also see alternating images. Idealization, suggested by the pretty, aristocratic woman, alternates with devaluation, represented by the ugly, monstrous man. This fabulized combination again suggests a breakdown of boundaries, though not as serious as previously noted. We also see the defenses that probably operate in the mother-child interaction, particularly splitting, projective identification and denial. Images are frozen and movement is blocked.

Cards VIII, IX, and X. These cards were not particularly noteworthy for the type of responses elicited, or for particular themes or content. Rather, they seemed to illustrate how each individual woman handled sustained emotional stimulation. They were generally characterized by a predominance of CF and C over FC.

W.D.'s responses indicated marked regression under stimulation; the imagery is developmentally arrested, and the tone is subjective. Her use of color is unintegrated and impressionistic.

On Card VIII her core conflict around intimacy is expressed. Activity is associated with separation and coldness, while passivity produces warmth, comfort, and fears of merger. The regressive cave response is denied and defended against with the percept of the cold ice mountain. It appears that under intense stimulation her only defense against being overwhelmed is to erect an icy facade and thereby deny feelings.

On Card IX we see her continued struggle to control affects and drives that are dangerously close to expression. Feelings are vague and poorly labeled. One gets the sense that the world is experienced as an unsafe place where good things suddenly turn bad. Shell imagery suggests that withdrawal is available as a defense against confusion.

On Card X she continues to focus on crustaceans, indicating her faulty attempts to defend against impingement. She deals with color arbitrarily and subjectively, and drive-dominated content breaks through with undertones of oral rage. Because the record ends on a note of tension and damage, one may infer that this woman continues to experience the world as dangerous and herself as its victim.

This record is representative of many incest victims in terms of ego weaknesses, intensity of drive, and thematic content. It also illustrates the mechanisms inherent in the intergenerational susceptibility to sexual abuse. Given the mother's defenses of projective identification, splitting, and denial, it is clear that the daughter has been assigned a fixed negative identity in her mother's psychic life. During the phases of separation-individuation in which issues of body boundaries, gender identity, and self-other differentiation are paramount, W.D., due to her own limitations, was a poor model for identification.

With the recrudescence of these issues in adolescence, there is again increased tension in the dyad. Both appear to be experiencing a developmental crisis at this time. As W.D. projects her own feelings of disgust for her body onto her daughter, the latter is prone to regression along the developmental lines of body independence (Freud, 1965). Her original difficulties with fecal soiling are superimposed upon later genital concerns regarding menstruation and sexual availability. She lacks a well-differentiated model to assist in the mastery of these developmental problems. Further, her underlying needs for approval and nurturance block appropriate action in sexual matters.

This Rorschach study also illustrates that the complicated clinical picture these women present often obscures the original sexual trauma. Presenting problems are frequently psychosomatic illness, eating disorders, multiple personalities, or depression. One woman was troubled by her "psychic" abilities and felt she was hearing voices. Actually she was experiencing a dissociative reaction related to the repressed aspects of the incest experience.

The personality profile described is strikingly similar to that of the infantile personality described by Sugarman (1979) in terms of ego weaknesses, orality, and depressive, masochistic, and paranoid fea-

tures. This raises an interesting question in terms of the borderline level
of personality organization found in these women and the relation of
sexual trauma to this diagnosis.

One possible explanation is that these women are products of
"borderline families." Their personality disturbances originated early
in life, and were closely tied to inadequate parenting. The ineffective
parenting left them vulnerable to victimization and emotionally ill-
prepared to master the sexual trauma. While this explanation implies
the intergenerational transmission of emotional disturbance, it does
little to elucidate the etiology of the original insult.

Another explanation could be that actual sexual trauma is the
basis of borderline functioning. Due to massive developmental interferences along the lines of sexual development, body management, and
object relations, the women are prone to the massive regressions
reflected in their records. Certainly, many of the hallmarks of a borderline level of functioning—hyperalertness, splitting, and dissociative
reactions—could be viewed as a stress response to threats in the
environment that are reality-based. The tendency to externalize could
be a means of alleviating guilt; boundary and body integrity difficulties,
an unfortunate legacy from real life experience. The content of their
records suggests that the actual experiences of these women cannot be
divorced from an analysis of their personality structures.

The reality basis of many of their current adjustment problems
poses many treatment challenges. These women are highly prone to
re-creating the dynamics of the incest situation within the clinical
setting, and transference and countertransference issues become
paramount.

The large oral component of their personality is often expressed in
unrealistic demands for care or proof of affection. This gets expressed
as well through seductive behavior, as they strive to please or become a
special person to the therapist. Smith (1984), in studying women who
had been abused by their therapists, found that all but one had been
sexually abused by their fathers. He finds in them a compulsion to
repeat in the treatment situation what had happened with their fathers,
this in the service of self-validation. The result is a vulnerability to
victimization.

This repetition compulsion need not take such direct expression.
Its derivatives can be found in a proclivity for intrusive medical procedures, or conversely, a sudden or abrupt halt to treatment when it is
perceived as too intense or penetrating. These patients also have a

knack for involving several professionals in their treatment. This serves to dilute the treatment alliance, split the therapists into good and bad representations, and enmesh and handcuff the professionals involved.

This raises issues as to treatment choice. While remediation has usually focused on group therapy techniques (Van Buskirk and Cole, 1983), one can question the long-term efficacy of this model. While such an approach appears to meet this population's needs for the immediate and safe expression of their rage and suffering, it does little for personality restructuring. Given their personality constellations, these women would perhaps benefit more from expressive, psychoanalytically oriented psychotherapy of the sort suggested by Kernberg for the treatment of borderline conditions (Kernberg, 1975).

Clearly, systematic longitudinal research is needed to bring more clarity to these diagnoses and treatment issues. To further understand the consequences of sexual abuse, an examination of the interaction between predispositional factors and the developmental stage during which the abuse occurred is needed. Controlled studies involving complete and detailed histories, the age of the child, the onset, duration, and nature of the incest relationship, the quality of care and experience with parents, and inherent vulnerability must be examined. This would then need to be integrated with assessments at developmentally critical periods. This type of research would not only increase our understanding of the long-term effects of sexual abuse, but would also contribute to our understanding of trauma in general. The Rorschach would appear to be an important instrument in this research.

REFERENCES

Appelbaum, S., & Holzman, P. (1962), The color shading response and suicide. In: *Handbook of Rorschach Scales*, ed. P. Lerner. New York: International Universities Press, pp. 430–440.

Bender, L., & Blau, A. (1937), The reactions of children to sexual relations with adults. *Amer. J. Orthopsychiat.*, 7:500–518.

Blatt, S. (1974), Levels of object representation in anaclitic and introjective depression. *Psychoanalytic Study of the Child*, 29:107–157. New Haven, CT: Yale University Press.

———— Brenneis, C., Schimek, J., & Glick, M. (1976), Normal development and psychopathological impairment of the concept of the object on the Rorschach. *J. Abnorm. Psychol.*, 85:364–373.

Cormier, B., Kennedy, M., & Sangowicz, J. (1962), Psychodynamics of father-daughter incest. *Can. Psychiat. Assn. J.*, 7:203–217.

Everstein, D. (1984), A systematic approach to the treatment of sexual trauma. Paper presented at Mental Research Institute, Second International Biennial Conference, Munich, Germany.

Exner, J. (1974), *The Rorschach: A Comprehensive System*. New York: Wiley.
_____ Weiner, I. (1982), *The Rorschach: A Comprehensive System: Vol. 3. Assessment of Children and Adolescence*. New York: Wiley.
Freud, A. (1965), *Normality and Pathology in Childhood: Assessments of Development*. New York: International Universities Press.
Gelinas, D. (1981), Identification and treatment of incest victims. In: *Women and Mental Health*, ed. E. Howell & M. Bayes. New York: Basic Books.
Heims, L., & Kaufman, I. (1963), Variations on a theme of incest. *Amer. J. Orthopsychiat.*, 33:311-320.
Herman, J. (1981), *Father-Daughter Incest*. Cambridge: Harvard University Press.
_____ Hirschman, L. (1977), Father-daughter incest. *Signs, 2*, 1-22.
Kaufman, I., Peck, A., & Taguiri, C. (1954), The family constellation and overt incestuous relations between father and daughter. *Amer. J. Orthopsychiat.*, 24:266-277.
Kernberg, O. (1975), *Borderline Conditions and Pathological Narcissism*. New York: Aronson.
Kwawer, J. (1980), Primitive interpersonal modes, borderline phenomena, and Rorschach content. In: *Borderline Phenomena and the Rorschach Test*, ed. J. Kwawer, H. Lerner, P. Lerner, & A. Sugarman. New York: International Universities Press, pp. 89-105.
Lerner, H., Sugarman, A., & Barbour, C. (1985), Patterns of ego boundary disturbance in neurotic, borderline, and schizophrenic patients. *Psychoanal. Psychol.* 2(1):47-66.
Luftig, N., Dresser, J. W., Spellman, S. W., & Murray, T. B. (1966), Incest: A family group survival pattern. *Arch. Gen. Psychiat.*, 14:31-40.
Meyers, J. (1979), Daughters at risk: Intergenerational transmission of impaired heterosexual functioning. Paper presented at the International Congress of Family Therapy, Tel Aviv, Israel.
Piotrowski, Z. (1957), *Percept-Analysis*. New York: Macmillan.
Rapaport, D., Gill, M., & Schafer, R. (1945), *Diagnostic Psychological Testing*. Rev. ed. New York: International Universities Press, 1968.
Smith, K. (1980), Object relations concepts as applied to the borderline level of ego functioning. In: *Borderline Phenomena and the Rorschach Test*, ed. J. Kwawer, H. Lerner, P. Lerner, & A. Sugarman. New York: International Universities Press, pp. 59-86.
Smith, S. (1984), The sexually abused patient and the abusing therapist: A study in sadomasochistic relationships. *Psychoanal. Psychol.*, 1(2):89-98.
Sugarman, A. (1979), The infantile personality: Orality in the hysteric revisited. *Internat. J. Psycho-Anal.*, 60:501-513.
_____ (1980), The borderline personality organization as manifested on psychological tests. In: *Borderline Phenomena and the Rorschach Test*, ed. J. Kwawer, H. Lerner, P. Lerner, & A. Sugarman. New York: International Universities Press, pp. 39-57.
Van Buskirk, S., & Cole, C. (1983), Characteristics of eight women seeking therapy for the effects of incest. *Psychotherapy: Theory, Research and Practice*, 20(4).
Weinberg, S. K. (1955), *Incest Behavior*. Secaucus, NJ: Citadel.
Weiner, I. B. (1964), On incest: A survey. *Excerpta Criminologica* 4:137-155.

Chapter 9

Body Representation in Paranoid and Undifferentiated Schizophrenics

Alan Sugarman, Ph.D.
Lee S. Jaffe, Ph.D.

Over the last decade psychodiagnosticians have come to realize the utility of attending to a patient's internalized representations of self and of others in making differential diagnoses as well as in devising treatment strategies (Athey, 1974; Krohn and Mayman, 1974; Blatt, Brenneis, Schimek, and Glick, 1976; Urist, 1977; Blatt and Lerner, 1983; Sugarman, 1986). This attention to the internalized relational paradigms by which a patient organizes his immersion in interpersonal reality has led to the recognition that a solely ego psychological emphasis on such personality variables as impulse-defense configurations, thought disorder, and reality testing obscures other key personality variables with important diagnostic implications. Therapists have known for years that two patients with the same diagnosis, based on ego organization, preferred defense mechanisms, and core libidinal conflict, can have very different treatment outcomes according to their capacity to form a treatment alliance. But ego psychological concepts offer no insight into this capacity; only an emphasis on the patient's internalized object relations can distinguish patients who can form and maintain such an alliance from those who cannot. Attention to a patient's self- and object representations thus complements the understanding of a patient's personality organization that may be gained from other perspectives.

229

This focus on the patient's representational world (Sandler and Rosenblatt, 1962) has proven particularly helpful in understanding and treating patients suffering from preoedipal pathology (Modell, 1963; Kernberg, 1967; Kohut, 1971; Rinsley, 1978). Such individuals have suffered such intense early trauma or were born with such serious constitutional impairments that they are unable to form the stable and integrated intrapsychic structures of the neurotic patient. Their nascent, vulnerable psyches have been so buffeted by painful experiences that their early internalizations cannot coalesce into the impersonal, hierarchically organized structures that make relating to the world an automatic and unreflective process, as it is for those who have been more fortunate in either constitutional endowment or facilitating environment. What tenuous organization has been accomplished soon gives way in the wake of increased drive pressures, developmentally mandated needs to individuate, and rapid changes in body image, especially during adolescence and early adulthood (Blos, 1962; Laufer and Laufer, 1984).

For the purposes of this chapter we will stress the body representation[1] as a key personality variable both affecting and reflecting an individual's capacity to adapt successfully to the added demands of the adolescent transition to early adulthood. Specifically, we will argue that the body representation is a core aspect of the structure of an individual's self-representation, and as such is crucial in facilitating the integration and regulation of the disparate personality dimensions that contribute to the eventual attainment of ego identity at the close of adolescence (Sugarman, Bloom-Feshbach, and Bloom-Feshbach, 1980). In severe psychopathology such an integration cannot occur, because the body representation is far too tenuously defined to withstand the reshaping and reorganizing called for by the maturational changes from a child's body to that of an adult. Frosch (1964) has realized the importance of the body representation and the way in which the body's surface helps to delineate the self/other boundary and maintain reality constancy. Complementarily, Lichtenberg (1978) has emphasized the vulnerability of the body representation to developmental difficulty: "body-self experience (and the non-experiential body schema) develops normally *only* when the phase-appropriate intensity of specific

---

[1]For the sake of conceptual clarity we prefer the term body representation to body ego. In this way the body representation is viewed as a schematic aspect of the self-representation without adding the conceptual framework of the structural model to the representational language of object relations theory.

stimulation occurs and the affective interchange between infant and mother supports and sustains the body response" (p. 366, italics ours). Mahler (Mahler and McDevitt, 1982) has also noted the importance of body/self disruptions in severe psychopathology.

Some time ago we noticed a peculiar tendency in paranoid schizophrenic patients to deanimate their human representations of body parts on the Rorschach (Sugarman, 1984). This tendency to blend animate body images with inanimate elements can be viewed as a manifestation of these patients' body representations. In contrast to Blatt (Blatt and Ritzler, 1974), we would argue that this human-inanimate blend is uniquely characteristic of paranoia and speaks to a defensive effort by these patients to devitalize or deanimate their body representations in a last-ditch effort to avoid its fragmentation as seen in undifferentiated schizophrenia. Attention to the vicissitudes of the body representation, as manifested on the Rorschach in the human body percepts of patients suffering from these different afflictions, can shed further light on their representational worlds and hopefully lead to more refined, diagnostically guided treatment strategies.

The little attention that has been paid to the body representation on the Rorschach has proven quite useful (Mahler and Silberpfennig, 1938; Schafer, 1960). Schafer, for example, has stressed the need to attend to many dimensions of the body representation, including its direction, differentiation, stability, vitality, and relationship to the environment. But these few papers on the body representation have failed to consider it in regard to differential diagnosis. Schafer, for example, talks about the human body percepts of schizophrenics as though they comprised a unitary diagnostic category. Similarly, Tausk (1919), who first recognized this deanimation process, discussed it summarily as characterizing the narcissistic neuroses. More recently, Mahler (Elkisch and Mahler, 1959; Mahler and McDevitt, 1982) noted the same phenomena in *psychotic* children, but she too failed to make crucial diagnostic distinctions.

A more differentiated approach to diagnosis is implicit in much of the recent work of object relations theorists and should expand the value of previous contributions. With this in mind, we will present Rorschach data to support the thesis that paranoid and undifferentiated schizophrenic patients show marked differences in their body representations. More specifically, the paranoid schizophrenic deanimates his body representation while the undifferentiated schizophrenic suffers a more profound fragmentation. Attention to these important differences can provide the basis for important diagnostic distinctions. But before presenting such data we will briefly elaborate the importance of the body representation in the development of the self-representation. It is this relationship which warrants such clear attention to vicissitudes of the body representation in severe psychopathology.

THE ROLE OF THE BODY REPRESENTATION IN PERSONALITY ORGANIZATION

An appreciation for the importance of the body representation arises out of the recognition that personality development involves the internalization of key regulatory functions (Sugarman and Jaffe, in press). Throughout the life span, most notably during nodal developmental stages, the illusion that internal need states will automatically summon satisfaction, and hence regulation, gives way to the reality principle (Freud, 1911; Winnicott, 1971; Krystal, 1978). There is in every human infant an innate potential for self-regulation, the development of which requires a facilitating environment. Through a reciprocal interaction between mother and infant, an ever greater capacity for self-regulation develops (Sander, 1983). In this way, as the infant grows into adulthood, the capacity to regulate inner states, provided initially by the environment, becomes "internalized," increasingly incorporated into the self-representation; omnipotence diminishes with this process. Intrapsychic structure may be conceptualized as containing more than the precipitate of abandoned object cathexis. It also includes a variety of drive-regulating, integrating, and adaptive functions performed previously by the caretaker. In part, this process of "transmuting internalization" involves a "depersonalizing" of the object representation with which the regulatory functions were associated (Tolpin, 1971). That is, the developing child's inner focus shifts from the global totality of the object representation to a differentiated emphasis on its specific functions. Consequently, the child's self-representation is enriched; the growth of intrapsychic structure allows him to perform the functions previously exercised by the other, in a fashion divested of the personal attributes of the other (Sander, 1983).

Thus there occurs a gradual accretion of self-regulating structure. The child becomes increasingly able to act on his own behalf, in response to both inner needs and environmental demands, thereby maintaining an inner-outer equilibrium. Under normal conditions the skills acquired compensate for the narcissistic deflating of the child's omnipotence; the child's burgeoning abilities to achieve real though limited satisfactions promotes the internal representation of self- as-agent (Schafer, 1960; Sander, 1983).

Despite the attractiveness of this formulation, we must keep in mind Krystal's admonishment (1978) to be aware of the universal human fantasy that the child has "literally" internalized these regulatory functions. Such a model (or fantasy) is only a metaphor for a much more complicated process in which "good enough" mothering promotes the maturation and utilization of regulatory functions. These capacities comprise part of the innate potential of the infant and yet require appropriate environmental stimulation. A more accurate model of this "internalization" process must stress "an adaptive relationship between organism and environment in which the organism establishes and maintains an internal equilibrium through active interchange with the environment" (Wolff, 1960, p. 11). Such interchanges mold the representational world to conform to external reality while simultaneously impacting the environment via the child's actions. Over the life span, the self-representation becomes increasingly more effective for adaptation, as both self- and object-representations become more differentiated and more integrated (Wolff, 1960).

Thus, the child's innate predispositions to become increasingly self-regulated is potentiated through subtle and complex interactions with the mother. These innate predispositions originate in stimulus-response reflex patterns which are present at birth and require environmental stimulation for their stabilization. This environmental stimulation then modifies these reflexes so that basic personality units become more complex (Wolff, 1960). Hence, self-representations derive from rudimentary body representations. This triadic combination of *inborn reflexes* affected by *past environmental demands* and by *present environmental constraints* forms a flexible mental organization which Piaget calls a schema (Wolff, 1960). Thus, existing mental organizations shape the infant's experience of the environment while the infant is simultaneously molded by events taken into the schema. Such schemas originate as sensorimotor, bodily ones, becoming more abstract as development and maturation proceed.

Piaget observed two interwoven processes, assimilation and accommodation, that promote the development of schemata (Piaget, 1954). Experience with the external world is registered through assimilation. A complementary process, accommodation, alters existing schemata to include the discrepant aspects of newly assimilated reality events; this reciprocal process allows the infant to adapt to experiences unlike those already internalized. The two processes spiral, forming higher levels of self- and object-representations, thereby advancing the child's ability to regulate the ever-increasing complexity of his developing world.

Initially, the infant's sensorimotor experience of the world is dominated by global, diffuse perceptions and actions (Piaget, 1954; Wolff, 1960; Blatt, 1974). There is minimal differentiation between inner and outer reality, with little capacity to differentiate self or other from the motor action that defines them. Early internal need states involve total somatic excitation. Empathic mothers attune themselves quickly to subtle variations in these global states and gratify the specific need in question. In this fashion the infant is enabled to differentiate subtle inner experiences by having been taught that the mother's response is determined by the specificity of a communication (Krystal, 1978). Furthermore, empathic ministrations prevent the trauma of the infant's being overwhelmed by intense need states. Though initially the libidinal object is experienced only as an extension of the infant's actions, an optimal degree of frustration allows differentiation of the object from its action context. In time, the act of obtaining gratification becomes more firmly located within the self-representation.

Such good enough mothering fosters the child's omnipotence while broadening his self-schema as he becomes aware of an increasingly differentiated array of inner states, as well as the reality requisites for their satisfaction. So long as excessive frustration does not occur, potentially shattering his emerging confidence and initiative, the young child retains the illusion that he is capable of self-care and self-regulation (Krystal, 1978). This belief allows the somewhat older child to feel capable of regulating even more complex inner states.

Without good enough mothering, premature and excessive frustration shatters the infantile omnipotence; the infant becomes aware that the true locus of gratification and regulation lies outside of the self, unfortunately independent of wish or desire. Given the partial lack of differentiation between self- or object-representations and their associated actions, the sensorimotor infant will experience regulating actions as belonging to the frustrating object. Hence the object-representation is not kept distinct from actions in which the self-representation plays, potentially at least, an equal role. In this way key regulatory functions become attributed to the object-representation, and aspects of inner reality become located outside the self-representation. In time such misattribution leads to a failure of internalization. Each developmental transition is characterized by a resurgence of internal demands to regulate increasingly complex needs. Should frustration become excessive, key regulatory processes can again be misattributed to the representation of the object.

This continued introduction of "just sufficient frustration" via early sensorimotor, bodily action promotes "internalization," resulting in continued expansion of the self-representation and an increasing sense of self-as-agent (Schafer, 1960). Through this expansion, a differentiated internal world is formed and separated from the external one via increasingly complex, developmentally induced boundaries. Without a sense of being willful, that is, of intentionally affecting the environment, little in the way of distinction between self and object, inner and outer, will emerge. Need gratification will remain experienced as magically present when desired or at arbitrary and meaningless times. In extreme cases of overly gratifying mothers, need gratification may be provided before awareness of an increasing need state is even registered. Such gratification can interfere with any experience of self-as-agent and secondarily with any distinction between inner and outer reality. Consequently, satisfaction and frustration remain experienced as arising from without, accompanied by an empty and tenuously defined self-representation.

There are stages which can be delimited in the development of this increasingly differentiated and integrated self-representation. These stages are not mutually exclusive, though each stage can be distinguished on the basis of shifts in the nature of needs and vehicles of need regulation. Each new awareness of a more differentiated internal state, and the ability to regulate it, develops slowly. Considerable developmental overlap can exist while such regulatory abilities are progressively emerging. Thus, although we are confident of the constant sequence of these stages, their exact timing and degree of overlap will vary with the individual.

Sensorimotor-Symbiotic Stage

During the initial stage of infancy characterized by oral primacy, the newborn's cognitive capacities are at a sensorimotor, need-satisfying level (Edgcumbe and Burgner, 1972). The infant responds to the object's actions but is unable to separate the object from its action. Consequently a failure to distinguish pleasurable sensations from the pleasing object ensues (Blatt, 1974). To the extent that mothering is not perfect, omnipotence wanes and the infant comes to recognize the separate existence of the external object of gratification from internal needs and satisfactions. The infant discovers with delight that auto-erotic behavior can also reduce tension. Later, even more advanced and coordinated motor movements will be used to reduce tension, to gratify inner needs, or signal others to meet those needs. Although a dawning awareness of self and of the caretaker emerges at this time, neither are distinguished fully from the environment. Self- and object-representations gain the foreground of dawning conscious thought only in the context of need gratification (Blatt, 1974).

Consequently the infant's fledgling sense of self remains ephemeral and tenuous. Bodily action, in the form of autoerotic stimulation, is necessary for the emergence of an inner sense of intentionality and mastery. Only through *being* willful, so to speak, can an awareness of willing develop, as actions are internalized to form thoughts. Consequently, *the earliest sense of self is as a body self.* In accordance with this conception Hoffer (1950) proposes that the infant's ability both to touch himself and to experience that touch "elicits two sensations of the same quality and these lead to the distinction between the self and the not-self, between body and what subsequently becomes environment. In consequence, this factor contributes to the processes of structural differentiation. Delimitation between the self-body and the outer world, the world where the objects are found, is thus initiated" (p. 19). Current researchers in the area of social cognition (Lewis and Brooks-Gunn, 1979) restate this point in a manner quite congruent with our view. They argue that the proprioceptive feedback of the infant's motor movements facilitates an early sense of self: "In fact from a definitional point of view, it is our strong belief that the first definition or feature of self is the simultaneity and identity of action and outcome. . . . Self is defined from action and reflects the identity of action and outcome in a specific locus of space" (p. 224). Autoerotic behavior, then, provides the most self-evident cause-effect relationship for the infant.

Function-Practicing/Rapprochement Stage

As the infant learns to anticipate and search for the desired object, an increasingly differentiated sense of self emerges. Motility with its pleasure at use of the body promotes excursions away from the mother. These excursions alternate with return trips for libidinal refueling

(Mahler, Pine, and Bergman, 1975). The early toddler gains a variety of visual and contextual perspectives on the mother in this fashion. Thus, the *interaction of cognitive and motoric maturation promotes more articulated representations of both self and other.* The libidinal object begins to take on greater stability for the toddler as it is observed and experienced in a variety of contexts. Simultaneously, each new excursion and additional perspective on the mother promotes an increased sense of self as the instigator of exploratory behavior.

During the early part of this stage, an initial capacity for symbolization is reflected in the achievement of both object permanence (Greenspan, 1979) and self-permanence (Lewis and Brooks-Gunn, 1979). However, genuine symbolism or representation cannot be considered dominant (Greenspan, 1979); action in the world of others remains a requisite for representing it. Although an understanding of causal relations begins to emerge, inner differentiation is still lacking in regard to an internalized sense of agency. Representations are static; they remain locked into the spatial and temporal contexts in which they were first encountered. The toddler remains dependent on tangible external feedback to experience a sense of agency or power. The representation of self remains defined by its immediate impact on the world, with minimal ability to develop a higher order image of self as the agent of various actions. Concrete feedback of the results of intentions is necessary to foster a sense of willing. From this perspective the toddler's love affair with the world can be seen as a love affair with the self, a fledgling realization (accompanied by awe) of the ability to impact the world. This dependence on the external world for confirmation of the sense of self-as-agent greatly limits the infant's ability to differentiate inner from outer reality. In fact, the egocentrism and omnipotence of the practicing toddler can be viewed as a maturationally imposed limitation.

As more experience and awareness of self-as-agent is gained, this initially ephemeral and unintegrated self-representation becomes more articulated. Further growth is promoted by the cognitive achievement of evocative object constancy.[2] This newfound ability to represent the libidinal object in its absence marks the emergence of genuine symbolic capacities. At this stage the child has learned to conserve the

---

[2]This form of object constancy is only one element contributing to Mahler's highly complex stage of object constancy. We concur with Edgcumbe and Burgner (1972) that the later stage is more accurately termed the capacity to maintain constant relationships, indicating a more complex array of developmental achievements.

environment without direct action in it. Such awareness of the external world independent of action promotes the awareness of being an independent agent; thus a sense of psychological causality is acquired (Wolff, 1960). These mental representations complement concrete action, facilitating further adaptation. As the toddler resolves the rapprochement crisis, the capacity for representing the mother's voice, image, feel, and smell allows refuge to be sought in her representational presence (Greenspan, 1979). The self-representation becomes distinctly more elaborated with this greater independence from the environment. A realization of self-efficacy occurs as the capacity to plan and modify goals is enhanced through the cognitive attainment of reversibility. On a concrete level, consequences can be anticipated and the planned sequence of actions can be reversed mentally, allowing a new sequence of acts to be considered.

The stabilization of this capacity for representation occurs slowly. Initially it remains tenuous and is disrupted easily by peremptory interpersonal experiences or drive intensification. Even under normal conditions, the post-rapprochement, preoedipal child needs periodic exposure to the objects represented in order to retain them in the inner world. Thus, the boundary between fantasy and reality remains tenuous. Egocentric modes of thought are evidenced in the magical and animistic thinking that characterizes this stage. Not until the structural accomplishments of the oedipal phase do representations gain greater stability and complexity. Although further stages in the development of self-representation have been delineated elsewhere (Sugarman and Jaffe, in press), we will defer their elaboration here; for the two earliest stages, just discussed, are most salient with regard to the psychopathological conditions we will present.

CLINICAL OBSERVATIONS

While our developmental framework describes the crucial role that the body representation plays in the evolution of the self-representation, the usefulness of this contribution rests on the extent to which clinical observations support the model. Further, the model should help organize and explain the clinical data so that treatment formulations are enhanced. In the next section we present the Rorschach protocols of two patients, one an undifferentiated schizophrenic, the other a paranoid schizophrenic, along with commentary that points out the relevant aspects of certain responses in understanding each patient's body representation. This is followed by a discussion that highlights key diagnostic variables revealed by the nature and function of their body representations. Although the next logical step would involve exploring the implications for treatment, this step is not included, as it is beyond the scope of this chapter.

Human Body Percepts of an Undifferentiated Schizophrenic Patient

The patient was an imposing, grossly obese young adult male with wild, unkempt hair and fingernails painted purple.

Card I

Protocol	Inquiry
1. A crab. What do you call it? (A horseshoe crab. What else?)	(Location?) Just in the shape, you know. (Where?) [He shows the location.] Sautaucket years ago, the Long Island Sound. (What part of the inkblot?) The whole thing (What about it made it look like that?), the shell shape [turns it over to show me despite my protestations].
2. John Shaw's pancreas pancreas. (Anything else?). Yeah. John Shaw's pancreas. Perhaps, gonads in some way. Perhaps, yeah, John Shaw pancreas. It looks like an X ray of John Shaw's pancreas.	(Location?) The whole thing. (What about it made it look like that?) Ah, what made it look like that? Ah, no, ah, the medicine he was on. I think cocaine, perhaps marijuana. (What made it look like his pancreas?) It just looked like his pancreas and he was working. (Who was he?) He's a friend, a monkey I know.

In the first card we already see a fragmented body part.

Card II

1. That looks like, uh, I'm not sure. It looks like completed surgery. Other than that, nothing. (Anything else?)

(Location?) Yeah, it looks like John Shaw's pancreas after surgery. I believe, I'm not positive. Other than that it looks like a good joint, too.

2. Okay, a flying saucer. Docking space ship, perhaps. It looks like a shot I took of the space ship when I was in the galaxy.

(Location?) Well, the dimensions itself. (Where was that?) A docking maneuver in deep space. [I lose most of his expansive rambling.] Call that reality. [He refers to the red part.]

Here, a fragmented body representation is linked to a sense of illness and dependence. The reference to surgery is also likely a metaphor for the testing situation. Expansive grandiosity quickly defends against this anxiety.

Card III

1. That also looks like John Shaw's pancreas. (What else?)

(What about it made it look like that?) What made it look like John Shaw's pancreas? I'm not sure. It's a different phase of surgery. It's completed surgery. It's a different view of John Shaw's pancreas. Knock it off, John. [Seems to be hallucinating.]

2. I'm not sure, schizophrenia. I'm not sure. I'll have to look at it more carefully. This also looks like John Shaw's pancreas and schizophrenia and nerves.

(Location?) Uh, it was a certain set of dimensions. Don't worry, John. (Was it the whole thing?) Basically.

The fragmentation of his body representation is tied into his own sense of being ill.

Card IV

1. It looks like John Shaw's liver. [He talks to John.] (What else?)

2. It looks like a bat. It looks like Bridget and Bernie's favorite trick. I thought you could appreciate the variation on it.

(Was it the whole thing?) Yeah, John Shaw's liver.

(The whole thing?) Yeah, that's Bridget and Bernie's favorite bat trick. (Who are Bridget and Bernie?) That shouldn't be defined. (What do you mean by favorite bat trick?) I don't know how it's done. It just is done. It's not to do with John Shaw's surgery.

The fragmentation of his body representation associated with inner visceral experience becomes perseverative.

Card V

1. Bridget and Bernie, both of them. (What else?)

2. John Shaw's liver before, I believe. And of Bridget and Bernie. I would suggest going home because there's a war going on.

(What made it look like Bridget and Bernie?) Two famous bats of the world. Quite willing. She being a foil for him.

Aggression is felt by him to disrupt his bodily coherence, eliciting wishes to return to the maternal orbit to regain cohesion.

Card VI

1. Perhaps none of your business. Probably should be conducted privately. The cat in the hat.

(Location?) The cat in the hat. (The whole thing?) [Silence.] (What about it made it look like the cat in the hat?) The whiskers. How long will this take? [He asks for a break and I agree to one once we complete

the Rorschach.] (What about it
made it look like the cat in the
hat?) Just does. You know, the
Dr. Seuss story.

Here the antagonism toward the examiner shown in the last two cards
becomes manifest and he tries to leave the scene.

Card VII

1. That looks like surgery in the
future. Not really. You're having
a nonreality on the basis of [he
laughs]. It's not funny. Yeah, I
know it but it's very uncool. I
don't know if you're the horse,
Dr. Sugarman, but it looks like
cancer surgery.

(What about it makes it look
like cancer surgery?) Uh,
nothing that's—I believe that's
completed surgery. (What about
it makes it look completed?) It
wasn't. It was diagnostically
uncorrectable. I corrected it. I
undid the surgery.

Here a sense of chronic inner deterioration of body representation
associated with pessimistic despair emerges. Grandiose defenses then
follow, and he devalues the body of the examiner.

Card VIII

1. Yeah, I know it's your colors.
(What does it look like?) It looks
like John Shaw's pancreas.
(What else?) It looks like many
things. It looks like John Shaw's
pancreas. It's your, it's the same
color.

Given the affective press of the colored card, boundaries between
separate objects blur and his body representation fragments.

Card IX

1. I love to do this kind of work.
Testing more than anything else.

Before and many things I'd
rather not. Top secret. (What
does it look like?) It's a police
secret. It looks like a child, like
them downstairs. (What else?)

2. It looks like the surgery of   (What made it look like
mankind, John Shaw's, well the   surgery?) It looks like John
combination of it.   Shaw's preexisting condition
                                                         without it.

His body representation disintegrates to the point that only an abstraction exists. Self and object blur under the impact of expansive grandiosity.

Card X

1. It looks like the measles.

2. On that being completed
surgery or a John Shaw II. That
being pancreatic cap. Completed
surgery.

The end of testing and having had his fragmented body ego exposed is expressed.

Human Body Percepts of a Paranoid Patient

This patient's physical appearance was "normal" and neat in contrast to that of the previous patient.

Card I

Protocol	*Inquiry*
1. It looks like a crab. (Anything else?) Or a lobster with its claws greatly dimininshed in size.	(Location?) Uh, well the shape sort of coming like this and then the body. And then it had two small things that looked like claws or pincers near the head

area. That's why I mentioned the lobster because crabs and lobsters are built on the same shape except the lobster is much larger. Except for the king crab. King crab is quite a lot larger than the regular crabs. They're more on the lobster size or even larger. (Is the lobster the same as the crab?) Yeah.

Although a human body is yet to be perceived, the patient's responses speak to a concern with his body representation in relation to its potency and its defectiveness.

Card II

1. Well, uh, sort of reminds me of the facial part of the schnauzer, which is a small type of dog. I think it's in the terrier family. Of course it's red and black. I don't know if you want me to show it to you now. (No.)

(Location?) Well, the two red parts at the top, the eye area. Of course the black part would be the nose and the lower portion of it was a schnauzer. Well, a neighbor used to have a lot of schnauzers and they would come over and play and it always looked like their mouths were way down low on their face. Almost looked like their mouths were on their necks. I always thought they were ugly dogs.

2. And then I could take the red section at the bottom which looks like a butterfly. Looks like two feelers in the back which of course in butterflies, I guess, are in the front.

(What makes it look like a butterfly?) Well, uh, I have to say the shape. Again, it was small. It sort of showed the form of wings and then the two where there were two feelers or antennas coming out of the back. I think they are some type of butterflies with feelers or antennas coming out of the rear part. It was greatly defined. It was the only thing I could say it looks like. (Anything else?) No.

3. Two red things at the top could be forms of seals.

(Forms?) Yeah, well their shape. They seem to be, you know, connected. Of course you have there, they are sort of defined heads. And the rest were the body. That's the way it was on the seals. They have undefined heads and the rest is their body. That's the way seals are. They sort of come down from the head and start sloping backwards. (What made them look connected?) No, no, not the seals, the rabbits. I mean there are two seals but they're looking at each other.

4. If I turn it, the black section on the sides look like rabbits. The dimensions are all that is complete to be a rabbit. The nose section is pushed in, the ears are a lot smaller unless it's in a reclining position. And of course they do have stubby tails, but their tails are usually bigger. That's about it.

(What makes it look like rabbits?) I get the rabbits from where I turn it sideways. The head seems to be well defined, as on a rabbit. The nose is well defined. The ears are there but I think the main thing about rabbits is their tail.

Here again, concerns about the potency of the body are evident. In addition, its definition and spatial coordinates are confusing.

Card III

1. Well, these are the same ones I had at Langley Porter. I can

(What makes it look like rabbits?) Oh this time it seemed like

make out a few things which may seem kinda, the two red things on the outside of the blot part or the black part here again look like rabbits. Of course the dimensions are overexaggerated. The ears are very large, the nose is very large, and the tail is very large.

they were sitting on their hind legs. They were standing up sorta as though they heard something and I mean one of the things that goes up first is their ears. Again, the type of rabbits we have around here. Their ears are not that big. The rabbits they have in the sub [sic] part of the country, I guess they call them long-eared jacks, their ears are very long. The tail is very large and the nose was very large also. And I think that it, the large ears and the oversized tail and nose would have to, I mean, maybe you could get it if you bred a long-eared rabbit from the south or southwest with a rabbit from around here. But it's got to be done that way.

2. And then the other red section in the middle, again I see a moth. Could be a gypsy moth.

(What makes it look like a gypsy moth?) The only thing I'm not worrying about is the color. But we've had a lot of gypsy moths and they're not really defined. But you can see a gypsy moth from a mile away. A white thing flapping. They have wings and a small body. They are playing.

3. And it could be a bowtie. That'all I can really see in that.

(What makes it look like a bowtie?) Well, the old-fashioned clip-on bow ties. It has two sides exactly alike and the snap underneath and it has some frilly thing in the middle. (Anything else?) No.

Once again questions about the potency of his body are raised. Is it strong or is it weak? Furthermore, exhibitionistic themes emerge around worries as to whether it is attractive or deformed. All these issues appear linked to latent homosexual impulses.

Card IV

1. This may sound weird. I don't want you to think I'm copying my answers from before, but I think I'm giving you the same answers as from Langley Porter. This, I'm turning it upside down, it looks like a platypus. I think it's an Australian mammal. It has big front flippers or paws or whatever you call them and they have small hind ones. Of course, the way I'm looking at this I see two, uh. On this one they have, they do not have feelers or antennas. The way I'm looking at this one it seems to have one. They do have a small tail. It's sort of like a miniature beaver's tail and it's sort of spread out and that's about all I see in this picture.

(What makes it look like a platypus?) Well, its massive body size. They are pretty big. Not in height, but their body seems like somebody stepped on them and then squashed them. The area where the head was. Definitely not the type of head they have. I can't remember much about their head.

Issues of potency and the power of his body become linked to sadomasochistic themes.

Card V

1. I think I've got a one-track mind today. This is definitely a beautiful picture of a butterfly. The defined wings, the antennas again. I can't remember. I can't recall. I think some butterflies

have some small feelers in the
back. That's all I can make of it.

Denial fails to conceal worries about potency and latent homosexual
themes.

Card VI

1. Well, um, I would like, this is going to sound funny, but to me it looks like an aerial view of an anteater with the long nose, the front legs, and the hind legs. You know, this is the sand or dirt. It looks like he's burrowing his nose to get some ants.

(What makes it look like that?) Well, it could be, you know you could be standing over it. You have the whole dimension if it, the nose, the front feet, the rear of it. It could possibly be looking through an infrared gun. I don't know if that can penetrate through the ground or not. It's definitely well structured as an anteater. (Part of it is in the ground?) Yeah. Part of his nose. They dig a hole with their front feet big enough to stick their noses in. And they have sort of like a suction setup, like a vacuum.

Oral and phallic themes intermingle and disrupt his understanding of
bodily function.

Card VII

1. This looks like two dogs. Uh, pretty large ears. The face is well defined. Well it's pretty well defined as two dogs. The ears are about right, the nose and face are about right, pretty short tail. Actually the body is not the right size.

(What makes it look like two dogs?) I saw two and you know the ears. It looks like they were looking at each other. The ears were pretty large. Most dog ears are usually erect. I guess not too many dogs outside of the spaniel and some terriers have drooping ears. To me it looked like a bunch of different dogs put together. The face of a boxer, the ears of a spaniel, and the tail of a French poodle.

2. Down at the bottom I see another butterfly. That's it.

An unintegrated body representation reflects conflicting impulses and anxieties about potency.

Card VIII

1. Again I see something here that I can't remember the name of it. It's the type of animal from South America. I don't know if it's an aardvark or what. From what I can remember the picture of them. Their tail is—they have a tail. They're mostly a ground animal. They have a small nose, they are small. That's it.

(What makes it look like an aardvark?) Well, I saw the defined outline and the four legs and the facial thing and the body minus a tail. And I like animals, like studying them. The most interesting animals come from South America and the animal is interesting to me because you don't see an animal without a tail.

The sense of body defectiveness finally emerges in themes of phallic insufficiency and/or castration.

Card IX

I can't make anything out of it.

Card X

1. Okay, there's a part in here which looks like it could probably be a human backbone. Greatly larger than it really is. It shows two ribs in there and a couple or organs off to the side, possibly the lungs. That's about it.

(What makes it look like that?) Well, I think the backbone is the most defined bone in your body and a lot of the other bones are connected to the backbone. And there are a lot of organs near the backbone, the backbone being one of the major parts of the

body. And it seemingly has great
strength in the picture, its size.
And to me it almost looked
metallic. You know it almost
looked. I could almost call it a
metallic rod that giant turbines
could be run by because it
looked so—that's how I relate to
the backbone because I've fallen
a lot and I always hurt the end of
my spine. It could also be the
intestinal tract which would sort
of mess up the whole picture.

Deanimation is turned to in an effort to integrate a sense of his body and
to reinstate a sense of its potency and effectiveness.

BODY REPRESENTATION IN PARANOID SCHIZOPHRENIA

The Rorschach of the paranoid patient illustrates the thesis of this
chapter. Virtually every card revealed some overriding concern about
his body representation—its potency, its masculinity, its integrity. But
not until Card X does he show the blending of the human and the
inanimate. Around the theme of his backbone, with all its phallic and
homosexual connotations, he borders on literally fusing it with a powerful machine. It is as though he must use this last opportunity in the test
(Appelbaum, 1961; Cerney, 1984; Jaffe, 1985) to communicate to the
examiner that he has mastered and can control the anxieties about his
body representation that were exposed on earlier cards. In essence, he
says that if he is machinelike, detached from human sensations and
feelings, he is powerful like a "giant turbine."

Although the most obvious anxieties in this patient's Rorschach
involved phallic and anal issues, we have found that the deanimated
body ego of the paranoid patient defends against a variety of regulatory
failures associated with further fragmentation of the body ego (Sugarman, 1984; Sugarman and Jaffe, in press). Such deanimation promotes
the well-documented ability of paranoid schizophrenics to outperform
undifferentiated ones on a multitude of cognitive and perceptual tasks
(Blatt and Wild, 1976).

These paranoid patients tend to be fixated at the transition point between the differentiation and practicing subphases (Sugarman, 1984). The developmental emphases on motoric development parallel the psychosocial struggles with autonomy versus shame and doubt, and make this stage crucial in regard to the body representation. Deanimation defends against the many anxieties associated with this stage and promotes some adaptation through maintaining self-regulation, however rigid and brittle. Narcissistic regulation is fostered through the icy disdain characteristic of such extreme detachment. Drive impulses are rigidly regulated. Sadistic, homosexual, and heterosexual impulses are inhibited via "mechanistic," devitalized representations of the body self. Object relations, with their threat of stimulating dependent longings, are regulated through the creation of a cold and sterile body-self representation devoid of needs for human contact. Lastly, ego functioning is enhanced. Secondary process thinking and reality testing are tenuously maintained, as all emotion or need which might disrupt these functions are rigidly constricted (Sugarman, 1979).

BODY REPRESENTATION IN UNDIFFERENTIATED SCHIZOPHRENIA

In contrast to the paranoid patient, the undifferentiated schizophrenic demonstrated gross and perseverative body fragmentation associated with numerous ego disruptions from Card I on. He was never able to muster sufficient intrapsychic wherewithal to integrate his self-representation. Of particular interest was his emphasis on internal visceral organs. Mahler (Mahler and McDevitt, 1982) has emphasized that the body self originates in early inner sensations before a shift to active perception occurs: "proprioception, with minimal influence from sensory inputs, conveys the first glimmerings of a primitive core of a body self" (Mahler and McDevitt, 1982, p. 829). We contend that this repeated emphasis on fragmented inner organs in the Rorschach of the undifferentiated schizophrenic man highlights his regression to the earliest stages of body ego and demonstrates a failure to retain homeostatic mechanisms (Sugarman and Jaffe, in press).

Such extensive regression has a profound effect in regard to a variety of self-regulatory failures. Ego functioning is so disrupted that only the most basic of self-preservative functions are left intact. With this patient, disrupted thinking and distorted reality testing intermingle with fragmented body percepts. His fluctuations between concreteness and undue symbolic abstraction gives his thinking a bizarre, ethereal, otherworldly quality. Drive regulation is also hampered by such fragmentation. In this patient's case, aggressive and sadomasochistic impulses are expressed around themes of war and surgery, which are symbolically related to his fragmented body ego. Libidinal regulation can also be troublesome for such individuals, often to the point that compulsive and conspicuous masturbation is commonplace. Object relations pose another difficulty in the face of such fragmentation. Because self- and object-representations lack stability, the self-other boundary becomes fluid and no cohesive sense of body self is maintained. Body parts and products are confused with persecutory introjects, and are viewed as powerful and dangerous. Lastly, narcissistic regulation is problematic. Their body self fragmentation contributes to an overwhelming sense of themselves as inadequate. Thus, a narcissistic struggle is revealed in the compensatory grandiosity that is apparent in this patient's test record.

CONCLUSION

The Rorschachs of two schizophrenic patients, one a paranoid type and one an undifferentiated type, demonstrate markedly different body representations. We have generalized this finding to differential diagnostic issues. Furthermore, we have presented a formulation of the vicissitudes of the body representations in these two types of psychopathology and clarified the overall impact of body representation on self-representation. Thus, attendance to such Rorschach indices can illuminate the structure of such patients' representational worlds and its relation to personality functioning more broadly.

REFERENCES

Appelbaum, S. A. (1961), The end of the test as a determinant of response. *Bull. Menn. Clin.*, 25:120

Athey, G. (1974), Schizophrenic thought organization, object relations, and the Rorschach test. *Bull. Menn. Clin.*, 38:406–429.

Blatt, S. (1974), Levels of object representation in anaclitic and introjective depression. *Psychoanalytic Study of the Child*, 29:107–157. New Haven, CT: Yale University Press.

———— Brenneis, C., Schimek, J., & Glick, M. (1976), Normal development and psychopathological impairment of the concept of the object on the Rorschach. *J. Abnorm. Psychol.*, 85:364–373.

———— Lerner, H. (1983), The psychological assessment of object representation. *J. Personal. Assess.*, 47:7–28.

_____ Ritzler, B. (1974), Thought disorder and boundary disturbances in psychosis. *J. Consult. & Clin. Psychol.*, 42:370–381.

_____ Wild, C. (1976), *Schizophrenia: A Developmental Analysis*. New York: Academic Press.

Blos, P. (1962), *On Adolescence*. New York: Free Press.

Cerney, M. (1984), One last response to the Rorschach test: A second chance to reveal oneself. *J. Personal. Assess.*, 48:338–344.

Edgcumbe, R., & Burgner, M. (1972), Some problems in the conceptualization of early object relationships: Part I. The concepts of need satisfaction and need satisfying relationships. *Psychoanalytic Study of the Child*, 27:283–314. New Haven, CT: Yale University Press.

Elkisch, P., & Mahler, M. (1959), On infantile precursors of the "Influencing Machine" (Tausk). *Psychoanalytic Study of the Child*, 14:219–235. New York: International Universities Press.

Freud, S. (1911), Psycho-analytic notes on an autobiographic account of a case of paranoia (dementia paranoides). *Standard Edition*, 12:9–79. London: Hogarth Press, 1958.

Frosch, J. (1964), The psychotic character. Clinical psychiatric considerations. *Psychiat. Quart.*, 38:81–96.

Greenspan, S. I. (1979), Intelligence and Adaptation. *Psychological Issues*, Monogr. 47/48. New York: International Universities Press.

Hoffer, W. (1950), Development of the body ego. *Psychoanalytic Study of the Child* 5:18–23. New York: International Universities Press.

Jaffe, L. S. (1985), The selected response procedure for the Rorschach. Paper presented at the annual meeting of the Society for Personality Assessment, May 1985, Berkeley, California.

Kernberg, O. (1967), Borderline personality organization. *J. Amer. Psychoanal. Assn.*, 15:641–685.

Kohut, H. (1971), *The Analysis of the Self*. New York: International Universities Press.

Krohn, A., & Mayman, M. (1974), Level of object representations in dreams and projective tests. *Bull. Menn. Clin.*, 38:445–466.

Krystal, H. (1978), Self-representation and the capacity for self-care. *Annual of Psychoanalysis*, 6:206–246. New York: International Universities Press.

Laufer, M., & Laufer, M. (1984), *Adolescence and Developmental Breakdown*. New Haven: Yale University Press.

Lewis, M., & Brooks-Gunn, J. (1979), *Social Cognition and the Acquisition of the Self*. New York: Plenum.

Lichtenberg, J. (1978), The testing of reality from the standpoint of the body self. *J. Amer. Psychoanal. Assn.*, 26:357–386.

Mahler, M., & McDevitt, J. (1982), Thoughts on the emergence of the sense of self, with particular emphasis on the body self. *J. Amer. Psychoanal. Assn.*, 30:827–848.

_____ Pine, F., & Bergman, A. (1975), *The Psychological Birth of the Human Infant*. New York: Basic Books.

_____ Silberpfennig, I. (1938), Der Rorschachse Formdeutversuch als Hilfsmittel zum Verstädnis der Psychologie Hirnkranker. *Schweiz. Arch. Neurol. Psychiat.*, 40:302–327.

Modell, A. (1963), Primitive object relationships and the predisposition to schizophrenia. *Internat. J. Psycho-Anal.*, 44:282–292.

Piaget, J. (1954), *The Construction of Reality in the Child*. New York: Basic Books.

Rinsley, D. (1978), Borderline psychopathology: A review of aetiology, dynamics, and treatment. *Internat. Rev. Psycho-Anal.*, 5:45–54.

Sander, L. (1983), Polarity, paradox and organizing process in development. In:

Frontiers of Infant Psychiatry, ed. J. Call, E. Galenson, & R. Tyson. New York: Basic Books.

Sandler, J., & Rosenblatt, B. (1962), The concept of the representational world. *Psychoanalytic Study of the Child*, 17:128-145. New York: International Universities Press.

Schafer, R. (1960), Bodies in schizophrenic Rorschach responses. In: *Projective Testing and Psychoanalysis*, ed. R. Schafer. New York: International Universities Press, pp. 170-196.

Sugarman, A. (1979), The infantile personality: Orality in the hysteric revisited. *Internat. J. Psycho-Anal.*, 60:501-513.

_____ (1984), The use of deanimated transitional phenomena in paranoid conditions. *Bull. Menn. Clin.*, 48:418-426.

_____ (1986), An object relations understanding of borderline phenomena on the Rorschach. In: *Assessing Object Relations Phenomena*, ed. M. Kissen. New York: International Universities Press, pp. 77-88.

_____ Bloom-Feshbach, S., & Bloom-Feshbach, J. (1980), The psychological dimensions of borderline adolescents. In: *Borderline Phenomena and the Rorschach Test*, ed. J. Kwawer, H. Lerner, P. Lerner, & A. Sugarman. New York: International Universities Press, pp. 469-494.

_____ Jaffe, L. S. (in press), A developmental line of transitional phenomena. In: *The Facilitating Environment: Clinical Implications of Winnicott's Theories*, ed. G. Fromm & B. L. Smith. New York: International Universities Press.

Tausk, V. (1919), On the origin of the "Influencing Machine." *Psychoanal. Quart.*, 2:519-556, 1933.

Tolpin, M. (1971), On the beginnings of a cohesive self: An application of the concept of transmuting internalization to the study of the transitional object and signal anxiety. *Psychoanalytic Study of the Child*, 26:316-352.

Urist, J. (1977), The Rorschach test and the assessment of object relations. *J. Personal. Assess.*, 41:3-9.

Winnicott, D. W. (1971), *Playing and Reality*. New York: Basic Books.

Wolff, P. (1960), *The Developmental Psychologies of Jean Piaget and Psychoanalysis*. Psychological Issues, Monograph 5. New York: International Universities Press.

Part III
Clinical Syndromes

Chapter 10

The Narcissistic Personality as Expressed Through Psychological Tests

Howard D. Lerner, Ph.D.

Recently, deepening investigations of the origin and nature of pathological narcissism have led to sharp differences among psychoanalytic theorists regarding the tasks and organization of early structural development. These differences have in turn clouded the diagnosis of the narcissistic personality by means of psychological tests. Clarification of the concept of narcissism and a reevaluation of the psychological test picture presented by narcissistic patients are necessary if differential diagnosis is to be facilitated.

CLINICAL DESCRIPTION OF THE NARCISSISTIC PERSONALITY DISORDER

The narcissistic personality disorder is an Axis II diagnostic category in DSM-III. There is a general consensus that individuals exhibiting pathological narcissism display disordered behavior involving a self-centered grandiosity, an inability to maintain loving relationships, and fluctuations in self-esteem. Their grandiosity may be blatant or subtle, either expressed openly, in exhibitionistic and often obnoxious plays for attention, or concealed through shyness and self-deprecation. All life events and relationships are seen in a self-centered fashion, and there is a craving for love and admiration as grandiose fantasies demand confirmation and mirroring.

257

Many patients with narcissistic personality disorders initially present with a charming and attractive facade, but they lack the capacity for sustained loving attachments or empathic concern for other persons. Interpersonal relationships are characterized by deep mistrust, angry and envious feelings toward the success of others (often expressed through spoiling and ruthless depreciation) and a virtual incapacity to experience positive feelings deeply or to genuinely share with others. Therapeutic relationships, especially in long-term expressive psychotherapy, tend to follow a pattern characterized by initial overidealization, accompanied by exaggerated and unrealistic expectations, followed by pessimism, depreciation, and, finally, festering anger and bitter disappointment as defenses are unmasked. Often beneath the facade of charm lurk exploitative demands and a "coldness" toward others—a chilling detachment and a solipsistic demand that others gratify their needs and ask nothing in return.

Their capacity to experience genuine depression, especially when confronted with loss, is questioned by Kernberg (1975) and Modell (1975, 1980), who maintain that this affect is defensively converted into resentment and vengeful fantasies. Nevertheless, fluctuations in self-esteem are apparent and are frequently linked to outside approval. Often genuine achievement and creativity provide no inner satisfaction, but instead seem geared to elicit admiration and applause from others. Experiences of boredom and anhedonia are common. Narcissists' emotional lives often lack depth, and drug addiction and perversion are frequently engaged in to enliven the sense of self. Depression or depressive equivalents are also common, especially bodily preoccupations and hypochondriasis, which often are precipitated by the narcissistic injury of being rebuffed or disappointed when exaggerated feelings of entitlement are not gratified. Such normal vicissitudes of the life cycle as advancing age and the loss of youthful beauty can pose a crisis, precipitating a profound sense of hopelessness and failure. Diagnostically, disordered or pathological narcissism can occur across a wide spectrum of severity, at one end of the continuum overlapping with borderline personality disorders and at the other blending with neurotic disturbances. Many variations in symptomatology are observed, including varying degrees of sociopathy, compulsiveness, and perversion.

NARCISSISM: HISTORICAL REVIEW OF THE CONCEPT

With the publication in 1914 of his classic paper, "On Narcissism," Freud laid the foundation for subsequent theoretical developments. In

Chapter 3 of this volume, Paul Lerner has outlined that paper's major contributions: (1) a definition of secondary narcissism as a withdrawal of libido from the outer world and a redirection of the libido onto the ego; (2) a designation of the ego ideal as the "heir" or adult version of infantile narcissism; (3) a recognition of the relation between self-esteem and narcissistic libido; and (4) the observation that there is a particular type of object choice and object relation that may be referred to as narcissistic on the basis of the quality of the need for the object and the psychic function that it serves. Freud's use of the term narcissism left many areas of ambiguity, which subsequent investigators have attempted to clarify. Pulver (1970) has reviewed these ambiguities. Clinically, Freud referred to narcissism both as a sexual perversion whereby one's own body is treated as a sexual object, and as the basis for a homosexual object choice (one seeks a body like one's own). Genetically, narcissism was used to refer to a developmental phase of libidinal investment in the self. Object relationally, narcissism referred either to a type of object choice in which aspects of the self predominate, or to the absence of object relations. Economically, Freud used the term to refer to self-esteem and to fluctuation in self-esteem as the ego/self is narcissistically cathected. Freud also used narcissism to refer to an infantile mode of thinking which is magical and omnipotent.

Although Freud did not use the term "self" in his writings, subsequent development of the concept of narcissism has replaced the concept of ego with that of self. The most widely used definition of narcissism was offered by Hartmann (1950): "the libidinal investment of the self." Hartmann's contributions and later elaborations by Jacobson (1964) distinguished the concepts of self as person, ego as structure, and self- and object representation as subsystems within the structural schema. Some recent attempts at redefinition have dispensed with the economic model and with it the concept of libido. Stolorow (1975) offers a functional definition of narcissism in terms of the "structural cohesiveness, temporal stability, and positive affective coloring of the self-representations" (p. 174); psychic functioning is seen as narcissistic to the degree that it serves to establish and maintain these conditions. Energic concepts are excluded.

Although in his earlier formulations Kohut (1971) retained the economic metaphor, he employed it rather differently. There narcissism was defined not by the "target" of libido (i.e., self instead of object), but rather by its quality. For Kohut, libido is narcissistic when it involves "idealizing" or "self-aggrandizing" features. If an attachment, whether to the self or to an object, serves idealization or self-aggrandizement, then that attachment is narcissistic. This formulation is in keeping with Kohut's clinical observation that patients with narcissistic disturbances do not withdraw their interest from objects but rather tend to relate to them in highly disparate and intense ways. According to Kohut, these disparate attachments can be understood in terms of the individual's needing the object to stabilize and bolster a self that is threatened in consequence of a defect in structural development.

Most authors implicate self-esteem in their formulations of narcissism (Freud, 1914; Kohut, 1971; Kernberg, 1975). Jacobson (1964) in particular, notes a relationship between ego ideal formation, narcissism, and self-esteem. According to her, self-representations are optimally and progressively based on representations of the real (not the fantasized) self as these gradually develop out of accurate perceptions of past and present experiences. By contrast, the ego ideal is based on the wished-for or "potential" self—the idealized self as it would like to be in the future. The ego ideal serves the function of holding up to the ego an idealized edition of the self-representation to be striven for. Out of this developmental matrix self-representations and the ego ideal evolve in tandem, and a cognitive-affective schema or attitude toward the self develops. This is what is called self-esteem. The nature of the "ideal self" subsumed by the ego ideal will influence the level of self-esteem as well as the libidinal investment of the self—that is, narcissism.

Since Freud, several theorists have attempted to formulate the relationship between narcissism and object relations (Jacobson, 1964; Modell, 1968; Schafer, 1968; Kohut, 1971, 1977; Kernberg, 1975). Schafer (1968) relates positive narcissism with the development of positive self- and object representations which arise from relatively positive experiences in infancy and childhood. Conversely, disturbances in narcissism involve primarily negative self- and object representations, which lead to the defensive expenditure of psychic energy for protection and for gaining satisfaction through revenge. Modell (1968) and Mahler, Pine, and Bergman (1975) observe that while the self emerges from a kind of merger with the object, paradoxically, it is only through the progressive separation of self from object that mature object relations develop. According to Modell (1968), "the awareness of the self as a discrete and beloved entity . . . may enable the individual to accept the fact that objects in the external world are separate and can be lost and destroyed" (p. 59). Individuals lacking a coherent, stable, and harmonious sense of self, as Kohut (1977) observes, cannot tolerate the separateness of the object. These individuals, according to Kohut, need the object for psychic survival—that is, for survival of the self.

NARCISSISM: CURRENT STATUS OF THE CONCEPT

A conviction has taken hold of late, both within and without psychoanalysis, and particularly among observers of culture, that pathological narcissism has become increasingly prevalent in our time. To some extent, it is argued, it has replaced the neuroses of Freud's time as the characteristic disorder of our age. Within psychoanalysis, central concepts and propositions stand in need of reformulation in the light of recent contributions from other disciplines (Eagle, 1984). Dissatisfaction with various aspects of current theory, especially metapsychology, has long been simmering, and the need to enhance therapeutic effectiveness with narcissistic disorders is keenly felt.

Despite recent developments in the theory and treatment of narcissistic patients, the field continues to be plagued by a lack of consensus as to what constitutes the "narcissistic patient." Kernberg (1975) is explicit in reserving the term for patients "in whom the main problem appears to be the disturbance of their self-regard in connection with specific disturbances in their object relationships..." (p. 227). Viewing most narcissistic patients as organized on a borderline level of personality organization, he describes such patients as exhibiting a heightened degree of self-absorption, an inordinate need to be loved and admired, an overinflated sense of themselves, and a desperate desire for adoration. He suggests further that their emotional life is shallow, that they show little empathy for others, and that they feel restless and bored unless their self-regard is being nourished. In relationships, potential providers of narcissistic supplies are idealized, while those from whom little is expected are depreciated and treated with contempt. Beneath their veneer of charm, Kernberg argues, such individuals are cold, arrogant, ruthless, and exploitative.

Although Kohut (1971, 1977) identifies a certain symptom complex as characteristic of the narcissistic patient (e.g., lack of enthusiasm and zest, perverse activity, subjective feelings of deadness), he regards such a symptom cluster as diagnostically insufficient. Rather, he uses the concept of the "cohesive self" as the guiding principle for differential diagnosis. The instability, or propensity for regression, of this nuclear psychic structure is regarded by Kohut as the leading diagnostic indicator of narcissistic personality disorder. In establishing a differential diagnosis, especially in terms of neurotic-oedipal conflicts on the one hand and what he regards as borderline states on the other, Kohut places major emphasis on treatment considerations. Kohut notes that with a neurotic patient disruption of the defensive narcissistic position will result in the emergence of a nuclear oedipal conflict. By contrast, the same type of intervention with a narcissistic patient will prompt a massive regression involving the breakup of the cohesive self. Kohut has also identified and described a constellation of atypical transference patterns which unfold in the treatment of patients with narcissistic personality disturbance. Kohut refers to these patterns as "selfobject" transferences and specifies, as subtypes, the "mirroring" and the "idealizing" transference. Each pattern contains regressive and progressive features, and treatment of the narcissistic patient consists of movement along one or the other of these developmental lines; alternatively, it may involve shifts between these transference configurations.

Because Kernberg starts from disturbances in object relations, and treats mainly hospitalized patients, while Kohut begins with disturbances in the cohesive self differences in the types of patients observed and sees mostly outpatients in psychoanalysis, the narcissistic patients they describe seem significantly different. Indeed, their major divergences have led Teicholz (1978) to question whether they are describing the same clinical entity. While Kernberg sees the narcissistic patient as organized on a borderline level, Kohut, by contrast, places the narcissistic patient closer to the neurotic end of the psychopathology continuum, clearly distinguishes between narcissistic and borderline patients, and conceives of the borderline as having a fundamentally psychotic makeup.

PSYCHOLOGICAL TEST MANIFESTATIONS
OF THE NARCISSISTIC PATIENT

While Chapter 3 of this volume examines the psychological test picture of the sort of patient described by Kohut, here the test manifestations of the narcissistic personality outlined by Kernberg will be delineated. The test battery used consists of the Wechsler Adult Intelligence Scale (WAIS/WAIS-R), Rorschach, and TAT. In some cases the Early Memories Test (Mayman, 1968) and Parental Descriptions (Blatt, Wein, Chevron, and Quinlan, 1979) were administered. The scoring system used for the Rorschach was that of Rapaport, Gill, and Schafer (1945). The author has had the opportunity to test and supervise a broad range of adolescents and young adults presenting with borderline and narcissistic pathology, both inpatients and outpatients. The ten individuals involved in the present study all meet independent DSM–III criteria for narcissistic personality disorder. They were evaluated either at the Psychological Clinic and Adolescent Inpatient Service at the University of Michigan or at the Yale Psychiatric Institute. The sample, all single, and middle to upper middle class, comprises five females and five males, ranging in age from sixteen to twenty-six.

Kernberg (1975) describes patients with narcissistic personalities as presenting

> excessive self-absorption usually coinciding with a superficially smooth and effective social adaptation, but with serious distortions in their internal relationships with other people. They present various combinations of intense ambitiousness, grandiose fantasies, feelings of inferiority, and overdependence on external admiration and acclaim. Along with feelings of boredom and emptiness, and continuous search for gratification of strivings for brilliance, wealth, power and beauty, there are serious deficiencies in their capacity to love and to be concerned about others. This lack of capacity for empathic understanding of others comes as a surprise considering their superficially appropriate social adjustment. Chronic uncertainty and dissatisfaction about themselves, conscious or unconscious exploitiveness and ruthlessness toward others are also characteristics of these patients. [p. 264]

Kernberg's clinical description of narcissistic patients can be divided into five areas based on level of object relations, defensive structure, internal object world, external presentation, and reality testing. The object relations of narcissistic patients are characterized by an apparent contradiction between a haughty, grandiose, and inflated self-concept and an inordinate need for tribute and administration from others. People are essentially viewed as need-gratifying or need-frustrating. Interpersonal relationships consequently have a parasitic and exploitative quality. The internal emotional life of these patients is actually shallow and empty, perpetually pursuing short-lived highs from their grandiose fantasies or external admirers. There tends to be little in the way of empathy for others and a striking absence of genuine feelings of sadness or depression. Affects tend to be relatively undifferentiated and revolve around anger, oral rage, resentment, envy, and revenge, which are often experienced as diffuse tension states in the form of a need to do things, to stay active, to act on the world. The defensive structure of narcissistic patients, according to Kernberg, belies an intense primitive oral rage that is central to their psychopathology. The narcissistic patient often exhibits, beneath the grandiose self, primitive borderline defenses such as splitting, projective identification, devaluation, idealization, and omnipotence; these ward off paranoid fears of projected oral rage and the development of any dependence on others. The narcissistic patient, however, fares better than most borderlines with respect to reality testing, which for the most part is preserved, and impulse control, which is better modulated. Compared with the ego boundaries of most borderline patients, those of narcissistic personalities are more stable, given the pathological fusion of ideal self, ideal object, and self-representations. Finally, the narcissistic patient often presents as a smooth-functioning, charming, and engaging person, a facade that often masks a cold and ruthless personality that calculates the "next lemon to be squeezed."

In general, the test features to be looked for in assessing narcissistic patients include a social facade characterized by egocentricity and self-references; an extreme personalizing of experience and discourse coupled with an almost rigid tendency to avoid anxiety and anxiety-arousing situations; and a solicitation of the examiner's affection, assistance, and admiration, often juxtaposed with subtle and not so subtle devaluations of the tests and the examiner. Representations of the grandiose self, of its constituent elements (a "shadowy" real self, an ideal self, and an ideal other), and of what this structure masks—intense narcissistic rage and a deep conviction of unworthiness and frightening images of barrenness, emptiness, and void—can be discerned on the Rorschach. Further, test representations of borderline defenses, boundary disturbance, and a preponderance of malevolent objects are frequently exhibited by these patients. In what follows, the test features of patients with narcissistic personalities will be considered in terms of specific and nonspecific manifestations of ego weaknesses, affect organization, pathology of internal object relations, defensive structure, and treatment considerations.

SPECIFIC AND NONSPECIFIC MANIFESTATIONS OF EGO WEAKNESS

Clinically, narcissistic patients may exhibit nonspecific manifestations of ego weakness, but their psychological test performance often reveals specific weaknesses as well, weaknesses suggestive of borderline personality disorder. According to Kernberg (1975), the integration of a highly pathological grandiose self compensates for the lack of integration of the normal self-concept, a lack that is part of an underlying borderline personality organization. The presence of this structure explains the paradox of relatively good ego functioning and surface adaptation in the presence of splitting mechanisms and a constellation of primitive defenses, an inner world populated with malevolent objects, and a lack of integration of object representations.

The paradox of a relatively stable surface adaptation, persona, and ego functioning superimposed upon more primitive structures is often subtle and requires astute perceptiveness and clinical sensitivity for its discernment. An outpatient graduate student was described as follows: "T seemed calm and cooperative over the phone when I contacted him. Appointments were set up early. He arrived on time for all three sessions, dressed casually with 'worn-in' sneakers. During the tasks he stretched his rather lengthy legs out in my direction so that they were nearly touching my legs. While he worked on the tasks, he assumed a relaxed, easygoing manner. Although he commented that the timed tasks were frustrating, he worked methodically and deliberately. He especially took his time on tests which required elaboration (i.e., Information, TAT) and seemed quite pleased with his performance. In the first session he struck me as trying to be clever, to outwit and impress me. In the following sessions, his manner became more subdued, sincere, and unassuming. He expressed his anger, frustration, and anxiety at various points very honestly. After we finished Early Memories, he asked if I was a psychologist in training. I said I was and asked if this was important to him. He replied that he felt some compensation for having been evaluated if he could evaluate me. On his way out, he stopped and walked over to me, warmly squeezing my hand in parting."

The clinical presentation and social facade of a twenty-two-year-old narcissistic inpatient was described as follows: "He is dramatic in an intense, frenzied manner, theatrical and highly exhibitionistic, revealing an admixture of masculine and feminine strivings; being verbose, at times disarmingly open, and highly self-centered, he readily attempts to seduce one into granting him permission to be flighty, arbitrary, and—most striking—to be special. Indeed, he is an individual who swiftly and astutely sizes up the situation and acts appropriately within it, while striving actively not to allow the situation to touch him. Hence, one sees an attunement to clothing, costumes, physical appearance, and other external, superficial attributes." The deceptively high level of social adaptation of these patients is often seen on their WAIS protocols in terms of elevated scores on Picture Arrangement (social anticipation) and Comprehension (social judgment and reasoning). Often these patients record higher scores on Picture Arrangement than Comprehension, reflecting a vigilant attunement to social cues as guides to behavior rather than a reliance on more abstract reasoning and conceptual abilities. Most narcissistic patients in the sample showed a pattern of lower scores on the Arithmetic and Digit Span subtests, which is characteristic of low anxiety tolerance and a tendency to avoid anxiety, especially when called upon to rely on internal resources. This anxiety is also demonstrated through comparatively lower scores on the Digit Symbol subtest, which is the only task on the WAIS which calls for new learning in the test situation. Again, the narcissistic avoidance of reliance on internal resources, of trusting themselves, and of learning from experience results in frequent checking-back to the standard, in anxiety, and, as a result, in poor problem-solving strategies and lower scores.

The porcelain veneer of narcissistic patients is often expressed through their flaunting a pseudosocial sophistication and through their responding to questions eliciting factual knowledge with excessive, often glittery elaborations which stripped of their window dressing actually reveal quite little. A twenty-year-old male student was asked, "Where is Brazil?" He responded with a smile, clasping his hands together, "Depends on the context you want: on planet Earth, on the lower hemisphere, next to Venezuela—which would you pick? I really pick? I really can't—continental South America. Usually the context, since the rest is assumed. You can see the kinds of methods I use." The same patient responded to the "What is the Vatican?" question with, "I don't know initially. An associative guess, it's a religious—what's the word?—some sort of religious building somewhere in Europe, contains religious treasures, a place of worship, where the Pope stays. That's all with 'perhaps' in front of it." As one clinician remarked of such patients, "There is less there than meets the eye."

Of the sample of ten narcissistic patients (five who were predominantly inpatient subjects) seven showed WAIS profiles of the Performance Scale equal or superior to the Verbal Scale. This discrepancy usually reflects a characteristic action-oriented style and emphasis on "doing things" shown by most narcissistic patients. One hospitalized patient's attempt at intellectual pretentiousness clashed with a poorly integrated, impulsive, action-oriented style when he composed a TAT story about aspiring to greatness as a symphony violinist. In it he referred to the violin as a fiddle. The degree to which this underlying impulsive, sensorimotor style breaks through more ideational defenses and the social facade to actually diminish performance and reality testing is the degree to which the character structure is unintegrated. The emphasis on action and on doing things may serve many functions: the maintenance of ego boundaries, the avoidance of debilitating self-doubts, a fuller affective experience, and the longings and fears that follow in their wake. The dynamics underlying this style were evident in one hospitalized patient's response to Card 5 on the TAT: "Jack and Bill took a pleasure cruise and the ship ran into a terrible storm and they were shipwrecked on an uninhabited island and they spent many, many years on the island helping each other survive. Soon, for their lack of planning the provisions ran out for lack of planning. What did I say? Eliminate the second 'lack of planning.' They started to become very hungry and wretched and they would fight over the little food which was left." Here one sees the convergence of homosexual impulses, devaluing defenses, anxiety, a flight from introspection, and the emergence of oral needs. Note that the frightening image of the world being devoid of food is activated by a relationship paradigm of dependency.

The reality testing of narcissistic patients seems more intact than it is. While they show neither the sharp, well-articulated, and creative responses of the more neurotic patient nor the severe reality distortions of hospitalized borderlines, their adequate but pedestrian F+ percentage (Schafer, 1954) is usually maintained by overarticulated, "showy" but mundane responses; not uncommonly, their form level exhibits striking departures from the norm where conflictual drive material is implicated. A twenty-one-year-old male inpatient's first response to Card I on the Rorschach was: "God this is dull. It looks like two Russian dancers—two male Russian dancers with hats on and Russian costumes. It's the clothing—big billowy sleeves, coat, big puffy pants reminded me of Russians, also the stiffened arm reminds me of Russian dancers." This well-articulated, flowery human movement response was soon followed by the more ambiguous and conflictual sexual stimuli of Card III: "Looks like two, everything is two, two native African women pounding on a drum. The red looks like some kind of animal that's being killed or hunted and being killed and being hung up. Looks like a combination between a sea horse and some kind of four-legged animal, a chicken. A sea horse head and like a calf's feet, two of them, and a chicken's body, and a monkey's tail." Here one sees a serious deterioration in reality testing under the impact of sexualized aggression, the emergence of powerful oral aggressive, possibly cannibalistic images, and the breakdown of the structural integrity or boundary of the object in the form of a fabulized combination–serious response, a blend of contaminationlike manifestation of thought disorder.

Paralleling most of these patients' ability to maintain a surface grip on reality is their tendency not to exhibit more florid signs of formal thought disorder. In this regard the concept of boundaries is important. Most developmental theories regarding borderline and narcissistic patients (Masterson, 1972, 1980; Kernberg, 1975; Mahler, Pine, and Bergman, 1975; Rinsley, 1977) emphasize that although these individuals have developed a rudimentary boundary between self- and object representations, this incomplete state of differentiation and boundary formation remains permeable because of an inability to fully integrate positive and negative affect states. Recent advances in theory and empirical research (Blatt and Ritzler, 1974; Blatt and Wild, 1976; Lerner, Sugarman, and Barbour, 1985) show that the concept boundary representation based on the object relations model is applicable to traditional notions of thought process and thought disorder based on the ego psychology model. Further, these formulations have been shown to have differential diagnostic and clinical utility.

Based on an integration of developmental psychology with object relations theory, Blatt and Ritzler (1974) initially suggested that intrapsychic development involves the formation of pivotal structural boundaries which promote the structuralization of self- and object representations that become progressively differentiated, articulated, and integrated along a developmental continuum. In applying this model to the Rorschach, the contamination response, implying a loss of between separate ideas, becomes reformulated as a fundamental loss of the self/other boundary. In turn, the confabulation response is recast as a loss of the inner/outer boundary. The fabulized combination response, an arbitrary combination of percepts based on spatial contiguity, is thought to involve a boundary laxness rather than overt disruption.

Lerner, Sugarman, and Barbour (1985) constructed a Boundary Disturbance Scale by applying the developmental continuum of boundary representation to the traditional ego psychological analysis of thought disorder. These investigators then applied the scale to independently diagnosed samples of neurotic, outpatient borderline, inpatient borderline, and schizophrenic patients. The results indicate that severe borderline psychopathology can be conceptualized as a failure to maintain the inner/outer boundary—that is, a loss of distinction between inner experience and external reality, with a propensity to overelaborate external reality with one's affective coloration of it. Schizophrenic patients showed the most severe form of self/other boundary disturbance. Narcissistic patients, because of the grandiose self, tend to conceal boundary disturbance on more structured tasks, not unlike borderlines, and to exhibit both subtle and more overt disruptions of boundaries on the Rorschach. Narcissistic patients can be expected to display a fairly wide range of boundary disturbance on the Rorschach, ranging from boundary laxness, through inner/outer boundary disturbance (seen in more labile, exhibitionistic patients), to some instances of highly condensed, blended (half-animal/half-human, parts of different animals, human-machine) fabulized combination–serious responses.

While there is no one type of thought disorder that characterizes the narcissistic patient as, for example, the contamination response characterizes schizophrenia, there are certain peculiarities of the response process (and, by extension, of thinking generally) which are common in the test protocols of narcissistic personalities. First, narcissistic thinking is remarkably egocentric and self-referential. Frequently test items become conduits for grandiose, self-aggrandizing statements about past accomplishments, experiences, or future plans. One often sees on the Rorschach a plethora of self-references. The self, for many of these patients, is the only frame of reference. For example, one outpatient responded to the "movie item" on the WAIS Comprehension subtest with, "Assuming I'm in a movie theater, first find a place of safety, say a door, then announce it." The same patient, after generating a fairly mundane, somewhat hostile response to another test item, observed, "I must say I'm pleased with that."

Egocentrism is an integral part of cognitive growth and psychological development in which the child, with progressive development, relates aspects of the immediate context to prior experience in order to understand reality in increasingly complex and sophisticated ways. Blatt (1983) has outlined three levels of egocentrism inherent in Piaget's developmental theory which have a bearing not only on normative development but on narcissistic cognition. Developmentally the child, through relinquishing succeeding levels of egocentrism, comes to comprehend actions and perceptions different from his own and is increasingly able to integrate and coordinate these actions and perceptions with his own viewpoint. According to Piaget (Inhelder and Piaget, 1958), succeeding levels of egocentrism are relinquished through a gradual process of "decentration"—the ability to shift from one aspect of a situation to another in a flexible, balanced fashion. In this way, cognitive processes are seen as reflecting greater maturity to the degree that conceptual thought or internalized abstract schemata gain ascendancy over immediate sense impressions and perceptions in structuring subject-object relationships. According to Blatt (1983), there are three successive levels of egocentrism, ranging from an initial state of total egocentrism to full objectivity. The first stage is characterized by a lack of differentiation between the self and the external world. Gradually, the developing child becomes reciprocally aware of himself and others. The first level of decentration occurs during the sensorimotor and preoperational stages, in which the child learns to distinguish his own actions from those of others. The child assumes that his viewpoint is the only one possible and that it is shared unquestioningly by others. Blatt cites the example of the child who covers his eyes and, because he can not see, assumes others cannot see him. At this initial stage of egocentrism the child confuses his actions and viewpoint with those of others.

The first stage of egocentrism is resolved at about six or seven years of age, when the child begins the period of concrete operational thought. At this second level of decentration, spanning the sixth through the twelfth year, the child gradually comprehends his own viewpoint more complexly but also becomes aware that different viewpoints are held by others. According to Blatt (1983), "he becomes aware of his subjective existence and of the multiplicity of other viewpoints. He becomes aware of himself as a unique object among other objects and of the relativity of his personal perspective" (pp. 297–298). The third level of decentration coincides, at approximately age twelve, with the emergence of formal operations. With an awareness not only of the independent existence of objects but also of the independence of his cognitive processes from the environment, the final form of egocentrism is relinquished. As Blatt states, "With this reflective self-awareness and appreciation of the nature of his own thought processes, as well as the viewpoints of others, the child can develop genuine social reciprocity in which he can maintain his own subjectivity while appreciating the subjectivity of others and differentiating it from more objective dimensions of reality" (p. 298).

Within this developmental schema, most narcissistic patients reflect egocentric thought processes characteristic of the first and second levels of decentration. Several patients in the sample used for this study exhibited behaviors demonstrative of sensorimotor, preoperational egocentrism. These patients often touch the test materials and run their hands across the shaded Rorschach cards. In describing what they see, they often depict part of the inkblots as missing or cover over those areas of the blots not included in their percepts. Kernberg-Bardenstein (personal communication) termed this behavior "tactile neediness"—a sensorimotor search for immediate sensate gratification or soothing which is rich in dynamic meanings. Many patients in this sample also manifested condensations in their word usage and thought processes which, though they do not quite qualify as contaminations, are reminiscent of autistic logic. One patient when given the proverb, "Strike while the iron is hot," responded, "Sounds like something out of an ironworker's vocabulary—don't wait too long or the tea will be cold, which is to say, act swiftly, or that on which you want to act may be *unactable*." Another patient referred to the TAT as "shrink cards." Often these overcondensed responses, perhaps a structural derivative of the fused real self, ideal self, and ideal other grandiose self, are embellished with oral and oral-aggressive content. One hospitalized patient offered the following response to Card IX on the Rorschach: "A weird-looking guy on the back of an eagle sniffing coke. The bird is part lion and part bird." A hospitalized patient responded to Card VI as: lion and part bird." A hospitalized patient responded to Card VI as: "Looks like a sword in a rock or crown, it looks like the crown of Hungry. There were two crowns—one in Vienna and the other in Hungry. Franz Josef was the Emperor of Austria and also the King of Hungry. The double sword is the symbol of the Hungarian crown. The of Card VII with "Looks like identical opposites, positive and negative." Egocentric cognition coupled with impaired object constancy is frequently exhibited on the TAT in the form of naming figures and/or in a devaluing way, spelling names or words for the examiner. A nineteen-year-old inpatient began a story to the TAT "graveyard" scene with "Barnaby, know how to spell Barnaby? B-A-R-N-A-B-Y. Let me think of a good last name. Slit. Barnaby Slit... was a very mean man."

Affect Organization

While the etiology of pathological narcissism is open to question in terms of the degree that the inborn intensity of the aggressive drive infiltrates the clinical picture, genetic reconstructions in the psychoanalytic situation often reveal a chronically cold, narcissistic, and vexingly overprotective mother as a central pathogenic agent. According to Kernberg (1975),

The inclusion of the child in the narcissistic world of mother during certain periods of his early development creates the predisposition for the "specialness" of the child, around which the fantasies of the grandiose self become crystallized. The narcissistic character defenses protect the patient not only against the intensity of his narcissistic rage, but also against his deep convictions of unworthiness, his frightening image of the world as being devoid of food and love, and his self-concept of the hungry wolf out to kill, eat, and survive. [p. 276]

In other words, beneath the protective structure of the grandiose self are to be found the typical conflicts and affects of borderline personalities. Not unlike patients functioning on an overt borderline level and often because of the early occurrence of psychic trauma, narcissistic patients have difficulty integrating affects with cognition and consequently experience difficulty in controlling and modulating affective expression. Because of the grandiose self-structure the clinical presentation of the narcissistic patient is, in contrast to the borderline patient, often one of a chilling or suave and smoothly blended-in self-sufficiency (Modell, 1975), an Olympian untouchability (Kernberg, 1975) concealing an underlying object-affect hunger, concomitant fear, and powerful affect block. Affects can be regarded as a leading diagnostic indicator of narcissistic personality disorders, particularly aggression, primitive sexualization, anxiety, and depression experienced as deadness, boredom, and narcissistic injury.

Narcissistic patients who present primarily with impulse disorders and affective lability often show characteristic ways of treating color on the Rorschach. These patients will often exhibit an experience balance skewed toward color, amassing a predominance of CF and C responses over FC, indicating a failure in integrating affect and ideation. According to Schafer (1948), "the genuine lability is likely to be displayed in dramatic, but none the less artificial over-responsiveness and over-demonstrativeness," in contrast to "more rigid narcissistic characters [who] tend to give few colors, perhaps one CF or one vague C, and one or no M's; in these instances, the histrionic, demonstrative quality of behavior is usually so shallow and transient that the entire person seems like a caricature" (p. 49). Despite the action orientation of many of these patients there is a basic passivity implicit in their protocols. Commonly one finds FC arbitrary responses in which color is ascribed to the percept solely on the basis of the color seen on the blot, regardless of whether that color actually fits the object in reality (e.g., a "pink wolverine"). One hospitalized male patient offered the following response to Card X: "It looks like a yellow-eyed man with blue hair and a green mustache." These responses reflect considerable passivity toward emotions, which, as with the hysteric, just happen, with little in the way of rhyme or reason, monitoring or modulation. The differential diagnosis from the low-level hysteric or infantile personality (Sugarman, 1979) can often be made on the basis of greater depth and object relatedness on the part of the infantile personality despite the presence of narcissistic features, particularly entitlement and rage.

The affect organization of one twenty-two-year-old hospitalized narcissistic patient was described in a test report as follows: "In keeping with his narcissistic character style the patient's affective life seemingly has an 'as if' insincere quality to it. Feelings have a dramatic, short-lived quality to them. Thus, his superficial hyperemotionality and excitability conceals a hyperalertness, vigilance, and anxious restlessness which serves as a defense against full-bodied emotions, especially feelings that would lead to greater closeness and hence mobilize fears of exploitation, inadequacy, and desires for merger. Underlying this avoidance of deeper levels of emotional experience is his need to avoid his depression. This depression is represented in experiences of emptiness and detachment, in a sense of loneliness, in his subtle thematic emphasis on the past, and finally in his complaints of boredom which can here be seen as a precursor of depression. The presence of depression, which is staunchly and at times rather cavalierly denied, appears rooted in fears surrounding object loss and the associated loss of oral supplies. It is not surprising that this patient uses anger, and especially oral aggression, as a defense against depressive affects. Other defenses noted were avoidance and intellectualization. As one might expect, when these devices fail the patient resorts to acting out. In addition, his emphasis on hedonism and glorification of the uninhibited provides a convenient rationalization for structured impulsivity such as drug ingestion. The modulation of his affects is fraught with difficulties, for on the one hand he is prone to a reckless exaggeration of his own capabilities, while on the other, he fears masculine competition (castration) and coming face to face with his sense of inadequacy, emptiness (loss), and alienation (self-experience)."

Aggression

The integration of aggression into the psychic structure has been identified as a prognostically crucial dimension for the treatment of narcissistic personalities (Kernberg, 1975, 1984). Aggression may be primitively split off or dissociated from libidinally invested object relations, condensed with sexual drive derivatives in the form of perverse sexual strivings, or sublimated into relatively adaptive ego functioning; each possibility represents a differential fixation/regression point, implies different clinical characteristics, and consequently calls for different treatment interventions and prognoses. In general, when aggression is integrated into existing superego structures and there is a capacity for depression, then a more uncovering or expressive treatment can be conducted and the prognosis is more favorable. Of great prognostic significance is the degree to which antisocial tendencies are embellished in the narcissistic character structure. Antisocial acts and the direct expression of sadism in sexual behavior reflect a lack of superego integration and of modulated capacity for depression, which are inversely related to the quality of object relations and thus to favorable prognosis. In general, the more aggression is integrated into the grandiose self-structure the more ego syntonic or characterological it is, and the more its sadistic expression will be accompanied by a sense of triumph or glee. Often in these cases self-esteem is enhanced by the direct expression of cruelty and by inflicting pain on others. These individuals, who essentially are in psychotherapy, often use the treatment situation as an outlet for their aggression and manifest an extraordinary capacity for projection and blaming. Not surprisingly, their Rorschach protocols reflect exploitativeness, sadistic pleasure in aggression, and a prevalence of paranoid features.

The repetitive activation of intense anger accompanied by ruthless demands and depreciating attacks in the treatment setting has been termed "narcissistic rage" by many clinicians (Kernberg, 1975). This excessive degree of preoedipal aggression can be gleaned from TAT stories that emphasize aggression and antisocial acts as well as sudden reversals involving retaliation and the talion principle (superego precursors of a primitive and sadistic nature). Rorschach responses involving explosions reflecting passivity as well as several "m" responses (inanimate movement) indicate that affects may be experienced as diffuse tension states and acted out. Often preoedipal aggression can be distinguished, on the basis of content, from a developmentally more advanced phallic aggression: Is the content more oral, involving teeth and mouths, or is it more phallic, involving rockets? Are themes of triangular relationships and object loss present on the TAT? How modulated is the expression of aggression?

The following examples illustrate various degrees to which aggression may be modulated on the TAT, Rorschach, and Early Memories tests. One hospitalized sixteen-year-old with a history of fighting, stealing, and drug abuse offered the following story to Card 15, the graveyard scene on the TAT: "Satan's child is standing in a graveyard trying to find out whose soul he is going to take. He is standing in front of a cross but he is going to take the soul. A big white hand comes down and crushes him. God's way—he was taking a soul." He offered the following story to the next card (14): "A guy just picked a door on the house and he is going in to rob it. He sees a case of beer—takes that—finds a whole mess of money—goes out and parties out. He doesn't get caught. It's his neighbor across the street." Oral aggression is expressed in his response to Card IX of the Rorschach: "Two wizards with machine guns in their mouths and they are shooting lightning out of their fingers."

The complex dynamic relationship between aggression, depression, and splitting defenses is illustrated in the response of a twenty-six-year-old female outpatient to Card II on the Rorschach. Her free association was, "An odd-shaped rocket blasting off into space" (m). This patient elaborated upon the response on inquiry: "Middle part, nose cone, odd-shaped. Not as streamlined as rockets. Fire coming out of it on the bottom. Could be a clown. A clown face or a mask. Eyes in consternation. Sadness. A mustache, no a beard and mouth. Hairy face. Red. Kind of looks like blood dripping but it doesn't fit in with sadness. Fits in with horror." This same patient's intellectualizing, distancing, paranoid, and devaluating defenses, her profound boundary disturbance, and her low self-esteem associated with intensely sexualized oral aggression are reflected in her second response to Card X: "Two animals holding up a long pole of some kind. Maybe rats or rodents standing on top of a pink cliff." On inquiry: "They're holding up a symbolic stake. It's like a fertilizing device and they're trying to aim it at the seed, but if they're successful the fertilizing of the seed will release the homunculi already released, but they were grabbed by the crab and ah, which killed them and you see blood dripping. It's dry blood now and you see this blue monster with a, could be a blue monster crab, trying to interfere with the two rodents. If it's separate from the picture it could be sad suns."

The condensation of aggression with sexual drive material can yield sadistically embellished polymorphous perverse activities, fantasies, and projective test content. A seventeen-year-old female patient with a history of sexual acting out and desultory relationships offered a Rorschach protocol replete with a counterphobic emphasis on sexuality associated with a confusion of intimacy and annihilation. On Card VI she responded, "A guy made love to a girl and he went in the belly button and came out where he was supposed to go in. Also it looks like it's on fire—the upper part is him, his genitals. The top part looks like it's on fire, actually the whole thing looks like it's burning. The heat of passion, pain; always liked that one, it always had possibilities." The representation of this compelling, sadomasochistic interaction is most likely rooted in this patient's early adoption and her core sense of self as rejected, unwanted, and powerless. This intensely affective response, bearing little relation to the stimulus properties of the blot, shows a confusion regarding body parts, a breach of the inner-outer boundary, and a general disregard of reality. Her frantic turning to men reflects a fear of her own rage, a fusion of early oral and genital urges, and a view of the penis as a breast providing nurturance to her stomach rather than to her vagina. The confused gender identification of this response reveals her fantasy that the sexual act is a conduit to her biological parents ("belly button"), as well as an identification with masculine strength and with the aggressor in order to defend against intense rage, rejection, and loss.

This patient absconded from the hospital with another patient in the sample used for this study. They eventually married. He offered the following response to the same card: "Oh my God! This looks like an inkblot. I get no response to this one—the parts don't remind me of anything—just a big stain. Is that possible? I see nothing—the second you gave it to me I didn't see anything. Wait a minute. Can I take part of a part away? If I take away these sides and these tentacles from here it reminds me of a penis. Other than that it reminds me of nothing. An atom bomb exploding." One sees in this response the immediate experience of being overwhelmed ("Oh my God!"), a massive defensive effort, based on denial, to regain a sense of reality by a cognitive regression to concreteness ("an inkblot"), and the breakdown of denial secondary to the emergence of highly charged aggression ("An atom bomb exploding"). The juxtaposition of penis with explosion suggests that sexuality is experienced as a highly aggressive, attacking, and destructive act.

Freud (1927) regarded fetishism, a perversion, as a complicated defensive denial of the lack of a female penis. In this regard, the fetish is thought to represent the female penis, one under the fetishist's control. The couple mentioned above engaged in polymorphously perverse sexual activities including fetishism. The male offered several Rorschach rare detail responses involving the vagina. On Card II he responded, "Looks like a vagina, a clitoris from the shape of it." On inquiry, "Just the separation where the blot was folded looks white—it's like light pink and the red is the majora and the light inside is the clitoris inside. The shape of the pink accented by the white." Again, on Card VII, "The bottom in the middle looks like another vagina and clitoris, except this one looks like you're looking at it from the woman's feet with her legs just slightly apart. Just seeing it from the upper thigh. I can also see her anus and that's because, not so much the shape but the coloring, the shading."

It should be emphasized that not all patients with pathological narcissism are affectively labile. Many patients are extremely inhibited, shy, and constricted in their approach to affective material and produce extremely meager, coarctated Rorschach protocols. These patients constrict their productivity in consequence of poor anxiety tolerance and a strong need to avoid nonstructured situations or any threat to emotional control. These inhibited patients, often confused with schizoid personalities, generate few responses, and these tend to be mundane, popular, and relatively non-articulated. Human or human detail responses tend to be of the quasi-human variety, involving a distancing of objects and affects in time and space. Color naming or color avoidance responses are common among these patients. They are extremely fearful of affects, they experience difficulty integrating affect with action and ideation, and they strive to contain affective expression through inhibition. The more constricted narcissistic personality often "tacks on" color to Rorschach responses in a half-hearted, rather bland way. The F/C response (e.g., "a gnarled tree trunk, it's a bluish green") often involves "cold" as opposed to "hot" colors, as well as lifeless, sterile content. With these patients both sides of the experience balance are constricted but weighted toward M.

Some constricted narcissistic patients maintain an illusion of self-sufficiency through aloofness and detachment (Modell, 1975; see also Chapter 3). These patients live in a cocoon where nothing leaves and nothing enters; they prefer to be left alone. One outpatient offered the following story to Card 8 on the TAT: "At the border of Russia and Poland there is a sentry guard that watches the gate. He spends all night watching the gate and nothing ever happens. No one ever comes and the guard gets very bored." The developmental origins and dynamics of this type of narcissistic character style is depicted in a sequence of three early memories offered by a twenty-three-year-old outpatient graduate student. "I was on the floor with my twin sister. We were crawling around before we were school age and I remember my two older sisters leaving for school or at least not being there. I felt very alone with my sister. I didn't experience Mother or Father or a baby-sitter, very much like I was in my own world. It was cartoony, like two kids crawling away from their parents. I feel myself being left. I'm feeling some independence, I didn't have to go to school. Fairly pleasant, kind of independent, no needs, just crawl around and scribble in the cubbyhole. And the sense of being left."

When asked to recall his happiest memory, this patient said: "I was in camp, there was a fellow who was a counselor or a cook. He operated these powered hand-controlled airplanes. He would take me on his airplane flying adventures. The first time he let me control one of his plastic planes—they're hand-controlled—there was a little fear that I was going to crash it, which I did. It was held together with rubber bands. When it was time to leave, I never said goodbye. I'm looking out of my eyes. I see parts of my own body. I see this man, don't remember his face, kind of tall. When I go to say goodbye, being ready to go, and deciding not to go up to him to say goodbye. It was a charged area, very uncomfortable, something like ambivalence with a charge. I was seven or eight."

When asked to recall a "special memory," he offered the following: "After I argued with my sister or was confined to my room when I was young, or for whatever reason I was forced to be alone. I have the fondest memory of playing with my Lego set, and a drawer with mechanical things, parts not wholes, things to be put together. It had a magical sense. It was never so bad to be sent to my room. I see my hands as I work." Asked what he was feeling then, he answered, "A little angry and sad but it all worked out in my hands. I was building. These fondest memories are building things, being off by myself. It comes back as pleasing."

Anxiety

Narcissistic patients have difficulty tolerating anxiety, which, when experienced, is extremely disruptive to their functioning. As Kohut (1977) observes, the subjective experience of anxiety in these individuals can readily lead to dissolution of the self-representation and, with it, a painful sense of disintegration and fragmentation. It is not surprising that the grandiose self-structure and associated borderline defenses found in these patients are extremely rigid. As mentioned previously, the ego functions of attention and concentration tapped by the Digit Span and Arithmetic subtests on the WAIS are acutely vulnerable to anxiety. The action orientation of these patients, frequently revealed by higher Performance than Verbal scores on the WAIS, reflect and in part serve to bind anxiety.

Traditionally, the way individuals experience anxiety on the Rorschach is determined by responses to shading (Ch), that is, by variations in lightness and darkness, distance or vista, or three-dimensionality. Interestingly, the presentation of dark or heavily shaded cards (IV, V, VI) frequently evokes a motoric response from narcissistic patients, such as picking up or rotating the card, touching the textured portion of the blot, or covering a segment of the blot with the hand (eliminating shading) in framing a response. As Sugarman (1980) notes, these patients often react to shaded areas of the blot without being able to integrate it into the response process. Thus, a response can obviously be determined by shading but not mentioned during inquiry. This reflects the difficulty narcissistic patients have integrating anxiety. When shading is used as a determinant, the content of the response can indicate the source of anxiety. An exhibitionistic, hospitalized male patient responded to Card IV: "Give me a break, it looks like a big-footed beaver hide with the inside of the hide facing up. The big foot, the beaver's big foot, it got mushed, squished." On inquiry: "A great big tail, tiny ears and head, and the light color of the top reminds me of a beaver's teeth or mouth. The shading made it look like a hide." This peculiar, shifting, and fabulized response blends phallic and orally aggressive themes, with the experience of anxiety about phallic prowess and integrity initially displaced to the foot counter-phobically ("big") and subsequently seen as secondary to a core sense of self as phallically damaged ("mushed, squished") and shamefully humiliated ("inside of the hide facing up"). The blend of "big foot" and "beaver" may also suggest perversion in general, and a foot fetish in particular, as a sexualized means of binding castration anxiety.

More commonly in seriously disturbed narcissistic patients one sees the experience of anxiety replaced by vigilance and hyperalertness. In terms of the response process on the Rorschach, anxiety is defensively modulated by using shading to carve out forms (c) frequently in rare and relatively undifferentiated areas of the blot (Dr). In Chapter 3 Paul Lerner describes experiential and structural aspects of the (c) Rorschach response in patients with narcissistic character pathology. Lerner relates this type of response to a number of dimensions of character pathology including self-system, defensive structure, affects, and cognitive regression. To achieve a (c) response one must seek out, scan, and attune to finer nuances as well as feel one's way into something that is not obviously apparent. Cognitively and stylistically, this requires a perceptual sensitivity and penetrating activity. According to Lerner, this hypervigilant and hypersensitive style is used defensively to ward off affects, especially those leading to greater intimacy or lowered self-esteem. Further, Lerner has found this style to be associated with depletion depression (Tolpin and Kohut, 1978), the use of projective identification and particular developments in treatment involving compliance and control of the therapist. Again, the content of the response can often indicate the source of anxiety. Frequently the content of (c) responses involves sexual or aggressive themes. An example of the (c) response can be gleaned from the Rorschach of the patient previously discussed. On Card X he responded, "It looks like two unicorn lice fighting each other." This percept was carved out of the middle of the upper center portion of the card. On inquiry, the patient stated, "Each one has little eyes and evil-looking mouths. Unicorns almost touch, looks like lice—it has horns. They're fighting because of the expression on their face." Here, one sees a vigilant cognitive style associated with a core sense of self as bad, as a louse. There is again a blending of oral and phallic aggression around which one can observe a contamination ("unicorn lice"), the structural equivalent of a disruption of the self/other boundary. One inference that can be drawn from this response is that the patient may resort to aggression and sexual activity, including homosexuality, as a paranoid defense against depletion and fragmentation experiences secondary to a structural weakness in his self-representation.

It should also be noted that the (c) response has been associated by several authors with the presence of suicidal tendencies (Appelbaum and Holtzman, 1962; Blatt, 1978). Lerner relates the (c) response with the precipitants of suicidal behavior in narcissistic patients. These precipitants relate to the nature of self-experience and the quality of object relations and include fear of impending fragmentation of the self, a dramatic or cumulative loss in self-esteem, and a yearning for symbiotic attachment with a lost or nonrepresented object.

The disruptive impact of anxiety on patients with narcissistic personalities can also become apparent in test-taking behavior and in the examiner-patient interaction. Under the protective shield of the grandiose self can be observed a motor restlessness as well as the presence of quick, tense movements, whether on the Block Design subtest of the WAIS, in manipulating the Rorschach cards, or in rather strained efforts to express affect. Some patients express anxiety through vigilance and a scrutiny of the examiner, sizing up critically any comment or action he or she may make. Such vigilance in the patient may evoke a countervigilance in the examiner, which can inhibit inquiry and other facets of test administration.

Depression

While the conceptual and clinical status of depression in narcissistic patients remains controversial, dysphoric affect and such equivalents as emptiness, deadness, and boredom are common subjective experiences of narcissistic patients and are manifested on psychological tests. Frequently, both in behavior and test responses, one can observe in the narcissistic personality powerful defenses against affects in general (Modell, 1975, 1980) and depression in particular. The grandiose self-structure of these patients provides a surface adaptation and pseudointegration of good and bad self-representations. The elements of this pathological structure (Kernberg, 1975) are the real self of childhood, the ideal self, and the ideal object (Sandler and Rosenblatt, 1962); these fuse defensively due to anxieties of the practicing substage. Confronted with the shocking awareness of separateness from the maternal object, the nascent narcissist is threatened with the loss of infantile omnipotence and the need-satisfying object. Formation of the grandiose self-structure fosters a compensatory illusion of self-sufficiency and a denial of true separateness. Projective tests permit a clinically rich glimpse of what underlies the grandiose self and constitutes the major source of depression for narcissistic personalities—representations ranging from profound oral neediness and hunger to poignant fears of smallness, inadequacy, and weakness. It is this author's opinion that depression, as both an affective experience and a clinical phenomenon is far more common in narcissistic personalities than is usually thought.

Our understanding of depressive experience in narcissistic personalities is limited by the lack of a unified psychoanalytic theory of depression and by unresolved conceptual issues regarding the question of separate developmental lines for narcissism and object relations. Blatt (1974), using a developmental model of object representation, articulated two types of depression—an oral, less structured anaclitic type of depression and a developmentally more advanced and structured superego or introjective type. According to Blatt, anaclitic depression evolves developmentally from a stage beyond the achievement of basic self/other differentiation, in which needs for nurturance and direct soothing contact with a need-satisfying part object are paramount. The object is experienced primarily at a sensorimotor pre-operational level, the other is valued for its need-satisfying functions, and its loss provokes experiences of abandonment and a search for immediate substitutes. Subjectively, anaclitic depression is characterized by feelings of weakness, helplessness, vulnerability, and depletion as well as intense desires to be loved, cared for, and fed in an immediate and direct fashion.

In contrast to the orality and relatively undifferentiated organization of anaclitic depression, introjective depression involves both a greater degree of self/other differentiation and struggles with a harsh, punitive, and critical superego. Objects in this configuration, according to Blatt, are represented as unintegrated, split-off, and ambivalent, based on exaggerated and overstated part properties. The depressive experience involves less a loss of need gratification than of the object's love, approval, and acceptance. There is an intense preoccupation with performance, achievement, and perfection as a means of achieving approval and recognition. Subjectively, introjective depression is characterized by feelings of guilt and worthlessness, and a sense of shame and failure in meeting expectations and standards.

Blatt and Shichman (1983) have broadened these formulations into a comprehensive developmental model of psychopathology based on two primary configurations or developmental lines—the anaclitic and the introjective—and draw important distinctions between these schemas along the dimensions of cognition, object relations, and defensive structure. This model has implications for conceptualizing depressive experience in patients exhibiting pathological narcissism. In general, the more impulsive, orally needy, and infantile narcissistic patients are (Sugarman, 1979), the more they can be expected to experience depression anaclitically. Conversely, the more phallic issues dominate the clinical picture, the more the patient can be expected to experience depression introjectively. Thus, the degree of ego structuralization and hence ego weakness, as well as self/other differentiation, may in the absence of other signs of depression be considered the leading test indicators of the developmental level at which dysphoric affect is organized. This is to say that a certain level of ego structuralization involving evocative object constancy is required for the reflective experience of depression, particularly object loss, in contrast to an affect state that is dysphoric but is experienced subjectively in a less articulated manner. Boredom, fatigue, feelings of meaninglessness, and somatic preoccupations are depressive equivalents commonly experienced by narcissistic patients, particularly when presented with depressive stimuli.

Equivalents of particular types of depression can often be gleaned from the content of TAT stories. A hospitalized adolescent male told the following story to Card 13 MF: "The guy just laid this chick after drinking the night before—he was supposed to be at home at ten last night. He goes home and gives his wife a big story. She kicks him out, he goes back to this woman and marries her and everything works out." Asked how the man feels about losing his wife, the patient answered, "He has another one." While this story may reflect the dynamic meaning of the separation-individuation process by which adolescents disengage from parental objects (Blos, 1979), the story illustrates the compelling anaclitic need for immediate gratification and the search for immediate substitutes when confronted with object loss. While little in the way of depressive affect is expressed in this story, one may infer from its structure that this patient is prone to anaclitic depression and to defend against profound feelings of emptiness, helplessness, and worthlessness through impulsive action, denial, and the virulent devaluation of objects.

As for the Rorschach, several authors have drawn a relationship between the use of achromatic color (C′), and depression (Rapaport, Gill, and Schafer, 1945; Schafer, 1948, 1954; Allison, Blatt, and Zimet, 1968; Mayman and Appelbaum, 1974). The use of any particular sign on the Rorschach must also be considered relative to other dimensions and variables. While some patients are drawn to black and gray areas of the blot and generate several C′ responses, others strenuously avoid mentioning C′ on inquiry, even when it is obviously used as a determinant. The degree of C′ avoidance can be taken as an indicator of difficulty with and defenses against depressive experience. It is not unusual to see a depressive structure in Rorschach responses (C′) coupled with nondepressive content. Again, this can be understood as a defense against dysphoric affect.

Narcissistic injury is the major source of depressive affect for these patients. An eighteen-year-old hospitalized girl offered several Rorschach responses indicative of a core sense of self as damaged, exploited, and victimized. These self-representations stood in stark contrast to her veneer of self-sufficiency as well as popularity and admiration. Rorschach images of a "bark chip or a moth trying to look like one, more like a flake," "an alligator coming out of the mud," and "a skinned cat" may be regarded as self-representations. On Card V she offered the following response: "A wet moth, a really tired wet moth. The wings were drooping—it looks bleak, like a foggy, wet day and it can't find some place to go." The structure of this response involves C′ used symbolically (distanced) and a transparency which is correlated with suicidality (Blatt and Ritzler, 1974). It appears that despite a facade of competence and of being socially accepted this patient experiences her self as nonexistent, hiding, stuck, and melting away.

A twenty-five-year-old hospitalized female patient offered a Rorschach protocol replete with responses depicting damage and decay. Her first response was, "A candle—just looks like one of those cheap candles you buy in a grocery store. Partially burned down." On Card IV this patient saw "a broken weathered leaf. A dead leaf." On inquiry she stated, "Looks like it died and it's all dry. Broken and torn in places." This response was followed by "A rusted, bent, broken crown, rusted away on the edges. Shading gives appearance of it being kicked or thrown around. Maybe it was in the sea and thrown around by the current." Further, "Maybe a bug crawling out from under a log—could be a shell. I think that's a slug. If you put salt on it they wither up." This patient's sadism and devaluing defenses can be understood as stemming from a core sense of self as discarded, devalued, and smelly.

PATHOLOGICAL INTERNALIZED OBJECT RELATIONS

The grandiose self-structure and its constituent elements of real self, ideal self, and ideal other, as well as what this structure compensates for and defends against, are the nexus for pathological internalized object relations in narcissistic patients. According to Kernberg (1975, 1980, 1984), this highly pathological structure is a defining characteristic of narcissistic personality disorders, distinguishes narcissism from borderline conditions while showing their relation, and is responsible for the social facade of narcissistic patients on the one hand and their fear of intimate interpersonal relationships on the other. Taking narcissistic resistance and related defenses in the course of psychoanalytic treatment as a point of departure, Kernberg (1975) notes:

> [N]arcissistic personalities repeat in the transference early processes of devaluation of significant external objects and of their intrapsychic representations as a secondary elaboration and defense against underlying conflicts around oral rage and envy. They need to destroy the sources of love and gratification in order to eliminate the source of envy and projected rage, while simultaneously withdrawing into the grandiose self which represents a primitive refusion of the idealized images of the parental figures and idealized images of the self, so that they escape from a vicious circle of anger, frustration and aggressive devaluation of the

potential source of gratification at the cost of serious damage to internalized object relations. In short, devaluation processes rationalized as "disappointment" reactions in the transference repeat pathological devaluation of parental images, while the defensive structure of the grandiose self actualizes the pathological condensation of components stemming from object relationships reflecting those conflicts. . . . The narcissistic character defenses protect the patient not only against the intensity of his narcissistic rage, but also against his deep convictions of unworthiness, his frightening image of the world as being devoid of food and love, and his self-concept of the hungry wolf out to kill, eat, and survive. [pp. 275–276]

The internal object world of the narcissistic personality is populated by the grandiose self and its numerous reciprocals—highly devalued, "shadowy" representations of self and others—and by persecutory objects (unintegrated sadistic superego forerunners), as well as by primitive, fantastically distorted object representations which contain intense projected sadism. The formation of the grandiose self allows for a certain degree of ego integration which in turn provides a higher level of social adaptation that is seen in more overtly borderline patients. According to Kernberg (1975), "The splitting of the self characteristic of borderline patients is thus compensated for, but at the price of a further deterioration of object relationships, the loss of the capacity to depend, and an ominous capacity for self-protection from emotional conflicts with others by withdrawing into the splendid, grandiose isolation which gives the specific seal to the narcissistic organization" (p. 282).

Patients with narcissistic personality disorders, like borderline patients in general and in contrast to their own social facade of charm and attractiveness, relate to others as part objects and have difficulty with object constancy—with experiencing others as whole, autonomous human beings, particularly in their absence. Primary manifestations of the internal object world of the narcissistic patient occur on the Rorschach test, can be seen in both the structure and the content of responses, and revolve around test expressions of the grandiose self as well as "shadowy" and devalued self- and object images underlying the grandiose self. Grandiose images of clowns, masks, coats of arms, medals, and other symbols of prestige, power, and importance are common. Whereas in narcissistic personalities functioning at a higher level these percepts can be understood as false self equivalents (see

Chapter 3), the more the response is embellished with aggression the greater the likelihood of more severe superego pathology and deterioration of internal object relations, as well as of paranoid manifestations in treatment. Grandiosity and representations of the grandiose self are intimately related to depreciation and envy. Lerner and Lerner (1980) consider Rorschach manifestations of devaluation to be a muted form of spoiling associated with envy. An example of this can be seen in the response of an Hispanic patient to Card II: "Two pigs dancing snout to snout or two Middle Eastern, not Middle Eastern, Middle European peasants dancing in a folk dance—women probably, peasants."

The need to spoil or devalue the object of envy can also work its way into the response process itself in terms of the form-spoil (Fs) response, by which an acceptable response (F +, Fo, Fw+) is spoiled by a perceptual oversight or distortion. An example of a form-spoil response is, "A person but instead of a mouth, there's a bird's beak." Spoiling can be manifested similarly on the WAIS when a correct response is changed, an easy question answered in a flip (1-point or 0) manner, or through intra-subtest scatter when easier questions are answered incorrectly while more difficult items are handled skillfully. More blatant grandiose, devalued, and spoiled content can be gleaned from the TAT, which, with more malignant forms of narcissism, may be infiltrated with sadism, sudden turns of events, and a generally depreciatory view of intimacy. Spelling words or punctuating stories is a way of "talking down to" or "giving dictation" to the examiner, and these patients also tend to give proper names to TAT figures (see the "Barnaby Slit" response reported above) by way of grandiose compensation for deficits in object constancy and confusion regarding object relations.

The complex interplay between the grandiose self-structure and the underlying "shadowy" object images can often be detected on the Rorschach through a sequence analysis. Using Blatt's Object Scale (Blatt, Brenneis, Schimek, and Glick, 1976), a research instrument designed to assess the representation of human figures on the Rorschach in terms of degree of differentiation, articulation, and integration. Blatt and Lerner (1983) analyzed the human representations of five prototypical patients, each representing a particular diagnostic category. The object representations of each case were analyzed in detail and conclusions were drawn about the developmental level and configurations of object representations in different forms of psychopathology. In describing the Rorschach object representations of a "borderline-narcissistic character disorder," Blatt and Lerner (1983) note:

> The initial object representation responses in this protocol are intact and accurately perceived, full human figures. As the record progresses, however, the representations quickly move to quasi-human and partial figures; and the last two responses are inaccurately perceived and inappropriately elaborated. Thus, throughout the protocol there is a gradual deterioration of the quality of object representations from initially accurate, well-differentiated and articulated full human figures to quasi-human or part properties, which are eventually inaccurately perceived and extensively elaborated in inappropriate ways. [p. 16]

Another object-relational phenomenon characteristic of some cases of narcissistic pathology are Rorschach responses involving twins, mirrors, and reflections. These responses convey a certain self-absorption and self-involvement in that the other either exists as an extension of the self or mirrors the self (Kwawer, 1980). One hospitalized sixteen-year-old girl offered several mirror-type responses to the Rorschach, the quality of which deteriorated over the course of the ten blots. She responded to Card II: "It looks like a clown going up to a mirror and putting his hand on the mirror and making a face of himself so it looks like there are two people, but there's really only one." On Card III she saw "two women throwing, picking things up from the ground and throwing them over their heads—both at the same time so that it looks like almost a mirror image." Her response to Card V was, "The character from Midsummer Night's Dream. Puck. He's resting against a tree and there is the water somehow being reflected in the water or a mirror so there's a double image." On Card VII she saw "a little girl with a big pigtail looking in the mirror and putting her arms in back of her. Sitting on the ground looking in the mirror—she has a sort of, like a turned-up nose." Her final response on Card X was, "Looks like a human rock 'n' roll show, it looks like an alien rock 'n' roll show." This patient was described as follows in the psychological test report: "the patient takes a detached stance which is impressively concealed by the use of her exquisite sensitivity to social norms and expectations and her remarkable capacity to present herself as she wishes to be perceived. The superficiality and 'as if' character of her interpersonal involvements is revealed in both the brittleness of the images she conveys and its overlearned quality. It is the consequence of this identity diffusion which is telling, however, for she has rather striking difficulty differentiating her actual internal states from images of herself that she creates in others. Her frequent perception of mirror images on the Rorschach speak quite graphically to both her reliance upon the reflection of herself in others in order to know herself and on the pseudomutual and need-gratifying quality of her relationships."

DEFENSIVE STRUCTURE

Theoretical Considerations

Based on a complex integration of ego psychology and object relations theory, Kernberg (1975, 1976, 1980, 1984) reconceptualized more traditional notions of psychic conflict as not simply a clash between impulse and defense, but as friction between two opposing units of internalized object relations. According to Kernberg, each set consists of a self- and an object representation linked by a drive derivative or manifested clinically as an affect disposition. Kernberg's theoretical formations and clinical illustrations are supported by research evidence (Lerner and Lerner, 1982) indicating that defensive functioning and representational capacity are inextricably related. This is to say that defenses are organized object relationally and consist of various constellations of self- and object representations.

Lerner and Lerner (1982) have outlined how defensive functioning and representational capacity can be conceptualized on a developmental-structural continuum. Defenses at the lowest developmental level (psychotic structure) are dominated by primitive, often somatically based drive-affective dispositions. Defenses on this level are pre-object representational and represent a fundamental failure in integration. As development proceeds and a representational capacity is achieved ("the psychological birth of the infant"), defenses increasingly assume an organizing function and protect the cohesion and integrity of poorly differentiated self- and object representations. Self- and object representations of this more borderline structural level are initially inconsistent and unstable owing to the permeability of the self/other boundary that will eventually form the chrysalis of the inner/outer boundary. Representations on this level are internalized as crude and global positive and negative images based on fantasy-drenched part properties of the object. In consequence of the polarization along drive-affective lines of self- and object representations, object relations have a "transitional object" quality characterized by a confusion among the external object, its inner representation, and the affective response to it. What are regarded as borderline defenses—splitting, projective identification, denial, primitive devaluation, idealization—are represented object relationally, serve a primitive organizing function, and simultaneously reflect the relatively undifferentiated, incompletely internalized or metabolized quality of the representation. At higher, more neurotic developmental and structural levels characterized by evocative object constancy (that is, enhanced affective-cognitive differentiation and representational capacity), more encapsulated defenses, limited in scope and related to specific drive-affective derivatives, function to protect a well-structuralized ego from anxiety stemming from conflict between intrapsychic structures composed of specific, more fully internalized self- and object representations.

While pathological narcissism can be conceptualized and is seen clinically on a structural continuum between borderline and neurotic levels, the following will focus on the defensive structure of more seriously disturbed, often hospitalized narcissistic patients. According to Kernberg (1975), the defensive structure of those patients is predominantly borderline; that is, underlying the facade of relatively good social functioning and beneath the grandiose self-structure, one frequently finds in long-term intensive psychoanalytic psychotherapy as well as on Rorschach test protocols manifestations of typically borderline defenses such as splitting, denial, projective identification, primitive devaluation and idealization, and omnipotence. In general, more malignant forms of narcissism involve chronic and intense envy and defenses against such envy, particularly devaluation. Less blatant expressions of devaluation, frequently replaced by distancing or narcissistic withdrawal, also defend against envy but represent a higher developmental level of disturbance and thus a better prognosis. In what follows, the narcissistic defenses of splitting, denial, primitive devaluation and idealization, and omnipotence will be briefly defined and Rorschach illustrations offered. Those interested in more detailed examinations of these defenses are referred to Lerner and Lerner (1980), Lerner, Sugarman, and Gaughran (1981), Lerner and Lerner (1982), Cooper and Arnow (1984), and Cooper, Perry, and Arnow (unpublished); those interested in projective identification are referred to Chapter 3. It should be noted that a major unresolved issue in the

Rorschach literature on defensive functioning involves the appropriate unit of analysis (human responses or all responses). In keeping with the object relations theory foundation of this review and the empirical relationship found to obtain between object relations and the spectrum of human responses (Lerner and St. Peter, 1984), the following illustrations revolve around Rorschach manifestations of defenses based largely on human (H and Hd) and humanoid ([H] and [Hd]) responses. The work of Cooper and his colleagues subsumes this approach and extends it to a consideration of all Rorschach responses and content.

Splitting

Splitting as a defense involves an admixture of separations of drives, affects, object representations, and external object relations (Robbins, 1976). According to Pruyser (1975), splitting involves a division of internal and external into (1) parts as distinct from wholes and (2) good and bad part objects. While splitting is characterized by a propensity to perceive and describe self and others in terms of overriding polarities, these divisions may take several forms—good-bad, frustrating-satisfying, dangerous-benign, friendly-hostile, strong-weak, close-distant. The tendency to polarize affective descriptions of objects underlies projective test manifestations of splitting.

Lerner and Lerner (1980) assess splitting on the Rorschach along four dimensions. First, in a sequence of responses, a percept described in terms of a specific, nonambiguous affect is immediately followed by another response in which the affective description is the opposite of that used in the preceding response. Examples of splitting include "Part of a skull covered by decay. Decaying flesh" followed by "a lady in New Orleans Mardi Gras costume." Second, in the description of one figure, a clear distinction is made so that part of the figure is seen as opposite to another part: "A giant. His lower part here conveys danger, but his top half looks benign" (Lerner and Lerner, 1980). Third, included in one response are two clearly distinguished figures, each described as opposite to the other: "Two figures, a man and a woman. He is mean and shouting at her. Being rather angelic, she's standing there and taking it" (Lerner and Lerner, 1980). Fourth, an implicitly idealized figure is tarnished or spoiled by the addition of one or more features or an implicitly devalued figure is enhanced by the addition of one or more features: "A headless angel."

Denial

Lerner and Lerner (1980), drawing on the work of Holt (1970) view denial in terms of a number of subsidiary defenses arranged on a severity continuum based on the degree of reality distortion in the Rorschach response. Manifestations of denial at a higher, more neurotic level involve adequate form level (F+, Fo, Fw+) and include negation ("virgin," "this person isn't angry"); intellectualization ("homunculi"); minimization ("a shadow cast by an evil person"); and repudiation (the patient retracts a response or denies having given it).

At a somewhat more severe middle level, denial takes the form of adequate form level or reality testing, but involved in the response is a fundamental contradiction. The contradiction may be logical, affective, or factual: "sad suns"; "two unborn fetuses"; "two pigs dancing snout to snout"; and "two sexy nuns."

At an even more severe level of denial, reality adherence is abrogated when an acceptable form level response is spoiled by adding something that is not there or by failing to take account of an aspect of the blot that is clearly to be seen. In keeping with middle-level expressions of denial, this more severe level also includes responses in which incompatible descriptions of the same object are offered. Lerner and Lerner (1980) advance the following examples: "two people, but their top half are female and bottom half male. Each has breasts and a penis"; "a person, but instead of a mouth there is a bird's beak"; "person sitting on their huge tail."

Devaluation

Devaluation is a central defense in more pathological forms of narcissism and refers to a tendency to depreciate, tarnish, and lessen the importance, and hence the danger, of one's inner and outer objects. It is closely linked to envy and has been conceptualized as both an aim of envy and as a defense against it. According to Segal (1973), envy aims at being as good as the object; when this is felt to be unattainable, however, it seeks to spoil that goodness and thus remove the source of the envious feeling. The amount of aggression manifested in the test situation may be considered a general barometer of devaluing processes; nevertheless, more subtle forms of devaluation can be seen in passive-aggressive interactions with the examiner, the patient's excessively critical attitude toward his own responses or the test materials, the use of idiosyncratic, intellectual, or technical language, etc. Lerner and Lerner (1980) assess devaluation along a continuum of severity involving three dimensions: (1) the degree to which the humanness of the response is retained (H, Hd, [H], [Hd], (2) a spatiotemporal dimension involving the degree to which the figure seen is contemporary or placed in past or future, and (3) the severity of depreciation as conveyed in the affective description of the object. Percepts described in more primitive, blatant, socially unacceptable ways are considered more pathological than those described in negatively tinged but modulated ways. The following examples illustrate the continuum and dimensional aspects of devaluation (Lerner and Lerner, 1980): "two people fighting"; "a diseased African child"; "cannibal standing over a pot"; "two people from Mars who look very scary"; "a woman with breasts, high-heeled shoes, and bird's beak for a mouth."

Idealization

Idealization involves a denial of unwanted characteristics of the self or object and the enhancement of the object by projecting one's own omnipotence onto it. Idealization is thought to be inextricably related to aggression and devaluation and aims to keep an object completely separate from internal persecutory objects, thus preserving the external object from harm and destruction. Idealization as a defense in narcissistic patients is precarious in that the more ideal the object becomes the more likely it is to arouse envy. Lerner and Lerner (1980) assess idealization along the same severity continuum and dimensions as devaluation. The following examples illustrate degrees of idealization: "a person with a happy smile"; "two handsome, muscular Russians doing that famous dance"; "Mickey Mantle"; "a warrior—not just any warrior but the tallest, strongest, and bravest"; "a bust of Queen Victoria."

Omnipotence

Cooper and Arnow (1984), drawing on the formulations of Kernberg (1975) as well as of Stolorow and Lachmann (1980), have operationalized Rorschach indices of omnipotence, a cardinal defense of narcissistic patients. Omnipotence as a defense is conceptualized by Cooper and Arnow as an idealization of the self "in which there is an unconscious conviction that one deserves to be lauded by others and treated as privileged" (p. 30). Omnipotence is also seen as a defense against aggression as well as its reciprocal—profound feelings of smallness, weakness, and ineffectiveness. As Cooper and Arnow note, omnipotence can be seen in the testing situation through comments on the patient's part regarding remarkable test-taking abilities, unique capacities outside the testing situation, and special powers and capacities. They offer the following Rorschach illustration of grandiose fantasies of magical omnipotence: "I think you are going to hear some very distinctive responses. My vocabulary is incredible." The compensatory nature of omnipotence was demonstrated by one patient who continually came to sessions after parking her car in front of the building in a parking zone for the handicapped. A fifty-dollar ticket occasioned narcissistic rage but did not change her behavior.

Cooper and Arnow (1984) further operationalized omnipotence through Rorschach responses in which the patient perceives himself in the blot and offers excessive, self-aggrandizing remarks following the response: "Looks like a beautiful woman with a full, formal gown, that looks like me when I was dressed up to go to the prom. I was the prettiest girl at the prom that night" (p. 32). Rorschach responses involving percepts of aggrandized, special, gifted, or treasured objects such as crowns, jewels, status symbols, and art objects may be associated with grandiose tendencies and omnipotence. Cooper and Arnow (1984) also consider the "editorial we" (Schafer, 1954, p. 241) a manifestation of omnipotence that takes the form of a pseudoidealized alliance with an object; in the test situation this may serve as a defense against being scrutinized by an inquiring examiner.

Narcissistic Withdrawal

While withdrawal or detachment has not been conceptualized as a defense, the clinical phenomenon of withdrawal is not uncommon in narcissistic patients and is frequently manifested in the patient-examiner relationship and the response process. Often stimulated by disappointment or anger in the test situation, prompted by a wrong answer, a difficult question, inquiry on the Rorschach, or some other form of "empathic failure," a certain decathexis, withholding, or letdown can be observed in the patient. Further inquiry or questioning distances the patient even more. Often this defensive response has a subtle intimidating quality that tends to pull (actually push) the examiner out of a position of neutrality into a more superego-like position of apologizing, being nice to the patient, and, in the process, away from a position of intellectual curiosity and active inquiry. In terms of the response process itself, it is not uncommon to see Rorschach responses of the quasi-human variety (clowns, witches, supermen, etc.) distanced in time and space. Often the distancing is into the future; "aliens from outer space" are not uncommon. Narcissistic withdrawal or detachment reflects a lack of authentic affective relatedness to the environment and a dynamic sense that these individuals feel that they were never known by their parents or understood by others.

TREATMENT CONSIDERATIONS

Just as psychopathology may be conceptualized along a continuum from psychosis to neurosis, so psychotherapy may be ranged along a continuum with ego-supportive and sealing-over measures at one end and expressive, uncovering, insight-oriented psychoanalytic psychotherapy and psychoanalysis at the other. Narcissism is a broad diagnostic category, narcissistic features can be found within many different character styles (e.g., obsessive compulsive–paranoid, hysterical-infantile, depressive-masochistic), and narcissistic personality disorders include near-psychotic, borderline, and neurotic levels of personality organization. The complex intersection between degree of psychopathology, level of personality organization, and questions regarding treatability and preferred treatment must be taken into account, along with degrees of specific and nonspecific ego weakness, disturbance in affective organization, pathology of internalized object relations, and defensive structure.

Kernberg (1984) uses the degree of aggressive infiltration of the grandiose self as the leading diagnostic indicator for type of treatment. The degree to which aggression is conscious, sadistic, accompanied by a sense of triumph, and ego-syntonic is the degree to which narcissism may be regarded as malignant and essentially untreatable by expressive, uncovering means. The antisocial personality and patients with sexual aberrations and perversions that are sadistic and life-threatening are unable to experience guilt, lack anxiety tolerance, are unable to place themselves, cognitively or affectively, in the position of the other, and are unable to maintain a realistic sense of time. In general, the prognostic picture improves for patients with narcissistic personality disorders with less severe superego pathology; here aggression is more ego-alien and conflict-ridden. The quality of object relations in general and the capacity to tolerate a dependent relationship and depressive affect can be regarded as important prognostic and treatment indicators. The greater the degree to which character defenses can be analyzed and the transference focused on, the better the prognosis; expressive and interpretive techniques and mutative change depend on these capacities.

REFERENCES

Allison, J., Blatt, S., & Zimet, C. (1968), *The Interpretation of Psychological Tests.* New York: Harper & Row.

Appelbaum, S., & Holzman, P. (1962), The color shading response and suicide. *J. Proj. Tech.*, 26:155-161.

Blatt, S. (1974), Levels of object representation in anaclitic and introjective depression. *Psychoanalytic Study of the Child*, 29:107-157. New Haven, CT: Yale University Press.

_____ (1978), Paradoxical representations and their implications for the treatment of psychosis and borderline states. Paper presented to the Institute for Psychoanalytic Research and Training, New York City.

_____ (1983), Narcissism and egocentrism as concepts in individual and cultural development. *Psychoanal. & Contemp. Thought*, 6:291-304.

_____ Brenneis, C., Schimek, J., & Glick, M. (1976), Normal development and psychopathological impairment of the concept of the object on the Rorschach. *J. Abnorm. Psychol.*, 85:364-373.

_____ Lerner, H. (1983), The psychological assessment of object representation. *J. Personal. Assess.*, 47:7-28.

_____ Ritzler, B. (1974), Thought disorder and boundary disturbance in psychosis. *J. Consult. & Clin. Psychol.*, 42:370-381.

_____ Shichman, S. (1983), Two primary configurations of psychopathology. *Psychoanal. & Contemp. Thought*, 6:187-254.

_____ Wein, S., Chevron, E., & Quinlan, D. (1979), Parental representations and depression in normal young adults. *J. Abnorm. Psychol.*, 88:388-397.

_____ Wild, C. (1976), *Schizophrenia: A Developmental Approach.* New York: Academic Press.

Blos, P. (1979), *The Adolescent Passage.* New York: International Universities Press.

Cooper, S., & Arnow, D. (1984), Prestage versus defensive splitting and the borderline personality: A Rorschach analysis. *Psychoanal. Psychol.*, 3:235-248.

_____ _____ (1986), An object relations view of the borderline defense: A Rorschach analysis. In: *Assessing Object Relations*, ed. M. Kissen. New York: International Universities Press, pp. 143-171.

_____ Perry, C., & Arnow, D., An empirical approach to the study of defense mechanisms: Reliability and preliminary validity of the Rorschach defense scale. Unpublished manuscript.

Eagle, M. (1984), *Contemporary Developments in Psychoanalytic Theory.* New York: Norton.

Freud, S. (1914), On narcissism: An introduction. *Standard Edition*, 14:73-102. London: Hogarth Press, 1957.

_____ (1927), Fetishism. *Standard Edition*, 21:152-157. London: Hogarth Press, 1961.

Hartmann, H. (1950), *Essays on Ego Psychology: Selected Problems in Psychoanalytic Theory.* New York: International Universities Press.

Holt, R. (1970), Manual for scoring of primary process manifestations in Rorschach responses. Unpublished manuscript, New York University Research Center for Mental Health.

Inhelder, B., & Piaget, J. (1958), *The Growth of Logical Thinking from Childhood to Adolescence: An Essay on the Construction of Formal Operational Structures.* New York: Basic Books, 1958.

Jacobson, E. (1964), *The Self and the Object World.* New York: International Universities Press.

Kernberg, O. (1975), *Borderline Conditions and Pathological Narcissism.* New York: Aronson.

———— (1976), *Object Relations Theory and Clinical Psychoanalysis.* New York: Aronson.

———— (1980), *Internal World and External Reality.* New York: Aronson.

———— (1984), *The Treatment of Severe Character Disorders.* New Haven: Yale University Press.

Kohut, H. (1971), *The Analysis of the Self.* New York: International Universities Press.

———— (1977), *The Restoration of the Self.* New York: International Universities Press.

Kwawer, J. (1980), Primitive interpersonal modes, borderline phenomena, and Rorschach content. In: *Borderline Phenomena and the Rorschach Test,* ed. J. Kwawer, H. Lerner, P. Lerner, & A. Sugarman. New York: International Universities Press, pp. 89–105.

Lerner, H., & Lerner, P. (1982), A comparative study of defensive structure in neurotic, borderline, and schizophrenic patients. *Psychoanal. & Contemp. Thought,* 5:77–115.

———— St. Peter, S. (1984), Patterns of object relations in neurotic, borderline and schizophrenic patients. *Psychiat.,* 47:77–92.

———— Sugarman, A., & Barbour, C. (1985), Patterns of ego boundary disturbance in neurotic, borderline, and schizophrenic patients. *Psychoanal. Psychol.,* 2:47–66.

———— Sugarman, A., & Gaughran, J. (1981), A comparative study of defensive structure in borderline and schizophrenic patients. *J. Nerv. & Ment. Dis.,* 169:705–711.

Lerner, P., & Lerner, H. (1980), Rorschach assessment of primitive defenses in borderline personality structure. In: *Borderline Phenomena and the Rorschach Test,* ed. J. Kwawer, H. Lerner, P. Lerner, & A. Sugarman. New York: International Universities Press, pp. 257–274.

Mahler, M., Pine, F., & Bergman, A. (1975), *The Psychological Birth of the Human Infant.* New York: Basic Books.

Masterson, J. (1972), *Treatment of the Borderline Adolescent: A Developmental Approach.* New York: Wiley.

———— (1980), *Borderline and Narcissistic Disorders.* New York: Brunner/Mazel.

Mayman, M. (1968), Early memories and character structure. *J. Proj. Tech. & Personal. Assess.,* 32:303–316.

———— Appelbaum, S. (1974), Rorschach Manual. Unpublished manuscript, Menninger Foundation.

Modell, A. (1968), *Object Love and Reality.* New York: International Universities Press.

———— (1975), A narcissistic defense against affects and the illusion of self-sufficiency. *Internat. J. Psycho-Anal.,* 56:275–282.

———— (1980), Affects and their non-communication. *Internat. J. Psycho-Anal.,* 61:259–267.

Pruyser, P. (1975), What splits in splitting? *Bull. Menn. Clin.,* 39:1–36.

Pulver, S. (1970), Narcissism: The term and the concept. *J. Amer. Psychoanal. Assn.,* 18:319–341.

Rapaport, D., Gill, M., & Schafer, R. (1945), *Diagnostic Psychological Testing.* Rev. ed. New York: International Universities Press, 1968.

Rinsley, D. (1977), An object relations view of borderline personality. In: *Borderline Personality Disorders*, ed. P. Hartocollis. New York: International Universities Press.

Robbins, M. (1976), Borderline personality organization: The need for a new theory. *J. Amer. Psychoanal. Assn.*, 24:831–854.

Sandler, J., & Rosenblatt, B. (1962), The concept of the representational world. *Psychoanalytic Study of the Child*, 17:128–145. New York: International Universities Press.

Schafer, R. (1948), *The Clinical Application of Psychological Tests*. New York: International Universities Press.

———— (1954), *Psychoanalytic Interpretations in Rorschach Testing*. New York: Grune & Stratton.

———— (1968), *Aspects of Internalization*. New York: International Universities Press.

Segal, H. (1973), *Introduction to the Work of Melanie Klein*. London: Hogarth Press.

Stolorow, R. (1975), Toward a functional definition of narcissism. *Internat. J. Psycho-Anal.*, 56:179–185.

———— Lachmann, F. (1980), *Psychoanalysis of Developmental Arrest*. New York: International Universities Press.

Sugarman, A. (1979), The infantile personality: Orality in the hysteric revisited. *Internat. J. Psycho-Anal.*, 60:501–513.

———— (1980), The borderline personality organization as manifested on psychological tests. In: *Borderline Phenomena and the Rorschach Test*, ed. J. Kwawer, H. Lerner, P. Lerner, & A. Sugarman. New York: International Universities Press, pp. 39–57.

Teicholz, (1978), A selected review of the psychoanalytic literature on theoretical conceptualizations of narcissism. *J. Amer. Psychoanal. Assn.*, 26:831–862.

Tolpin, P., & Kohut, H. (1978), The disorders of the self: The psychopathology of the first year of life. In: *The Course of Life. Vol. I. Psychoanalysis and the Life Cycle*, ed. G. Pollock & S. Greenspan. Washington, DC: NIMH, pp. 425–458.

Chapter 11

Differential Diagnosis of Borderline and Narcissistic Personality Disorders

Michael A. Farris, Psy.D.

Over the last fifteen years the fields of clinical psychiatry and psychology have expanded to include the study of the personality disorders as well as the more traditional neuroses and psychoses. This shift is evident in the most recent revision of the American Psychiatric Association's *Diagnostic and Statistical Manual* (DSM–III), which, for the first time since the inception of the DSM, has a section specifically devoted to these disorders. Current theorists have addressed themselves more and more to the study of character disorders as discrete from other forms of psychopathology. Kernberg, Stone, Kohut, Masterson, Grinker, and others have expanded on the writings of Freud, the neo-Freudians, and the ego psychologists, as well as such prominent object relations theorists as Klein, Mahler, and Winnicott, to develop a theoretical framework in which to describe these disorders. Diagnostic criteria for character disorders have been a focus of investigation, as have their psychodynamics and genetic and etiological determinants. In this regard, the borderline and narcissistic disorders have far outstripped the other personality disorders in terms of popularity, interest, research, and publication. Yet, despite this intensive study, more questions than

The author wishes to express his gratitude to Stanley Moldawsky, Ph.D., of the Graduate School of Applied and Professional Psychology at Rutgers University and to Arthur Carr, Ph.D., of the New York Hospital–Cornell University Medical Center for their support and guidance in the implementation of this study.

answers have been generated, and the field remains rife with debate as to whether these disorders exist, whether we can reliably diagnose them, and how to treat them if they can be diagnosed.

The current classification system, as delineated in DSM–III, includes nine personality disorders; these are conceptually linked in that each is a consistent, inflexible, and maladaptive pattern of interaction with the environment and oneself. Much criticism has been directed against the DSM–III position, including the argument that the conceptual link is spurious and ignores accepted psychodynamic, developmental, and biological assumptions about such disorders (Gunderson, 1980; Kernberg, 1981). A further criticism, and the one perhaps most relevant to the present study, is that DSM–III contains no explicit indication of the relative severity of these disturbances. Instead the various disorders are grouped together on the basis of whether they are manifested in anxious/fearful, dramatic/histrionic, or odd/eccentric clinical presentations. The clinical utility and theoretical consistency of such a grouping has been seriously questioned. It is suggested that a system stressing severity of disturbance would have greater prognostic value and would be of greater use to clinicians attempting to treat individuals with such disorders (Kernberg, 1981).

In the present study an attempt was made to demonstrate, via the use of several scoring indices applied to Rorschach data, that the borderline and narcissistic personality disorders may indeed differ from one another in terms of severity of disturbance. An attempt has also been made to integrate the historical underpinnings of the current nosology with the present-day body of psychoanalytic literature on the two disorders. Specifically, differences in the areas of object relations, defensive organization, developmental level, and character style/prominent psychodynamics are addressed, both in terms of how these differences are reflected in current psychoanalytic thinking, and how they manifest themselves on the Rorschach. This was done in order to illustrate some of the salient differences between these two disorders, with specific reference to severity of disturbance.

In the area of psychopathology and diagnosis, research may be conceptualized in terms of levels, distinguished by the state of knowledge and precision with which hypotheses can be generated and expressed. Four levels of scientific inquiry can be generated. At level one, the aim is hypothesis finding; variables are as yet undefined and methods are mainly descriptive and classificatory. At level two, classification and tentative formulation of relationships between variables discovered at the first level are subjected to more systematic study, correlation, clinical prediction, and crude quantification. At level three, hypotheses are generated with greater precision, research designs are more systematic, relevant variables may be controlled, and specific results are predicted. Finally, at level four, invariant relationships are postulated and through deliberate control are tested. Within this scheme, the present study, centered primarily around level two, rests upon previous research at level one, and is equipped to generate hypotheses for inquiry at level three (Howard Lerner, personal communication). Hopefully, the guidelines regarding use of the Rorschach in the diagnosis and assessment of these personality disorders will prove useful to researchers, diagnosticians, and clinicians.

DESCRIPTIVE-PHENOMENOLOGICAL FEATURES

Narcissistic personalities have been described as grandiose, self-centered, exhibitionistic, and arrogant (Masterson, 1981) and as overly dependent on external validation (Kernberg, 1975). They have been described in DSM-III as having a grandiose sense of uniqueness and preoccupation with fantasies of unlimited success. Along with these fantasies is a driven, ambitious quality which affords no pleasure and cannot be satisfied. Masterson has described these individuals as being in pursuit of power and perfection, which may be concomitant with the painful self-consciousness and preoccupation with grooming and youthfulness listed in the DSM-III. In contradistinction to this picture is the borderline, with chronic feelings of dysphoria (Stone, 1980) and a pervasive sense of futility (Perry and Klerman, 1978). Unlike the grandiose inflated self-image seen in the narcissist, the borderline views himself as inadequate, masochistic (Sugarman and Lerner, 1980), and self-deprecatory (Masterson, 1981).

The social adaptation of the borderline has been described in DSM-III as marked by social contrariness. By contrast, this adaptation in the narcissist has uniformly been described as positive. In fact, descriptions of narcissists often include their ability to charm and entertain people (Meissner, 1978a). Along with this charm is the sense that it is in the service of exploiting and manipulating others for one's own needs (Kwawer, 1979; Bursten, 1982). The manipulation of the borderline, on the other hand, is marked by its self-destructive features (Stone, 1980; Kernberg, 1981), and is most often in the service of clinging and demanding wishes for nurturance (Masterson, 1981). Both are described as having shallow, uninvolved relationships with the general public (Grinker, Werble, and Drye, 1968; Perry and Klerman,

1978), but the borderline is described as having close relationships that are intense, unstable, and marked by alternating clinging dependency and hostile distancing (Kernberg, 1975; Masterson, 1981; DSM–III). In contrast, it is doubtful that the narcissist forms close relationships; instead he forms relationships marked by cool indifference and self-absorption (Masterson, 1981; DSM–III). There are some similarities and several striking differences when the two are compared along affective lines. Both are thought to have depressive tendencies (DSM–III), but the narcissist is more likely than the borderline to defend against depression with hypomanic denial (Kernberg, 1975). Anger and rage are characteristic of both types, yet Masterson (1981) makes a distinction between the cool, detached rage of the narcissist and the object-related desperate quality of borderline anger. Dysphoria and loneliness in the borderline are replaced with fantasies of unlimited success and admiration from others in the narcissist (Kernberg, 1975; DSM–III).

A diminished capacity to work and achieve has been noted in the vast literature on the borderline patient (Knight, 1954; Kernberg, 1975). The narcissistic personality, in marked contrast, rarely shows impairment in this area, and is in fact often more talented and success-ful than the general public (Kernberg, 1975). Acting out (promiscuity, substance abuse, antisocial behavior, etc.) is thought to be characteris-tic of both (Kohut and Wolf, 1978; DSM–III), yet both Masterson (1981) and DSM–III emphasize the self-destructive aspects of this behavior in borderlines as opposed to the gratifying, manipulative quality to the acting out in narcissistic individuals. Masterson further suggests that for these reasons the differential diagnosis between anti-social and narcissistic personality disorders is far more difficult than that between antisocial and borderline personality disorders.

Disruptions in ego functioning such as a distorted sense of reality, depersonalization, derealization, and dissociation are mentioned fre-quently in the literature describing borderline pathology (Knight, 1954; Perry and Klerman, 1978). Such distortions and perceptions are strik-ingly absent from the literature on narcissistic pathology. In extreme form, these disturbances in the borderline are described as transient psychotic episodes, a notion which, although present in the DSM–III criteria for both disorders, is typically emphasized in the theoretical and clinical literature on the borderline, and omitted or excluded from that describing the narcissistic personality disorder (Kohut, 1963; Kohut and Wolf, 1978; Masterson, 1981). Similarly, cognitive disruption, such as thought-blocking, impaired integrative and conceptual capacities, and peculiar use of language, have been noted as common among borderlines (Rapaport, Gill, and Schafer, 1945; Knight, 1954), especially in unstructured settings (Gunderson and Singer, 1975). These impairments are not referred to in the literature on the narcissistic personality disorder, and are in fact unlikely, given the at least modal if not superior academic and professional achievement noted among narcissistic patients.

Finally, several authors have discussed these two disorders in terms of response to and motivation for treatment. Both Kernberg and Kohut have commented on the analyzability of at least some narcissistic personalities, and the relative unanalyzability of the borderline. In fact, Kohut has suggested that this factor may be a primary means of differential diagnosis between them. Masterson (1981) has suggested that the motivation for treatment differs between the two groups. He suggests that the pursuit of "perfect mirroring" is primary for the narcissist, whereas "bare acknowledgment of their existence" is the motivating force for borderlines (p. 30). This last concept also relates to the notion of "identity disturbance," found in the descriptive literature on the borderline but absent from that on narcissistic pathology, and also discussed in detail in the respective bodies of literature on object relations in the two groups.

OBJECT RELATIONS

The issue of object relations in borderline and narcissistic pathology is directly linked to and, indeed, at the root of, many of the descriptive-phenomenological notions above, including interpersonal relationships, self-cohesion, relationship to reality, and response to treatment. Object relations theorists have proposed an incompleteness of differentiation of self from other in the borderline (Mahler, 1971; Kernberg, 1975; Rinsley, 1977; Olesker, 1980). Meissner (1978b) has asserted that borderlines respond to environmental and intrapsychic objects in a manner suggestive of Winnicott's notion of the transitional object (1951); i.e., the object possesses the qualities of the nurturant object while at the same time being part of the self. Kernberg (1975) has referred to borderlines as being constantly on the border between object cathexis and identification. Manifestations of this failure to completely differentiate are described above, in terms of the borderline's absence of a cohesive identity and the tendency toward clinging, demanding, and intense interpersonal relationships. The unstable and vacillating quality of these relationships has been accounted for by the borderline's intense wish for merger with the object (leading to markedly dependent, clinging behavior) and the concomitant fear of engulfment (leading to the dissolution of the self and, hence, the distance-creating rage).

The narcissistic personality, on the other hand, is thought to have a less fragile sense of self (Bursten, 1982), and a typically different pattern of interpersonal relationships. In contrast to the borderline, the narcissist "maintains a sense of separateness ... and has considerable difficulty in developing meaningful or mutually gratifying relationships" (Meissner, 1978a, p. 178). Kohut (1971) has stated that narcissists, unlike borderlines, have "in essence attained a cohesive self and have constructed cohesive idealized archaic objects. And, unlike the borderline, these patients are not seriously threatened by irreversible disintegration of the archaic self or of the narcissistically cathected archaic objects" (p. 4). This vulnerability is consistent with the vulnerability of borderline patients to psychotic regression, as noted above. As Rinsley (1977) suggests, "The persistent denial of separateness is paradigmatic for the impairment of the sense of reality and capacity for reality testing, which finds such protean symptomatic expression in the daily life of borderline personalities" (p. 57). While Rinsley is suggesting a link between disturbances in object relations and disturbances in other ego functions, implicit in his statement is the notion that the maintenance of primitive defenses (in this case denial) impedes the sense of reality and the ability to test reality. Kernberg has made similar statements regarding the use of splitting and its effects on ego functioning. This notion will be discussed in detail below.

DEFENSIVE ORGANIZATION OF BORDERLINE AND NARCISSISTIC PATHOLOGY

Differences between the two types of pathology in this area may be differences in degree and effectiveness rather than in kind. Kernberg (1975), for example, refers to a constellation of primitive defenses found in both disorders, including splitting, primitive denial, projective identification, idealization, and devaluation. Smith (1980) notes, however, that use of primitive defenses is in the service of protecting the newly emerging sense of self, an issue which may be of greater concern to the borderline than to the narcissist. This may necessitate more frequent or exclusive use of such defenses in the former group. Similarly, Modell has linked the use of primitive denial to separation anxiety, and has suggested that quantitative factors (the extent of the anxiety) may determine the extent of the denial (Meissner, 1978b).

Given the greater centrality of separation issues in the borderline described above, it would follow that these individuals may well use denial more extensively than do narcissists. Olesker (1980) and Meissner (1978b) have also addressed the issue of the ineffective use of defenses in the borderline. Meissner adds that splitting contributes to ego weakness and necessitates further splitting, with an ensuing spiral effect. The manifestations of ego weakness described earlier may well be the consequences of such a process, of which the psychotic regression mentioned above may be the most severe. Kernberg (1975) notes that the use of splitting precludes the use of higher-level defenses in individuals at the lower end of the borderline spectrum. Lerner and Lerner (1980) have also suggested that different forms of psychopathology are related to specific levels of defensive organization. Given the descriptive and object relations literature reviewed above, specifically the generally held notions that borderline pathology may represent a more severe disturbance in both its presentation and its relation to environmental and intrapsychic objects than narcissistic pathology, one might assume that this would be reflected in the respective defensive organizations of the two groups. Inversely, one might expect to see more frequent use of higher-level defenses in the narcissistic personality, a notion consistent with the position that narcissists may achieve aspects of oedipal resolution not found in borderlines. Such developmental issues are addressed in greater detail below.

DEVELOPMENTAL ISSUES

The intersection of developmental theory with the body of knowledge described above seems to lie in the realm of explanatory or heuristic formulations about the complexity of borderline and narcissistic pathology. While somewhat inferential, current developmental speculations regarding these types of pathology represent the combination of theory with clinical observation of adults thought to demonstrate this pathology, and longitudinal observations of children who later develop these disturbances. Most current theorists concur that borderline and narcissistic pathology results from an interplay of environmental (specifically parent-child interactional) and constitutional factors (predominance of aggression). The crucial period for observation of these factors is generally held to fall somewhere between the second and third years of life, corresponding to Mahler's separation-individuation phase of development. Specifically, most authors agree that such disturbances arise out of the rapprochement subphase of development (18 to 24 months), with unsuccessful negotiation of the practicing subphase (8 to 16 months) sometimes setting the groundwork for such rapprochement disturbances (Kohut, 1963; Mahler, 1971; Kernberg, 1975, 1976; Sugarman and Lerner, 1980). In this process, inappropriate parental response to individuative strivings in the rapprochement child precludes the integration of libidinally determined internalized self-and object images. What results are aggressively tinged, undifferentiated self- and object representations, in which benevolent and malevolent aspects remain unintegrated. A manifestation, and indeed the maintenance, of such undifferentiated and unintegrated self- and object images is the defense of splitting, a central feature of the borderline's defensive organization (Kernberg, 1975). Phenomenological manifestations of splitting have been described above, including alternating affective states, unstable interpersonal relationships, and various forms of ego weakness. Object relations manifestations of this process include the vulnerable self-identity found among borderlines and their tendencies toward unrealistic distortion of others. Failure to complete these early stages of development successfully taints the negotiation of subsequent psychosexual tasks, resulting in a condensation of pregenital and genital conflicts, manifested in the "polymorphous perverse" sexuality seen in such patients (Kernberg, 1975; Masterson, 1981; DSM–III).

The narcissistic personality, on the other hand, is not commonly believed to show these disturbances in functioning to the same degree as the borderline. Meissner (1978a) accounts for this difference as follows:

> The narcissistic personality has been shaped by different developmental experiences. The passage through separation and individuation has not been contaminated to the same degree by aggressive derivatives. The narcissistic child does not meet the same degree of parental rejection, disapproval, hostility, or destructiveness. . . . The narcissistic personality is [thus] left with a greater sense of individuation and correlative self-cohesion. [p. 198]

He goes on to add that "the generally held clinical impression that borderline disorders are more severe than narcissistic disorders may be accounted for by a developmentally earlier, and therefore more devastating, trauma in the borderline disorder" (p. 198). Rinsley (1978) concurs, and posits that borderline pathology may originate in the early rapprochement subphase (18 to 22 months), whereas narcissistic pathology has its roots in the late rapprochement, early object constancy phase (24 to 36 months). Mahler and Kaplan (1977) and Olesker (1980) have arrived at similar conclusions from their longitudinal research observing the development of borderline and narcissistic children. Mahler and Kaplan commented on the contributions of even earlier phases of development (symbiotic phase, practicing subphase) in the evolution of borderline pathology, and in all of their borderline children a tendency toward regression, primary process dominance, and disorganization was noted; all of these features were found to be absent among narcissistic children.

What emerges from these observations and investigations is a picture which points to early developmental distortions and failures as germane to the evolution of borderline and narcissistic pathology. Additionally, it appears that the timing of these traumata or fixations determines the severity of disturbances manifested in later life. Observations of the phenomenology, defensive organization, and object relations of borderline and narcissistic individuals is consistent with the notion that borderline pathology may well originate at an earlier developmental point than does narcissistic pathology.

Stylistic and Prominent Psychodynamic Differences

The literature cited above regarding the phenomenology, object relations, defensive organization, and developmental levels of the two types of pathology is primarily quantitative in nature. This view, however, does not take into account some of the more qualitative differences between the two groups, as manifested in variations of character style and prominent psychodynamic issues. Proponents of the structural diagnosis of borderline conditions (Kernberg, 1975; Spear, 1980; Carsky and Bloomgarten, 1981) advance convincing arguments to suggest that differences in style and central dynamics may be some of the most salient variables in distinguishing one form of character pathology from another. Shapiro (1965) has dealt with such issues in the neurotic realm of psychopathology, and has similarly argued that a patient's clinical presentation may vary considerably regardless of his basic structural configuration.

Several important differences between the narcissistic and borderline personality disorders emerge as the focus shifts from structural to dynamic and stylistic issues. Tolpin and Kohut (1980) have made the distinction between structural deficits (absence of structures essential for self-cohesion) and structural conflicts (conflicts between existing structures). Stylistic and dynamic differences in the two types of pathology may be accounted for, at least in part, by the respective combinations and permutations of structural deficits and conflicts in the two groups. An example may be the narcissist's extreme involvement with self-esteem regulation, a necessary precondition of which is the existence of a cohesive sense of self. In the borderline, however, these issues are subordinated to concerns over existence and annihilation, reflecting the absence of this self-identity. Another manifestation of the interaction of structural deficits with conflicts can be seen in the types of relationships formed by the two groups. The borderline's use of transitional objects, as mentioned above, may reflect a deficit in the differentiation of self from other, whereas the narcissistic personality's tendency to relate to others as mirrors of the self presupposes the existence of differentiated self- and object representations. The two examples cited above may reflect the mechanism by which differences in style, such as a tendency to be preoccupied with appearance and perfection, or the tendency to exploit others, can be understood in terms of the interaction of structural deficits and structural conflicts.

Other differences in style and dynamics may reflect the degree to which oedipal and preoedipal issues are condensed. Mahler (1971) has noted the narcissistic personality's greater likelihood of achieving aspects of an advanced oedipal resolution than the borderline's. This would imply the substitution of castration for annihilation anxiety, as well as a general trend toward genital as opposed to oral and anal eroticism. Historically, descriptions of the narcissistic personality have included allusions to exhibitionism, power, conquest, and urethral eroticism (Reich, 1933; Fenichel, 1945; Harder, 1979), all of which are suggestive of at least some degree of prominence of phallic-oedipal themes. These descriptions are also consistent with those found in the current descriptive literature (DSM–III). By contrast, however, are the descriptions of borderline individuals as clinging and dependent, with polymorphous perverse sexuality and sexual identity confusion. Behavioral concomitants of these differences may also be seen in the exploitive, self-serving behavior of the narcissist, reflecting this preoccupation with power and conflict, as opposed to the borderline's masochism and self-destructiveness.

Finally, the metabolism and expression of affect may account for some of the dynamic and stylistic differences noted between the two disorders. Borderlines have been described as prone to depression (Grinker, Werble, and Drye, 1968; DSM–III), whereas an incapacity to experience depression and the use of hypomanic denial to defend against it is thought to be characteristic of the narcissistic personality. A biological link between the narcissistic personality disorder and manic psychosis has also been proposed (Sugarman and Lerner, 1980), presumably as a reflection of this difference in affective experience. Similarly, Masterson suggests that envy, a significant dynamic for the narcissist, is subordinated to emptiness and depression in the borderline as a consequence of this affective difference.

In summary, whereas many of the distinctions between the borderline and narcissistic personality disorders have been made on quantitative grounds, there exist, as well, qualitative distinctions which reflect variations in character style and the prominence of different psychodynamic issues. These differences reflect the interplay of structural deficits and conflicts, the relative impact of psychosexual development subsequent to the preoedipal core conflict, and issues surrounding the metabolism and expression of affect.

REVIEW OF THE PSYCHOLOGICAL TEST LITERATURE

Relatively little has been written on the psychological test performance in narcissistic pathology. The borderline personality, however, and its nosological variants have received considerable attention in the psychological test literature. Stern commented in 1938 that borderline psychopathology is more apparent in psychological test performance than in clinical interaction. Knight (1954) noted the presence of cognitive peculiarities in borderlines that were not apparent in clinical interviews. In fact, Rorschach himself predicted that diagnosis "in the borderland" between schizophrenia and the neuroses would be his test's area of greatest utility (Fried, 1980). Urist (1980) has similarly proposed that the Rorschach, because of its unique sensitivity to primary-process material, has unique utility in the diagnosis of borderline pathology.

The movement response (M) has received considerable attention in the literature, and has been described as especially relevant to borderline pathology (Stern, 1938; Fried, 1980; Smith, 1980; Carr and Goldstein, 1981). The M response has been linked with impulse control, empathy, and identity integration, concepts which are thought to represent central deficits in borderline pathology. Perhaps even more widely accepted is the relevance of the borderline patient's response to varying levels of structure on psychological tests. Gunderson and Singer (1975) have observed that borderlines tend to function well on relatively structured tests, such as the Wechsler tests, which is in sharp contradistinction to their performance on relatively unstructured tests, such as the Rorschach. Singer (1977) has commented that disruptions noted in borderlines' Rorschach protocols may be even more severe than those of schizophrenic subjects. Singer and Larson (1981) have reported the interesting finding that borderline responses to Rorschach cards deteriorate with each subsequent response to the card, and improve when a new card is presented, presumably because structure increases.

Another feature observed in borderline Rorschach performance is the tendency to overelaborate responses with affective and thematic material (Singer, 1977; Smith, 1980; Spiro and Spiro, 1980; Singer and Larson, 1981). Often seen in conjunction with peculiar verbalizations and circumstantiality, this overelaboration is thought to represent an "inner preoccupation . . . at the expense of objectivity and responsiveness to the outer world" (Olesker, 1980, p. 436), and may reflect an inability to distinguish internal from external stimuli (Carr and Goldstein, 1981). In addition to the fabulized and confabulated responses described above, several authors have commented on the borderline's proclivity to ego-syntonic fabulized combination responses, or responses combined merely on the spatial contiguity of the percepts (Rapaport, Gill, and Schafer, 1945; Schafer, 1948; Fisher and Cleveland, 1958; Stone and Dellis, 1960).

Other aspects of Rorschach performances of the borderline patient include strong regressive tendencies. Regressions are seen in reversions to primitive modes of thought (Friedman, 1952; Urist, 1980), and in the fusion of oral and genital drives. Smith (1980) noted that oral and genital content is frequently attributed by borderlines simultaneously to the same area of the blot. Olesker (1980) noted these regressive tendencies in a decline of form-dominated and human responses over time. These test manifestations of regression parallel the clinical observations described above of cognitive disruption and diffuse ego weakness in borderlines.

There have been some attempts to evaluate the Rorschach performances of subjects thought to represent subtypes within the borderline realm. Rapaport, Gill, and Schafer (1945), for example, studied two groups of individuals who may well correspond to schizotypal and schizoid personalities (using the current nomenclature). The former group, which they call "overideational," showed high response productivity, high rate of response to rare details, and a preoccupation with self- and body representations. The latter group showed evidence of inhibition, constriction, and anxiety and was called "coarctated." Sugarman, Bloom-Feshbach, and Bloom-Feshbach (1980) similarly compared the Rorschachs of adolescents diagnosed as either having borderline features or being borderline psychotic. These authors were able to distinguish between the two groups on the basis of reality testing (F+ percentage), regressive trends, and condensations of oral and genital imagery, and the integration and modulation of affect (response to color) in their Rorschach protocols. Using content-analysis, Carsky and Bloomgarten (1981) were able to discriminate between Spitzer's odd/eccentric and affectively unstable borderlines, finding a greater incidence of schizophrenic-like "otherworldly" response in the former group. Additional attempts at subtyping within the borderline realm have addressed themselves specifically to the areas of object relations, defensive organization, developmental issues, and, to a lesser degree, stylistic or psychodynamic themes.

Within the realm of object relations, Spear (1980) was able to discriminate groups of schizophrenics, hysterical/impulsive borderlines, and obsessive/paranoid borderlines on the basis of both structural and thematic aspects of object representations on the Rorschach. Other studies examining object relations on the Rorschach have yielded similar results. Sugarman (1980) noted that, consistent with clinical observations, borderlines relate to objects on the Rorschach as part (Hd) objects rather than whole objects (H), and also noted the relative dearth of M responses in such subjects. Similarly, Spiro and Spiro (1980) discriminated between schizophrenics and borderlines on the basis of human face responses, of which borderlines reported significantly greater numbers. They noted further that these human face responses accounted for a sizable portion of fabulized and fabulized combination responses, consistent with the findings of Singer (1977) and Singer and Larson (1981). From these data, Spiro and Spiro hypothesized the use of faces on borderline Rorschachs as transitional objects. Carr and Goldstein (1981) have described similar disturbances in object relations evident in the Rorschachs of borderlines as "fluctuating and poorly delineated percepts of people" (p. 565). Related disturbances were manifested in responses permeated with themes of engulfment, merger, incorporation, and intrauterine experience. He also (Kwawer, 1979, 1980; Smith, 1980). Kwawer noted that such disturbances were manifested in response permeated with themes of engulfment, merger, incorporation, and intrauterine experience. He also noted, similar to Carr and Goldstein (1981), the presence of percepts with weak, permeable boundaries and concomitant autistic elaboration of such responses. Smith has also noted the presence of symbiotic images in lower-level borderlines, and found greater numbers of pair and reflection responses, with a greater attention to differences within pairs in higher-level borderlines, suggesting a higher degree of object differentiation. Blatt, Brenneis, Schimek, and Glick (1976) have demonstrated the utility of object relations measures in discriminating between the Rorschachs of psychotic and normal subjects. These investigators developed a detailed structural scoring system for evaluating the formal aspects of inner object relations as manifested on the Rorschach, which has demonstrated high reliability and validity. This scoring system is unique in that it represents one of the few empirical attempts to address the relationship between thought organization and object relations; it is used as a measure of object relations in the present study.

Relatively less research has directly addressed the use of primitive defenses in the Rorschach. Carr and Goldstein (1981) have noted the use of splitting and projective identification primarily, and devaluation and idealization secondarily, in borderline Rorschachs. Sugarman (1980) describes in detail the borderline's use of projective identification and splitting as manifested in test behavior, formal features, and content on the Rorschach. Borderlines using projective identification tend to look similar to paranoid schizophrenics in terms of test behavior, and yet do not show the formal features commonly associated with them. The content of borderline projective identification responses is typically of a threatening nature, of poor form quality, and often confabulated. As regards splitting, Sugarman notes the presence of alternating negatively and positively tinged percepts, and also frequent global/impressionistic or distorted/combinatory whole responses in the presence of an unremarkable W percentage. Sugarman hypothesizes that these difficulties in forming adequate whole responses are reflective of deficient integrative capacities secondary to the use of splitting. Smith (1980) and others (Carr and Goldstein, 1981) have also addressed the use of splitting in the Rorschachs of borderlines. Splitting is noted in the presence of objects seen in strong affective terms, as well as aggressively weighted self- and other representations. Toward the higher levels of the borderline spectrum, Smith (1980) notes a replacement of splitting with repression, "reflecting the growing discomfort with and need to resolve such discrepant views of reality" (pp. 74–75). Smith also notes a reluctance in individuals employing splitting to identify concepts as actual things rather than as "creatures" or "beings," reflecting an avoidance of the unpleasant affect associated with the integrated whole-object view. Lerner and Lerner (1980), in perhaps the most comprehensive study of defensive operations on the Rorschach to date, attempted to discriminate between borderlines and neurotics on indices of splitting, projective identification, idealization, devaluation, and denial. Borderlines were found to manifest all of these defenses, with the exception of idealization, more frequently than neurotics, splitting and projective identification being used exclusively by borderlines. The authors also found that neurotics modulated their use of idealization and devaluation with a concomitant use of high-level denial, lending support to the notion that the absence of splitting allows for the invocation of higher-level defenses.

Friedman (1952, 1953) has developed, and others have modified (Becker, 1956; Hemmendinger and Schultz, 1977), what has become the most widely used measure of developmental level as applied to Rorschach data. Based on Werner's principles (1948, 1957) that development proceeds from a state of relative globality to states of increasing differentiation, articulation, and hierarchic integration, Friedman examines standard Rorschach locations for evidence of the flexibility, variability, and mobility of cognitive functioning which characterizes healthy adult cognition and perception. Subsequent revisions have added the dimension of reality testing (F+ level) and thought disorder (Fabulized Combination, Confabulation, Contamination, etc.). What has evolved is an index of cognitive/perceptual development with demonstrated high reliability and validity, which has successfully discriminated between varying levels of pathology (Frank, 1951; Pena, 1953; Siegal, 1953). This scoring system, used in the present study as a measure of development, is described in greater detail below.

The Rorschach, in addition to its use in assessing object relations, primitive defenses, and cognitive/perceptual development, has been found to be an effective tool for the assessment of stylistic/thematic issues. Spear (1980) applied Shapiro's notion of character style (1965) to the Rorschachs of schizophrenics, obsessive/paranoid borderlines, and hysterical/impulsive borderlines using Krohn and Mayman's scale (1974), and found that thematic-dynamic issues could successfully discriminate character typology. Spear reported that although all of his borderline subjects displayed "classic defensive organization (Gunderson and Singer, 1975; Kernberg, 1975), including splitting, projective identification, primitive idealization, grandiosity, and denial, they were also differentiated along a second psychological dimension generally reflective of Shapiro's (1965) conceptualization of neurotic character styles" (p. 332). Smith (1980) has found the Rorschach similarly useful in the area of typology and noted that narcissistic characters tend to respond overinferentially to small details, possibly reflecting a hyper-vigilance to the environment that enables effective manipulation of others. Sugarman (1980) has also noted that an individual's "personal-ity constellation," determined by the individual's defenses, psychosex-ual conflicts, and cognitive style, affects the degree of intensity with which drive-laden thematic material is expressed. He noted an explicit-ness and exhibitionism in such subjects absent in the Rorschachs of more constricted borderlines. Kwawer (1980) has suggested that the Rorschach may be a useful measure of narcissistic personality style in that it offers the opportunity for "narcissistic mirroring responses." In one study, Exner (1969) was able to discriminate among hospitalized homosexuals, sociopaths, depressives, and college student controls on the basis of these mirror images and reflection responses. Similarly, Harder (1979) demonstrated the utility of the Rorschach in discriminat-ing between subjects rated on independent measures as either "ambitious-narcissistic" or "nonambitious-narcissistic." He developed scales of ambitious-narcissistic character style for the Rorschach, TAT, and Early Memories Test, using the theoretical concepts of Reich, Green, Fenichel, Murray, and Bibring, and found the Rorschach scale to be the most highly reliable and valid index of the three in discriminating among his groups. This scale, used in the present study, is discussed in greater detail below.

In summary, a review of the clinical, theoretical, and research literature on the borderline and narcissistic personality disorders has allowed for the generation of some preliminary hypotheses regarding the severity of the respective disturbances on a variety of parameters: the areas of object relations, defensive organization, developmental level, and stylistic or prominent psychodynamic issues. The present study is an attempt to investigate the preliminary hypothesis that on the Rorschach borderline personality disorders will show greater distur-bance in the areas of object relations, defensive organization, and developmental level than narcissistic personality disorders, and that narcissistic personalities will show greater evidence of phallic-oedipal thematic material than will borderlines.

METHOD

Subjects

Subjects were drawn from a population of patients who received in- or outpatient treatment at a university-affiliated psychiatric hospital in suburban New York City between 1978 and 1982. Groups of borderline and narcissistic subjects were formed on the basis of the patients' meeting the DSM–III criteria for one or the other disorder as assessed both by the treating clinician and an independent chart review. All subjects received a standard psychological test battery while in treatment. Pairs of borderline and narcissistic subjects were matched for age, sex, socioeconomic level, inpatient or outpatient status, and the presence of DSM–III Axis I diagnosis. Subjects were eliminated who met DSM–III criteria for more than one Axis II diagnosis. Table 1 lists each of the $N = 9$ matched pairs and the variables on which they were matched.

Collection of Data

Subjects had been administered standard psychological test batteries (WAIS or WAIS-R, Rorschach, TAT, Human Figure Drawings) during treatment by pre- or postdoctoral clinical psychology trainees or by junior or senior faculty members. Rorschachs, administered according to the guidelines set forth by Rapaport, Gill, and Schafer (1945), were extracted from the batteries, coded, and divided into cards by a colleague unaffiliated with the study, in order to reduce the experimenter bias effect of scoring Rorschach batteries in toto. Before scoring, the author and a co-rater scored practice Rorschach responses until a minimum Kappa statistic of interrater reliability (Fleiss, 1981) of $K = .60$ was achieved on each of the four scales described below. Scoring was then performed by the author, assuming that the $K = .60$ insured that the scales were being employed reliably.

Developmental Analysis of the Concept of the Object on the Rorschach

This measure, devised by Blatt, Brenneis, Schimek, and Glick (1976), is an attempt to assess the state of internal object representations according to the orthogenetic principles of Werner (1948, 1957) and Werner and Kaplan (1963). Blatt and his colleagues attempt to measure the degree to which human objects as perceived on the Rorschach are differentiated, articulated, and integrated, with the underlying assumption that increasing degrees of these processes are indicative of psychological health.

Friedman's Developmental Level Scoring

Although also based on Werner's orthogenetic principles, this

MICHAEL A. FARRIS

TABLE 1

Composition of Groups by Sex, Age, Religion, Marital and Socioeconomic Status, and
DSM–III Axis I Diagnoses

	Sex	Age	Religion	Marital Status	S.E.S.	DSM–III Axis I Diagnoses
Borderline Subjects						
1	M	20	Roman Catholic	Single	Middle	305.92 Alcohol Abuse, Episodic 296.82 Atypical Depression
2	F	39	Protestant	Married	Upper Middle	296.82 Atypical Depression
3	M	35	Jewish	Single	Middle	296.30 Major Depression w/o Melancholia
4	M	25	Greek Orthodox	Single	Middle	No Axis I Diagnosis
5	F	22	Protestant	Single	Middle	307.92 Anorexia Nervosa
6	M	19	Protestant	Single	Upper Middle	296.32 Major Depression w/o Melancholia, Recurrent
7	M	27	Jewish	Single	Middle	296.26 Major Depression, Single Episode, in Remission
8	F	26	Protestant	Single	Middle	296.82 Atypical Depression 305.91 Unspecified Drug Abuse, Continuous

	Sex	Age	Religion	Marital	Class	Axis I Diagnosis
9	M	21	Jewish	Single	Middle	No Axis I Diagnosis
Narcissistic Subjects						
1	M	19	Roman Catholic	Single	Middle	305.91 Alcohol Abuse, Continuous 296.36 Recurrent Major Depression in Remission 315.00 Attention Deficit Disorder, w/o Hyperactivity
2	F	51	Protestant	Married	Upper Middle	296.82 Atypical Depression
3	M	51	Protestant	Single	Middle	396.30 Major Depression w/o Melancholia, Recurrent
4	M	23	Jewish/RC	Single	Middle	No Axis I Diagnosis
5	F	27	Roman Catholic	Single	Middle	307.51 Bulimia
6	M	45	Protestant	Married	Upper Middle	296.32 Major Depression w/o Melancholia, Recurrent
7	M	27	Jewish	Single	Middle	296.26 Major Depression, Single Episode, in Remission
8	F	18	Protestant	Single	Middle	296.82 Atypical Depression
9	M	21	Jewish	Single	Middle	No Axis I diagnosis

measure differs from the Blatt et al. scale in that the emphasis is on the cognitive-perceptual functioning of the individual as seen in location scores only, rather than on how the higher-order concepts of differentiation, articulation, and integration are seen in human percepts. Reliability of this system has been demonstrated to be quite high. In several studies using two judges, mean percent agreement was 93.5 (Friedman, 1953; Hurwitz, 1954; Misch, 1954; Lofchie, 1955; Goldfried, 1962; Zimet and Fine, 1965). With three judges, mean percent agreement was 93.6 (Frank, 1951; Siegal, 1953). Validity research on this scoring system has been extensive. Several criterion-related (Hemmendinger, 1953; Levine, 1959) and construct validity studies (Frank, 1951; Pena, 1953; Becker, 1956; Wilensky, 1959; Lebowitz, 1963) have demonstrated the system's utility in differentiating among normals, brain-damaged, neurotic, and mentally defective subjects according to theoretical expectations.

Harder Scale of Ambitious-Narcissistic Character Style

Harder (1979) relies on the theoretical notions of Green (1967) and Shapiro (1965) for his definition of character style and on Reich's description of the phallic-narcissistic character (1933) in the formulation of this scale, applied to content and movement aspects of Rorschach responses. Harder conducted both reliability and validity studies on this scale, and it was found to be both highly reliable and valid. Table 2 lists reliability and validity figures for both the scale as a whole and the individual subscales of which it is comprised. Table 3 lists results of a one-way ANOVA, comparing the scale to a criterion-measure of the same construct and shows the Rorschach scale to be a highly valid index.

Assessment of Primitive Defenses in Borderline Patients

Based on the theoretical formulations of Kernberg (1975), Lerner and Lerner (1980) have devised a scoring system for the assessment of primitive defenses (splitting, projective identification, denial, idealization, and devaluation) as seen in full human responses, either static or in motion, on the Rorschach. Reliability and validity studies on the scoring system have shown favorable results. Lerner and Lerner (1978) applied this system to the Rorschachs of ten borderline and ten neurotic subjects and found interrater percent agreement ranging from 83 to 100 on the various scales (see Table 4). Table 5 shows the result of a chi-square

TABLE 2

Reliability of Projective Test Ambitious-Narcissistic Style
Scales in Terms of Percentage Agreements and
Reliability Coefficients

	Rorschach Percentage Agreements
Percentage Acceptance Agreements	82
Percentage Exact Agreements	76
Percentage Agreements on Use of "0"	73

	Reliability Coefficient of Computed Variables
Ambitious-Narcissistic Style	.87
Intrusive/Thrusting	.84
Exhibition/Voyeurism	.70[a]
Urethral Excitation	.53[a]
Mastery/Competence/Power	.77
"Self-Potency"	.73

From Harder (1979).
[a] These categories were used infrequently by raters so that distributions of these
variables for each rater were heavily skewed toward "0."

TABLE 3

Mean Scores and One-Way Analyses of Variance for Three
Projective Scales by Ambitious Style Group Variables

	Definitely Ambitious Style Group ($N=12$)	Possible Ambitious ($N=6$)	Nonambitious Style Group ($N=22$)	F Value
TAT Scale	6.75	5.67	3.36	6.33*
EMT Scale	9.83	7.67	5.23	8.00*
Rorschach Scale	54.58	35.00	31.00	8.99*

From Harder (1979).
df for F tests$=2.37$.
*$p < .005$
*$p < .001$

analysis, in which the scoring system was found to be successful in
discriminating between the two groups in all the primitive defense
categories except idealization, with splitting and projective identification being the most highly discriminative indices.

TABLE 4

Agreement Between Raters for Major Defense Categories

Defense	Number of Times Rated	Percentage of Agreement
Splitting	5	100%
Devaluation	43	91%
Idealization	16	87%
Projective Identification	5	100%
Denial	24	83%

From Lerner and Lerner (1980).

TABLE 5

Chi-Square Value Between Groups for Defense Scores

Defense		Frequency Borderline	Neutoric	X^2	P
Splitting		9		9.00	.01
Devaluation	1	8	15	2.20	NS
	2	12	6	2.00	NS
	3	19	18	.02	NS
	4	3	2	.06	NS
	5	19	4	7.20	.01
Idealization	1	6	8	.28	NS
	2	2	5	1.28	NS
	3	4	7	.82	NS
	4	2	1	.32	NS
	5	5	5		NS
Projective Identification		10		10.00	.01
Denial	1	7	14	2.40	NS
	2	8	3	2.20	NS
	3	13	2	8.00	.01

From Lerner and Lerner (1980).

RESULTS

Interrater reliability studies were conducted on each of the four scales before scoring of the actual data. Kappa statistics (Fleiss, 1981) were computed for each scale and Kappa $\geq$ .60 was considered adequate agreement between raters. Kappa statistics for each scale are reported below. A total of 564 Rorschach responses were then scored on each of the four scales. Table 6 shows the breakdown of total R for each subject. Three hundred twenty-seven of these responses were produced by the borderline group and 237 were produced by the narcissistic group. Mean numbers of responses for each group were 36.3 (SD = 16.95) and 26.3 (SD = 8.90), respectively. Comparisons of total R for the two groups yielded a $X^2 = 3.32$, which is significant at the .1 but not at the .05 level. Total scores for all subjects on all scales were corrected for the differences in R between the two groups by dividing each raw score by R for that subject. Findings are reported by individual scale below.

TABLE 6

Total Number of Rorschach Responses (R) Produced by Subjects

Borderline	R	Narcissistic	R
1	16	1	12
2	42	2	26
3	25	3	48
4	57	4	25
5	49	5	15
6	38	6	29
7	17	7	19
8	23	8	27
9	60	9	31
Total Group R = 327		Total Group R = 237	
M = 36.33		M = 26.33	
SD = 16.95		SD = 8.9	

Developmental Analysis of the Concept of the Object on the Rorschach

Interrater reliability studies conducted on 18 responses yielded a level of agreement between raters of K = .654. A total score for each subject was computed reflecting scores on the categories of differentiation, articulation, and integration. Table 7 reflects a comparison of the

TABLE 7

Level of Performance on Blatt et al.'s Developmental
Analysis of the Concept of the Object on
the Rorschach

Diagnostic Group	M	SD	t
Borderline	1.827	1.07	−2.48*
Narcissistic	2.915	0.76	

*$p < .01$.

borderline and narcissistic groups' mean scores. The borderline group achieved a mean score of 1.827 ($SD = 1.07$), and the narcissistic group had a mean score of 2.915 ($SD = 0.76$). Comparing the two means, t tests yielded a value of $t = -2.48$, which suggests that the narcissistic subjects showed a significantly higher ($p < .01$) level of object differentiation, articulation, and integration than did borderline subjects.

Friedman's Developmental Level Scoring

Interrater reliability studies conducted on 16 responses yielded a level of agreement with raters of $K = .662$. A total score for each subject was computed, reflecting the summation of weights assigned to each percept according to Becker's modification (1956) of Friedman's scoring system. Total scores were multiplied by a factor of $1/R$. Results of a t test comparing corrected scores for each group are found in Table 8. Mean corrected score for the borderline group was 3.206 ($SD = 0.34$). Mean corrected score for the narcissistic group was 3.706 ($SD = 0.19$). Comparison of the two groups yielded a value of $t = 3.83$, suggesting that narcissistic subjects achieved significantly higher scores ($p < .002$) than borderline subjects on the Developmental Level Scoring System.

TABLE 8

Level of Performance on Friedman's Developmental
Level Score

Diagnostic Group	M	SD	t
Borderline	3.206	0.34	−3.83*
Narcissistic	3.706	0.19	

*$p < .002$.

Harder Scale of Ambitious-Narcissistic
Character Style

Interrater reliability studies conducted on 16 responses yielded a level of agreement between raters of $K = .923$. A total score for each subject was computed and total ambitious-narcissistic scores were multiplied by a factor of $1/R$ for each subject. Results of a t test comparing mean corrected scores for each group are found in Table 9. Mean corrected score for the borderline group was 0.787 ($SD = .36$). Mean corrected score for the narcissistic group was 0.788 ($SD = .33$). Comparison of the two groups yielded a value of $t = -0.011$, suggesting that borderline and narcissistic subjects did not differ significantly in their overall performance on this measure of ambitious-narcissistic character style.

TABLE 9

Level of Performance on Harder's Scale of
Ambitious-Narcissistic Character Style

Diagnostic Group	M	SD	t
Borderline	0.787	0.36	−.001 NS
Narcissistic	0.788	0.33	

On closer inspection, however, differences between the two groups' scores on specific ambitious-narcissistic categories emerged. Results of a chi-square analysis comparing the performance of the two groups on each of the seven categories are presented in Table 10, in which total group frequency scores were compared with expected frequencies for that group, the latter reflecting a correction for R by a factor of $n_B = 0.725$ or $n_N = 1.380$. No significant differences between borderline and narcissistic subjects were found for the Phallic Mastery, Phallic Exhibitionistic/Voyeuristic, Phallic Urethral, or Sex categories, however. For the Phallic Organ category, narcissistic subjects produced a number of ambitious-narcissistic responses reflecting a greater departure in the positive direction from the expected frequency than did borderline subjects ($X^2 = 4.55, p < .05$). Similarly, narcissistic subjects produced a relatively greater number of Body Narcissism responses than did borderline subjects ($X^2 = 32.63, p < .001$).

TABLE 10

Chi-Square Values Between Groups for Ambitious-Narcissistic Category Scores

Ambitious-Narcissistic Category	Frequency		X^2	p
	Borderline	Narcissistic		
Phallic Thrust	29	19	1.65[a]	NS
Phallic Mastery	27	15	0.43	NS
Phallic/Exhibition-istic/Voyeuristic	27	16	0.77	NS
Phallic Urethral	18	3	2.75	NS
Phallic Organ	47	34	4.55	.05
Sex	31	13	0.04	NS
Body Narcissism	65	74	32.63	.001

[a]Expected frequencies (not listed) reflect correction for R by a factor of $n_B = .725$ or $n_N = 1.380$.

Assessment of Primitive Defenses in Borderline Patients

Interrater reliability studies conducted on 26 responses yielded a level of agreement between raters of $K = .859$. A total score for each subject was computed and total scores were multiplied by a factor of $1/R$ for each subject. Results of a t test comparing mean corrected scores for each group are found in Table 11. Mean corrected score for the borderline group was 2.32 ($SD = 1.24$). Mean corrected score for the narcissistic group was 0.54 ($SD = 0.38$). Comparison of the two groups yielded a value of $t = 4.11$, suggesting that borderline subjects produced a significantly greater number of responses reflecting the use of primitive defenses than did narcissistic subjects ($p < .0005$).

TABLE 11

Level of Performance on Lerner and Lerner's Scale for the Assessment of Primitive Defenses

Diagnostic Group	M	SD	t
Borderline	2.32	1.24	4.11*
Narcissistic	0.54	0.38	

*$p < .0005$.

Additional differences between the two groups emerged when the data were examined for each of the individual primitive defense categories. A chi-square analysis comparing the performance of the two groups on each of the 15 categories is presented in Table 12. No significant differences between borderline and narcissistic subjects were found for any of the Devaluation, Idealization, or Denial categories. There were significant differences in the remaining two categories, however. In the Splitting category, borderline subjects produced a significantly greater number of primitive defense responses than did narcissistic subjects ($X^2 = 4.16, p < .05$). Similarly, borderline subjects produced a significantly greater number of Projective Identification responses than did narcissistic subjects ($X^2 = 4.16, p < .05$).

In summary, t tests comparing total or overall scores on the Blatt et al., Friedman, and Lerner and Lerner scales revealed significant differ-

TABLE 12

Chi-Square Values Between Groups for Primitive Defense Scores

Defense		Frequency		X^2	p
		Borderline	Neurotic		
Splitting		6 (5.5)[a]	0 (.5)	4.16	.05
Devaluation	1	4 (3.5)	1 (1.5)	0.80	NS
	2	5 (4.5)	2 (2.5)	0.57	NS
	3	5 (4.5)	2 (2.5)	0.57	NS
	4	4 (3.5)	3 (3.5)	0	NS
	5	7 (6.5)	1 (1.5)	3.125	NS
Idealization	1	3 (3.5)	4 (3.5)	0	NS
	2	0 (.5)	1 (.5)	0	NS
	3	5 (4.5)	1 (1.5)	1.50	NS
	4	2 (.5)	0 (.5)	0.50	NS
	5				
Projective Identification	1	6 (5.5)	0 (5.5)	4.16	.05
Denial	1	7	6	0.08	NS
	2	2 (1.5)	1 (1.5)	0	NS
	3	5 (4.5)	1 (1.5)	1.50	NS

[a]Numbers in parentheses reflect the use of Yates correction for continuity in cells where expected value (not listed) < 5.

ences between borderline and narcissistic subjects. Total scores on the Harder scale did not differ for the two groups. Chi-square analyses performed on the individual category scores for the two groups on the Harder and Lerner and Lerner scales revealed significant differences between groups in the Phallic Organ and Body Narcissism categories of the former scale, and in the Splitting and Projective Identification categories of the latter scale. These results will be discussed in detail below.

DISCUSSION

Although not a significant difference at the predetermined $p < .05$ level, a greater response productivity in the borderline group ($R = 327$) than the narcissistic group ($R = 237$) was noted. This finding was surprising in that it is discrepant both with theoretical assumptions about psychodynamic and biological links in the two groups to the major affective disorders, and with the literature based on the performance of the two groups on psychological tests. Borderlines have been described as prone to periods of depression, whereas an incapacity to experience depression and the hypomanic denial of depression are believed to be characteristic of the narcissistic personality. Biological links to depression in the borderline personality have been postulated, as have been similar ties to mania in the narcissistic personality (Sugarman and Lerner, 1980). Since response productivity is thought to be a direct correlate of mood and affect (Rapaport, Gill, and Schafer, 1945), one would expect greater response productivity in the narcissistic than in the borderline group. And, in fact, the literature on the test performance of the two groups has borne out these predictions (Sugarman, 1980).

The present study, however, does not bear this out. It is possible, since the difference between the groups is significant only at the $p < .10$ level, that it can be accounted for by chance occurrence. Given the small sample size in the two groups, this is perhaps the most likely explanation for such a phenomenon, and is further supported by the large variance found relative to the mean of the two groups. Another possible explanation relates to the notion that borderlines may not have the degree of impulse control found in narcissistic personalities (DSM–III). This lack of impulse control may contribute to borderlines' inability to regulate and limit their responsivity to these relatively unstructured stimuli (Gunderson and Singer, 1975). Two of the borderline subjects produced more than fifty responses to the Rorschach, which may also reflect a lack of awareness of social norms or the social contrariness mentioned earlier (DSM–III). Because the greater response productivity of the borderline group is possibly not attributable to chance occurrence, R was controlled for in the analysis of the data generated on all four scales.

The prediction that borderlines would show greater disturbance on a measure of object relations than narcissistic subjects was confirmed by the performance of the two groups on the Developmental Analysis of the Concept of the Object on the Rorschach (Blatt et al., 1976). Narcissistic subjects showed greater degrees of object differentiation, articulation, and integration on this scale than did borderlines. The finding that narcissistic subjects produced responses with higher degrees of differentiation than did borderlines is consistent with Sugarman's suggestion (1980) that borderlines perceive part rather than whole objects in the environment, as manifested in the predominance of Hd over H responses in their Rorschach records. Spiro and Spiro (1980 also noted that human faces predominate in the Rorschach records of borderline patients. Faces are scored as Hd rather than H on the Blatt et al. scale and would therefore account, at least in part, for the lower scores of the borderlines on object differentiation. Scores on object articulation and on object integration were similarly lower in borderline than in narcissistic subjects, consistent with past observations of test performance (Blatt et al., 1976; Carr and Goldstein, 1981).

Kohut and Wolf (1978) and Mahler (1971) have argued that the narcissistic individual has a greater degree of cohesiveness of the "self" than does the borderline individual, and Mahler and others have also suggested an incomplete differentiation of self from object in the latter group (Kernberg, 1975; Rinsley, 1977; Olesker, 1980). Meissner (1978a, 1978b) has also commented on the greater sense of separateness in the interpersonal relationships of the narcissistic personality than in those of the borderline personality. Results of the present study support these clinical observations, and suggest also that the Rorschach may be especially useful in assessing the state of object relations of such patients.

The hypothesis that borderlines would score lower on a measure of developmental level than would narcissistic personalities was also confirmed by the results of the present study. The total scores of borderlines on Friedman's Developmental Level Scoring System were significantly lower than those of narcissistic subjects, lending support to observations of current theorists that the borderline personality disorder represents a fixation or developmental arrest at an earlier point than that of the narcissistic personality (Meissner, 1978a; Rinsley, 1978). Lower scores on the Friedman scale reflected the presence of poorly structured, amorphous responses, as well as those manifesting evidence of contamination and fabulized combination. These findings corroborate Sugarman's observation (1980) that borderlines tend to produce an abundance of global, impressionistic whole responses, and lend additional support to the finding that the fabulized combination response is particularly common in the Rorschach records of borderline patients (Stone and Dellis, 1960; Singer, 1977; Singer and Larson, 1981). The findings are also consistent with Smith's observation (1980) that narcissistic and other "higher-level borderline" personalities tend to produce fewer merged or fused responses than do lower-level borderline personalities. The generally lower scores of borderline subjects as compared to narcissistic subjects on the Friedman scale in the present study similarly point to the presence of transient disturbances in reality testing and stronger regressive tendencies in borderlines, as noted elsewhere (Perry and Klerman, 1978; Urist, 1980).

Total scores on the Harder Scale of Ambitious-Narcissistic Character Style did not support the hypothesis that borderlines would show a relative absence of phallic-oedipal themes in comparison to narcissistic personalities on a measure of ambitious-narcissistic character style. In the present study there was no difference between the two groups for total scores on this measure. This is discrepant with most current theoretical and clinical observations of the two disorders. It is generally accepted that the dynamics of the borderline individual lie at the separation-individuation stage of psychological development, specifically in the rapprochement subphase of this stage. In contradistinction are the dynamics of the narcissistic personality, which are thought to lie at a later point, specifically the late separation-individuation/early object constancy phase. It has been asserted that this relatively more advanced point of fixation allows for the achievement of at least some aspects of an oedipal solution in the narcissistic personality. This view is supported by observations of other theorists who point to the predominance of oedipal and specifically phallic and urethral dynamics in the narcissistic personality (Reich, 1933; Fenichel, 1945; Harder, 1979). The borderline, however, is thought to show a predominance of both types of responses within an individual record, or in the attribution of both oral and genital thematic content to single percepts (Smith, 1980). This tendency would also be expected to manifest itself on the Rorschach in the substitution of castration themes for themes of annihilation.

This was apparently not the case in the performance of the two groups on the Harder scale in the present study. One possible explanation for this finding is that the borderlines and narcissistic personalities may be concerned with similar psychodynamic issues and themes, but may manifest these concerns differently as a consequence of varying levels of object relations, defensive organization, and developmental level. It is unlikely, however, that phallic-oedipal themes play as central a role for the borderline as for the narcissistic personality in pure form; as the literature suggests, these are more apt to be fused or condensed with preoedipal issues.

On closer inspection, examination of the performance of the two groups on individual subscales of the Harder scale revealed significant differences in the categories of Phallic Organ and Body Narcissism. Narcissistic subjects scored significantly higher on these indices of ambitious-narcissistic character style than did borderline subjects. On all other subscales, no significant differences between the groups emerged. One possible explanation for this phenomenon is that out of the seven subscales developed by Harder, these two are the most closely related to phallic imagery and the body proper, as well as to the maintenance of self-esteem, commonly thought to be central dynamics of the narcissistic personality. As Kohut and others have suggested, the maintenance of self-esteem is central to the dynamics of the narcissistic personality, but is subordinate to concerns over existence and annihilation in the borderline.

The Body Narcissism category showed the greatest differences between the two groups. This category is most concerned with the adornment of the body proper, and with mirror and reflection responses. The performance of the two groups in this category is consistent with descriptive notions about the preoccupation of the narcissistic personality with youth and beauty (DSM–III) and also with previous research noting an abundance of reflection responses in the Rorschach records of narcissistic individuals (Exner, 1969). The Phallic Organ category is concerned with phallic imagery and relates to the exaggeration and glorification of symbolic phalluses. This is consistent with the theoretical assumption that the narcissistic personality attains at least a partial oedipal resolution, whereas the borderline personality remains fixated around issues of separation-individuation.

With the exception of the Phallic Urethral category, the remaining Harder subscales reflect derivative and symbolic rather than direct, concrete expression of phallic themes. It may be that borderlines and narcissists do not differ in these more derivative forms of presumably oedipal features. The categories of Sex and Phallic Exhibitionistic/Voyeuristic may be measuring something other than, or in addition to, phallic-oedipal dynamics. It has been noted elsewhere that borderline patients tend to overelaborate their responses with primary process material. Kernberg and others have noted that the failure of the borderline to successfully complete early stages of development leads to a failure in negotiating subsequent psychosexual tasks, leading to polymorphous perverse sexuality (Kernberg, 1975; Masterson, 1981). It is quite likely that the Phallic Exhibitionistic/Voyeuristic and Sex categories are measuring, in addition to phallic-oedipal dynamics, elements of this primitive, polymorphous perverse primary process material. It is difficult to determine to what extent the performance of the two groups on these scales is accounted for by this primary process material and what can be accounted for by the predominance of phallic-oedipal strivings. It may be useful in future studies to examine the extent to which the Harder scale is affected by the presence of primary process material in patients who show a predominance of this type of material on other measures, but who are not considered narcissistic.

The prediction that borderlines would show more exclusive or prominent use of primitive defensive operations than would narcissistic personalities was borne out by the performance of the two groups on the Lerner and Lerner Scale for the Assessment of Primitive Defenses. This was reflected in significant differences between both group mean total primitive defense scores and on group frequencies of Splitting and Projective Identification responses. Very similar to Lerner and Lerner's comparison of borderlines with neurotic individuals (1980), splitting and projective identification emerged as the best discriminative indices between the two groups. The results of the present study lend support to their assertion that different forms of psychopathology are related to specific levels of defensive organization. In contrast to Lerner and Lerner's findings, however, borderline subjects did not use lower level devaluation or denial more frequently than did narcissistic subjects. These findings are not surprising in view of the fact that borderlines in the present study were compared with narcissistic personalities, as opposed to neurotics in the Lerner and Lerner study. It would follow that the indices found to be their strongest discriminators would similarly discriminate between groups with less striking differences in level of pathology, whereas their less potent indices would not make distinctions where relative levels of pathology reflected subtler differences. In addition, several authors have placed the narcissistic personality on a continuum reflecting degree of pathology (Kohut, 1963; Kohut and Wolf, 1978; Rinsley, 1978), and it would follow that narcissistic pathology would manifest itself as similar to both borderline and neurotic pathology but as identical to neither. The findings are also consistent with Kernberg's notion that primitive defenses are used by both narcissistic and borderline individuals, and that the differences between the two groups may be quantitative rather than qualitative.

The finding that borderlines use splitting more predominantly than narcissists contributes to an understanding of the descriptive literature on the two disorders. Kernberg has noted that splitting precludes the use of higher-level defenses. Meissner has related the psychotic regression seen in borderline patients to a defensive failure resulting from ego weakness caused by excessive use of splitting (Meissner, 1978b). The transient psychosis, impaired vocational functioning, and peculiarities in cognition and perception found in descriptions of borderlines and absent from descriptions of narcissists may be directly related to this more exclusive or prominent use of splitting in the borderline.

The present study showed also that borderline subjects use projective identification more than narcissistic subjects. The index of projective identification in this scale is sensitive to location, form level, and confabulation. Sugarman, Bloom-Feshbach, and Bloom-Feshbach (1980) have noted reality distortions as well as cognitive and perceptual difficulties in borderline Rorschachs, which would account for the inadequate form level and rare detail locations of these projective identification responses. Several other authors have commented on the tendency of borderline patients to overelaborate their responses with affective and thematic material. This may account for the confabulatory aspects of the projective identification responses. Smith has commented further that as one ascends from low-level to higher-level borderline pathology, percepts remain aggressively tinged but with decreasing intensity. The data in the present study suggest that narcissistic individuals are less likely than borderlines to produce responses with inadequate form, with rare locations, and with striking overelaboration with drive-laden thematic material.

Some Possible Methodological Limitations

The greatest limitations to the present study relate to generalizability and external validity, though some threats to internal validity exist as well. By virtue of the subjects' affiliation with the hospital setting, they may differ from individuals with similar psychopathology diagnosed by other clinicians, living in other geographic areas, or receiving other forms of treatment or no treatment at all. The fact that most subjects also had Axis I diagnoses also limits generalizability to individuals with exclusively Axis II pathology.

Similarly, the presence of Axis I pathology also represents a threat to internal validity insofar as these disorders may have interacted differentially with each subject's Axis II diagnosis. Matching was done to minimize this effect, but exact matching was difficult in a small number of cases. Instrumentation may pose a minor threat to internal validity in that subjects were tested and diagnosed by numerous clinicians. This is one reason for the chart review, and why the data collection for this study was done by one individual. The latter precaution, however, itself represents a hazard in terms of experimenter bias. For this reason, all data were coded by an unaffiliated colleague and Rorschach protocols were not examined in toto. Additionally, the validity of the Rorschach scales used as a "battery" may be questioned. There are several areas in which the scales show considerable overlap, and constructs and concepts are all subject to the operational definitions of the author. This overlap is understandable, given the overlap in the theoretical and clinical literature, and given the relative youth of some of the concepts, yet raises the question of whether in fact we are measuring what we intend to measure. Finally, although the results of the present study allow for speculation about the differences and similarities in borderline and narcissistic pathology, the lack of a control group may make it considerably more difficult to place the results in the broader context of psychopathology in general.

CONCLUSION

The present study has attempted to address some of the uncertainty and confusion regarding the borderline and narcissistic personality disorders in current psychoanalytic and descriptive literature. Despite a century of study on borderline phenomena and over half a century on the concept of narcissism, this uncertainty and debate continue in the fields of clinical psychiatry and psychology to the present day. Although implicit in much of the literature is the notion that the borderline personality disorder represents a more severe form of psychopathology than does the narcissistic personality disorder, this has been explicitly stated by only a few current theorists, and remains an issue of disagreement among others. The present study has attempted to address these issues directly, and the results suggest that, at least as measured by the four scales applied to Rorschach data, the borderline personality may indeed represent a more severe disturbance than the narcissistic personality disorder. The results are consistent with both the psychoanalytic and descriptive literature on the two disorders, and have heuristic value for understanding the respective presence or absence of many of the descriptive observations of the disorders.

Several authors have commented recently on the relevance of this type of research for the differential diagnosis and treatment of individuals suffering from character pathology (Berg, 1983; Blatt and Lerner, 1983; Lerner, 1983). Kernberg (1975, 1976) has stressed the importance of careful diagnostic assessment of these individuals, including psychological tests, for treatment planning and the management of transference and countertransference issues. Kohut (1963) and Masterson (1981), on the other hand, have asserted that the primary means of differential diagnosis between the two disorders is the response to psychoanalytic treatment. This type of post hoc evaluation is unfortunate in that it can be costly and inefficient. Having a means of accurately distinguishing borderline from narcissistic pathology specifically, and of assessing severity of character pathology in general, would enable practicing clinicians to make more thorough and judicious decisions in choosing treatment strategies for such persons.

Clearly, there are limitations to this present study. It would be useful to study similarly character-disordered individuals who do not present with Axis I diagnoses as well. More information could also be gleaned from studying larger numbers of borderline and narcissistic personalities than the present study was able to. In addition, controlled studies may enable researchers to place their findings in the broader context of psychopathology and make informed suggestions about where these two types of psychopathology lie in the continuum of individuals presenting both more and less severe disturbances. It would also be useful to study the Rorschach scales individually and collectively, in order to assess their validity in the measurement of the actual concepts of object relations, defensive organization, developmental level, and character style. At the outset, it was hoped that the present study would serve to sharpen and clarify some of the salient variables in looking at the two disorders consistent with the "level two" type of hypothesis generation and testing described earlier. The objective of this level of inquiry is the stimulation of additional research, the end goal of which would be the more accurate assessment and effective treatment of individuals suffering from these types of psychopathology.

REFERENCES

Becker, W. (1956), A genetic approach to the interpretation and evaluation of the process-reactive distinction in schizophrenia. *J. Abnorm. & Soc. Psychol.*, 65:229–236.

Berg, M. (1983), Borderline psychopathology as displayed on psychological tests. *J. Personal. Assess.*, 47:120–183.

Blatt, S., Brenneis, C., Schimek, J., & Glick, M. (1976), A developmental analysis of the concept of the object on the Rorschach. Unpublished manuscript, Yale University.

———— Lerner, H. D. (1983), The psychological assessment of object representation. *J. Personal. Assess.*, 47:7–28.

Bleuler, E. (1924), *Textbook of Psychiatry.* New York: Dover.

Bursten, B. (1982), Narcissistic personalities and DSM-III. *Comprehensive Psychiat.*, 23:409–419.

Carr, A., & Goldstein, E. (1981), Approaches to the diagnosis of borderline condition by use of psychological tests. *J. Personal. Assess.*, 45:563–574.

Carsky, M., & Bloomgarten, J. W. (1981), Subtyping in the borderline realm by means of Rorschach analysis. *Psychiatric Clinics of North America*, 4:101–116.

Exner, J. (1969), Rorschach responses as an index of narcissism. *J. Proj. Tech. & Personal. Assess.*, 33:324–330.

Fenichel, O. (1945), *The Psychoanalytic Theory of the Neuroses.* New York: Norton.

Fisher, S., & Cleveland, S. (1958), *Body Image and Personality.* New York: Von Nostrand.

Fleiss, J. (1981), *Statistical Methods for Rates and Proportions.* 2nd ed. New York: Wiley.

Frank, I. K. (1951), Conceptual Structuralization in Certain Psychoneurotic Disorders: A Genetic Evaluation by Means of the Rorschach Test. Unpublished doctoral dissertation, Boston University.

Fried, R. (1980), Rorschach and Icarus. In: *Borderline Phenomena and the Rorschach Test*, ed. J. Kwawer, H. Lerner, P. Lerner, & A. Sugarman. New York: International Universities Press, pp. 107–132.

Friedman, H. (1952), Perceptual regression in schizophrenia: An hypothesis suggested by the use of the Rorschach test. *J. Gen. Psychol.*, 81:63–98.

———— (1953), Perceptual regression in schizophrenia: An hypothesis suggested by the Rorschach test. *J. Proj. Tech.*, 17:171–185.

Goldfried, M. R. (1962), Rorschach developmental level and the MMPI as measures of severity in psychological disturbance. *J. Object. Tech.*, 26:187–192.

Green, B. A. (1967), Character structure and its functions. *Psychoanal. Rev.*, 54:329–354.

Grinker, R. R., Sr., Werble, B., & Drye, R. C. (1968), *The Borderline Syndrome.* New York: Basic Books.

Gunderson, J. G. (1980), DSM-III diagnoses of personality disorders. Paper presented at McLean Hospital Symposium on DSM-III, October 15.

_____ Singer, M. T. (1975), Defining borderline patients: An overview. *Amer. J. Psychiat.*, 1975:1–10.

Harder, D. W. (1979), The assessment of ambitious-narcissistic character style with three projective tests: The Early Memories, TAT, and Rorschach. *J. Personal. Assess.*, 43:23–32.

Hemmendinger, L. (1953), Perceptual organization and development as reflected in the structure of Rorschach test responses. *J. Proj. Tech.*, 17:162–170.

_____ Schultz, K. D. (1977), Developmental theory and the Rorschach method. In: *Rorschach Psychology*, ed. M. A. Rickers-Ovsiankina. Huntington, NY: Krieger, pp. 83–112.

Hurwitz, I. (1954), A Developmental Study of the Relationship Between Motor Activity and Perceptual Processes as Measured by the Rorschach Test. Unpublished doctoral dissertation, Clark University.

Kernberg, O. F. (1975), *Borderline Conditions and Pathological Narcissism*. New York: Aronson.

_____ (1976), The diagnosis of borderline conditions in adolescence. Paper presented at the Eastern Seaboard Regional Meeting, American Society for Adolescent Psychiatry, Washington, DC: October 8.

_____ (1981), Problems in the classification of personality disorders. Paper presented at the New York Hospital–Cornell University Medical Center, Westchester Division, September 10.

Knight, R. (1954), Borderline states. *Bull. Menn. Clin.*, 17:1–12.

Kohut, H. (1963), The psychoanalytic treatment of narcissistic personality disorders. *Psychoanalytic Study of the Child*, 23:86–113. New York: International Universities Press.

_____ (1971), *The Analysis of the Self*. New York: International Universities Press.

_____ Wolf, E. S. (1978), The disorders of the self and their treatment: An outline. *Internat. J. Psycho-Anal.*, 59:413–425.

Krohn, A., & Mayman, M. (1974), Object representations in dreams and projective tests. *Bull. Menn. Clin.*, 38:445–466.

Kwawer, J. S. (1979), Borderline phenomena, interpersonal relations, and the Rorschach test. *Bull. Menn. Clin.*, 43:515–524.

_____ (1980), Primitive interpersonal modes, borderline phenomena, and Rorschach content. In: *Borderline Phenomena and the Rorschach Test*, ed. J. Kwawer, H. Lerner, P. Lerner, & A. Sugarman. New York: International Universities Press, pp. 89–105.

Lebowitz, A. (1963), Patterns of perceptual and motor organization. *J. Proj. Tech.*, 27:302–308.

Lerner, H. (1983), An object representation approach to psychostructural change: A clinical illustration. *J. Personal. Assess.*, 47:314–323.

_____ Lerner, P. M. (1978), The Rorschach assessment of defensive structure in borderline and neurotic patients. Paper presented at the Annual Convention of the Society of Personality Assessment, Tampa, FL.

Lerner, P. M., & Lerner, H. D. (1980), Rorschach assessment of primitive defenses in borderline personality structure. In: *Borderline Phenomena and the Rorschach Test*, ed. J. Kwawer, H. Lerner, P. Lerner, & A. Sugarman. New York: International Universities Press, pp. 257–274.

Levine, D. (1959), Rorschach genetic level and mental disorder. *J. Proj. Tech.*, 23:436–439.

Lofchie, S. H. (1955), The performance of adults under distraction stress: A developmental approach. *J. Psychol.*, 39:109–116.

Mahler, M. (1971), A study of the separation-individuation process and its possible application to borderline phenomena in the psychoanalytic situation. *Psychoanalytic Study of the Child*, 26:403-424. New York: Quadrangle Books.

———— Kaplan, L. (1977), Developmental aspects in the assessment of narcissistic and so-called borderline personalities. In: *Borderline Personality Disorders*, ed. P. Hartocollis. New York: International Universities Press, pp. 71-86.

———— Pine, F., & Bergman, A. (1975), *The Psychological Birth of the Human Infant*. New York: Basic Books.

Masterson, J. (1981), *The Narcissistic and Borderline Disorders*. New York: Brunner/Mazel.

Meissner, W. W. (1978a), Narcissistic personalities and borderline conditions: A differential diagnosis. *Ann. Psychoanal.*, 7:171-201.

———— (1978b), Theoretical assumptions of concepts of the borderline personality. *J. Amer. Psychoanal. Assn.*, 26:559-598.

Misch, R. C. (1954), The Relationship of Motoric Inhibition to Developmental Levels and Ideational Functioning: An Analysis by Means of the Rorschach Test. Unpublished doctoral dissertation, Clark University.

Olesker, W. (1980), Early life experience and the development of borderline pathology. In: *Borderline Phenomena and the Rorschach Test*, ed. J. Kwawer, H. Lerner, P. Lerner, & A. Sugarman. New York: International Universities Press, pp. 411-439.

Pena, C. D. (1953), A genetic evaluation of perceptual structuralization in cerebral pathology: An investigation by means of the Rorschach test. *J. Proj. Tech.*, 17:186-199.

Perry, C. J., & Klerman, G. I. (1978), The borderline patient: A comparative analysis of four sets of diagnostic criteria. *Arch. Gen. Psychiat.*, 35:141-150.

Rapaport, D., Gill, M., & Schafer, R. (1945), *Diagnostic Psychological Testing*. Rev. ed. New York: International Universities Press, 1968.

Reich, W. (1933), *Character Analysis*. 3rd ed. New York: Noonday.

Rinsley, D. (1977), An object-relations view of the borderline personality. In: *Borderline Personality Disorders*, ed. P. Hartocollis. New York: International Universities Press, pp. 47-70.

———— (1978), Borderline and narcissistic disorders: Clinical and developmental aspects. Unpublished manuscript.

Schafer, R. (1948), *The Clinical Application of Psychological Tests*. New York: International Universities Press.

Shapiro, D. (1965), *Neurotic Styles*. New York: Basic Books.

Siegal, E. L. (1953), Genetic parallels of perceptual structuralization in paranoid schizophrenia: An analysis by means of the Rorschach technique. *J. Proj. Tech.*, 17:151-161.

Singer, M. T. (1977), The borderline diagnosis and psychological tests: Review and research. In: *Borderline Personality Disorders*, ed. P. Hartocollis. New York: International Universities Press, pp. 193-212.

———— Larson, D. G. (1981), Borderline personality and the Rorschach test. *Arch. Gen. Psychiat.*, 38:693-698.

Smith, K. (1980), Object-relations concepts as applied to the borderline level of ego functioning. In: *Borderline Phenomena and the Rorschach Test*, ed. J. Kwawer, H. Lerner, P. Lerner, & A. Sugarman. New York: International Universities Press, pp. 59-87.

Spear, W. E. (1980), The psychological assessment of structural and thematic object representations in borderline and schizophrenic patients. In: *Borderline Phenomena and the Rorschach Test*, ed. J. Kwawer, H. Lerner, P. Lerner, & A. Sugarman. New York: International Universities Press, pp. 321-340.

Spiro, R. H., & Spiro, T. W. (1980), Transitional phenomena and developmental issues in borderline Rorschachs. In: *Borderline Phenomena and the Rorschach Test*, ed. J. Kwawer, H. Lerner, P. Lerner, & A. Sugarman. New York: International Universities Press, pp. 189–202.

Stern, A. (1938), Psychoanalytic therapy in the borderline neuroses. *Psychoanal. Quart.*, 14:190–198.

Stone, H. K., & Dellis, N. P. (1960), An exploratory investigation into the levels hypothesis. *J. Proj. Tech.*, 24:333–340.

Stone, M. H. (1980), *The Borderline Syndromes*. New York: McGraw-Hill.

Sugarman, A. (1980), The borderline personality organization as manifested on psychological tests. In: *Borderline Phenomena and the Rorschach Test*, ed. J. Kwawer, H. Lerner, P. Lerner, & A. Sugarman. New York: International Universities Press, pp. 39–57.

_____ Bloom-Feshbach, S., & Bloom-Feshbach, J. (1980), The psychological dimensions of borderline adolescents. In: *Borderline Phenomena and the Rorschach Test*, ed. J. Kwawer, H. Lerner, P. Lerner, & A. Sugarman. New York: International Universities Press, pp. 469–494.

_____ Lerner, H. D. (1980), Reflections on the current state of the borderline concept. In: *Borderline Phenomena and the Rorschach Test*, ed. J. Kwawer, H. Lerner, P. Lerner, & A. Sugarman. New York: International Universities Press, pp. 11–37.

Tolpin, M., & Kohut, H. (1980), The disorder of the self: The psychopathology of the first year of life. *The Course of Life: Psychoanalytic Contributions Toward Understanding Personality Development. Vol. 1, Infancy and Early Childhood.*, ed. S. I. Greenspan & G. H. Pollock, Washington, DC: Government Printing Office, pp. 425–442.

Urist, J. (1980), The continuum between primary and secondary process thinking: Toward a concept of borderline thought. In: *Borderline Phenomena and the Rorschach Test*, ed. J. Kwawer, H. Lerner, P. Lerner, & A. Sugarman. New York: International Universities Press, pp. 133–154.

Werner, H. (1948), *Comparative Psychology of Mental Development*. New York: International Universities Press.

_____ (1957), *The Comparative Psychology of Mental Development*. Rev. ed. New York: International Universities Press.

_____ Kaplan, B. (1963), Some experiments in support of an organismic theory of symbol formation. *Psychologische Beiträge*, 5(3/4):484–491.

Wilensky, H. (1959), Rorschach developmental level and social participation of chronic schizophrenics. *J. Proj. Tech.*, 23:87–92.

Winnicott, D. W. (1951), Transitional objects and transitional phenomena. In: *Collected Papers: Through Paediatrics to Psycho-analysis*. London: Tavistock, 1958, pp. 229–242.

Zetzel, E. (1971), A developmental approach to the borderline patient. *Amer. J. Psychiat.*, 127:867–871.

Zimet, C. N., & Fine, H. J. (1965), Primary and secondary process thinking in two types of schizophrenia. *J. Proj. Tech. & Personal. Assess.*, 29:93–99.

Chapter 12

Transference and Countertransference in Psychological Testing of Patients with Eating Disorders

Susan Bram, Ph.D.

As an eating disorder is by definition a behavioral syndrome, it is readily diagnosed according to descriptive criteria, such as those found in the Diagnostic and Statistical Manual (DSM–III) of the American Psychiatric Association (1982). The classification of eating disorders according to that schema includes two major syndromes—Anorexia Nervosa, marked by severe weight loss and fear of becoming obese, and Bulimia, marked by recurrent episodes of binge eating.

Despite the relatively high degree of consensus as to the general definition of these disorders, there is still ongoing discussion regarding some of the inclusion criteria (Dally, 1969; Feighner, Robins, Guze, Woodruff, Winokur, and Munoz, 1972; Garrow, Crisp, Jordan, Meyer, Russell, Silverstone, Stunkard, and Van Itallie, 1975; Morgan and Russell, 1975; Rollins and Piazza, 1978). There is even greater controversy regarding the distinctions among various subtypes of eating disorders (Crisp, Harding, and McGuinness, 1974; Beumont, George, and Smart, 1976; Boskind-Lodahl, 1976; Beumont, 1977; Garfinkel and Garner, 1982) and whether or not there are common personality traits, types, or disorders among patients with eating disorders (Garfinkel and Garner, 1982).

The issue of subtypes of eating disorders has emerged with the increasing recognition among clinicians that many patients do not fit precisely into the two syndromes described in the DSM–III. For example, there are bulimics who are as preoccupied with weight loss as anorexics, though "pursuit of thinness" is not a requisite for this diagnosis. Similarly, anorexics may vary considerably in their choice of method for losing weight; some simply restrict intake, others exercise and diet, and others employ laxatives or purgatives. Furthermore, throughout the course of the illness, patients may develop different methods to control their weight. Garfinkel and Garner (1982) attempt to resolve these diagnostic complexities by employing the label *anorexia nervosa* for all their patients with eating disorders and dividing them according to whether or not they are "restricters" or "bulimics" (gorgers). Other diagnostic issues have not yet been resolved—for example, how to label patients with eating disorders whose weight does not fluctuate significantly.

The wide variety of patients with eating disorders has contributed to the longstanding confusion as to whether or not they have personality traits, types, or personality disorders in common. Because most practitioners over the years have used slightly different diagnostic criteria and have had access to distinct patient populations, the findings to date have been equivocal and there is little consensus in this area. For example, two types of patients with eating disorders were identified by Janet in 1919—hysterics and obsessives. Half a century later, Dally (1969) studied his patients and subdivided them into Hysterics (H), Obsessives (O), and Mixed (M). Struck by the prevalence of bodily delusions among anorexics, others have emphasized schizophrenia (Binswanger, 1944) or suggested that there is a psychotic-like process underlying the syndrome (Bruch, 1973; Selvini-Palazzoli, 1978). Masterson (1977), Stone (1980), and others claim that patients with eating disorders meet the criteria for the diagnosis of borderline personality.

Whether or not there is a common personality type or disorder associated with anorexia and bulimia is a debatable question in its own right. For example, Morgan and Russell (1975) point out that use of the term "personality disorder" for adolescence (the predominant age period for the onset of eating disorders) may be inappropriate, as character formation is still under way until adulthood. Others have emphasized that research and clinical data yield such a variety of personality types and psychopathologies that it is more accurate to speak of heterogeneity, rather than homogeneity, among patients with eating disorders (Bram, Eger, and Halmi, 1982; Swift and Stern, 1982). If it is true that the incidence of eating disorders is on the increase, as some authors suggest (Schwartz, Thompson, and Johnson, 1982), and that it is crossing class and cultural lines, then one could expect the syndrome to become even more diversified in the future.

Speculation about personality development and psychodynamics among patients with eating disorders is thus likely to continue along the tortuous path it has followed so far during this century. As Kernberg (1980) and others (Sugarman, Quinlan, and Devenis (1981), Swift and Stern, 1982; Lerner, 1983) have pointed out, theorizing about the psychology of eating disorders has paralleled the evolution of psychoanalytic theory itself. For example, early formulations centered on psychosexual issues such as fear of oral impregnation (Benedek, 1936; Lorand, 1943). Bruch (1973) introduced the notion of cognitive impairments and deficits in autonomy, in line with her interest in ego psychology and interpersonal psychiatry. Others have interpreted eating disorders as a deficit in the development of the self (Goodsitt, 1977), while object relations theorists have delineated difficulties in separation and individuation (Masterson, 1977; Selvini-Palazzoli, 1978). Recently, Sugarman et al. (1981) and Lerner (1983) have attempted to integrate the contributions of cognitive theory, developmental research, self psychology, and object relations theory in their formulations.

Given the rich and extensive literature on diagnosis, personality, and dynamics of patients with eating disorders, it is remarkable that so little attention has been paid to the contribution of psychological testing. Very few studies have been published that draw on psychological assessment techniques. Those that do have emphasized descriptive, structured instruments such as the MMPI and the Eysenck Personality Instrument, self-report measures, or observer rating scales (Crisp, Harding, and McGuinness, 1974; Stonehill and Crisp, 1977; Ben-Tovim, Marilov, and Crisp, 1979; Crisp, Hsu, and Stonehill, 1979; Gomez and Dally, 1980; Hood, Moore, and Garner, 1982; Small, Teagno, Madero, Gross, and Ebert, 1982; Solyom, Freeman, and Miles, 1982; Piazza, Rollins, and Lewis, 1983; Weiss and Ebert, 1983; Katzman and Wolchik, 1984; Nagelberg, Hale, and Ware, 1984). It is not surprising, given the nature of the instruments utilized and the character of the syndrome, that these studies have so far added little to our understanding of the underlying dynamics or treatment of eating disorders. For example, patients with eating disorders are found to be "compulsive" and "introverted" on such scales, traits which would seem to be implicit in the diagnosis of anorexia. In fact, despite high levels of "objectivity" and standardization of such measures, the findings are quite inconsistent (Small, 1984).

Studies using projective tests, such as the Rorschach, TAT, or figure drawings, have been rare and often suffer from small samples, lack of control groups, or a limited focus on a few variables (Thielgard, 1965; Selvini-Palazzoli, 1969; Wagner and Wagner, 1978; Strober and Goldenberg, 1981; Bram, Eger, and Halmi, 1982; Kaufer and Katz, 1983; Wallach and Lowenkopf, 1984). Although some of the findings have been valuable, they represent but a small example of the insight and understanding that can be generated by responses to unstructured instruments designed to tap intrapsychic life.

Some of the practical reasons for the neglect of psychological testing are obvious. For example, the medical urgency that accompanies the severely emaciated anorexic when brought to the office or hospital precludes lengthy psychological assessment at intake. In addition, many researchers and practitioners have found that a patient's mental status is impaired by the physical effects of starvation or purgation and thus prefer to defer assessment of personality until adequate weight has been achieved.

Beyond these practical concerns, however, there are psychological factors that may contribute to the neglect of diagnostic testing in work with eating disorders. Since some of the aspects of eating disorders (e.g., emphasis on fitness, pursuit of thinness) are syntonic in our culture, there may be a hesitancy on the part of clinicians to acknowledge the possibility that serious psychopathology underlies the ailment. Indeed, patients often try to convince family and friends that their problem is only a "diet gone awry," a "bad habit" that needs to be broken. Moreover, the discrepancies among appearance, ideation, and affect in these patients can be confusing to clinicians. For example, a patient who looks frail may have a high level of energy and be preoccupied with jogging. A patient who has regained her normal weight may still harbor bodily delusions or depressive affect, even though she appears healthier than on admission. Ironically, it is just this dissociation of internal and external world that psychological testing, particularly the Rorschach, is well suited to investigate if administered expertly by a trained diagnostician.

The fact that psychological testing has been given short shrift in the field of eating disorders is as much the fault of the psychodiagnostician as of the clinician. Brief, superficial, or unintegrated test reports can severely hinder assessment and treatment and discourage practitioners from relying on this nonmedical procedure (Appelbaum, 1970). Many factors contribute to the optimal administration, interpretation, and reporting of psychological tests and have been amply discussed elsewhere (Rapaport, Gill, and Schafer, 1945; Schafer, 1954; Appel-baum, 1972). In recent years however, one set of variables has begun to emerge as pivotal to the psychological test process: the relationship between patient and examiner and the feelings this relationship evokes in each, in the form of transference and countertransference.[1]

Early contributors to the development and refinement of psycho-logical testing gave heed to the importance of the interpersonal rela-tionship and the testing situation (Schachtel, 1945; Schafer, 1954; Appelbaum, 1959; Schlesinger, 1973). However, the emphasis was more often on the transference, that is, the feelings and attitudes of the patient toward the examiner, than on the countertransference, the emotional responses of the examiner to the patient. One approach to this issue is found in Schafer's classic discussion of interpersonal aspects of the test situation (1954).

In describing the testing situation, Schafer outlines various con-straints on the psychologist, such as professional demands and the relationship to the referring therapist. He then enumerates ways in which the role of diagnostician can evoke various aspects of a psychol-ogist's personality—the "voyeur," the "autocrat," the "oracle," the "saint." These situational factors can in turn elicit a range of responses from the patient. Depending on various personality factors, the patient may feel exposed, threatened with loss of control, confronted with disconcerting aspects of the self, encouraged to regress, or over-

---

[1]The terms transference and countertransference have a history that is beyond the scope of this paper (Racker, 1968; Epstein and Feiner, 1979). Both concepts were originally used to describe phenomena that interfered with psychoanalytic treatment. The discovery that transference (the projection of feelings, thoughts, and wishes by the patient onto the analyst as though he or she is a significant person from the past) could be a source of important data, rather than an obstacle, marked a turning point in Freud's work. Countertransference was initially defined in like manner, as the unconscious projection of thoughts, feelings, and wishes by the analyst onto the patient; the analyst was obligated to eliminate such feelings through self-analysis. In recent years, the meaning of countertransference has been broadened by some to include feelings evoked by the patient directly, as well as via the analyst's past. In our discussion we have chosen to employ the broadest and least inferential meaning of the terms. Thus, "transference" is used here to describe any emotional response to the analyst (or diagnostician) expressed by the patient through words or behavior, and "countertrans-ference" to describe any emotional response to the patient expressed by the psycholo-gist. Since the testing situation does not allow thorough analysis of the sources of these reactions, our discussion is limited to a description of partial transferences, most aptly thought of as transference *reactions*. Furthermore, as diagnosticians we obviously have more data on countertransference than transference and have therefore made the former our focus, although in our view they are interdependent phenomena.

whelmed by the "freedom" of the unstructured test setting. Although Schafer offers a full description of these variables, he stops short of suggesting that the interpersonal responses on the part of psychologist or patient may be of diagnostic value.

It is only in recent years, with an expansion of interest in counter-transference in treatment (Epstein and Feiner, 1979) and the development of an object relational approach to psychodiagnostics, that the countertransference aspects of testing have been given greater attention. Sugarman (1981) reviews the development of this concept in psychoanalytic theory and, through case presentations, makes it clear that countertransference material can be a valuable source of data for diagnosis and formulation. I believe, with Sugarman, that a more careful examination of feelings expressed by the patient, as well as those evoked in the tester, can contribute to a richer descriptive and psychodynamic understanding of patients. Whereas in the past such aspects of the testing situation have been treated as epiphenomena or sources of interference to be discussed only in seminars or supervision, some now suggest that psychologists include them in their total evaluation and in the test report. This would seem to be a particularly useful approach in assessment of patients whose feelings and thoughts are not easily expressed in words because they are split off from their verbal responses to everyday behavior and may not be fully tapped even in projective testing. Inclusion of countertransference and transference material can also provide a direct linkage between testing and treatment, as Gorney and Weinstock (1980) point out in their description of testing with borderline patients.

In the discussion that follows I will draw on my experience in testing and treating patients with eating disorders, and in supervising their testing and therapy, during the past seven years. My observations are based on a careful review of test reports and Rorschach protocols, as well as notes on the testing process. Particular attention has been paid to that section of the test report that traditionally has been the vehicle for describing interpersonal aspects of the test situation: Description of the Patient and Test Behavior. The focus of the discussion will be on the following aspects of the testing situation: sociohistorical context; setting; physical appearance of the patient; mood, affect, and attitude of the patient; and patient-tester interaction. Although most of the comments concern anoretic patients, a separate section will review these variables as they affect the testing of patients with bulimia or anorexia with bulimic features.

SOCIOHISTORICAL CONTEXT

The sociohistorical context of testing patients with eating disorders is itself a contributor to the interpersonal situation. The work described here was carried out during the first half of the 1980s, a decade during which public awareness of eating disorders was beginning to rise and the incidence of anorexia and bulimia was apparently on the increase (Schwartz, Thompson, and Johnson, 1982). As a result, there was a certain "cachet" to having one of these disorders, and an aura was sometimes passed on to those who worked with the syndrome. Adding to the glamour of eating disorders was the fact that in the United States they had been seen predominantly among the upper and upper middle classes, although during the time period described there were indications that this was changing. In addition, the high mortality and morbidity rates among patients with eating disorders—an estimated mortality rate of 12 percent among anorexics, according to Garfinkel and Garner (1982)—created a sense of urgency that was particularly great on an inpatient unit which admitted patients in states of severe emaciation and sometimes in great medical danger. Although high levels of anxiety could sometimes masquerade as excitement and provoke feelings of heroism among staff, more often they exacerbated the usual tensions that surround testing and treatment. Furthermore, since there had been little professional agreement as to optimal treatment, testing referrals were often made in a state of confusion, with the hope of resolving unresolvable conflicts about the level of psychopathology, the personality diagnosis of the patient, and the indications for treatment modality.

Despite diverse backgrounds and a wide range of ages among patients *admitted for treatment* to the inpatient unit discribed below— they ranged from eleven to forty-three—there was actually a great deal of homogeneity in age among the patients *tested*. The age of onset for eating disorders has been described as bimodal—peaking at about age fourteen and again at age eighteen. Since the psychologists testing in the described setting tend to be between twenty-five and thirty-five years of age, there was often a maximum age difference between patient and clinician of about two decades and in some cases, patient and tester belonged to the same age cohort.

There was even greater homogeneity in gender. The patients discussed here are all female, representing the fact that anorexia and bulimia have to date been found primarily in women. [According to Garfinkel and Garner (1982), an estimated 4 percent of eating disorder patients are males, and only one was tested during the period described here.] Indeed, although the sociology of the syndrome is still poorly understood, many observers have remarked that its increased incidence and emergence in the media occurred during a period in which the effects of the second wave of feminism had begun to be felt in the culture at large: changing sex role definitions, affirmative action programs, expanding opportunities for women in education and work. Thus, one could hardly ignore the fact that we were seeing a large segment of a cohort of women who were passing through their adolescence during a period of upheaval in sex roles and mores. They were evidently conflicted about their sexual identity or, at a minimum, were suffering from an illness that has an impact on sexual development. For female psychologists conscious of the contemporary social context, this was a challenging and at times ironic situation. Were we in effect "sisters" to these patients? Role models? The "enemy"? For male psychologists these factors posed different, but often intense, dilemmas about their view of females.

In summary, the psychologist evaluating patients with eating disorders in the first half of this decade could hardly carry out the work in a vacuum. In the context of great public and individual concern about the health of a generation of young women, of professional disagreement about the level of psychopathology (or social pathology) represented by the syndrome, and about the appropriate approach to treatment, testing could not be administered without strong transference and counter-transference feelings.

THE SETTING: INPATIENT AND OUTPATIENT TESTING

The inpatient unit on which most of the testing described here took place is an intermediate-stay unit (three to six months) that is part of a large psychiatric hospital. Treatment was provided by an interdisciplinary team composed of psychiatrists, psychologists, social workers, nurses, and mental health workers. Individual therapy carried out by professionals from the first three groups was combined with group, family, and milieu treatment. Because of its reputation in the treatment of eating disorders, the unit attracted patients who were in some degree of medical danger and had a chronic history of eating disorders; often they had been in a variety of previous treatments with little success. Thus, they were admitted to the unit because of a legitimate concern on the part of referring clinicians, family, friends, or school personnel. The policy on the unit was to attend first to medical concerns and to defer testing until some weight gain had occurred in order to eliminate the effects of cognitive impairment resulting from emaciation. As a result, patients were usually close to their medically approved weight by the time they reached the diagnostician's office. However, as is usually the case with rapid weight gain, it tended to be uneven and often would fluctuate over the course of the psychological testing.

Psychological testing was carried out by the psychologists at the request of the therapist or the treatment team. The explicit referral questions tended to focus on degree of psychopathology (e.g., is there a psychotic process underlying the disorder?), potential for psychotherapy (e.g., uncovering or supportive work), existence of intellectual impairments or learning disabilities, confusion about the response to treatment, and, occasionally, recommendations for placement.

Implicit in many of the testing referrals on the unit were requests that the examiners participate in the evaluation and treatment of the patient in one of the ways described by Schafer (1954)—as "oracle," "autocrat," or "saint"—or in a role that is particularly important on an inpatient unit, that of "referee." The "oracle" was called upon to look beneath the surface of the behavior disorder and determine if the "resistance" to weight gain was willful, malicious, or crazy. The "autocrat" was called in to "get the patient organized" through a series of encounters that would impose order on an otherwise unruly or recalcitrant patient. The "saint" role was often evoked when negative countertransference pervaded the team's view of the patient and a dispassionate observer was desired to "calm the waters" by reminding the staff how truly vulnerable the patient was. The "referee" role, a combination of all three of these, was often derived from clashes among staff about the best way to understand the patient and, more often, about where to send the patient upon discharge: home, a residential placement center, or another hospital.

At first glance, the outpatient setting would seem to be less complicated a context for psychological testing, since usually the referral involves only two people, rather than an entire treatment team. Thus, only one person's agenda is conveyed to the psychologist, and communication can proceed more directly. Furthermore, patients in an outpatient setting are usually less disturbed than those who have been admitted to the hosptial. Nevertheless, when outpatient testing is requested, it is often to determine if inpatient treatment is indicated. Thus, the "oracle" must be called upon to clarify the level of functioning and depth of pathology in a patient who may, for example, be slowly but steadily losing weight. Indeed, when the outpatient treatment begins to feel rocky, the examiner may be called in to give order to both therapist and patient in the role of "autocrat." (Referrals that emphasize intellectual difficulties in a patient who appears to function adequately in this domain may signal such a need as most therapists associate cognitive tests with authoritarian notions of school and schoolteachers.) Although the role of "referee" may be less appropriate in the outpatient setting, very often the tester is called in to participate in decisions regarding placement, prognosis, or adequacy of the treatment. Some patients will use this situation to pit the psychologist against the therapist, who may even covertly collaborate with the fantasy of giving up the patient to someone else's care. In sum, although the stakes seem higher on an inpatient unit, and there are more personnel with whom to communicate, countertransference feelings can be generated in the outpatient setting as well as on the inpatient unit.

PHYSICAL APPEARANCE

It is an indisputable fact that patients with eating disorders are concerned with their physical appearance and engage in behaviors that have an impact on how they look. When underweight, not only do they appear emaciated; they may in addition be edemic or pallid and frail from the cumulative effects of their peculiar eating habits, purging, and exercising. Their skin may appear sallow, and their hair may be thin or dull.

In light of this, it is of particular interest that of thirty-five test reports reviewed for this chapter only three gave any indication of the physical state of the patient. It is as if the patient's own denial had so pervaded the testing situation that even the examiner, sitting face-to-face with the patient, was blinded to a very obvious reality; covertly, the examiner seemed drawn into colluding with the patient in a belief that there was nothing wrong with her weight. Indeed, the refusal to acknowledge the existence of a problem in anorexia nervosa and in bulimia has had a major impact on the treatment of such patients. Family, friends, spouses, and even school and medical personnel are often unwitting participants in a "conspiracy of silence" which can result in delayed treatment and the development of a life-threatening situation. Even when the patient is in ongoing psychotherapy, the denial of weight loss or illness can persist to a dangerous degree.

In like manner, the test reports reviewed made little mention of the patients' style of dress, even though this is another domain in which eating disorder patients often stand out. Most typically, patients with anorexia have in the literature been noted to overdress: to wear bulky sweaters, jackets, and sweatpants, even in warm weather or well-heated offices. Although some believe that overdressing is a result of hypothermia resulting from weight loss, the persistence of this style of dress well after weight gain suggests that it serves psychological purposes as well. Obviously, because of its inappropriateness, overdressing brings attention to the patient. When asked their reasons for dressing as they do, however, patients often indicate that such clothing serves to hide the body. Some clinicians have speculated that heavy clothing serves as a reinforcement of tenuous ego boundaries (Strober and Goldenberg, 1981). Viewed from an interpersonal perspective, the wearing of heavy clothing may act as a protective barrier between self and others.

In contrast, a less frequent but not atypical style of dress seen among patients with eating disorders is that of underdressing. Here the message seems less ambivalent at first glance, as the style obviously draws attention to the skin and bones of the emaciated patient. For example, one patient on the unit, who was tall, lanky, and grossly underweight, started a fad among the other patients by wearing short shorts and a tank top even in cool weather, apparently enjoying the dramatic effect it had on others. When confronted about this provocative behavior, this patient and the others denied that they wanted people to look at them. Nevertheless, underdressers do seem to be engaged in a more direct form of exhibitionism than do overdressers.

What is not clear is the fantasy behind the two styles of presentation and how they affect the observer so that appearance is not mentioned in the test report. We have found that the psychologist working with such patients is often struck by a mixture of conflicting feelings. The overdresser may at first make the examiner feel uncomfortable because of the peculiarity of the costume. In the mild case, it is as if the patient were preparing for a quick getaway by holding onto her coat or sweater. In the extreme, it is as if one were sitting with a teenage "bag lady." The tester who is naive regarding this characteristic of eating disorder patients may be tempted to offer to reduce the heat or open a window to make the patient feel more comfortable. The shrug of the shoulders or verbal protest that usually follows quickly enlightens the tester, may discourage further nurturant behavior, and creates a distance between examiner and patient.

A more complex set of reactions may be generated by the underdresser, who is often experienced as simultaneously seductive and repulsive. The fact that underdressers are exhibiting their emaciated bodies may draw one toward them out of curiosity or a desire to help, but the ugliness of the transformed body pushes one away. Although the psychologist's gender may have some impact on which response predominates, we have found that both men and women are often left with a sense of pathos for the patient, who seems unaware of the self-defeating nature of her attempt to get attention.

Although the visual modality is primary in the response to the patients, other senses come into play as well—auditory, olfactory, and kinesic. In general, the eating disorder patient is extremely quiet, certainly in contrast to her adolescent peers. Her voice may be low, her verbal output sparse, and one might find oneself leaning closer or lowering one's own voice in her presence. In an otherwise calm office one is often struck by the silence during pauses between responses or when the patient is working on her own, e.g., during certain subtests of the WAIS. Although with some patients such quiet can be experienced as calm or soothing, the quality of the interaction with the anoretic patient is such that the silence can leave one feeling quite alone and empty.

Smells can be a prominent part of the experience of working with eating disorder patients as well. The anoretic habit of chewing gum to avoid fattening food may carry with it the characteristic odor of spearmint, which adolescent therapists know well but may still find sickening. A more dramatic parade of smells will accompany the anorexic or bulimic who vomits. These patients are often preoccupied with hiding the telltale odor that accompanies their purging by liberal use of chewing gum, hair spray, or perfume.

The activity level of the anorexic also contributes to the testing situation. Many anoretic patients respond lethargically to personal interactions, move slowly, as if in a trance, and thus underline the feeling that something is physically wrong with them or that they are depressed. Once in the testing room, however, they may engage in compulsive rituals that have been developed ostensibly in the service of weight loss. For example, one patient surreptitiously tapped her foot throughout the testing, even when asked to stop, while another drummed her fingers on the desk. Another subtle maneuver has been observed in patients who change their position in the chair a number of times during the hour. Since in conventional situations these habits are usually signs of nervousness, impatience, or rudeness, the psychologist must make a special effort to understand them as symptomatic of the syndrome and strive to be sympathetic despite the irritation they can provoke.

Although the specific sensual aspects of interaction with eating disorder patients are rarely a source of direct comment in test reports, the overall image conveyed by the patient is often discussed. Anoretic patients are usually described as looking younger than their age, but on occasion may also appear haggard, wrinkled, and eerily older than expected. Sexual attributes and style (or their lack) is also a source of comment and often causes discomfort among testers. Although the awkward combination of exhibitionism and withdrawal described above is common among adolescent patients generally, those with eating disorders often seem to be playing out conflicts over secondary sexual characteristics in a more dramatic manner than is usual. For example, descriptions of the patient in test reports may mention the lack of the usual feminine accoutrements seen on adolescent girls—jewelry, colorful hair ornaments, makeup. The absence of such signs of sexual stereotyping may cause the anoretic patient to seem unfeminine in comparison to her peers. Ironically, however, the childlike appearance, coupled with frailty and a superficial passivity, can convey an image of traditional femininity that is still part of the Western stereotype of females. Differences in the responses to this aspect of the patient's image were noted between the male and female psychologists whose reports were reviewed for this chapter. For example, one severely emaciated older anoretic woman was described by the male psychologist who tested her as feminine and seductive, whereas to the female staff she appeared prim and asexual.

In summary, the patient with an eating disorder presents herself in a dramatic fashion, evoking a variety of responses in the examiner. Nevertheless, her own denial, deflection, repression, and isolation of affect often cause the psychologist to ignore many of these elements in writing the test report despite the fact that they have an insidious effect. One may initially feel kindly, protective, and nurturant toward the patient with an eating disorder. On the part of the male psychologist, these feelings may even be confused with a sexual response. However, such proactive feelings are usually followed in rapid succession by discomfort, irritation, and anger. The implications of this for understanding the dynamics of eating disorders and for treatment will be discussed below.

MOOD, AFFECT, AND ATTITUDE

One of the most palpable aspects of testing patients with eating disorders is the air of constraint that fills the room. It is evident in body posture, movement, verbal output, affect, and attitude toward testing. The factors described above, such as physical appearance, clothing, and image, set the stage for a drama that is played out in microcosm within the testing situation and has implications for treatment. The affective tone that is conveyed can be quite mystifying at first, and the psychologist is likely to go through a variety of moods in response to this drama. Indeed, the armamentarium the patient brings into the testing room may act as a shield for her and serve to disarm the psychologist, at least initially. Thus, quietly, subtly, and relentlessly, the patient's internal struggle for autonomy becomes manifest as a struggle for self-control, and ultimately for power within the dyad.

The arrangement of psychological testing is one arena in which the struggle takes place. Traditionally, psychologists set the terms of an appointment, carry out testing on their own turf (the office), administer test materials in a systematic way, and request of patients only that they respond freely. Since the patient with an eating disorder has usually gone to great lengths to avoid any revelation of herself in her recent life, and to ward off intrusions, even this relatively benign situation can create a high level of tension. The aspect of give-and-take in the testing dyad can be an additional threat. Through the struggle over her weight the patient with an eating disorder has let it be known that she does not like people to tell her what to do; she certainly does not like people to "feed" her. In our experience, the struggle around these issues is alternately expressed by the patient herself and projected onto the examiner throughout the test process. For example, the patient may at first be concerned about her own punctuality and then induce apprehension about lateness in the examiner.

Among the themes that emerge throughout the testing are self-consciousness, perfectionism, exigence toward others, and self-involvement. The patient with an eating disorder is often caught up in perfectionism, self-consciousness, and compulsive attention to detail that is evident both in her attitude and in actual test answers. For example, she will try to follow all instructions to a T, and to answer all questions with exactness, especially on the WAIS or the WISC; she will rarely refuse a task or a card on the Rorschach. Indeed, on the IQ test her attention to detail may result in "spoiled" answers. Her responses to the Rorschach are often prefaced with such comments as "I'm not sure this is correct, but . . . ," alerting the examiner to her high standards of performance and her feelings of inadequacy, as well as her distortion of the test situation (i.e., there is no correct answer on the Rorschach). This attention to detail reflects rigidity and illustrates the desire for perfection in these patients.

One could at first feel sympathy for someone so caught up in trying to be perfect in an otherwise imperfect world if these demands were limited to the self. However, the ambivalent aspect of the perfectionism among patients with eating disorders is expressed through the highly critical attitude focused on others, in this situation on the examiner. Thus, she not only expects punctuality, tidiness, and perfection of herself, but of the examiner as well. If the psychologist is a few minutes late or the test sessions run over, the patient will not hesitate to look at her watch or let the psychologist know quite directly what is wrong. Not surprisingly, this exigent attitude is most dramatically expressed in the arena of food. Psychologists dealing with these patients may often find themselves confiscating all evidence of lunch and hiding the cup of coffee that usually sits on the desk in order to avoid a patient's scorn. Test materials will be prepared in advance, and the female psychologist may find herself smoothing out wrinkles in her clothing before approaching the patient for testing. Underlying this emphasis on self-consciousness and appearance is a superficiality of focus and a concreteness in thinking. Both patient and examiner may thereby become immersed in attention to relatively minor details and diverted from more significant concerns such as feelings, relationships, or pathology of thought. It is consistent with this style that Rorschach responses are often illustrated by actual references to items on the desk or parts of the body. For example, a patient may say, "This is like the book I have" or point to a part of her own body to explain her response to the Rorschach. An extension of this self-consciousness and perfectionism is a self-involvement that borders at times on self-referential thinking. For example, in the Rorschach responses mentioned above, answers were often explained in terms of "my neck," "my spine," "my home."

Again, one could imagine psychologists feeling a bit like the mother duck in her ducklings' imprinting stage when the patient attends to details of her self and of the "caretaker" in an attempt to model herself and develop her own identity. When this dynamic is experienced in work with children or adolescents, it is often relatively easy for the empathic clinician to feel nurturance toward the patient and to participate in this process in a warm and generous manner. Yet, this aspect of the interaction with eating disorder patients is often laced with hidden competitive strivings and aggression that make the examiner feel vulnerable rather than helpful.

PATIENT-TESTER INTERACTION

As a result of the factors just described, there are many levels of interaction going on during the testing process. On the surface a psychologist may find the patient with an eating disorder "simple to test." She is organized, punctual, neat, seemingly cooperative, and well-controlled. She is of at least average intelligence and seems to understand instructions and the requirements of the test situation readily. Thus, testing with such patients is relatively easy initially, certainly in comparison to testing with adolescents who have other sorts of disturbances, such as conduct disorders. But though the anoretic patient is superficially cooperative, even compliant, beneath the surface one senses a struggle for control that feels at times like defiance, hostility, and even rage at those whom she perceives as more powerful than herself. If one has not already sensed the seething aggression beneath the surface, a careful examination of test responses will indicate its presence. For example, one patient had an otherwise unremarkable Rorschach that proceeded with a variety of popular responses— "moth," "bat," "dogs," "tree"—and then, on Card X, "a whole bunch of insects, two long pink objects like centipedes, two blue objects like spiders, two gray objects that look like bugs, and *the whole picture looks like hostility.*"

Similarly, on the surface the patient with an eating disorder seems respectful, even deferential toward adults such as the psychologist. Again, however, beneath this facade one senses a disdain for others which may be directed at adults in general or at women in particular. This hostility may be most evident at moments when the examiner expresses aspects of the nurturant role or conveys feelings of tenderness toward the patient by reassuring her about her test performance, by attempting to help her relax, or, as described above, by trying to make her more comfortable in the testing situation. One finds simple gestures of kindness rebuffed and it is easy to feel rejected, invalidated, and left with a sense of helplessness as one is prevented from carrying out the role of helper.

Indeed, as the work of testing proceeds it becomes clear that the process of testing is itself threatening to the patient. Although the patient may seem cooperative, she is made uncomfortable by both cognitive and projective questions and will let the psychologist know this by her comments and by vigilance about what is written. Thus it becomes increasingly evident that the patient feels untrusting, and there is little that can be done to reassure her.

In sum, the patient with an eating disorder may let the psychologist have control at first and play the role of adult, expert, and professional. However, in subtle but insidious and relentless ways she slowly chips away at the psychologist's status and self-esteem as she aims to wrest control for herself. Since this power struggle is of a different order from that usually experienced in work with adolescents, and because it is so well-camouflaged, it is difficult to interpret early in the work in order to stabilize the testing relationship. The lack of a more palpable engagement with the patient can leave the examiner feeling quite bereft of human contact despite the interpersonal engagement. After testing a patient with an eating disorder, one may long for the gratification of testing patients whose emotional life is more accessible. It can in fact be quite a relief to evaluate a patient who is more overtly "difficult" after one has done this sort of work.

TESTING THE BULIMIC AND THE ANOREXIC WITH BULIMIC FEATURES

As noted above, there are indications in the literature that the bulimic patient and the anoretic patient who binges or purges make up a subtype of eating disorder with characteristic personality dynamics and a distinct history and etiology (Garfinkel and Garner, 1982). Our experience as diagnostician corroborates this notion. It is therefore of interest to examine the test protocols and reports of this subgroup in order to investigate their presentation in the testing and the countertransferences evoked by them. Several pertinent findings emerge.

In striking contrast to test reports on patients who were purely anoretic, reports on patients with bulimia tended to include more elaborate descriptions of physical status and appearance, with comments such as "the patient is slender." There were more references to stereotypical female sexual attributes, e.g., a barrette in the hair. As with anorexics, there was also mention of patients looking younger than their chronological age.

Another distinguishing feature of the reports on patients with bulimia or anorexia with bulimic features was that the patients were described as being "difficult" to test. In many cases the difficulties were attributed to lability and moodiness, with words such as "petulant" and "histrionic" being used. Many of the bulimic patients were described as actively negativistic toward both the testing and the examiner. For example, in one case a patient made the psychologist wait while she finished drying her hair. In another instance, the psychologist was asked to come back on a different day when the patient had found her glasses. In a third case, the patient was described as "dawdling in her room past the appointment time." Thus, there was more direct mention in these reports of how frustrating the experience of testing was for the psychologist.

With all these difficulties, then, it is of particular interest to us that the psychologists tended to conclude that, although testing was a frustrating experience, the patient was "overall cooperative." Indeed, cooperativeness was sometimes taken to the extreme of overcompliance; patients were described as giving overelaborate answers in response to structured as well as unstructured questions. One wonders if the conclusion that the patient was cooperative is an indication of the relief felt by the psychologist after the initial opposition early in the sessions.

Although a struggle for control was waged via overt behaviors described in the test reports, it seems that the directness of resistance to testing was easier to handle than the more subtle struggle waged by the anorexic. The relationship between the bulimic patient and the psychologist seems to be one in which the patient was more open to receiving help. For example, some patients were described as saying they "felt illiterate" or "weird," or that they were "going crazy." One patient who was giving elaborate, rapid-fire answers to the Rorschach looked up from the protocol and said to the examiner, "Am I in a race?" Another bulimic patient, who gave a thirty-response Rorschach, recognized that she was unable to stop turning the card and seeing more answers; she communicated this to the examiner, who then was in a position to offer reassurance. Thus, although bulimic patients appear to have more difficulty with impulse control than do anorexics, they are also more open to the possibility of using others to enhance their internal organization.

The other distinguishing feature that emerges from a review of the reports has a direct bearing on the treatment of patients with bulimia or bulimic symptoms. It is very evident from the anoretic reports that the major relationship, such as it was, was limited to the dyad of patient and tester. By contrast, several of the test reports of the bulimic patients made mention of the fact that they brought other individuals into their relationship with the psychologist. For example, one patient is described as being particularly concerned that Dr. S. would think she was "stupid and that the results of testing would jeopardize her chances for college." Another is described as stating that she was angry because her therapist was away during the time of the testing, and yet another patient feared that the psychologist was going to say something to her therapist about the findings of the tests. A bulimic patient was preoccupied throughout testing with how she had missed a group activity because of testing and that she felt guilty about disappointing the group therapist. On the one hand, this may give evidence of more object relatedness among bulimics than among the anorexics described here; on the other hand, the style of relationship that emerges suggests an ambivalence which is handled through the use of splitting.

CONCLUSIONS

In summary, the testing of patients with eating disorders can be a highly dramatic event marked by strong transference and countertransference reactions. The sociohistorical context, the setting of the testing, the physical appearance of the patient, her mood, attitudes, and affect, as well as the actual interaction between patient and tester, all contribute to the data yielded by the test material itself. Although a full understanding of the implications of transference and countertransference in testing is beyond the scope of this chapter, some tentative conclusions can be drawn.

The behavior of the patients described here was marked by a pervasive use of denial, isolation of affect, perfectionism, and an extreme emphasis on control—of body, of verbal responses, and of the environment. The central conflicts that these defenses seem to protect against are those concerning nurturance, selfhood, and aggression. The extent to which such conflicts are intolerable to these patients is evidenced by the additional use of idealization and devaluation, splitting, and projective identification, defenses that have an interpersonal focus and are thus revealed in transference and countertransference responses more readily than in test responses per se. It is because of this that a description of the phenomenology of testing from the point of view of the examiner is of particular importance with these patients.

At first, as described above, the examiner may feel an expectable level of apprehension and concern when approaching the patient with an eating disorder who appears physically as well as emotionally ill. One may also feel bolstered to a level of self-importance by the patient's deference and respect. It soon becomes clear, however, that playing one's role as caretaker is not acceptable to the patient who rebuffs gestures of caring. The patient's critical stance vis-à-vis the examiner, her scorn at various "misdemeanors," and her questioning of the testing procedure may have the insidious effect over time of leaving the examiner feeling devalued rather than idealized. Furthermore, in the case of bulimics, when other people are brought into the dialogue, one begins to feel oneself part of a competition over who is to be the "good" object and who the "bad." Finally, and most important, psychologists may find themselves experiencing various feelings of insecurity, emptiness, competitiveness, and anger that seem to be induced by the patient's projective identification. What makes contending with these dynamics particularly difficult in the testing of anorexics is that the struggle about these conflicts seems to be "underground." Thus, it is only upon reflection that the examiner can recognize the extent to which issues of differentiation were being addressed throughout the interaction. For example, the emphasis on appearance and on concrete details of presentation of self in patient and in examiner can be understood as part of the effort on the part of the adolescent or young adult female patient to both identify with and distinguish herself from the other person.

By contrast, the struggle fought by the bulimic patient and the anoretic patient with bulimic features tends to be less subterranean. Here there is apparently less ability to control affects and impulses and thus much less use of isolation and restraint as defense mechanisms. Indeed, although denial is used among these patients, it is expressed more through avoidant behavior than through the passivity and constraint of the anorexic. Thus, although the prognosis for bulimic patients has been found to be less positive, the dynamic struggles may seem more accessible to the examiner and in turn to the therapist. A reflection of the extent to which the bulimic's emotions are palpable is the style of the test reports: more elaborate detail is given in describing the patient, and more direct expression of the examiner's affect is in evidence. One result of these dynamics is that the examiner is more able to play the role of psychologist and is less invalidated, as happens in work with the anorexic. In other words, the active resistance of the bulimic patient opens channels of communication (although the communication may be of hostile and aggressive feelings) that are not available in the passive resistance of the anorexic. Following the testing of a bulimic patient, one is likely to feel drained, as if "eaten up" by the interchange and by the competitive struggle both with the patient and with the others drawn into the dialogue. In contrast, following work with anorexics, one typically feels that the patient has "bitten the hand that feeds." The contrast between these two overlapping dynamics suggests to us that, while the anorexic is struggling with issues of individuation and differentiation of self from others, the bulimic is struggling more actively with how it feels to be separate and yet dependent.

What has been said here concerning transference and countertransference in the testing of patients with eating disorders has many implications for treatment. It is evident that work with these patients is fraught with difficulties because of the various levels of functioning represented by the disorder. It is also clear that looks are indeed deceiving, i.e., that there is much more to this disorder than a difficulty with food or eating as such. Rather, concern about food symbolizes issues of nurturance and dependency and serves as a defense against the more fundamental issues of selfhood, differentiation, and separation. The use of denial, isolation of affect, and projective identification can keep therapist and patient away from the rage these issues evoke. Thus, attention to countertransference reactions is particularly important. Although in testing one is not usually in a position to interpret such concerns, in treatment it is most important to delve beneath these defenses and to encourage the intrapsychic struggle to emerge in the interpersonal domain as early as possible. For example, struggles about treatment arrangements, scheduling, or family and peer issues can be the focus of productive investigations into the patient's hostility and rage. Allowing discussion of issues other than food can free the patient from the struggle about weight and may facilitate medical care. When a patient discovers that the therapist can withstand the anger earlier caretakers could not, and will allow the patient to be her own distinct and separate person, ego boundaries can be strengthened and some of the sources of cognitive disorganization eliminated. It is evident that such work is greatly facilitated by using the content of patients' transference material and the countertransference reactions elicited by the patient in examiners and therapists alike.

REFERENCES

American Psychiatric Association (1982), *Diagnostic and Statistical Manual of Mental Disorders, Third Edition*, Washington, DC: APA.

Appelbaum, S. A. (1959), The effect of altered psychological atmosphere on Rorschach responses: A new supplementary procedure. *Bull. Menn. Clin.*, 23(5):179–189.

_____ (1970), Science and persuasion in the psychological test report. *J. Consult. & Clin. Psychol.*, 35(3):349–355.

_____ (1972), A method of reporting psychological test findings. *Bull. Menn. Clin.*, 36(5):535–545.

Ben-Tovim, D. I., Marilov, V., & Crisp, A. H. (1979), Personality and mental state (P.S.E.) within anorexia nervosa. *J. Psychosom. Research*, 23:321–325.

Benedek, T. (1936), Dominant ideas and their relation to morbid cravings. *Internat. J. Psycho-Anal.*, 17:40–56.

Beumont, P. J. V. (1977), Further categorization of patients with anorexia nervosa. *Austral. & N.Z. J. Psychiat.*, 11:223–226.

_____ George, G. C. W., & Smart, D. E. (1976), "Dieters" and "vomiters and purgers" in anorexia nervosa. *Psychol. Med.*, 6:617–622.

Binswanger, L. (1944), Der Fall Ellen West. Schweiz. *Arch. Neurol. Psychiat.* 54:69–117.

Boskind-Lodahl, M. (1976), Cinderella's stepsisters: A feminist perspective on anorexia and bulimia. *Signs: Journal of Women in Culture and Society*, 2:342–356.

Bram, S., Eger, D., & Halmi, K. (1982), Anorexia nervosa and personality type: A preliminary report. *Internat. J. Eat. Dis.*, 2(1):67–74.

Bruch, H. (1973), *Eating Disorders*. New York: Basic Books.

Crisp, A. H., Harding, B., & McGuinness, B. (1974), Anorexia nervosa: Psychoneurotic characteristics of parents: Relationship to prognosis. A qualitative study. *J. Psychosom. Research*, 18:167–173.

_____ Hsu, L. K. G., & Stonehill, E. (1979), Personality, body weight and ultimate outcome in anorexia nervosa. *J. Clin. Psychiat.*, 40:332–335.

Dally, P. (1969), *Anorexia Nervosa*. New York: Grune & Stratton.

Epstein, L., & Feiner, A. H., Eds. (1979), *Countertransference*. New York: Aronson.

Feighner, J. P., Robins, E., Guze, S. B., Woodruff, R. A., Jr., Winokur, G., & Munoz, R. (1972), Diagnostic criteria for use in psychiatric research. *Arch. Gen. Psychiat.*, 26:57–63.

Feinstein, S. C., & Giovacchini, P. L., Eds. (1977), *Adolescent Psychiatry*, Vol. 5. New York: Aronson.

Freud, S. (1915), Observations on transference-love. *Standard Edition*, 12:157–171. London: Hogarth Press, 1958.

Garfinkel, P. E., & Garner, D. M. (1982), *Anorexia Nervosa: A Multidimensional Perspective*. New York: Brunner/Mazel.

Garrow, J. S., Crisp, A. H., Jordan, H. A., Meyer, J. E., Russell, G. F. M., Silverstone, T., Stunkard, A. J., & Van Itallie, T. B. (1975), Pathology of eating, group report. In: *Dahlen Konferenzen, Life Sciences Research Report 2*, ed. K. T. Silverstone. Berlin.

Gomez, J., & Dally, P. (1980), Psychometric rating in the assessment of progress in anorexia nervosa. *Brit. J. Psychiat.*, 136:290–296.

Goodsitt, A. (1977), Narcissistic disturbances in anorexia nervosa. In: *Adolescent Psychiatry*, Vol. 5, ed. S. C. Feinstein & P. L. Giovacchini. New York: Aronson, pp. 304–312.

Gorney, J. E., & Weinstock, S. J. (1980), Borderline object relations, therapeutic impasse and the Rorschach. In: *Borderline Phenomena and the Rorschach Test*, ed. J. S. Kwawer, H. D. Lerner, P. M. Lerner, & A. S. Sugarman. New York: International Universities Press, pp. 167–187.

Hartocollis, P., Ed. (1977), *Borderline Personality Disorders*. New York: International Universities Press.

Hood, J., Moore, T. E., & Garner, D. M. (1982), Locus of control as a measure of ineffectiveness in anorexia nervosa. *J. Consult. & Clin. Psychol.*, 50(1):3–13.

Janet, P. (1919), *Les Obsessions et la Psychasthenie*. Paris: Felix.

Katzman, M. A., & Wolchik, S. A. (1984), Bulimia and binge-eating in college women: A comparison of personality and behavioral characteristics. *J. Consult. & Clin. Psychol.*, 52:423–428.

Kaufer, J. F., & Katz, J. L. (1983), Rorschach responses in anoretic and nonanoretic women. *Internat. J. Eat. Dis.*, 3(1):65–74.

Kernberg, O. (1980), Foreword. In: J. A. Sours, *Starving to Death in a Sea of Objects.* New York: Aronson, pp. ix–xi.

Kwawer, J. C., D. Lerner, H. M., Lerner, P. S., & Sugarman, A., Eds. (1980), *Borderline Phenomena and the Rorschach Test.* New York: International Universities Press.

Lerner, H. D. (1983), Contemporary psychoanalytic perspectives on gorge-vomiting: A case illustration. *Internat. J. Eat. Dis.*, 3(1):47–63.

Lorand, S. (1943), Anorexia nervosa: Report of a case. *Psychosom. Med.*, 5:282–292.

Masterson, J. F. (1977), Primary anorexia nervosa in the borderline adolescent: An object relations view. In: *Borderline Personality Disorders*, ed. P. Hartocollis. New York: International Universities Press, pp. 475–494.

Morgan, H. G., & Russell, G. F. M. (1975), Value of family background and clinical features as predictors of long-term outcome in anorexia nervosa: Four year follow-up study of 41 patients. *Psychol. Med.*, 5:335–372.

Nagelberg, D. B., Hale, S. L., & Ware, S. L. (1984), The assessment of bulimic symptoms and personality correlates in female students. *J. Clin. Psychol.*, 40:440–445.

Piazza, E., Rollins, N., & Lewis, F. S. (1983), Measuring severity and change in anorexia nervosa. *Adolescence*, 18:293–305.

Racker, H. (1968), *Transference and Countertransference.* New York: International Universities Press.

Rapaport, D., Gill, M., & Schafer, R., (1945), *Diagnostic Psychological Testing.* Chicago: Yearbook.

Reich, A. (1960), Further remarks on counter-transference. *Internat. J. Psycho-Anal.*, 41:389–395.

Rollins, N., & Piazza, E. (1978), Diagnosis of anorexia nervosa: A critical reappraisal. *J. Amer. Acad. Child Psychiat.*, 17:126–137.

Schachtel, E. G. (1945), Subjective definitions of the Rorschach test situation and their effect on test performance. *Psychiat.*, 8:419–448.

Schafer, R. (1954), *Psychoanalytic Interpretation in Rorschach Testing.* New York: Grune & Stratton.

Schlesinger, H. J. (1973), Interaction of dynamic and reality factors in the diagnostic testing interview. *Bull. Menn. Clin.*, 37:495–517.

Schwartz, D., Thompson, M. G., & Johnson, C. L. (1982), Anorexia nervosa and bulimia: The socio-cultural context. *Internat. J. Eat. Dis.*, 1(3):20–36.

Selvini-Palazzoli, M. (1969), Psychopathology of bodily experience: II. Contributions of a new Rorschach scoring. *Psychother. & Psychosom.*, 17:241–256.

———— (1978), *Self-Starvation: Individual to Family Therapy in the Treatment of Anorexia Nervosa.* New York: Aronson.

Singer, M. T. (1977), The borderline diagnosis and psychological tests: Review and research. In: *Borderline Personality Disorders*, ed. P. Hartocollis. New York: International Universities Press, pp. 193–212.

Small, A. (1984), The contribution of psychodiagnostic test results toward understanding anorexia nervosa. *Internat. J. Eat. Dis.*, 3(2):47–54.

———— , Madero, J., Gross, H., Teagno, L., Leib, J., & Ebert. M. (1981), A comparative analysis of primary anorexics and schizophrenics of the MMPI. *J. Clin. Psychol.*, 37:733–736.

———— , Teagno, L., Madero, J., Gross, H., & Ebert, M. (1982), A comparison of anorexics and schizophrenics on psychodiagnostic measures. *Internat. J. Eat. Dis.*, 1(3):49–56.

Solyom, L., Freeman, R. J., & Miles, J. E. (1982), A comparative psychometric study of anorexia nervosa and obsessive neurosis. *Can. J. Psychiat.*, 27:282–286.

Stone, M. (1980), *The Borderline Syndromes: Constitution, Personality and Adaptation.* New York: McGraw-Hill.

Stonehill, E., & Crisp, A. H. (1977), Psychoneurotic characteristics of patients with anorexia nervosa before and after treatment and at follow-up 4–7 years later. *J. Psychosom. Research*, 21(3):189–193.

Strober, M., & Goldenberg, I. (1981), Ego boundary disturbance in juvenile anorexia nervosa. *J. Clin. Psychol.*, 37:433–438.

Sugarman, A. (1981), The diagnostic use of countertransference reactions in psychological testing. *Bull. Menn. Clin.*, 45:473–490.

Sugarman, A., Quinlan, D., & Devinis, L. (1981), Anorexia nervosa as a defense against anaclitic depression. *Internat. J. Eat. Dis.*, 1(1):44–61.

Swift, W. J., & Stern, S. (1982), The psychodynamic diversity of anorexia nervosa. *Internat. J. Eat. Dis.*, 2(1):17–35.

Thielgard, A. (1965), Psychological testing of patients with anorexia nervosa. In: *Gottingen*, ed. J. E. Meyer & H. Feldman. Stuttgart: Thieme, p. 122.

Wagner, E. E., & Wagner, C. F. (1978), Similar Rorschach patterning in three cases of anorexia nervosa. *J. Personal. Assess.*, 42:426–432.

Wallach, J., & Lowenkopf, E. L. (1984), Five bulimic women: MMPI, Rorschach and TAT characteristics. *Internat. J. Eat. Dis.*, 3(4):53–66.

Weiss, S. W., & Ebert, M. H. (1983), Psychological and behavioral characteristics of normal weight bulimics and normal weight controls. *Psychosom. Med.*, 45:293–303.

Chapter 13
Borderline Phenomena in Anorexia Nervosa and Bulimia

Niva Piran, Ph.D.

Clinical reports of patients suffering from the eating disorders of anorexia and bulimia suggest that such patients are organized at a primitive level of personality organization. Authors treating these patients have stressed their overcompliance and lack of spontaneous expression (Bruch, 1978), symbiotic attachments and problems separating from parents (Masterson, 1977), the presence of anaclitic depression with experiences of abandonment and rage (Sugarman, Quinlan, and Devenis, 1981; Lerner, 1983), and a transference in which the therapist performs functions that should be managed internally, such as the "holding" function (Lerner, 1983). In a comprehensive review of recent psychoanalytic perspectives on bulimia, Lerner (1983) comments that the major deficits found in the underlying psychological structures are conceptualized differently depending on theoretical orientation. For example, eating disorder patients have been described in terms of psychoanalytic developmental theory as manifesting problems in the separation-individuation process (Masterson, 1977); in self psychology terms, as lacking parental confirmation at the mirroring stage of the patient's psychological self (Rizzuto, Peterson, and Reed, 1981) and as revealing problems in self-regulation (Goodsitt, 1983); and, in terms of object relations theory, as identifying the body with the bad maternal object (Selvini-Palazzoli, 1974) and as using the bodily action of eating as a vehicle for a somatosensory representation of the mother (Sugarman and Kurash, 1982).

These clinical observations apply to both anorexic patients, who exclusively restrict their diet, and to bulimic anorexic patients, who, in addition to the dieting, also binge and purge. Questions arise as to what might account for the different eating behaviors of these two patient groups. For example, do these phenomenological differences reflect differences in the severity of psychological disturbance, or do they reflect the fact that developmental arrest has occurred at different stages? The few authors who have dealt with these issues have suggested interesting formulations. Rizzuto, Peterson, and Reed (1981) consider anorexics as manifesting an earlier and a more severe disturbance of self in which they have never been mirrored or responded to beyond physical needs, and which has resulted in a schizoid personality organization and a style of communication in which the body is the major mode. Bulimia is seen as a consequence of later interactional failures with the maternal object, resulting in a tendency to get involved in "dissociated" oral pleasures that do not involve the representation of the "bad" mother (Rizzuto, 1983). These failures are viewed as creating a fear of the monstrous, bad, and hungry part of the self, which, threatening to take over, gives rise to the need to vomit and expel that part. Sugarman and Kurash (1982) disagree with this line of thinking. They consider bulimia the more primitive disturbance, and suggest that bulimics are arrested at the practicing subphase of separation-individuation. This arrest in turn occasions an arrest in cognitive development such that such patients function at the sensorimotor level. For these patients, binges are a vehicle for representing the maternal object, while vomiting represents its repudiation. Other authors (e.g., Russell, 1979) have used follow-up studies associating bulimia with a less favorable prognosis to infer a more severe disturbance; their methodology, however, has been questioned (Toner, Garfinkel, and Garner, 1985).

The present study examined borderline phenomena in the Rorschach protocols of a large sample of consecutively referred anorexic and bulimic patients on the hypothesis that this material would reflect the heterogeneity of these disorders (Sours, 1974) and allow an unbiased comparison of the two groups. To that end their protocols were compared on scales reflecting reality testing (Mayman, 1962); integrity of thought processes (Watkins and Stauffacher, 1952); primitive defenses (Lerner and Lerner, 1980); and object representation (Blatt, Brenneis, Schimek, and Glick, 1976). Included, as well, were content indices suggested by Kwawer (1980) as reflective of the primitive interpersonal modes of the borderline patient, namely, difficulties in separation-individuation vis-à-vis a primary object. Two additional content scales were included. One registered references to fatness, while the second scored aggression content according to Holt's manual (1970). The latter subdivides aggression responses into those reflective of sadistic aggression, victimization and aftermath of aggression.

METHOD

Subjects

Subjects were eating disorder female patients, ranging in age from sixteen to thirty-five, referred consecutively to an eating disorder unit in a major Toronto hospital. Thirty-one subjects met the DSM–III criteria for anorexia nervosa; thirty-four met those for bulimia. The two groups did not differ in age ($x = 22.3$), chronicity ($x = 4.9$ years), or socioeconomic status. Initially, a third group of patients, referred because of personality disturbances but without eating difficulties, was to be included as a control. These patients met the DSM–III criteria for borderline personality disorder, as well as those of Gunderson. However, comprehensive assessment of these patients, as part of a larger research project, revealed that seven of the thirteen in fact had eating disorders themselves. As this group was therefore disqualified as a control, norms or results obtained in other studies were used as a basis for comparison.

Measures

All Rorschach protocols were scored using the following scales:

1. Form Level scale (Mayman, 1962).
2. Delta Index scale (thought disorder) (Watkins and Stauffacher, 1952).
3. Primitive Defenses scale (Lerner and Lerner, 1980).
4. Developmental Level of the Concept of the Object scale (Blatt et al., 1976). These include Accuracy of Response, Differentiation (human, quasi-human, human details, and quasi-human details), Action responses, and Content of Action (Malevolent/Benevolent).
5. Indices of Primitive Interpersonal Modes (Kwawer, 1980). These include content indices of engulfment, symbiotic merg-

ing and separation, uterine, birth and transformation themes, and narcissistic mirroring.
6. References to Fatness.
7. Aggressive Content (Holt, 1970), including attack (sadistic), victimization (masochistic), and results of aggression (masochistic).

Frequency counts for the content categories (4–7) were analyzed for human and animal responses together and separately.

Procedure

All patients were independently interviewed by two clinicians to derive DSM–III diagnoses. Rorschach protocols were administered by a doctoral candidate in clinical psychology using the method described by Rapaport, Gill, and Schafer (1945). The author scored the protocols on the Primitive Defenses and Concept of the Object scales. The doctoral candidate scored the protocols on the Form Level and Delta Index scales. Protocols were scored blindly, separately for each scale so that scores on one scale would not affect scores on the other. Fifteen protocols were randomly selected for reliability check and independently scored by the two raters. The results on the different scales were Form Level $r = .88$; Delta Index $r = .78$; Primitive Defenses—Splitting 90 percent, Projective Identification 100 percent, Devaluation 96 percent, Idealization 90 percent, Denial 88 percent; Concept of the Object Indices—Action responses 96 percent, Malevolent/Benevolent 91 percent; Primitive Interpersonal Modes 100 percent; Fatness Indices 100 percent; Aggressive Content 89 percent.

Statistical Analysis

Student's t-tests and χ^2 tests were used to compare the two groups on quantitative and qualitative measures, respectively. All results reported are for two-tailed tests.

RESULTS

Reality Testing and Integrity of Thought Processes

Table 1 details results related to the quality of reality testing and the integrity of thought processes. No significant differences were found on the Form Level measure, reflecting reality testing, though bulimics tended to show a lower form level ($p < .1$). The Delta Index, reflecting integrity of thought process, showed no significant differences between the two groups; 85.3 percent of bulimics and 80.6 percent of anorexics obtained Delta Index scores within the cut-off point of .1 suggested for the differentiation of normals and neurotics from psychotics. Using chi square, on the Delta Index, bulimics were found to have a higher number of Fabulized Combination Not-Corrected responses ($\chi^2 = 8.73$, $p < .01$) and queer verbalization extreme responses ($\chi^2 = 6.15$, $p < .01$), while restricters showed a higher use of Overelaborate Symbolism, moderate ($\chi^2 = 3.96$, $p < .05$).

TABLE 1

Measures of Reality Testing and Integrity of Thought Processes
in Anorexics and Bulimics

Measure	Bulimics $N = 34$		Anorexics $N = 31$			
	X	SD	X	SD	t	p
Form Level	4.87	.50	5.08	.43	1.81	.1
Delta Index (%)	.22	.15	.19	.12	.62	NS

Primitive Defenses

Bulimics and restrictive anorexics were found not to differ significantly on test indices of splitting, projective identification, devaluation, and low-level idealization (see Table 2). Restrictive anorexics were found to use indices of high-level idealization and middle-level denial significantly more often. Bulimics tended to use more projective identification, high-level devaluation, and high-level denial (implying a tendency to more severe disturbance). The total number of devaluation responses did not differ between the two groups. Restrictive anorexics gave a significantly greater number of idealization responses ($\chi^2 = 8.69$, $p < .01$). Comparisons of the number of protocols in which each of the test indices of primitive defenses appeared in the two groups yielded no significant differences except for test indices of Denial. More anorexics than bulimics used middle-level denial ($\chi^2 = 5.14$, $p < .05$), while significantly more bulimics used low-level denial ($\chi^2 = 3.95$, $p < .05$).

TABLE 2

Comparison of Bulimics and Anorexics on the Primitive
Defense Scale[a]

| | Frequency | | | |
| | Bulimics | Restricters | | |
Defense	$N = 34$	$N = 31$	X^2	p
Splitting	20	20	.39	NS
Projective	37	22	2.00	NS
Identification				
Devaluation:				
1	22	16	.20	NS
2	24	22	.12	NS
3	3	8	3.43	.10
4	8	5	.27	NS
5	34	18	3.01	.10
Idealization:				
1	7	15	4.96	.05
2	8	15	3.94	.05
3	3	4	.39	NS
5	10	9	.03	NS
Denial:				
1	19	25	2.71	.10
2	8	18	6.52	.05
3	21	9	3.23	.10

[a]The X^2 were calculated out of the total number of scorable Human Responses, 156 for bulimics, 130 for restricters. The average number of whole Human Responses per protocol did not differ between the two groups: Bulimics ($x = 4.59 + 4.34$), Anorexics ($x = 4.19 + 3.67$), $t = .39$.

Representation of the Object

Table 3 details results obtained with indices from the Concept of the Object scale. No differences were found between the two groups on the frequency of accurately articulated versus inaccurately articulated human responses. This was true for the total of human responses, and separately for full human responses, full quasi-human responses, human details, and quasi-human details. Nonsignificant results were obtained when the hierarchically organized subcategories of the Human Differentiation index were compared between the two groups, together and separately for accurately and inaccurately articulated responses. When bulimics and anorexics were compared on the number of human responses in which any action was elaborated, bulimics were found to incorporate action in their responses more often than anorexics. A striking difference was found in the distribution of aggressive or destructive content versus neutral or positive content within the Action category. While in the bulimic group malevolent actions constituted half of the action responses, they occurred in only one-fifth of the Action responses among anorexics.

TABLE 3

Comparison of Bulimics and Anorexics on Indices from the Concept of the Object Scale[a]

	Frequency			
Index	Bulimics $N = 34$	Restricters $N = 31$	X^2	p
Number of Responses with Positive Articulation[b]	174	135	2.107	NS
Number of Human versus Quasi Human Responses[c]	175	127	.076	NS
Action Responses	177	109	4.78	.05
Malevolent (versus Benevolent Actions[d]	86	24	20.12	.001

[a]The X^2 were calculated out of the total number of scorable responses, i.e., the total H, (H), Hd, and (Hd) responses—241 for bulimics and 172 for restricters.
[b]Same nonsignificant results were obtained for comparing H^+ vs. H^-, Hd^+ vs. Hd^-, $(H)^+$ vs. $(H)^-$, and $(Hd)^-$ vs. $(Hd)^+$.
[c]Same nonsignificant results were obtained for comparing Hd vs. (Hd), H vs. Hd, (H) vs. Hd, and (H) vs. (Hd), together and separately for accurately and inaccurately articulated responses.
[d]X^2 was calculated out of the total number of Action Responses.

Aggressive Content

Table 4 reveals the distribution of aggressive content in terms of sadistic ("attacks"), masochistic ("victims," "results of aggression"), or both. A significant difference was found in the distribution of aggressive responses. Not one exclusively sadistic response was found in the anorexic group, whereas ten such responses were found in the bulimic group ($\chi^2 = 8.145$, $p < .05$). In the anorexics, all sadistic responses included the victim. Examples of sadistic responses in the bulimic group include the following: "two animals climbing up to destroy it" (Card VIII); "bunnies sacrificing something" (Card II): "the raccoon is vicious when provoked" (Card V); "somebody ready to shoot" (Card IV).

TABLE 4

Distribution of Aggressive Content Responses in
Bulimics and Anorexics

	Bulimics $N = 34$	Anorexics $N = 31$
Sadistic	10	0
Sadistic and Masochistic	7	6
Masochistic	15	15

$X^2 = 8.145, p < .05$

Primitive Interpersonal Modes

When the summation frequencies in which the indices of engulf-ment, symbiotic merging and separation, uterine, birth, and transforma-tion themes, and narcissistic mirroring occurred in the two groups, no significant differences were found (see Table 5). However, the percen-tage of protocols with such indices was significantly higher in bulimics: 75 percent of bulimics versus 38 percent of anorexics. Examples of such responses are "joined fetal humans" (Card IX); "babies attached to the body of a woman" (Card IX); "funny-looking guy looking in the mirror deformed" (Card II); "a wicked witch looking into the mirror and looking very ugly" (Card X); "two heads back-to-back stuck together, trying to rip apart" (Card VI).

Fatness

Sixty-five percent of Rorschach protocols in the bulimic group and 71 percent of protocols in the anorexic group contained human or animal references to fatness or thinness. In two additional protocols (6 percent) in the anorexic group, there was no perception of fatness, but people were seen as exercising, a frequent expression through action of the fear of being fat.

TABLE 5

Frequency of Responses Reflecting Primitive Interpersonal
Modes in Bulimics and Anorexics

Mirroring, Symbiosis, Uterine Indices	Frequency		X^2	p
	Bulimics $N = 34$	Anorexics $N = 31$		
Total Human Responses[a]	28	24	.50	NS
Total Animal Responses[b]	18	11	1.77	NS
Total Human and Animal Responses	46	35	.28	NS
Number of protocols with at least one such Human Response	16	10	1.48	NS
Number of protocols with at least one such Human or Animal response	24	12	6.67	.05

[a]Total Human Responses was 241 for bulimics and 172 for restricters.
[b]Total Animal Responses was 233 for bulimics and 232 for restricters.

References to fatness carry a variety of meanings. There were expressions of the bad and angry self-object: "puffed-up body, plump, full of poison" (Card X) or "two girls, dumpy stomach, dark tough face, not delicate" (Card VII). There were expressions of self-deprecation, poor self-esteem, and dysphoria: "stupid fat bird caricature" (Card VIII); "huge ugly fat body, I detest bugs" (Card I). Sexual and instinctual fears were expressed through fatness: "a stripper, not graceful; two fat legs here; grossly overweight woman; how could she split apart that way; very ugly and expressing herself; she is shielded by material fat" (Card V). There were indications of communicating through the emaciated body: "the arms sticking out; the thinness of it reaching out" (Card VIII). The regressive aspect of the emaciation was found as well: "a little figure, a child, skinny, innocent; it then grows into this huge thing with tons and tons of organic material." Worries about intactness of the boundaries of the self were expressed: "the body is a mass, shapeless, just spread" (Card II). The primitive and magical quality of exercise in these patients was expressed by one patient: "skinny legs; these legs look like my legs after I swim."

An interesting finding related to this index is its relation to the presence of anorexia and bulimia. The index identified five of the seven borderline controls later found to have anorexia and bulimia (see Table 6).

TABLE 6

The Relationship between the Fatness Index and the Presence of Aneroxia and Bulimia in a Borderline Sample ($N = 13$)

Presence of Anorexia/Bulimia	Fatness Index	
	+	−
+	5	1
−	1	6

$X^2 = 6.198, p < .05$

DISCUSSION

The study included Rorschach measurement of thought processes, primitive defenses, object representation, primitive interpersonal content, aggressive content, and reference to fatness. In comparing the abstaining anorexic and bulimic patients, it is instructive to look at each of the measures separately as well as at their interrelation.

On the measures reflecting reality testing and thought organization, anorexics and bulimics showed a similar range and type of difficulties. Most responses were of good form level, but were ordinary and almost never creative. Articulations with either positive or negative form level were often confabulatory and idiosyncratic, somewhat more disruptive of form level in the bulimic group. Such a pattern of performance on the Rorschach has been reported in borderline patients (Sugarman, 1980) and, as Sugarman notes, reflects the weaknesses of their self-object boundary and their need to rely on external cues for a reality-oriented response. On the Delta Index, a measure sensitive to a confabulatory mode of response and to a boundary disturbance, most anorexics and bulimics scored within the "psychotic" range. Small, Teagro, Madero, Gross, and Ebert (1982) found that anorexics obtained the same Delta Index values as did schizophrenics.

Lerner and Lerner (1980, 1982) operationalized Kernberg's constellation of lower-level primitive defenses (Kernberg, 1975). In two validation studies of their scale, the authors found that the defenses of splitting, projective identification, low-level devaluation and low-level denial differentiated borderlines from both neurotic and schizophrenic patients. The defense of projective identification occurred only in the borderline group. The frequency counts of the bulimic and anorexic groups in the present investigation on the Primitive Defenses scale were almost identical to those reported by Lerner and Lerner for the border-line group and markedly different from the neurotic and schizophrenic groups. This confirms clinical observations suggesting that anorexics and bulimics are both at the borderline level of personality organiza-tion, using Kernberg's three-level schema of personality organization (Kernberg, 1970). The comparison with Lerner and Lerner's borderline and neurotic samples reveals two interesting differences. First, bulimics tended to use projective identification more often than either anorexics or Lerner and Lerner's borderline group. These scored precepts involved confabulatory responses of human figures, typically with an aggressive content in which the real properties of the blot were discarded.

A second difference related to the defense of denial. In their method of scoring, Lerner and Lerner divided this defense into higher-level denial, including negation, intellectualization, minimization, and repudiation; middle-level denial, involving a basic contradiction on affective, logical, or reality grounds; and lower-level denial, in which reality adherence is abrogated as indicated by responses in which incompatible descriptions were made of the percept. Anorexics showed as frequent a use of high-level denial and as infrequent a use of low-level denial as the reported neurotics, but they used middle-level denial as often as the reported borderlines. Lerner and Lerner observed that their neurotics appeared to mitigate extreme devaluation through higher-level denial, while borderlines did not. In their 1982 paper, Lerner and Lerner suggest that their data support Kernberg's formula-tion (1975) that primitive splitting in borderline patients is supplanted by higher-level defenses in neurotics. The authors posit an inextricable relationship between object representation capacity and available defenses, which would support a developmental view of defenses. In this manner the limited availability of high-level defenses to the border-line would be related to the low level of representational capacity. However, Lerner and Lerner note that clinical observations (Sugarman and Lerner, 1980) and theoretical discussions (Lustman, 1977) ques-tion the supplanting theory of defense. The findings of the present study would also question this formulation. Among the anorexics, who used splitting and projective identification as often as the reported border-lines, deprecated images were found to be modulated by high-level denial. The Concept of the Object scale yielded findings regarding the object representational capacities of anorexics and bulimics that also question Lerner and Lerner's hypothesis; both groups obtained similar scores on the Differentiation dimension of the scale, which assesses the degree to which humanness is maintained in the Rorschach human percept. A difference in the content of human representations was found, rather than developmental differences in the level of representation. Bulimics gave significantly more malevolent responses. Considering this finding together with the greater tenency of bulimics for disruption in reality testing, their lack of higher-level defenses, and their less extensive use of idealization one can infer that bulimics' defensive structure is weaker than that of anorexics, especially in dealing with the bad object. The extensive and concomitant use of denial and idealization (being pure, ethereal, angelic, etc.) has been observed among anorexics (Wilson, 1982). These results resemble those obtained by Lerner and St. Peter (1984) in their comparison of in- and outpatient borderline samples. They found that the inpatient borderlines were unable to escape from malevolent objects, while the outpatients dealt with them through distancing in time and space.

The results obtained from Holt's Aggression scale point to differences between the groups in dealing with aggression and this could relate as well to the greater disturbance exhibited by bulimics in reality testing and their greater use of the confabulatory mode of response. While anorexics express their rage through masochistic means, often bolstered by idealization and denial, bulimics experience and express their aggression in a more erratic yet direct way. The differences in handling aggression within an interpersonal contact is likely to become manifest in the therapeutic transference relationship. While anorexics develop and rigidly maintain a masochistic approach to therapy, whereby the therapist is perceived as a sadistic attacker, bulimics develop rapidly changing transferences in which the containment of their aggression by the therapist is the crucial aspect. (It has been my experience in treating bulimic patients that their aggressive fantasies are immediately present from the outset of therapy. By contrast, anorexics inhibit such expressions; when the fantasies do emerge, they may be taken as a sign of therapeutic progress.)

Primitive interpersonal themes of merger, fusion, separation, and individuation were found more frequently in the records of the bulimics. This is consistent with the finding that bulimics exhibit a weaker defensive structure and hence cannot protect themselves, as can anorexics, from regressive experiences and micropsychotic episodes.

The fear of fatness, despite its being an inseparable part of both anorexia and bulimia, is often not mentioned in clinical descriptions of these patients. Yet their Rorschach protocols reveal the importance of looking at fatness responses and their elaboration as a means of identifying and better understanding these disorders. The "fat" object, it would seem, is often a way of representing the "bad" object in body image terms. The present study suggests the possible heuristic value of such an index in making diagnoses.

In conclusion, it appears that anorexics and bulimics both display a borderline level of personality organization, as formulated by Kernberg. The integration of measures of thought processes, reality testing, primitive defenses, object representation, and aggression suggests that a major difference between anorexics and bulimics is the way in which they handle bad objects. While anorexics display the defensive operations of idealization and high-level denial and defend against the experience of aggression through a rigidly maintained masochism, bulimics show a weaker defensive operation and thus are more vulnerable to bad objects, regressions, and disruptions in reality testing.

REFERENCES

Blatt, S. J., Brenneis, C. B., Schimek, J. G., & Glick, M. (1976), A developmental analysis of the concept of the object on the Rorschach. Unpublished manuscript, Yale University.

Bruch, H. (1978), *The Gold Cage: The Enigma of Anorexia Nervosa.* Cambridge: Harvard University Press.

Goodsitt, A. (1983), Self-regulatory disturbances in eating disorders. *Internat. J. Eat. Dis.*, 2:51–60.

Gunderson, J. (1977), Characteristics of borderlines. In: *Borderline Personality Disorders*, ed. P. Hartocollis. New York: International University Press, pp. 173–193.

Holt, R. R. (1970), Manual for the Scoring of Primary Process Manifestations in Rorschach Responses. Unpublished manuscript, New York University Research Center for Mental Health.

Kernberg, O. (1970), A psychoanalytic classification of character pathology. *J. Amer. Psychoanal. Assn.*, 18:800–822.

———— (1975), *Borderline Conditions and Pathological Narcissism.* New York: Aronson.

Kwawer, J. S. (1980), Primitive interpersonal modes, borderline phenomena, and Rorschach content. In: *Borderline Phenomena and the Rorschach Test*, ed. J. Kwawer, H. Lerner, P. Lerner, & A. Sugarman. New York: International Universities Press, pp. 89–105.

Lerner, H. (1983), Contemporary psychoanalytic perceptive on gorge-vomiting: A case illustration. *Internat. J. Eat. Dis.*, 3:47–63.

———— Lerner, P. M. (1982), A comparative study of defensive structure in neurotic, borderline, and schizophrenic patients. *Psychoanal. & Contemp. Thought,* 5:77–115.

———— St. Peter, S. (1984), Patterns of object relations in neurotic, borderline and schizophrenic patients. *Psychiat.,* 47:77–92.

Lerner, P. M., & Lerner, H. D. (1980), Rorschach assessment of primitive defenses in borderline personality structure. In: *Borderline Phenomena and the Rorschach Test,* ed. J. Kwawer, H. Lerner, P. Lerner, & A. Sugarman. New York: International Universities Press, pp. 257–274.

Lustman, J. (1977), On splitting. *Psychoanalytic Study of the Child,* 32:119–154. New Haven: Yale University Press.

Masterson, J. (1977), Primary anorexia in the borderline adolescent: An object relations view. In: *Borderline Personality Disorders,* ed. P. Hartocollis. New York: International Universities Press, pp. 475–494.

Mayman, J. (1962), Rorschach form level manual. Unpublished manuscript, Menninger Foundation.

Rapaport, D., Gill, M., & Schafer, R. (1945), *Diagnostic Psychological Testing.* Rev. ed. New York: International Universities Press, 1968.

Rizzuto, A. M., Peterson, R. K., & Reed, M. (1981), The pathological sense of self in anorexia nervosa. *Psychiatric Clinics of North America,* 4:471–487.

———— (1983), Eating and monsters. Conference, Harvard Medical School, Department of Continuing Education, Boston, June.

Russell, G. F. M. (1979), Bulimia nervosa: An ominous variant of anorexia nervosa. *Psychol. Med.,* 9:429–448.

Selvini-Palazzoli, M. (1974), *Self-Starvation: From the Intrapsychic to the Transpersonal Approach to Anorexia Nervosa.* New York: Aronson.

Small, A., Teagro, L., Madero, J., Gross, H., & Ebert, M. (1982), A comparison of anorexics and schizophrenics on psychodiagnostic measures. *Internat. J. Eat. Dis.,* 1(3):49–55.

Sours, J. A. (1974), The anorexia nervosa syndrome. *Internat. J. Psycho-Anal.,* 55:567–579.

Sugarman, A. (1980), The borderline personality organization as manifested on psychological tests. In: *Borderline Phenomena and the Rorschach Test,* ed. J. Kwawer, H. Lerner, P. Lerner, & A. Sugarman. New York: International Universities Press, pp. 39–57.

———— Lerner, H. D. (1980), The current state of the borderline concept. In: *Borderline Phenomena and the Rorschach Test,* ed. J. Kwawer, H. Lerner, P. Lerner, & A. Sugarman. New York: International Universities Press, pp. 11–37.

———— Kurash, C. (1982), The body as a transitional object in bulimia. *Internat. J. Eat. Dis.,* 1(4):57–67.

———— Quinlan, D., & Devenis, L. (1981), Anorexia nervosa as a defense against anaclitic depression. *Internat. J. Eat. Dis.,* 1(1):44–61.

Toner, B. B., Garfinkel, P. E., & Garner, D. M. (1985), Long-term follow-up of anorexia nervosa. Manuscript in preparation.

Watkins, J. G., & Stauffacher, J. C. (1952), An index of pathological thinking in the Rorschach. *J. Proj. Tech.,* 16:276–286.

Wilson, A. (1982), A Developmental Approach to the Assessment of Levels of Internal Object Relations in Borderline as Contrasted with Neurotic and Psychotic Patients. Unpublished doctoral dissertation, Temple University.

Chapter 14

A Specific Category of Borderline Conditions: Perverse Personality Organizations and the Rorschach

Colette Merceron, M.A.
Odile Husain, M.A.
Frieda Rossel, M.A.

In a previous study (Merceron, Ponce, and Rossel, 1983) we described perverse signs among psychopaths; although that study was limited to psychopaths, in our view such signs exist in all borderline conditions. This means that one can find on the Rorschach particularities related to perverse defense mechanisms without necessarily inferring that obvious perverse behaviors exist. Nor do we conclude that such behaviors do not exist. Indeed, we want to make it clear that we do not believe in deductions and "guesses" concerning reality.

In addition to the well-known sexual perversions (homosexuality, fetishism), perverse character organizations have been studied by various authors including Bergeret (1974, 1980), McDougall (1978), David (1972), and Dorey (1981).

Following Bergeret's views, we agree with the concept of personality structure in the sense of a basic and permanent organization. We consider psychopathic and perverse personalities as stable organizations within borderline conditions. In these cases fragmentation anxiety has been overcome, whereas the developmental level proper to castration anxiety has not been attained. The major anxiety in these patients is anaclitic; it relates to object loss, to the unbearable feeling of incompleteness, and hence to narcissistic disturbance.

377

Such an understanding of perversion may be compared to what Winnicott (1951) says in "Transitional Objects and Transitional Phenomena." He merely touches on the topic, but his hypothesis is a very attractive one: the fetishistic object would be the successor of the transitional object; at the adult stage, the transitional object of normal childhood development would have changed into a perverse sexual relationship with human and nonhuman objects.

Although perverse signs are found in all borderline conditions, we believe it possible to circumscribe within that broad category a specific perverse organization, i.e., an organization based on disavowal, as described by McDougall (1978).

We approach the Rorschach from a psychoanalytic perspective but do not adhere to a specific scoring system. In our view, the various systems tend to be reductionistic and fail to take into account comments accompanying contents or the grammatical particularities of speech. It is these latter elements which we use in differentiating personality levels. That is, we place great importance on the elements of speech. In what follows we will outline and then discuss the prominent elements, as manifest on the Rorschach, indicative of perverse personality organization.

PROMINENT ELEMENTS IN PERVERSE ORGANIZATIONS

Emphasis on certain postures. Overemphasis on certain body parts or postures; gestures limited to and located in the body part (i.e., behinds sticking out); and unrealistic postures.

Fetishistic contents. (1) Attunement to specific elements of the body such as "beard" or "mustache," as well as references to "hairs" or "a hairy skin." (2) Objects accepted as fetishes in the psychoanalytic literature—feathers, fur, shoes, leather, collars, vests, shorts, bras.

Defensive reactions to eventual perception of deficiency (disavowal). This phenomenon is reflected on the Rorschach in a tendency to compensate for inadequacy. As opposed to psychopaths, who deal with their own limitations by criticizing and placing blame on external factors, perverts spontaneously attempt to compensate.

Distortion of the patient-examiner relationship. (1) A tendency to reverse roles as regards knowledge. (2) A search for complicity (resulting from disparagement of knowledge) and control by arousing the examiner's curiosity (enigma). (3) Responses related to the type of object relation described by Dorey (1981)—the mastery relation.

Suppression. In contrast with conventional notions of repression, this involves the use of conscious or preconscious mechanisms in an attempt to prevent the emergence of a fantasy, idea, or affect.

Characteristics of knowledge cathexis related to disorders of the symbolic function. (1) Class blending: the blending of conventional classes—characteristics wrongly assigned to a person, animal, or object (e.g., "the hands of an animal") and shifts from nature to culture. (2) Class misuse: tautological formulations ("a woman with breasts") and impaired relationships between whole and part. (3) Distortion of established speech rules: particular use of certain words with distortion of form ("boilizing" instead of "boiling," "genetic" instead of "genital," an "animalist" figure) and of certain phrases ("I don't know whether I have a particular liking for animals but . . . ").

Object categories. The object contents recorded are mostly functional (corkscrew, brush), consistent with a frequent emphasis on the possible use of these objects.

EMPHASIS ON CERTAIN POSTURES

Six types of statement on the Rorschach reflect this emphasis.

1. Statements referring to particular body postures (e.g., specifying that the figures on Card III have "their behinds sticking out" or "their legs apart"). Having noticed, at first, that such responses are typical of confirmed perverse characters, we then wondered what specific meaning could be assigned them. In most cases the accompanying comments emphasize the unusualness of these postures ("an animal in a *strange posture*"). Such hints seemed to us intended to create an enigma and to arouse the examiner's curiosity. Considering the manner in which the examiner is referred to, as an accomplice, one may wonder whether this category of comment is related to what McDougall (1978) calls "the fantasy of the anonymous onlooker" (p. 222).

2. Statements involving movement of parts of the body (perceptions of parts of the body such as feet, thumbs, or legs, these being given a great deal of power by being seen as having the capacity to move independently of the object as a whole). Examples include "legs together, woman's legs, because of the thick calves"; "ballerina's feet dancing on toes"; and the following response, given by a drug addict: "a thumb hitchhiking." Common to the above examples is a marked tendency to attribute causality and intentionality to part rather than full objects. This tendency, as noted on the Rorschach in terms of

attributing action to body parts, has been repeatedly emphasized in the clinical literature.

3. Statements referring to a particular perspective (e.g., "an animal seen from behind"). The pervert's particular apprehension of space generally consists of a back-to-front inversion (thus a subject told us that the popular animal on Card VIII could also be an anteater, provided that head and tail were reversed). On occasion there is a top-to-bottom inversion. These inversions should be distinguished from the inside-outside confusions that are more particular to the psychotic structure. In our opinion, this phenomenon relates to a basic mechanism at work in fetishism whereby a hypertrophied meaning is assigned to one part of the body in order to conceal the significance of another part. For example, the response "a woman seen from behind" may be viewed as defensive, for if the woman was viewed from the front sexual differences would have to be acknowledged. Thus, implicit in the perspective is an element of disavowal.

4. Statements showing extreme concern for "placing" objects. Among the many details used to describe posture are details that are unnecessary because of their obviousness. For example: "two bodies of similar animals, back to back, with their faces facing outward." If the animals are back to back, their faces must obviously be looking in opposite directions. In addition, one should stress that such postures generally refer to the closeness of "doubles" ("two guys leaning against each other," "two men leaning against a rock," or "two bodies of similar animals"). We view the appearance of "doubles" as reflecting a need for support, a search for anaclisis, and a need to establish a mirror relationship in order to compensate for a specific narcissistic failure.

5. Statements involving impossible postures associated with the idea of balancing. For example, a female swindler saw on Card VII "a small trinket, two fish, one on top of the other, placed on a pebble or something of that kind." During the inquiry she added that the two superimposed fish "are holding each other's fins, in the middle." In real life such an assemblage (such a "posture") is impossible; fish do not stand on pebbles. They would have to be glued together for such a construction to be possible. Nevertheless, one can note that this woman grants little importance to the support ("a pebble or something of that kind"), as if only the construction matters. This again reveals the need for anaclisis, and for omnipotent handling and juggling of reality (conflict of the ideal ego with reality). These tricky postures imply an idea of achievement—"two individuals in a sort of rocky gorge, carry-ing something, hard for me to define, something akin to equilibrism

(sic)"—since the idea of balancing is given greater value than the gesture or even the identity of the object. In addition to an exhibitionistic connotation, law-infringing elements are equally present; laws of balance are being infringed by an omnipotent, ego-challenging reality.

6. Statements referring to bird's-eye views. This type of comment is not limited to perverse organizations, but is found in all borderline conditions. The subject places himself above his perceptions ("I could perhaps see a very beautiful butterfly, seen from above"; "a long road, seen from an aerial view"). Reference is made here to a special viewpoint that would provide a better picture. Such details concerning the possibility of dominating the object reflect both the constant endeavor to control and the grandiose narcissistic aspirations of these organizations.

FETISHISTIC CONTENTS

Unlike other prominent elements of perverse organizations, contents of a fetishistic nature can be found in all borderline conditions as defined by Bergeret (1980). The presence of such contents appears consistent with traces of less well-organized perverse fixations.

Freud considered fetishism the prototype of perverse organizations; cathexis of the fetishistic object is linked with the basic mechanism at work in perversion (i.e., denial of women's castration, and denial of only part of reality, as opposed to the massive denial observed in psychosis). The following contents appear to reflect this mechanism. (Nowadays the expression "denial of sex difference" is more commonly used than "denial of women's castration," in order to emphasize the fact that the disturbance is that of incompleteness.)

Four points will be considered:

1. Contents of a fetishistic nature in the literal sense of the word. These include very specific contents such as furs, shoes, underwear, panties, or bras, objects commonly used as fetishes by sexually perverse subjects. This is not an exhaustive list; it is often in the particular nature of the comment that one sees the subject's interest in these details. For instance, instead of the animal skin usually seen on Card VI, one subject spoke of "the inside of a coat lined with fur." Reference is made to a part of the object that must be given special attention in order to be seen; this implying a scopophilic component. Also, reference to the "transparency" of clothes ("a see-through skirt") may be present, as well as an emphasis on certain items of clothing: "shoes, because of the heels" for the "feet" of the figures on Card III; "sticking-out lapel of a

jacket," seen at the height of the women's breasts on the same card; or "edge of a lace frill" seen at the height of the figure's head on Card IV.

It also is important to note the insistence on such elements as "a beard" or "hair" or details such as "hairs" or a "hairy" animal (e.g., on Card IV "a wild animal, certainly hairy, shaggy") as well as details regarding texture, such as "a black leather coat."

2. Explanations justified by fetishistic details. Sometimes these details suffice to justify, in the eyes of the subject, the sexual identity of the figures. The details play a great part in his argument, often upsetting the scale of values normally assigned things. Certain sexual interpretations are considered part of perverse denial when, through arbitrary equivalences, they are linked with alternatives or justifications: "the genitals of a woman or an anus" (Card VII bottom) or "the genitals of a woman; one can see the clitoris and there are hairs around it" (Card II).

Here the confusion is not total as in psychosis. Psychotics establish aberrant causal links; for instance, a response such as "skeleton of a woman's pelvis" (Card II) is absurd, as nothing on the Rorschach can justify the femaleness of this pelvis. Also, a statement like "Here I recognize the anus of a chicken" (lower red detail on Card II) is an absurd deduction, a totally arbitrary "recognition." One cannot grasp the meaning of such autistic perceptions, for they reflect massively impaired reality testing.

In perverse organizations fetishistic details are often part of a distorted argumentation which attributes an essential significance to elements which normally have but secondary value: "women with hair hanging down their back, hair which would give the impression which I had already compared to ears" (Card II); "red elements here featuring hair and the top of the ear" (Card III). Subjects occasionally mention a female silhouette merely because of clothing details: "the hem of a miniskirt sticking out" (Card III, lower black tip, "penis" of the figures); "hair coming halfway down the arm" (Card III, red side detail). Similar justifications are sometimes given on the TAT, particularly for Card 3: the figure is a woman "because the shoes are ladies' shoes and no trousers are to be seen"; or else the "shoes" are no doubt men's shoes. Only perverse subjects can notice on Card 5 of the TAT, in the lower part of the picture, a kind of lighter shade which they perceive as "a naked thigh" or "an open skirt"; the woman would thus be wearing a "split skirt."

3. Inverted sexual characteristics. Schafer (1954, p. 446) in mentioning responses manifesting sex identity disorders, emphasizes the male/female inversion of sexual contents (e.g., subjects seeing the

black tip on Card II as "a vagina" or the lower part of Card VII as "a penis"). In our opinion, such examples characterize psychotic rather than borderline structures, as they reflect totally impaired reality testing. Partial denial, which is specific to perverts, is expressed through distortions that often consist of substituting a fetishistic object for what may be felt as a deficiency. For instance, a subject sees the middle detail at the bottom of Card VII as "part of a half-open zipper." The detail at the top of that same card (women's heads) is not seen according to the usual pattern (woman's head with a ponytail or headdress, seen as a whole), but the top part might be detached from the global perception and be interpreted separately as a "bushy foxtail."

4. Elements indicating a fixation on component instincts. We find in this category responses that involve references to sight or touch ("animals rubbing against each other") or sometimes to smell ("animals sniffing each other"). For example, if the crab on Card III is described as "the bottom part of a crab, seen through a glass pane," we obviously take into account the importance of the scopophilic component. As for responses referring to the sense of touch, we have often noted substantial deviations in perverse personalities when it comes to the object of appeal or repulsion. In such cases one often finds that the most common repulsions or attractions are reversed. These subjects may scorn the rather unpleasant sensation usually associated with touching insects or bats. They will talk about the softness of the "hairs of a bumblebee" and the extremely pleasant feel of the skin of reptiles—"a snakeskin, it's soft to the touch" (Card VI)—or they will find the animal skin on Card VI disgusting and slimy. Active handling of the objects described often has overt masochistic or sadistic implications. For example: "a brush which has been trodden upon, one can see the hairs spread apart on both sides" (Card VI, upper detail).

Defensive Reactions toward Eventual Perception of Deficiency (Disavowal)

In our view, the "incompleteness" disturbance, as explained by Bergeret (1974) and Kernberg (1967), represents a major concept in the understanding of perverse organizations. This disturbance underlies most perverse productions. Although it is shared by all borderline conditions, its expressions are nonetheless manifold. For instance, whereas psychopaths systematically react to deficiency with critical statements involving external factors, perverts make every effort to deny it.

The concept of "deficiency denial" is consistent with what McDougall (1978) calls the "disavowal mechanism." What is being described is an "avowal" followed by the destruction of meaning due to a break of the associative chain. The perverts perceive a deficiency they will then deny. The prototype of this is the denial of sex difference. This is reflected on the Rorschach by the subject's spontaneously making up for the deficiency.

Indeed, in comparison with psychopaths, perverts do not criticize. By contrast, they occasionally pay compliments, emphasizing the good quality of the cards, at the same time trying to improve on the imperfections of what they see. These improvements enable them to entertain the illusion that they can control the object they please, by handling reality at their convenience.

Seen from the vantage point of psychosexual development, such alterations involve a fixation at the anal-retentive stage, characterized by an endeavor to control objects. This should be differentiated from the self-mastery of obsessional subjects, the latter occurring at the level of thought and, consequently, at the symbolic level.

Since formulations concerning deficiency denial are extremely complex, we will attempt to examine first the locations that promote this mechanism, then the processes, and finally the contents provided by perverts in order to make up for the deficiency.

Locations

Some cards or portions of them provide more opportunities than others for reacting to deficiency. The following details particularly promote the emergence of deficiency denial:

1. White details. We have been struck by the way many perverts interpret white first, focusing all their attention on it, though there is absolutely nothing there: "a kind of mine, with somewhat rugged walls, a very important brightness in the middle" (white detail, Card II); "Bonaparte's silhouette which would be encrusted in an armchair" (white detail, Card VII).

2. Small gaps between blots "filled" by responses such as "a sword," "the pistil of a flower," or "a bell clapper" (axis of the white detail on Card IX); "the Rolls Royce emblem" or "feet showing ten past ten" (small white detail on Card VII—the feet are seen in the position of the hands of a clock).

3. Prominent features of certain details: "heads of mammals with short trunks" (inquiry) "I first thought of an elephant but the trunk

being too short, I fell back on a wild boar" (Card VII). Here the special emphasis on the trunk obviously carries a fetishistic connotation. With respect to the deficiency, it should be mentioned that the subject is not satisfied with merely stating it, for this would mean accepting its possibility. However, he does not blame it on external factors, as would a psychopath, by saying that it is "badly done": "a crab, the two pincers and the body, but two legs are missing, there should be eight, not six" (Card I). Instead he makes every effort to make up for the deficiency by stating that the animal is probably "a wild boar." First a deficiency is perceived ("the trunk being too short"), and only then is the supposedly incomplete object (the elephant) transformed (into a wild boar), enabling the subject to deny the initial deficiency.

Processes

Although we are still dealing here with alterations of reality, these do not always bear their author's signature. Some subjects claim themselves as authors of the proposed alterations, while others designate an anonymous author. The following is an example of the former: "I don't find it very inspiring, perhaps well, a not very elaborate hairstyle on a head. I don't know, I would like to draw eyes, to complete it, maybe I would like to draw a face" (white detail, Card VII). To illustrate the latter, we shall quote a homosexual's response to Card VI: "a skin of—ugh, it could look like the skin of a wild animal, which might have been slightly modified, one would have taken out some parts." Here the deficiency is the result of an actively but anonymously imposed transformation. Maybe the subject thinks of an "improvement"; the skin may have been modified in order to give it a more pleasant appearance or to show that it has been worked upon. The change being wanted, it is no longer a deficiency; it has been intentionally achieved, and hence controlled.

We shall leave unanswered the question as to whether claiming the authorship of such alterations is developmentally more evolved, showing enhanced self-awareness, or whether, on the contrary, it is less evolved, showing a marked omnipotence.

Another possible distinction can be made between alterations in which the subject adds something (e.g., when he fills the white spaces) and those where he removes something (e.g., the skin: "one would have taken out some parts"). We observed that the same subjects perform both sorts of alteration. What matters is the process: the attempt to modify, to control, whether by adding or by removing.

Contents

Deficiency and deficiency denial are expressed by perverts through contents which are not meaningless, for they are usually supported by various partial drives.

"Mirror" and more often "light" are among the most frequent themes used to fill the gap of white details. Here we are dealing with arrangements related to the setting, the aim being either to be seen or to watch: "a kind of mine, of course it is vague, and a very important brightness in the middle" (Card II); "a disproportionate spider, also a ceiling light" (Card VII). Besides the scopophilic connotation of these two responses, we notice that in both cases the content that enables the subject to "see better" ("brightness," "ceiling light") comes as a reaction to the blank space and immediately follows a statement regarding the object's inadequate constitution ("vague," "disproportionate"). By means of a clever trick, the deficiency is denied; it is replaced by light or even by a decorative object such as a lamp.

Among other favored themes intended to compensate for an object likely to restore deficiency is the introduction of fetishistic contents. On Card I the female figure in the central detail is often seen by perverts as "a woman with her head tilted backward" or "a woman with a hat" or "a woman because there is a dress." No reference is made to the absence of a head, no criticism is expressed, in contrast to the typical response of a psychopath: "a woman, but it won't do, there is no head." However, perverts compensate for the deficiency by adding "a hat," "a dress," or sometimes, as in the case of one homosexual subject, a veil: "maybe people wearing costumes, different from ours, kind of African, even veiled." As the veil is used to hide and screen nudity, it relates to the concealment of sex difference (which we shall deal with later).

In the meantime, as regards the same detail, it seems important to differentiate such formulations from responses which, though apparently similar, are fundamentally different in terms of the underlying mechanism. In "a two-headed figure," for instance, the content is also the result of a denial, but since it is impossible or at least senseless for somebody to have two heads in real life, this necessarily implies a denial of a more psychotic nature. On the other hand, in a genitalized organization of the hysterophobic type, one can find statements such as: "a woman, although one doesn't see the head." Objectively, it is indeed difficult to find a "head," but for these organizations this does not prevent representation of the total object, since the female figure is apprehended globally. Consequently, it can be "seen," imagined. The capacity for symbolic representation is sufficiently developed to enable the subject to refer to a well-constructed mental image and to "tolerate" an eventual deficiency in reality, without it upsetting the representation. In the case of perverts, however, object representation is impaired and they are therefore obliged to resort to reality in order to reinforce and support the deficient representation. "A silhouette, I would rather say a woman because of the hips and the legs seen in transparency": here the female figure (the idea that it is a woman) is substantiated by "visible" elements (the "hips," the "legs"), such elements being taken as signs of femininity.

Perverts therefore can rely only on what is visible. Only the visible exists; what cannot be seen is nonexistent. The following is a response of an exhibitionist on Card III: "two women, one cannot see the second leg, therefore they are one-legged." This is a very good illustration of a deficient representation. Since the women on Card III are implicitly seen in profile, most people never mention the absence or potential presence of that "leg." For this particular subject, however, the leg is of capital importance, since its absence—on the card—implies an impaired whole object representation. On Card III one may also have "two women with their legs apart." Both responses convey the same meaning. In both cases the subject assigns a predominant function to the detail, which can be seen as a "penis" if the figures are seen as men, but becomes negligible when they are seen as women.

In the underlying chain of associations, such operations as justifying the sex by the "dress" (or the one-leggedness by the missing "second leg") can rest only on a denial of the difference between whole and part. Overestimating the accessory implies the denial of fundamental sex differences. The same mechanism appears to be at work in the blendings and shifts that perverts perform within species, categories, and logical classes.

Deficiency denial, which, as we have just seen, includes denial of sex difference, is well expressed through the perception of bisexual figures: "men with breasts" or "women with penises" (Card III). But, like other mechanisms, denial may be expressed by the formulation alone; perception need not be involved. Examples of this are "a man's male genitals" and "a woman's vagina," which would imply that there also exist women's "male genitals" as well as men's "vaginas." Such tautological precisions also contain the assertion of bisexuality and a clear denial of sex difference. Describing men with breasts or women with penises means that completeness is engraved in the speech (rather than being elaborated on the symbolic level). In other words, the disturbance is that of narcissistic failure and not of a castration complex.

DISTORTION OF THE PATIENT/EXAMINER RELATIONSHIP

The perverse characteristics of the organization of the self/other relationship can be clearly defined; the elements we will describe all include evidence of a perverse "mastery" relationship. Dorey (1981) distinguishes the "mastery" relationship of perverts from that of obsessionals; the latter implies a clear self/other distinction, whereas in the perverse mastery relationship the other is captivated through a seduction process that assigns him a role of "double" or "mirror." Perverts deny the value of the other's desire. They accept only the reflection of their own desire and simultaneously play a subtle game of denying what is known by both parties.

We have chosen the word "distortion" as regards the testing relationship because we are dealing here with very subtle ways of denying the other's knowledge. Perverse personalities do not manifest the massive opposition of character-disordered organizations. In the case of perverts there is neither the violent struggle for power nor the general devaluation of the usefulness of the tests. Psychopaths, for example, devalue continuously in order to maintain a permanent conflict in the relationship. By contrast, the "double" game played by perverts in the relationship implies submission to the given rules. These subjects are cooperative; they even try to prove their acceptance of instructions in a very artificial manner, assuring the interviewer that they are doing their best to please. A remark typical of the pervert is the following: "No matter how hard I try I just can't compare it with anything. I can see nothing else in this drawing." Nevertheless, perverts constantly infringe the rules, in one way or another. Such a distortion, in Dorey's opinion (1981), is present in all their relationships and tends to be cleverly hidden.

We have outlined three categories:

1. Denial of the other's knowledge. Perverts deny the interviewer's knowledge. Although the psychologist's professional status implies a superiority in understanding his particular field, perverts cleverly try to arrogate this knowledge to themselves, pretending it is theirs. They explain with great authority how the Rorschach cards are made: "inkblots folded in two and one has added color." Such explanations are given repeatedly during the test, as if the examiner was not the best

expert on the matter. They also tend to deny his competence by skillfully reversing the roles. They actively reshape the rules, asking for example, "I believe it is the first idea that matters, isn't it? Because one can always have other ideas, but they always revolve around the first one, I think." They also anticipate any possible question and forestall what they believe to be the other's desire: "Now I am going to make a comment with relation to your profession, just to please you!" They deny the value of any deduction that might be drawn from their responses, resenting it as an intrusion. They mistrust intrusions, even though they provoke them, and therefore try to preempt them: "I don't know whether I have a special liking for animals, but this is what I see" or "two human beings—yes, I insist," as if the interviewer had raised an objection.

The inquiry, as we practice it, sheds more light on the patterns of the perverse relationship. We usually draw the subject's attention to details he has not noticed on his own. Without being included in the list of popular responses for all authors, these details are often interpreted (for instance, the detail in the middle of Card I seen as "a female silhouette"). We suggest the common interpretation when the subject fails to see it spontaneously. Psychopaths reject these suggestions altogether, without any justification ("can't see anything there") or else, taking reality as their support, they criticize what is suggested (Figure ? "Not at all! He'd be pretty awful then!"). Perverse personalities show much more ambiguity. At first they seem to agree, which can be explained by their intense search for narcissistic anaclisis; but later on they reshape the interpretation in such a way that it ends up being extremely different from the initial suggestion ("A woman here ? No, yes—well, yes, not quite, or else in the lower part, hips and legs, with the edge of a fur coat, in that case, yes!"). Such alterations result from a need, typical of this personality organization, to deny deficiency and the anxiety created by its perception. They add elements. For example, on Card I for the middle detail: "A human figure, you mean ? Yes, if you put legs and a head on it!" They impose modifications in order to confirm their illusion of omnipotence and reinforce their sense of power when faced with the latent threat of narcissistic impairment.

In addition, they frequently repeat the instructions and questions of the inquiry. These repetitions may lead one to believe that the interviewer was not clear enough. On the other hand, it may create the illusion that it is they who are conducting the test. In the same vein, one can easily understand why, during the inquiry, they often respond to white when asked to comment on red, and vice versa.

2. Distortion of knowledge cathexis in general. Denial of knowledge extends to many other fields. As explained by McDougall (1978) and other authors, perverts are convinced of being in on the secret of sexual matters, completely denying the value of "normal" sexuality. Consequently, they deny the value of knowledge in general, even while developing a marginal knowledge of their own, using it to seduce and subjugate. Drug addicts, for instance, often try to impose their very special knowledge as if it was shared by all. They nearly always quote an author of comic books named Druillet, as if such works were part of humanity's cultural treasures. However, anything related to universal knowledge is frequently treated with circumspection and skepticism, for example: "It looks like the genetics (sic) of a woman, I am being influenced by a television program I watched, it looks very much like that, according to what had been shown in that documentary" (Card IX). The "according to what had been shown in that documentary" seems to question the value of established knowledge.

One indirect way of defeating the other is by mentioning elements taken from real life that are unknown to him. The other is thereby denied any possibility of control or judgment. For example, "It looks exactly like a book I saw. There were animal carcasses just like these." The subject is referring to a totally personal knowledge on which he has a hold the other has not.

3. A search for mastery, correlated with denial of knowledge. Denial of knowledge goes along with the mastery that perverts try to exercise over others. To this end they aim at arousing in the other a desire complementary to theirs, by awakening the component instinct. Such a scheme is based on the fantasy of omnipotence, which is obviously correlated with deficiency denial. On the Rorschach test, as elsewhere, the use of "they," "we," and "you" instead of "I" implicates the other without soliciting his opinion. It is as if it were natural that he should be in collusion with the subject and in no case experience things differently.

The alteration and reshaping of reality described in the preceding section belong to the same type of relational perversion. They are a way of offering the untrue for the true, the fictitious for the real, thus hoping to gain the audience's approval. We have found many examples of this in confabulatory responses throughout the protocols: "two bears which produce, through contact of their limbs, a kind of fictitious flame, but done on paper." This is an attempt to suggest as possible what is impossible. It implies an attempt to create an illusion of omnipotence that is confirmed by the seductive captivation of the other's attention.

On Card X a reference to "a fan which would open and show all its colors" rests on a denial similar to that described previously for the movement of parts of the body: as if an inanimate object could open on its own and intend to exhibit its colors. This is one of the many cases of shifts from animate to inanimate (and from human to animal) that we shall describe at length further on. It is an attempt to force the other into the illusion of omnipotence.

SUPPRESSION

We have often found, among perverse organizations, special formulations that lead us to wonder what defense mechanism is involved. These formulations contain hints and suggest a possible extension of the commenced interpretation by means of a sentence interruption or an interposed "I don't know." For instance, referring to the animals on Card II: "two bears holding each other—no, not holding—sniffing each other. I don't know." Or, for the popular figures on that same card: "two figures who are—nothing, that's all."

One can find somewhat similar reactions in other contexts, for example among obsessional personalities, but here they occur in another form. Again on Card II, an obsessional patient may say: "two bears or two—no, excuse me, I was thinking of two wild boars, but it does not seem to be really appropriate, after all." The inhibition of the second response derives from an obsessional perfectionism. The subject clearly verbalizes his explanations, as opposed to perverse personalities, who maintain the suspense and entertain doubt: "a thing that looks—although, no, rather like a furry animal" (Card IV) or "This seems to me—no, I would rather say elephants" (Card VII).

Obviously we are not dealing here with repression, as that mechanism prevents any kind of representation: "the red here, I can't see what it could be, I am looking, but I see nothing" (Card II) or "I don't see anything. It can probably represent something, but I don't know what I could imagine here" (Card VI).

The observations made among perverse personalities apparently relate to the conscious or at least to the preconscious; it is a hardly elaborate retentive movement which easily disappears, either during the test or during the inquiry. Sometimes a clear perverse content then emerges. Here is a typical example, taken from the protocol of a young drug addict with very blatant psychopathic and perverse characteristics. He first rejects Card VII and then says, with a faint smile, "A woman, no, I don't know." He ends up by adding, somewhat hesitantly,

"Yes, I was thinking—I wanted to say a willing woman from behind, her legs apart." His response is a good example of the perverse equivalence between part and whole objects, since he says "a woman" although he means only part of the body (buttocks and legs). Such responses are considered by some authors to be a "return of the repressed." We do not share this view, because repressed elements, when they tend to reappear, do so "in a distorted fashion in the form of a compromise" (Laplanche and Pontalis, 1973, p. 398).

On the contrary, the protocols to which we are referring here contain very direct, at times even crude statements. Most of the expressions collected from a large number of protocols are much more subtle than the relatively crude example quoted above, yet they are absolutely equivalent as to what is insinuated. To cite a rather typical example: "It is somewhat—smutty, isn't it?" No true response is provided though evidently the subject has something in mind; he is able, however, to express it clearly enough to arouse sexual fantasies in the other and to keep things in suspense, deliberately it would seem.

We believe that the defense mechanism at work here is that of suppression. In order to avoid any confusion due to translation, we will recall a few definitions: the process referred to here corresponds to the French word "répression," which translates as "suppression" in English and "supresión" in Spanish. Laplanche and Pontalis (1973, pp. 438–439) describe it as a conscious or preconscious mechanism that can obstruct the emergence of a fantasy, an idea, or an affect, as opposed to the English "repression" and the Spanish "represión"; these correspond to the French "refoulement," a mechanism through which "the subject attempts to repel, or to confine to the unconscious, representations (thoughts, images, memories) which are bound to an instinct" (p. 390).

Suppression therefore does not involve "a translation from one intrapsychic system (the preconscious-conscious) to another (the unconscious)" (p. 439). It would imply a low-level censorship of representations, and this is precisely what we observe in a large number of examples.

Studying the important role of suppression among perverts led us to notice that it plays a crucial role in their handling of relationships. Indeed, perverts behave as if they were exhibiting the fact that an idea or fantasy is being suppressed, as if they were showing that something is being hidden, something that can, at will, either be revealed to or concealed from the onlooker. A female swindler made the following final statement on Card VI: "I believe it is the first idea that matters isn't it? Because one can always have other ideas, but they always revolve around the first one, I think." She suggests that she might, if she wished, have "many more ideas," but that she tries to maintain her mastery through an arbitrary "agreement" concluded as part of an omnipotent move to deny the examiner's knowledge.

One might recall here the "manipulation of the secret" among perverse personalities that some authors, such as McDougall, connect with fixations at the anal stage. McDougall (1978) specifies that the important point is the "play" established around the possession of a secret and its subsequent "erotization" in relationships with others. By playing with what is left unsaid, perverts create an enigma in order to fascinate others and to evoke in them a complementary fantasy. But in order to exercise their mastery, they must *reveal* that everything has not been said. Here is another example: the female impersonator mentioned above said of the animals on the sides of Card VIII: "Two animals trying to climb, not at all like a wild beast, no, nothing of that kind. How do you call them—those ferreters?" One may infer that a suppression mechanism is operating, and is immediately used to handle the relationship ("How do you call them?"). The curiosity aroused by such ambiguous statements is further reinforced by an obscure reference to an activity that may be understood as conveying a perverse connotation ("those ferreters"); in French the term used was "fouineurs," which refers to no specific animal and is in fact inappropriate when applied to animals generally; some animals are "fouisseurs" (burrowers) but not "fouineurs" (nosy ones), the latter describing inquisitive *persons* who poke their noses into other people's business.

This play with the unsaid goes along with infraverbal expressions, such as knowing looks and smiles, which incite the examiner to ask questions; the latter is supposed to guess that a perverse hint is implied in the withholding process.

CHARACTERISTICS OF KNOWLEDGE CATHEXIS RELATED TO DISORDERS OF THE SYMBOLIC FUNCTION

In this section we shall deal with a number of observations related to the symbolic function. As a basic component of representation, the symbolic function is "necessary to render possible the interaction of thought among individuals and consequently, the constitution or acquisition of collective meanings" (Piaget, 1945, p. 429). Although disturbance in representation is found in various personality organizations, perverts in particular reveal multiple disturbances in symbolization.

One can immediately differentiate perverts from psychotic and psychopathic personalities. Perverts show neither the totally impaired reality testing nor the autistic cathexis of hermetic knowledge found among psychotics, and they do not massively disparage knowledge, as psychopaths do. In fact, we have noticed that in Switzerland, a country with high economic standards, psychopaths rarely complete officially approved training programs. This can be understood as a noncathexis of knowledge and its rules and a preference for leisure activities which involve a strong pleasure principle (at school they prefer drawing classes and gymnastics to subject areas with strict rules, such as French or arithmetic). Perverts, by contrast, nearly always have a professional qualification, but their cathexis of knowledge is very particular. This will be examined below.

Class Blending

Perverts frequently blend classes (by "class" we mean established categories as defined by social consensus). Two main categories of blending may be noted.

1. Qualities or characteristics wrongly attributed to a class of entities or objects. Confusion may first of all occur in the description of the entity or object and of its components; for instance, mentioning "the arms of an owl" or "the hands of an animal" reflects confusion between human and animal classes. The subject may also mix several animal species: a female swindler spoke of a wasp's "spine." As wasps are invertebrates, the idea is inappropriate. The above process, which is quite frequent, may be correlated with deficiency denial. In describing the wasp with a spine, she denies the hierarchies of the animal kingdom by placing vertebrates and invertebrates on a single level.

Class blending of this sort is sometimes more subtle and is conveyed by verbal lapses from one species to another. Presumably unsatisfied with the smallness of a rat, a homosexual comments: "If I should compare them to a species, I would say they are rats, but that is not quite accurate"; the interviewer then expects a change within the same species, but the subject carries on: "some kind of bird, owl, church-owl, eagle-owl." The way he changes from a rat to a bird is probably a way of denying incompleteness, particularly since the subject shifts from a negatively connoted rat to a bird bearing a name of power (in French "eagle-owl" translates to "grand-duc").

Still another variety of such blending consists in attributing an impossible activity to the person or thing being considered. For example: "Figures busy with a gambling wheel. I mean in a casino, with small animals performing somersaults all around" (Card III). Such an arrangement is impossible: first, animals seldom do somersaults spontaneously, unless they have been specially trained; second, there are no animals in casinos. However, despite its being unfeasible, the arrangement is maintained, which again signifies the omnipotent handling of reality.

2. Subtle transitions from nature to culture. In this second category we shall cite cases which reveal confusion between two very different types of object—the natural object and the artifact. We have frequently observed among perverse organizations shifts from one type to another. Examples include the following: "an abstract work of art where one would have included two animals" (Card VIII). The confusion here is twofold. "An abstract work of art" implies precisely the absence of any natural object, yet the subject introduces one. This reveals representation disorders (i.e., disturbances in the relation between signified and signifier).

Regarding this point, psychotics make very odd statements. They ignore the identity and nature of both signified and signifier, and in consequence produce concretized abstractions. Perverts, by contrast, handle these two components of representation as if they were equivalent—that is, as if each could simultaneously represent and be represented. This is illustrated in the following example: "a small trinket, two fish, one on top of the other, placed on a pebble or something of that kind. It is as if there was a mirror in the middle and they are looking at themselves. They are holding each other's fins, in the middle" (Card VII). Here too there is a transition from artifact to natural object, as the fish, initially described as "a small trinket," finally come to life.

Examples such as these are typically quite puzzling to the examiner. In addition to the very particular and misleading shift described earlier, the subject creates even more confusion by giving absolutely no indication of the transformation rules that might enable the interviewer to grasp what object category is being referred to (abstract or figural in the first example, animate or inanimate in the second).

One also finds blendings among psychopaths; but in their case the process is more straightforward. For example, in the response "men with birds' heads" (Card III), the subject seizes two existing classes and then combines them to produce a hybrid class in violation of reality. As for perverts, they resort to a more clever and complex stratagem: nonexplanation of the rules of transformation. This is used also as but one of many ways of maintaining the enigma. Such an explanation is compatible with the fact that these shifts also reflect disturbances in representation.

Class Misuse

Having dealt with class contents, we shall now focus on the question of how class is handled (i.e., study of form as opposed to substance). The most salient features in this regard were (1) tautological statements and (2) difficulties concerning the relation between whole and part.

In contents such as "a wasp with its sting at the back" or "a woman with breasts," emphasis is laid on details inherent in the object. These formulations are tautological, because the "with" phrase, instead of drawing attention to a contingent fact, is superfluous: the "sting at the back" belongs necessarily to the wasp, just as breasts are part of the woman. Yet perverts will mention these parts as if their presence could not be taken for granted; they are like fetishistic objects, to be added or removed at will. Thus words like "wasp" and "woman," which normally refer to precise representations, are here given partially different meanings.

These responses should be distinguished from those of obsessional subjects, who often take great care in detailing their responses ("and the two large black areas are like two animals, two bears, one can see the eye, two ears and two paws, yes, the forelegs"), and from the seemingly similar descriptions provided by psychotics. Despite the apparent similarity of "a woman with breasts" (perverse response) and "a standing figure with legs" or "a torso with eyes" (schizophrenic responses), the latter express glaring absurdity as well as a lack of body integrity. A struggle against fragmentation is suggested, the word "with" being used in an attempt to stick parts of the body back together. By contrast, the perverse response ("a woman with breasts") underlines the priority of part object cathexis.

The tendency to add appendages as if they were not integral parts of the body reflects disorders in the relation between whole and part; the part object stands in metonymic relation to the whole object, and becomes its equivalent. In other words, there is a distortion of hierarchical values in which the part is oversignified at the expense of the whole.

Distortion of Language

Here we shall present only a few examples, since those we can cite are taken from the French language and it may be difficult to find equivalents. Furthermore, depending on the language considered, these errors might give rise to different formulations. However, we do want to mention these speech errors, because we assume that they are not purely accidental.

Sometimes existing words are used incorrectly: "genetic" instead of "genital," an "animalist" figure, etc. We were struck by a homosexual's repetitive use of the word "reference": "not bears, but an animal reference" (Card II); "animal references placed around that coat of arms" (Card VIII). It was as if the subject wanted to cover the real meaning of the word and the subordination involved; in fact, reference is generally made to something or references are obtained from somebody else, but here the subject expresses himself as if a reference could refer to itself. On other occasions the radical of the word exists but is reshaped in an idiosyncratic way ("boilizing" instead of "boiling") or is given an innovative touch ("fulgurance" instead of "fulguration"). Often an expression is used ambiguously in justifying a response. A female impersonator declares on Card II, "I don't know whether I have a particular liking for animals, but I seem to see two kinds of bears." In French, the phrase translated here by "to have a liking for" may take on a sexual connotation. Here, however, the sense is left ambiguous, which can only arouse curiosity and create a climate of enigma. Lastly, we often notice mistakes in the use of formulations related to reciprocity. In the phrase "I am going to counteract myself" (instead of contradict), the confusion is certainly not meaningless: generally, one counteracts the actions of another or is oneself subjected to counteraction from without. Here the expression implies a defensive reaction to the risk of being counteracted by the other. This may be understood as a denial of the other's narcissism (the other is denied the power to counteract or oppose the self).

These examples are by no means exhaustive. What we wish to show is that distortions of form and meaning in the speech of perverts are meaningful, and that they differ from psychotic neologisms involving hermetic thinking. Comparative observations have led us to conclude that speech errors are more peculiar among psychotics than among perverts.

Moreover, we want to make it clear that these examples are to be distinguished from slips of the tongue. In slips of the tongue, the speaker corrects himself and restores the right word. In addition, the underlying mechanism differs. In slips, "suppression of the speaker's intention to say something is the indispensable condition for the occurrence of a slip of the tongue" (Freud, 1916–1917, p. 66).

Perverts, by adding a personal touch to certain words, oblige the interlocutor to adjust to their manner of speaking, to their idiosyncrasies of style. As language involves collective conventions that encourage compliance, distortions in the form or meaning of certain words might well result from a disavowal of current rules governing linguistic structures. Such distortions may be regarded as infringements of these rules (in the present case, we are dealing with the rules of speech, but the same holds for the laws of balance, etc.). As a result, a so-called new language is "created" and hypercathected at the expense of the norm, the value of which is denied. Similar mechanisms would seem to exist both for language and for fetishes. Regarding this point, René Major in "Langage de la perversion et perversion du langage" (1972) recalls that the main function of language is its binding activity; this can be achieved only by means of acoustic images linking word presentation with thing presentation. But with perverse subjects the visual image confuses the acoustic image, sight is focused on part, not whole, objects.

In short, unlike psychotics, who misapprehend reality and social consensus, and unlike psychopaths, who reject knowledge in toto and consider it useless, perverts show disruptions in symbolic processes and in the cathexis of particular bits of knowledge.

Regarding these disruptions, most authors speak of symbolic process disturbances. We have seen that in perversion words fail to act as a bond between instinctual energy and the representational world; this failure is caused by the prevalence of the visual image over the acoustic image. This obstruction of the auditory field has an impact on the subject's psychic development, as it plays a role in superego formation. As for psychosexual development, McDougall (1978) considers disavowal of the father's phallic function the first "gap in knowledge," the prototype of a screening process which in perverts extends to other fragments of human knowledge.

Nevertheless, the pervert cathects certain fields of knowledge. Characterized by the "art" of juggling elements of knowledge (conventional classes, turns of speech) and infringing rules, the pervert aims to "create," according to Chasseguet-Smirgel (1973), an area of knowledge all his own. This area, though somewhat marginal, is highly prized by the pervert; it remains his exclusive property.

OBJECT CATEGORIES

Perverts often provide responses in which the utilitarian and functional aspects are emphasized: "a corkscrew" (white detail, Card IX); "the leg of a table" or "a pen nib" (upper detail, Card VI). Furthermore, their manner of describing these objects focuses on the way they are handled: "that miner's tool is used to break stones when digging tunnels." The sole worth of the object lies in its possible handling. One can understand this as another manifestation of the search for mastery.

In our opinion, this type of content relates to the symbolic process disturbances discussed in the preceding section. For the pervert these objects have never acquired the full symbolic status accorded them in collective representations. Instead a concrete connection is immediately made with an often prosaic and utilitarian function of these objects: a "brush" can be used only to do one's hair, "eyeglasses" to see better, etc. However, it would be wrong to assume that objects with symbolic value in collective thinking are necessarily absent from the speech of perverts. Yet, depending on the structure of the personality, these objects are very differently commented on. The content "totem" is a good example. Whereas an obsessional will describe it as "an object of worship in Indian civilizations of North America," a perverse subject will rather say: "that piece of wood, you know, a stick, with feathers hooked up on top and the bottom is covered with a skin." For the former, it is the value of the collective religious symbol that predominates; for the latter, it is the artifact that is first manipulated and then displayed. It might be said that perverts ignore the symbolic meaning of the totem, which is reduced to a mere assemblage of elements to be manipulated. We have often made similar observations about other objects to which a recognized symbolic value is attributed ("vase," "coat of arms," etc.).

Although contents identical to those described above may be found in different organizations, we believe that they do not always convey the same meaning. For neurotic personalities (centered around the castration complex), participation in collective representations allows objects to be integrated with their symbolic value. As for perverse personalities, objects remain closely related to their concrete function. This function is very often highlighted by the subject's insistence on the handling or use of the object in daily life: "a cat skin, like the one my parents have on their bed"; "an oilcan for machines, it has that shape, it is soft and there is oil coming out here" (he makes the gesture). One can often observe a tendency to mime the actions mentioned. This too reflects impaired representation and shows that words have taken the place neither of objects nor of the actions that may be performed on them or with them.

It seems that the object's entire importance derives from the mastery that can be exerted on it. Indeed, when referring to the animal skins seen on Cards IV and VI, many perverts specify: "skins to be hung on a wall" or "to be put in front of the fireplace in a sitting room." Furthermore, they often isolate from the object a specific partial function, as in the following example: "a, you know, one of those things you put in the fields, to scare sparrows." There is a distortion in this definition of a scarecrow, a contrivance basically designed to protect crops. Its main purpose is not to scare birds but to keep them away. Yet the pervert insists on this negatively connoted correlative function.

Such distortions involving the use of objects are frequent. We mentioned earlier the example of the "brush" response to Card VI: "a brush which has been trodden upon, one can see the hairs spread apart on both sides." As a rule, a brush is not meant to be walked on. These comments on the "brush" and the "scarecrow" bear the stamp of the sadistic drive. Other contents, such as "a keyhole," a "misty pane of glass" through which things can be seen, "spectacles," or "a pair of eyeglasses," are directly related to the component instinct these objects can help satisfy, i.e., the scopophilic instinct.

CONCLUSION

It may seem surprising that the present study should contain examples taken from the protocols of transvestites, drug addicts, and homosexuals. However, if their speech is analyzed in the light of the criteria we have presented, it seems obvious that these protocols exhibit comparable configurations, regardless of the manifest perversion.

Indeed, all perverts have in common a fixation on component instincts, an attachment to the fetishistic object, the disavowal of sex difference, and recourse to the mechanism of suppression. In addition, their symbolic function is disturbed.

Psychoanalysts have tried to provide theoretical explanations for the "choice" of perversion. There may indeed exist subtle differences between one form of perversion and another, but we are not yet in a position to differentiate them on the basis of projective tests.

In clinical practice we often as a group discuss our protocols, with no hint or indication concerning the subject's history or the reason for psychological assessment. After brief discussion we usually manage to agree on a diagnosis of perverse personality organization in a given case, but seldom "guess" the specific type of perversion involved. Thus, we may all agree on a diagnosis of perverse personality organization without knowledge of any manifest perversion. But this is not a reason to question the value of diagnoses made on the basis of projective tests. Many of our examinations are court-ordered assessments, in which case we are often apprised in advance of some perverse behavior or ideation. However, where this is not so, as with military referrals in cases of insubordination, we are not prevented from diagnosing perverse organization. Perverts, after all, seldom speak of their perversion—not because they try to hide it but, rather, because they are deeply convinced that their sexuality represents normality (McDougall, 1978). We have in fact learned from experience that those who speak very freely of their perversion are often prepsychotic.

In this chapter we have excluded from consideration all prepsychotic subjects with perverse defense mechanisms. Such subjects present some of the above characteristics, object responses in particular, though often these are objects that are relatively mechanical. In any case, this type of pathology may easily be differentiated from perverse organizations. First, in prepsychotics these common characteristics often appear in an absurd context; second, the underlying anxiety relates to fear of fragmentation. The essential difference is that we do not observe among prepsychotics the main criteria used to determine perverse personality organizations: suppression and the major handling of relationships dominated by the striving for mastery. One may therefore find similar perverse behaviors both in lower-level borderline conditions (genuine perverse organizations) and in more archaic organizations. It is important to distinguish these conditions; indeed, identical behavior does not have the same meaning in the two contexts. It does not defend against the same type of anxiety.

Finally, since perverse organization is a subcategory of borderline personality and since a problem common to all borderlines is the inability to overcome a feeling of incompleteness, it is hardly surprising that perverse characteristics such as fetishistic contents and posture responses (e.g., the "seen from above" response) are found also among so-called higher-level borderline conditions (character neuroses, narcissistic personalities, and dependent personalities).

REFERENCES

Bergeret, J. (1974), *La Personalité Normale et Pathologique.* Paris: Dunod.
————— (1980), *La Dépression et les États-Limités.* Paris: Payot.
Chasseguet-Smirgel, J. (1973), Essai sur l'idé*al du moi. In: Revue Francaise de Psychanalyse.*
David, C. (1972), La perversion affective. In: *La Sexualité Perverse: Études Psychanalytiques.* Paris: Payot, pp. 195–227.
Dorey, R. (1981), La relation d'emprise. In: *Nouvelle Revue de Psychanalyse,* 24:117–139.
Freud, S. (1916–17), Introductory lectures on psycho-analysis. *Standard Edition,* 15/16:15–239, 243, 463. London: Hogarth Press, 1963.
Kernberg, O. (1967), Borderline personality organization. *J. Amer. Psychoanal. Assn.,* 15:641–685.
Laplanche, J., & Pontalis, J.-B. (1973), *The Language of Psycho-Analysis,* tr. D. Nicholson-Smith. New York: Norton.
Major, R. (1972), Langage de la perversion et perversion du langage. In: *La Sexualité Perverse: Etudes Psychanalytiques.* Paris: Payot, pp. 97–117.
McDougall, J. (1978), *Plaidoyer pour une Certaine Anormalité.* Paris: Gallimard.
Merceron, C., Ponce, L., & Rossel, F. (1983), Aménagement particulier des états-limités: Les troubles du comportement à caractère délictueux. In: *Psychologie Francaise,* 28:(2):156–163.
Piaget, J. (1945), La formation du symbole chez l'enfant. Neuchatel: Delachaux et Niestlé.
Schafer, R. (1954), *Psychoanalytic Interpretation in Rorschach Testing.* New York: Grune & Stratton.
Winnicott, D. W. (1951), Transitional objects and transitional phenomena. In: *Collected Papers.* London: Hogarth, 1958, pp. 229–242.

Chapter 15

Transsexualism and Disturbances in Genital Symbolization: An Exploratory Study

Richard L. Karmel, Ph.D.

Mitchell (1976) and Limentani (1979) express the viewpoint that transsexuals, male transsexuals in particular, suffer from a disturbance in "genital symbolization." Their position contrasts with that of Stoller (1975), who views transsexualism as the concomitant of a primary, nonconflictual cross-gender identity—i.e., an irreversible, fundamentally female gender identity brought about in a male by a particular set of family dynamics. The male infant is "feminized" within the context of a pathological family constellation and never acquires a masculine core gender.

This conflict-free, nonpathological view of transsexualism is disputed by Mitchell, who argues that for the male transsexual severe psychopathology is indeed present. Mitchell's argument centers around the male transsexual's relationship to his genitalia and his capacity to appreciate its significance in self-gender differentiation. According to Mitchell, "the male transsexual has been unable to symbolize the penis" (p. 359), a deficiency that constitutes an important if not critical component of transsexualism—a sense of discomfort and inappropriateness regarding one's anatomical sex and the wish to be rid of one's genitals and live as a member of the other sex. For Mitchell, the transsexual's inability to acquire a realistic sense of his biological-anatomical nature suggests a reality deficit and the presence of psychosis.

Limentani continues this line of argument, stating that in the transsexual's early life history there has been a "faulty appraisal of the genital organs and genitality" (p. 147), resulting in a disturbance in symbol formation. This disturbance develops as a consequence of early failures in separation, failures whose repetition can be observed in the course of the psychoanalytic process. Ongoing interviews with these patients reveal marked anxieties over separation from primary objects, anxieties that manifest "the severity of the projective and introjective identificatory processes" (p. 148). The intensity of these processes renders the child confused about his genitals: they may be felt to be not his own. This will alter if not abort the child's capacity to develop or form "genital symbols," that is, to utilize the genitals for purposes of symbolic thinking and symbol formation (language, play, and fantasy). In the place of symbolization, more concrete forms of mental development and mental processing, such as fetishistic attachments, will emerge. The clinical-theoretical formulations of Segal (1957) provide a major conceptual framework for the formation or construction of this explanatory model and will be more fully discussed below.

To summarize, on the basis of arguments posed by Mitchell (1976) and Limentani (1979), a challenge is posed to Stoller's nonconflictual cross-gender identity formation view of transsexualism (1975). Mitchell and Limentani argue that transsexuals suffer from a disturbance in genital symbolization capacities and, by the same token, in reality sense, body image, and body ego. By emphasizing the presence of such a disturbance in transsexuals, they provide conceptual clarification of what DSM–III calls a "gender identity disorder."

Symbolism and Symbol Formation

In order to apply the genital symbolization defect hypothesis, it is first necessary to consider symbol theory and its evolution within what is often referred to as the British or Kleinian school of psychoanalysis. In earlier presentations (Karmel, 1981, 1982), I have discussed the relevance of Kleinian symbol theory for the Rorschach method and its specific applicability to the study of transsexualism.

The views of Melanie Klein, as outlined in a 1930 paper, "The Importance of Symbol-Formation in the Development of the Ego," marked the beginning of what can be thought of as a departure from the more "classical" position on symbolism: that the symbol stands for "conflict and prohibition," since it functions as a camouflage deflecting conflict-laden affect away from the primary object onto a secondary or substitutive object (Jones, 1916). This would permit conflict associated with the original object to remain hidden, dissociated, and essentially unattended to, relegated to the province of the unconscious, Intrapsychic conflict, it was held, produced symbolism; avoidance of painful affect was the motivating factor behind symbol formation.

Klein presented a contrasting position, introducing the developmental-ontogenetic view that "symbolism is the foundation of all sublimation and of every talent, since it is by way of symbolic equation that things, activities and interests become the subject of libidinal phantasies" (p. 220). She shifted emphasis away from a conflict-repression model of symbolism to a developmental model, though it should be noted that conflict continued to play an important role. Significant emphasis, for example, was placed on the role of "early infantile" conflict in psychological development. In this she followed the lead of her mentor, Sandor Ferenzci, who had postulated, in Klein's words, "that identification, the forerunner of symbolism, arises out of the baby's endeavour to rediscover in every object his own organs and their functioning" (p. 220). Klein emphasized the infant's "early anxieties" and made the point that symbol formation serves to alleviate them. Arising from the infant's sadism and the need to deactivate or neutralize conflict brought about by emotions, such as retaliatory anxiety. In the mind of the young child "equations" are formed between body parts, body organs (of mother, father, and self), and external objects. In turn, these equations may themselves become the source of anxiety owing to the underdeveloped ego. New equations or a straining of equations may thus emerge as the child attempts to alleviate anxiety; yet each new equation may bring with it additional conflict. The overall effect is one of propulsion; the child is propelled to search out new objects and to engage in symbol formation.

Klein's emphasis on the centrality of symbolism can further be noted in her statement "not only does symbolism come to be the foundation of all phantasy and sublimation but, more than that, it is the basis of the subject's relation to the outside world and to reality in general" (p. 221). Anxiety, as pointed out, is a necessary prerequisite; anxiety tolerance an essential requisite for the working through of early anxieties; and there is a close interrelationship between symbol formation, phantasy, and ego development. The latter is actually quite dependent on symbol formation in Klein's scheme, as it is the means by which early anxieties (sadistic and libidinal) are mastered. Symbol formation is therefore an indication of ego development, ego capacity (anxiety-conflict tolerance), and ego mastery (sublimation).

While Klein's views on the centrality of symbolism and symbol formation are of general psychological significance, applicable to a wide range of patient populations, her emphasis on the role of sadism is of particular relevance in the study of transsexualism. Referring to the problems confronting the male child—the erection of defenses against his destructive impulses—she states, "In the boy this strong defence is also directed against his penis as the executive organ of his sadism and it is one of the deepest sources of all disturbances of potency" (p. 232).

What is at issue is the "excess and prematurity" of the child's defensive operations against his sadism since they have the potential to alter and disturb normal ego development. Since it is by way of fantasy and symbol formation that the ego develops, providing for anxiety tolerance and the working through of sadism, fantasy and symbol formation are seen as critical components enabling the individual to have a relationship with the environment. Furthermore, again bearing on the question of transsexualism, it is the means by which body parts and body organs can be brought into such relationships.

Klein's innovative theorizing about the nature, function, and formation of symbols led to a series of papers by her colleagues. Milner (1952) was also of the opinion that symbol formation was critical to reality adaptation, and pointed out the importance of noting how symbolization might be used: as a creative link to new discoveries and identifications or as a means of obscuring and distorting reality. The latter is related to what Fenichel (1945) called "archaic symbolism." In other words, symbolism may be used in two distinctly different ways. For example, in the more advanced adult context, a phallic symbol is employed, say, a snake or an airplane, to hide an objectionable idea, that of the penis. In this case, the genital reference will be rejected, though a connection may seem plausible. However, in what Fenichel refers to as archaic symbolism—a component of prelogical thinking— the symbol "snake" evokes the emotion originally connected with the penis; in fact, penis and snake may be essentially without distinction. The snake is treated as a representation of its genital referent in this instance and no separation is intended.

Where archaic symbolism and prelogical thinking motivate symbol formation, Milner (1952) conceived of there being a state of fusion between primary and secondary objects, or what might be termed a *fusion fantasy*. This requires as well that there be an illusion operative such that "the person producing the fusion believes that the secondary object *is* the primary one" (p. 183).

Finally, there are the views of Rycroft (1956), who took the position that "symbolization is a general capacity of the mind which is based on perception and which may be used either by the primary or the secondary process" (p. 137). As such, symbolization is a feature of both conscious and unconscious mental activity.

This position argues that all levels of symbolic thinking and symbol formation are accessible to the conscious mind, regardless of diagnosis, and whether or not artistic creativity is highly developed. Put another way, there is no simple relationship between accessibility to one's symbolic processes, no matter the level, and mental illness or artistic capacity. Rycroft (1956) believes that the strength of the Kleinian viewpoint lies in its emphasis on the fact that "unconscious symbolic and imaginative processes underlie the development and maintenance of a sense of reality just as much as they do neurosis" (p. 141). That there exists a "reciprocity between fantasy and reality," as opposed to an antithesis, is also underscored—note the usefulness of the role of illusion. As with Milner, there is reference to problems created by an absence of imaginative processes in fully appreciating reality. In essence, symbolization may serve a variety of functions, enhancing reality adaptation and self-expression or, by contrast, limiting and curtailing psychological growth and development.

In order to clarify his viewpoint, Rycroft offers the following formulations: "A symbol may (a) resemble the primary object in appearance, function, or capacity to arouse an identical affect, or (b) be part of the primary object, or (c) have been experienced in spatial or temporal contiguity with it" (p. 143). "A symbol carries affect displaced from the object it represents." (The symbol is chosen specifically for its affect-aptness.) Therefore, with regard to *phallic* symbols, the choice of symbol—dagger, gun, plane, snake—corresponds to an "affective conception of the penis" as well as to a "functional conception."

Displacement may be repeated indefinitely, moving further and further away from the primary object, a process first noted by Jones (1916): "Symbolism is a centrifugal, one-way process." Nonetheless, the direction may be reversed—"centripetal displacement" or, more commonly, regression. Rycroft introduces the term "desymbolization" and notes that under certain conditions involving regression "word-images are replaced by visual-images." This is termed "regressive visualization."

The Rorschach and the Process of Symbolization

Schafer (1954) has discussed at length the nature of the Rorschach response process, citing the manifold "levels of psychic functioning" called into play. Assuming an ego psychology viewpoint, his approach emphasizes a balanced view in evaluating the symbolic properties of any Rorschach response.

The Rorschach test situation induces what Schafer terms "temporary creative regression" (p. 112), although counterregressive forces are also operative. The specific conditions surrounding administration of the test and the test stimuli themselves constitute "the Rorschach frame" (see Milner, 1952). The fact that creative regression is facilitated suggests that the Rorschach will set into motion the process of symbolization or at least provide an excellent opportunity for symbol formation to occur. However, depending on the nature and degree of regression induced, one may also see evidence of desymbolization. Regression may be "creative," "neurotic," or "psychotic," or, using Fenichel's terms "adult" or "archaic" (prelogical).

Jones (1916), as Rycroft (1956) notes, held the view "that each individual re-creates his symbolism anew by perception" (p. 144). Once a symbol is formed, a number of possible mental operations may ensue. If a primary process operation is activated, the symbol "is treated in exactly the same way as the memory-imago of the primary object" (Rycroft, 1956, p. 144). In such instances, the "manifest" meaning and its significance is obvious even if the symbol in external reality could not perform that function. Where secondary process operations are operative, satisfaction is directly associated with the symbolization process and a broadening of symbolizing capacities will ensue. This will extend into external reality, object relatedness, and the maintaining of one's relatedness to one's own symbolic productions (as opposed to their disavowal).

Disturbances in Symbolization: Criteria

The presentation thus far has reviewed the theory of symbol formation as formulated by Klein (1930) and developed by Milner (1952) and Rycroft (1956). Both normality and abnormality have been considered, referred to in terms of "true" symbols versus "archaic" symbols or "symbol equations." The question of how to judge the quality of a Rorschach response—a Rorschach symbol—remains.

Segal (1957), while citing clinical examples to explain disturbances in symbolization, offers a number of possible criteria which may be applied to an analysis of Rorschach data. A disturbance in symbolization should result and be identifiable when a symbol is felt to be the primary object rather than its representation. In such instances, the affective tone or coloring associated with the primary object, which would normally remain unconscious (adult symbolism), is consciously experienced. This affective experience is usually quite disturbing to the subject and is likely to produce the following reactions.

Some subjects will react to the inkblot stimuli in a manner denoting marked self-restraint. They will demonstrate an abrupt shift in their freedom to respond (following Card V) and will display massive inhibition in relation to the blot. They will seem blocked and will limit themselves to a type of "perceptual recognition" shutting off any expression of fantasy. This manner of responding represents one type of disturbance.

The subjective reaction of the subject can also be noted on the basis of subsequent reactions within the card proper, i.e., through sequence analysis. This has been alluded to above in regard to one's acceptance or disavowal of own symbolic productions. Again, since the subject is unable to differentiate between the original object and the response produced—there is an obscuring of boundaries between the original object and the subject's own projections—a strong affective reaction will appear as well as a sense of confusion. Furthermore, if the symbol produced is connected to a "bad object" (a persecutory or guilt-evoking image), anxiety will be further aggravated. This will in turn result in attempts by the subject to annihilate the symbol, either totally or partially. In other words, one will see a destructive reaction take place, a destruction of the symbol.

The production of "equations" or, more accurately, "symbolic equations" may, then, result in a number of possible reactions, including a variety of Rorschach responses, all of which constitute disturbances in symbolization. These reactions may be summarized as follows: (1) a marked inhibition in responding and exaggerated avoidance of the inkblot stimuli; (2) a conspicuous avoidance of symbolic imagery with close attention paid to the more concrete perceptual qualities of the stimuli; (3) a conspicuously strong affective reaction whereby the symbol does not function as a symbol, that is, does not contain the affect associated with the original object and thus fails to become an acceptable symbol substitute. In such cases, the symbol equation will be (4) annihilated, attacked, or undone. Finally, one may observe (5) the phenomenon of scotomization, a highly selective, delimited manner of perceptual screening whereby the perceptual field is greatly reduced. A "blurred" perceptual experience may appear concomitantly in which perceptual focusing cannot be achieved (as it might result in a symbol equation and too powerful an affective experience).

On a more evolved level of ego development, disturbance may be reflected in ambivalence with the accompanying affects of guilt, fear of loss or the actual experience of loss and mourning, and a striving to re-create the object (Segal, 1957, p. 394). In such instances, a clear distinction is drawn between self and object, between primary objects and symbols; in consequence, attempts at retaining relatedness and reactions to loss of relatedness are in ascendance. This is the impetus for symbol formation and permits symbols to take on new functional status. Displacement of affects is now possible as retaliatory anxieties are lessened and symbols are now valued for their ability to re-create primary affective states and for enhancing object relatedness.

The production of symbol equations constitutes a significant disturbance in symbolization. Clinical findings suggest that transsexuals suffer from such disturbances, particularly in the area of genital symbolization; this in fact may be the most basic form of symbolic expression and symbolic disturbance. It remains to be seen whether such responses will be found among a population of male transsexuals in response to the inkblot stimuli.

METHOD AND RESULTS

In this exploratory study, genital symbolization among male transsexuals was evaluated by examining responses to Card VI, the inkblot stimulus which has the greatest potential for eliciting a response pertaining to the male genitalia (Shaw, 1948; Pascal, Ruesch, Devine, and Suttell, 1950). Rorschach protocols were obtained from the files of thirty-five male patients requesting sex change at the Montreal General Hospital since 1973. Linguistically and culturally, many were French Canadians, coming from all walks of life in terms of education, occupation, and social class. Ages ranged from nineteen to fifty. At the time of testing, many appeared as transvestites, often taking hormone drugs. Their responses to Card VI are presented in Table 1 and are broken down by category in Table 2.

TABLE 1
Card VI Responses of 35 Male Transsexuals

Performance	Inquiry
1. The middle of a person cut down the middle; dorsal passage	It's not the design; I thought of me and remembered the inside looks different from outside. The penis and scrotum; in fact it protrudes from this.

Comment: Self-object fusion fantasy male genitalia seen as "real" (symbolization defect)

2. Looks like a . . . skin, a pelt; whiskers, e.g., a weasel.	Like a rug, legs, head, whiskers, pointy, weasel Q shading here . . . fur.

That's all I see.

Comment: Popular (Weasel phallic symbol?)

3. I don't know . . . a bird right top or an eagle standing on a hill.	Bird giving us his back; his wings open. Its shape.

An upside-down jacket.

Comment: Phallic symbol (eagle) → anal homosexual image

4. Looks like . . . a humanoid that has lots of accessories, just standing there.	Can see through it; circulation; X ray. No eyes, no mouth.

Comment: Highly distorted self-representation; no genital symbol

5. Another fur skin, a fox cut in half, been opened in front.	Fox skin.

Comment: Popular; castration fantasy

(Continued)

TABLE 1 (Continued)

Performance	Inquiry
6. Top, cat head; rest—got to use imagination.	Little whiskers in cartoon, caricature; funny design, not really thing.

Comment: Symbol ambivalence emphasized

7. Looking down on cat lying down, flames upper part.	Cat sprawling out Jaggedness, flicker.
Two people reaching out, back to back.	In a protective position, someone coming from behind. Add: now cat more savage, a panther rug. Color of leopard.

Comment: Genital symbol = "flames" → anal homosexual fantasy → symbol equation emerges

8. Cannot imagine anything, unless this could be a piece of leather.	I've seen pieces of leather that shape, raggedy-looking or pelted. Looks like stretched but don't know what they do with it.

Comment: Symbol equation defended via "impotence"

9. Can't...	Looks like a gray blotch on white piece of paper.

Comment: Symbol equation defended via scomotization.

10. Crab legs.	Looks like small legs, uneven.
Animal skin, spread out, entrance, a hole.	Looks like big bear skin; entrance.
Profile of a penis.	Obviously the shape.

Comment: Popular + female genital image + male genital (bisexual)

TABLE 1 (Continued)

Performance	Inquiry
11. Looks like reflection of meadow and lake.	Blurry, not clear, faded, really gray.

Comment: Scotomization as defense

| 12. Guitar, violin, any stringed instrument. | Shape. |

On TV, an alley cat, uncut, unmanaged, doesn't have a tail.

RM top of a totem pole.

Comment: Genital symbol → castrated image → phallic symbol reinstated

| 13. Looks like radiography, those kinds of pictures. | Black and gray
Add: canal, an operation. |

Comment: No genital symbol; female genital image added

| 14. Head of a snake, then it becomes a mess. | The head and the body; the rest is just a mess.
Add: two gorillas, back to back. They're crushing the snake, but it doesn't seem to be in pain. |

Comment: Symbol equation

| 15. It's a bear fur, laid on the floor. It's split. | The hunter's cut the fur in middle. Two front paws, back paws, The head cut in middle. Shading. |

| A girl sitting at the side of the river on the grass doing her exercises. | Shape of gown (beginning of twentieth century). |

Comment: Popular + masochistic fantasy → feminization

(*Continued*)

TABLE 1 (Continued)

Performance	Inquiry
16. I really don't see anything at all. Sorry, I can't make anything out of that.	(Rejects popular.)

Comment: Scotomization

Performance	Inquiry
17. A cat, flat cat.	Flattened, run over, cartoon.
Crooked version of Europe.	Coastline only, map, Spain.
Clouds.	Gives you thunder; shape.
Mouth of some type of animal, with four very sharp teeth.	Spider.
An explosion.	Dynamite, an oil refinery, pieces of metal shooting away.
Face of a hamster.	Roundish, swimming.
Lake reflection when sun going down.	Water very still, cloud cover, peaceful.

Comment: Masochistic images + vagina dentata + orgastic image

Performance	Inquiry
18. A dead animal carved up. What's left is the skin. Wolf, not a hen (joke).	

Comment: Symbol equation

Performance	Inquiry
19. This is a statuette. A man (not human). I think it's a man's body.	Egyptian statuette with a big hat head. Artistic sculpture. Man or woman, not able to say. On a stand.

TABLE 1 (Continued)

Performance	Inquiry
This way I see a torch.	A trophy. The torch shines for me, gives me light. From a victory when all is over with what I need—surgery.
I see woman's body. I've just seen it.	Difficult to tell difference between man and woman. Same for statuette.

Comment: Feminized male; gender ambiguity → transsexual fantasy resolution

20. Again, the same thing. Fur skin spread on the floor. Nothing else.	Middle lifted up; swelled up. Short hair, not very thick.

Comment: Popular

21. A person's face with eyes, nose, mustache. Only the head.	Male, mustache, big nose, statue. Handicraft. Wood? Plastic with feathers. Plastic pendant.
Bearskin without head	Head is missing. Back paws are missing too. Claws. Been damaged, beat up, thrown away, discarded.

Comment: Emasculation of symbol → symbol equation

22. Person's face, but a funny kind of person.	Add: What's left? Makes me think of a bearskin which doesn't have head. Paws, body.

Comment: Emasculation as defense against symbol equation

(Continued)

TABLE 1 (Continued)

Performance	Inquiry
23. I don't know. Same kind of cowhide that you put on a wall or floor.	This is the head; top is nose and mouth part. A goat or zebra, like a hide. Way it's spread out.

Comment: Popular

24. A penis.

Neck of the uterus, the ovaries, the lips, the tubes.

Comment: Bisexual genitalia

25. A savage beast.	It's a beast that has just been torn apart in order to remove the skin. That is the skin that is to be displayed.

Comment: Symbol equation

26. REJECTION	Serpent's head with two eyes. Because of the form.

Comment: Rejection suggests symbol equation

27. Fur skin stretched on the floor.	It's the way in which it's spread out. It's on the floor and not on the wall.

Comment: Popular

28. A masculine phallic symbol.	It's an erection. You can even see the testicles. It's the shape, the texture that struck me.
The leg of a table.	It's the black.

TABLE 1 (Continued)

Performance	Inquiry
Two profiles of older people.	Again very abstract, like when you see children's books, everything is exaggerated in order to show something. In this case, old age.

Comment: Male genital image → phallic symbol → hypermasculinity as defense → ambiguity in identity

29. Looks like skin that has been stretched and put on wood to dry out. You know, they take out the fat.	An animal from the back. Fur. Differences in color.
Looks like an Indian totem pole with a strict face and mustache. Looks serious.	From close you can see the eyes, the nose, the mouth, a beard.
Looks like a spine with coccyx. The X ray of the pelvic area.	Different tones of color. Line in middle.
In every design they have the genitals: the exterior and interior lips, the vagina, the passage.	Same thing as before. The lighter color makes me see the passage. Form of the lips.

Comment: Popular → genital symbol humanized ("strict face") suggests symbol equation + self-object fusion, i.e., "in every design . . ."

30. A human face with a body that doesn't exist. Like a Martian, like somebody of another planet; he is not of the Earth. He is not normal. He is a man that doesn't exist on Earth.	The head, chin, arms. Arms are not arms, not realistic. Two legs are not normal in my opinion. It's in another planet. Color makes me think he is a man that does not live on Earth. It's black, white, gray—not a man that lives on Earth.

(Continued)

TABLE 1 (Continued)

Performance	Inquiry

Comment: Symbol equation (probable psychosis)

31. I've made a dissection in a laboratory before. Looked like an animal that has been emptied after being opened. They only kept the nervous system and the skin that covers it.	The brain of an animal cut in two. The skin has been opened to take a specimen between the bones and skin and hair. To examine the spine. This could be the trachea. This is a picture and it's treated with colors to see the different parts of tissue because they react differently to the liquids.

Comment: Emasculation of symbol = symbol equation

32. An animal skin. We can can put it on the end of the bed or on the floor somewhere. I can't see what else.	The form, it's unequal. The skin without the legs. They have massacred the nose of the animal. They couldn't save the paws.

Comment: Symbol equation

33. Variations on a theme. I can make very little of . . . a flying insect. I like it the least. It doesn't speak to me of anything definite.	I can see a highly distorted bear or dog. It's a dog more than a bear. I don't know what to make of it—channel and thing on top could be a missile launched and trail left behind. This card is more farfetched than the rest. Don't see it now; it was the shape.

Comment: Ambivalence + anxiety suggests symbol equation

34. A bear skin stretched on a table.	The whole stretched: paws outstretched. I have a similar one in my basement.

TABLE 1 (Continued)

Performance	Inquiry
A part of a sponge; I don't see anything else.	A part of a sponge, broken, torn, way it stands out, texture of a sponge.
A part of a bone. I can't recall the scientific name. The tip at the top.	What part of flesh—no, it's not flesh, but cartilage. Human bone around the thorax or the neck.

Comment: Popular → desymbolization suggests symbol equation

35. A highway.	Like in a helicopter; mountains, hills.
A bug	Shape Add: eel, fist, sword, face.

Comment: Female genital symbol → male genital symbols appear as additionals (fist, sword)

TABLE 2

Types of Response to Card VI[a]

	No.	Percentage
1. Symbol equation	12	34
2. Popular	9	26
3. Impotence-emasculation-castration	7	20
4. Homosexual-bisexual-feminine	6	17
5. True genital (phallic) symbol	5	14
6. Male genitalia	4	11
7. Scotomization	3	09
8. Self-representation disturbance	2	06
9. Rejection	1	03

[a]Responses are assigned to more than one category where appropriate.

Discussion

The male transsexuals under investigation gave a wide variety of responses to Card VI of the Rorschach. Responses which might be considered representative of "true" genital (phallic) symbols are notably few in number, only two in the entire sample: the eagle standing on a hill of subject 3 and the totem pole of subject 12.

In attempting to distinguish "true" genital symbols from genital symbol equations in order to establish the presence of a disturbance in genital symbolization, it became clear that it would be necessary to consider the card as a whole. This approach goes beyond content analysis and concentrates instead on the sequence of responses and reactions, from performance through inquiry, with an attempt to grasp the subjective and experiential aspect as well as the content or final product. The objective is to gain an understanding and clarification of the process of symbolization. Thus, there is the initial reaction, the response, reactions to the response, and, as will be discussed, acts of destruction and/or reparation. In many instances it is the subject's reaction to his own responses that provides the key to the nature, function, and effectiveness of his symbolizing capacities.

To repeat: a true symbol functions as an anxiety container and as an affect container. When operating successfully, the process of phallic-genital symbolization permits the male (or the female) to use the male genitalia in symbolic fashion through the avenue of symbolic representation. Card VI should mobilize the subject's symbolizing capacity and allow the genital symbolizing function of the ego to be scored. That is our working hypothesis. To illustrate:

The absence of a genital symbol, determined on the basis of card rejection at the level of "perceptual blindness" or scotomization, was observed for five subjects (8, 9, 11, 16, 26), though their rejections were of varying quality. For instance, although subject 26 initially rejected the card outright, he was able, upon inquiry, to produce the response "Serpent's head with two eyes." This sequence may be taken as reflecting (a) an inhibition in genital symbolization, due to anxiety, and its eventual containment and/or (b) a successful struggle to overcome the emergence of a symbol equation. Subjects 8, 9, and 11 are less successful. None can produce a genital symbol, and 8 produces responses suggestive of "symbolizing impotence." Such responses, denoting impotence and blurred perceptions, are taken to be defensive responses against the production of symbol equations. Here the symbolization process of the individual is disrupted, if not rendered completely ineffectual, in the sense that the perceptual apparatus has become nonfunctional so as to protect the transsexual from more actively expressing the symbolic meaning of his genitalia. It is theorized that this mental operation occurs because a symbol equation would otherwise likely emerge that would increase anxiety beyond the level of perceptual-affect containment—conscious awareness of a general representation is too discomforting and disturbing.

An example of a symbol equation is provided by subject 14. Here we see how a "classic" phallic symbol, the snake, functions in fact as a symbol equation. We may note also how the lower portion of the blot, potentially evoking a female genital representation, may present significant difficulty for the subject: perceptual blurring is combined with an "anal" symbolic reference. In the inquiry the subject successfully introduces "gorillas" to perform an act of symbol destruction ("crushing the snake"), which is then defensively negated ("it doesn't seem to be in pain"). The point to be made is that symbol-destruction must necessarily occur when the symbol is in fact a symbol equation. Taken at face value, the snake would seem to be a phallic symbol. However, the sequence of the subject's associations makes it clear that the snake does not function as a true symbol; in the end it receives the treatment reserved especially for symbol equations—sadistic attack.

Other symbol equations may be noted in the sample and are associated with varying degrees of symbol-destroying ideation. Subject 18 acts upon an implied symbol equation by "deadening" the animal, that is, by annihilating the potential symbol equation. This ensures total and complete destruction of the phallic-genital symbol equation. Subject 19 introduces an elaborate, complex fantasy about a "feminized male"—a "statuette." The feminized male is ambiguous in gender identity, yet is not without a phallus—the "torch." However, the phallus is given to the surgeon; that is, it is the phallic surgeon who in the end will give "light"—the wished-for well-articulated gender identity. This elaborate attempt at self-transformation, operative at a conscious level, is not unusual for (though not exclusive to) transsexuals, particularly where the male has been "feminized." This can result only in gender ambiguity at a conscious level, it is argued, as the phallic representation continues to be actively operative on a conscious level but takes the form of a symbol equation. In this instance a form of "concretized splitting" can be observed: the surgeon has been given the magical, all-transforming phallus. Subject 21 affords additional insight into how potentially disturbing genital symbolization is dealt with. Again a response has been subjected to what might be termed "desymbolization": the active obliteration of a phallic representation because it functions as a symbol equation. Deactivation of the symbol equation is achieved in this instance quite remarkably. The subject moves from "statue" to "handicraft" to "plastic pendant" (that the phallus may not completely be forgotten); the final version then dramatizes, through its imagery of escalating destructiveness toward the symbol (subtraction of the bearskin's dangerous head, back paws, and claws, then damage to what remains, finally its utter disappearance) the degree to which self-directed phallic-symbolic destructiveness is required when genital symbol equation is operative. In order that the symbol equation not emerge into consciousness, active attempts are made to desymbolize via the destruction of all forms of phallic imagery.

Another variant, even more conspicuous in its meaning and implication, is presented by subject 25: "a savage beast." It is only by virtue of the inquiry—"a beast that has just been torn apart" (the passive mode is quite typical, which may represent the "acting in" of a masochistic wish)—that we are alerted to the presence of a symbol equation. This argument is consistent with the view, held by both Jones (1916) and Klein (1930), that the "true" symbol—in this case, the true genital symbol—successfully deflects and/or contains the affective discomfort first associated with the original object—in this case, the male genitalia. True symbolization enables one to take a relatively impassive attitude toward the symbol rather than making a strenuous protest. Yet there may be more to this protest than is clearly evident. For example, subject 32 begins with the popular precept ("an animal skin"), only later to indicate that "they have massacred the nose of the animal. They couldn't save the paws." This subject demonstrates quite clearly that a popular response does not necessarily contraindicate the presence of a symbol equation. The annihilation of the phallic-genital component, assumed to be a symbol equation, is still required.

What seems to provoke such reactions may be the male transsexual's inability to contain his genital sadism through its symbolic transformation. In this study, it can be observed how failures in genital symbolization may set off strong sadistic-destructive reactions among a good number of male transsexuals. Among this group, it is hypothesized, subjects are "fused" with their genital sadism and are unable to distance themselves from it by way of symbolization; they are thus highly susceptible to consciously experiencing pronounced inner tension with regard to this genital sadism. As a result of an inability to tolerate such tensions, to recognize that a disturbance in genital symbolization is a fundamental aspect of his dilemma, the male transsexual strives for a solution, however misdirected and misplaced. Genital sadism remains closely associated with the genitalia, probably in consequence of early developmental failures in its symbolic transformation; despite its apparently benign status, it can be reactivated in the psyche under external conditions such as administration of the Rorschach. Ultimately, the male transsexual wishes to destroy the destroying aspect of himself with which he feels fused—his destructive genitalia. It is therefore argued that Card VI is capable of evoking "genital fusion fantasies" whereby self-object boundaries become blurred, resulting in attacks upon one's own projections. In the context of fusion and merger, strong retaliatory reactions are inevitable. For example, subject 7, upon producing an anal homosexual attack fantasy, says, "now cat more savage." The "flames" of the cat indicate the affective tone of the genital symbol. Here it can be observed how Card VI reevokes a homosexual fantasy and the sadism associated with the male genitalia. The emphasis on "a protective position" points to a close if not intense involvement with the homosexual fantasy, which suggests that a fusion fantasy has been set off. Gradually, as the narrative progresses, the percept takes on a more savage form. This phenomenon is common to disruptions in the symbolization process, where symbol equations are exerting pressure on the subject's symbolizing capacities; this often creates a need to protect oneself from one's sadistic genital projections.

In conclusion, this chapter is intended as an initial exploration of the clinical observation that transsexuals suffer from a disturbance in genital symbolization. It has not invoked the more stringent methodological conditions necessary to establish the Rorschach phenomena in question as distinctive for a clinical population of male transsexuals. For example, no attempt has been made to distinguish between "primary" and "secondary" transsexuals (Ovesey and Person, 1974; Person and Ovesey, 1974) or to separate male transsexuals as a group from other clinical populations in which gender dysphoria and related disturbances may operate. Given the paucity of Rorschach-based reports on transsexualism, however, it is hoped that this presentation will encourage greater implementation of the Rorschach method as a means of further clarifying and delineating the nature and meaning of transsexualism.

References

Fenichel, O. (1945), *The Psychoanalytic Theory of Neurosis.* New York: Norton.

Jones, E. (1916), The theory of symbolism. In: *Papers on Psycho-analysis.* London: Bailliere, Tindall & Cox, 1948, pp. 87–144.

Karmel, R. (1981), Genital symbolization and male transsexualism: Preliminary remarks. Paper presented at the Tenth International Rorschach Congress, Washington, D.C.

———— (1982), The Rorschach test and the British school of psychoanalysis. Paper presented at meeting of Society for Personality Assessment, Tampa, Florida.

Klein, M. (1930), The importance of symbol-formation in the development of the ego. In: *Love, Guilt and Reparation and Other Works: 1921*–1945. New York: Delacorte Press, 1975, pp. 219–232.

Limentani, A. (1979), The significance of transsexualism in relation to some basic psychoanalytic concepts. *Internat. Rev. Psycho-Anal.,* 6:139–153.

Milner, M. (1952), Aspects of symbolism in comprehension of the not-self. *Internat. J. Psycho-Anal.,* 33:181–195.

Mitchell, J. (1976), Book review, *The Transsexual Experience. Internat. J. Psycho-Anal.* 57:357–360.

Ovesey, L., & Person, E. (1974), The transsexual syndrome in males: II. Secondary transsexualism. *Amer. J. Psychother.,* 28:174–193.

Pascal, G., Ruesch, H., Devine, C., & Suttell, B. (1950), A study of genital symbols on the Rorschach test: Presentation of a method and results. *J. Abn. & Soc. Psychol.,* 45:286–295.

Person, E., & Ovesey, L. (1974), The transsexual syndrome in males: I. Primary transsexualism. *Amer. J. Psychother.,* 28:4–20.

Rycroft, C. (1956), Symbolism and its relationship to the primary and secondary processes. *Internat. J. Psycho-Anal.,* 37:137–146.

Segal, H. (1957), Notes on symbol formation. *Internat. J. Psycho-Anal.,* 38:391–397.

Schafer, R. (1954), *Psychoanalytic Interpretation in Rorschach Testing.* New York: Grune & Stratton.

Shaw, B. (1948), Sex populars in the Rorschach test. *J. Abn. & Soc. Psychol.,* 43:466–470.

Stoller, R. (1975), *Sex and Gender: Vol. II. The Transsexual Experiment.* London: Hogarth Press.

Chapter 16

The Rorschach and Affective Disorders: The Role of Projective Testing in a Descriptive Psychiatric Model

Randy S. Milden, Ph.D.
Pamela S. Ludolph, Ph.D.
Howard D. Lerner, Ph.D.

Psychoanalytic psychologists working with seriously ill patients in psychiatric hospital settings increasingly find themselves confronted by the primacy of the biological psychiatric model. In many institutions, patients with affective disorders, schizophrenia, and even characterological disturbances are discussed in psychobiological rather than psychodynamic terms. Treatments, somatic rather than psychotherapeutic, proceed not from dynamic formulations but from assessments based on descriptive symptom tallies and hypothesized biological "markers." Family history is reduced to a count of first- and second-order relatives who have been mentally ill, relevant diagnostic information because an inherited component is assumed in many of these disturbances.

In this context the traditional role of psychoanalytic psychology is challenged. Biological psychiatry is active and descriptive, aimed at the alleviation of symptoms. Psychoanalytic psychology is receptive and dynamic, with insight the main goal. A persuasive argument could be

The authors would like to acknowledge the support of the Clinical Studies Unit and Clinical Psychobiology Program. Department of Psychiatry, University of Michigan.

425

made that these models are incompatible. To those who explain affective disorder neurobiologically, evaluate it by symptom constellation and laboratory studies, and treat it pharmacologically, a psychodynamic explanation, assessment, or intervention may seem beside the point. Correspondingly, psychoanalytic psychologists may throw up their Rorschach cards and declare psychotherapy impossible when faced with patients who explain their mood as a "chemical imbalance," documented by a quantity of hormones secreted in the blood and correctable by a provident and potent medication regime.

What place does a psychoanalytically oriented psychologist have in this biological climate? In particular, what is the utility, in a biological psychiatric setting, of assessment techniques which, like the Rorschach, are grounded in psychoanalytic assumptions? It is the premise of this chapter that although the psychobiological and psychoanalytic approaches may be antithetical on a number of significant dimensions, there are meaningful ways in which the two approaches can and should be integrated. More specifically, the use of projective measures like the Rorschach can increase our understanding of the psychological aspects of biologically defined psychiatric illness, while our involvement in biological psychiatric domains provides a unique opportunity to expand our knowledge of Rorschach psychology.

It is easy to make the abstract claim that models of affective illness should integrate psychoanalytic and psychobiological perspectives, and draw on both projective and descriptive data. More confounding is the complicated question of how and when to apply psychodynamic thinking and projective assessment, particularly in the evaluation of these disorders. One approach, using the Rorschach to identify personality traits that may underlie or respond to affective states in patients with unipolar and bipolar affective illness, is outlined by the authors in Chapter 18. The present chapter will elaborate another way in which the two viewpoints, psychoanalytic and psychobiological, can be profitably joined. We will explore the impact of recurrent affective episodes on the patient's sense of self through an analysis of relevant Rorschach responses. Further, we will suggest that the features observed may be not only primary to the endogenous affective illness but also secondary, both to the illness and to psychobiological treatment.

THE CLINICAL IMPACT OF ENDOGENOUS ILLNESS

In the classical biological perspective, affective disorders are viewed as episodic. Although recent psychobiological thinking (Akiskal, Hirschfeld, Yerevanian, 1983; Hirschfeld, Klerman, Clayton, and Keller, 1983; Mattussek and Feil, 1983) suggests that patients with endogenous affective disorders have psychological symptoms between episodes of illness, most discussions of affective illness assume that there is a pattern of affective episodes distinct from more normative interepisode periods. This course is posed in contrast to that of a psychiatric disease like schizophrenia, in which the pattern after onset is more continuous and deteriorating, or a characterological depression or dysthymic disorder, continuous though relatively stable.

Between episodes, patients with endogenous unipolar or bipolar depression may seem "back to normal" or at least back to their old selves, which may of course manifest neurotic or characterological difficulties. However, Milden (1984) has suggested, based on clinical evaluation and ongoing psychotherapy with such patients, that on a deeper level, once they have had a major depressive or manic episode, patients with endogenous affective disorders will not be the same as they were prior to the onset of the illness. As a result of the experience of somatically explained and treated affective episodes, these patients have a residual vulnerability in their sense of themselves which is refractory (and to some extent secondary) to psychobiological intervention.

The problems in self-representation which many of these patients develop appear to be specific to the illness and different from those experienced by patients with other psychiatric or medical diseases. They are also distinct from the "premorbid" difficulties in self-representation that the patient brings to the illness. Many of these patients surely have problems in self-structure which predate the onset of the affective disorder, and one might predict that preexisting problems of self-representation could place a patient at a higher risk for developing an affective disorder. A sense of loss of coherence in self-representation expressed by a patient with a history of endogenous depression, either directly in a clinical interview or projectively in a Rorschach response, may be in large measure a function of an earlier, primary problem in this area. Nonetheless, it appears also to be the case that longstanding psychological difficulties are reshaped with the experience of the biologically framed affective illness, such that they now have a form and content in some part defined by that experience. Thus, in evaluating the performance of these patients on the Rorschach, it is important to consider expressions not only of enduring personality features but also of the psychic toll this illness often, and perhaps inevitably, takes.

The experience of an endogenous affective illness is powerful. By definition, patients in depressive episodes have emotions and thoughts different from what they would normally experience—depressed mood, guilt, negativism, hopelessness, and suicidal ideation. Their thinking may be psychotic, with what are termed mood-congruent delusions of hopelessness, poverty, guilt, hypochondriasis, or nihilism. They have different behaviors and personality traits: anhedonia, social withdrawal, decreased concentration, and diminished motivation. Physiological rhythms and drives are dramatically altered. Patients experience insomnia or hypersomnia, decreased appetite or hyperphagia, weight loss or gain, low energy, psychomotor retardation or agitation, loss of libido, and diurnal variation (mood worse in the morning, improving over the course of the day). They often look physically ill, gray, and cadaverous. The symptom constellation shows little reactivity to environmental stimuli or internal will.

Manic or hypomanic patients present an equally dramatic shift in personality from the normal or euthymic state. Characteristically they display some combination of the following symptoms: unrealistically elevated mood, grandiosity, racing thoughts, pressured speech, increased libido, decreased need for sleep. They may spend money with abandon and in general act recklessly, frequently coming into conflict with the law.

These depressive or manic changes can occur relatively late in life, to people who have lived for decades without significant psychiatric difficulties. Endogenously ill patients are told they have a biological illness, not unlike diabetes: chronic, episodic, and out of their psychological control. Medication is duly prescribed, and they are told they will soon feel "back to normal." Patients must somehow cope with the likelihood that there will be periodic recurrences in which they will shift into another state, or, in the patient's experience, another persona. Unipolar depressives must struggle with two personae, depressed and nondepressed or euthymic. Bipolar depressives have three: depressed, manic or hypomanic, and euthymic.

Many affective patients acknowledge this experience of a change of persona, and they struggle to reconstruct a relatively coherent and intact self-representation after the onset of affective episodes. Some can discuss these struggles directly in a clinical interview or in conversations with other patients, family, or friends. They tell what it feels like to become "not yourself" and then "yourself" again and not be certain who the "real you" might be. Is the real self the euthymic self? Or can you put together, out of the self-in-episode and the self-out-of-episode, a self-representation that lets you feel whole? In an episode, some patients, particularly those with a retarded depression, describe feeling "dead"; they relate these feelings to their sense that the self they know has disappeared or died, that they have become no one. It may be the case that for some patients suicidal ideation is an indirect expression of these feelings, communicating not a wish to die but a sense that the self is already dead. Others, usually presenting with agitated depression or mania, say they feel "crazy," a term that captures for them the sense of having become someone strange and unfamiliar, someone else.

For still other patients, especially when a significant amount of time has passed since an episode, the emphasis is less on the loss of self as a whole and more on the loss of vital, organizing aspects of the self. As they reflect on their being told that these changes of state are caused by neurobiological alterations or dysfunctions, they often speak of a powerful sense of loss of control or mastery. Many describe a feeling, which may persist out of episode, of their lives happening *to* them. Control is now exercised by medications that regulate their states, and some of these patients describe feeling incomplete, requiring a steady addition of an exogenous substance in order to be whole and functional. Self-sufficient before the onset of the illness, they are now dependent on the pills and the prescribing physicians, ambivalently embraced self-objects. They tell you about their difficulty reintegrating a normal range and intensity of affect when they emerge from an affective episode. Thus, euthymic mood, defined as normal, is not normal at all. Strong emotions are more often than not consciously disowned or blunted by the out-of-episode self because of anxiety that any intense affect may spiral, out of control, into another full-blown affective episode. The out-of-episode sense of self seems empty and flat, lacking the unifying and motivating force of emotional vitality and expressiveness.

Many affectively ill patients, however, do not spontaneously verbalize these reactions. In some cases, depending on the patient and the nature of the illness, there may be no significant or protracted response to report. The quality and intensity of the impact of the illness may be mediated by such variables as the quality of the illness experience (episode severity, treatment type and efficacy, age of onset, frequency of recurrence), premorbid personality (ego organization, early history of loss or trauma, narcissistic integrity), and environmental support (family, work). A relatively benign illness experience would presumably be less assaultive, particularly in patients with sufficient intrapsychic and interpersonal resources. For example, a forty-five-year-old woman who suffered a single and rather mild depressive episode, who responds well to the outpatient trial of an antidepressant, and who has significant psychological strengths, solid family ties, and a satisfying career might experience relatively little enduring psychological fallout from the illness and treatment. On the other hand, a sixty-five-year-old widowed housewife with a forty-year history of mild intermittent trouble with her "nerves," even before she began, at the age of sixty, having yearly delusional depressions that remit only partially after inpatient ECT, would be at significant risk for severe difficulties in reintegrating a stable sense of self.

Nevertheless, it seems to be the case that some patients in whom one would predict a noticeable, even impressive change in self-representation as a result of the experience of an endogenous affective disorder do not easily discuss it in clinical interviews. These are patients who often are good interviewees in the descriptive psychiatric sense, offering precise columns of symptoms, present and absent. But they have less access to spontaneous self-descriptions, which require more depth and elaboration, even when the cognitive impairments of a severe depression or mania have apparently cleared. The preliminary results of an ongoing investigation of affective disorders and self-representation, using the same patient sample described in this chapter and various quasi-objective measures derived from social psychological research on self-schemas, confirm our clinical sense that many of these patients have more difficulty elaborating their mood and sense of self in unstructured, open-ended situations than in forced-choice tasks (Milden, Pietromonaco, Markus, and Newman, 1985).

Keeping in mind these two clinical observations, the residual problems in self-representation which some patients with affective disorders describe and the difficulty many of these patients seem to have with elaborated self-description, we will consider the Rorschachs of these patients. We suggest that, in addition to its more traditional function as a vehicle for the expression of enduring personality traits, the Rorschach may be used to tap indirectly the effects of recurrent, biologically defined state changes, effects that are difficult for many of these patients to convey directly.

We will present clinical examples of these problems of self-representation, drawn from Rorschachs administered to unipolar and bipolar depressives on the Clinical Studies Unit, an inpatient and outpatient clinical research center for psychobiological affective disorders at the University of Michigan. These patients were diagnosed according to the Research Diagnostic Criteria (RDC) (Spitzer, Endicott, and Robins, 1978) based on a structured descriptive interview, the Schedule for Affective Disorders and Schizophrenia (SADS) (Spitzer and Endicott, 1978). The authors reviewed approximately one hundred Rorschach protocols of unipolar and bipolar patients for the present chapter, including both Rorschachs administered clinically and Rorschachs that were part of our ongoing formal research study of affective patients tested first in and then out of depressive episode. In line with our interest in the lasting effects of affective episodes after symptoms have lifted and the patient is apparently "well," the chapter focuses on protocols collected after a successful course of pharmacotherapy or ECT, when patients were euthymic, as defined by therapist-administered Hamilton Depression Inventory scores (Hamilton, 1960) of less than ten. The clinical examples we will present to illustrate these patients' experience of a biologically defined affective disorder will include both the responses of these patients to the administration of a Rorschach and the thematic content of their Rorschach percepts. Our aim is not to suggest that the response these patients have to the Rorschach setting or these Rorschach percepts themselves are unique to this patient group, or that they are a reflection of the impact of an endogenous affective illness and nothing more. What we want to communicate is that a Rorschach can provide a vehicle through which patients can express the experience of having a recurrent affective disorder; in listening to their Rorschachs, clinicians should be attuned to manifestations of the impact of the disorder along with more fundamental aspects of personality organization.

Response to the Rorschach Setting

Like all testing patients, those with biologically defined affective disorders bring to the task and to the relationship with the examiner transference attitudes which we assume relate to enduring conflicts and internalized object representations. Thus, we build our inferences about a patient's personality not only on an analysis of what the patient sees on the Rorschach cards but also on responses to the examiner and to the experience of being tested. There may also be aspects of the "testing set" of endogenous patients that are a function of the experience of their affective illness and the treatment of this illness in a biologically oriented facility. In assessing their behavior and attitudes regarding the administration of the Rorschach, one needs to consider the expression of longstanding intrapsychic issues and conflicts even as one keeps in mind issues secondary to the assault of the biological disorder.

Some patients with affective disorders respond to the process of a Rorschach, whether clinical or research, with a fairly neutral attitude. This is in part a reflection of personality and in part a function of their illness and psychobiological clinical care. Their treatment includes no exploration of the personal meaning of experience and does not encourage the elaboration of transference reactions. While there is surely at least some meaning and transference stirred up by the testing, these responses, typically, are not shared. Patients complete the task in a straightforward manner whether depressed or euthymic, and it is often difficult to glean the less conscious impact of the task and interaction.

Occasionally patients in this setting are more forthcoming. Typically, these are patients who express disappointment with their invasive, omnipotent physicians in a seductive bid for attention and rescue by the receptive examiner, who becomes the caring maternal object in the splitting—"the only one who wants to hear what I feel and think." While the use of splitting in involvements with staff members is hardly unusual for seriously ill patients in an inpatient treatment facility, the internal defense in this case finds a compatible external reality in which there is a striking philosophical difference between examining and treating professionals.

Most patients with affective disorders are actively or passively negative about Rorschach testing. Although some participate cheerfully in testing and enjoy the attention and concern of the psychologists, they demean the process as they would occupational or recreational therapy: as diverting, engaging, and basically incidental to the evaluations and interventions of the "real," biological doctors. Some do not really want to be tested, but uneasily comply. Others do not see the point of being tested, given the biological explanation and treatment of their disorder. One patient midway through a Rorschach testing session commented, "Of all the research, this is the only part I don't like." Asked why, he replied, "I don't see the meaning." Still others are at the corner store buying cigarettes at the time they agreed to meet the examiner for a testing session. A number of patients compare the Rorschach unfavorably with various biological studies, enthusiastically signing consent forms for two-day catheter studies involving serial blood draws after the infusion of powerful experimental drugs, but refusing to participate in a study in which they are given a Rorschach when depressed and then again when the depression has lifted.

While resistance to an instrument like the Rorschach may be part of a longstanding characterological stance, we are suggesting that there is another aspect. Affective patients who have experienced the loss of a stable sense of self in recurrent depressive and manic episodes find solace and strength in the high-tech activity of the psychobiological model. Repeated blood draws are paradoxically less painful to them than are inkblots. Patients experience the needle-stick in an endocrine study as a penetrating, omnipotent self-object, taking their blood as it imbues them with medical magic; the Rorschach, by contrast, is experienced as disappointingly passive and soft. A catheter study binds bad feelings, providing masochistic distraction and promising to be a positive step on the way to a drug therapy guaranteed to still any emotional upheaval. Patients complain that the Rorschach does the opposite, stirring them up affectively and occasioning images, thoughts, and feelings that are uncomfortable or even overwhelming. One patient accusingly remarked to the Rorschach examiner, "Boy, you beat my brains out here!" As noted earlier, many patients with an endogenous unipolar or bipolar depressive disorder are very frightened of affective arousal, fearing any challenge to what seems to them a very fragile defensive equilibrium; it might at any unguarded moment collapse, catapulting them into another affective episode. In this context, then, the Rorschach is perceived as a threat, and the psychological examiner as the only professional on the ward who wants to rile the patient rather than soothe.

Here we might note parenthetically, if rather obviously, that the countertransference problems experienced by Rorschach examiners in this setting and with this patient population are impressive. In addition to managing the countertransference responses one might expect in work with seriously ill depressives, one must also come to terms with the differences between the goals of a clinical or research Rorschach testing and the primary psychobiological orientation of the ward. Feelings of depression and of envy of the more powerful physicians typically alternate with a devaluation of the more concrete and symptom-focused psychobiological program. The internal conflict between competitive and collaborative motivations can chafe. Often, the psychological examiner has the only nondescriptive data on these patients, and it is possible for the Rorschach to become the field for a heated battle between biological psychiatrists and psychoanalytic psychologists in decisions regarding clinical management, a struggle that frequently leads to more general debate involving broadly framed philosophical differences. It is ironic that at a time when psychoanalytic psychologists feel themselves in political jeopardy at these institutions, worrying about challenges to the role of psychodynamically based instruments like the Rorschach in clinical decision making, in practice the psychological test report, particularly in the relative absence of dynamic interviews and histories on psychobiological services, can become a rather prominent, authoritatively quoted, and passionately supported or reviled document.

RORSCHACH CONTENT CATEGORIES

To illustrate the assault on the sense of self inflicted by recurrent affective episodes, we will describe categories of thematic content in Rorschach percepts of patients with endogenously defined unipolar and bipolar affective disorders. Based on our diagnostic testing experience with various patient populations, including affective patients, we are suggesting that the themes we will describe are not peculiar to this group, nor are they necessarily seen more frequently in the protocols of such patients. We would predict no significant differences in any formal analysis of these themes, reliably coded with a validated scale which would correspond to the problems of self-representation we are describing, in the protocols of patients of different affective subtypes (unipolar, bipolar, nonendogenous depressive) or with other psychiatric or medical disease. What is unique is the meaning these Rorschach themes may have for this patient group. It is our sense that the themes convey something of significance regarding these patients' experiences in struggling with recurrent affective disorders. This is particularly the case with those patients who have difficulty in more directly expressing their feelings about who they are and who they have become in the wake of their affective illness. The Rorschach themes then become a good starting point as therapist and patient endeavor to bring these feelings into awareness in order to work them through.

A prominent thematic feature of the Rorschachs of patients with endogenous affective disorders is a relative dearth of lively, evocative images, with a reliance instead on flat, unimaginative percepts. The examiners who administered our research Rorschachs, whose main prior testing experience had been with outpatients presenting for psychodynamic psychotherapy, remarked on this dullness of thematic content in many of the protocols, and we have certainly wondered about it as we have begun to make sense of the data collected. Redundant images of unelaborated, static bats or bugs may tell us various things about the patients who describe them. One would consider the possibility of a residual depressive damper, even in patients who met our technical out-of-episode Hamilton Depression Inventory criteria.

Other likely explanations might be a mild organicity, particularly in patients who have just completed a course of ECT, relatively low intelligence, or an hysterically or obsessionally inhibited underlying personality style that precludes freer play with the inkblots.

Still another possibility involves the effects of affective disorders that we have elected as our focus. What is often mistaken for residual depression or a more fundamental cognitive or defensive problem might well have an explanation more specific to the experience of the affective disorder. We have spoken of the difficulty these patients have in expressing intense feelings or thoughts in an open and relaxed manner. Although the Rorschach may be useful in providing an indirect vehicle for affective patients who have trouble talking about themselves in a clinical interview, these patients' worries about affective arousal in the wake of affective episodes may in some cases inhibit direct self-expression significantly and projective material to a somewhat more limited degree. Schafer (1967) speaks about the requirement of regression in the service of the ego in projective testing, noting that what is demanded of the patient is "a partial and fluctuating relaxation of ordinary ego controls and orientation to allow normally preconscious or unconscious material some access to consciousness. . . ." He continues: "without this regression, subjects would do little more in the Rorschach situation than describe the blots or cling to the most obvious forms, as some indeed do if they experience their own equilibrium as too precarious to tolerate any degree of regression" (p. 11). Most patients with endogenous affective disorders have the ego capacity to manage impulses and emotions when out of an affective episode. Understandably, however, they do not trust that they will have that capacity when an episode overtakes them. The defensive flexibility required on the Rorschach is difficult for these patients, who worry that if they let down their guard, delving into emotion or fantasy, they will lose control and be hopelessly, helplessly trapped in another endogenous episode of depression or mania.

Another recurrent theme in the euthymic protocols of affective patients is an allusion to the affective episode. Although their episodes have resolved by the time of the testings, the spectre of their recent and possibly repeated experience of being ill is very much on their minds, projected readily onto the shapes on the inkblots. For example, they see on the Rorschach heavy, immovable weights, reminiscent of descriptions of endogenous depressive mood by some of the more articulate patients.

A euthymic bipolar patient describes an image of "a moth stuck on a display card—it could fly—a flying insect, as opposed to one that doesn't fly, meaning it could fly." One hears this patient's struggle regarding her illness, particularly her mania, and her decidedly ambivalent stance toward the potential that is always there for her to "fly." For her, "flying" is a state counterposed to one in which she is caught and exposed, pinned to a piece of paper and used for show. This image of a moth on display, pinned and observed, may reflect, in part, the patient's response to her role as a subject in the seemingly relentless series of biological and psychological studies conducted on a psychobiological clinical research unit. In the response of another bipolar patient we see a similar opposition of passivity and flight: "An angel, like a Christmas tree ornament hanging on a tree. I thought of an angel because of wings. It is flying around." The contrast between a suspended inanimate bauble and a winged angel in flight seems again to reflect a struggle to accept not only the highs but possibly what seems to be the even more troubling lows or middle (euthymic) episodes. One would infer from this response that these affective states are not yet well integrated for this patient, mania possibly representing a welcome escape or respite from the deadness of euthymia or depression. In considering the tension and apparent lack of integrated resolution expressed in this percept, one wonders if this kind of struggle is seen typically on Rorschachs administered shortly after an episode, with the patient gradually resolving the conflict so that a Rorschach administered later might reflect more stable integration. Unfortunately, we do not yet have enough Rorschachs administered at such later dates to know the answer to such a question.

Another theme in out-of-episode protocols that can be understood as reflecting the effects of recurrent affective disorders is that of false, hidden, or alternate selves. Although our focus here is on the narcissistic assault of endogenous affective disease as an explanation of these images, this in no way precludes the contribution of more primary or fundamental narcissistic problems (see Chapter 10). Masks are images perceived by these patients with relative frequency and vividness. In one particularly evocative percept, a euthymic patient described, on Card III, "a face mask in the light color, with the darker objects covering up each side of the face mask—your comedy and tragedy face masks that symbolize the theater." Asked which of the two this one was, the patient replied, "Well, actually it's sort of in between." The mask image in this response conveys the patient's sense of an affectively toned persona (comic or tragic) that is superimposed on the normal self in an episode. Now, out of episode, though the mask has not been discharged, the affective valence is "in between." Another patient, also out of episode, perceives a mask which is not at all an expression of "in-between," neutral, or euthymic emotion. His mask is a representation of a malevolent "alien creature, its face all distorted and contorted and irregularly shaped and —black. And his eyes, sunken into his head. Looks like a death mask." The horror of the recent depressive episode is gruesomely portrayed by this "alien" object that covers the familiar face, much as the self-in-episode obscures the out-of-episode persona. One wonders what might account for the striking differences between the masks in these two euthymic patients' protocols. While we can suggest such factors as underlying personality, severity of the affective disorder, and proximity to the heart of the episode (the more benign response reflecting greater distance from the recent depression), such inferences must be speculative. Other thematic content images which speak to the idea of false or buried self-representations are portrayals of human figures hidden behind structures and references in a number of protocols to real versus unreal objects. One such mention, where the patient wonders aloud, "maybe it's not sure if it's what it really is," seems to convey concisely this patient's struggle to master the disruptive changes in self-representation that accompany an endogenous affective illness.

We have been intrigued with the images of rebirth and reemergence seen in a number of protocols of patients tested after their recovery from an acute depressive episode. Caterpillars with "exposed and rough edges, jagged around the outside" emerge from cocoons, and flowers sprout imperfectly shaped new buds. While these may be seen as images of promise or hope, concerns about vulnerability and damage in these representations of an emerging, post-episode persona come through clearly as well. One patient describes the birth of baby animals on Card VIII, "still attached [to the placenta], struggling to get out, but it is a good thing. It was safe inside, but it will be safe outside." Another patient sketches a poignant farewell scene on Card I, "two people, embracing and holding one another. They're embracing as if someone just left and they're waving goodbye, waving at someone leaving on a train. This is the smoke or steam from the train as it pulls away." The attachment-separation issues expressed in both images may again speak to earlier concerns which, according to traditional psychoanalytic theories, might leave these patients vulnerable to depression. More immediately, however, these are patients who are both relieved and anxious about their recovery from a major depressive episode and who are anticipating discharge from the hospital to return to their homes and out-of-episode lives. Although there is certainly a positive feeling in leaving the acute phase of the disease behind, readjustment to a normal life, haunted by the possibility or likelihood of recurrence, makes the step out of the hospital a tentative one. As another patient observed, describing an animal crossing a stream in Card VIII, "It's kind of not too stable an area for their first time going across. He's approaching, looks like a small limb on his front paw and being as small as it is, you could understand precaution."

Images of body damage and fragmentation are also noteworthy in these Rorschach protocols of patients coming to terms with the impact of recent affective episodes and psychobiological interventions. There are repeated references in many of these protocols to missing body parts (no head, brain, ears, eyes, insides of the body, outside of the body, limbs), deformed or grotesque bodies, disembodied anatomical parts, bodies sadistically pulled apart or torn. Flesh or skin is pulled off, in percepts like that of a "walrus, separated from its carcass." Some creatures projected on the cards are left without "an outer coating strong enough to survive." There are numerous skeletal images of ribs and body frames. One patient saw, on Card VIII, "some kind of partial coat covering some ribs and a backbone—part of a skeleton with part of a coat." It is hard to imagine an image which might more graphically convey a primitive feeling of somatic fragmentation and the breakdown of the sense of having a protective and binding body ego. Whatever basic issues of body damage these patients may bring to the illness, we are also convinced that a recurrent affective disorder and invasive biological studies and treatments can dramatically assault a patient's sense of bodily integrity.

We might add, in this context, that medical procedures often find their way into the protocols. Patients see in the Rorschach cards images of X rays, tests, specimens, dissections, CT scans. These medical images are, not surprisingly, prominent also in the protocols of nonendogenously depressed patients treated on psychobiological units. It would make sense that these images, at least insofar as they reflect immediate rather than longstanding preoccupations, would characterize patients undergoing similar treatments, regardless of differences in clinical diagnosis. In fact, some patients with characterological rather than affective disorders may, as a function of these character problems, be the most enthusiastic regarding active, invasive psychobiological procedures and therapies. One of the most heartfelt expressions of a patient's experience of the psychobiological model appears in the protocol of a patient with a Borderline Personality Disorder, also meeting the criteria for Major Depressive Disorder, nonendogenous type, by RDC categories: "Two pigs trying to separate a person's mind from his heart, shoulders and arms outstretched in a helpless fashion. Bruised—very depressed, confused, and hopeless."

CONCLUSION

Biological psychiatry is effective in helping to regulate the states of patients with unipolar and bipolar affective disorders. There is, however, a psychological cost attendant on the illness and on psychobiological treatment, and many of these patients have a residual vulnerability regarding their sense of self after the onset of the affective illness. As psychoanalytic psychologists working in biologically oriented hospital settings and involved in the care of these patients, we can make a significant contribution in helping them with this secondary psychological aspect of their difficulties. In particular, given the problems many of these patients have with spontaneous self-expression, a psychoanalytically oriented psychological assessment such as the Rorschach provides a useful vehicle through which these issues can be projectively brought together. Once these secondary problems with self-representation are identified, therapist and patient can begin the task of understanding and working through in order that patients are more stable while out of episode, not only in how they feel but also in how they view themselves and their recurrent illness.

REFERENCES

Akiskal, H. S., Hirschfeld, R. M. A., & Yerevanian, B. I. (1983), The relationship of personality to affective disorders: A critical review. *Arch. Gen. Psychiat.,* 40:801–810.

Hamilton, M. (1960), A rating scale for depression. *J. Neurol. Neurosurg. Psychiat.,* 23:56–62.

Hirschfeld, R. M. A., Klerman, G. L., Clayton, P. J., & Keller, M. B. (1983), Personality and depression: Empirical findings. *Arch. Gen. Psychiat.,* 40:993–998.

Mattussek, P., & Feil, W. B. (1983), Personality attributes of depressive patients: Results of group comparisons. *Arch. Gen. Psychiat.,* 40:783–790.

Milden, R. S. (1984), Affective disorders and narcissistic vulnerability. *Amer. J. Psychoanal.,* 44:345–353.

———— Pietromonaco, P., Markus, H., & Newman, J. (1985), Cognitive-affective self-schemas in affective disorders. Unpublished preliminary research findings.

Schafer, R. (1967), *Projective Testing and Psychoanalysis.* New York: International Universities Press.

Spitzer, R. L., & Endicott, J. (1978), *Schedule for Affective Disorders and Schizophrenia.* 3rd ed. New York: New York State Psychiatric Institute.

———— ———— Robins, E. (1978), *Research Diagnostic Criteria.* New York: Biometrics Research, Evaluation Section, New York State Psychiatric Institute.

Chapter 17

Levels of Depression and Clinical Assessment

Arnold Wilson, Ph.D.

An emerging body of clinical evidence concerning anaclitic depression and archaic transferences is linked in this chapter to newly conceptualized diagnostic testing indices. Anaclitic depression is also distinguished from the more traditionally understood notion of guilty depression. Diagnostic testing, in the Rapaport, Gill, and Schafer (1945) tradition, can be no more valid or elegant than the theory informing the interpretation of evidence and the skill of the examiner in managing and evaluating such evidence. Thus, any advance in testing acumen must be parallelled by an advance in clinical theory construction. This inquiry will address; first, the clinical and theoretical relationship between anaclitic depression and archaic transference configurations, each with its roots in the repetition of archaic mental states; second, the implications of such a view for diagnostic psychological testing, utilizing the standard testing procedure described by Rapaport, Gill, and Schafer.

Schafer (1954) has described the necessity of supporting the diagnostic inference process with evidence from three converging streams of test data: The thematic (content and sequence analysis), interpersonal (transferential and observational data), and structural scores and summary. This is a helpful framework for organizing and contrasting the clinical data and theory with the psychological testing

The author would like to thank Steven Passik and Laurie Newman for their generous assistance with this paper.

indices and is used here to present the evidence in support of the argument.

It is important that the concept of depression be clearly defined before taking up a discussion of its testing indices. Often it is difficult to understand clinical reports concerned with the theory and treatment of depression because of a lack of agreement with an author's tacit definition of depression. The word depression, depending upon the preference of the clinician, at times can be alternately held to refer to a symptom, an affect, a mood, a syndrome, or a character style. This lack of clarity has forced psychoanalysts to be more explicit in definitions and to further refine thinking. One very promising theoretical path begins with the idea of locating depression within the realm of the basic affects, with its earliest roots in prerepresentational psychobiological life, and subject to permutations throughout the human life span (Anthony, 1975; Basch, 1975; Bemporad and Wilson, 1978). Based on the early theoretical work of Bibring (1953), such a view considers depression a basic affect conceived of neither in abstract metapsychological terms nor as emerging out of intrapsychic conflict as a drive discharge epiphenomenon. Rather, the origin and consolidation of depression as a basic affect is to be found in normative developmental events, it is viewed as arising out of early object relating and being transformed by such early social experiences as the multiple ambivalences of the rapprochement subphase (Mahler, 1966), the inevitable calamities of childhood (Brenner, 1974, 1983), or early narcissistic aspirations conjoined with actual experiences of helplessness within the immature ego (Bibring, 1953). This view lends a new conceptual clarity to the examination of the phenomenon of depression within the context of the psychoanalytic method and the study of the emergence of psychic conflict (Wilson, 1986). This concept of depression as a basic affect lends itself evidentially to both observations of children and generalizable reconstructions from the psychoanalytic case situation. This definition of depression is employed in this paper.

The psychological test battery contains powerful tools for the diagnostician to assess the level and quality of affective development of an individual, to unveil a personality structure. For example, the Rorschach assumes the projection onto the inkblots of unconscious templates—affective, cognitive, and enactive coded representations of stored information and action tendencies. These templates can be interpreted within the normative perspective of human development as well as highlight individual variants akin to reconstructive evidence.

LEVELS OF DEPRESSION AND TRANSFERENCE

In the diagnostic testing interview, inferences are often made on the basis of informed observations of the patient's transference to the examiner. Many archaic transferences (Gedo, 1981) form with amazing rapidity over the course of the testing, and color the generation and interpretation of the actual responses. Anaclitic depression is often accompanied by an archaic transferential style, so that manifestations of one are often diagnostic of the presence of the other.

In recent years, numerous reports have appeared about narcissistic, borderline, and psychotic patients that describe the following constellation of dynamics: An underlying mental state of primary depletion, an "abandonment depression" (Masterson, 1972), a sense of overwhelming emptiness with a resulting panic-driven object seeking, and a profound despair and hopelessness concerning the possibility of need gratification. This depressive-like affective experience has been described as the "core" of such personalities, and it has been alternatively conceived of as both a developmental precursor to guilt ridden depression and as a unique form of depression. These manifestations of anaclitic depressive affect can be conceptually distinguished from those of guilt ridden depression, which includes the fear of loss of the object's love, a sense of self-condemnation, and feelings of worthlessness.

A review of the relevant literature suggests a growing consensus that depression can be dichotomized into guilty and empty forms. In order to understand the underlying empirical similarities in the clinical description of depression to be offered, the reader should be prepared to see beyond the divergent metapsychological accounts provided by these analytic theorists. From their varying perspectives, each have also pointed to a number of different maturational attainments that are used to explain and differentiate the depressive experiences.

Blatt (1974), for example, distinguishes between "anaclitic" and "introjective" depression. The former is characterized by dependency, helplessness, weakness, depletion, and overriding fear of loss of the loved object, and the latter by self condemnation, guilt, and overriding fear of loss of the object's love (rather than of the object itself). In this view, anaclitic depression results from impairments of self- and object-representations at a sensorimotor cognitive-structural level of organization, in which representations are drive laden and organized in accordance with action schemas. The patient is thereby predisposed to actual experiences of loss of the object due to impairment in evocative memory and libidinal object constancy. Introjective depression, too, is a result of impairment in representations, but this occurs at a higher cognitive and affective developmental level. Characteristic introjective issues include feelings of being unworthy and unlovable, and of failing to live up to others' expectations—hallmarks of phallic oedipal dynamics.

Kohut (1977), too, draws a distinction between "empty" and "guilty" depressions. For Kohut, empty depressions are particularly characteristic of disorders of the self, and derive from an impairment of self-cohesiveness on the self/narcissistic line of development, while guilty depression derives from conflicted psychosexual experiences on the object/libidinal line of development. The dominant types of psychopathology associated with the self/narcissistic line of development, according to Kohut and Wolf (1979), are narcissistic, borderline, and psychotic states; thus, if we may extrapolate from Kohut's inferences, we would expect empty depression to predominate in these conditions. Kohut's distinction between signal anxiety and disintegration anxiety is also relevant here, disintegration anxiety predominating in those self disorders characterized by depletion and emptiness. Kernberg (1975) utilizes one developmental line instead of two, yet reaches similar empirical conclusions, especially regarding the equation of empty depression with severe forms of psychopathology. In assessing levels of character pathology, he notes that the greater the capacity for mature guilt as a manifestation of superego integration, the greater the probability that there is present a higher level of personality organization. The less adequate the integration of the superego, the more likely it is that the patient will experience empty rather than guilt-ridden depression, as well as oral rage, anxiety and affect intolerance, splitting and its derivatives, and harsh projected paranoid trends, all characteristic of borderline personality organization.

Whether the particular focus is superego integration, level of object relations, representational capacities, or the attainment of a cohesive self, the common thread is of two general forms of depressive experience. The developmental factors of their etiological significance should be considered for the specification of psychodiagnostic test indices.

The distinction between depressive subtypes may in part be understood through the application of maturational principles. Brenner (1975) has described how depressive affect and anxiety, both basic affects, possess a signal function (Freud, 1926) and as such are fundamental and irreducible building blocks of human experience. In his view, both anxiety and depression arise out of early object-relational experiences; however, anxiety is associated with an internalized and unconscious thought that something bad will soon happen, whereas the signal function of depression is associated with the thought that something bad has already occurred.

While such a retroflective signal function is characteristic of guilty depression, a developmental analysis suggests it is unlikely that anaclitic depressive affect possesses the identical function. The signal that something bad (a correctable wrong) has occurred presumes a capacity to discriminate good from bad as well as a motivation to rectify what is wrong. It is guilt-ridden depression that lends itself to such sophisticated ideational activity. Depressive affect originating in traumata or fixation prior to the acquisition of these cognitive abilities will perform a function other than that of retroflective signaling.

I hypothesize that within a psychic economy in which true separateness has not been realized, in which the child remains dependent on the caregiver for the optimization of regulatory activity, manifestations of depressive affect will be organized according to the function of *self-regulation* rather than the signal of danger. In a similar manner, Gedo (1984) has described what he terms "l'espace blanc" as the phase-specific depressive experience during the early period in which the superordinate developmental task is regulation of the infant's level of arousal and management of traumatic overstimulation within the caregiver-infant matrix. Numerous other clinical and research reports have described how the child, in the presence of the as yet inadequate ability to self-regulate, is psychobiologically programmed to periodically reach out to and rely upon the caregiver for external help in being optimally stimulated and maintained (Bowlby, 1969; Mahler, Pine, and Bergman, 1975). Although detailed discussion of self-regulation is beyond the scope of this chapter, it is important to note that this developmental principle finds support both in the work of clinical psychoanalysis (see Gedo, 1979, 1981) and in the burgeoning literature on direct infant and child observation, as summarized by Sander (1980) and Stern (1983, 1985). These latter analytically informed infancy researchers report a fascinating "dance of attunement" between infant and primary caregiver in which the only context for understanding the psychological life of the infant is that of "interindividuality." Caregiver and infant together construct the infant's patterning of social reality and creation of core selfhood through their joint understanding of optimal levels of internal stimulation across a variety of psychosocial contexts, with a complexity and subtlety previously suspected by few.

A developmental context for two types of depression emerges; a guilt ridden form characterized by depression that signals something bad has occurred; and anaclitic depressive affect that marks a failure in self-regulatory activity consequent to a primary caregiver-child misattunement.

This developmental perspective, which highlights levels of depression, also brings into focus a view of transference as a multilevel phenomena. Sander discusses the relevance of infancy research to clinical psychoanalysis and the theory of transference:

> these adaptive configurations constitute the strategies that give us what we are now calling the "archaic transference." The importance of psychoanalysis—of an understanding of early development, its variations and the uniqueness of each adaptive mother-infant system—lies in the clues it gives us as to how to begin to recognize in the transference the archaic nature of the regulatory process that was unique for that system as it was consolidating. [p. 198]

The psychological testing indices of anaclitic depressive affect, it will be seen, in part grow out of the specific relationship of the levels of depression to levels of transference.

Transference has traditionally been understood as reexperienced affects, wishes, fantasies, and defensive styles, mobilized toward a particular person, which repeats a dynamic configuration established through personal history toward an earlier significant figure, usually but not always a parent (Greenson, 1965). In the recent literature, it has become increasingly clear to psychoanalytic clinicians that the generic term could be further honed by examining several more specific dynamic processes. Thus, a number of concepts evolved that were intended to bring clarity and order to these critical phenomena. Such terms as the rational alliance (Sterba, 1934), the therapeutic alliance (Zetzel, 1970), the working alliance (Greenson, 1965), the holding environment (Winnicott, 1960), and the various self-object transferences (Kohut, 1971, 1977) were introduced to refine and deepen our understanding of complexities within the transference concept. Most of these concepts emphasized the preoedipal determinants of the personality organization.

Many of these contributions focused on experiential factors above and beyond the acquisition of insight, in keeping with the technical problem of treating patients who at early stages of their treatment can make little or no therapeutic use of self-understanding. Many patients whose object relations tend to be organized at a need-gratifying senso-rimotor level often have difficulty with the benevolent neutrality of the analytic therapist, because he is not of explicit immediate importance. One of the goals of treatment in such instances is to facilitate the establishment of a therapeutic climate in which the patient might be better able to use the therapist in a more advanced form of object relating. In seeking to account for such transference configurations, variants and modifications in analytic procedures have led clinicians to coin a multitude of specific terms while describing issues of technique with generally treatment refractory patients. For example, the interpersonal transaction with such patients has been characterized as "holding" the narcissistic patient through turbulent crises and through fantasies of merger, oneness, and fusion (Fleming, 1972; Modell, 1976). The separation-individuation theory of Mahler has been brought to bear on the analytic treatment of seriously disturbed adults, with the hypothesis that the substages become reenacted in the context of the transference through various verbal, nonverbal, and sensorimotor reenactments (Kramer, 1979). Pine (1979) has elaborated this conception and described what he refers to as "transference to the undifferentiated other"; he also notes various similarities between the therapist-patient relationship and that between parent and child.[1]

These studies, as well as many other inquiries into the problem of how transferences of severely disturbed patients unfold, extend the meaning and implications of the concept of transference; we can now understand that it is based on a repetition of affect, need, and misat-tunement states grounded in a preoedipal context. What these clinicians hypothesize as being subject to repetition are patterns of expectations arising from a lack of self-other differentiation or the psychic structuralization that supports individuation and self stability. Adler (1980) has recently examined this problem and speculated that self-object transferences are manifest in all analytic treatments. He suggests that in all analytic contexts, and not exclusively in the treatments of severely disturbed patients, there are two distinct forms of transference. The first, a neurotic/triadic transference, is based on a

---

[1]Pine (1985), like Schlesinger (1969), has also questioned the applicability of supportive *versus* expressive modes of psychotherapy. Pine's discussion of "interpretation in the context of support" highlights Schlesinger's concern that a consistent supportive psychotherapy shortchanges the difficult patient, because it deprives him of the opportunity to do expressive work in areas in which he is capable.

repetition of oedipal anxieties, and is dependent for its visible emergence in the analytic hour upon the successful resolution of a self-object transference that tends to be either very "noisy" (in severely disturbed patients) or very "quiet" (in neurotic patients). The self-object transference Adler refers to implicates a constellation of fantasies that promote the patient's wish for others, especially the empathic analyst, to perform those subtle ministrations that provide an attunement to assure the patient that he is being understood and can be helped. This is often necessary, with narcissistic and borderline patients, for the establishment in the treatment hour of the self-stability that forms the foundation of a therapeutic alliance allowing treatment to proceed. Adler suggests that such a transference is present in neurotics but is often left unspoken but assumed; it is the essence of those fantasies through which the holding environment is created and maintained as a backdrop for analytic neutrality. In fantasies of likeness, similarity, and mutuality a basis of object relating is created that allows the belief in safety and the potential to trust a benevolent stranger. It is assumed by most neurotics and is therefore not spoken of, but the severely disturbed patient cannot assume it, and it therefore noisily dominates many aspects of long-term treatment with such patients. Extensive work is required simply to forge a therapeutic climate in which continuity of care can be maintained.

The notion of the self-object transference may be an oversimplification of a complicated matrix of as yet unclassified repetitions of preoedipally derived mental states patterned in the nexus of dyadic rather than triadic object relations, which after Gedo (1979, 1981) we might refer to as archaic transferences. The self-object transference is one archaic transference—perhaps the most visible and readily conceptualized, due to the work of Mahler, Pine, and Bergman (1975), Stolorow and Lachmann (1980), and Kohut (1971, 1977) all of whom stress the significance of the notion of *separateness*—among a multiplicity of other such repetitions. Such archaic transferences, in need of systematic and scientific classification, may subsume the individual case of the self-object transference. Thus, the fantasies of one archaic transference (the self-object transference) may serve to establish a holding environment, in that it bonds the patient to the therapist, while those of other archaic transferences may serve a more disruptive function. There is no reason to believe that all archaic transferences are ipso facto pathological; in this case, the self-object transference may be understood as performing a salubrious and necessary psychic function.

In this light, Adler (1980) notes that the successful engagement of a self-object transference "may coincide with the analyst's sense that the patient is 'settling down' to analysis and is comfortable enough to be able to begin to work collaboratively" (p. 551).

What has been described are distinct levels of depression (anaclitic and guilt-ridden) and of transference (archaic and oedipal). Both unfold along what we usually think of as independent axes, yet in fact are intertwined. What is the specific relationship, then, between these levels of depressive affect and transference? The affect of depression is interpersonally manifest in its anaclitic form through certain archaic transferences, including the self-object transference, while guilt-ridden depression is manifest in the neurotic or triadic transference based on repetition of the childhood neurosis, castration reactions, self-directed aggression and the recognition of the object as separate from the self and as not susceptible to loss when proximity is not possible. Anaclitic depressive affect, like the archaic transferences, can be traced to preoedipal structural development. Both are based upon a preoedipal frame of inherent interindividuality and are phenomenologically related through experiences of depletion, helplessness, weakness, and actual struggles to maintain physical and emotional contact with the need-gratifying object lest it be lost. Guilt-ridden depression, like the transference neurosis proper, is characterized by ego ideal conflicts, a sense of perpetually failing to live up to both internally and externally imposed standards, worthlessness, self-directed aggression, hostility and self-reproaches, and fears of loss of the object's love and approval.

An important psychodiagnostic problem lies in the lack of correspondence between visibility of anaclitic depressive affect and a singular conception of "level of pathology." As previously described, anaclitic depressive affect seems to be almost unanimously viewed as a derivative of a primitive mental state. My clinical experience does not support this view; the appearance of anaclitic depressive affect in psychodiagnostic practice does not necessarily suggest a primitive mental state (Blatt, Quinlan, Chevron, McDonald, and Zuroff, 1982). I have found that neurotics with high-level functioning often present clinically with anaclitic depressive concerns; contrary to expectation, patients with low-level functioning often do not. Since anaclitic depressive affect is a normative affect arising out of particular object-relational interactions, it is not in and of itself pathological. It is usually recognized and diagnosed when it occurs in an archaic transference amid the multiple impairments found in narcissistic, borderline, and psychotic psychopathology. When anaclitic depressive affect is present in most neurotic organizations, it tends to be quiet. For most neurotics, it seems to be the ambiguity and safety of the controlled analytic regression that elevates it to a central role in the analytic discourse. Likewise, in the psychological test battery, the test stimuli with high amounts of ambiguity are more likely to prompt the appearance of anaclitic depressive issues, even in high functioning patients. For neurotics, anaclitic wishes and longings can ordinarily be gratified by such expected life experiences as mature love, marriage, hobbies and interests, and career success, gratifications that are often not possible, for severely disturbed patients given their structural organization. Anaclitic depressive affect can and does occur in any level of psychological organization—neurotic, borderline, or psychotic—its preoedipal origin does not necessarily imply pathology.

CASE ILLUSTRATION

I would like to enliven the theoretical discussion by presenting a case that illustrates many of the points made here.

B. was a nineteen-year-old white Protestant female referred for long-term residential inpatient treatment due to a series of suicide attempts, promiscuity, and progressively worsening interpersonal relationships. From ages sixteen to nineteen she had been a chronic drug and alcohol abuser, and had been hospitalized on three occasions after impulsive overdoses. Her cognitive orientation was predominantly hysterical, although organized on a borderline level; she presented a diagnostic picture similar to what used to be called the "bad" hysteric (Zetzel, 1970) and is now often termed the infantile personality (Kernberg, 1975). She was prone to dramatic outbursts of tears and rageful temper tantrums when she could not have her way with people, a situation often triggered by her inability to empathically "read" other people's motives. This led to paranoid projections and a chronic inability to observe her own self. Although she did not have delusions or hallucinations, she was subject to eerie and frightening periods of depersonalization and derealization during which the subjective experience of the flow of time slowed down and she perceived the world in slow motion. B. fancied herself as a soon-to-be-famous punk rock singer, and enjoyed shocking her parents and other "straights" with her demonstrations of punk garb and manners.

Her parents, part of the upwardly mobile suburban middle class, presented a picture of studied blandness. Their rigidity stood in sharp contrast to their daughter's flamboyance. By the time she was an adolescent, the patient was dominating her family with verbal abuse and violent aggressive acts, as well as by instilling in them a constant fear of her self-destructiveness. Her parents would go along with almost anything she wished rather than confront her when she was throwing a tantrum. B.'s father was a stoic and passive man who seemed bewildered by his daughter's provocations and signs of abnormality. B.'s mother was both nurturer and disciplinarian when B. was growing up, but she too was cold and nondemonstrative. She was also more clearly depressed than was her husband. Overburdened by her child, she indulgently provided anything material her daughter wanted amid a mother-child context of emotional barrenness.

B.'s childhood was marked by repeated attempts to act like a baby and thus arouse other people to care for her as if she were one. Issues of body integrity abounded throughout the early years, such as her near-delusional belief as a latency child that her parents were in collusion with a neighbor to cut parts out of her body and out of other children in order to eat them. Shortly after treatment was begun, the patient wrote her therapist the following poem:

> i see things sometimes   i black out most times
> > in fact, i think i'm crazy
> its still a mystery to me   why things i see
> > disappear into the walls
> am i a grownup or a child? you "see" me laugh you "hear" me
> > smile
> > but inside i hurt
> > > alot
> he's figuring me out   and i have to pout
> > 'cause i'm dying inside
> i guess i'm just scared to "get well" 'cause you never can tell
> > what normal really is
> (i know that) he's trying to help me but i think he can see
> > that i'm dying inside

During early therapy hours, B. was pseudocooperative. Her unquestioning compliance with the goals and rules of treatment constituted a resistance, as she agreed with everything the therapist said, even when she did not, and even when she did not so much as grasp the issues. This compliance turned out to represent an unconscious scenario of how she and the therapist might benefit each other, a quid pro quo whereby she would agree with everything the therapist said and he, in turn, would magically prevent her from regressing to the level of disorganization where the core of her disturbance was to be found.

It quickly became clear that the patient possessed a dramatic capacity for regression, which at times made it appear as if she were under the influence of multiple dissociated ego states. At her best, she participated in imperious adolescent sexual fantasies; she was flamboyant, flirtatious, and competitive, and fantasized that she was so important that others meant nothing to her, that she needed nothing from them—she could scorn or adore them as she pleased. Her anaclitic depressive neediness was largely denied or counteracted. For example, one recurrent fantasy she had when at her best was that she was a famous and glamorous rock singer. She had just finished a concert and, surrounded by adoring fans and reporters, announced that she was moving to a desert island to live alone because nobody could ever nor would ever be able to know her. When frustrated, stressed, or otherwise unable to maintain such illusions, she regressed to a level where she acted like a passive-aggressive child, and sought safety and stability in overconventionality. She experienced herself as an "ant" in a world of gigantic and monstrous grown-ups, and strove blithely to simply love and be loved—which led her ardently to seek a child or a substitute for one. Such overconventionality represented a desperate struggle to meld with those around her, who might shelter her from the devastating experiences associated with the anaclitic depressive issues at the heart of her disturbance. When unable to maintain this intermediate level of organization B. would regress to her lowest level of functioning, characterized by severe oral rage, thought and associative disturbances, suicidality, and feelings of unreality. At this level, anaclitic features starkly predominated. She displayed evidence of an internal emptiness and a longing to be emotionally and physically filled up, but her hunger was too great and she would rather die than ask for nurturance. She experienced herself as heroically suffering, alone in a world of bountiful supplies withheld from her by sadistic adults. During a series of hours, B. developed the fantasy that she would never be able to return to her bedroom in her parents' house unless she was successful at "filling the room up" with her own possessions. This seemed to represent a condensation of the equation body equals room, as if the room, like her body, was so frighteningly empty that it needed to be filled before it would stop exerting an overpoweringly incorporative longing. Intolerable feelings of loneliness and helplessness led to prolonged periods of crying, tantrums, and at one point a physical assault on another patient. Her wish for a person to stabilize her was so overpowering and important that minor imperfections in others led to contemptuous dismissal of their importance. After one session in which such anaclitic depressive themes predominated, she wrote her therapist the following poem:

power

i'm only a little girl
but one day, someway, i'll own the (whole) fuckin' world
(and everybody in it . . .)
they know now, i'm a child of might
born on a star, a wonderful sight
although they thought i'd try in vain
they knew in their hearts that i'd live again
they'll bow at my feet and beg for a kiss
they'll think me a saint but they don't know this:
> that i'd crush their tiny hands as they scream "merci beaucoup"
> and let me tell you a "secret"—i'd do it to you
>> *too!*
>>>> no thanks to "them" . . .

This case of an impulsive borderline young woman illustrates the etiology, clinical factors, and transference implications of severely disturbed patients whose psychopathology includes an anaclitic depressive affect component. Such features are a regularly occurring "noisy" phenomenon among severely disturbed patients. In the case of B., dissociative defenses mobilized against the yearning to be helpless, filled-up, and dependent on an emotionally constant object resulted in a layering of personality structure which resembled multiple ego states. Anaclitic depressive affect was present at each level of organization, but was handled and defended against in diverse ways which had dramatic implications for the treatment. At her highest level, her imperiousness, denial, and grandiose fantasies made it virtually impossible to engage her analytically. When this level and the level of overconventionality and compliance (a last-ditch mobilization of psychic resources against regression) failed her, her overwhelming anaclitic depressive neediness emerged, along with untrammeled rage, a limited capacity for affect tolerance, and pananxiety, resulting in a withdrawal from gratifying communicative interpersonal contact unless others obeyed her every whim and caprice. Thus, in this case, the archaic transference that carried the anaclitic affect stabilized the patient at higher levels of organization, but when this failed to ward off events which precipitated frustration and rage, she withdrew from an interpersonal context into another phase of archaic transference, one more starkly narcissistic, in which only she herself could fulfill the task of meeting her thwarted needs; only to the extent that others obliged her could they be perceived and tolerated. Hopelessness superseded her agonizing struggles over dependency, and B. returned to the only person whose ministrations could fill the emptiness of her own loneliness—herself.

DIAGNOSTIC TEST INDICES OF THE DEPRESSIVE TYPOLOGY

In this section I shall take up the issue of the differential diagnosis of anaclitic depression in clinical practice. The discussion and examples follow from the clinical/theoretical perspective presented above.

In general, when nonspecific indices of depression (such as lower Performance than Verbal IQ scores, suppressed DSym and DS, slow reaction times, paucity of productivity, distractibility, dysphoric thematic content, and limited or unusual use of color and movement) are present, the examiner may wish to attempt a subtyping of the depression into its guilt-ridden or anaclitic forms, so that appropriate treatment and diagnostic conclusions may be drawn. It is important to stress that anaclitic and guilt-ridden depressive affects are not mutually exclusive; they can and frequently do occur within the same personality structure. The indices outlined below have proved useful in making these distinctions.

The Test Interview

1. Suggestions of the establishment of an archaic transference in which there are indications of fantasies of merger, fusion, or extreme forms of dependency or counterdependency. Primitive affect states may predominate. The particular fantasies characteristic of anaclitic depression may be manifested by signs of increased depressive emptiness and apathy in the absence of the examiner (or his support) rather than in his presence (or lack of support). In consequence, the examiner should be careful not to overcontrol the testing situation or to avert prematurely the transference themes that arise during the interview. Rather, he might consciously vary the amount of support he lends the patient while carefully observing the patient's reactions. This is to be monitored while bearing in mind too that the tests themselves are

varied in the amount of external structure they provide. Too much support, which can emerge in the presence of the examiner's anxiety to obtain a rich protocol, can allay the very fantasies and behaviors that are diagnostically most useful.

2. The examiner's countertransference reactions to the patient (Sugarman, 1981) should be monitored for reactions to the patient's success, or lack of it, at mobilizing the examiner to help him contain or manage the anaclitic depressive affective experience.

An example of this interview process involved a twenty-seven-year-old female with an hysterical personality structure and a history of occupational, social, and psychological competence. She had recently left her therapist while moving to a new city, and was anxiously seeking a new therapist. She had begun suffering panic attacks following the move, and unfortunately fate found her alone and without a job in an unknown and alien New York City. During her first interview, she described the panic attacks she was experiencing as "a feeling of emptiness, like I was going to disintegrate. I felt abandoned." Eager to enlist the therapist's emotional support, she voiced an immediate and urgent need for a therapist who would give her extensive feedback and who would talk to her and prevent her from feeling like she would have "an attack right in the office." Uninterested in exploratory psychotherapy, she likened the therapeutic process of exploring dynamics and feelings to "a walk through the mud—you'll just get dirty." She insisted on a phone number to call at times when she feared an anxiety attack was imminent. This patient was searching for a person who could help her contain and define overwhelming feelings of abandonment and anaclitic depressive concerns. Her panic attacks seemed to be archaic repetitions geared toward drawing in the other in order to stabilize and regulate herself. That she had no previous history of psychological disorder is an example of how activation of an archaic transference within a higher-functioning individual can occur under extreme regressive conditions. An archaic mode of relating had become noisy.

The Wechsler Adult Intelligence Scale

1. Low I and high C may suggest a histrionic character style, which lends itself to demonstrations of visibility of the anaclitic type of depression (Blatt and Shichman, 1983), while guilt-ridden depression is more likely to be visible in patients with an overideational paranoid/obsessive character style.

2. Idiosyncratic responses on Comprehension and stories on Picture Arrangement, especially FLIRT or TAXI, which reflect thematically the issues discussed in this paper.

3. Overexaggerated libidinal object seeking on Picture Completion, e.g., seeing as missing human figures or objects whose function is to hold up an object in need of support. For example, a hand may be seen as missing in the water pitcher card rather than the water flow. Others include a rider for the horse, or a rower for the boat.

4. Block Design and Object Assembly should be evaluated closely to determine if they are impaired by poor frustration or affect tolerance, characteristic of anaclitic depressive affect, rather than psychomotor retardation or poor attention or concentration.

The Thematic Apperception Test

1. Stories with predominant themes of emptiness, worthlessness, loss, desertion, aloneness, and loss of the object rather than loss of the object's love. In those cards on which a single character is depicted, themes may focus around the isolation of the character as opposed to the introduction of nondepicted ones. This is due to an inability to evoke or introduce new characters (especially the libidinal object), at times, in the case of severely disturbed patients, as a result of a lack of evocative memory (see Adler and Buie, 1979).

2. The presence of harsh criticism of self and others rather than a more mature and modulated guilt.

3. Self and other figure carriers who may be described as bored, apathetic, or listless, or as feeling nothing.

4. Hypercritical or abandoning representations of authority figures.

5. One or more of the characters possess the potential for, or is in the midst of, an explosive expression of affect or impulsive action.

With these indices in mind, the TAT can be quite useful in thematically inferring the presence of anaclitic depression. In the examples that follow, predominant themes are of loss of the object, where others are seen only in terms of ability to gratify or frustrate needs, indicative of the early ontological focus on self-regulation and its failings.

Card 6BM: Nineteen-year-old male, schizoid personality. This is a woman who doesn't know what to do. She feels very sad and helpless. She's collapsed on the floor and is just sobbing. She'll make it all right but will be sad for the rest of her life.

Card 14: Eighteen-year-old female, infantile personality. This person is all alone, doesn't have any friends or family or anything, and he's just looking out the window watching his life go by, and wondering where everybody went. He just feels really lousy. He just thinks about it and gets all bummed out and depressed.

Anaclitic themes predominate in these two examples. Striking is how in each case others are not evoked. Rather, there is no press to introduce the libidinal object; it is merely lost, leaving the self carrier alone and hopeless in a state in which time is inexorable and unchanging. Compare the tone to that of the following example:

Card 5: Thirty-eight-year-old female, reactive depression. It's a mother opening the door to a child's bedroom, to see what they're doing. To see if they're doing what they're supposed to be doing. And she looks annoyed because she knows they weren't. She had dinner ready and came up to get the kids, but she's annoyed.

In this example, guilt feelings are presented. There is indication of loss of the object's love, as well as failure to live up to the object's expectations. Evocative memory is intact; indeed, the self carrier is not depicted here and must actually be introduced. A time continuum is implied. Finally, in the next example, note the unintegrated quality of the parental representation and how this is defensively compensated for via grandiose, magical thinking.

Card 15: Eighteen-year-old male, narcissistic personality. This man's son just died in a car accident and he happens to be a warlock. He has been going to the graveyard every night to mourn his son, so one night he comes out to the graveyard and pours some magic potion on the grave and rises his son from the dead. They bring the rest of the family up from the dead—it would be nice to do that. When the family is reassembled, they have a reunion, big party, lots of dancing.

Hypomanic denial, grandiosity, and magical thinking are used here to gloss over and actively organize an experience of what is otherwise a macabre, gloomy tale in which real objects do not exist, and in which basic human needs are associated with the hopelessness of death and the desperation implicit in a resort to the supernatural as the only way to obtain gratification.

6. A preponderance of two- rather than three-character stories, as the triadic stories would be more apt to contain themes of jealousy, competition, or guilt over failing to live up to expectations of the significant other.

7. A characterization of others primarily in relation to need gratification, i.e., primarily in terms of their ability to please or frustrate, with no true recognition of their separate existence as persons.

Following are some examples of TAT stories which illuminate the nature of the two-character, dyadic themes and the focus on finding stability and support, often by an undifferentiated other.

Card 10: Thirty-eight-year-old male narcissistic personality. A lonely, middle-aged man, widowed, and a lonely middle-aged old maid, meet at a lonely hearts dance. They dance together and realize how much they need each other, converse, find each other. Something happens and they marry. It was just a magic night and they got lucky. She's thinking all she had to do was be held and she was amazed at how much so little contact could console her.

Note how the theme of a genital male-female encounter veils what is essentially a focus on abandonment (widowed), loneliness (three times in the first sentence the word "lonely" appears), and the need for physical proximity to mitigate such feelings. The defense against the "noisy" quality of these concerns gives the overall story a glib and strangely casual tone, which barely disguises what is a very shallow understanding of mature love or male-female relationships. There is a magical denial of the suffering induced by loneliness. Finally, the defensive grandiosity in this male narcissistic individual is witnessed in his projection of these needs to the female figure; thus, instead of presenting as in need of, he is the supplier of, love and stabilization.

The Rorschach

1. Lowering of form level around oral incorporative themes.
2. The presence of two or more (c) responses, in the context of other severe pathognomic signs. These (c) percepts are often of a low form level. The (c) response refers to the articulation of an object on the inkblots based on clearly definable and highly differentiated forms which are made possible through the juxtaposition of light and dark. This response was held by Schactel (1966), in his discussion of shading responses, to imply a stretching out of psychic feelers in order to navigate within the emotional and at times anxiety-filled worlds of self and others. At his best, a patient who employs this skill will display a higher-level capacity for empathy, which at his worst becomes paranoid scanning with the use of primitive projective and introjective defenses. The anaclitic depressive may perceive the (c) response as a

reflection of his wish to omnipotently control the object, by self-regulating through honing in to the world of the other in order to control him so as to avert loss or impel him to lend tolerance of the depressive affect.

The theoretical bifurcation of depressive affect into empty and guilt-ridden forms may find a concrete analogy in the Rorschach indices used for inferring depressive affect. The traditional C' Black response,[2] as described by Rapaport, Gill, and Schafer (1945), has been thought to represent the equivalent of depressive affect. However, this traditional use of C' Black no longer appears adequate, as it fails to account for the interpretation of anaclitic depressive affect. The interpretation of the C' response implies a capacity for guilt, knowledge of right and wrong, and time orientation, a signaling capacity. The C' response refers to a white-black-gray area identified by its achromatic coloring. The ability to articulate black dimensions out of the shading is representative of the acknowledgment of a despair that is lived with and recognized. Acknowledging the blackness reveals the response process as depressive affect construed as a guilt-ridden reaction to something disturbing that has already occurred. Such a conceptualization of depression is similar to guilt-ridden depressive affect, but fails to capture the emptiness, depletion, and object longing of anaclitic depression. The (c) response, when given by a severely disturbed patient or when characterized by a poor form level, ties into the more central anaclitic depressive issues of self-regulation and object seeking. An example of each should help to illuminate this thesis.

Card VI: C' Black: Thirty-two-year-old male, manic depressive in remission. This looks like a black pelt of some kind. Sometimes when people shoot a small animal, like a woodchuck, they cut off the hide and dry it out and hang it on the wall. It seems to have a nice color to it, black, and a lot of nice contrasts. A beautiful skin.

(Card VI) (c): Eighteen-year-old male, narcissistic personality. The darkest section up the middle here looks like the leg which supports a table. One made on a lathe. The tip of the leg would have to be attached.

---

[2]Although the C' response technically also includes other achromatic colors, usually white, many clinicians prefer to limit the interpretation of depressive affect to the C' Black response.

The first example, in which a defensive disavowal is immediately evoked, is organized around the depressive idea of killing something small, expiation for aggressive wishes, and a notion of right and wrong. The (c) response in the second example, however, finds the patient perceptually "working" to carve out a coherent image amid the ambiguity of the light and dark. Rather than resigning himself to being lost in the ambiguity of shading, he seeks support by overarticulating the ambiguities around him. It is no accident that he perceives a structure whose function is to "support a table," in which attachment "would have to be" as a necessary condition. The patient's wish to enlist external support through attachment is exemplified in this example, both structurally and imagistically.

3. Fluctuations between signs that affects must be contained and overcontrolled and signs that one is in imminent danger of being overwhelmed by them. This is reflected in such determinant responses as F/C, C—F, FC(c), and especially FCarb., which may suggest an intolerance of or a surrender to affects such as rage that the patient is desperately striving to control.

Another area where we may see these trends is on Rorschach movement responses. As Mayman (1976) and others have noted, the human movement responses can be seen as cognitive templates that reflect and determine self- and object-relational paradigms. There the patient with anaclitic depressive concerns may demonstrate a preponderance of passive movement responses (Rorschach's original so-called flexor). To the extent that they can perceive movement at all, this may reflect the degree to which they are passively involved with the object world. Central to these different levels is the victimized, starved position these patients at times assume—that things happen to them as opposed to being initiated by them.

REFERENCES

Adler, G. (1980), Transference, real relationship, and alliance. *Internat. J. Psycho-Anal.,* 61:557–558.
———— Buie, D. (1979), Aloneness and borderline psychopathology: The possible relevance of child development issues. *Internat. J. Psycho-Anal.,* 60:83–96.
Anthony, E. J. (1975), Childhood depression. In: *Depression and Human Existence,* ed. E. J. Anthony & T. Benedek. Boston: Little, Brown, pp. 231–278.
Basch, M. F. (1975), Toward a theory that encompasses depression: A revision of existing causal hypotheses in psychoanalysis. In: *Depression and Human Existence,* ed. E. J. Anthony & T. Benedek. Boston: Little, Brown, pp. 485–534.
Bemporad, J., & Wilson, A. (1978), A developmental approach to depression in childhood and adolescence. *J. Amer. Acad. Psychoanl.,* 6:325–352.

Bibring, E. (1953), The mechanism of depression. In: *Affective Disorders,* ed. P. Greena-cre. New York: International Universities Press, pp. 13–48.

Blatt, S. (1974), Levels of object representation in anaclitic and introjective depression. *Psychoanalytic Study of the Child,* 29:107–157. New Haven, CT. Yale University Press.

_____ Quinlan, D., Chevron, E., McDonald, C., & Zuroff, D. (1982), Dependency and self criticism: Psychological dimensions of depression. *J. Consult. & Clin. Psychol,* 50:113–124.

Blatt, S., & Shichman, S. (1983), Two primary configurations of psychopathology. *Psychoanal. & Contemp. Thought,* 6: 187–202.

Bowlby, J. (1969), *Attachment and Loss: Vol 1. Attachment.* New York: Basic Books.

Brenner, C. (1974), On the nature and development of affects: A unified theory. *Psychoanal. Quart.,* 43:532–556.

_____ (1975), Affects and psychic conflicts. *Psychoanal. Quart.,* 44:5–28.

_____ (1983), *The Mind in Conflict.* New York: International Universities Press.

Fleming, J. (1972), Early object deprivation and transference phenomena: The working alliance. *Psychoanal. Quart.,* 41:23–49.

Freud, S. (1926), Inhibitions, symptoms and anxiety. *Standard Edition,* 20:87–174. London: Hogarth Press, 1959.

Gedo, J. (1979), *Beyond Interpretation: Toward a Revised Theory for Psychoanalysis.* New York: International Universities Press.

_____ (1981), *Advances in Clinical Psychoanalysis.* New York: International Universities Press.

_____ (1984), *Psychoanalysis and Its Discontents.* New York: Guilford Press.

Greenson, R. (1965), The working alliance and the transference neurosis. *Psychoanal. Quart.,* 34: 155–181.

Kernberg, O. (1975), *Borderline Conditions and Pathological Narcissism.* New York: Aronson.

Kohut, H. (1971), *The Analysis of the Self.* New York: International Universities Press.

_____ (1977), *The Restoration of the Self.* New York: International Universities Press.

_____ Wolf, E. (1979), The disorders of the self and their treatment. *Internat. J. Psycho-Anal,* 59:413–425.

Kramer, S. (1979), The technical significance and application of Mahler's separation-individuation theory. *J. Amer. Psychoanal. Assn.,* 27(suppl.):241–262.

Mahler, M. (1966), Notes on the development of basic moods: The depressive affect. In: *Psychoanalysis: A General Psychology,* ed. R. M. Loewenstein, L. M. Newman, M. Schur, & A. J. Solnit. New York: International Universities Press, pp. 152–168.

_____ Pine, F., & Bergman, A. (1975), *The Psychological Birth of the Human Infant.* New York: Basic Books.

Masterson, J. (1972), *Treatment of the Borderline Adolescent: A Developmental Approach.* New York: Academic Press.

Mayman, M. (1976), A multidimensional view of the movement response. In: *Rorschach Psychology,* ed. M. Rickers-Ovsiankina. Huntington, NY: Krieger, pp. 229–250.

Modell, A. H. (1976), The holding environment and the therapeutic action of psycho-analysis. *J. Amer. Psychoanal. Assn.,* 24:285–307.

Pine, F. (1979), On the pathology of the separation-individuation process as manifested in later clinical work: An attempt at delineation. *Internat. J. Psycho-Anal.,* 60:225–242.

_____ (1985). *Developmental Theory and Clinical Process.* New Haven, CT: Yale University Press.

Rapaport, D., Gill, M., & Schafer, R. (1945), *Diagnostic Psychological Testing.* Rev. ed. New York: International Universities Press, 1968.

Sander, L. (1980), New knowledge about the infant from recent research: Implications for psychoanalysis. *J. Amer. Psychoanal. Assn.,* 28:181–198.

Schactel, E. (1966), *Experiential Foundations of Rorschach's Testing.* New York: Basic Books.

Schafer, R. (1954), *Psychoanalytic Interpretation in Rorschach Testing.* New York: Grune & Stratton.

Schlesinger, H. (1969). Diagnosis and prescription for psychotherapy. *Bull. Menn. Clin., 33,* 5:269–278.

Sterba, R. F. (1934), The fate of the ego in analytic therapy. *Internat. J. Psycho-Anal.,* 15:117–126.

Stern, D. (1983), Implications of infancy research for psychoanalytic theory and practice. *Psychiatry Update: 1983.* American Psychiatric Association, pp. 8–21.

———— (1985). *The Interpersonal World of the Infant.* New York: Basic Books.

Stolorow, R., & Lachmann, F. (1980), *Psychoanalysis of Developmental Arrests: Theory and Treatment.* New York: International Universities Press.

Sugarman, A. (1981), The diagnostic use of countertransference reactions in psychological testing. *Bull. Menn. Clin.,* 45:473–490.

Wilson, A. (1986). Archaic transference and anaclitic depression. *Psychoanalytic Psychology,* In press.

Winnicott, D. W. (1960), The theory of the parent-infant relationship. *Internat. J. Psychoanal.,* 4:585–595.

Zetzel, E. (1970), *The Capacity for Emotional Growth.* New York: International Universities Press.

Chapter 18

Rorschach Profiles of Depressives: Clinical Case Illustrations

Pamela S. Ludolph, Ph.D.
Randy S. Milden, Ph.D.
Howard D. Lerner, Ph.D.

The episodic aspect of unipolar and bipolar depressive illness naturally gives rise to questions about the relationship of the illness to the patient's premorbid and interepisode personality. These questions are of significance in a number of respects. As Chodoff (1972) has pointed out, there is considerable theoretical interest in these issues as the two major schools of thought on depression—the psychoanalytic/environmental and the psychobiological—would predict different findings. On the one hand, psychoanalysts propose a continuous relationship between the interepisode personality and the depressive illness, consonant with a more environmentally based notion of etiology. On the other hand, the more biological theories of the genesis of depression would predict a healthier interepisode adjustment on which the illness is superimposed as an unfortunate, genetically determined twist of fate. Of course this dichotomy is oversimplified. The ranks of psychoanalysts have always held those who strongly believe in the significance

The authors would like to thank the following individuals and groups for their support: the staffs of the Clinical Studies Unit and Clinical Psychobiology Program, Department of Psychiatry, University of Michigan; Dr. Irene Fast; Dr. Naomi Lohr; Dr. Martin Mayman; Ms. Anath Golomb; various University of Michigan Clinical Psychology graduate students who commented on the draft of the paper.

of constitutional predisposition, including Freud (1914), writing on the libidinal drive in general, and Jacobson (1953), on depression in particular. In addition, modern psychoanalysts have had to consider the very real effectiveness of psychopharmacological agents like lithium carbonate: such a consideration promotes a more biological view of at least certain types of depression. And, of course, the most recent psychobiological thinking admits personality factors to some extent, especially as they reflect attenuations of the same constitutional endowment that produces the episodes, or complicate recovery from the illness (Akiskal, Hirschfeld, and Yerevanian, 1983). Nonetheless, psychobiologists and psychoanalysts for the most part see themselves as very much at odds on the issue of the primary genesis of depression and its relation to personality.

Questions of interepisode personality also have notable implications for treatment and prognosis. Once the relevant personality traits are elucidated, effective psychotherapeutic strategies can be evolved to modify characteristics which seem to presage depressive episodes (Mattussek and Feil, 1983). Psychotherapy can also intervene to address the narcissistic injury inherent in the experience of the affective illness (Milden, 1984). Further, to the extent that personality variables can be added to clinical-descriptive (Biegel and Murphy, 1971), psychopharmacological (Klein, Gittelman, Quitkin, and Rifkin, 1980), and neuroendocrine (Carroll et al., 1981) features, psychobiologists can refine their capacities to accurately diagnose and assign appropriate treatment. The work of Donnelly and his colleagues (Donnelly, Goodwin, Waldman, and Murphy, 1978; Donnelly, Murphy, Waldman, and Goodwin, 1979) is particularly promising in this regard; this group has been able to predict differential responses to classes of antidepressants on the basis of MMPI findings.

The significance of these theoretical and clinical issues has led our group into an investigation of the personalities of these patients. Our tool is the Rorschach test, the most extensively used projective measure of intrapsychic processes. Our diagnostic groups are defined by the stringent criteria of biological psychiatry, certainly not the only way to think about diagnosis, but one which is readily replicated and widely accepted in general psychology and psychiatry.

At present we are analyzing Rorschach data on over fifty inpatients, while continuing to collect protocols from others. This chapter thus cannot be a definitive compilation of our findings. Rather it will report preliminary results, primarily through the medium of a detailed examination of the Rorschachs of two depressed patients—one bipolar and one unipolar. In each case Rorschach data will be presented from the acutely depressed period at the time of hospitalization, from the time of discharge after somatic treatments had been employed and the patients were seen (and operationally defined) as recovered from their episode of illness (euthymic), and from a period several months after hospitalization, when the patients remained without symptoms of major affective disorder. We hope to be able to use these protocols to trace the recovery process in these patients, to address the completeness or incompleteness of the psychobiological cure, and to compare, in a limited way, the modes of adjustment of the patients as they exemplify their diagnostic groups. A review of the relevant literature and a brief statement of our research methodology will provide a context within which the protocols can be understood.

REVIEW OF THE LITERATURE

Personality Traits of Depressives

Many of the earlier studies on the interepisode personalities of depressives tended to group patients homogenously and then compare them to normals or other patient groups on the basis of personality inventories. Using this method, one study determined that depressives were more rigid and prone to anxiety than normals (Julian, Metcalfe, and Coppen, 1969). Other such studies attempted to distinguish anxious and depressed patients, with inconclusive results. Some researchers found no significant differences between these patient groups (Mendels, Weinstein, and Cochrane, 1972), while others found anxious patients to be significantly more neurotic both at the time of hospitalization and at follow-up some years later (Roth, Gurney, Garside, and Kerr, 1972; Schapira, Roth, Kerr, and Gurney, 1972).

An additional level of sophistication was added to this method when distinctions began to be made among groups of depressives. One general distinction separated reactive or neurotic depressives from endogenous or biological ones. This approach served to validate the long-held clinical assumption that some depressives were primarily reacting to environmental stress or internal neurotic concerns, while others had a more physiologically based illness with fewer apparent reactive components and more vegetative signs. Thus, one study found that reactive depressives scored higher than endogenous patients on Maudsley Personality Inventory measures of general neuroticism, and lower on an extraversion factor (Kerr, Schapira, Roth, and Garside,

1970). Another study found that while obsessional traits and symptoms were common in both groups of depressives while they were ill, reactive depressives had more obsessional symptoms on recovery (Kendell and DiScipio, 1970). A third group of workers used an interview technique to determine personality correlates of an independent diagnosis of reactive and endogenous depression. Reactive illness was related to feelings of self-pity, inadequacy, hysterical features, obsessionality, irritability, and hypochondriasis. Endogenous illness, on the other hand, was unrelated to neurotic qualities, and more tied to such signs as early awakening, diurnal variation, psychomotor retardation, and weight loss (Kiloh and Garside, 1963; Kiloh, Andrews, Neilson, and Bianchi, 1972).

In the course of investigating the distinctions between reactive and endogenous depression, some researchers began to be struck by the relative heterogeneity of the reactive group as compared to the endogenous. Paykel (1971) used a cluster analysis technique to derive four subgroups of depressives, one corresponding to the traditional endogenous category, and three being subtypes of the reactive group. The first of the reactive subgroups comprised anxious depressives, with high loadings of psychic and somatic anxiety, depersonalization, and obsessional symptoms. The next subgroup, hostile depressives, were generally somewhat less depressed, with personality concomitants of hostility and self-pity. The third subgroup was the least depressed, and was made up of relatively young patients with high neuroticism and a disturbed life pattern and social relations suggestive of personality disorder. Paykel used these subgroups in later studies as a basis for predicting differential response to amitriptyline (Paykel, 1972; Paykel et al., 1973) and analyzing discordance between self-report and interview data on depression (Paykel and Prusoff, 1973). Paykel's findings on the subtypes have also been replicated by a second group (Kiloh, Andrews, Neilson, and Bianchi, 1972). Another researcher has used cluster analysis to derive three somewhat different categories of neurotic depression. One of these groups was characterized by anxiety and extraversion, another by self-criticism and relatively mild depression, and a third by the most disturbed, neurotic, and hostile features (Roy, 1979).

By far the most common pair of groups compared in studies of depression are the unipolar and bipolar types. Investigations of premorbid personality differences in these groups have produced a number of interesting findings. A trend in the literature has been to see manic-depressives as relatively healthy when they are recovered, while unipolars seem more disturbed. Researchers have found euthymic bipolars to be relatively normal in a study based on chart review (Titley, 1936) and in several investigations using personality measures (Perris, 1966, 1971; Murray and Blackburn, 1974; MacVane, Lange, Brown, and Zayat, 1978). This view has been challenged by psychoanalysts in particular, who see the euthymic bipolar patient as only superficially well functioning, with a more disturbed underlying personality. The classic paper here is that of Cohen, Baker, Cohen, Fromm-Reichmann, and Weigert (1954). They describe the manic-depressive as follows:

> a person who is apparently well adjusted, between attacks, although he may show minor mood swings or be chronically overactive or chronically mildly depressed. He is conventionally well-behaved and frequently successful, and he is hard-working and conscientious. . . . He is typically involved in one or more relationships of extreme dependence, in which . . . [he] seeks to control the other person in the sense of swallowing him up. His inner feeling, when he allows himself to notice it, is one of emptiness and need. . . . His principal source of anxiety is the fear of abandonment. . . .
>
> . . . interpersonal relations have been arrested in their development at the point where the child recognizes himself as being separate from others, but does not yet see others as being full-sized human beings; rather he sees them as entities who are now good, now bad, and must be manipulated. . . . [He] sees relationships as all-or-none propositions. . . . [pp. 120–121]

We have quoted liberally from this early report to indicate the extent to which this description corresponds to the concept of the narcissistic character disorder in modern dynamic psychology, and in particular to Greenson's account of the screen personality (1958). It should be noted also that two studies replicated the findings of Cohen and her colleagues concerning the superficial conventionality and success orientation of bipolar individuals (Gibson, 1958; Spielberger, Parker, and Becker, 1963). Anthony (1975) in a prospective study of the children of bipolar parents, supported several of Cohen and colleagues' findings about the narcissistic psychodynamics and fears of abandonment in children constitutionally at risk for bipolar illness. He makes the point that these personality characteristics seem determined both by genetic loading and by early experiences of narcissistic injury in households where a parent was often either manic or depressed.

An interesting hypothesis on the premorbid personality of bipolar depressives comes from von Zerssen (1977). He postulates two contrasting premorbid personality styles for depressives with a continuum of traits in between. He labels these types "Typus melancholicus" and "Typus manicus," but goes to lengths to indicate that there is no absolute concordance between the types and the symptomatic presentation of bipolar and unipolar groups. Those with the pure "Typus melancholicus" personality are seen as constant, dependent, conventional, meticulous, unimaginative, conscientious, and cautious. By contrast, the "Typus manicus" patients are inconstant, independent, unconventional, broadminded, imaginative, generous, and daring. Von Zerssen finds that unipolars most often do have a melancholic disposition, as described above. Bipolars, however, are a more heterogeneous group, with premorbid personalities ranging from the pure melancholic to the pure manic type, with many graduations in between. Interestingly, von Zerssen sees the frequent finding that bipolars appear normal when euthymic as reflecting this heterogeneity; it is not so much that the group is really normal, as that it is bimodal, with the melancholic personalities balancing out the manic ones.

Donnelly and his colleagues have published a series of papers which address personality differences between bipolar and unipolar patients. Overall, this work lends support to the notion that bipolars appear more healthy on the surface than unipolar patients, as measured by the MMPI (Donnelly and Murphy, 1973a; Donnelly, Murphy, and Goodwin, 1976; Donnelly, Murphy, Waldman, and Reynolds, 1976) and the Rorschach (Donnelly, Murphy, and Scott, 1975). Closer examination of these data, however, reveals a number of interesting departures from expectation. For one thing, bipolar patients consistently underestimated the severity of their depression while in episode and appeared to amend their responses to self-report instruments in the direction of social expectation (Donnelly and Murphy, 1973b). This finding was interpreted as supporting the ideas of Cohen and colleagues concerning the social conformity of bipolars; in these and other studies Donnelly and his group also point to the pervasive use of defensive denial in these patients. He describes them as attentive to external rather than internal stimuli (Donnelly, Murphy, and Scott, 1975) and overactive and impulsive, as measured by both the MMPI (Donnelly, Murphy, and Goodwin, 1976) and a perceptual-motor task (Donnelly and Murphy, 1974).

The most recent studies of the interepisode personalities of bipolar patients continue to provide equivocal conclusions. Hirschfeld and

Klerman (1979) found that manics had much more normal personality profiles than unipolars, though manics scored significantly higher on a measure of obsessionality than normals. Hirschfeld and Cross (1982) confirmed these findings on the relative normalcy of bipolars in a survey of the epidemiological literature on affective disorder. Thus, the idea that bipolars are relatively normal when euthymic remains a prevailing trend in the literature. The opposing trend largely supports the ideas of Cohen and her colleagues. Mattussek and Feil (1983) tested euthymic bipolars with a variety of self-rating questionnaires and characterized them as compulsive, aggressive, and driven to success and achievement. In a critical review of the literature, Akiskal, Hirschfeld, and Yerevanian (1983) similarly concluded that "bipolar affective psychoses often arise from the soil of extraverted, cyclothymic, and related dysthymic temperamental disorders; a driven, work-oriented obsessoid quality is often present in such temperaments" (p. 808).

Akiskal, Hirschfeld, and Yerevanian (1983) attempt to skirt the evident inconsistency in the literature concerning the presence of an obsessional personality in bipolars by using the rather vague appellation, "obsessoid." In fact obsessional characters are rarely "extraverted," nor do they show the impulsivity and pervasive denial noted by Donnelly and his colleagues. Cohen et al. (1954) specifically note that the bipolar, while possessing compulsive traits, "does not show the obsessional's typical need to control the other person for the sake of power, but instead seeks to control the other person in the sense of swallowing him up" (p. 120). They also point out that the bipolar takes on the opinions of others in an "as if" way and "this contrasts with the outward conformity but subtle rebellion of the obsessional" (p. 120). In addition, the issue of the obsessionality of bipolars is complicated by confusion of obsessional symptoms and character traits in the measures used in some of the studies. Perhaps we would be safest in concluding that while there is a trend to find euthymic bipolars compulsive and driven, there is much uncertainty about whether the underlying personality should be characterized as obsessional.

There is much less dissension in the literature regarding the interepisode personalities of unipolar patients; most researchers find introversion, obsessional traits, and substantial psychopathology in these patients when they are euthymic. Freud (1917) first noted that obsessional individuals are particularly predisposed to serious depression, a finding supported by many subsequent workers. One early researcher, for instance, described involutional (unipolar) melancholics as having "a narrow range of friendship, intolerance, and uniformly poor adult

sexual adjustment . . . , a pronounced and rigid ethical code, the proclivity for saving, the marked sensitivity, the outward evidence of anxiety, the notable stubbornness, the overconscientiousness and the
meticulosity . . ." (Titley, 1936). This description closely corresponds
to the "Typus melancholicus" of von Zerssen (1977), described above.
Personality inventory studies have regularly found unipolar patients to
be significantly neurotic and disturbed (Perris, 1966, 1971; Murray and
Blackburn, 1974; Hirschfeld and Klerman, 1979). Compared with the
MMPI profiles of bipolars, those of unipolars show significantly elevated psychopathology while in episode, on scales measuring obsessionality, paranoia, hysteria, hypochondriasis, schizoid tendency, and
introversion; these differences tend, however, to dissipate considerably
upon recovery (Donnelly, Murphy, and Goodwin, 1976). The Donnelly
group also reports that these patients are more attentive to inner
experience than are bipolar patients (Donnelly, Murphy, and Scott,
1975); as opposed to bipolars, they accurately reflect on the severity
of their depression while in episode (Donnelly, Murphy, and
Goodwin, 1976).

For the most part, recent reviews and studies have confirmed
earlier findings on the personalities of unipolars. Hirschfeld and Cross
(1982) noted the association of dependency, low self-esteem, and
obsessionality with nonbipolar depression. Another study used self-
report personality inventories to assess female nonbipolar patients and
concluded they were introverted, submissive, and passive, with increased
interpersonal dependency (Hirschfeld, Klerman, Clayton, and Keller,
1983). Mattussek and Feil (1983) found that endogenous unipolar
patients lacked autonomy, while nonendogenous unipolars were over-
autonomous and aggressive. Akiskal, Hirschfeld, and Yerevanian
(1983) concluded that introversion is the trait most strongly associated
with nonbipolar depression. They felt that other characteristics noted in
the literature, such as dependency and low self-esteem, might well
reflect the persisting influence of the depressive state on the post-
episode personality.

The Rorschach Test as a Measure of Personality
Traits of Depressives

One more study exists in the literature assessing personality variables in unipolar and bipolar depressives using the Rorschach (Donnelly,
Murphy, and Scott, 1975). Although this study is notable for having
initiated an exploration into the usefulness of the Rorschach in examin-

ing the depressive patient group, it is flawed by several methodological problems. First, this study attempts to predict euthymic personality from testing in episode, by generalizing rather freely from behavior observed while the patients were depressed. Second, the administration of the Rorschach was unusual in that no inquiry procedure was used; such an approach simplifies the data, but at the expense of considerable clinical richness and detail. Third, the Rorschach was scored on only seven idiosyncratic characteristics as determined by an ill-described pilot study that led to the hypotheses that bipolars would exceed unipolars on such hysteriform characteristics as color responses, amorphous percepts, and low rate of response; unipolars were to exceed bipolars on movement responses, sexual percepts, and remarks on the integration of the blots. Although these hypotheses were supported, indeed to a remarkable extent, the study did not take advantage of the clinical complexity of the Rorschach and the many excellent systems that are used to interpret and code it. Further, in interpreting the data it was not specifically noted that aspects of hysterical and obsessional style were being assessed (Ludolph, 1981). Thus, investigation of the interepisode personalities of depressives using improved methodology seems indicated.

General Methodological Considerations

A number of methodological difficulties recur in the literature and require our attention. First is the issue of accuracy and replicability of diagnosis. In many of the studies we have cited, diagnostic criteria for depressive types are left incompletely specified. This is evident particularly in the near-tautological examinations of neurotic depressives who are first diagnosed according to unspecified criteria for neurosis, and then assessed experimentally using the same criteria. In addition, distinctions between endogenous and nonendogenous unipolar patients are often not made.

A second major problem, possibly the most serious one, is the tendency of many researchers to use examination of the patient in episode to evaluate the post-recovery personality. This approach is justified on the basis of studies which have shown that aspects of the basic personality do manifest themselves in episode (Coppen and Metcalfe, 1965) and that patients' self-reports of their premorbid personalities while in episode correlate adequately with post-recovery reports (Kendell and DiScipio, 1968). Nonetheless, as recent authors have pointed out, this methodological approach is fraught with hazards in the potential confounding of the depressive state with the basic personality (Hirschfeld et al., 1983). Also, the use of retrospective self-reports with patients in episode seriously limits the kinds of personality measures that can reasonably be employed; though there is some reason to believe that a patient can be induced to report in a straightforward way on his premorbid personality, it would be entirely unrealistic to ask him to respond to a projective device like the Rorschach as if he were not in episode.

A related problem arises when researchers try to generalize too freely from interepisode personality to premorbid personality. Milden (1984) points out the evident narcissistic vulnerability that proceeds from the diagnosis and treatment of these disorders; some patients must also integrate the disorganizing effects of psychosis. Akiskal, Hirschfeld, and Yerevanian (1983) have suggested research strategies that might be employed to assess premorbid personality more accurately. At present, however, we have no such studies, so we are impelled to generalize at times from interepisode data to premorbid personality; we do so with caution, and with awareness of the methodological and conceptual difficulties inherent in this approach.

Finally, we must note the conceptual limitations of studies of personality based primarily or exclusively on self-report inventories. Such instruments do little justice to the complexities of the human mind, making it impossible to begin to address unconscious dynamic issues. Additionally, there is evidence that the major types of depressives vary considerably in the accuracy of their self-reports and their use of distorting defenses like denial; bipolars are particularly unreliable reporters (Donnelly and Murphy, 1973b). Thus, one can never be sure whether reported differences between unipolar and bipolar groups reflect variance in personality or variance in proclivity to distortion. The argument put forth for such scales inevitably has to do with their increased reliability (Akiskal, Hirschfeld, and Yerevanian, 1983). This argument neglects both problems regarding the validity of such measures and recent advances in Rorschach rating scales that meet more than acceptable criteria for reliability and validity.

Our study addresses the methodological difficulties of previous studies by using careful, standardized diagnostic techniques, by assessing patients when recovered from their depressive episodes, and by using the Rorschach test, combining more qualitative, dynamic interpretation with quantitative analysis of established rating scales (for example, Krohn and Mayman, 1974; Blatt, Brenneis, Schimek, and Glick, 1976; Lerner and Lerner, 1980).

METHODLOLGY OF THE PRESENT STUDY

Subjects were inpatients hospitalized for acute episodes of Major Depressive Disorder, subtyped according to Spitzer's Research Diagnostic Criteria (Spitzer, Endicott, and Robins, 1978). Diagnoses were arrived at by consensus of the treatment team, including a senior psychologist or psychiatrist, and after administration of the Schedule for Affective Disorder and Schizophrenia (SADS) (Spitzer and Endicott, 1978). Patients were tested both while they were drug-free and in an episode of depressive illness, and after they were treated by medication or electroconvulsive therapy, such that their depressions remitted according to the Hamilton Rating Scale for Depression, a widely accepted clinician-administered interview for symptoms of depression (Hamilton, 1960). To examine patients who are in a more stable euthymic state, a small subgroup was also tested a third time, at least a year after discharge and still without signs of major affective illness.

Patients were administered all ten Rorschach cards, given in the standard order, with inquiry after all cards. Testers were advanced graduate students in clinical psychology with substantial experience in Rorschach administration. Protocols were then rated according to the Klopfer scoring system (Klopfer, Ainsworth, Klopfer, and Holt, 1954) and various other Rorschach rating scales; interrater reliability for Klopfer scoring was assessed and found acceptable, ranging from 75 to 92 percent. Examiners, raters, and principal investigators were all blind to the diagnoses of the patients.

Case Illustrations

As indicated, this chapter will not present the comprehensive results of our study, but rather an intensive examination of two cases, with brief reference to our preliminary findings. A full presentation of our results will appear in subsequent papers. The following is a synopsis of the histories of the two patients who will serve as illustrations of the Bipolar Endogenous and Unipolar Endogenous groups. The patients were selected from among subjects with three test administrations.

Mrs. A., a seventy-two-year-old widow, was admitted for her first psychiatric hospitalization. On admission she was depressed and lethargic, with sleep and appetite disturbances. She spoke of wishing to die in a car accident to end her psychological pain, and ruminated endlessly about minor past indiscretions. No psychotic processes were observed, however. She reported similar periods of depression beginning approximately at age thirty-five; her depressions alternated with hypomanic periods in which she would feel elated, irritable, creative, and overactive. At these times she could spend money foolishly, and would work frenetically at her hobbies until near collapse. She thus met the criteria for a diagnosis of Bipolar Disorder II (with Hypomania), Depressed State.

The patient's age and tendency to present herself as relatively free of emotional problems made it difficult to obtain a history. She recalled being a shy early adolescent who became so panicked in the presence of a certain male teacher that she obtained a transfer to another class. She was married to a factory worker in her late teens, and remained married until his death forty years later. She seemed to receive gratification from her roles as homemaker and mother of six children; in addition, she is a talented and successful musician. In recent years, her greatest trials are her social isolation and her protracted mourning for her husband.

Mrs. A. was treated with antidepressant medication and supportive psychotherapy while in the hospital, showing a good treatment response: her Hamilton Rating Scale for Depression moved from a substantial score of 21 to a normal range 5.5 during the course of her two-month hospitalization. She was tested a third time fourteen months after discharge, and judged still euthymic by her psychiatrist; at that time she remained on antidepressant treatment.

Mr. Y. was a fifty-four-year-old married man who was admitted suffering from his first episode of major depressive illness. He had been depressed for over a year, with symptoms of low mood, poor concentration, and lethargy. A recovered alcoholic, his desperation led him to occasional bouts of drinking and barbiturate abuse; his irritability and lack of efficiency at work decreased to the point that he had to be relieved of many of his responsibilities. In the month preceding admission his condition worsened substantially. He claimed to have virtually stopped sleeping; he was never hungry and precipitously lost ten pounds; he wished to die. Most strikingly, Mr. Y. developed a number of persistent and mood-congruent delusions: he was certain that his family had become impoverished, that his wife was dead (her daily visits altered this belief only temporarily), that he was dying, that he had intolerable body odor, and that his future was hopeless. His thinking was loose and his speech was sometimes only marginally coherent, so great was his depressive agitation and preoccupation.

Again, little history could be obtained. Mr. Y. had been employed for thirty years as a bookkeeper for a small firm. He had been married for twenty-five years to a troubled woman, with whom he had three children. Until three years previously he had drunk upwards of a fifth of alcohol daily; he stopped drinking precipitously when one of his children confronted him about it. His family described him as something of a worrier, "the sort of man who keeps everything inside." He had persistent problems with impotence and claimed to have had no sexual relations at all for the two years preceding hospitalization.

Mr. Y. was treated with a course of eight electroconvulsive therapy treatments (the standard treatment for psychotic depression), which rapidly ameliorated his condition. All signs of psychosis disappeared within two weeks and his Hamilton Rating dropped from 29 to 9. He was retested eighteen months after hospitalization while maintained on a moderate dose of a tricyclic antidepressant. His psychiatrist felt that his improvement had continued steadily in the post-hospitalization period.

RORSCHACH FINDINGS

The following discussion will focus on four aspects of the Rorschach performance of our bipolar and unipolar depressives. First we will examine the initial protocol of the unipolar patient, to see how he presented when severely depressed and psychotic. Next we will look at specific percepts longitudinally, through the three testings, in order to observe the recovery and reintegration process. Third, we will examine defensive adaptation and defensive style, using percepts from the two post-episode testings and comparing the two subjects to a limited extent. Finally, we will attempt to address the question of their degree of psychopathology when euthymic, this time using the post-hospitalization testing.

The Depressive Psychotic Episode of Mr. Y.

Constriction is the most striking aspect of the protocol of the in-episode testing of our unipolar, patently delusional patient (see Table 1). The protocol shows no bizarre imagery and an emphasis on popular responses. Six of the ten responses are of acceptable form, three would best be characterized as of weak form, and only one, that of Card

TABLE 1
Rorschach Protocol: Unipolar Endogenous Depressive while in Episode and Psychotic

Card		Inquiry
I.	1.Λ	Bat.
		[(?) The wings. (Points) The body. (?) Feelers. (?) No.]
II.	1.Λ	Elephants.
		[Trunks. The shape of the head. (?) Ears. (?) No.]
III.	1.Λ	Dancing girls. (You may turn the cards if you wish.)
		[The way they are shaped . . . and their breasts. (Dancing?) They don't look like they're dancing . . . (?) they're in a peculiar position. (?) That's all.]
IV.	1.Λ	Bug.
		[Just the shape . . . feelers. Head . . . mouth. (Any special kind of bug?) No. (?) There are the legs here.]
V.	1.Λ	A bat again.
		[Wing, and antennae. (?) Tail.]
VI.	1.Λ	Bearskin.
		[It's stretched out. (?) It just looks like a bear skin. (Any particular parts?) It's just the skin stretched out.]
VII.	1.Λ	Three girls.
		[Just the face . . . and the bust line. (?) No . . . they've got a funny hairdo. (?) No.]
VIII.	1.Λ	A bug.
		[It's just a peculiar shape . . . I can't describe it. I don't know what kind of bug it is. (Parts of the bug?) Not really. Why are you writing? Are you writing down the things I say? (Yes, to help me remember later.)]
IX.	1.Λ	Sea horses.
		[It's the shape here . . . and it looks like coral here. (?) Just shape . . . face and body. (Coral?) It's the color and the shape.]
X.	1.Λ	A pagoda. Do you know what that is? (Tell me.) It's a temple, oriental.
		[Temple—here . . . it looks oriental. (?) It's just the shape that does. Here's the temple and these are the decorations . . . oriental.] (Dr)

VIII, is of vague or poor form. The responses are unelaborated and simplistic, with vagueness in the inquiry that makes one wonder what is being concealed. There is a preoccupation with sexual content, but the imagery is relatively restrained, unlike the unfettered libidinal displays of many psychotic protocols. More worrisome signs include a moderate amount of suspiciousness about the verbatim recording procedure, voiced on Card VIII, and the emphasis on Card VI on the animal skin which is "stretched out," in a way that may bespeak an anxious loss of control.

Certainly this is a protocol that most clinicians would see as distinctly psychopathological, with its impoverishment of response, sterotypy, perseveration on poorly seen "bugs," and its scant use of color and movement. The bleak monotony of the tone of the protocol might well make one pick up on the centrality of depression in this clinical picture. One would probably not be so certain, however, that the patient was psychotic. The power of the depression seems to take precedence over that of the psychosis in this case. Indeed, this protocol looks remarkably like the constricted record of our similarly depressed but nonpsychotic bipolar patient. She too produced only ten responses, with seven of them being of acceptable form, five populars, and eight F responses. These data give rise to at least some question about the way a psychotic Rorschach can look in a depressive. Rapaport, Gill, and Schafer (1945) do note that the retardation of depressive psychotics leads to stereotyped response, a high F percentage and low M production, all of which are present in Mr. Y.'s protocol. On the other hand, these authors also suggest that a substantial degree of psychotic idiosyncrasy is often present, for instance pure C responses or entirely arbitrary form; nothing like this can be seen in Mr. Y.'s record.

The Recovery and Reintegration Process

A second major point illustrated by these protocols is the dramatic enlivening of the perceptual processes as the patients recover. The hesitancy, constriction, and generally retarded quality of response lift palpably through the three testings. The monotony is shed, and the defensive uniqueness of the individual returns. The Card V responses of each patient amply illustrate this point (see Table 2).

The unipolar man when acutely ill produces an absolutely unelaborated popular bat. His discharge percept is of "another bat," indicating at least some conscious awareness of his tendency to stereotyped, perhaps perseverative response; it should be noted that the recent ECT treatments could be contributing to organic signs like perseveration at this testing (though some perseveration was also present at the first testing). There is an obvious lifting of psychomotor retardation in the patient's willingness to turn the card, though he produces no additional response. On inquiry, the locations are elaborated this time. As yet, however, no determinants besides form contribute to the percept. In contrast, the post-hospitalization administration yields two animal movement responses. Again, the first response is a bat, which may to some extent be perseverative. Then the patient apparently twirls the card around with a flourish, a testament to his lively approach to the task. In 180° rotation the blot becomes a butterfly, perhaps a significant metaphor for the complete transformation the patient feels he has made. On inquiry, the shapes of the percepts are more articulated than in the second administration. The bat is seen flying. Most interesting is the butterfly, which is clearly elaborated as a Monarch butterfly, certainly one of the showiest, most self-satisfied creatures ever to emerge from a cocoon. This butterfly, however, is still on the verge of its rebirth: "Poised, as though it's on the edge of waiting to take off." So it would seem that the somber bat has flown off, with a butterfly on the edge of full vitality replacing it.

The bipolar patient first sees the card vaguely as a "bird of some kind." On inquiry the form is very little elaborated. A question presumably designed to test the limits of the patient's flat, stereotyped response pattern asks for a particular kind of bat. To this the patient responds with what appears to be a neologism, telling the examiner that the percept is "a vulcan." Interestingly, this patient, who seemed nonpsychotic to the large team of clinicians working with her, produces a neologism. Even if the neologism does not connote frank psychosis in this case, it does indicate the substantial level of defensive disorganization present during the acute depressive episode. One might further surmise that a "vulcan" is a close relative of a vulture, with all the grisly, oral aggressive, and depressive connotations of a bird that feeds on carrion. At the discharge testing, the Card V percept is firmly, perhaps peremptorily delivered: "That's one bat." The elaboration is fuller than in the first testing, though still idiosyncratic. There is an emphasis on legs sticking out, which may have a phallic meaning. The head has "some kind of prongs," again potentially phallic, while adding an oral aggressive element. In general, the patient finds the percept "repulsive," and lends bats a foreboding and pathologically personalized quality as she describes them flying at dusk and hitting her in the hair. This bat is "batty," she adds, indicating a defensive vagueness, perhaps about its sinister quality; a perceptual diffuseness and possibly a continuing trend to misuse language; and, finally, a likely colloquial self-description of a woman in her seventies in her first psychiatric hospitalization. This patient's response to Card V at the post-hospitalization testing is a more equivocal "bat, I think." The inquiry then proceeds in a straightforward manner. She points out the legs, wings, and head, and then, on further questioning, says the bat is flying. Thus, as she recovers, this patient, like the last, proceeds from an unelaborated, motionless creature, to an elaborated one, to one clearly in flight. Data such as these seem to support the convincingness of the psychobiological cure in enlivening the self- and object world of depressives.

TABLE 2

Card V Responses at Each Testing for Both Subjects

Mr. Y. (Unipolar Endogenous Depressive)

Depressed State:

1.Λ   A bat again.
      Wing, and antennae. (?) Tail.

At Discharge, in Remission

1.Λ   Another bat. (Turns card sideways, then right side up again.) Again, it's the shape of the wings. Here are the feet going out . . . Head . . . Antennae. (?) The shape of the wings, feet, head, antennae.

Post-Hospitalization, in Remission

1.Λ   A bat. I see a bat again. (He twirls the card around.)
2.V   And this way a butterfly, and that's all I see.
      Again the outline. This one is more distinguished. There's the elongated tail, large wings, and head and antennae. And it's flying. (Butterfly?) The wings. It's in a different position from the bat and the antennae is different from the bat. It looks like it could be a Monarch butterfly. (?) The general shape of it. (?) Poised, as though it's on the edge of waiting to take off.

(Continued)

TABLE 2 (Continued)

Mrs. A. (Bipolar Endogenous Depressive)

Depressed State

1.Λ   A bird of some kind.
       The legs and the wings. (?) No. (Any particular kind of bird?)
       Oh . . . a vulcan? . . . or something . . . (?) I guess that's a
       kind of bird. (?) No.

At Discharge, in Remission

1.Λ   That's one bat.
       Yes . . . Here's the legs. The head with some kind of prongs.
       The legs are out here. They must have legs. Anyway . . . it
       looks a little repulsive. (?) Just the batty look. If you've ever
       seen them flying at dusk . . . It would be awful if one were to
       hit your hair.

Post-Hospitalization, in Remission

1.Λ   That's a bat I think. (?) No. That's it.
       Here are the legs. Here are the wings, and this is the head.
       (And how do you see the bat?) I would say it would be flying.
       Yes, I see it flying.

Defensive Adaptation and Style

     The next aspect of the functioning of depressives to be illustrated is that of defensive adaptation and style. This aspect of the data will be examined with primary reference to the two remission testings, in that the initial protocols seem too colored by depression to accurately characterize defensive style. Specifically, we will consider Card VI in both patients (see Table 3).

     The bipolar patient rejected Card VI entirely at the first testing, perhaps indicating a profoundly complete and primitive denial operating against the phallic properties of the blot. When she was recovered enough for discharge, she delivered a relatively disturbed response, setting the stage with an affectively laden exclamation. The first percept is an animal skin, seen in the usual location. On free association, she sees the skin improbably "clinging," indicating a likely confusion between hides and animals, things dead and alive. On inquiry, the clinging aspect is not elaborated, but the furry texture and "stretched" quality are, in a way which gives a dependent and anxious cast to her state at this time. Again, her explanations are personalized, even somewhat autistic: the percept is the way it is "because that's how I've seen them." The "snake's head [with] bulging eyes and so on" is a patent and phobic phallic response defended against by the previous denials and anxious, dependent themes. At the post-hospitalization testing the tone is angry and externalized. After the longest latency to any card, she poses an oppositional, irritated question: "Are we supposed to see living things?" Perhaps this reflects a suppressed percept with the animate-inanimate confusion described above, or perhaps it is a reference to an all-too-alive erect penis in the area where the snake's head was previously seen. The exclamations, externalizations, and denials then proceed almost humorously from the mouth of this feisty, somewhat prim elderly woman: "I see nothing else. I don't know what you get out of

TABLE 3

Card VI Responses at Remission Testings for Both Subjects

Mrs. A. (Bipolar Endogenous Depressive)

At Discharge, in Remission

1.Λ   Oh . . . oh dear! A skin or hide of some kind of animal . . . but I don't know what it's clinging to.

2.V   That looks like the head of a reptile.
   I think it's with the furry side up, probably stretched to dry. I don't know why there's a snake's head up here . . . I can't figure it out. (Furry?) It's got a furry texture, that you can see. (Stretched?) That's the way I've seen them tacked up on barn doors to dry. (?) That's how I've seen them. (Snake's head?) Up here. This part looks like a reptile. (?) I don't know. Something about the bulging eyes and so on. (?) No.

Post-Hospitalization, in Remission

1.Λ   Are we supposed to see living things? (Whatever it looks like to you.) I don't care for this one. It doesn't look like anything to me but an inkblot. Those might be legs and that might be a head, but I don't know what it is.
   (?) Those are the legs and the head but I see nothing else. I don't know what you get out of these, but they're certainly tiresome for me. I really would like lunch.

(Continued)

TABLE 3 (Continued)

Mr. Y. (Unipolar Endogenous Depressive)

At Discharge, in Remission

1.Λ   Bearskin rug.

It's the general shape. This looks like the front paws. That's about it. (Anything else other than the shape that made it look like a bearskin rug?) No. (?) Just the four feet. (?) This could be the head.

Post-Hospitalization, in Remission

1.Λ   A bearskin. Not a beerskin, but a b-e-a-r skin. (Laughs.)

2.V   An old man with a beard. And that's all I see.

It's the outline. And the coloring I'd say too, and the fur. (What made it look like fur?) Well, the shades in it, and this is the backbone, and it's in a different color coming into the legs, and the head is also missing. (What made it look like an old man with a beard?) Well, the bulk of the head, and the long beard and shaggy hair. (Shaggy?) The irregularities in the back of his head. He has a shaggy head and shaggy beard. And it looks like he's sitting at a table eating. Not on the table, but sitting on a chair. (Can you show me how you see that?) I can't explain it. But, well, there's the position of his head and arms. His head is tilted back and his arms are leaning forward and he's getting food. (Dr: Side projection is the table, beard slightly above it in inverted position.)

---

these, but they're certainly tiresome for me. I really would like lunch." This woman seems to have reconstituted with a set of primitive hysteriform defenses, helped along with an externalized irritability.

In a number of respects, this patient is stylistically characteristic of our bipolar group, which now numbers eleven. Generally, the records of our recovered bipolars showed some aspects of the superficial adaptation with which other authors have credited them. Their responses were frequently stereotyped, with many populars or near-populars, and primarily animal content. Defensively, reaction-formation and denial were prevalent; primitive denial was sometimes reflected in responses in which acceptable percepts were spoiled (Lerner, Sugarman, and Gaughran, 1981). Overall, their percepts had much of the vagueness, phobic quality, emotionality, personalization, and color reactivity that other authors have found characteristic of the hysterical personality style (Ludolph, 1981). In this regard, our findings parallel those of Donnelly, Murphy, and Scott (1975) to a considerable extent.

Turning now to our unipolar patient, we find that he sees Card VI as a bearskin when depressed. His anxiety and general distress emerge in an elaboration of the bearskin as "stretched." At discharge, the patient gives the same response in a somewhat more comforting form: "Bearskin rug." On inquiry, he makes clear that the only determinant at this point is form. At the post-hospitalization testing, he begins with a "bearskin" and moves to an idiosyncratic percept (Dr) of "an old man with a beard." He first remarks that it is "not a beerskin, but a 'b-e-a-r skin,'" an ironic reference to his history of alcoholism, with an intellectualized, somewhat controlling, and demeaning flourish in his spelling of bear. On inquiry, he starts well, omitting the "stretched" aspect which characterized his second response, and adding a clear reference to the furry texture. He then elaborates that there is a backbone and that the hair is missing. The presence, and certainly the visibility, of a backbone in a bearskin is improbable; the missing head likely indicates either castration anxiety or more primitive concerns with part objects, or both. The percept of the old man also contains perceptual inaccuracies, in that it is elaborated without due concern for the realities of the form of the blot. The man is seen "eating," one of several percepts involving orality and oral aggression. Overall, the post-hospitalization responses to Card VI do portray a man with obsessional traits such as intellectualization and meticulousness. Unfortunately, what is elaborated seems to spoil the responses rather than complete them, or to add more primitive oral concerns. The emphasis on shading and body damage also lends a depressive cast to the profile.

Our sixteen unipolar endogenous patients were more difficult to characterize than the bipolars, in part because they seemed to represent a more diffuse group. Stylistically, they appeared more obsessional than the bipolars, with evidence of isolation of affect around themes of sexuality, body damage, and oral aggression. In this respect, Mr. Y.'s protocol is illustrative of the group. In other ways, however, it is unusual. Most significantly, Mr. Y.'s protocol seems to us healthier than many in his cohort, and this despite his evident tendency to spoil responses. Many of the other remitted unipolar protocols show much more patent defensive failure, which makes stylistic issues difficult to assess. We plan further data analyses to try to draw more definitive conclusions about the defensive adaptation of the unipolar group.

Interepisode Psychopathology

The final issue we wish to address involves the level of characterological psychopathology these patients manifest after recovery. As we stated at the outset, this is a matter of considerable theoretical interest, as psychobiologists would prefer to see these patients as well functioning, while psychoanalysts would postulate an euthymic condition more continuous with the depressed state. Our preliminary data seem more in line with the predictions of the psychoanalytic group. While far more lively and engaging in euthymia, these patients manifest distinct indicators of psychopathology. Responses to the Rorschach at the posthospitalization condition will illustrate our point for both these patients (see Table 4).

The bipolar patient begins with a percept which illustrates the oral dependent and aggressive strivings which Cohen et al. (1954) attributed to this group. The response seems to start as an attempt to produce some kind of popular winged creature, but it quickly deteriorates as the patient focuses on the way the creature is "hanging onto something." This forces her to a somewhat peculiar fabulized combination, involving a birdlike creature with "two pairs of paws," (Klopfer d3 and d5) "all gripping the center thing." Exactly what is being grasped remains unclear, but it seems an intangible, not very trustworthy source of support. The creature, too, becomes an insubstantial shadow: this could well indicate a difficulty in seeing objects as whole and fleshed out, in separating the abstract and intangible from the concrete and solid (Fast, 1969).

The bipolar patient again produces a mildly fabulized combination to Card II: "two animals with funny turbans and blank faces." She appears relatively comfortable with her unusual juxtaposition of human and animal traits: indeed, when asked about the turbans, she snaps, "It's just the way it looks." She thus twists reality around to suit her in a manner that certainly has an externalized, characterological feel to it. Secondly, the faces are "blank," further pointing to the dehumanized object world this woman lives in. Not only is her own experience pervaded by repressed and denied feelings, but others are blankly anonymous and inaccessible to her. The justification for the blank appearance of the faces seems to be that "it doesn't show their faces," another piece of peculiar logic which indicates a difficulty in object constancy and a pathologically personalized viewpoint; presum-

TABLE 4

Selected Responses, Post-Hospitalization Testings

Mrs. A. (Bipolar Endogenous Depressive)

I.   1.Λ   Some kind of funny bird hanging onto something. (Turns card.) And that's all I can see. Maybe they're creatures instead of birds. They have more limbs than birds. Yes, yes, it looks like two pairs of paws, all gripping the center thing. (You said it was funny at first?) Well, it's just the shadow of the whole creature, not the whole thing.

II.   1.Λ   It seems like there are always two of something. These look like animals of some kind, two animals with funny turbans and blank faces, I guess. (Some people see more than one thing. Do you see anything else?) No, I don't think so. (?) Well, it doesn't show their faces. They have blank faces, but the turbans are up here. (What made it look like a turban?) It's just the way it looks. Two animals wearing turbans.

IV.   1.V   I guess that might be an eruption, but I don't know what it is.

       2.V   Maybe some kind of animal. (Briskly returns card to the table.) (Eruption?) Just here. It isn't really an eruption . . . but that's what I see. (?) The whole thing would be the eruption, like what comes out of an eruption. (Animal?) Oh, I don't think so. No.

IX.   1.Λ   Oh, how fancy . . . well the colors are so pretty, but I don't see anything. I don't see any animals. It's blue-green. Green-blue. If this were in the sky it would be a cloud. That's all. It's pretty like clouds. (What made it look like a cloud?) Just the color. It's like the blue you sometimes see: a shadowed cloud, a heavy cloud. Underneath is the shadows from the clouds. That's what you see when you're on the ground.

(Continued)

TABLE 4 (Continued)

Mr. Y. (Unipolar Endogenous Depressive)

III.   1.Λ   (In a booming voice) Dancing girls! (He twirls the card around.) I forgot I could turn it.

2.V   Oh, I see . . . well, it could be a pair of deer heads . . .

3.V   And palm trees. There's a lot in this one.

4.Λ   And a butterfly. (He twirls the card around again.) That's about it.

First girls because they have breasts and they look like they have slender legs, the way dancing girls do. (Chuckles.) And the outline of the head. And in that position they look like they're dancing. (?) No details. (Deer?) Why, those two there. The antlers are up in there. (What made it look like deer?) The antlers. Their heads are pointing toward each other like they might be in a battle of some kind. (Palm trees?) This one and that one. In the wind. The wind is blowing them over. (What made it look that way?) The silhouette. I've seen them in Florida. Florida, the land of palm trees. The shape looks like the wind's blowing it, the leaves, and the trunk, and bending it over. (Butterfly?) Yep. Right here. Just the shape of it, the shape of the wings. (How do you see it?) Flying. And that's it.

IX.   1.Λ   (He twirls the card around again for some time before beginning.) Crabs.

2.V   And buffaloes. And that's it. (Turns over the card.) The crabs are right here. (?) The outline of it, with no detail. (How did you see it?) With its antennae protruding and searching for food. (Searching?) The general position of the antennae. It looks like they're extended. It's feeling for something, and it probably will be food. (Buffalo?) Just the outline. And the shagginess of the head that the buffalo has. And the bump underneath is its mouth. They always have that too. (Shaggy?) The irregularity of the outline, you know. It's poised, still poised.

X.   1.Λ   That's pretty! I see crabs again.

(Continued)

TABLE 4 (Continued)

2.Λ   And sea horses. And that's all. (He turns the card and places it on top of the others, neatly arranging the pile.) (Crabs?) Just the general outline. (How do you see them?) They're eating. There's the food. They have it in their claws. (Sea horse?) The countours . . . upright. It's elongated, with a long snout and a curled tail. (What makes it look curled?) Because it goes around like that and sea horses are in an upright position. Sitting still . . . sitting very still.

---

ably, the patient feels that if faces are out of view, if she cannot see them, then they must be expressionless.

To Card IV Mrs. A. gives a tentative response of an amorphous "eruption." On inquiry, she seems to try to reject the response, but cannot, so instead resorts to one of her pathologically personalized justifications: "It isn't really an eruption . . . but that's what I see." Another response, of "animals of some kind," is then retracted. The eruption response stands as a testament to this patient's ego weakness, her lack of affect modulation and perhaps of impulse control. That the response worries her indicates her marginal contact with nonpsychotic reality, but she stands in unsteady balance, reminding us of those shadowy Card I creatures grasping for an ephemeral support. One wonders whether this response reflects this patient's enduring struggle with hypomania and depression, with an accompanying sense that her psychic structure might "erupt" at any moment. One also notes her likely difficulty with the phallic properties of this blot, similar to the conflict on Card VI; the hysteriform edge to her personality thus surfaces again.

Card IX also displays this patient's difficulty modulating and integrating affect, this time in her unrestrained response to color. She begins with a hysteroid exclamation about the pretty colors. She continues with a negation of animal content, which conveys a mildly perseverative trend in that, of course, no one told her to see animals. The percept she ultimately delivers is somewhere midway between a pure color response and a color-form response, only taking on the vague shape of a cloud after considerable color naming. The elaboration seems to indicate that shading is also a determinant, making this a color-shading response of the kind Appelbaum and Holzman (1962) have associated with suicidality. This particular patient does not support their hypothesis, however, in that she produced color-shading responses to Card IX at discharge and post-hospitalization testings, when she was not depressed or suicidal. When she was depressed and preoccupied with thoughts of death, the protocol was very constricted, and there were no color-shading responses. Thematically, the response does have a distinctly depressive mood, as Mrs. A. describes a "shadowed cloud, a heavy cloud," perhaps reflecting an enduring depressive cast to her personality. Additionally, she sees a shadow, once again indicating her preoccupation with the insubstantial rather than with the tangible.

In sum, this patient seems to be functioning at a borderline level, with evidence of primitive defenses like low-level denial and suppression of response; instances of defensive failures; lack of affect modulation; conflicts concerning oral dependent strivings; marginal difficulties with reality testing; and an impoverished, inaccessible object world (Lerner and Lerner, 1980; Smith, 1980; Sugarman, 1980).

The unipolar patient is expansive and very pleased with himself as he approaches the post-hospitalization Rorschach; sometimes his excitement almost seems to have a counterdepressive, hypomanic edge, though this patient has no history of mania. Despite this, one sees a number of areas of intrapsychic conflict in his percepts. On Card III he sees dancing girls, identified most prominently by their breasts. This sexual content, together with a number of other percepts of animals with protruding snouts and tails, indicates a substantial degree of preoccupation and conflict around sexual themes; this finding makes sense in light of the patient's ongoing impotence. The next percept of Card III is deer heads, not well seen, with "heads pointing toward each other like they might be in a battle of some kind." Themes of phallic aggression and castration seem patent here. Then Mr. Y. sees palm trees "in the wind. The wind is blowing them over." Here is the tension of inanimate movement, and one wonders about his anxious experience of the affective winds that buffet him.

Card IX illustrates another side to this man's conflict. He sees crabs with "antennae protruding and searching for food . . . feeling for something." We see the concern with things protruding, but here in a distinctly oral aggressive context. There is a starkness to this image that evokes a primeval, omnivorous hunger. The buffalo which are seen next have three major characteristics. First, they are shaggy around the edges, a response that does not quite admit texture, reminiscent of the shaggy beard on Card VI. Likewise the buffalo are "poised," in other words, not quite moving. And finally, they have very distinct mouths. Most of the same themes are then repeated on Card X, where there are crabs eating with their claws, and sea horses "sitting still . . . sitting very still." One can surmise that this man exhibits a characterological isolation and constriction of affective experience that will not admit sensual or vulnerable feelings into consciousness. His sexual life is barren underneath his hearty bravado, and he finds any degree of dependency threatening. Objects in his world seem real and available, but the idea of full emotional engagement with them is frightening; thus, he and his objects must remain poised on the edge of full engagement. Sometimes more intense involvement seems imminent and possible, as with the Card V butterfly waiting to take off; other times Mr. Y.'s object world appears more static and less hopeful, for instance when he portrays the starkly immobile sea horses. One remains unsure here how much this patient is still in the process of recovery from depression, and how much his defensive stance is more entrenched and characterological. Speaking to the more characterological hypothesis is the degree of orality in the protocol, particularly the oral aggression. To fully feel his interpersonal world might well mean the unleashing of raw, omnivorous impulses that would threaten to overwhelm him.

Our sense is that Mr. Y. is a severely neurotic man with largely obsessional defenses and conflicts centering on both oral and phallic aggression. He seems to have a predominantly sound self-structure, but is plagued with defensive inhibitions that render him unable to experience fully the vitality of human relationships and gratifications. As noted earlier, he cannot be seen as characteristic of the unipolar group, as many subjects in his cohort showed flaws in self-structure, with substantial deficits in reality testing, affective integration, and defensive organization.

TENTATIVE CONCLUSIONS

Although this data analysis is preliminary and relies mostly on anecdotal evidence, we may draw certain tentative conclusions from the Rorschachs. First, we examined the record of the psychotically depressed unipolar patient while he was ill, and found it simplistic and constricted. Interestingly, it was without bizarre imagery, arbitrary form, or most other standard indices of psychotic decompensation. This case would indicate that the Rorschach presentation of psychotic depressives merits further study.

Second, we used a longitudinal analysis of the Rorschach percepts of each patient (at admission, discharge, and at least a year after discharge) to observe the recovery process after severe depression. Detailed examination of percepts to Card V revealed a clear enlivening of the self- and object worlds of these patients as they reintegrated. When depressed they saw unelaborated, motionless creatures, which were elaborated by discharge, and seen in motion by the post-hospitalization testing. Since both patients were treated almost exclusively with somatic treatments, these data speak to the clear and positive effect of such treatments on intrapsychic representation as measured by the Rorschach.

The third issue addressed in the findings concerns the defensive adaptation and style of the two patients. We found the unipolar patient obsessional in style, with defenses involving meticulousness and intellectualization. This finding generally supported the literature on the interepisode personality style of unipolar endogenous depressives. The bipolar patient was hysteroid in style, with relatively infantile defenses centering on denial and externalization. As such, she typified the subgroup of bipolars in the larger study we are conducting; these data also supported the findings of the Donnelly group on the interepisode personalities of bipolar patients.

Last we briefly examined the level of psychopathology indicated on the third testings, when the patients had been nondepressed for at least a year. While more lively and engaging at this time, our subjects still manifested distinct indicators of psychopathology. The bipolar patient appeared to be functioning at a borderline level in terms of defenses, conflicts, and object relations. The unipolar patient seemed a severe obsessional neurotic with much defensive inhibition. This finding suggests that in at least two cases the psychobiological cure is not as complete as some would argue. Clearly, much more data must be collected before this finding can be safely generalized. Further investigation is also indicated to determine how much of the post-episode psychopathology arises from premorbid disposition, and how much from the disorganizing effect of the episode itself.

References

Akiskal, H. S., Hirschfeld, R. M. A., & Yerevanian, B. I. (1983), The relationship of personality to affective disorders: A critical review. *Arch. Gen. Psychiat.,* 40:801–810.

Anthony, E. J. (1975), The influence of a manic-depressive environment on the developing child. In: *Depression and Human Existence,* ed. E. J. Anthony & T. Benedek. Boston: Little, Brown, pp. 279–315.

Appelbaum, S. A., & Holzman, P. S. (1962), The color shading response and suicide. *J. Proj. Tech. & Personal. Assess.,* 26:155–161.

Biegel, A., & Murphy, D. (1971), Unipolar and bipolar affective illness. *Arch. Gen. Psychiat.*, 24:215–220.

Blatt, S., Brenneis, C. B., Schimek, J. G., & Glick, M. (1976), Normal development and psychopathological impairment of the concept of the object on the Rorschach. *J. Abnorm. Psychol.*, 85:364–373.

Carroll, B. J., Feinberg, M., Greden, J. F., et al. (1981), A specific laboratory test for the diagnosis of melancholia. *Arch. Gen. Psychiat.*, 38:15–22.

Chodoff, P. (1972), The depressive personality. *Arch. Gen. Psychiat.*, 27:666–673.

Cohen, M. B., Baker, G., Cohen, R. A., Fromm-Reichmann, F., & Weigert, E. V. (1954), An intensive study of twelve cases of manic-depressive psychosis. *Psychiatry*, 17:103–138.

Coppen, A., & Metcalfe, M. (1965), Effect of a depressive illness on MPI scores. *Brit. J. Psychiat.*, 111:236–239.

Donnelly, E. F., Goodwin, F. K., Waldman, I. N., & Murphy, D. L. (1978), Prediction of antidepressant responses to lithium. *Amer. J. Psychiat.*, 135:552–556.

———— Murphy, D. L. (1973a), Primary affective disorder: MMPI differences between unipolar and bipolar depressed subjects. *J. Clin. Psychol.*, 29:303–306.

———— ———— (1973b), Social desirability and bipolar affective disorder. *J. Consult. Clin. Psychol.*, 41:469.

———— ———— (1974), Primary affective disorder: Bender-Gestalt sequence as an indicator of impulse control. *Percep. & Mot. Skill*, 38:1079–1082.

———— ———— Goodwin, F. K. (1976), Cross-sectional and longitudinal comparisons of bipolar depressed groups on the MMPI. *J. Consult. & Clin. Psychol.*, 44:233–237.

———— ———— Scott, W. H. (1975), Perception and cognition in patients with bipolar and unipolar depressive disorders. *Arch. Gen. Psychiat.*, 32:1128–1131.

———— ———— Waldman, I. N., & Reynolds, T. (1976), MMPI differences between unipolar and bipolar depressed subjects: A replication. *J. Clin. Psychol.*, 32:610–612.

———— ———— ———— Goodwin, F. K. (1979), Prediction of antidepressant responses to imipramine. *Neuropsychobiology*, 5:94–101.

Fast, I. (1969), Concrete and abstract thought: An alternate formulation. *J. Proj. Tech. & Personal. Assess.*, 33:331–335.

Freud, S. (1914), On narcissism: An introduction. *Standard Edition*, 14:73–102. London: Hogarth Press, 1957.

———— (1917), Mourning and melancholia. *Standard Edition*, 14:243–258. London: Hogarth Press, 1957.

Gibson, R. W. (1958), The family background and early life experience of the manic-depressive patient: A comparison with the schizophrenic patient. *Psychiatry*, 21:71–90.

Greenson, R. (1958), On screen defenses, screen hunger, and screen identity. *J. Amer. Psychoanal. Assn.*, 6:242–262.

Hamilton, M. (1960), A rating scale for depression. *J. Neurol. Neurosurg. & Psychiat.*, 23:56–62.

Hirschfeld, M. A., & Cross, C. K. (1982), Epidemiology of affective disorders: Psychosocial risk factors. *Arch. Gen. Psychiat.*, 39:35–46.

———— Klerman, G. L. (1979), Personality attributes and affective disorders. *Amer. J. Psychiat.*, 136:67–70.

———— ———— Clayton, P. J., & Keller, M. B. (1983), Personality and depression: Empirical findings. *Arch. Gen. Psychiat.*, 40:993–998.

Jacobson, E. (1953), Contributions to the metapsychology of cyclothymic depression. In: *Affective Disorders*, ed. P. Greenacre. New York: International Universities Press, pp. 49–83.

Julian, T., Metcalfe, M., & Coppen, A. (1969), Aspects of personality of depressive patients. *Brit. J. Psychiat.*, 115:587-589.

Kendell, R., & DiScipio, W. (1968), Eysenck Personality Inventory scores of patients with depressive illnesses. *Brit. J. Psychiat.*, 114:767-770.

——— ——— (1970), Obsessional symptoms and obsessional personality traits in patients with depressive illnesses. *Psychol. Med.*, 1:65-72.

Kerr, T., Schapira, K., Roth, M., & Garside, R. (1970), The relationship between the Maudsley Personality Inventory and the course of affective disorders. *Brit. J. Psychiat.*, 116:11-19.

Kiloh, L. G., Andrews, G., Neilson, M., & Bianchi, G. N. (1972), The relationship of the syndromes called endogenous and neurotic depression. *Brit. J. Psychiat.*, 121:183-196.

——— Garside, R. (1963), The independence of neurotic depression and endogenous depression. *Brit. J. Psychiat.*, 109:451-463.

Klein, D. F., Gittelman, R., Quitkin, F., & Rifkin, A. (1980), *Diagnosis and Drug Treatment of Psychiatric Disorders: Adults and Children*, 2nd ed. Baltimore: Williams & Wilkins.

Klopfer, B., Ainsworth, M. D. Klopfer, W. G., & Holt, R. R. (1954), *Developments in the Rorschach Technique: Vol. 1*. New York: Harcourt, Brace.

Krohn, A., & Mayman, M. (1974), Object representations in dreams and projective tests. *Bull. Menn. Clin.*, 38:445-466.

Lerner, H., Sugarman, A., & Gaughran, J. (1981), Borderline and schizophrenic patients: A comparative study of defensive structure. *J. Nerv. Ment. Dis.*, 169:705-711.

Lerner, P., & Lerner, H. (1980), Rorschach assessment of primitive defenses in borderline personality structure. In: *Borderline Phenomena and the Rorschach Test*, ed. J. Kwawer, H. Lerner, P. Lerner, & A. Sugarman. New York: International Universities Press, pp. 257-274.

Ludolph, P. S. (1981), The dissociative tendency: Its relationship to personality style and psychopathology. Unpublished dissertation, University of Michigan.

MacVane, J., Lange, J., Brown, W., & Zayat, M. (1978), Psychological functioning of bipolar manic-depressives in remission. *Arch. Gen. Psychiat.*, 35:1351-1354.

Mattussek, P., & Feil, W. B. (1983), Personality attributes of depressive patients: Results of group comparisons. *Arch. Gen. Psychiat.*, 40:783-790.

Mendels, J., Weinstein, N., & Cochrane, C. (1972), The relationship between depression and anxiety. *Arch. Gen. Psychiat.*, 27:649-653.

Milden, R. S. (1984), Affective disorders and narcissistic vulnerability. *Amer. J. Psychoanal.*, 44:345-353.

Murray, L., & Blackburn, I. (1974), Personality differences in patients with depressive illness and anxiety neurosis. *Acta Psychiatr. Scand.*, 50:183-191.

Paykel, E. S. (1971), Classification of depressed patients: A cluster analysis derived grouping. *Brit. J. Psychiat.*, 118:275-288.

——— (1972), Depressive typologies and response to amitriptyline. *Brit. J. Psychiat.*, 120:147-156.

——— Prusoff, B. A. (1973), Response set and observer set in the assessment of depressed patients. *Psychol. Med.*, 5:13-17.

——— ——— Klerman, G. L., Haskell, D., & DiMascio, A. (1973), Clinical response to amitriptyline among depressed women. *J. Nerv. & Ment. Dis.*, 156:149-165.

Perris, C. (1966), A study of bipolar (manic-depressive) and unipolar recurrent depressive psychoses: IV. A multidimensional study of personality traits. *Acta Psychiatr. Scand.*, 42:68-82.

_____ (1971), Personality patterns in patients with affective disorders. *Acta Psychiatr. Scand.,* 47:43–51.

Rapaport, D., Gill, M., & Schafer, R. (1945), *Diagnostic Psychological Testing.* Rev. ed. New York: International Universities Press, 1968.

Roth, M., Gurney, C., Garside, R., & Kerr, T. (1972), Studies in the classification of affective disorders: The relationship between anxiety states and depressive illnesses—I. *Brit. J. Psychiat.,* 121:147–161.

Roy, A. (1979), Are there different types of neurotic depression? *Brit. J. Med. Psychol.,* 52:147–150.

Schapira, K., Roth, M., Kerr, T. A., & Gurney, C. (1972), The prognosis of affective disorders: The differentiation of anxiety states from depressive illnesses. *Brit. J. Psychiat.,* 121:175–181.

Smith, K. (1980), Object relations concepts as applied to the borderline level of ego functioning. In: *Borderline Phenomena and the Rorschach Test,* ed. J. Kwawer, H. Lerner, P. Lerner, & A. Sugarman. New York: International Universities Press, pp. 59–87.

Spielberger, C. D., Parker, J. B., & Becker, J. (1963), Conformity and achievement in remitted manic-depressive patients. *J. Nerv. & Ment. Dis.,* 137:162–172.

Spitzer, R. L., & Endicott, J. (1978), *Schedule for Affective Disorders and Schizophrenia.* 3rd ed. New York: New York State Psychiatric Institute.

_____ _____ Robins, E. (1978), *Research Diagnostic Criteria.* New York: Biometrics Research, Evaluation Section, New York State Psychiatric Institute.

Sugarman, A. (1980), The borderline personality organization as manifested on psychological tests. In: *Borderline Phenomena and the Rorschach Test,* ed. J. Kwawer, H. Lerner, P. Lerner, & A. Sugarman. New York: International Universities Press, pp. 39–57.

Titley, W. (1936), Prepsychotic personality of patients with involutional melancholia. *Arch. Neurol. & Psychiat.,* 36:19–33.

Zerssen, D. von (1977), Premorbid personality and affective psychoses. In: *Handbook of Studies on Depression,* ed. G. Burrows. New York: Excerpta Medica.

Chapter 19

Transmission of Psychopathology

Mary M. Gallagher
Barbara R. Slater

It is possible to perceive of pathological thought processes as an adaptation to disordered transactions within the family context across generations, and to trace the origins of later borderline characteristics to pregenital problems in the psychological processes of separation-individuation. In order to maintain fragile object constancy in adult social relations, the grown child may extend the original mother-child interactions by selecting a spouse possessing essential personality characteristics of the mother. Within the alcoholic family constellation, this reenactment process can be exaggerated as a result of the personality characteristics of the alcoholic. To illustrate these concepts, the Rorschach protocols of a mother-adult son-son's spouse triad are presented and analyzed.

TRANSACTIONAL NATURE OF PSYCHOPATHOLOGY

Psychopathology has traditionally been perceived as an outcome of insoluble intrapsychic conflicts. In contrast, the dialectical or transactional orientation concludes that psychopathology may be the manifestation of a disordered relationship with symptomatology existing as a function of the relationship context and, therefore, as an interpersonal resolution of inner conflict (Boszormenyi-Nagy, 1965; Bowen, 1965). The assignment of a role of projective transference distortions in a family or a social transaction represents an unconscious attempt "to master, reenact, or externalize their intrapsychic conflicts" around needs stemming from "relationship experiences in the family of origin" (Framo, 1965, p. 274). Wolin, Bennett, Koonan, and Deltenbaum (1980) expressed the opinion that, from a family systems perspective, the pathology associated with alcoholics "becomes so intertwined with the functioning of the family that the pathology cannot be isolated from family interaction and behavior" (p. 200).

Psychoanalytic theory, while emphasizing that the preservation of the family is assured by the resolution of the Oedipus complex (Freud, 1913), has failed to examine sufficiently the transaction dynamics of the family and its impact on the individual (Boszormenyi-Nagy, 1965; Framo, 1965). With the evolvement of object relations theory, an explanation for the source of irrational family role assignments and intrafamilial transferences is available. Fairbairn (1952) contended that the fundamental motive of life is man's need for a satisfying object relationship, and Boszormenyi-Nagy (1965) noted, "mutual related-ness, through an alternation of subject and object roles, is a vital structural component of the personality" (p. 50).

Individuals may seek representations of their inner psychologi-cally split libidinal and antilibidinal introjects in their external relation-ships (Framo, 1972). Other persons are then conceived of mainly in terms of personalized needs resulting in distorted expectations and in unconscious attempts to fit others into internal role models. According to Framo (1972), "Just as a phobia, in intrapsychic terms, is an attempt to localize anxiety within a single situation while saving the ego from recognizing the real problem, and just as an obsessional isolates his symptoms from the rest of his personality and does not feel them as his own, so will people isolate, localize, and place forbidden tendencies and anxieties onto their intimates, manipulating others into expressing and carrying their problems for them" (p. 298).

Wolin and Bennett (1983) proposed that "spouse selection is a critical intermediate step in the process of generational transmission [of alcoholism]" (p. 274). According to their study of the adult children of alcoholics, spouse characteristics can reduce or increase the likelihood of continued alcoholism.

The dialectical or transactional theory examines the role of rela-tionships in self-delineation experiences (Boszormenyi-Nagy, 1965). Each transaction between subject and object, real or anticipated, rede-fines personality boundaries, implying that the experience of selfhood is dependent of the intactness of the boundary between self and other. The reciprocal alternation of subject and object is the dialogue of the relationship which prevents symbiotic merger and, when achieved, makes possible the growth of ego strength and autonomy. Failure to obtain a mature dialogic relationship can result in the regression of either or both partners, "reviving their non-reciprocal needs for a parent, i.e., a captive supporting (anaclitic) object" (Boszormenyi-Nagy, 1965, p. 52). This author claimed that the dialectical or transactional orientation to psychopathology focuses on the dynamic factors that prevent a self-other distinction between parent and child, typically mother as parent, rather than focusing on intrapsychic conflicts behind the adult child's personality problems and behavioral abnormalities.

Because of the heavy predominance of men over women in much of the research on adult children of alcoholic parents[1] it was decided to limit this study to intergenerational transmission of pathology to sons. It is important to understand that the authors are not implying that adult daughters of alcoholic parents escape negative influence or that they are not important subjects of research.

Stanton (1983) provided support for use of the transactional theory within the family context in his discussion of the triadic family structure of drug abusers. His delineation of factors distinguishing addict families from other dysfunctional families included: "higher frequency of multigenerational chemical dependency (particularly alcohol among males) . . . ," "more primitive and direct expression of conflict . . . ," "mothers of addicts display 'symbiotic' child-rearing practices further into the life of the child . . . ," [and] "a form of 'pseudo-individuation' at several levels" (p. 255).

OBJECT RELATIONS, TRANSACTIONAL
THEORIES, AND ALCOHOLISM

Boszormenyi-Nagy's (1965) work integrated, in a highly logical manner, essential aspects of transactional or dialectical theory and object relations theory. He concluded that "all relationships go through phases of unrelatedness (autistic phase), affiliative overinvolvement (symbiotic phase), growth of autonomy in members (individuation

---

[1]In the 1980 volume (Volume 41) of the *Journal of Studies on Alcoholism,* eighteen research studies were fully reported. Of these, eight reported all male subjects, three reported all female subjects, two failed to report subject sex, and five reported mixed subjects. In this last category, 329 males and 143 females were noted.

phase), and dissolution (separation phase) leading to re-involvement" (p. 76). In order for the self to be released from dependency on particular external objects, it is necessary that infantile and early childhood relationships be transformed into a structural relational context, involving intrapsychic self- and object representations. Wood (1984) mentioned that the lack of stability and the erratic behavior related to vocational and interpersonal matters common to many adult children from alcoholic families was related to the parents' inability to attend to their needs. These unmet needs then motivate the formation of dependent adult relationships inhibiting mature interpersonal interactions of alternating subject-object roles because of continued separation-individuation problems.

According to Shapiro (1978), three of the major tasks in the developmental shaping of internal representations are "self-object differentiation," "integration of loving and hating images and the development of object constancy," and "further integration of these images into flexible psychic structures (for example, superego and ego ideal)" (p. 1309). He also stated, in a discussion of separation-individuation, that "successful completion of this developmental period results in the capacity for frustration tolerance, the mastery of separation anxiety, and the maintenance of self-esteem" (p. 1311). When the mother maintains an unconscious conflict with specific attributes of the infant, age-appropriate symbiosis is blocked, leading to flaws in the early dependency on mother and in impaired separation-individuation. The mother's inability to respond empathically to the infant may also provoke an inappropriate premature ego development (Shapiro, 1978). In addition, achievement of a mature dialogic relationship may be prevented. As a result, rigid projections and transferences are maintained and directly related to unconscious configurational requirements for individuation and for avoidance of the ever present fear of depersonalization. If an individual's "intrapsychic mastery is tenuous, he will fortify it at the expense of another member's autonomy" (Boszormenyi-Nagy, 1965, p. 40).

Stanton's view (1983) of spouse selection in adult children of addictive families was that "dyadic relationships that abusers, especially addicts, become involved in are a repetition of the nuclear family of origin, with roles and interaction patterns similar to those seen with the opposite-sex parent" (p. 260). This certainly is consistent with the carrying forward of dependency mechanisms.

Wood (1984) expanded Jacobson's (1971) work on depression to the alcoholic family. She felt that the son, confused by a lack of clear parent-child boundaries, seeks the perfect protection of an ideal object by investing in an imperfect object and then elevating this object to a state of perfection. Spouse selection and later spouse treatment may fulfill this early defective separation-individuation. Wood (1984) also addressed the instability of such a relationship and the resultant vacillations between idealizing and disparaging the object. This too is consonant with object relations theory and with the polarization typical of the borderline patient.

Both characteristics of involvement and self-other differentiation of the individuals need to be considered in any full dialectical assessment of relatedness. The more pathology present, the less is the person's ability to perceive persons as they are or as they actually behave toward that person, and the more projective identification is employed. By attending to others' messages that are congruent with the introject, the self employs the internal dialogue as a means for regulating the interpersonal dialogue (Boszormenyi-Nagy, 1965). The mixing of internal-external relating is based on the projection of the split-off bad aspects of an internalized partner.

For example, in situations where the mother perceives her own needs as "bad" and therefore unacceptable, she may project such needs onto the infant, reject them in the infant, and then become neglectful of the infant's real needs because of her attention to her own projected needs (Shapiro, 1978). As a result of this process, the external other "is seen in a scapegoat-like 'bad' role so that the remaining internal parental image can remain 'good'" (Boszormenyi-Nagy, 1965, p. 48). Mutual relatedness, achieved through alternation of subject and object roles, is an essential structural aspect of the personality. This alternation of roles among individuals assists in avoidance of fusion or vague, undifferentiated interchanges. The unconscious struggle with incorporated objects is acted out with a variety of family members in "endless attempts to change real others into unconditionally loving parents" (Framo, 1965, p. 158).

According to Davis and Wallbridge (1981), if the father is unable to offer support and protection to the mother during the period following the birth of her baby, then she cannot devote anxiety-free attention to the infant. Her anxiety may result in flaws in handling the infant, in turn leading to inefficient adaptive behavior on the infant's part. If the infant complies with the mother's symbolic behavior rather than developing his or her own needs system, the lack of good enough mothering can result in the earliest stages of the false self (Winnicott, 1965). False interpersonal relationships are developed and introjects of major personality aspects of the mother, healthful or pathological, may result in the child's later close resemblance to the mother (Winnicott, 1965; Mahler, Pine, and Bergman, 1975).

During the separation phase of development, the ambivalent mother, who both rejects and depends upon her child to fill the gap left by the nonattentive alcoholic father, sets down a pattern of conflicted approach-avoidance interpersonal involvements in the child. According to Masterson and Rinsley (1975), the mother who exhibits borderline characteristics may experience considerable gratification from the child's symbiotic dependence on her, but she may have difficulty tolerating the child's increasing need for independence and expression of aggression. This would result in a push-pull interaction between mother and child, further complicating the child's overall emotional development.

The alcoholic mother, neglecting her child during alcoholic phases, would provide yet another aspect, that of erratic rejection. In turn, the child, caught between support for dependent regression, punishment for independence, and sporadic rejection, may oscillate between extreme dependence, rage, and fear of closeness (Kwawer, Lerner, Lerner, and Sugarman, 1980).

In the rapprochement phase, the quality of the mother's availability is important if her toddler is to achieve optimal capacity in the autonomous ego. If her availability is of poor quality, the toddler may increase efforts to win her undivided attention (Mahler, Pine, and Bergman, 1975), thereby establishing further dependency. Attention to the father also becomes quite evident during this phase. Alcoholic parents are generally unable to provide needed availability or attention to an infant because of the interruption of their own distorted needs. Thus, realistic identifications with the attitudes and values of mother and father are blocked and the earlier introjects survive into later life, particularly inhibiting affective object constancy associated with internalized positive parent images (Mahler, Pine, and Bergman, 1975). Because full individuation is not achieved, early infantile needs are carried forward into adult life and affiliative overinvolved relationships are established.

In situations such as the one described above, early object representations would be impaired and widely divergent. Need gratification would become of primary importance and a son would be apt to develop rigid defenses against the perceived potential mother-son merger as well as against feared isolation. In order to achieve a clear separation among internalized affective components of the self and among mother-father-son object representations, the son may engage in splitting, which in turn may lead to ego weakness or an arrest of ego development. In order to function within the family and in social situations, the resultant borderline individual may require affiliative overinvolvement in interactions with significant others so that affective experiences of self and object representations can be maintained (Kwawer et al., 1980).

In order to achieve a fit between internal self- and object representation and external relationships, the conflicted son may select a mate possessing major traits similar to those of his mother. This enables him to plan out or to reenact the conflicts related to needs developed within the earlier disturbed family relationships in his current family relationships (Wolin et al., 1980; Stanton, 1983; Wolin and Bennett, 1983). This also permits the necessary direct contact which facilitates some degree of object constancy in the higher-level borderline individual.

PSYCHOPATHOLOGY AND ALCOHOLISM

The literature on sons of alcoholics suggests that certain personality traits of the sons may predispose them to become alcoholics. Such traits, as presented by Aronson and Gilbert (1963), include acquisitiveness (such as oral demanding, insatiable demands and impulsive grasping activity patterns), inappropriate emotional expression (essentially emotionally immature expression as manifested by an impulsive, excessive, and inappropriate response to emotional stress), dependence (passive and dependent, either alone or together), evasion of unpleasantness (inability to cope, with the addiction serving as a direct means of evading responsibility and reality), and self-dissatisfaction (seen in the presence of dysphoria and low self-esteem).

Jones (1968) has noted the presence of underlying conflicts around dependency, with overcompensatory strivings for "maleness." Both Aronson and Gilbert (1963) and Mik (1970) described alcoholic sons as ambivalent toward the father/authority figure, as identifying with the providing sphere/mother fixation, as having a questionable identification, and as manifesting dominant passive-dependent traits. It has been reported that affected boys were most often the oldest sibling (El-Guebaly and Offord, 1977). Extensive psychopathology in general, with repression and denial as highly characteristic defenses, were reported in alcoholics by Eshbaugh, Tosi, and Hoyt (1968). Clearly major conflicts clustered around male-female gender identity aspects are characteristic of alcoholic sons.

Others (Woitiz, 1983; Perrin, 1983, 1984) have proposed that children of alcoholics, as adults, may have marked problems in the areas of love and work. It would be anticipated that, because of distortions of self and of relationships with others, the alcoholic would be more focused on control of relationships than on the development of the effective interpersonal interchanges necessary for consistent love or work relationships of a successful nature.

As discussed earlier, many of the children of alcoholics in adulthood continue to experience separation-individuation conflicts because of an inability to maintain an attachment to, and a regard for, an individual in the face of inevitable disappointments, conflicts, and disillusionment (Wood, 1984). Without an integrated sense of self, these adults also have difficulty tolerating differences and separateness from significant others. This difficulty may be because their relationships tend to be formed in terms of their complementation to antilibidinal and libidinal introjects. According to Wood (1984), "When the process of separation-individuation is impeded, a distorted, false self arises, which is a collection of reactions to, and partial incorporation of, disappointing parents and compensatory ideal figures" (p. 15). Such conflicts further complicate an already confused attempt to adjust to self and to others.

It seems quite clear that the sons of alcoholic parents experience unique stresses and interactions which frequently lead to adult psychopathology. This is particularly true in cases where the mother herself is pathological, passing on to her son major pathological characteristics which increase the likelihood of his becoming both pathological and alcoholic. While the choice of a spouse with a more healthful life style might permit him to move away from alcohol, his own pathology may necessitate the choice of one who will facilitate the reenactment of the family of origin.

CASE STUDY

In order to more clearly develop the preceding materials on pregenital development of psychopathology as an adaptation to disordered family transactions and on transmission of such pathology through the psychological process of identification with parental introjects and through spouse selection, a mother-son-wife triad of Rorschach protocols will be discussed. Projective techniques are a most useful means of tracing psychopathology, and the Rorschach is particularly efficacious in exploring the dynamics of atypical family thought patterns (Loveland, Wynne, and Singer, 1963; Wynne and Singer, 1963; Boszormenyi-Nagy, 1965; Singer and Wynn, 1975; Framo, 1979).

Kwawer et al. (1980) have edited an excellent volume on the use of the Rorschach in examining borderline phenomena, an area highly relevant to this study. As will be seen, the triad of protocols is most logically tied together by the thread of borderline characteristics pervasive across all three. Alcoholism in the family of origin serves to compound the existing psychopathology. Thus we have, as salient features, alcohol abuse, disordered family transactions, borderline characteristics, and reenactment of early object relations in spouse selection.

Subject Characteristics

The mother, a white woman in her mid-fifties and in her third marriage, was employed in the retail area. While reportedly a heavy drinker, she was not diagnosed as alcoholic. Her first spouse, father of the son we are considering, was reportedly an alcoholic who was physically abusive to family members during episodes of drinking. At other times he tended to ignore his wife, two sons, and daughter. This marriage lasted approximately twenty-four years and was terminated by the husband's desertion following a particularly brutal altercation. The mother's second marriage lasted only a few months and was terminated by mutual agreement. Her third husband was reportedly a heavy alcohol user who had recently been fired for "drinking on the job."

The son, oldest of the siblings, was in his mid-thirties, married with two children, and in military service. He had a history of two voluntary short-term hospitalizations for the treatment of alcoholism, and of infrequent and brief contacts with Alcoholics Anonymous. He had been denied an anticipated military promotion and had been transferred to a less desirable post because of intoxication on duty.

The son's wife was the middle of three siblings and did not have a history of alcohol abuse. She was, however, a frequent "recreational" drug user and used alcohol "moderately." Strong interdependence was noted between this woman and her mother. She also had a history of unstable extramarital relationships.

None of the triad had experienced a psychotherapeutic relationship other than the alcohol treatment program of the son. The mother and her daughter-in-law maintained an amiable relationship, with frequent exchanges of confidences. Son and mother remained unengaged as much as possible, with the son relatively resistant to his mother's twice-yearly visits. The wife and her own mother maintained their interchanges by means of frequent correspondence, telephone communication, and yearly visits. These interchanges tended to be warm and close, although the mother continued to disapprove of her daughter's marital choice. The son maintained a rather aloof relationship with his mother-in-law during her visits, and spent as little time as possible at home. Both the wife's father and the son's stepfather appeared to be relatively innocuous members of the family.

Rorschach Presentation and Interpretation

To illustrate the personality dynamics through which the adult alcoholic son takes on essential characteristics of the symbiotic mother and through which that son adjusts to his pathology by spouse selection, three Rorschach protocols will be presented and compared. While the basic method of scoring was Rapaport, Gill, and Schafer (1945), Mayman's form level (1957) was also used, as were aspects of the Exner system (1974) and of the Holtzman Inkblot Test (Holtzman, 1961; Hill, 1972).

Such a combination of techniques might be considered suspect in a psychodiagnostic situation, but it is an appropriate means of highlighting the richness of the protocols. Because many borderline features were found in all three protocols, these features will be discussed first, with other pathological elements following. A description of mechanisms for the transmission of pathology through family transactions and the ultimate step of spouse selection will follow.

Tables 1 and 2 present selected psychometric aspects of the protocols. Because of the extensiveness and richness of responses, some of the characteristics which are not specifically addressed in the text may provide the reader with a more complete comprehension of the triad. The current focus in no way should be interpreted to mean that the authors saw these elements as the sole points of importance in the protocols.

According to Kwawer et al. (1980), borderline phenomena on the Rorschach may be exhibited by a number of distinctive characteristics. If we were to limit ourselves to Lerner and Lerner's (1980) defensive criteria, then splitting, devaluation, idealization, projective identifica-

TABLE 1
Selected Rorschach Characteristics

	Mother (R 44)		Son (R 29)		Wife (R 64)	
	Number	%	Number	%	Number	%
Mode of Approach						
W	4	9	11	38	12	19
D	30	68	14	48	33	52
A	0	0	0	0	2	3
Dr	10	23	4	14	12	19
s (not included in R)	0	0	3	10	1	2
Determinants						
M	4	9	2	7	0	0
M tend	0	0	2	7	1	2
FM (humanized)	0	0	1	3	1	2
FM (pure animal)[a]	8	18	5	17	2	3
m	0	0	1	3	3	4
Total of neutral or benevolent movement	10	—	5	—	6	—
Total of malevolent movement	2	—	6	—	1	—
FC	9	20	5	17	13	20
FC(c)	0	0	0	0	3	5
C(c)F	0	0	1	3	0	0
CF	2	4	1	3	0	0
C	0	0	0	0	0	0
FC'	1	2	4	14	3	5
FCh	2	4	4	14	6	9
ChF	0	0	2	7	0	0
F(c)	7	16	4	14	0	0
Quality of Form Perception						
F%		52		34		61
F'%		95		93		100
F+%		52		60		49
F'+%		48		52		41
Chromatic Reaction Time	$\bar{X}$ 11.20		$\bar{X}$ 61.00		$\bar{X}$ 15.80	
Achromatic Reaction Time	$\bar{X}$ 9.75		$\bar{X}$ 62.60		$\bar{X}$ 11.00	
Content						
H	2	4	2	7	1	2
Hd	2	4	4	14	8	12
(H)	1	2	1	3	0	0

(*Continued*)

TABLE 1 (Continued)

	Mother (R 44)		Son (R 29)		Wife (R 64)	
	Number	%	Number	%	Number	%
(Hd)	1	2	0	0	1	2
A	20	45	8	28	13	20
Ad	2	4	5	17	10	16
(A)	1	2	0	0	0	0
(Ad)	2	4	0	0	0	0
Blood	1	2	0	0	0	0
Sex	0	0	0	0	2	3
Anatomy	0	0	1	3	5	8
X ray	0	0	1	3	1	2
Fire	1	2	1	3	2	3
Pair (2)[a]	22	50	13	45	27	42
Twins	0	0	0	0	1	2
Pregenital references						
Oral	5	11	4	14	2	3
Anal	0	0	2	7	2	3
Phallic	0	0	1	3	4	6
Affect Arousal[b]	+3		−4		−6	
Barrier[b]	7	16	9	31	10	16
Penetration[b]	4	9	8	28	10	16
Affective Tone[b]						
Aggressive	7	16	11	38	3	4
Extreme	1	2	3	10	0	0
Moderate	6	14	8	28	3	4
Impotent	1	2	3	10	0	0
Positive	6	14	1	3	0	0
Type of Animal Used[c]						
(A + Ad)						
Aggressive	8	18	7	24	6	10
Nonaggressive	15	34	6	21	17	26
Experience Balance	5/8.5		2.5/6.0		.5/6.5	
Responses to Cards VIII–X	50		24		30	
Evidence of Thought Disorder						
Self-reference	1		1		0	
Peculiar Verbalization	0		4		0	
Fabulized Combinations	1		0		3	
Confabulization Tendency	0		3		1	
Contamination Tendency	2		0		1	
Contamination	0		1		0	

(*Continued*)

TABLE 1 (Continued)

	Mother (R 44)		Son (R 29)		Wife (R 64)	
	Number	%	Number	%	Number	%
Perseveration	0		1		1	
Autistic Logic Tendency	1		1		0	
Autistic Logic	3		2		1	
Fluidity	0		1		0	
Fabulized	11		7		2	
Total	19		21		9	
Borderline Defensive[d]						
Characteristics (All						
human responses)						
Splitting	0		0		2	
Devaluation	4		5		5	
Idealization	2		0		1	
Projective Identification	0		1		0	
Denial	2		2		0	
Total	8		8		8	
Borderline Defensive[e]						
Characteristics						
Applied to Animals						
Splitting	2		0		0	
Devaluation	5		5		3	
Idealization	3		0		0	
Projective Identification	1		3		0	
Denial	7		0		2	
Total	18		8		5	

[a]Exner
[b]Holtzman
[c]Includes all animal responses, separate or part of other response
[d]Derived from Lerner and Lerner (1980)
[e]An informal inspection of data at a primitive level

tion, and denial relating primarily to whole human responses would be examined. However, because of regressive tendencies and the strong use of part objects, insufficient whole human percepts were available for analysis (mother 2; son 2; wife 1).

Sugarman (1980) referred to the borderline tendency to relate to others as part objects rather than totalities, which may be reflected in Hd Rorschach responses and in a predominance of H over M responses. Kernberg (1975, 1976) discussed the borderline's typical part object

TABLE 2

Selected Atypical Responses

Mother

Two dogs fighting, maybe they're in an act

A circus act with a bird head on a dog

Oh dear, two little puppies making love, no koala bears hanging onto a tree and wanting to make love, they're lovable, one's sad

Oh dear, a piece of watermelon

Oh, two cupids kissing only they're not together

This is the man in the moon with green eyes, coming up from behind clouds

Two french-fried shrimp

A peacock upside down

Butterflies on top of dogs

Weird-looking, strange animals with horns and big green eyes

Son

Two persons, back to back, probably females with distinct busts

Two rabbits eating a carrot, in a cage with the carrots dangling above their heads

Looking down someone's mouth, seeing tonsils and white teeth

Santa Claus's elves' boots, not standing up but flopped. Santa Claus has black shiny boots. Elves have boots that don't fit and are not neat

Two court jesters, a hat that flops and long noses, slouching over

Two men, with beards, reclining against a pillow

Ruined Xray of a spinal cord

Two rats with teeth bared, snarling

Wife

Praying hands, two of them

I forget what it is, your bum with red paint on it

Two space ships, one being emitted from the other

A penis, the same part as the praying hands but longer

Where I saw the penis, an Xray of the liver

Rear end of an ostrich, I see double but not connected

Female organs, looking up through the vagina—two of them

Siamese twins, joined together on the sides and distorted

A bug stuck in tar

A big penis, coming out of the sun (hot rays of the sun)

relations and the failure to integrate "good" and "bad" self and other aspects adequately into the personality organization. Blatt, Brenneis, Schimek, and Glick (1976) attended to the developmental decline in normal adolescents and young adults of distorted or partial human percepts and the increase in accurately perceived whole human figures. The importance of differentiation of human figures was further elaborated by Blatt and Lerner (1983). Rausch de Traubenberg and Boizou (1980), in their discussion of prepsychotic children's responses, referred to the use of animals in affective positions, and Hill (1972) discussed Holtzman animal responses in immature adults. In line with the above material, it was decided to analyze, not only whole human responses, but also humans seen as part objects and in distorted ways. It was also decided to examine the use of animals, particularly those animals seen in humanlike activities and those where affective components were present.

The overall pattern of strong animal use and of insufficient differentiation of human figures may be seen on all three protocols, with the proportion of fully differentiated human percepts "H" to poorly differentiated human percepts Hd, (H), (HD) being: mother 2:4; son 2:5; wife 1:9. Complete human to complete animal percept proportions were: mother 2:20; son 2:8; wife 1:13. While the wife was more marked in immaturity of object representations, mother and son also displayed the immaturity typical of borderlines.

As mentioned previously, lack of sufficient differentiated human data for adequate analysis led the authors to a modification of traditional interpretation. The reader will need to keep in mind that, in presenting borderline characteristics, part object human, quasi-human, and full human responses were considered. As may be seen from Table 1, each person displayed eight of Lerner and Lerner's defensive characteristics (1980). While most of these defenses were not at the more severe levels of organization, the striking aspect is the similarity among the protocols. When we informally applied these criteria to animal percepts, the infantilization of the mother became much more evident. Under the stress of affect, she became much less able to maintain stable percepts at a mature level, demonstrating lack of ego strength. A similar pattern of animal use was seen in both the son and his wife, although the degree of infantilization was much less marked.

Examination of the use of color and shading and of the quality of form perception of all three persons reveals that they all experienced impaired reality testing under affective circumstances. At such times, strong but largely ineffective defenses of a primitive nature were employed. Effective adaptive mechanisms would also be negatively affected under affective stress, resulting in even lower levels of functioning.

Smith (1980) mentioned the strong use of pairs as another borderline characteristic. He indicated that over 40 percent of lower borderline responses were in pairs according to his observations, a figure close to the present data from all three persons. The preponderance of pairing of percepts is related to the balance concept and may represent the inner insecurity and fear of impulsivity discussed by Hill (1972) in relation to the Holtzman Inkblot Test. Pairing is also related to Exner's Egocentricity Index (1974). According to Exner's data, a normal score range is .25–.40, with a mean of .37 and with higher scores representing excessive self-concern. This difficulty in differentiation represents an ego weakness and may reflect "the openly dependent infantile character" (Smith, 1980, p. 72). Pregenital responses on all three protocols support the presence of immature personality development with separation-individuation problems.

When each of the protocols is examined individually, other borderline characteristics and signs of psychopathology are evident. The mother was frequently unwilling to classify percepts as actual things, modifying potentially threatening ideas by downgrading them into acts, games, halloweeners, cupids, etc., or by employing reaction-formation to avoid negative impact. This was particularly true with percepts of an aggressive (fighting, bleeding) or sexual (kissing, making love) nature and is related to a reluctance to acknowledge unpleasant aspects and a tendency to split images in order to avoid such acknowledgment.

While she was stimulated by the environment, she was also disturbed by it and tended to distance herself and to exhibit primitive defenses. According to E. F. Hill (personal communication, February 8, 1983), an informal application of the Holtzman concepts of barrier, penetration, balance, and attribution of affect arousal is appropriate to highlight data in the form of estimates. Barrier refers to the degree of definiteness of the body-image boundary and represents the individual's sense of being an entity separate from the environment (Hill, 1972). Penetration refers to the permeability of the body boundary, and a preponderance of these scores is negatively correlated with maturity and tolerance of stress (Hill, 1972). The mother's adequate barrier and low penetration profile indicates her sense of herself as separate from the environment and minimally vulnerable to environmental stress. Pairing, which is related to balance, has already been discussed. A hysteroid quality was reflected by strong affect arousal of an artificial positive quality and by conflicted positive-negative affective designations. Hill (1972) felt that high affect arousal was a sign of loss of distance and a tendency to discharge inner drives impulsively.

The mother's preponderance of animal over human responses is indicative of her regressive tendencies, and the number of borderline defensive characteristics applied to such animal percepts further delineates her immaturity and faulty object relations. In addition, she typically devalued males while infantilizing them, and she presented an inadequate view of female sexuality. Evidence of thought disorder was quite clear (19 instances) and, combined with other evidence of psychopathology, gives us a picture of a seriously impaired family member.

The son's long reaction times, rejection of one card, and various spontaneous comments during testing illustrate his caution and may be related to projective identification. Destroyed percepts, malevolent movement, strong shading, and use of many negative affective tones may imply the mechanism of splitting and are indicative of his difficulty in modulating affect and his inability to integrate cognitive and affective components of reality effectively.

Confabulation tendencies, manifested by unrealistic elaboration, and the relatively high barrier and penetration scores point to boundary problems, with the need to defend against threat of impingement. While this was not clear, there may have been some fear of merger with others. Strong oral needs, with conflicts over acceptance of and control of such needs, were present, and oral aggression seemed to be blocked as unacceptable. In addition, the son included anal percepts and at times combined oral and anal content, demonstrating conflicts around sexual identification and lack of appropriate developmental progress. Male percepts were impotent or lacking in vitality, while female percepts were embodied with considerable vitality. These characteristics have been related to homosexuality, which is consistent with the son's history. High penetration, problems in acceptance of dependency, and negative male percepts have also been associated with alcoholism (Hill, 1972; Khantzian, 1983).

The son appeared to be using repression and primitive defenses to counter his mother's hysteria and impingement upon him, although such mechanisms were not effective in reducing anxiety. Evidence of thought disorder was extremely strong (21 instances) and, combined with the history of alcoholism, provides a picture of cross-generational disturbed personality development.

Last to be presented is the son's wife. While her protocol is the richest of the three, it also contains the most varied evidence of pathology. Her total of sixty-four responses is quite high, particularly when the suspect quality of many responses is considered. She had only one fully articulated human response, and that was of distorted Siamese twins, possibly an indication of symbiotic merger (Kwawer, 1980). Also present were examples of engulfment (bug stuck in tar), malignant internal processes (a severed kidney), separation-division (rear end of an ostrich but not connected, paws that aren't connected now), and boundary disturbances (a fuzzy picture; a cloud formation—reminds me of looking at clouds; colored tissue paper—fragile and thin). All of the above have been described by Kwawer (1980) as images related to early symbiotic experiences. She also demonstrated mechanisms of splitting and polarization of part objects.

Stress on oral and anal aspects, faulty phallic aspects, and male-female confusion illustrate her lack of adequate individuation and the primitive nature of her personality development. A number of responses reflected a fear of males mixed with attraction, and rather labile sexuality. This material points to strong pregenital issues and may be noted in combination with the partial fusion of oral and genital components.

Perhaps most dramatic was the amount of symbiotic imagery, with shifting percepts, peculiar combinations and sequences, and loss of distance associated with the more striking responses. Her relatively high barrier profile with higher penetration, the presence of balance (symmetry) percepts, and high levels of anxiety assist us in seeing the results of her fear of impingement and incorporation. With strong id impulses and lack of appropriate inner controls, her fear of environmental stimulation and her strong reaction to such stimulation seem consistent with her development of primitive defense mechanisms rather than the development of higher-level, more effective defenses. Clearly this is the protocol of a woman with relatively severe problems in personality development.

Discussion

Mother-son-wife protocols have been presented and discussed, and the presence of strong pregenital characteristics within their borderline personality organizations has been clarified for all three members of the triad. The next step is to explore the transactional nature of pathology transmission across generations and the mechanisms of spouse selection that permitted the son to function, however minimally.

Characteristics within the alcoholic family and the assumption, by the son, of pathological aspects of his mother's personality have already been discussed. In the current constellation, an abusive, alcoholic father caused the son to turn to his mother for support and identification. Her degree of pathology, the strength of her dependence needs, and her extreme approach-avoidance conflicts created a unique environment for the son's early development. It is likely that she engaged in the symbiotic aspects of early interchanges in order to buffer herself from her husband's neglect and abuse. Her son would have been caught between a desire to comply with his mother's needs and the need to separate from her, a conflict resulting in rage and guilt. In addition, her approach-avoidance behaviors would have forced him into a vacillating situation, confusing the development of object constancy and requiring him to develop an ideal object by elevating aspects of the mother to a state of near-perfection. The development of a false self would permit him to adapt to this chaotic situation.

The mother perceived herself as having "bad" feelings and thoughts, but also engaged in the devaluation of males. A combination of introjection and projection resulted in her son's perception of himself and of women as negative in nature but also of women being more dynamic. Thus we see the groundwork for the assumption of pathology by the son, in relation both to his father's alcoholism and his mother's heavy drinking, and to the unhealthy traits in the mother-son interactions.

The son carried on the family alcoholism within the context of personality disturbance into his adult life. When he began living apart from his family of origin, it became necessary for him to stabilize his life to some degree. One avenue open to him was to select a spouse who would replicate the original family transactions, who would permit the false self to continue to function, and who would permit him to identify with the oral-dependent needs unacceptable in him but acceptable in a wife.

The similarities between mother and wife are quite remarkable, allowing for a symbolic merger that would bring family-of-origin transactions to the fore. Because of the son's similarities to his mother, this would also encourage further symbiotic interchanges between the son and his wife. The latter's own pathological needs and defenses allowed her to accept this immature and destructive relationship as a means of maintaining some degree of fragile object cathexes while protecting her from a feared merger with others.

The entanglement of pathology and alcoholism with the family structure provides an excellent illustration of the transactional nature of pathology as an adaptation. It is both frightening and intriguing to consider the fate of the next generation within this pathological matrix. Unless the chain of pathology can be interrupted by powerful intervention, it is likely that the two children of this couple will carry forth a heritage of borderline characteristics into their own transactions.

REFERENCES

Aronson, H., & Gilbert, A. (1963), Preadolescent sons of male alcoholics. *Arch. Gen. Psychiat.,* 8:235–241.

Blatt, S. J., Brenneis, C. B., Schimek, J. G. & Glick, M. (1976), Normal development and psychopathological impairment of the concept of the object on the Rorschach. *J. Abnorm. Psychol.,* 85:364–373.

_____ & Lerner, H. D. (1983), The psychological assessment of object representation. *J. Personal. Assess.,* 47:7–28.

Boszormenyi-Nagy, I. (1965), A theory of relationships: Experience and transactions. In: *Intensive Family Therapy,* ed. I. Boszormenyi-Nagy & J. L. Framo. New York: Hoeber/Harper & Row, pp. 33–86.

Bowen, M. (1965), Family psychotherapy with schizophrenia in the hospital and in private practice. In: *Intensive Family Therapy,* ed. I. Boszormenyi-Nagy & J. L. Framo. New York: Hoeber/Harper & Row, pp. 213–243.

Davis, M., & Wallbridge, D. (1981), *Boundary and Space: An Introduction to the Work of D. W. Winnicott.* New York: Brunner/Mazel.

El-Guebaly, N., & Offord, D. R. (1977), The offspring of alcoholics: A critical review. *Amer. J. Psychiat.,* 134:357–365.

Eshbaugh, D. M., Tosi, D. J., & Hoyt, C. (1968), Personality patterns of male alcoholics. *J. Personal. Assess.,* 48:409–417.

Exner, J. E. (1974), *The Rorschach: A Comprehensive System.* New York: Basic Books.

Fairbairn, W. R. D. (1952), *An Object Relations Theory of the Personality.* New York: Basic Books.

Framo, J. L. (1965), Rationale and techniques of intensive family therapy. In: *Intensive Family Therapy,* ed. I. Boszormenyi-Nagy & J. L. Framo. New York: Hoeber/Harper & Row, pp. 143–212.

_____ (1972), Symptoms from a family transactional viewpoint. In: *Progress in Group and Family Therapy,* ed. C. Sager & H. Kaplan. New York: Brunner/Mazel, pp. 271–308.

_____ (1979), Family theory and therapy. *Amer. Psychologist,* 34:988–992.

Freud, S. (1913), Totem and taboo. *Standard Edition,* 13:1–161. London: Hogarth Press, 1955.

Goodwin, D. W. (1983), The genetics of alcoholism. In: *Etiologic Aspects of Alcohol and Drug Abuse,* ed. E. Gottheil, K. A. Druley, T. E. Skoloda, & H. M. Waxman. Springfield, IL: Charles C Thomas, pp. 5–13.

Hill, E. F. (1972), *The Holtzman Inkblot Technique.* Washington: Jossey-Bass.

Holtzman, W. (1961), *The Holtzman Inkblot Technique: Administration and Scoring Guide.* New York: The Psychological Corporation.

Jacobson, E. (1971), *Depression.* New York: International Universities Press.

Jones, M. (1968), Personality correlates and antecedents of drinking patterns in adult males. *J. Consult. & Clin. Psychol.,* 32:2–12.

Kernberg, O. F. (1975), *Borderline Conditions and Pathological Narcissism.* New York: Aronson.

———— (1976), *Object Relations Theory and Clinical Psychoanalysis.* New York: Aronson.

Khantzian, E. J. (1983), Psychopathological causes and consequences of drug dependence. In: *Etiological Aspects of Alcohol and Drug Abuse,* ed. E. Gottheil, K. A. Druley, T. E. Skoloda, & H. M. Waxman. Springfield, IL: Charles C. Thomas, pp. 89–140.

Kwawer, J. S. (1980), Primitive interpersonal modes, borderline phenomena, and Rorschach content. In: *Borderline Phenomena and the Rorschach Test,* ed. J. Kwawer, H. D. Lerner, P. H. Lerner, & A. Sugarman. New York: International Universities Press, pp. 89–105.

———— Lerner, H. D., Lerner, P. M., & Sugarman, A., Eds.(1980), *Borderline Phenomena and the Rorschach Test.* New York: International Universities Press.

Lerner, P. M., & Lerner, H. D. (1980), Rorschach assessment of primitive defenses in borderline personality structure. In: *Borderline Phenomena and the Rorschach Test.,* ed. J. S. Kwawer, H. D. Lerner, P. M. Lerner, & A. Sugarman. New York: International Universities Press, pp. 257–274.

Loveland, N. T., Wynne, L. C., & Singer, M. T. (1963), The family Rorschach: A new method for studying family interaction. *Family Process,* 2:187–215.

Mayman, M. (1957), Form Level Scoring Manual. Unpublished manuscript.

Mahler, M. S., Pine, F., & Bergman, A. (1975), *The Psychological Birth of the Human Infant: Symbiosis and Individuation.* New York: Basic Books.

Masterson, J., & Rinsley, D. (1975), The borderline syndrome: The role of the mother in the genesis and psychic structure of the borderline personality. *Internat. J. Psycho-Anal.,* 56:163–177.

Mik, G. (1970), Sons of alcoholic fathers. *Brit. J. Addict.,* 65:305–315.

Perrin, T. W. (1983), Issues for children and alcoholics. *COA Review,* 5:9.

———— (1984), Psychotherapy with Adult Children of Alcoholics: A Structured Group Model. Unpublished manuscript.

Rapaport, D., Gill, M., & Schafer, R. (1945), *Diagnostic Psychological Testing.* Rev. ed. New York: International Universities Press.

Rausch de Traubenberg, N., & Boizou, M. F. (1980), Pre-psychotic conditions in children as manifested in their perception and fantasy experiences on Rorschach and thematic tests. In: *Borderline Phenomena and the Rorschach Test,* ed. J. S. Kwawer, H. D. Lerner, P. M. Lerner, & A. Sugarman. New York: International Universities Press, pp. 395–409.

Shapiro, E. R. (1978), The psychodynamics and developmental psychology of the borderline patient: A review of the literature. *Amer. J. Psychiat.,* 135:1305–1315.

Singer, M. T., & Wynne, L. C. (1975), Principles for scoring communication defects and deviances in parents of schizophrenics: Rorschach and TAT scoring manuals. In: *Handbook of Rorschach Scales,* ed. H. D. Lerner. New York: International Universities Press, pp. 361–405.

Smith, K. (1980), Object relations concepts as applied to the borderline level of ego functioning. In: *Borderline Phenomena and the Rorschach Test,* ed. J. S. Kwawer,

H. D. Lerner, P. M. Lerner, & A. Sugarman. New York: International Universities Press, pp. 59–87.

Stanton, M. D. (1983), A family theory of drug abuse. In: *Etiological Aspects of Alcohol and Drug Abuse*, ed. E. Gottheil, K. A. Druley, T. S. Skoloda, & H. M. Waxman. Springfield, IL: Charles C Thomas, pp. 249–270.

Steinglass, P. (1976), Experimenting with family treatment approaches to alcoholism, 1950–1975: A review. *Family Process,* 15:97–123.

Sugarman, A. (1980), The borderline personality organization as manifested on psychological tests. In: *Borderline Phenomena and the Rorschach Test,* ed. J. S. Kwawer, H. D. Lerner, P. M. Lerner, & A. Sugarman. New York: International Universities Press, pp. 39–59.

Winnicott, D. W. (1965), *The Maturational Processes and the Facilitating Environment.* London: Hogarth Press.

Woitiz, J. G. (1983), *Adults Children of Alcoholism.* Hollywood, FL: Health Communications.

Wolin, E. J., & Bennett, L. A. (1983), Heritage continuity among the child of alcoholics. In: *Etiological Aspects of Alcohol and Drug Abuse,* ed. E. Gottheil, K. A. Druley, T. E. Skoloda, & H. M. Waxman. Springfield, IL: Charles C Thomas, pp. 271–284.

Wolin, S. J., Bennett, L. A., Koonan, B. B., & Deltenbaum, M. A. (1980), Disrupted family rivals. *J. Studies on Alcoholism,* 41:199–214.

Wood, B. L. (1984), Children of alcoholics: Patterns of dysfunction in adult life. Unpublished manuscript.

Wynne, L. C., & Singer, M. T. (1963), Thought disorder and family relations of schizophrenics: I. A research strategy; II. A classification of forms of thinking. *Arch. Genl. Psychiat.,* 9:191–206.

Chapter 20

Changes in Rorschach Percepts of Four Schizophrenic Patients

Mary S. Cerney, Ph.D.

In a recent study, Spohn, Coyne, Mittleman, Larson, Johnston, Spray, and Hayes, (1985) questioned the effects of neuroleptic medication on information processing and thought processes in chronic schizophrenics. Their findings suggest that there are possibly two kinds of thought disorder, one that does not respond to neuroleptic medication and one that does. According to this study, neuroleptic medication may normalize "situation-bound, intercurrent disruption of communication process" while the "long enduring etiologically rooted thought pathology" may remain untouched (p. 584).

Cerney, Poggi, Mittleman, Zee, and Coyne (unpublished) have found that select chronic schizophrenic patients show significant internal structural changes as measured by repeat psychological testing at strategic points in their treatment. These changes appear in Rorschach protocols obtained at intervals of one to two years during treatment.

These two studies raise interesting diagnostic questions. One can rather quickly ascertain which individuals can benefit from medication, but how one predicts which individuals can benefit from long-term treatment, and from what kind, is a far more difficult question.

I wish to thank Dr. Herbert Spohn and his co-researchers for generously and graciously making their research data available for my examination and use in this paper. Also I would especially like to thank Mrs. Judy Spray for her help in locating the data that I used for my comparisons and for her helpful comments in regard to the Spohn et al. (1985) study.

In this chapter I will study the characteristics and diagnostic implications of thought disorder as seen on the Rorschach protocols of two patients taken from each of the two studies mentioned. The patients chosen were those showing the most significant change during the course of study. The patients from the Spohn study are Jack, who after medication withdrawal needed to resume its use, and Jane, who continues to improve behaviorally while remaining on placebo. The two patients from the Cerney study are Jay, whose overall treatment included medication as an important component, and Alan, who because of his extreme paranoia could use medication only intermittently, until the latter phase of his long-term inpatient hospitalization.

THOUGHT DISORDER

For years researchers have struggled to achieve a clear and comprehensive view of all that is embraced by the term "thought disorder." The result has been an overwhelming and entangling array of confusing theoretical assumptions and empirical data, a phenomenon which seems akin to schizophrenia itself. In an attempt to make sense of this massive volume of research, Athey (1974) points out that authors make "various assumptions which, unfortunately, are not always explicit and may covertly affect conceptualizations of the schizophrenic process" (p. 406). He identified two such covert assumptions: the assumption of deficit and the assumption of undimensionality. The former postulates a loss of some crucial function that results in or defines the psychosis, and the latter negates differentiating distinctive patterns of organization that may exist in a patient's disordered thinking.

After an exhaustive review of the literature, Johnston and Holzman (1979) concluded that "no single unitary measure can adequately reflect the complexity and variation of thought disorder" (p. 56). From their studies, they selected and concentrated on five areas of thinking in the development of their measure of thought disorder. By employing a multidimensional model of thought they hoped not only to develop an index which would measure the subtleties inherent in what is called schizophrenic thinking, but to go beyond the label and classify subjects on the basis of various quantities and qualities of thought disorder. Using data from both the Rorschach and the WAIS, their Thought Disorder Index (TDI) covers five important areas of thought functioning. Since this index was used in the Spohn et al. (1985) study, I will review in detail the aspects of thought included in their five areas.

1. *Concept formation.* This includes concreteness, overinclusion, and richness of association. (a) Concreteness is defined by Johnston and

Holzman (1979) as "the tendency of a subject to stay within the bounds either of the immediate specific stimulus situation or of his or her own personal experience" (p. 20). This aspect of concept formation has long been considered a pathognomonic indicator of schizophrenia (Vygotsky, 1934; Benjamin, 1944; Goldstein, 1944). (b) Overinclusion is more accurately defined as "conceptual overinclusion" and involves an assessment of the level of abstraction of concepts used. According to Harrow, Himmelhoch, Tucker, Hersh, and Quinlan (1972), this concept is frequently confused with "behavioral overinclusion," which refers to the quantitative aspects of the subject's overt behavior, and "stimulus overinclusion," which consists of difficulty in attending to relevant stimuli. This concept of overinclusion, first presented by Cameron (1944), is, according to Weiner (1966), one of the "distinctive and diagnostically useful features of schizophrenia concept formation" (p. 94). (c) Richness of association refers to "responses indicating originality and awareness of a variety of possible categorizing principles" (Johnston and Holzman, 1979, p. 23).

2. *Cognitive focusing.* Weiner (1966) noted that schizophrenic patients have difficulty focusing on relevant stimuli, appropriately changing a mental set, and inhibiting extraneous associations. Under this category Johnston and Holzman (1979) include the following. (a) Stimulus overinclusion, defined by Shield, Harrow, and Tucker (1974) as "perceptual experiences characterized by the individual's difficulty in attending selectively to relevant stimuli, or by the person's tendency to be distracted by or to focus unnecessarily on a wide range of irrelevant stimuli" (p. 2). (b) Idiosyncratic thinking, which "refers to content that deviates from the usual social norms or expectations, is inappropriate to the task at hand, and thus appears confused, contradictory, or illogical" (Johnston and Holzman, 1979, p. 24). (c) Excessive yielding to normal biases: for schizophrenic patients, strong associations frequently replace correct responses. How this process takes place is not clearly understood and present theory does not account for the bizarre and autistic quality of many schizophrenic patients' thought. (d) Looseness of association, that is, thought that has few apparent causal links in a train of associations so that "the speaker appears to lose the focus of thought and expresses lines of irrelevant and loosely connected associations" (Johnston and Holzman, 1979, p. 25). (e) Overspecific responses, which Quinlan, Harrow, Tucker, and Carlson (1972) define as irrelevant, personalized, and tangential associations, with elaboration beyond what is justified by the qualities of the stimulus.

3. *Reasoning.* This area includes the following. (a) Overgeneral-

ized thinking, defined by Weiner (1966) as "jumping to erroneous conclusions on the basis of minimal evidence and investing experiences with elaborate meanings not justified by their actual stimulus properties" (pp. 63–64). (b) Combinative thinking, which refers to "a condensation of perceptions and ideas in a way that appears to disregard usual conceptual boundaries between ideas and objects" (Johnston and Holzman, 1979, p. 26). (c) Circumstantial thinking, in which incidental aspects of a situation are used as a basis for fallacious conclusions (Arieti, 1974). Although circumstantial thinking is implicit in overgeneralization and combinative thinking, when "it occurs explicitly as a state of purposeful, faulty logic cast in syllogistic form, it is called autistic logic" (Johnston and Holzman, p. 27).

4. *Modulation of affect.* Although schizophrenics experience difficulty in modulating affect, this problem is not specific to schizophrenia.

5. *Reality testing.* This is defined by Freud (1911) as the process by which a person is able to distinguish between stimuli originating in the outside world and stimuli emanating from internal bodily sources.

Johnston and Holzman's review of the empirical literature convinced them of the concept of a continuum of thought disorder ranging from mild slippage to bizarre verbalization. They concluded that it should be possible to place individuals at different points on its continuum and to compare severity of thought disorder not only within a single individual over time but also across individuals. This index was constructed to be applicable to both psychotic and nonpsychotic conditions (Holzman, 1978).

THE SPOHN STUDY

The subjects of the Spohn et al. (1985) study were one hundred patients diagnosed as chronic schizophrenics using the Research Diagnostic Criteria (RDC) (Spitzer, Endicott, and Robins, 1975) who had previously manifested a therapeutic response to neuroleptic treatment. Their mean age was 32.6 years with a mean duration of illness of 9.7 years. The subjects were randomized to two conditions: one group remained on medication, and another group were withdrawn from it and placed on a placebo without their knowledge. All subjects were tested, with an extensive battery in a baseline test session prior to experimental assignment, and four sessions at two-week intervals thereafter. In this chapter, I will discuss only the first three testings involving the Rorschach.

THE CERNEY STUDY

The Cerney et al. study (in progress) includes twenty DSM–III diagnosed chronic schizophrenic patients who also fit the RDC. They were admitted consecutively to a long-term treatment unit noted for its work with chronic schizophrenic patients. The age range at admission was 17 to 38 with a mean age of 24.9. The mean duration of illness was 8.9 years.

The purpose of the study is to assess why certain chronic schizophrenic patients who present similar clinical pictures at admission are quite different at discharge or at follow-up three to five years later. The Rorschach protocols used in this chapter are those of two patients who were administered complete test batteries as part of diagnostic assessments at appropriate points in their inpatient treatment programs and whose Rorschach protocols evidenced considerable improvement in their thinking at termination.

During their hospitalization the patients participated in a program of milieu therapy and psychotherapy. The milieu therapy included daily meetings with their hospital doctor, team meetings and community meetings as the patients became able to participate, regular contacts with an assigned nurse or licensed mental health technician, and a program of activity therapy designed to meet their particular needs. A social worker made weekly contacts with the patient's family, with family meetings scheduled every four to six weeks depending on the needs of the patient. When ready, the patient was assigned a psychotherapist who met regularly with the patient. These meetings might be one half hour daily or a few times each week, or one hour sessions one to three hours weekly, depending upon the needs of the patient. Initially these contacts were supportive and became more expressive as the patients became stronger. Chemotherapy was used if clinically indicated and if other interventions failed to reduce the patient's anxiety and psychotic symptoms.

TESTING INSTRUMENTS EMPLOYED IN
THE PRESENT STUDY

The Thought Disorder Index. To assess thought disorder the Spohn study used the Thought Disorder Index (TDI) developed by Johnston and Holzman (1979). The TDI recognizes that a variety and range of thought disturbances exist and that some categories (such as contaminations and neologisms) are more serious indicators of psychosis than are others (such as peculiar word usage). The TDI assigns weighted scores reflecting four degrees of severity of thought disorder to pathological verbalizations as manifest on the WAIS and the Rorschach. Scores are summed to arrive at a composite thought disorder score. The higher the score, the greater the pathology present. Spohn et al. employed two TDI scores in their data analysis: one representing the sum of severity-weighted pathological verbalizations on the Rorschach corrected by the number of Rorschach responses (TDR) and the other representing the sum of weighted pathological verbalizations on four verbal subtests of the WAIS (TDW). Johnston and Holzman used the WAIS and the Rorschach in the TDI to elicit verbal samples from which thought disorder is measured because the verbalizations for each of these tests are produced under different conditions. The WAIS calls for habitual reactions with the frame of reference implicitly dictated. With the Rorschach, the social expectations are less obvious, with broad guidelines leaving patients ample opportunity to form their own expectations.

The Rorschach. Although the administration for the Rorschach is standardized, subjects are asked to choose a frame of reference to organize their perceptions. Rapaport, Gill, and Schafer (1945) described this process: "In the first phase, the salient perceptual features of the blot initiate the associated process; in the second, this process pushes beyond these partial perceptual impressions and effects a more or less intensive organization and elaboration of the inkblot; in the third, the perceptual potentialities and limitations of the inkblot act as a regulating reality for the associate process itself" (p. 276). These authors emphasize that the task is neither a purely perceptual one nor solely one of free association. Subjects who experience difficulty with the normal process of organization and regulation as described above will evidence faulty reasoning, unusual concept formation, and failure to focus or to attend in appropriate ways on their Rorschach protocols.

The Wechsler Adult Intelligence Scale (WAIS). The WAIS measures an individual's efficiency in intellectual functioning at the moment and is particularly suited to examine forms of psychopathology that fluctuate and selectively encroach upon certain intellectual functions. As the subject performs tasks for which there is wide social agreement, it is possible to observe the individual's knowledge of social expectations, reactions to those expectations, and compliance with them.

The Brief Psychiatric Rating Scale (BPRS). Spohn et al. also obtained ratings on the BPRS (Overall and Gorham, 1962) at each testing session, in part to determine whether patients who had relapsed in Sessions 2 and 3 manifested an increase in severity of symptomatic behavior due to a reduction in neuroleptic influence. This scale was developed to provide a rapid assessment technique to evaluate treatment change in psychiatric patients while at the same time to yield a rather comprehensive description of major symptom characteristics. It includes ratings based on observations of the patient and ratings based primarily on the patient's verbal report. The higher the summed total of ratings, the greater the pathology in evidence.

Although additional scales were used in the Spohn study, those mentioned above are the only significant ones for the study reported here.

PROCEDURE

Patients in both the Spohn and the Cerney studies were administered the Rorschach according to the method of Rapaport, Gill, and Schafer (1945), in which inquiry is made after the patient has completed his responses to a card. Card II responses from the Spohn study include patients' Rorschach protocols given just prior to withdrawal from medication (baseline), six weeks later or when withdrawal appeared to occur (withdrawal status), and then four weeks later (remedication or continuance of off-medication status). Subjects from the Cerney study were administered complete batteries of tests at critical points in their treatment as part of diagnostic procedures. Their Card II Rorschach responses are taken from these testings.

Card II responses were used for several reasons: (1) Card II is the first Rorschach card that has some color added to it and would therefore test not only the black-and-white effect but also the color effect upon the subject; (2) Card II frequently creates difficulty for many patients; (3) Card II responses appear, after an examination of the protocols, to be representative of the test responses given by the subject to the other cards; and (4) the Spohn study did not administer all ten Rorschach cards at the second administration, but did include Card II.

The subjects from the two studies are not comparable except in diagnosis and age. They come from different socioeconomic conditions and different family situations. This examination of Rorschach protocols reveals the kinds of changes that can occur on the Rorscach and the diagnostic implications of such changes.

THE CASE OF JANE: PLACEBO MAINTENANCE

Jane, a thirty-four-year-old single woman, had been hospitalized almost continuously since the age of nineteen. Adopted at age six by parents who are now considered to be alcoholics, she had been setting fires since she was twelve. She had assaulted a stranger with a knife outside an ice cream store when she was twenty-six and was reported to have stabbed a young woman. She was also a self-mutilator, frequently sticking herself with needles, safety pins, or bobby pins. Jane enjoyed the research—she participated in the Spohn study—and wanted the research assistants who administered the tests to adopt her. She grieved when the study was completed.

Card II: Baseline (5/30)

Response. You must have thought of animals on these today. It looks like dogs. (Anything else?) They're eating something. No, it looks like their heads, it looks like they are dogs and it looks like when they have puppies, they are all bloody and everything. The back part of them is where they just had puppies and that is the blood still on them. These things here are still part of the puppies, still in their bag. They haven't broken the bag. (Anything else besides the dogs?) Praying hands—and also right in there, you can see all the different things that pertain to the same thing but all different kinds of things. Okay, I can see, you know, the little tiny magnets. I see two small magnets coming together. Now I see they are different shades of dark and light gray. (What are different shades?) Their bodies are different shades of gray, different shades of gray. Their bodies are a different color. (The color of what?) The dogs. It could be either praying hands or, you know, those hedge clippers. It could either be either praying hands or hedge clippers. (Anything else?) I'm trying to think what kind of terrier. I think they are those Scottie dogs. Scottie terriers. That's all I see.

Inquiry. (What made them look like Scottie terriers?) Because that is the color and that is—I have seen them this kind of, that is the shape and the kind they are. Because that is what the real Scotties, the Scottie terrier look like. (Show me any features?) Well, the whole body, this whole body like, that is the way they are, they are small and the ears and that way their face is shaped, their heads and face are shaped. (Where?) Right here, there are the ears and it goes around like that and down like that. They are very small dogs. (All bloody?) Yeah, they are just having puppies. (What makes it look bloody?) Because, like, it is hard to explain but, you know, a lot of dogs when they have puppies get blood all over the back when they come out and everything. And that is the blood still coming out of them because they just had puppies. (This here?) Yeah, that's when they are still having puppies and you know like, dogs get together and help have their babies. Okay, they are both having babies and they're trying to help them. (Where are the praying hands?) Right here. (What made it look like they are praying?) See, like I said. All animals and all different things in the same thing. Because like this, see, like they are like this. That is the way they used to make the molds. (Hedge clippers?) Right there. (Tell me how it looked like that?) Well, see like they—grass not hedge. Because it's kind of scissors, things you clip them with. That's the clipper part, and right there those are the handles to them. (Magnets?) Right there. Those little tiny things. (What made them look like magnets?) That is the way they are shaped, you know, they are kind of magnets, not the big ones but those tiny ones you stick together. They are slowly coming together. I told you it takes a big imagination, that's what they have been looking like. I hope you got something, don't look like [laughs] They're so many different shaped ones.

Commentary. "You must have thought of animals on these today" is a projection and Jane's first comment suggests that she thinks the examiner is responsible for what is seen on the card. Although Jane's form level was generally good, she had difficulty controlling the fluidity of her thinking. She fabulizes her response, going far beyond the stimuli of the blot. The examiner's "Anything else?" appears to be an invitation to let down the barriers, and she becomes immersed in issues of eating and giving birth. Immediately after saying "They're eating something," she continues with "No, it looks like their heads," a statement that is unclear and jarring, particularly in context. Jane's thoughts are loosely connected; from eating she slips into issues of giving birth, but a birth which is incomplete ("They haven't broken the bag"). Interrupted by the examiner, she sees praying hands and then makes a bewildering statement: "and also right in there, you can see all the different things that pertain to the same thing but all different kinds of things."

Jane is vague and frequently unclear. "Scottie terriers" was a reasonably good response initially, but Jane seems mesmerized by the blot as she attempts to integrate all parts. The birth scene comes from her own inner world, and one wonders how long she would have continued if not interrupted by the examiner. Dogs, however, have long been a preoccupation for Jane. In the course of treatment she had reported to her hospital doctor that she goes into "heat," has had sex with dogs, and has tried to have puppies herself.

Jane's logic is not always easy to follow. One sees this in her comment, "All animals and all different things in the same thing." This suggests that more is going on within her inner world than is actually being stated. Diagnostically, Jane is very ill. Her thinking is psychotic and confused even with the help of medication.

Card II: Withdrawn status (6/25)

Response. It looked like newborn babies the last time. (What?) The same thing looked—miscarriage. These are two Scottie terriers. (Anything else?) They both lost a baby. One's the mother and her daughter, each had puppies and both lost them. (Anything else?) I'm not sure if they are mother and daughter or mother and baby. I'm not sure. I'm not sure if they are mother and daughter or mother and baby or two babies, dogs. (Anything else besides the dogs?) I see the blood. And that's their paws. That's all.

Inquiry. (When you first saw the card, I'm not sure I heard what you said. Did you say newborn?) I'm not sure if they are mother and daughter or mother and baby. (What kind of babies did you first see?) Scottie terriers. (What made them look like Scottie terriers?) That's what Scottie terriers look like. They got the heads of Scottie terriers and bodies of Scottie terriers. (Outline one?) This is the feet, right there, this is the head. (What made it look like they lost the babies, the puppies?) It is confusing. I can't tell if it is a mother or grown dogs and puppies. But I think they are newborn puppies. (What makes them look newborn?) Because, like, you know, when a baby, a puppy, is born, they come out in a sack. That looks like the sack. (There?) Uh-huh. See, they are not completely out of the sack. See this red part is part of the sack they're coming out of. (What makes the red look like a sack?) I'm not sure, but see, like, you can see the red on them. That is apparently the sack they are still coming out of. You can tell I live on a farm. (The blood?) It is like this, this red on this one, that's the sack they are coming out of. That is the front, like they are starting head first, that is the front of the sack and this is the back of the sack they are coming out of. They're not Siamese twins because like, when they are first born they are still coming out of the sack, like that's the way they are. (?) No, it is like when they are first born they're still coming out of the sack, they're not completely out of it. It is trying to get hot in here. (Going to be all right?) Yeah, I'll cool off. [Whispers something about cool with the curtains open.] (Feel like doing one more?) Yeah.

Commentary. Jane is more constricted in her initial response to the card than she was previously. She begins by repeating the response from the earlier testing. If she had stopped there, all might have been well, but she goes far beyond the stimuli to report a "miscarriage." This time Jane is so caught up in the birth-miscarriage percept that she cannot extricate herself even with the help of the examiner. In the inquiry she continues to be caught up in this response. Nor does she respond to the examiner's questions. Ultimately Jane appears to forget the task or needs to escape from it, and her thoughts center upon herself and her own discomfort. She does not offer any of the other responses she had given earlier. Jane's later responses to other cards become even more distant, bearing little relation to the stimuli. As on this card, she frequently sees blood, which she attempts to integrate into the context of her response. Her logic becomes more difficult to follow as she attempts to explain her responses and how and why she sees them. Although the examiner struggles to clarify the meaning, Jane easily slips away into another equally confusing comment. The fluidity noted in the previous testing is even more pronounced, with confabulation far afield from the stimulus of the card. Diagnostically, Jane's thinking appears more seriously disturbed than in the previous testing. Without medication, her fragile controls give way to the overwhelming pressure from her psychotic thought. Remedication is indicated, but Jane refuses and insists she be allowed to continue her current regimen—in reality, a placebo.

Card II: Withdrawn status (7/9)

Response. They are noting on the order of the movie. [Saw the first card as the movie *Airplane.*] That is off the ground, oh, that's not off the ground, that is not the shape of the airplane but it doesn't look like the shape of an airplane, but that is the way the very front part right there, see, right there, that is part of the airplane, that is the nose of the airplane. I'd describe it but I can't describe it by the colors in it because the colors don't match it. If I look at it close, it looks like those two airplanes side by side, they weren't taking off. I can see the two wings, but not the way airplane wings look. The reason I describe it because the colors don't match in it. Things in front and back, are the lights on the runways. (Anything else?) It's got the tail of an airplane in a way. I describe parts of an airplane, I'm not sure what some of them are called. And like I said the two front, these two front parts are part of it, with the lights on the runway, and it's got the exhaust or whatever they call it coming out of the end of the plane. (Anything else?) That's all.

Inquiry. (Where are the two planes you say are side by side?) Still the same ones. They are still in the same position. (Same position as what?) That is still the main plane. (What makes them look like planes? Is that the nose of one of those planes?) See, see, like they are not touching but like I said it was on a very close, tight runway. That is the way that the point of an airplane looks like. (Where are the wings?)

Right here. (The exhaust?) Right here. (What made that look like the exhaust?) That's just the way they look like when they come out in an airplane. (Where are the lights?) There, these two large front parts. And these two parts at the back. See, the reason they look so blurry in the picture is because it is right in the middle of the worst snowstorm in history. (What makes those parts look like the lights on the runway?) Because that is the way it looks in the middle of a bad blizzard. They are not all together, it is not one spot, it looks foggy and they look that way in a snowstorm. All spread out and streaky. All I can remember, it has same parts as telling these inkblots have just like the movie.

Commentary. Jane had seen the movie *Airport* the evening before and continued to perseverate on the film, seeing each card as another aspect of the film. This thought overrode anything that could come from the blots themselves. Her narrative is one long confabulation in which she has totally lost distance from the response. She is over-whelmed with a proliferation of ideas, with little attention to how her percepts fit the blot itself. In this testing, Jane was frequently incoherent, as she eagerly responded to each of the Rorschach cards by incorporat-ing them into her *Airport* narrative. Autistic logic, confabulations, confabulized combinations, poor form level, and incoherent speech characterized her response to this and succeeding cards. Jane's thinking has progressively worsened.

Summary

Jane was delighted to be a research subject and thrived on the attention she received. Her self-esteem improved and she was quite pleased and proud that she could do the tests. She boasted to everyone on the unit that she was doing so much better without Thorazine, even before she was informed that she was on a placebo. When officially informed she was on one, she was delighted and requested her unit doctor to continue her on the placebo rather than on her previous medication.

Jane was a very sick patient on active medication before the research began. As she was so disturbed when first tested, it was difficult to determine whether she had relapsed on the placebo. Jane was always very talkative and became progressively more difficult to follow at each succeeding testing. She felt that she was so helped by the placebo, however, that she has insisted on remaining on it to the present time.

Since the end of the research program, Jane has continued to improve and now has a paid job at a hospital workshop. She is proud of her progress in the last few months, having lost forty pounds, is on the highest level of responsibility she has ever been able to achieve at the hospital, and remains off medication. She misses her involvement in the research program and all the people who were so interested in her.

Discussion

One is not surprised, reading Jane's Rorschach Card II responses, that her TDR (Rorschach: 5.645; 65.62; 80.83) increased throughout the three testings. Jane is floridly psychotic and has an inner reality untamed by convention. Her TDR scores were not paralleled in the TDW (WAIS: 6.00; 0.75; 3.00) or BPRS (22; 31; 24).

In light of her increased pathology on the TDR (5.645–65.62), the decline on the TDW (6.00–0.75) is surprising and puzzling. Closer examination of the WAIS subtests reveals that the 0.75 TDW score does not capture specific aspects of what happened to Jane's thinking. Her more pathological responses in the first testing were on the Comprehension subtest, which was not administered in the second testing; hence the lower pathology score. Her responses on the third testing appear somewhat improved over the first testing. This improvement does not parallel the Rorschach, which worsened with each of these administrations, but showed some slight improvement thereafter.

The Comprehension subtest taps into an individual's ability to apply judgment to concrete everyday situations. It also contains proverbs that assess an individual's ability to abstract a generalized meaning from a concrete expression. We will sample each of those aspects in two questions from the Comprehension subtest illustrating Jane's more pathological responses on that test.

Why are child labor laws needed? (3/26) Too many young girls getting pregnant and get married. Because, like you sometimes hear about a twenty-two-year-old guy marrying a two-year-old girl and also besides that I read about this four-year-old girl and also an eight-year-old girl got pregnant and had babies. Child labor is to prevent young children like that who are working and are getting married. *Commentary*. Pregnancy is clearly on Jane's mind, as we saw in her Rorschach protocols. Her thinking is loose and her response is governed by her own inner associations.

(4/19) Abuse from their parents. (Explain?) Child labor laws. Is that the kind of laws for children working? Well, that would be about the same thing, parent abuse, because it would keep the parents from making their young children work to support the parents' smoking and drinking. It's like the shows I have been watching, like *Airport.* The last of these shows I have been watching on TV have to do with a lot of these questions you are asking, like the movies that these specials they have been having. *Commentary.* Jane does not quite answer the question, but this response suggests she has some understanding of the topic. However, the film *Airport* manages to get into her response. On the Rorschach she was unable to speak of anything else.

What does this saying mean? "Shallow brooks run noisily." (3/26) I don't know, but what still water means, you know the Bible says, sheep drink beside the still waters. It is noisy also because of rocks that is also sheep drink. *Commentary.* This response is pure confusion. Jane remembers something from the Bible but cannot articulate a clear concise response. One becomes bewildered attempting to following her reasoning.

(4/19) Because the water is shallow and it is noisily running over the rocks. *Commentary.* This response is essentially a repetition of the proverb concretely stated, but it is not as confused as the earlier response.

No examples of pathological verbalization were found on the Information subtests and there were only a few minor difficulties on Vocabulary. Jane improved her score on each successive administration of these tests, answering questions correctly on the second and third administrations that she could not respond to on the initial administration. The kinds of changes noted suggest a lifting of repression.

The WAIS Similarities subtest taps into an individual's ability to conceptualize. Generally Jane's responses during the second administration are more pathological than the first. The third administration produces a mixture: some responses are better or at least clearer, while others reveal more pathology, particularly when questioned. Some of Jane's more pathological responses are listed below:

In what way are a dog and a lion alike? (3/26) Pekingese are part—a wildcat and lion are the same thing, isn't it? Pekingese is a dog and a cat is—a lion is like a wildcat and back in the seventeenth century those little Pekingese are part wildcat so back in the seventeenth century they were three feet tall, so they are like about the same size and everything. *Commentary.* Here is an example of autistic logic and some very loose associations.

(4/11) A Pekingese is a dog and they are part, well, catlike, wildcats and lions are about the same thing. Pekingese is part wildcat, wildcats and lions are about the same thing, that is what Pekingese is a part of. *Commentary.* This response is similar to the previous one and does not answer the question. However, Jane does not elaborate to the degree she did in the previous testing, so there is some improvement.

(4/19) They are kinds of dogs that are related to the lions. *Commentary.* If this statement had been questioned, would Jane's response have been as confusing as before? Jane appears to be controlling the elaboration of her illogical thinking, but her thinking is still quite autistic.

In what way are air and water alike? (3/26) Rain comes from the air and makes the water. (4/11) Water comes from moisture in the air. *Commentary.* Although this response does not answer the question, it is an accurate statement and better stated than the 3/26 response.

(4/19) They are both made out of the same thing. (Tell me more?) Air is made out of water and water is made out of air. The water comes from the air and the air comes from the water. *Commentary.* On the surface the first part of the 4/19 response appears to be a potentially acceptable answer. Inquiry reveals a kind of thinking which Arieti (1974) describes as paleologic and quite characteristic of schizophrenia. In paleologic thinking "a class is a collection of objects that have a predicate or part in common; by virtue of having such a predicate or part in common, these objects become identified or equivalent" (p. 230). We see, more simply, a type of circular thinking that was more incipient in the two earlier responses.

In what way are an egg and a seed alike? (3/26) They are food. *Commentary.* Correct, but not an acceptable response.

(4/11) I never heard that one. I don't know. I know one thing comes from animals and that is part of a fruit or something, I don't know. I don't know how they are alike. *Commentary.* Jane's thinking is slipping, but she is not exposing the pathological content, only her confusion.

(4/19) Well, eggs, lots of baby animals come from eggs and the baby animals come from seeds and the mother. *Commentary.* Jane appears to have pieces of information that she cannot integrate.

In what way are a poem and a statue alike? (3/26) There's poems about famous statues. (4/11) Well, one is by a sculptor and one is by a poet and different poems are about sculptures. (4/19) They both come from the same thing. Poems are written about statues and statues come from different kinds of poems. *Commentary.* Again, as we've seen repeatedly on this test, the patient's thinking is circular. Contiguity influences her associations rather than an ability to abstract.

In what way are a fly and a tree alike? (3/26) I don't know. *Commentary.* Jane is cautious and does not reveal her inner thoughts.

(4/11) I don't know. (Want to think about it awhile?) I don't know how some of the sayings compare, about the same. It might be a fly lives on trees. You can tell I don't know much about science. (That's all right, kind of a tough question.) That was my worst subject in high school, science. (4/26) I don't know, but flies land on trees. That's all I know. *Commentary.* Jane's Similarities responses parallel her Rorschach responses in that they appear to worsen progressively, but not all of them. Some, as noted above, indicate her capacity for greater control.

The changes in the BPRS are more understandable. Jane's behavior does seem to worsen when medication is withdrawn, as revealed in the second BPRS score (22; 31; 24). Although her third score improves, considerable behavioral psychopathology is still present. We might ask if this improvement may have been influenced by her wanting to please the examiners, whom she liked so much she wanted them to adopt her.

Discussion

The overall worsening of Jane's psychopathology is not surprising following her withdrawal from medication. What is surprising is the improvement we see on the TDW and the BPRS. One wonders if the placebo has not become a "transitional object" linking her with her beloved research team and, as described by Winnicott (1951), giving her the security and stability to permit improved behavioral functioning. Could the enhanced self-esteem and importance Jane experienced in being part of a large research study, and the attention and care she received from sensitive caring researchers, have generated sufficient hope and a change of attitude to alter her behavior but not the thought disorder itself? Some clinicians are fearful that permitting their patients to participate in research will disrupt or interfere with treatment. Yet for Jane, participation in the research appears to have been a potent adjunct to treatment that helped to facilitate significant behavioral change.

The results in Jane's case raise more serious questions: How much voluntary control can a patient exercise in regard to expressions of psychopathology? This question can ordinarily be answered within a diagnostic assessment. If we look at Jane's Rorschach responses, she appears to be unable, even with the help of the examiner, to monitor or control the expression of psychotic thought. Even though one might say she uses denial in her assessment of her internal functioning (BPRS), there is nevertheless considerable behavioral improvement evident in her ability to lose weight, get a job on grounds at the hospital, and move up in the hospital status structure. Jane's behavior, as observed by others and as seen in her self-report (BPRS), indicates improvement, even though the Rorschach score indicates greater internal psychopathology at each of the three testings.

THE CASE OF JACK: A RELAPSE

Jack, a twenty-one-year-old single male, had managed despite his tragic history of shuttle parenting to complete his eleventh year of school. The current hospitalization was his third; his first occurred when he was sixteen. He stated that he was an habitual drug user, although he was not currently on drugs. As an automobile accident had earlier affected his right leg and arm and his speech, the staff initially questioned his eligibility for the research.

Jack thought medication slowed him down, and he liked "feeling high." Three days after being put on the placebo he began to experience insomnia and racing thoughts, though he denied having hallucinations. He was on the placebo a total of seven days before requiring remedication with Haldol; his condition was worsening and he feared losing control.

Card II: Baseline (4/28)

Response. Two people—two bears dancing. Throwing up this white stuff—for attention, the red stuff. And a shell. And a moose. And an ape. And two bears [laughs], and big hands in the middle, and these tongs looks like a spaceship. That's about it.

Inquiry. (Can you point out any features of the first bears you saw?) There's a bear and there's a bear. And there's a hand. There's a butterfly. (You said the bears were dancing?) Yes. (Why did they look like they were dancing to you?) Because they were together. (Do you see all of them or just part of the bears?) I see all of them, most of them. Except not the nose. (And you said they were throwing up?) Yes, this and this hands and this has shoes. (What was that?) Shoes. (Is this with something else?) No, the bears. The butterfly. (Now what were you saying about the bears? They were doing what?) Putting a shoe up there, tapping it. And they're touching hands here. And the legs are shown, but they're apart. (And you said a shell?) Butterfly. And a shell. (Are they both in the same place?) Yes. (What made it look like a shell?) It's this part broke open. (How did it remind you of the butterfly?) This split and the wings and the body of the butterfly. (And you said a moose?) A bear. A bear is more accurate. (Where is it?) There's the bear. And they have nothing on except for a handkerchief, so I don't know. (What do you mean they have nothing on but a handkerchief?) There's a handkerchief. And a spaceship inside there. (Inside the bears?) Well, in the ornament they make. (Do you see these as different bears than the ones in the beginning?) Yes. (Why don't you outline around one that you see now? Okay, that's the one with the handkerchief?) Yes. (And then you also saw an ape?) Well, I just said that. (Do you see the ape there on the card?) Either one of these could be an ape, I guess.

Commentary. Jack's form level for his responses is generally acceptable. His thoughts, however, were fluid, as they move from one response to another with no clear transition. Two people quickly become two bears dancing. But in the inquiry autistic logic is more clearly evident: the bears were dancing "because they were together." Attempting to integrate other aspects of the blot with this percept, he goes beyond the stimulus to interpret "throwing up this white stuff" as an attempt to attract "attention." Jack experiences difficulty responding to the examiner's structured questions. In the inquiry Jack's fluidity of thought became even more apparent. His language is somewhat peculiar: he describes the space between the bears as an "ornament they make." The percepts in this space have little stability, beginning as "tongs that look like a spaceship" and emerging on inquiry as "a spaceship inside there. . .in the ornament they make."

Card II: Withdrawn status (5/10)

Response. Looks like two boots. Two praying hands. Two bears putting their paws up to each other. And a butterfly, a very pretty butterfly. Or a moth or whatever the hell it is. And there's a line that's got to be broken. That's why I'm saying—and a top. There's a top. I see a smile. And there's a big butterfly if you want to look at it that way—it's a soul. That's why it's a butterfly. I guess souls don't have to be in any shape. They're just free and running around. Well, you know what I'm saying. Reincarnation in animals are spirits. Ghost. But everyone doesn't have to see the ghosts, because they could run up to me when they wanted to and now I'm here and they're going to have to—well, I've seen them already. I'm doing right by telling you all this. Okay. I'm just scared. That's all. (Something about that card makes you feel scared?) Well, it's God. He wants to sleep but he wants to see me and him both got—we were in heaven all this time. I been in heaven since I was born and you know I had to put a human inside Jack to let him live. Right? And he enjoyed everything that he did because he planned it at birth. And Jack he's me you know. I got two personalities. He's me.

Inquiry. (What was it about the card that made you think of the boots?) They're up here. Right there. And they have on ties like the old-time people used to wear back in the country. Might put that in the bank for a while. It's a wishbone and they wish for what they got. I like the butterfly and flowers. (What reminded you of the butterfly?) Because of this right here. It's just the hidden butterfly. (What makes it hidden?) Life. He's just afraid to jump into life. He can enjoy it but it's going to take time to take the pressure off of him. He is a hulk and that's why I like the Hulk series because that's the way I am and if anybody fucks with me they're going to get it. And I don't know if I should be locked up now or just free. I just want to be free. Like a big-ah-silly guy if they want to so, that's all. If they push me I will snap and I want you to know it now because their day will come. It don't matter, but guns won't kill me so their day, their number, is going to be up if they fuck with me—you know what I'm saying? I don't want to be locked up in prison forever. If they're going to shoot me they deserve to die and that's why they choose or mistaken me with chosen and maybe their life is so hard maybe they think that's the only way out, but their day will come. Know what I'm saying? I'll go back and judge them when the time is right. (Sounds like you have a lot on your mind.) Yes, I do. (Let's get back to the card. Did you say you saw a smile on the card? Where is it?) Right here. That's just a smile on a top. You know, a top. That's what I used to play with when I was a kid. That's why I'm this way because I just had to make a top to enjoy the speed. And I don't need drugs but it's a way of releasing the energy I have and I gotta have them so please allow me to do it with my own house. My dad smokes marijuana and he ain't been busted yet and he grows it out in the country and—hey! It's cool because it's a way of relaxing. And it's cool. It's cool. They ought to legalize it. Bust him. But don't lock him up. Don't lock him up 'cause he's already tried. (Can you point out any features of the bears on the card?) They're people and souls. They're spirits and just setting there holding their hands up together because that's why I mean people.

Commentary. Jack's responses speak for themselves. At the beginning of the card Jack exercises some control over his thoughts, but they soon overwhelm him and he speaks of a "line that's got to be broken," a response pressured by forces from within himself. He recovers and again slips into his own inner world, becoming self-referential, slipping into and out of reality. His thoughts, governed by their own inner logic, are difficult if not impossible to follow. He loses distance from the card and becomes frightened as his inner world becomes more and more chaotic and less under his control.

Thought merges into thought with little regard for how ideas actually relate to each other. Even the examiner's efforts to structure him are of little help. Any stimulus sends him off into a confabulized monologue beginning with self-referential fears and paranoia that feed upon themselves, becoming ever more frightening to the patient. He lets others know of his fragility while exposing a world that becomes increasingly more bizarre. Boundaries crumble before the onrush of primitive ideation, which is only marginally related to the stimulus of the card.

Only Cards I, II, and VIII of the Rorschach were administered at this testing. Responses to the other two cards were similar to those to Card II, although the fluidity and autistic logic became even more bizarre on Card VIII. On that card Jack became so absorbed within his confabulized narrations that he began to cry, fearing he was going to be sent to jail and killed.

Card II: Remedicated status (5/25)

Response. It's a spirit with a collar because it wanted to be a butterfly. And I see two things putting their hands together. Bears. And I see some old-time boots. I see a mouse. And a snake. And a top. And two things getting ready to hit each other. And blood, splat. And that's about it.

Inquiry. (So how much of this card is the spirit?) The whole thing except the paper. [Laughs] (And you said it was with a collar?) Yes, butterfly. I don't know what the collar is. (Was it color you said?) I guess. I don't know. (What made it look like the butterfly?) Right here. (What is it about that part that reminds you of one?) Shaped like a butterfly. (You said two things putting their hands together?) Yes, right here. (Can you describe them?) Bears right here and they're putting their hands together like this. (Putting their hands together as if?) Yes. (As if what?) Communication. (Do you see the rest of it?) Yes. (Is it the whole body?) Yes. Except for their feet. (And where's their head?)

Right here. Stuck behind their arm. (What made those boots look like they were old-time boots?) Right here. (The boots, what made them appear old-time?) They look that way. (Is there something you can show me that made them look that way?) Ties and ankle-high. Can I get up and walk around? (Okay, you can take a break.) (Where did you see the mouse?) Mouse? Right in here. If you want to say that. (Can you point out any of the mouse's features?) The head and feet and tail. (And where did you see the snake?) Right here. (And a top?) Right here. And there's an island with a tree on it, too. (And the two things getting ready to hit each other? Where were those?) Their arms are pulled back to here. They're going to make contact right here. And the blood's splatting. (Do you see that these two things that are going to hit?) Yes. (Can you tell what the things are?) Bears. (Which way are you holding the card when you see the bears?) This way.

Commentary. Jack's first response suggests that he has not yet regained his former control over his internal thought. It is not clear whether he means "collar" or "color," and he does not give the examiner much help in clarifying this ambiguity. His confused first response suggests that he is experiencing what is frequently termed "color shock," that is, a disorienting experience which can be inferred from a rather long delayed response or a confused first response. Jack does recover and although he seems to jump randomly from section to section on this card, he does continue with acceptable form level responses. Nevertheless, there is a fluidity of conceptual boundaries seen in Jack's increasing inability to keep percepts and their corresponding concepts distinct from each other. Thus, following Jack's train of thought is a difficult task.

Looking at the three responses over the experimental period, one is struck by the effect medication has in enabling Jack to exercise more control over his responses. Medication, however, cannot obscure the underlying pathology of thought as evidenced in his fluidity of thought, his approach to the card, and in his use of autistic logic. Jack's use of language is somewhat peculiar, as in the first testing: "This split and the wings and the body of the butterfly." Exactly what split is unclear and unexplained. Was it the shell or something else? Jack appears to be fighting some inner battle. Even in the third administration we have glimpses of the violence that exists within his mind: "And the blood's splatting." Further inquiry would no doubt have elicited even more pathological responses, but the roots are evident in the material presented.

Summary

Jack's relapse after the second testing was thought to be due to lack of medication, his assumption about the study that he was on the placebo, and his fear of not being released from the hospital at the time he had hoped to leave, all of which served to increase his agitation. Although Jack's initial motivation for participating in the study was money (each participant received ten dollars), he began to relate more warmly to the research assistants. At termination of the study he had not quite reached his preresearch level of functioning, but he was continuing to show improvement and reported he was happy and felt like laughing a lot. He had unrealistically high hopes that he would soon be living with his dad on the farm. It would take some time before Jack could accept that his dad did not want him coming back to the farm, and that the next step for him was a halfway house in which he would have to learn to rely more on himself.

Discussions

When Jack's medication was withdrawn, his pathology became more apparent as his ability to suppress more blatant psychotic ideation decreased. When medication was reinstituted, his pathology scores began to lower dramatically (Rorschach: 12.90; 50.00; 15.57; WAIS: 0.00; 3.50; 1.25; BPRS: 5; 31; 21). In these scores we see the effect of withdrawal from medication (Rorschach: 50.00; WAIS: 3.50; BPRS: 31). With remediation, all three scores begin a downward trend (Rorschach: 15.57; WAIS: 1.25; BPRS: 21). A few of Jack's responses on the WAIS Similarities subtest will illustrate the kinds of changes seen there.

In what way are a dog and a lion alike? (4/16) Just because they look alike and they're just the same thing except for being wild lions. *Commentary.* "They're just the same thing" could refer to a dog and a lion being animals but Jack does not explicitly say so.

(5/29) They've both got tempers. They've got four legs and they have fur and they both got faces. *Commentary.* In this session Jack himself was quite belligerent at times. He is quite concrete in his description.

(11/29) They're animals. *Commentary.* A perfectly acceptable response.

In what way are a fly and a tree alike? (4/26) A fly? They both grow. *Commentary.* This is an acceptable answer.

(5/29) They're both parts of life and flies got life and trees got life and they're both beautiful if you look at them in the right way. That's why they have so many eyes so they can see. They just can't see through. *Commentary.* This response illustrates how one idea gets associated to another, starting another train of thought. From people seeing flies as beautiful comes the need of the flies to have many eyes for them to see. But even so they can't see enough.

(11/29/82) They're both alive.

The changes from medication status to withdrawal status to remedicated status are quite striking. The responses given during the withdrawal status are characteristically loose, while responses given before medication was withdrawn and after it was reinstated are much more concise. With medication Jack is better able not only to attend to the question but also to control the expression of extraneous thoughts.

Medication in Jack's case was an important adjunct to treatment. Although it allowed him to function more appropriately within the social context, it did not eliminate the underlying pathology, which although not initially evident on the WAIS (0.00) and BPRS (5) was quite clearly captured on the Rorschach (12.90). Medication allowed Jack to maintain sufficient control over his illness so that with treatment he could begin to approach near-normal functioning in his day-to-day behavior.

THE CASE OF JAY: MEDICATION PLUS LONG-TERM TREATMENT

Jay was eighteen when first admitted to long-term treatment but had been seeing mental health professionals since grade school; the first of four brief hospitalizations occurred at age sixteen. He was quite paranoid and fearful that there was a conspiracy to destroy him, since he had a unique plan to save the world and only he could do it. The admission process took over a week, and he struggled over whether he should enter the hospital voluntarily. Finally his parents gave him an alternative; either he would sign himself in voluntarily or they would take him back home to have him committed. Jay seemed relieved as he signed the admission papers.

Medication was an important part of Jay's overall treatment plan throughout his hospitalization. After one year of long-term hospitalization he was discharged and functioned relatively well in a halfway house setting for almost a year. On his own he decided he no longer needed medication and discontinued it. He became progressively more paranoid, psychotic, and behaviorally unmanageable within the half-

way house structure. Jay was rehospitalized and remained within the
hospital for almost two more years.

Card II: Three weeks after admission (5/4/1974)

Response. [49-second delay] One sort of ah, a vase in the middle
here [shakes head "no"]. (Anything else?) That's about it. (Take your
time.) [2-minute silence as patient looks at card and at examiner,
frowns and grimaces frequently while looking furtively at the examiner.] Two feet. I'm talking about the white part—red and black.
That'd be, that would be, nothing that comes right off hand, and a blot
of ink, I guess [holds the card and looks at it for another minute]. [Time:
4 minutes, 15 seconds.]

Inquiry. (What made it look like a vase?) Uh, uh, in the red, by the
black. The red part and the feet were by the red part. (What made it
look like feet?) The space, uh white part, by the red at the top.

Commentary. Jay was not telling all he saw, as his behavior clearly
indicated. It took him considerable time to respond, and there were
many silences between his responses. Although his form level for the
responses was reasonably good, the inquiry and his long delay in
responding to this card revealed that he was experiencing considerable
difficulty with the color on the card. Observing his facial reactions, one
could only guess at the frightening content of his thoughts. At times he
would turn his head as though listening to someone and then shake his
head as if attemping to get rid of something. The Rorschach became
increasingly difficult for Jay and his responses more difficult to follow.
Each successive card resulted in increased grimacing and shaking of
his head. After examining Card VI for over three minutes, he said he
couldn't see anything. Neither could he see anything on Cards VIII and
IX. However, before laying them down he looked at each of them a very
long time, becoming increasingly uncomfortable. On Card IX he
trembled and exclaimed "No!" as he laid the card down with considerable force. When the examiner asked what he had seen, he laughed,
somewhat embarrassed, and said, "Only just orange, green, blue."
Later he was able to tell his hospital doctor of the voices who told him
all kinds of terrible responses; he didn't know which were his and which
weren't, so he didn't say much.

Card II: Six weeks after rehospitalization (1/5/1976)

Response. [5-second delay] Two men dancing and clapping their
hands coming in contact with each other's hands with the clap . . . I

also see the outline of a camel and there's a man that's yelling. [Time: 60 seconds.]

Inquiry. (What made it look like two men were dancing?) Well, you can see it looks like men and it appears they're in some sort of movement like dancing. Here you can see the outline of a camel. It's not very big, but on the edge here, and there's a man yelling like I yell at times. One thing I'm going to do is give up responsibility for taking over for the family. They're going to have to take care of themselves. They've depended on me to get them the help they need, but I'm not going to do that anymore.

Commentary. Jay seemed to be doing very well in controlling his inner thoughts but the last response opened a whole reservoir of feeling. The self-referential paranoid style came sharply into focus and continued onto the next card. Jay became so anxious that he said he felt he couldn't hold the card and didn't want to look at it. He began to accuse the examiner of judging him by his actions rather than by what he said. On Card III he said he saw a fly magnified and spent time associating to "fly" and how annoyed he was with flies and how wonderful it would be to fly. Clang associations launched him into verbal flights of fantasy, a rather frequent occurrence in this testing. He spoke of the girl who abandoned him, and of staff who wanted to make contact with him on a different level, but he didn't want a social relationship with them. He then launched into a continuation of his comments from the previous card about assuming responsibility for his family, especially for his father's health or death. He told the examiner how angry he was with her but he did manage to control his anger and then expressed considerable loneliness and fear of abandonment. Jay reorganized and gave some more appropriate responses but there were frequent lapses as he completed the testing. One became aware of the inner turmoil he was experiencing and his difficulty in maintaining boundaries as he lost distance from the cards. This protocol contained many contaminations, expressions of his inability to keep percepts and their corresponding concepts distinct from each other.

Diagnostically, this testing was very important in enabling the treatment team to plan a treatment strategy. Jay had initially been rehospitalized on the emergency unit because it was thought he would reorganize quickly once his medication was reinstituted and readjusted. But Jay did not reorganize and required transfer to a long-term unit. Because of his paranoia he would frequently refuse medication; eventually, however, he realized he needed it to function more appropriately. What was most distressing to the treatment team was that Jay seemed more disturbed than he was when first admitted. One thing was

most certain: he was more clearly showing the pathology he could not
express openly during the previous testing.

Card II: Prior to discharge (10/24/1977)

Response. [7-second delay] This looks like two Oriental, Chinese
men dancing, like way back in the old days. Then if you look in the
middle it looks like a spaceship, one that is taking off, as you can see the
thrust that powers it up. [Time: 2 minutes.]

Inquiry. (What made it look like two Chinese men dancing?) The
way they're clapping makes it look like an old dance or the way some
ceremonial dances are done. They also look like they have robes on.
The shape makes it look like the garments do not cling to the body. You
see these lines in between? What made them look Oriental was the way
the heads were shaped. (Spaceship?) The space in the center looks like
a spaceship and the red beneath that area looks like an explosion such
as is used for thrust to get a spaceship off the ground.

Commentary. Jay's responses were creative, with appropriate
elaboration. He appeared comfortable in making his responses and did
not exhibit the constriction or looseness found in previous administrations. He spoke quite freely with the examiner and appeared to have
greater control over his functioning. His responses flowed easily one
from another so that one had little difficulty following his thinking. On
Card VI his initial response was a malignant cell because of the texture
and color. (He was concerned about his mother, who had just been
diagnosed as having cancer.) Although there was some loosening
around this response, he quickly recovered. Only one other response
was of questionable merit, and that was on Card X, where he saw
"Cinderella with no head." Jay's ego functions seemed considerably
strengthened and only under stress did some of the underlying pathology seep through. He exercised considerable control throughout the
testing, while permitting some playfulness and some spontaneity
(which had never been characteristic of him previously).

Diagnostically, this testing was very important for the treatment
team. Remembering how Jay had appeared ready for discharge in his
previous hospitalization, they had been somewhat suspicious that Jay's
underlying pathology had not been touched. Now, however, they felt
more comfortable with his impending discharge and had information
from the testing to permit more appropriate discharge planning. Jay
underwent vocational testing and was accepting of the fact that he

required an environment that would minimize stress; he had already given up his ideas of becoming president of his father's company.

Summary

After his first admission to the hospital, Jay took considerable time before he was comfortable enough to participate in group activities. As he began to trust the treatment team, he began to improve ever so slightly. His treatment was an up-and-down affair with many setbacks, but after a year of treatment he seemed ready for discharge. He had been out of the hospital for almost a year when he relapsed and required rehospitalization. This second treatment effort was more stormy. After almost two years of additional treatment, Jay was considerably improved. Many staff members remarked how mature he had become and how helpful he was to others, both patients and staff members, while never seeming to lose a sense of boundary and appropriate assertiveness. It was evident, however, that Jay could not handle great stress, and he changed his aspirations from becoming a contractor and taking over his parents' company to working as a laborer with a construction firm. He continued in an after-care program in his own city and is now self-supporting, working with a construction company. Jay has been out of treatment for over seven years.

Discussion

Psychological testing was helpful in diagnostically examining Jay's internal world to facilitate appropriate treatment planning. Deterioration was evident in the second testing, which occurred shortly after his readmission, and indicated a need for structure and, because of Jay's heightened suspiciousness, a nonintrusive treatment strategy. The treatment team found the test report useful in helping them predict how Jay would respond in particular situations. They knew the kinds of situations that tended to disturb Jay and helped him avoid them. From the testing they learned how to keep his behavior from escalating. For example, during the testing, he suddenly became quite angry with the examiner. Instead of responding or questioning him, she empathically stated how hard it must be for him to come back into the hospital. He immediately became calm and almost tearful as he spoke of his embarrassment and concern that everyone would leave him. This tactic was repeated many times in the course of treatment and averted many potentially violent interactions. Testing in the latter stage of treatment enabled the treatment team to feel more comfortable with their plan for discharge.

Some of the changes that occurred on the WAIS are of equal importance in demonstrating the kinds of changes occurring within Jay. Although his overall IQ increased significantly during the latter phase of treatment, more interesting are the subtest scores, which indicate where some of the more significant changes occurred. Jay's ability to understand (Vocabulary) and think abstractly (Similarities) and to apply his judgment to concrete everyday situations (Comprehension) indicated the most striking changes (see Table 1).

TABLE 1

	5/4/74	1/5/76	10/24/77
Information	10	11	11
Comprehension	6	7–11	13
Similarities	12	10	14
Verbal IQ	96–102	96–104	111–118
Performance IQ	109–111	109–111	110–115
Full Scale IQ	100–105	102–108	110–116

The information subtest scores did not change appreciably over this period. Some examples from other tests show the kinds of changes that occurred within Jay and were diagnostically important for the staff in assessing his action orientation and the quality of his thinking. For example, his responses over this period to a question within the Comprehension subtest:

What should you do if you were the first person within a theater to smell smoke or see a fire? Illustrate the change in his action potential: (5/4/74) Oh, yell out fire or put it out, I guess. (1/5/76) Put it out. (Q) I don't know if I'd get the management or yell fire. (Q) Panic, so get the management. People would burn. Like the mattress fire, it starts slow and then it's on you. (10/24/77) Find the management and report it to them. *Commentary.* Jay's action potential can be inferred from his earlier responses to this question. He appears to be struggling with what to do in the 1/5/76 response, but his looseness of thought has him associating to the possibility of people burning and a way fire can start, as in a mattress. In the 10/24/77 response, he appears to have his impulses and associations under control.

Similar changes are evident in how he handles a question from the Similarities subtest:

In what way are an egg and a seed alike? (5/4/74) Umm—I don't know. I couldn't comprehend the two of them together. (1/5/76) Both yield one kind of produce. (10/24/77) Birth. They are both life-giving, the beginning of new life reproducing themselves. *Commentary.* Jay doesn't even attempt to respond to the question in the 5/4/74 testing. The response for 1/5/76 might have been questioned, as it is not quite clear what he meant. It was in this testing, however, that Jay became very hostile when questioned or asked to explain responses. The third testing (10/24/77) elicits a quite acceptable response, comfortably given.

The freeing of Jay's potential is evident in the WAIS results. Examining his WAIS results alone, however, one might be deceived into thinking that Jay could handle much more in the workplace than one might expect when the results of his Rorschach are also considered. Because of the structure inherent in the WAIS, even psychotic patients can function much more appropriately than on unstructured tests like the Rorschach. Both tests, however, indicate Jay's significant intrapsychic change during the course of his long-term treatment.

THE CASE OF ALAN: INTERMITTENT MEDICATION PLUS LONG-TERM TREATMENT

Alan, age twenty-two, entered a long-term psychiatric hospital after failure of three previous short-term hospitalizations. He was acutely suicidal and quite delusional, thinking that he had to return his body to the earth so that it could be recycled and someone else could use it. Alan's troubles apparently began at birth. He was colicky during his first four months of life and had difficulty eating. When older he became fearful that he would be castrated by his father. Alan was first referred to mental health professionals when he was eight years old, for provocative behavior and stealing from his father.

Alan's long-term treatment lasted a total of seven and a half years, about half of this time being spent within the long-term unit and the other half within the day hospital program. Progress was slow, with many setbacks. Although medication was a part of the physician's orders from the very beginning of treatment, Alan was too paranoid to use it consistently until the latter phase of his inpatient hospitalization.

When Alan first entered the hospital, he was too ill to be tested. Attempts at testing resulted in long, loose associations, even to the

WAIS, with the patient becoming very anxious, very paranoid, and quite upset. Testing was therefore interrupted. The first complete testing occurred when he had been hospitalized almost one year. (For a more complete discussion of Alan and his treatment see Cerney, 1984.)

Card II: 1971

Response. [17-second delay; took card and laid it down immediately.] A space capsule. A penis entering a vagina. A bird. Two faces facing each other. That's all. [Time: 1 minute, 20 seconds.]

Inquiry. (What made it look like a space capsule?) The white portion inside the black. It had fire coming out of the bottom. (What about the blot made it look like a space capsule?) The general space, shape of space capsule. (Anything else?) [Yawns.] Not much, really, just a black ring around the top of it, kind of like a decoration. (What about the penis?) At the top of the picture it looks like a penis entering a vagina. Two red lips and a black proturberance. (What made it look like a vagina?) Well, it had the two major lips of the vagina, that I saw there. (What made it look like a penis?) That looks like a penis, a short [laughs] stubby penis. Can I get a match? [Lights a cigarette.] (What made it look like it was entering a vagina?) Nothing except the fact it was faced that way, toward the vagina. (Lips were red?) Uh-huh. (What about that?) Just that the lips of a vagina are red. (You saw a bird?) Uh-huh, the black area and red area had the wings of a bird with the beak jutting out, and the white were areas on the wing like a decoration, so the wings were white and black and red. (How much of the blot did you use?) Everything excluding the two lips at the top. (And what about the two faces?) I forget. (Any idea?) I think it was the two lips facing each other. (What made it look like faces?) Can't remember it clearly. I don't know if I can go on. I'm really getting depressed. I'm getting nowhere. Dr. X is talking about I'll have to stay for fifteen years. I'll never get better. I'm just wasting my parents' money. And the tests aren't doing any good because I'm not applying myself, but I want to [support by examiner; looks at card again]. Oh, now I remember, yeah, the deeper red parts, there are the eyebrows, the eyes, nose, lighter parts, chin jutting out, the teeth; two pairs, neck going down.

Commentary. Alan's thought was still quite fluid as he jumped from one section of the card to another, rapidly giving percepts. He quickly got rid of the card, as if it were contaminated, something that needed to be avoided. His struggle with sexual issues indicating the pressure of internal thought forced its way into his narration of what he saw. His description of the penis was not only derogatory but also expressed in peculiar language: "black protuberance." His language became vague and he became more clearly disturbed, revealing his paranoia, projection ("Dr. X is talking about I'll have to stay for fifteen years"), depression, and sense of hopelessness. On succeeding cards, Alan's associations loosened and many of his percepts were of poor form level. His language became ever more peculiar and vague. He saw "monsters facing me about to attack" and began to expose more and more of his frightening inner world.

Card II: 1973

Response. [10-second delay] At the top I see two faces looking at each other just about to kiss. I can see their eyebrows, eyes, noses, mouths, chins, some portion of their necks. I also see our space capsule in flight. White space in charcoal gray, red-orange and flames are shooting out of the bottom. . . . I also see some prehistoric creature. I can see its eyes, its beak, its wing and tail feathers [turns the card around]. And I see a rabbit with his nose pressed up against a window. I see two heavyset men dancing with one another. I can see their arms, their heads, and their noses. They're in tunics and involved in a folk dance. That's all. [Time: 4 minutes.]

Inquiry. The fact that they were colored red made me think they were going to kiss each other. The shape of the nose reminded me of people I know that look like that, and the space was white on black, hurling through outer space. (What made it look prehistoric?) White on the back, black and irregular on edges made it seem prehistoric and red feathers here made it all seem like a prehistoric creature. (Rabbit?) It looks like he were coming at me, but he didn't because the glass is in the way. (Men?) Both of them were heavyset, made me feel like they were male rather than female; also the shape of their hands made me think that.

Commentary: Although Alan's form level has improved considerably, autistic logic is apparent in his reasoning of why the two faces were going to kiss each other—because "they were colored red." Nevertheless there was a smoother transition from percept to percept and Alan did exert greater control over his thought. On other cards his preoccupation with sexual issues continued to emerge, with poor form level responses as previously. He saw lost children and images of death and giving up. Alan's depression became even more apparent in the rest of the test. There was considerable fluctuation between primary and secondary process thinking as Alan struggled to remain with the test and not allow his internal fantasies to override the task. Contamination responses were notably absent in this administration.

Card II: 1975 (Discharge from inpatient treatment)

Response. [20-second delay] Two bears wearing human masks and walking along together with one arm upraised, space capsule taking off going up. There's a crab at the bottom facing me. No, it's a bunny rabbit not a crab. I can tell the bears are wearing masks. They're not smiling although they're having a good time. They have human masks, bears don't have human features. Also a pair of white feet stuck in between their faces. [Time: 2 minutes, 35 seconds.]

Inquiry. (Bears?) They had large black bodies with legs and arms and they were shaped like a bear. (Anything else?) The tuft of hair between their legs—bears have that when they stand. Their bodies are very bulky. They looked very powerful. (Space capsule?) The shape looked like a UFO. It was white, I guess. America is always sending up a white spaceship. It also has orange exhaust. (Crab?) Looks like a crab from a different angle, but from this way it looks like a rabbit. You can see his body and his ears here. (Feet?) It's the shape of the space between the red part.

Commentary. A further strengthening of Alan's ego structures is evident in his responses to this card. His form level was consistently good on this card and although there was some fabulized content it was not so ominous as before. Even percepts seen in the same area were more clearly justified, such as the crab and rabbit. There was occasional slippage evident on the other cards, but generally Alan's Rorschach did not speak to an underlying florid psychosis ready to break through. However, his controls were rigid and he was quite constricted, particularly on Cards VI and IX, which suggested that some of his difficulties, though controlled, were not too far from the surface.

Card II: 1978 (Discharge from day hospital service)

Response. [30-second delay] It looks like two fellows with their right hands pressed up against each other in some sort of contest. That looks like a spaceship taking off, and there's a crab. That's all. [Time: 90 seconds.]

Inquiry. (Men?) I imagine so. It looks like men from the profile, their heads in particular, their features, their noses, eyes. They seemed to have masculine faces and you don't see women involved in that sport—I've stereotyped. Good Lord, I'll never take a job like that. Too much writing [referring to the examiner writing everything down]. (Spaceship?) It's the shape and the color of the exhaust. (Crab?) Again it's the shape and color. For some reason I picture crabs as being reddish.

Commentary. Alan's form level was good on this card and throughout the test, with the exception of Card X. His first response there was, "This looks like some nightmare, an outer space being held together by some mass." (What makes it look like an outer space being held together by some mass?) "It's the colors and the shape. It's energy more than mass." But he immediately recovers from that response and the rest of the responses have excellent form level. On Card II we see evidence of strengthened ego functions. Alan is flexible, more self-reflective ("I've stereotyped") and more sensitive to others. Frequently during the testing he would ask if he were speaking too fast for the examiner and would ask if she needed to rest her hand from writing. Although his attention on the examiner could be seen as a diversion from the task, it did not seem to be. Alan was becoming more other-centered in all his interactions with others. He appeared less suspicious of what was being written, which had been quite an issue in other testings. There is a flow in his responses but not the fluidity once noted. Alan could joke about what he remembered from his previous responses, commenting that he didn't understand how he saw such things, as he doesn't see them now. Alan seemed to enjoy this testing. He asked about the results and wondered if the examiner would talk to him about the changes in his testing over the years. He then commented on the changes he felt he had made. Alan's internal ego structures were significantly strengthened. He was aware, however, that stress could undo some of what he had worked so hard to achieve. He was determined not to allow that to happen.

Summary

Alan's treatment at times seemed to go nowhere. Finally he began to improve to the point that discharge seemed appropriate. He was out of the hospital only a short time when he decompensated. After a serious suicide attempt, he asked for readmission and completed a treatment that turned out to be quite successful in the end, but was marked by severe regressions in its beginning stages. After returning home, Alan continued his studies, graduating with honors, and was hired by a prestigious company. After a time with the company, he realized that the work was too pressured for him and resigned. He quickly found a similar job with less pressure within a smaller firm. Alan lives independently, is self-supporting, and has continued his studies along with his work. He has been out of treatment for almost seven years.

Discussion

Psychological testing was used effectively in helping the treatment team plan Alan's treatment. The first testing (1971) pointed to the need to maintain the firmness of structure that had been instituted. Testing went further, however, in helping the treaters to understand what lay behind the difficulties he had with his parents. With a better diagnostic understanding of the symbiotic tie to his mother and his envy and fear of his father, they could plan a more appropriate strategy to assist the patient in working with these issues.

The 1973 testing alerted team to how seriously the treatment depressed and suicidal Alan had become. He was at the point of giving up, and if this attitude had not been altered Alan might have become unreachable. These are important diagnostic issues that can easily be missed but, if recognized, can make a difference in treatment. Alan's Rorschach was particularly helpful in revealing his internal world. He was like the lost children he saw on Card X of the Rorschach, who found peace in the oceanic experience of death.

The 1975 testing gave the treatment team confidence in their plans for discharge. Although they knew Alan was ready for discharge, they were cautious and helped him structure an environment that would avoid the consequences of his previous discharge. Alan worked slowly through the after-care service, and the testing that preceded his discharge from that service indicated he was indeed ready to be on his own.

Alan made some significant changes in his WAIS scores during the course of his treatment (see Table 2).

All Performance subtests were not given at each administration and therefore no Performance IQ is computed. The drop in Alan's 1973 Picture Arrangement subtest score, which taps into an individual's ability to assess social situations, is quite remarkable and mirrored the difficulties he was having in interpersonal situations: farting in public, being incontinent, and generally behaving inappropriately. It was only

TABLE 2

	1971	1973	1975	1978
Information	11	13	15	16
Comprehension	15–16	16	16	16–17
Similarities	17	17	17	17
Picture Arrangement	11	5	14	15
Verbal IQ	125–132	135	136	140–143
Performance IQ	121			132
Full Scale IQ	126–130			141

on this subtest that he gave evidence of bizarre thinking and a fluidity of thought with loose associations.

Alan's 1978 information subtest score suggests a lifting of repression. More information was now available to him. Although his Comprehension and Similarities subtest scores did not change appreciably, the manner in which he responded did. His answers were more elaborate in the initial testings and more simply stated in the later testings. For example, he responded in the following manner to a question on the Similarities subtest:

In what way are air and water alike? (1971) Air and water? How are they alike? They're both fluids. (How are you using the term "fluid"?) As matter which has indefinite shape. Chemistry and physics both define it that way. I should be giving the best answer or just what comes to mind? (The best answer). (1973) Air and water are necessary for human survival. (1975) Both contain hydrogen and oxygen and both are fluids. (What would be the most important?) I can't really say. Probably the most important is that they are necessary for life. They're needed by living tissue. (1978) Both are chemical constituents necessary for human life. *Commentary.* None of these answers are incorrect nor do they speak to the underlying thought disorder. They speak to the intellectual ability of this patient and how he could (and did) use his superior ability very defensively.

In general, one does not see on Alan's WAIS the evidence for thought disorder that is clearly evident on the Rorschach.

CONCLUSION

Before clinicians can decide what to do in regard to helping individuals in psychic pain, they must first find out what is wrong. Giving the problem a DSM–III diagnostic classification code is not the solution.

Already in 1963, Menninger, Mayman, and Pruyser wrote, "Diagnosis has gradually become a matter less of seeking to identify a classical picture and give it a name than of understanding the way in which an individual has been taken with a disability, partly self-imposed and partly externally brought about" (p. 35).

Diagnosis and treatment planning are inseparable. Diagnosis involves, according to Menninger, Mayman, and Pruyser, "understanding just how the patient is ill and how ill the patient is, how he became ill and how his illness serves him. From this knowledge one may draw logical conclusions regarding how changes might be brought about in or around the patient which would affect his illness" (p. 7). It was in this sense that psychological testing was used throughout the treatment of both Jay and Alan. When questions arose that could not be adequately addressed by other means, treaters consulted the psychological testing and at critical points asked for repeat testing to further their understanding.

Diagnosis is not a solo task involving only the professional, but a partnership in which the patient is an active participant. Partners together, patient and professional try to understand the symptoms, what has caused them, and what, if anything, should be done. Pruyser asserts that "the ideal diagnostic team leader should be the patient" (Pruyser, 1984, p. 12). Patients are not helpless victims but human beings in pain who have taken the first step toward healing by approaching a mental health professional. It is up to the mental health professional to enlist the resources of these patients in their own diagnostic understanding of what their problems are and what are the salient issues. That process in itself can be a very healing venture, raising self-esteem and revitalizing self-confidence. Jane, the first patient discussed, made significant behavioral changes after her participation in the research. Perhaps her improved sense of self came from feeling she was a partner making a significant contribution in a large research study.

Psychological testing involves the willing partnership with a patient who responds to specific test questions. How this partnership evolves is in itself diagnostically significant and paradigmatic for treatment. The psychological test reports of Jay and Alan were part of a more comprehensive diagnostic evaluation. Testing was utilized throughout treatment, guiding interventions and continually reminding the treatment team of the significant characteristics of each patient.

Of all diagnostic procedures, the Rorschach is especially revealing of a patient's inner life. This test can reveal not only the pathology present, but also the inner resources at the patient's disposal. As noted earlier, Johnston and Holzman (1979) have combined the Rorschach with the WAIS in developing a Thought Disorder Index which covers verbalization produced under both structured conditions and less structured conditions.

Part of the diagnostic procedure is ascertaining which patients can benefit from the use of specific medications. The Spohn et al. research (1985) has made a significant contribution in delineating what aspects of thought disorder are amenable to medication. With the help of medication, some patients become better able to utilize their own resources and those available through treatment. Jane and Jack, two patients discussed in this paper, illustrate not only the effect of medication on the thinking of schizophrenic patients, but also how powerful something other than medication—the placebo and all the meanings attached to it—can become for a patient.

Some pessimism exists about the therapeutic outcome with individuals suffering from a schizophrenic illness, regardless of the intervention or combinations of interventions used. Cerney, Schroder, Coyne, Frieswyk, Newsom, and Novotny (1984) in their study of ego function assessment—its relation to psychiatric hospital treatment outcome and follow-up adjustment—found at follow-up that schizophrenic patients did improve significantly in the area of reality testing, that is, in being able to detect the difference between inner and outer reality and in their accuracy of perception. There was also significant improvement noted in the areas of judgment, autonomous functioning, synthetic-integrative functioning, and in the patient's ability to conceptualize and to control primary process thinking. Positive outcomes, when they occur, are frequently labeled as misdiagnoses rather than as healing generated by a dedicated treatment team, loyal parents, and cooperative patients.

This chapter has examined the Card II Rorschach responses of two schizophrenic patients from the Spohn et al. study (1985) on the effects of neuroleptic treatment and the Card II Rorschach responses of two schizophrenic patients from the Cerney et al. study (in progress) on the effects of long-term treatment. These patients were selected because of the significant changes they manifested.

Although medication apparently helped to control the patients' distractibility and fluidity of thought, it did not conceal residual thought disorder as seen on the Rorschach. The Rorschach responses of two patients who received long-term treatment in addition to medication had quite different Rorschachs at the end of their treatment. Ego functions were strengthened, and there was greater flexibility in defenses, an increased attunement to the dictates of reality, and a greater sensitivity to interpersonal relationships. Although the underlying thought disorder was not completely absent, it emerged only under stressful conditions, from which the patient could more easily recover. Not all patients, however, are responsive to all treatment interventions. Research would help the clinician immensely if it could define accurately the profiles of patients most responsive to particular treatments or combinations of treatments.

REFERENCES

Athey, G. (1974), Schizophrenic thought organization, object relations, and the Rorschach Test. *Bull. Menn. Clin.,* 38:406–429.

Arieti, S. (1974), *Interpretation of Schizophrenia.* 2nd ed. New York: Basic Books.

Benjamin, J. D. (1944), A method for distinguishing and evaluating formal thinking disorders in schizophrenia. In: *Language and Thought in Schizophrenia,* ed. J. S. Kasanin. New York: Norton, pp. 66–71.

Cameron, N. (1944), Experimental analysis of schizophrenic thinking. In: *Language and Thought in Schizophrenia,* ed. J. S. Kasanin. New York: Norton, pp. 50–63.

Cerney, M. (1984), Unraveling the symbiotic bond: Psychotherapeutic change in a schizophrenic patient. *Bull. Menn. Clin.* 48:479–500.

————— Poggi, R., Mittleman, F., Zee, H., & Coyne, L. (unpublished), Twenty schizophrenic patients: Treatment and outcome.

————— Schroder, P., Coyne, L., Frieswyk, S., Newsom, G., & Novotny, P. (1984), Ego function assessment—Its relationship to psychiatric hospital treatment outcome and follow-up adjustment: The follow-up study. In: *The Broad Scope of Ego Function Assessment,* ed. L. Bellak & L. A. Goldsmith. New York: Wiley, pp. 121–149.

Feinsilver, D., & Gunderson, J. (1972), Psychotherapy for schizophrenics: Is it indicated? A review of the relevant literature. *Schizophrenia Bull.,* Fall:11–23.

Freud, S. (1911), Formulations on the two principles of mental functioning. *Standard Edition,* 12:218–226. London: Hogarth Press, 1958.

Friedman, R., Gunderson, J., & Feinsilver, D. (1973), The psychotherapy of schizophrenia: An NIMH program. *Amer. J. Psychiat.,* 130:674–677.

Goldstein, K. (1944), A Methodological approach to the study of schizophrenic thought disorder. In: *Language and Thought in Schizophrenia,* ed. J. S. Kasanin. New York: Norton, pp. 17–39.

Gunderson, J. (1978), Defining the therapeutic processes in psychiatric milieus. *Psychiatry,* 41:327–335.

Harrow, M., Himmelhoch, J., Tucker, G., Hersh, J. & Quinlan, D. (1972), Overinclusive thinking in acute schizophrenic patients. *J. Abnorm. Psychol.,* 79:161–168.

Holzman, P. S. (1978), Cognitive impairment and cognitive stability: Towards a theory of thought disorder. In: *Cognitive Defects in the Development of Mental Illness,* ed. G. Serban. New York: Brunner/Mazel, pp. 361–376.

Johnston, M. H., & Holzman, P. S. (1979), *Assessing Schizophrenic Thinking,* Washington: Jossey-Bass, pp. 1–310.

Menninger, K., Mayman, M., & Pruyser, P. (1963), *The Vital Balance.* New York: Viking.

Overall, J. E., & Gorham, D. R. (1962), The Brief Psychiatric Rating Scale. *Psychol. Reports,* 10:799–812.

Pruyser, P. (1984), The diagnostic process: Touchstone of medicine's values. In: *Diagnostic Understanding and Treatment Planning,* ed. F. Shectman & W. Smith. New York: Wiley, pp. 5–17.

Quinlan, D., Harrow, M., Tucker, G., & Carlson, K. (1972), Varieties of "disordered" thinking on the Rorschach: Findings in schizophrenic and nonschizophrenic patients. *J. Abnorm. Psychol.,* 79:47–53.

Rapaport, D., Gill, M., & Schafer, R. (1945), *Diagnostic Psychological Testing.* Rev. ed. New York: International Universities Press.

Schooler, C., & Spohn, H. (1982), Social dysfunction and treatment failure in schizophrenia. *Schizophrenia Bull.,* 8:85–98.

Shield, P., Harrow, M., & Tucker, G. (1974), Investigation of factors related to stimulus overinclusion. *Psychiat. Quart.,* 48:1–8.

Spitzer, R. L., Endicott, J., & Robins, E. (1975), *Research Diagnostic Criteria.* New York: Biometrics Research, Evaluation Section, New York State Psychiatric Institute.

Spohn, H. E., Coyne, L., Mittleman, F., Larson, J., Johnston, M., Spray, J., & Hayes, K. (1985), Effect of neuroleptic treatments on attention, information processing and thought disorder. *Psychopharm. Bull.,* 21:582–587.

Vygotsky, L. (1934), *Thought and Language,* trans. E. Hanfmann & G. Vakar. Cambridge, MA: M.I.T. Press, 1962.

Weiner, I. B. (1966), *Psychodiagnoses in Schizophrenia.* New York: Wiley.

Winnicott, D. W. (1951), Transitional objects and transitional phenomena. In: *Collected Papers,* New York: Basic Books, 1958.

Part IV
Primitive Mental States
in Children
and Adolescents

Chapter 21

When Does the Rorschach Become the Rorschach?
Stages in the Mastery of the Test

Martin Leichtman, Ph.D.

Insofar as the psychological concept of "primitivity" is associated with early periods of normal development or severe forms of psychopathology, studies of young or profoundly disturbed children should provide the basis for significant contributions to an understanding of the relationships between the Rorschach test and "primitive mental states." Yet for such contributions to have a solid foundation, it is necessary to confront a paradox. This chapter is about that paradox, a way of dealing with it, and the consequences of this solution not only for clinical work with children but, even more, for our understanding of the nature of the Rorschach test itself.

The paradox facing those who would use the Rorschach to study primitive mental states in children can be stated simply: The more primitive the children's mental states, the more reasons there are to question whether the Rorschach can or should be used with them. To review the literature on the extension of Rorschach technique to preschool children is to recognize that there is no area in the Rorschach literature in which there is less agreement over such fundamental issues as how the test should be administered, scored, and

I am indebted to Dr. Maria Luisa Leichtman for her helpful critical comments on drafts of this manuscript.

interpreted or, indeed, whether it should be given at all (Klopfer, Fox, and Troup, 1956; Klopfer, Spiegelman, and Fox, 1956; Ames, Metraux, Rodell, and Walker, 1974). The testing of severely disturbed children, while subject to less debate, involves many of the same methodological problems encountered with preschoolers. For example, it is often extraordinarily difficult to administer psychological tests in their standard forms to children who manifest what have been labeled "borderline conditions" (Leichtman and Shapiro, 1980; Leichtman and Nathan, 1983). If one considers an even more disturbed population and restricts attention to the Rorschach, frequently the most difficult test in the battery for children, the range and intensity of these problems increase markedly.[1] Because of methodological issues of this kind, studies of the application of the Rorschach to young or deeply troubled children might aptly be subtitled "The use of the Rorschach test with children for whom it may be inappropriate."

The main thesis of this essay is that coming to terms with this paradox requires moving back from the question of what the Rorschach can contribute to the study of primitive mental states to a more fundamental question, that of how children come to be able to take the Rorschach test at all. The first section will review the literature on the use of the Rorschach with preschool children in order to clarify methodological conflicts, outline differing views of stages in early Rorschach reactions, and suggest the manner in which these controversies contain within them the seeds of a new synthesis. Assuming that the basis for this synthesis lies in considering the behavior of both preschool children and examiners as they negotiate the test situation, the second section will propose a model of how children come to master the Rorschach that integrates earlier concepts of stages of Rorschach performance and provides a way of understanding, if not resolving, controversies regarding method. The concluding section will explore the implications of this model for the

---

[1]For example, of the 3300 Rorschach records of children over the age of six collected by Exner and Weiner (1982) for their standardization sample, only 74 cases required substantial alterations of their test procedure or had to be discarded. Almost all of these cases were children under the age of eight who manifested schizophrenic symptoms or marked behavior problems. Although the behavior problems are not specified, the extent to which they interfered with the test process suggests that in many cases they are probably consistent with a "borderline personality" diagnosis.

use of the Rorschach with preschool and severely disturbed children and for Rorschach theory in general.

CRITICAL ISSUES IN THE PRESCHOOL RORSCHACH LITERATURE

The Rorschach and Young Children

Because the Rorschach test has not been used widely with young children for clinical purposes, the literature on preschool Rorschach performance is relatively limited. Works devoted to this group constitute only a small fraction of the publications on the use of the test with children, and these in turn constitute only a small fraction of the Rorschach literature as a whole (Levitt and Trauma, 1972). Nonetheless, because the manner in which preschool children take the Rorschach provides a developmental perspective on the test itself, the subject is one that has captured the interest of such major Rorschach authorities as Rorschach himself (1964), Klopfer (Klopfer and Margulies, 1941; Klopfer, 1956), Piotrowski (Piotrowski and Lewis, 1950), and Ernest Schachtel (1966) and one that has a significance beyond what the number of publications alone might suggest.

Rorschach practitioners have from the first been intrigued by children's responses to the test. Even before Rorschach's work, studies had been undertaken of children's associations to inkblots (Kirkpatrick, 1900; Whipple, 1910; Pyle, 1915; Parsons, 1917); Rorschach (1964) commented in passing on developmental changes in children's responses to the test; and, in the decade and a half following his death in 1922, the relatively small group of European clinicians and researchers who kept interest in his test alive gradually applied the technique in a more systematic way to studies of children and, on occasion, very young children (Bohm, 1958).

Use of the Rorschach with preschool children increased with the test's growing popularity. As the Rorschach took root in the United States in the 1930s, the enthusiasm it generated led to considerable curiosity about how early the test could be administered and what kinds of results could be obtained from young children. This interest is best seen in the Klopfer and Margulies paper, "Rorschach Reactions in Early Childhood" (1941), a study drawing on material gathered by collaborators in a half-dozen nursery schools and child study centers in the East. By the early 1940s a modest stream of works on preschool Rorschachs began to appear and, within ten years, two books presenting normative data on the subject were published (Ford, 1946; Ames, Learned, Metraux, and Walker, 1952).

A steady flow of articles dealing with early Rorschach performance from a variety of perspectives continued through the next two decades. For example, Allen (1951, 1954, 1955) published a series of longitudinal studies of Rorschachs given repeatedly to individual youngsters between the ages of two and five; Halpern (1953, 1960) explored clinical applications of the test with young children; students of Heinz Werner, following a line of experimental research initiated by Dworetzki in the 1930s (Meili-Dworetzki, 1956), studied children's Rorschachs in terms of the principles of perceptual development (Hemmendinger, 1953, 1960; Goldfried, Stricker, and Weiner, 1971); Amers (1959, 1960a, 1060b, 1965, 1966) extended her work on clinical and developmental applications of the test; and Klopfer and his colleagues examined a host of methodological and theoretical problems related to preschool Rorschachs (Klopfer, 1956). More recently, Nordland (1966) published a longitudinal study of responses of Norwegian children; Francis-Williams (1968) devoted significant sections of her book on children's Rorschachs to preschoolers; and Ames et al. (1974) offered a third edition of *Child Rorschach Responses* with extensive data from new normative samples.

Although this body of literature is not large, it is distinguished by the fact that there is probably no other area of Rorschach research in which there are wider disagreements over fundamental methodological and substantive issues. These differences of opinion can best be appreciated if consideration is given to controversies around issues of technique and interpretation, on the one hand, and characterizations of patterns of developmental change in children's Rorschachs, on the other.

Methodological Issues

Age at first administration. An initial question facing those who would give the Rorschach to children is the age at which children can begin to take the test in an "appropriate" manner. Those expressing opinions on the matter fall into two groups. A heterogeneous group of experts who believe that the Rorschach can and should be given to relatively young children agree that, while records can be obtained from two-year-olds, the test is better suited to children three years of age and older (Ford, 1946; Klopfer, Fox, and Troup, 1956; Ames et al., 1974). The Ames and Klopfer groups acknowledge that there is another group of experts who are convinced that the Rorschach technique is not appropriate until children are of school age. Members of the latter group are not named and there is in fact little argument in the literature opposing the use of the Rorschach with preschoolers. This silence itself makes a statement however, as does the fact that the Rorschach is used so infrequently with young children. Two recent and otherwise comprehensive books on the Rorschach with children (Levitt and Trauma, 1972; Exner and Weiner, 1982) make no reference to the subject and consider the test only with children five or older.

A rationale for restricting the use of the Rorschach to older children and adults can be found in three points articulated by Ames et al. (1952), who were concerned chiefly with refuting them. These points are worth considering in some detail because they touch on methodological issues that divide all major authorities on preschool Rorschachs and allow opposition to the use of the Rorschach with young children to be seen as a logical extension of a wider body of opinion.

Questions regarding technique. The first objection to the use of the Rorschach with preschool children is that "the test is difficult to administer to young children" (Ames et al., 1952, p. 29). This fact is beyond dispute. All who work with preschoolers agree that they present a host of problems that interfere with test administration. These include problems raised by children's difficulty grasping the nature of the test task, their readiness to redefine the task in their own way, their disinterest, their difficulty sustaining a set, their distractibility, their impulsivity, their capriciousness, their resistance to the inquiry process, and simply their readiness to ignore adults' wishes and do whatever happens to intrigue them at any given moment. The Ames group tries to counter objections based on difficulties in test administration by noting that the Rorschach can nonetheless be given to children if suitable adaptations are made. However, methodological questions cannot be dismissed so easily. The critical problem is that the difficulties encountered in administering the Rorschach to young children are such that there is no consensus on whether and how the test should be adapted. Indeed, no two major authorities on preschool Rorschachs seem to agree on the way the test should be given.

Almost all differences of opinion regarding technique revolve around one general question: in order to remain faithful to "the spirit of the Rorschach," is it necessary to alter the method of its presentation to accommodate the characteristics of preschool children, or do such alterations so change "*the* Rorschach" that it is preferable to give the test in its standard form and accept problems in administration and uncertainty about results as unavoidable consequences of working with young children? Those inclined to the former position have recommended such changes in technique as the use of a trial blot to help children understand the nature of the task (Ford, 1946), restricting rotation of the cards to prevent children from becoming distracted by their interest in manipulating objects (Ford, 1946), conducting inquiry after each card (Ford, 1946; Ames et al., 1952) or even after each response (Halpern, 1960) to offset boredom or limitations in memory, limiting inquiry to avoid frustration or distraction (Ames et al., 1952), and relying heavily on examiners' sensitivity to nonverbal cues and intuition in scoring responses (Ames et al., 1952). Those inclined to the latter position, such as Klopfer, Fox, and Troup (1956), argue that major changes in technique with young children are probably unnecessary and, even if necessary, alter the nature of the test and undercut its interpretation. Consequently, they contend, while minor adaptations in test administration may be made to establish rapport or help a child understand the test's language, the Rorschach should be given in essentially the same manner to both children and adults.[2]

Some of the problems and trade-offs in each position are illustrated by the argument between the Ames and Klopfer groups as about various scoring issues. Ames et al. (1952) believe that, in order to keep preschoolers involved with the Rorschach and obtain as full a record as possible, it is desirable to conduct inquiry after each card, to "not force" the inquiry process unnecessarily, and to rely instead often on the content of responses and nonverbal cues (e.g., the "direction of the child's regard") to determine such matters as location (p. 27). By contrast, Klopfer, Fox, and Troup (1956) advocate conducting the inquiry process after the presentation of all cards has been completed, engaging in more extensive inquiry, and relying on explicit indications of location and determinants in scoring. They argue that "guesswork" should play little part in scoring and that it is better to attempt a rigorous

---

[2]It is easier for Klopfer to advocate such methodological purity than for most other Rorschach authorities. Although the investigation of determinants of percepts is restricted to a formal inquiry process in most Rorschach systems, Klopfer's standard procedures also include an "analogy period" and "testing-the-limits" (Klopfer, Ainsworth, Klopfer, and Holt, 1954). Klopfer, Fox, and Troup (1956) acknowledge that it is the latter procedure that often provides the basis for scoring the responses of young children.

inquiry and content oneself with question marks in scoring than to rely on intuitions about what children may have meant by their responses.

While the gap between the Ames and Klopfer positions can be narrowed to some extent,[3] the two approaches constitute opposing tendencies that can be recognized by all who give the Rorschach test to young children. On the one hand, it is possible to obtain more responses and produce more comprehensive scores with modifications of technique designed to engage children more fully, with special efforts to encourage the production of responses, and with the use of intuition in making decisions about the meaning of particular responses that young children have difficulty explicating. To the extent to which such changes in technique are introduced, examiners will be prepared to use the Rorschach with children at earlier ages and to make more elaborate interpretations of personality development on the basis of test results. However, they are also more likely to be confronted by questions from colleagues about the appropriateness of their procedures, the soundness of their data, and the value of their conclusions. On the other hand, the more examiners hold to a standard set of procedures used with adults as well as children, the more likely they are to obtain sparser test records, to have more questions about scoring, to be more cautious about interpretations, and to prefer to use the Rorschach with children at older ages. Practitioners who favor using the test only with children of school age or older represent an extreme version of the latter position, one that assumes that the data obtained from younger children are so dubious that it is simply not worthwhile to administer the test to them.

Validity. A second argument against preschool Rorschachs addressed by Ames et al. (1952) is that test results may not be valid because "determinants which indicate disturbance appear in children who on other grounds are considered quite undisturbed" (p. 29).[4] Cast in this form, the criticism is easy to handle. If interpretations of protocols are made with reference to children's norms rather than adult ones, there is no more reason for considering children's immature responses pathological than there is for assuming that a mental age of "only" 36 months on the Stanford-Binet is a sign of retardation when it is achieved

[3]For example, Ames et al. (1974) later stressed some of the "objective" bases of judgments about determinants relying on nonverbal cues and pointed out that a degree of judgment or "guesswork" is present in any decision about scores, using examples from Klopfer's work to illustrate their point (p. 13).

[4]Carrying this line of thought to an extreme, Halpern (1953) notes: "In fact, children of the age of two to four-and-a-half have been characterized as 'healthy schizophrenics,' and their Rorschach protocols bear out this description" (p. 69).

by a three-year-old. However, the criticism is not so easily dismissed when it is recognized that the "pathological" features under consideration are, above all, the perservative and confabulatory thinking that seems to pervade the Rorschachs of young children (Klopfer, Spiegelman, and Fox, 1956). To the extent to which such modes of thinking do not represent isolated departures from "higher level" approaches to the Rorschach but instead constitute characteristic ways of dealing with the task, it can be argued that the processes underlying the Rorschach responses of preschool children are fundamentally different from those of older children and adults. If this is true, such basic scores as those for location and form level with young children may well be artifacts of different approaches to the test and have different meanings from those usually given them in the Rorschach literature. Even if the argument is not carried this far, it can be contended, nonetheless, that these early forms of "concept formation" are of such significance that they eclipse any other consideration in the interpretation of preschool children's Rorschachs (Klopfer, Spiegelman, and Fox, 1956).

Meagerness of data. A third type of objection to the use of the Rorschach noted by Ames et al. (1952) concerns the "meagerness" of the data obtained. Even if questions about methodology and validity are ignored, such an argument runs, preschool Rorschachs still yield too little information to allow for the kind of differentiated analyses one expects from *the* Rorschach.

How rich or meager test results are, of course, depends upon who is making the judgment and on what basis it is being made. For example, while acknowledging that preschool Rorschachs may be far less revealing than those of adults, Ames et al. (1952, 1974) are able to point to the fact that extensive data can be derived from the Rorschachs of young children, and offer table after table showing changes over age in each Rorschach scoring category. Moreover, the Ames group advance detailed analyses of these trends, seeking to demonstrate the manner in which Rorschach performance correlates with the major developmental characteristics of each age as outlined by Gesell and Ilg (1943, 1946).

At the same time, even recognizing that the Ames data is biased in the direction of fuller and more differentiated Rorschachs because of an overrepresentation of bright children from upper socioeconomic classes in their sample, a case can still be made on the basis of that data that the Rorschachs of most preschoolers are too limited to permit the analyses typically done with older subjects. For example, at two years of age, Ames's children produce only about ten Rorschach responses, and the extent of perseveration is such that it is likely that there are only one or two true responses. Even at the age of five, the children give an average of only fourteen or fifteen responses, including some perseverations. Equally important, while Ames found consistent statistical trends across age for most basic determinants, the actual differences are often so small that the tables are of little value as normative data against which to judge individual performance. For example, the average number of M responses in a record changes from .1 at two years to .6 at five years; m from .1 to .2; shading responses from .2 to .4; achromatic color responses from .1 to .2; FC responses from .1 to .2; and C from .4 to .2. While more significant shifts over age occur with some determinants (CF responses, animal movement responses, and form level), the most marked changes in Rorschach performance in the sample lie in such relatively simple factors as number of responses, number of different content categories used, total time required to administer the test (four minutes at two; about eight minutes at five), number of cards refused, and number of words used in giving responses—hardly the material on which most Rorschach practitioners would like to base their analyses. In addition, although the Ames group offers comprehensive interpretations of characteristics of children of different ages on the basis of such Rorschach signs, serious questions have been raised about the validity of their analysis by psychologists sympathetic to the use of the Rorschach with preschool children (see Klopfer, Spiegelman, and Fox, 1956). Finally, while prepared to make bold generalizations about age groups on the basis of Rorschach data, even Ames and her colleagues are quite cautious about clinical use of the test with children under five.

Conceptions of Developmental States in Preschool Rorschach Performance

Models of developmental change. Although there is no consensus in the Rorschach literature on how best to characterize changing patterns of Rorschach responses across the preschool years (Klopfer, Spiegelman, and Fox, 1956), disagreements over these substantive issues have been far less intense than those over methodological issues. For example, in spite of their arguments over Rorschach administration, the Ames and Klopfer groups often seem to agree on the main types of responses characteristic of different periods of early childhood. The perseverative tendencies stressed by Klopfer and Margulies (1941) in their description of the "Rorschach reactions" of two- and three-year-olds figure prominently in the work of Ames et al. (1952), while the Ames group's observations of confabulatory phenomena in Rorschachs of three- and four-year-olds are used by Klopfer in advancing his later conception of stages in Rorschach responses (Klopfer, Spiegelman, and Fox, 1956). Moreover, differing conceptions of such stages are generally presented in modest ways. As a rule, they are offered as attempts to highlight salient features of a developmental process rather than as definitive treatments of the subject that preclude others.[5] Consequently, the four major approaches that have been adopted in describing developmental changes in the Rorschach performance of young children need not necessarily be seen as antithetical; rather, they may be viewed as models organized around different principles, each model having its own particular strengths and limitations.

The perseveration model. One of the first and most influential conceptions of stages of "early Rorschach reactions" centers on the handling of a strong initial predisposition toward perseverative responses. An early version of this scheme advanced by Klopfer and Margulies (1941) described three successive "patterns of reactions": the first, encountered typically in two-year-old children, consists of pervasive perseverations in which an initial response is repeated on all subsequent cards as if it were a "magic key" that allows children to make a difficult problem disappear; the second, common in children between two and a half and three and a half, consists of modified perseverations in which children refuse some cards or give a few different responses; and the third, often emerging between three and a half and five, is one in which the hold of the perseverative tendency is broken and different responses are given on a majority of the cards. Ford (1946) elaborated this view, renaming the patterns (the "pre-logic," "confused-logic," and "true-logic" stages) and suggesting an additional pattern between the latter two, a "perseverated-logic" stage in which children make an effort to find characteristics of each blot that fit the repeated concept.

Two aspects of these conceptions of stages in early Rorschach responses are noteworthy. On the one hand, by focusing on perseverative tendencies, the schemes highlight what is undoubtedly the most salient feature of the Rorschach performance of children between the

---

[5]For example, before presenting their own conception of patterns of early Rorschach preformance, Klopfer, Spiegelman, and Fox (1956) write, "Future Rorschach research with children will have to contribute a great deal for the clarification and conceptualization of such phases of development. At the present stage of knowledge, or lack of it, it is difficult to give a systematic presentation of interpretation problems connected with age patterns" (p. 25).

ages of two and three-and-a-half. All who write about preschool Rorschachs recognize the prominence of these tendencies and, if they disagree to some extent about the timing of shifts from stage to stage, they nonetheless make use of these concepts of stages in doing so. On the other hand, conceptual schemes focused on perseveration alone are too narrow to do justice to the range of phenomena encountered in preschool Rorschachs, especially among three- to five-year-olds. Recognizing this limitation, Klopfer himself later proposed a broader position (Klopfer, Spiegelman, and Fox, 1956).

The Ames approach. A second major effort to describe developmental changes in preschool Rorschachs is that of Ames et al. (1952). Working with groups of fifty children spaced at half-year intervals between the ages of two and six, the Ames group traces changes in a range of test behaviors and almost every scoring category. Correlating these test signs with traits ascribed to children at each level by Gesell and Ilg (1943), they suggest that striking transformations in personality can be seen in Rorschach performance at each six-month interval.

Although this research provides a rich description of a wide array of changes in the ways in which preschool children handle the Rorschach, it is subject to three sets of criticisms. First, because it describes such a multiplicity of continuous and discontinuous developmental trends, the Ames approach makes it difficult to see which aspects of Rorschach performance are most significant at each stage. Second, rather than deriving characteristics attributed to a developmental stage from children's Rorschach performance, Ames and her colleagues begin with the Gesell and Ilg scheme and search for Rorschach signs at each age that correlate with it. Third, objections can be raised to that model of personality development itself. For example, in their critique of the Ames position, Klopfer, Spiegelman, and Fox (1956) note, "One wonders what kind of creature it is that in the space of six months changes its rigidity into flexibility, its inadaptability into adaptability. Perhaps this chameleon wasn't really 'rigid and inadaptable' at all . . ." (p. 22).

The perceptual development model. A third approach to children's Rorschachs seeks to understand change in terms of general principles of "perceptual development." Drawing upon Gestalt theory and the genetic psychology of Claparède, Meili-Dworetzki (1956) views the Rorschach as a perceptual task on which change follows the principle that development proceeds in the direction of increasing differentiation, complexity, and integration. In analyzing children's Rorschach responses, she utilizes a model in which an initial stage of "syncretic perception" consisting of a "general and confused perception of the whole" gives way to a second stage of "distinct and analytic perception of the parts" that is in turn superseded by a final stage in which there is a "synthetic recomposition of the whole with awareness of the parts" (p. 112). Hemmendinger (1953) proposes a closely related position, contending that children's Rorschachs follow a course of perceptual development embodying Werner's orthogenetic principle, the principle that development proceeds from relatively global, undifferentiated states to increasing levels of differentiation and integration (Werner, 1961). Hemmendinger (1953) holds that (1) three-year-olds are "whole-perceivers" whose mode of experiencing the inkblots is "immature, inflexible, and undifferentiated"; (2) four- and five-year-olds stilll exhibit relatively immature modes of perception but take more notice of details; (3) six- to eight-year-olds notice parts in a more differentiated way but do not integrate them into wholes; and (4) older children are increasingly capable of this integrative process (p. 168).

Among the strengths of these positions are their emphasis on the manner in which children's Rorschach performance follows general developmental principles; Meili-Dworetzki's detailed analyses of the genesis of particular Rorschach determinants; and Hemmendinger's use of a scoring system that combines location and form level scores in a way that helps reveal basic developmental trends. Among the potential problems in using these schemes alone to characterize changes in preschool children's Rorschachs is that they may be too limited. Meili-Dworetzki's stages are relatively undifferentiated in the sense that all preschool Rorschachs are included in her first stage; children do not typically reach her second stage until they are six or seven. More important, both schemes focus chiefly on perceptual development and underestimate the significance of other aspects of the response process.

The "concept formation" model. Finally, Klopfer, Spiegelman, and Fox (1956) propose a conception of stages in preschool Rorschachs oriented around shifts in "concept formation," the "only" area in which they believe "clear age patterns" have emerged in research (p. 25). The first stage, that of "magic wand perseveration" is attributed to children from two to four and incorporates Klopfer's earlier perseveration model. The second stage, held to be characteristic of children from three to five, is distinguished by the predominance of confabulatory thought processes. The final stage, typically found in four- to six-year-olds, is one of "confabulatory combinations" in which confabulations now involve multiple elements.

This view of successive stages in "concept formation" has a number of attractive features. In emphasizing modes of thinking, it highlights processes which, there is good reason to believe, lie at the core of developmental changes in Rorschach performance; it subsumes Klopfer's earlier perseverative model, while offering a richer character- ization of the test performance of three- to five-year-olds; and, although focused on test responses, it nonetheless suggests, at least occasionally, that the same concepts can be applied to the test process as well. However, this stage concept has limitations as well. In its emphasis on concept formation alone the scheme is too constricted to encompass many phenomena that deserve attention at each stage; there are only hints of relationships between changes in test behavior and test protocols, relationships that warrant systematic elaboration; and ques- tions can be raised about whether the third stage, combinatory confabu- lations, is a qualitatively different one or whether it represents a sophisticated variation of the processes encountered in the second stage.

The Preschool Rorschach Literature: Consensus, Controversy, and Synthesis

To survey studies using the Rorschach test with preschool children in this way is to become acutely aware of the persistent and unresolved conflicts around most basic methodological issues and the diversity of opinion around many substantive ones. In a sense the situation could hardly be otherwise. When an instrument already subject to dispute is used with a group on the fringe of the population to which it is usually applied, attention inevitably focuses on conflicts about how and with whom the test should be used.

Yet for all of the disagreements that have been characteristic of these studies, the preschool Rorschach literature contains within it the possibility of a synthesis that encompasses these antithetical positions and reveals an order and regularity in the phenomena to which they have been applied. The basis for this synthesis may be appreciated if the literature is reconsidered in terms of areas in which there is consensus, in which there are simply differences of opinion, and in which there appear to be unbridgeable disagreements.

In spite of their often intense conflicts around other issues, most Rorschach authorities agree about how young children of different ages behave in the test situation and about the kinds of protocols they produce. Those who have given the test to preschool children describe that process, especially the problems encountered in it, in remarkably similar ways. As has been noted, differences of opinion about technique center chiefly on how to cope with these problems. Similarly, although different techniques cannot but have some effect on test results, there is a surprising degree of agreement about the kinds of test protocols obtained from children of different ages. For all of their conflicts around scoring and interpretation, for example, the Ames and Klopfer groups accept each other's test records as characteristic of particular groups of preschool children. At the very least, their arguments are about the same children.

While differences of opinion exist regarding how best to characterize developmental changes in Rorschach performance across the preschool years, for the most part, these differences are not divisive. Beginning with the work of Klopfer and Margulies (1941), descriptions of "stages in early Rorschach reactions" have typically been presented as tentative efforts to articulate salient features of children's test performance. How such stages are delineated and whether they are best understood in terms of perceptual development, concept formation, or broader developmental transformations that encompass both types of processes are generally treated as open questions. In any case, such problems are subordinate to methodological ones, since there can be little certainty about characterizations of data as long as major questions exist about the nature of the data and the means by which they should be gathered.

The basic, seemongly irreconcilable conflicts about preschool Rorschachs are the methodological controversies about whether and how the Rorschach may be used with young children. These are controversies that center on the definition of the test—on the purposes for which it can be used, the ways it should be administered, the manner in which it should be interpreted, and the value of its results. Those who have least questioned the applicability of the test with small children have been clinicians ready to use an individualized, impressionistic mode of analysis (A. Schachtel, 1944; Halpern, 1953, 1960) and researchers for whom the Rorschach represents an experimental task that can be scored and analyzed in terms of a developmental scheme oriented as much around the primitive responses of preschoolers as around the more advanced responses of adults (Hemmendinger, 1953; Meili-Dworetzki, 1956). Those who have most questioned its use with young children are practitioners committed to sophisticated Rorschach systems developed for use with adult populations; these clinicians doubt that their norms and modes of analysis can be extended to a population that may have difficulty taking the test in a standard way, engaging in a demanding inquiry process, or responding to central aspects of the Rorschach task in ways that make it safe to assume that scores have the same meaning they do for adults. Between these extremes are a variety of other positions that involve some degree of adaptation of administrative or scoring procedures to special problems presented by children. The arguments among these groups are, above all, arguments about criteria for what constitutes "the Rorschach" and about the strictness or leniency with which such criteria are to be applied.

Whether a synthesis of these positions can be achieved hinges on the manner in which areas of consensus and controversy are related. If the problem of preschool Rorschach performance is approached from the standpoint of what the Rorschach can reveal about young children, conflicts are inevitable, as it is necessary to begin by making a commitment to a methodological stance about which there is a maximum of controversy in order to explain phenomena about which there is considerably more agreement. However, if the terms of the problem are reversed, if the performance of preschool children is used to examine the Rorschach test, a very different situation arises. No longer is there a need to decide among competing methodologies. Instead, conflicts about technique can simply be accepted and used as a basis for inquiring into what there is about the manner in which young children take the Rorschach that makes it so difficult for experts to agree about how the test should be given. Moreover, even a cursory consideration of children's behavior in the test situation is sufficient to answer such a question: differences in method arise because children do not take the test in the same way as do older children and adults. They are only gradually coming to understand and respond to the requirements of the Rorschach task. Controversies about method are thus primarily controversies about strategies for dealing with these limitations. Although the strategies may differ radically, the phenomena with which they seek to cope are the same.

What is most important about this view of disputes over technique is that it provides the key to understanding "stages" in early Rorschach performance. It becomes clear that the fundamental problem to be addressed is not simply that of describing patterns of preschool Rorschach responses, but rather that of articulating the stages through which children come to master the test itself. It also becomes clear that different aspects of the Rorschach literature have distinct contributions to make toward dealing with this problem. On the one hand, observations about test behavior and test protocols around which there is broad consensus can now be emphasized properly. On the other hand, methodological controversies can receive equal attention, for, to the extent to which these controversies involve something more than factional disputes, to the extent to which they represent genuine efforts to respond to the ways in which children approach the Rorschach, it becomes possible to read back from these divergent strategies to the common characteristics of children's test behavior with which they are intended to cope.

STAGES IN CHILDREN'S MASTERY OF THE RORSCHACH

Characteristics of the Model

The approach to describing the steps in children's mastery of the Rorschach that will be advanced here has the following rationale: If the Rorschach is given to normal children of younger and younger ages, a point will be reached at which they are so unable to grasp the task or to respond to its demands that the test appears to be meaningless for them. If the test is given to children at later and later ages, another point will be reached at which youngsters are able to understand the nature of the task, to give a variety of responses to different cards, and to respond to an inquiry process sufficiently well that protocols can be scored and interpreted in what most Rorschach examiners would take to be a standard way.[6] Because the Rorschach involves a complex, multifaceted intellectual task and requires that

---

[6]Use of the term "standard way" with regard to the Rorschach requires some clarification. In a sense, there is no standard form of the test. In the 1930s and 1940s, five major Rorschach systems evolved, each differing from the others to some extent in how the test is presented, how inquiry is conducted, what scores are used, and how these scores are interpreted (Exner, 1969). In the last several decades, other, more specialized approaches to the test have been developed (Goldfried, Stricker, and Weiner, 1971) as well as one other major system (Exner, 1974, 1978). Yet, for all of their differences, versions of the test used with adults share many common features. Certainly all assume that subjects understand a similar set of instructions, that they can participate in an inquiry into the basis of their responses, and that it is possible to score and interpret the test with a reasonable degree of consistency. Because the manner in which young children take the Rorschach frequently departs markedly from the expectations of all major systems, the term "standard form" will be used here to denote adult forms of the test collectively. To say that subjects are able to take the Rorschach in its "standard form" means that they are capable of taking the test in any of its various incarnations, including the most demanding and commonly used ones involving a detailed inquiry process conducted after responses are obtained to all ten cards.

children engage in a demanding interaction with examiners, the distance between these two points will not be transversed quickly or in a single step. To the contrary, it is to be expected that mastery of the Rorschach task will occur over a considerable period of time—the preschool years and beyond—and that it will be reflected in a series of increasingly complex, qualitatively different patterns of test performance. The task of describing the manner in which children come to be able to take the Rorschach thus consists of delineating these patterns or stages.

The approach to be taken to this task is based on a number of assumptions. First, it is assumed that the manner in which the test is given provides the best general indicator of these stages. Although Rorschach authorities are committed to different conceptions of the test, to the extent to which a new stage is present it is anticipated that each approach to giving the test will register this change in its own way. Second, it is assumed that distinctive patterns of test performance can be delineated within each stage with regard to both children's and examiners' behavior in the test situation, on the one hand, and characteristics of test responses, on the other. Third, it is assumed that the latter characteristics can be described in ways that subsume the main features of earlier models of stages in children's Rorschach reactions. Finally, it is assumed that qualitative differences in the kinds of change occurring over this period warrant the use of a concept of transitional periods or substages to encompass more modest shifts in Rorschach performance that reflect a modification of principles characteristic of a given stage rather than a transformation of those principles. Hence, the model will consist of three basic stages with two intermediate transitional periods.

These stages, it should be stressed, are "ideal types." They are intellectual constructs intended to highlight and clarify qualitative differences in phenomena. Although to help appreciate stages, estimates of the ages at which they typically emerge will be offered, stages are defined by patterns of test performance, not age. As will be seen, a three-year-old can provide a prime example of Stage I phenomena usually found in children a year younger. Furthermore, it is not assumed that particular children of any given age will display pure characteristics of a stage; they may well present a "mixed" picture. The concept of stages is intended to clarify theoretical issues, in this case steps in a developmental process; whether and in what ways the concept applies to any given youngster or group of youngsters are empirical questions.

Stage I: Perseverative Approaches to the Rorschach

The test process. The initial stage in the mastery of the Rorschach is that at which Rorschach responses, or something resembling them, are first elicited from children. Although such responses have been obtained from subjects as young as fifteen to eighteen months (Klopfer, Fox, and Troup, 1956), it is not until the age of two that records have been gathered from significant numbers of children. There is a remarkable degree of agreement among those who work with this age group about what the test process is like and about the kind of Rorschach records produced. Ford (1946), Allen (1951), and Ames et al. (1952, 1974) concur that the pattern of pervasive perseveration described by Klopfer and Margulies (1941) represents the earliest form of Rorschach performance.

The test process in this stage is exemplified well by one of the first cases in the American literature, that of Colin reported by Anna Schachtel (1944). At the age of three, Colin was tested by his nursery school teacher, who approached him asking if he would like to see some pictures. When he indicated an interest, she tried to lead him to a quiet office, but remained instead in a corner of the playroom when Colin insisted on working there. Asked what he saw on the first card, the child replied that it was a mountain and immediately asked to see the next card. On that card he saw a red mountain and demanded the third card. On each succeeding card he again insisted that he "saw" a mountain, at times noting different colors. However, by the fifth card he noticed a girl nearby pretending some chairs were a train. After giving one more response, he pushed away Card VI and went off to join in her play. Over the next hour and a half, the teacher coaxed Colin to return to the test, but he refused, feeling he had more interesting things to do. Finally, in an interlude while awaiting his turn to paint, he agreed to resume the testing. On Cards VI, VII, and VIII, he saw more mountains before discovering that the Rorschach cards could stand on edge if placed in a crack in the table. Both he and his teacher found this activity hilarious and it was repeated with Card IX until the card slipped through the crack and fell to the floor. He continued playing in this manner on the last cards, also managing two more responses, both mountains, before completing the test.

While this case cannot be used to illustrate the finer points of test administration, it does reveal distinctive aspects of the test process noted by most of those who have administered Rorschachs to two-year-olds. First, because the nature of relationships can easily overshadow the activities conducted within them, most of the Rorschachs obtained from young children have been given by parents, nursery school teachers, and other familiar figures. Second, even under these conditions, whether or not a youngster responds to the test depends on the "spirit of the moment"; a child may cooperate with the test one day and not the next or even one moment and not the next (Klopfer and Margulies, 1941). Third, examiners typically have great difficulty keeping two-year-olds focused on the test or keeping the Rorschach card from being transformed into a toy. For example, Ford (1946) notes:

> Early in the preliminary experimentation it was evident that the young child was unduly concerned with the manipulation of the Rorschach card. He felt it, patted it, smelled it, and sometimes kissed it. Occasionally he pushed it off the table or threw it on the floor. More often he became engrossed in the manipulative possibilities. Not only did he inspect the card from all angles, but he was equally concerned with examining the back of the card. In fact, his interest in manipulation became primary and only secondarily, if at all, was he concerned with meanings. [p. 33]

Indeed, Ford was so sensitive to the play potential of the Rorschach card that she recommended prohibiting children from turning it. Finally, as was the case with Colin, most examiners have not found the inquiry process with very young children worth the effort. For example, describing the typical test process with two-year-olds, Ames et al. (1952) note:

> Any effort on the part of the Examiner to clarify the response by getting the child to indicate exactly where he sees something or to point out which part of the blot is the doggie or kitty, usually only confuses matters. The 2-year-old appears to be very suggestible, and at the same time quite unclear as to what he has seen or where he has seen it. If asked where he has seen something, he will point to some part of the card, apparently at random, to satisfy the Examiner; and if the Examiner departs from proper procedure to the extent of making a specific suggestion, the child is almost certain to accept it. [p. 110]

Hence, while Colin's teacher might have been firmer about structure (e.g., taking Colin into a quiet room or trying to get him to focus on the task more) or might have undertaken a fuller inquiry, and while such interventions may have elicited different behavior in Colin, it is unlikely she would have obtained a very different Rorschach protocol.

Test responses. Although Colin was approaching the upper age at which children typically produce such protocols, his Rorschach responses are characteristic of the "magic repetition" taken by Klopfer and others to represent the earliest type of Rorschach protocol. Klopfer and Margulies (1941) note that this pattern consists of an undifferentiated reaction to the test in which there is an "utter disregard for the difference between the ten cards," as "the child simply repeats the same word as his reaction to each card" (p. 4). They note also that the first response, that which is perseverated, "may or may not be determined by some vaguely perceived features of the first card" (p. 4). For example, Schachtel believes that Colin's response of "mountain" was probably based on the upward slope of certain areas of Card I, a belief that may well be correct, but which, in the absence of an inquiry process, remains little more than speculation. Indeed, the vagueness of children's responses during this stage and the seeming lack of congruence between responses and blot characteristics often leave examiners with little more than hunches about what led to the response; in some cases they have a strong suspicion that the response may in fact have little to do with the blot at all.

The transition from Stage I: partial perseverations. Often by two and a half years of age, children move away from the total perseveration of Stage I to modified patterns in which perseverations alternate with children (1) refusing particular cards, (2) perseverating on most cards but still giving new responses to a few, or (3) searching later blots for characteristics that justify the use of the perseverated concept (Klopfer and Margulies, 1941; Ford, 1946; Ames et al., 1952). For example, of ten two-and-a-half-year-olds in the original Klopfer and Margulies sample, four perseverated on a single response, while the other six engaged in the modified forms of perseveration; of twenty-seven three-year-olds, only 11 percent engaged in pervasive perseveration, 33 percent engaged in modified forms, and a majority now gave a variety of responses to seven of ten cards. Ford (1946) encountered no cases of pervasive perseveration among the three-year-olds in her group, although a third still engaged in Klopfer's modified forms. By four years of age, Klopfer and Ford found, only about a fifth of their groups still engaged in even modified forms of perseveration. Hence, although limited samples and methodological problems dictate a need for caution in dealing with such statistics, the Rorschach literature leaves no doubt that the earliest form of Rorschach responses are pervasive perseverations which by the time children are three increasingly give way to more limited and modified forms of perseveration that remain common in children through their fourth birthday.

Stage II: Confabulatory Rorschachs

General indicators of change. Around the age of three or shortly thereafter, there is a major qualitative shift in how children take the Rorschach. One general marker of this change is the fact that all Rorschach experts who are inclined to give the test to young children, despite major differences among them, now believe the test is applicable. For example, although Ames et al. (1952) give the test to very young children out of scientific curiosity, they recognize that "at 2½ years as at 2 years, it does not seem that the Rorschach is a uniquely useful tool for determining intellectual and emotional characteristics of the child or for revealing the characteristic individuality of the child *or* of the age" (p. 122). By contrast, they believe children's responses at three years of age become complex and varied enough that they begin to allow for judgments about whether an individual's performance is above or below age level and for giving a more differentiated picture of children as a group. Having conducted pilot studies with younger children, Ford (1946) believes that only at three do children show sufficient interest that the Rorschach becomes an appropriate instrument. Klopfer, Fox, and Troup (1956) also hold that the test can be administered to any child with a mental age of three or over. Similarly, Hemmendinger (1953) begins his developmental study of the Rorschach at this age. The reasons such experts start to see the test as appropriate at this age can be understood in the light of shifts in how children take the test and in the nature of the test protocols they produce.

The test process. The test process in Stage II differs from that in Stage I in that the Rorschach can now be administered in a form that bears some resemblance to the test given adults. Two-year-olds may or may not do the test as the spirit moves them; three-and-a-half-year-olds come to scheduled test sessions and produce protocols at that time. Two-year-olds perseverate and often treat blots in such arbitrary ways that examiners are left in doubt about whether the children are truly looking at and responding to the Rorschach cards; three-and-a-half-year-olds clearly give responses of some kind *to the cards.* Above all, with two-year-olds the inquiry process is a pointless exercise that is typically omitted; with children in Stage II it becomes possible to undertake such a process, at least in a rudimentary form.

Stage II is distinguished from Stage III by the work examiners must do to maintain a test process that resembles later forms of the Rorschach and by the fact that, even with this effort, the result is often only a crude approximation of the test as it is given to older children and adults. To read between the lines of any discussion of preschool Rorschachs is to sense how important it is for examiners to accomplish two sets of divergent tasks. On the one hand, they must establish rapport with children, providing extensive support, encouragement, and help in dealing with anxiety, distractions, and a host of other factors that interfere with test performance. On the other, they must provide a high degree of structure, maintaining the boundaries of the test and dealing with children's readiness to avoid or utterly transform the task. To be sure, empathy, sensitivity, and firmness with regard to test demands are important with subjects of all ages. However, whereas with older children and adults these qualities affect chiefly the inquiry process and determine how good an understanding of the basis of test responses is gained, with children in Stage II such qualities in the examiner may be a prerequisite for obtaining test protocols at all.

The distinctive character of the test process in this second stage can be seen in the debates over whether to institute special testing procedures. It is with children in this group that consideration is given to (1) using familiar figures as examiners, as children are extremely sensitive to the social situation; (2) restricting manipulation of cards in order to reduce distraction and decrease the play value of the test material; (3) inquiring after each response or after each card to reduce frustration, distractibility, and disinterest or to compensate for problems with memory; (4) limiting inquiry to maintain interest in the test and avoid excessive frustration; and (5) relying heavily on examiners' sensitivity to the shared context of the test situation for scoring responses where explicit verbal indications of determinants is lacking. For present purposes, what is most significant about the methodological controversies around these issues is not which position is best, but rather that the manner in which children approach the test in Stage II is such that these controversies exist at all. Opposing positions on each issue represent plausible alternative strategies for coping with how children take the test, and choices in one direction or another will have both costs and benefits. In Stage III children are able to take the Rorschach in a different manner and these debates simply evaporate.

Two aspects of the test process at this time warrant particular attention. First, for these children the relationship with the examiner is primary and the test task is often only a peripheral concern. In part this is a reflection of the fact that the requirements of the Rorschach are not clear to children and the task is not an especially appealing one for them (Halpern, 1953, p. 7), but this situation is to some extent true of all tests with preschool children. The children have not come to "do tests," to enter a situation defined primarily by the objective requirements of tasks, but rather to "do something with the examiner," something often described as "games." Consequently, motives related to the relationship with the examiner—whether that relationship is seen as one in which there is an opportunity for play with a friendly parental surrogate or an anxiety-filled encounter with a frightening stranger—heavily influence what occurs in the test situation. Recognizing this fact, skilled examiners know that, in order to keep preschoolers engaged in the testing, it is essential to develop what each child, in his or her own way, will experience as a benign, supportive relationship. On their parts, children are equally interested in using the relationship for their own ends. While examiners are "giving tests," children are bombarding them with questions about every topic under the sun, taking associations to any aspect of the test process as an opportunity to tell stories or recount interesting events in their lives, changing the test into a game, or bartering the "work" they are doing for a chance to play with toys around the room. In contrast to two-year-olds, who may simply stop the test and play, children at Stage II can typically be kept at or brought back to tests because of the character of their relationship with the examiner. However, in a sense, it is the interest derived from the capital that examiners invest in that relationship that allows them to initiate and maintain the test process.

The other distinctive characteristic of the test process in Stage II is simply that children often do not treat the Rorschach as an objective task warranting serious consideration. Ames et al. (1952) note that, beginning at about three and increasing over the next year, children engage in a good deal of silly behavior that can be seen in their language, percepts, and attitudes toward the test. For example, children in this period give responses such as "a gumba, a gunga," "a broken bee bee bla," "a silly old moo coose," "a parade bee bee bee," or "a krozokus." Similarly, Allen (1954) notes that his son, a bright, charming youngster who had already had extensive experience with the Rorschach, began giving silly responses at this time. In addition to perfectly adequate percepts, at three and a half the child's protocol contained such responses as a "sisser," a "piadigat," a "schniatz," and a "poopoohead"; three months later he reported seeing a "red foomba" on Card II, "booms" on Cards VI and VII, a "soom" on Card VIII, and a "boonji" on Card IX; at four, although such responses had by then diminished, he nonetheless managed to find two "boo-carriers" on Card VII. (Although Allen does not score the protocols, one cannot help but be curious about what content categories he would use for these responses.) Related problems are encountered in the inquiry process. In Stage II, while it is often possible to obtain a clear idea of the location and determinants of responses, percepts may at times be described in such garbled or arbitrary ways that one has no confidence in scores. In a vivid description of the test process with a typical four-year-old, Klopfer, Spiegelman, and Fox (1956) observe that "frequently, the child may choose any of his favorite animals, point out one of its properties . . . and gleefully assign the rest of the blot material to the same concept. He merely *points* vaguely all over the card when the cruel examiner tries to pin him down as to the parts of the animals" (pp. 27–28). Hence, although children in Stage II are beginning to take the Rorschach in a recognizable form, there is often reason to doubt that they do so with the dedication and seriousness so important a task undoubtedly warrants and that older youngsters and adults are usually prepared to give.

Test responses. Rorschach test protocols in Stage II differ fundamentally from those in Stage I. Perseverative tendencies recede and children produce different responses on most cards. Moreover, because a rudimentary inquiry process is now possible, it makes sense at least to try to score responses. Hence, Rorschach protocols begin to resemble those obtained at later ages.

At the same time, test protocols in Stage II differ significantly from those of Stage III. Although many responses can be scored with some degree of confidence, others cannot. In some cases, responses are such that examiners must question whether and in what ways they represent genuine responses to the blots. In other cases, the ability or willingness of children to participate in the inquiry process is still so limited that examiners either score many responses with question marks (Klopfer) or rely on their own intuition (Ames). Moreover, since investigators differ on criteria for administration and scoring, data across systems is far less comparable than it will be later. Consequently, although responses may be scored and tabulated in Stage II, such data is likely to look "soft" to any but the most committed preschool Rorschach practitioners.

In spite of the "softness" of the data and differences in procedures across studies, a number of generalizations can be made with a reasonable degree of assurance, generalizations which define the salient characteristics of Rorschach protocols in Stage II.

1. *Number of responses.* When perseveration is taken into consideration, Rorschach protocols during Stage I typically contain one to three distinct responses. In contrast, the average number of responses elicited in various studies of three- and four-year-olds range from ten to twelve (Kay and Vorhaus, 1943) to sixteen to nineteen (Meili-Dworetzki, 1956), although, because these figures still contain some perseverations, a reasonable estimate of distinct responses in the stage is probably ten to thirteen. It is likely that the lower end of this range is representative of responses obtained under conditions comparable with those forms of the Rorschach used most widely with adults, ones in which inquiry is conducted after responses are obtained on all ten cards.[7] In Stage III, children's Rorschachs using the latter procedure will typically contain sixteen or more responses (Levitt and Trauma, 1972; Exner and Weiner, 1982).

2. *Range of responses.* In Stage I the same response is simply repeated. In Stage II a variety of responses begin to appear. In most studies, about half of these responses are animals, although, through the period and into the next stage, there is a steady expansion of the range of responses given and the number of content categories into which they fall.

3. *Location.* The predominant response during Stage II is the whole response. Most investigators report that half to two-thirds of the responses of three- and four-year-olds are W's, with the remainder consisting chiefly of large details. By six, the percentage of W's is reduced by half, large D responses predominate, and smaller and rarer details become more prominent. For example, Hemmendinger (1953) notes that three- and four-year-olds in his study gave between 55 percent and 63 percent W responses, whereas by six the figure falls to 30 percent.

[7]Exner and Weiner (1982) report that among a group of five- to seven-year-olds a procedure similar to that of Ames, in which inquiry is conducted after each card, yielded an average four more responses than procedures involving inquiry after responses are elicited to all cards.

4. *Form level.* In spite of marked variations across studies in how form level is measured, each study in its own way reports major changes on their measures between Stages I and II. For example, Kay and Vorhaus (1943) report that the three- and four-year-olds in their study gave only 24 and 34 percent W+ responses respectively, in contrast to the 50 percent by five-year-olds; conversely, "crude," "arbitrary," "perseverative," and "pseudopsychotic" W's fell from 76 percent to less than 50. Hemmendinger (1953) found that 55–60 percent of the W responses among his three- and four-year-old groups were poor or vague in contrast to only 30 percent among his five- and six-year-olds. Even using a considerably more generous system basing form level scores in part on the frequency of responses among children, Ames et al. (1952) found that the F+ percentage rose from 60–67 among three- and four-year-olds to 78 and above after the age of five.

5. *Confabulatory whole responses.* Klopfer, Spiegelman, and Fox (1956) argue that the most salient aspect of children's Rorschachs in the three- to five-year-old period is a confabulatory mode of concept formation reflected chiefly in confabulatory whole (DW) responses. In such responses "the subject generalizes from one detail to the whole card, but he is able to justify his response only in terms of the one clearly seen detail, and insists that the whole card is used when it is impossible to reconcile the concept with the shape of the whole blot" (Klopfer et al., 1954, p. 64). At first it appears difficult to reconcile this finding with that of other experts, who place the incidence of DW responses among three- and four-year-olds at 10 percent (Hemmendinger, 1953) or a bit lower (Kay and Vorhaus, 1943). However, the basis for Klopfer's assertion becomes clearer when it is recognized that he uses a more stringent inquiry process than that of most other investigators and a somewhat broader conception of the confabulatory whole response, one in which any single aspect of the blot, including color, is overgeneralized and overrides all other constraints of the stimulus material. Used in this manner, the concept may be seen as an effort to conceptualize the process underlying the crude or arbitrary W response Kay and Vorhaus see as characteristic of the period, or the Wv and W− responses emphasized by Hemmendinger. It is also consistent with Meili-Dworetzki's concept (1956) of the syncretistic character of perception as the dominant characteristic of the period and with the stress Bohm (1958) and Meili-Dworetzki (1956) place on *pars pro toto* thinking in preschool Rorschach responses.

6. *Confabulation.* Klopfer, Spiegelman, and Fox (1956) make it clear that, in characterizing children's thinking in this stage as predom-

inantly confabulatory, they are also using the term in the broad sense described by Rapaport (1946). Confabulations, in this sense, constitute a class of phenomena in which, instead of a balance being maintained between "perceptual" and "associative" aspects of the response process, "objective" characteristics of the blot do little more than serve as a springboard for subjective processes that seem to take flight. As in the case of DW responses, some aspect of the blot initiates the process, but instead of simply overgeneralizing, the subject gives free rein to fantasies, wishes, or ideas that result in responses that have little to do with the stimulus.

Used in this more elastic fashion, the concept of confabulation covers many of the more extraordinary aspects of the Rorschach performance of normal three- and four-year-olds. First, the silly language highlighted by Ames et al. (1952) may be seen to represent a behavioral confabulatory response to the blot. For example, something about the Rorschach cards may have started Allen's three-year-old son talking about "boonjis," "pink sissers," and "piadigats" (1954) but only God and perhaps the youngster at that time had any idea of what it was. Second, Klopfer, Spiegelman, and Fox (1956) suggest that what Ames describes as the "confused percepts and concepts" of three- and four-year-olds (e.g., "a fireplace with feet") are confabulatory in nature. Third, even more striking manifestations of confabulatory tendencies may be seen when children transform the Rorschach into a CAT, noting an animal on the card and proceeding to give a long story about it (Ames et al., 1952). Fourth, children of this age may enact fantasies that are so vivid that Ames et al. (1952) feel they exhibit "some confusion between reality and pictured items" (p. 127). For example, a youngster notes upon seeing bears on Card VIII, "Ouch, they bit me!" or, seeing snow on Card VII, talks about making snowballs with it. Finally, children in this period give that purest of confabulations, the response seemingly stimulated by no characteristics of the blot whatsoever. For example, describing the three-and-a-half-year-old, Ames et al. (1952) note, "the child seems to feel perfect freedom to introduce objects and animals which do not actually exist in the blot" (p. 140). Hence, on Card X, a youngster may refer to a cow that has walked onto and off of the card, a response that poses interesting problems for those trying to score location not to mention form level.

Emphasizing aspects of Stage II protocols related to location and form level, Hemmendinger (1953) and Meili-Dworetzki (1956) suggest that the distinguishing characteristic of the period is children's tendency to perceive wholes in syncretistic ways. Focusing on "concept formation," Klopfer and his colleagues (1956) take confabulation as the most salient feature of the period. Both groups agree that qualitative differences distinguish this period from those before and after.

The transition from Stage II. As children reach school age, a number of changes can be seen in the manner in which they approach the Rorschach. First, although testing four- to six-year-olds continues to be difficult, problems encountered in the test process are usually far milder than earlier. For example, Klopfer, Fox, and Troup (1956) note that with children over the age of four they use few question marks in scoring, whereas their relatively demanding scoring criteria made these common with younger children. Second, there is a gradual increase in the number of responses and the number of large detail responses. Hence, Hemmendinger (1953) suggests a new stage is reached, although one in which children's perception is still "immature" and "syncretistic." Finally, Klopfer, Spiegelman, and Fox (1956) suggest a new stage is reached, that of "confabulatory combinations." On the one hand, such combinations can be seen in broadened confabulatory whole responses in which two details (e.g., the head and the tail of a dog) are used as the basis for a response that still bears little resemblance to the blot. On the other, although other forms of confabulation begin to decline, Ames et al. (1952) note that four and a half is the "high point for the giving of extremely confused or unrelated concepts" (p. 168), responses in which elements are combined in an odd, idiosyncratic fashion. For example, children may see a fish with two heads, a person with several pairs of arms, or a dog with a head at each end. The phenomena Hemmendinger and Klopfer describe are treated here as "transitional" because, while marking significant changes in how children perform on the Rorschach, they can nonetheless be viewed as sophisticated variations of the syncretistic modes of perception or confabulatory modes of thought that are characteristic of Stage II.

Stage III: "The Rorschach"

In one way or another, most of those who give Rorschach tests to children recognize another major qualitative shift in performance in the five- to seven-year-old period. It is with this period that a new group of authorities, e.g., Exner and Weiner (1982) and Levitt and Trauma (1972), begin to present norms and trace developmental trends. At this point, Klopfer, Spiegelman, and Fox (1956) become comfortable applying standard modes of interpretation of Rorschach data rather than emphasizing the development of "concept formation" alone. Similarly, even Ames and her associates (Ames et al., 1952), the group making the heaviest use of Rorschach scores and signs in their interpretation of preschool protocols, now have confidence in the test as a clinical instrument rather than one to be used chiefly for scientific purposes. Perhaps most important, there is now a consensus among these diverse experts that the Rorschach can be used with children in the same form it will be used with adolescents and adults.

In part, this change is a result of the way in which children are able to take the test. Examiners can now give the test in its most complex forms and expect that children will respond in ways roughly comparable to those of older individuals. For example, while Exner and Weiner (1982) recognize that some difficult five- and six-year-olds may still require a modified test procedure in which inquiry is conducted after each card, they note that, with most normal children of these ages, the Rorschach can and should be given with all ten cards presented first, followed by a relatively demanding inquiry process. Of course, establishing rapport and the conduct of the inquiry process may still require extra effort even with older children. Nonetheless, the test process is now perceived as one that is similar to that with adults.

The shifts characteristic of Stage III are even more apparent in examiners' confidence in the test protocols they obtain. The fundamentally different "modes of concept formation" that governed the response process at earlier stages decrease markedly and come to represent signs of pathology. For example, Klopfer, Spiegelman, and Fox (1956) hold that "if a seven-year-old child still gives responses based on any of the three steps of perseveration, confabulation, and confabulatory combination, we may assume that he functions below his age level. The reason for this may lie in mental retardation, emotional infantilism, or a temporary emotional disturbance" (p. 28). Equally important, it is now assumed that tests can be scored and analyzed in the same way with both children and adults and that basic scoring categories and relationships between scores have the same meaning at all ages. While rules of interpretation vary from one Rorschach system to another, within each system the same rules are utilized with children in Stage III and with adults. To be sure, significant changes across age may be seen on the Rorschach. For example, throughout middle childhood there is a steady rise in the number of detail responses and a decrease in the number of whole responses, with this trend reversing later. Similarly, as children become older they give more movement responses, FC responses, human responses, and so forth. However, it is now assumed that the Rorschach remains an invariant instrument and that scores on it register changes in children faithfully.

In effect, as children reach this stage in the early school years, the Rorschach becomes "the Rorschach."

IMPLICATIONS OF THE MODEL

Conclusions and Beginnings

It is reasonable to expect that so extended a discussion of patterns of preschool Rorschach performance should conclude by bringing closure to the problems raised in the course of the essay. It is reasonable, for example, to expect answers to clinical questions of whether and how the Rorschach can be used with young children and to theoretical questions about the nature of the phenomena encountered in each stage of the model. Lest more be promised than delivered, it should be stressed that these expectations will not be met. The implications of the model that will be emphasized center less on the problems this concep-tion of stages in the mastery of the Rorschach solves than on the ones it poses.

To conclude in this manner is not to deny that the need to find answers to these clinical and theoretical questions is pressing. On the contrary, the methodological controversies that have been described stand in the way of the use of the Rorschach not only with preschool children, but also with severely disturbed children who take the test in a similar manner; these controversies cannot be resolved until there is a better understanding of how children come to be able to take the test; and the understanding of this developmental process will be a major contri-bution to one of the most fundamental yet neglected questions in the general Rorschach literature, that of the nature of the psychological processes underlying the formulation of Rorschach responses. How-ever, before solutions to problems can be proposed, it is necessary to focus on the right problems, to appreciate their nature, and to consider the directions in which solutions may be found. It is with issues of this kind that these concluding remarks will be concerned.

On the Use of the Rorschach with Preschool Children

On the surface, the conception of stages in children's mastery of the Rorschach that has been advanced seems to point toward a negative verdict on the question of whether the test can be used in a consistent, effective way in the study of the "mental states" of young children. The model underlines methodological problems that confront all efforts to extend techniques and modes of interpreting the Rorschach used with older subjects to the study of young children. Among the points it emphasizes are (1) there are marked qualitative differences in how the Rorschach is taken in each of the three major stages; (2) in the first two stages, children approach the task in erratic, shifting, and problematic ways; (3) examiners adopt a variety of quite different strategies to cope with such behavior; (4) Rorschach protocols in the first two stages are usually sparser than in the last stage; and (5) perseverative and confabulatory responses are characteristic of early Rorschach performance. Given such circumstances, it is to be expected that (1) there will not be a consensus among authorities regarding appropriate techniques for testing young children; (2) there will be controversy over whether conditions presupposed by standard interpretations of the Rorschach are met when the test is used with preschoolers; (3) individual examiners may often be uncertain about whether particular children have taken the test in ways that meet their own criteria for valid testing; (4) even advocates of preschool Rorschachs will acknowledge that protocols of preschool children are "less revealing" than those of older subjects (Ames et al., 1974, p. 27); and (5) doubts will be present about whether the same processes underlie Rorschach responses of young children and adults and about whether test scores can be interpreted in the same way with each group. These conditions, in turn, make it easy to understand why the Rorschach is not used extensively with young children and why strong supporters of the test, such as the Ames group, are conservative in recommending its clinical use. In short, the model provides a theoretical basis for accounting for the maze of controversies, questions, and uncertainty surrounding use of the Rorschach with preschool children.

At the same time, if one sets aside questions of whether the Rorschach should be administered and analyzed in the same ways with both children and adults, if one does not worry about whether the test is "the Rorschach" and simply treats the task as an opportunity to observe behavior, the model lends support to Ames's conviction that the Rorschach can be used to investigate children's "developmental status" and aspects of their personalities (Ames et al., 1974, p. 27). At each stage, interesting observations can be made of children's attitudes and response to the task, their ways of interacting with examiners around it (e.g., who defines the test situation in which way for how long), and the nature of their test responses (e.g., the degree to which perseveration prevails, the number and types of confabulatory responses, and the extent to which children can participate in the inquiry process). Moreover, as has been seen, qualitative changes in such test behavior and responses occur in a regular developmental sequence. Hence, while the ways in which preschool children perform on the Rorschach cannot be encompassed readily by standard approaches to interpretation, there is reason to believe that the test can make useful contributions to an understanding of preschool children if an appropriate interpretive framework is found.

The conception of children's Rorschachs that has been put forward suggests that "appropriate" frameworks will differ from those currently used in at least two ways. First, in stressing that the process of testing preschool children involves a complex, shifting negotiation of definitions of the test situation between children and examiners, the model makes it clear that analyses of test behavior, attitudes toward the test, and "the interpersonal dynamics of the test situation" (E. Schachtel, 1945, 1966; Schafer, 1954) must be emphasized far more heavily than is typically the case. Indeed, as much attention should be paid to how children take the test and relate to the examiner as to the nature of their test responses. Second, in stressing "stages" in children's Rorschach performance, the model points to the need for developmental interpretations that focus on the principles governing children's approaches to the Rorschach situation and on transformations of these principles across the preschool years.

While suggesting characteristics of such interpretive systems, the model cannot by itself provide a sufficient basis for their derivation. In a sense, finding the means for clinical interpretation of young children's Rorschachs is one aspect of a broader set of theoretical problems. To describe stages in children's mastery of the Rorschach is not to explain the phenomena encountered in this process; rather, it is to raise a host of questions requiring explanation. For example, how are children's different modes of relating to examiners in each stage to be understood? What is the meaning of such phenomena as perseverations and confabulations? How do children move from one stage to another? It is answers to these theoretical questions that provide the basis for analyzing the test performance of individual children.

However, by raising questions of this kind, the problem of accounting for the Rorschach performance of young children takes on a significance that extends well beyond potential applications to empirical research or clinical work with children. At this point the problem of preschool Rorschachs touches on issues at the heart of Rorschach theory and poses major challenges to theories of the Rorschach response process.

Preschool Rorschachs and Rorschach Theory

In order to formulate explanations of how children take the Rorschach, it is necessary to come to terms with the fundamental questions in Rorschach theory: What is the nature of the Rorschach task and what psychological processes underlie responses to that task? One contribution of the study of children's Rorschachs to Rorschach theory lies simply in raising such questions, since to do so forces a recognition of how little attention has been paid to these issues in the Rorschach literature as a whole.

Rorschach himself devoted only a few pages of *Psychodiagnostics* (1964) to outlining his view that the test measured a particular form of perception. In the introduction he stressed that the book was "empirical" in nature, an attempt to describe a technique and the results of its application, and acknowledged that "the theoretical foundation for the experiment is, for the most part, still quite incomplete" (p. 13). Subsequent work on the test conformed closely to this initial paradigm. Over the next several decades, with only a few notable exceptions (e.g., Frank, 1939; Rapaport, 1946), major systematizers of the test accepted Rorschach's formulation that the test was based on a form of perception, sidestepped serious discussion of the response process, and focused on issues of administration and scoring, interpretations of scores and patterns of scores, and ways of using such a framework to understand personality and psychopathology. Consequently, in 1954 Holt could begin a discussion of the theoretical rationale of the test by quoting Rorschach's statement about its "incomplete" theoretical foundation and observe: "When one considers the fact that these words were written more than 30 years ago, and that some thousands of persons have worked with Rorschach's test since then, producing a bibliography that now runs to over twelve hundred items, it is sobering to note how well the last sentence quoted could describe the situation today" (p. 501). A dozen years later, Ernest Schachtel (1966) opened his *Experiential Foundations of Rorschach's Test* with the same quotation and the same observation about the state of Rorschach research.[8] In the next decade, Exner (1974) began the most influential recent

---

[8]"Of the extensive literature on the test, by far the greatest part has been devoted to adding to these [Rorschach's] empirical observations and to refinements of technique; relatively few attempts have been made to inquire into the rationale of the test and to contribute to its theoretical foundations" (E. Schachtel, 1966, p. 1).

work of the Rorschach in a characteristic fashion—with a volume devoted entirely to administration and scoring of the test. Only in his second volume (Exner, 1978) did he offer a chapter on "the response process" and there, after also quoting Rorschach's introductory remark, he made a statement that, coming after fifty years of Rorschach research, can only be viewed as extraordinary:

> Whatever might have been had Rorschach lived longer, the question of how a Rorschach answer is formed and delivered remains one of the fundamental mysteries of the test. It is an area of research that has been sorely neglected in the Rorschach literature; and this neglect may well have contributed considerably to the broad divergence that occurred among those attempting to extend Rorschach's work and "complete" the test. [p. 37]

While the theoretical situation may not be quite so bleak, there can be little doubt about the relative paucity of studies of the Rorschach response process.

Consideration of the Rorschach performance of young children can help remedy this state of affairs. Rorschach researchers have been able to ignore basic theoretical issues because adults take the test in more or less predictable ways and produce test records that can be scored and interpreted without practitioners experiencing a need to inquire into the presuppositions underlying their analyses. By contrast, the atypical ways in which children take the test and the curious kinds of protocols they produce stimulate questions about the nature of the test and almost demand an examination of the assumptions on which it is based.

As these assumptions are examined, preschool Rorschachs present a more serious challenge to Rorschach theory, for they call into question the adequacy of those conceptions of the response process that have provided the foundation of major Rorschach systems. Nowhere is this challenge greater than with regard to what has been the central tenet of Rorschach theory, the conviction, expressed in the subtitle of *Psychodiagnostics,* that the Rorschach is "a diagnostic test based on perception" (Rorschach, 1964).

If it is assumed that the Rorschach response process is chiefly perceptual in nature, then the perseverative and confabulatory responses of young children appear to be anomalous. What is most striking about these responses is how little they are based on perception. As has been seen, in working with children in Stage I examiners often have difficulty determining the perceptual roots of the initial test responses and, at times, doubt there are any. The essence of the perseverations that follow is that these first responses are repeated regardless of the stimulus characteristics of subsequent inkblots. In Stage II, some perceptual bases of responses can be discerned, yet confabulatory responses are distinguished by how rapidly and how far they depart from this starting point. Recognizing these qualities of children's test responses, Klopfer, Spiegelman, and Fox (1956) organize their conception of stages in children's Rorschachs around changing modes of "concept formation," not around perceptual development.

Of course, ways can be found to extend theories of the Rorschach as a "perceptual" or "perceptual-cognitive" task to account for such phenomena. Whether these explanations are adequate is doubtful, although a critique of them is beyond the scope of this essay. What is important for present purposes is that anomalies of this kind constitute a challenge to existing Rorschach theories; it is in this very fact that the significance of the study of preschool Rorschach lies. Because theories of the Rorschach response process have been developed with adults in mind and more or less fit the manner in which the test is usually taken, these theories have rarely been subjected to critical analysis. By contrast, because the phenomena encountered with young children require that theories of the response process be extended beyond their usual, familiar domain, they represent an ideal ground for testing the adequacy of particular theories and for deciding among competing theories.

The ways in which young children take the Rorschach do more than provide a testing ground for theories of the response process; they also constitute a fertile field in which new theories can germinate. Paradoxically, the promise the study of preschool Rorschachs holds for Rorschach theory resides precisely in the fact that the test is being used with "children for whom it may not be appropriate." As has been seen, difficulties in test administration and questions about the validity of the test arise because young children are only in the process of grasping the Rorschach and becoming able to respond to its demands. Consequently, every way in which children's test behavior and responses raise doubts about whether the test is appropriate for them constitutes an opportunity to investigate the developmental processes through which they come to understand and master it. In effect, the problems preschoolers experience in taking the Rorschach and the problems examiners experience in giving and interpreting the test afford a unique perspective on the evolution of the processes that enable individuals to take the Rorschach in "standard ways."

The Rorschach and Primitive Mental States

If the preeminent issue in the study of preschool Rorschachs is that of understanding how children come to master the test, questions involving the relationship of "the Rorschach" and "primitive mental states" assume a distinct form. The primary theoretical task becomes one of finding ways of using theories about primitive mental states to explain children's Rorschach performance and the Rorschach response process itself.

How this task is approached depends heavily on the manner in which "primitive mental states" are defined. Construed broadly, the term may refer to almost any aspect of the behavior or personality of young or profoundly disturbed individuals; construed narrowly, it may refer only to forms of cognition encountered early in development or in states of marked regression. It is "primitive mental states" in the latter sense that have most to contribute to an understanding of the Rorschach, because to define the concept in this way invites a consideration of ways in which such theories of mental development as those of Piaget and Werner can be applied to the problem.

Students of preschool Rorschachs have, in fact, made some use of these theories. Meili-Dworetzki (1956) draws upon the ideas of Claparède, Piaget, and the Gestalt theorists to illuminate the manner in which aspects of perceptual development bear upon children's handling of the Rorschach; Fox (1956) bases some of his speculations on the meaning of young children's approaches to the Rorschach on Piagetian ideas; and Hemmendinger (1953) organizes his conception of children's Rorschach performance around a Wernerian theory of perceptual development. However, the fruitfulness of these applications of developmental theories is limited because, for the most part, the analyses begin with the assumption that the Rorschach is chiefly a perceptual task.

Only when the nature of the Rorschach task itself becomes the object of inquiry can the potential contributions of these theories be appreciated fully. When the Rorschach response process is assumed to be a predominantly perceptual one, theories of early mental development contribute relatively little to understanding the stages in children's Rorschach performance. The points at which children begin to give Rorschach responses or exhibit marked, qualitative shifts in their handling of the task do not correspond to any major, well-defined changes in perceptual development, certainly none sufficient to account for these shifts. By contrast, when the Rorschach is defined in a more open-ended way as simply a cognitive task "of some kind," it is difficult to ignore correlations between stages in children's Rorschachs and significant points of transition in developmental theories such as those of Piaget. For example, children give their first Rorschach responses at the very point at which Piaget locates the beginning of a new epoch in intellectual development, the shift from the sensorimotor period to the early stages of representational thought (Piaget and Inhelder, 1969; Flavell, 1977; Ginsburg and Opper, 1979); confabulatory responses become prominent in the same period that symbolic play is at its height and children are relatively indifferent to distinctions between play and reality (Flavell, 1963, p. 161; Piaget, 1951, 1973; Piaget and Inhelder, 1969); and children typically cease giving confabulatory responses, produce more "realistic" responses, and are able to reflect on their responses and participate more fully in the inquiry process in the same period that they are moving beyond preoperational stages of intellectual development (Piaget and Inhelder, 1969). Such correlations suggest that the most significant components of the Rorschach response process may well be forms of cognitive activity and, specifically, forms of representational thought.

If the Rorschach is viewed from the standpoint of representation, new applications of Wernerian theory become possible. In particular, whereas Hemmendinger (1953) drew on Werner's conception of perceptual development, the later work of Werner and Kaplan (1963) on symbol formation, especially on the formation of symbols in nonverbal media, can be seen to be more germane to the study of the Rorschach. Advocating such an approach, Leonard Cirillo (personal communication) has argued that the Rorschach inkblot provides the material for the creation of a symbolic vehicle and that ontogenetic and other variations in the response process are best analyzed in terms of Werner and Kaplan's conception of developmental differences in symbolization.[9] This model posits (1) that symbol formation involves a subject shaping a medium into a symbol that represents a concept or object to another or others and (2) that the development of this process is governed by the orthogenetic principles and consists in a progressive differentiation and integration of the four components of the symbol situation—symbol and referent, addressor (self) and addressee (other).

---

[9]To the best of my knowledge, a series of lectures given by Dr. Cirillo as part of a course on clinical methods at Clark University in the early 1970s has been the only systematic effort to apply Werner and Kaplan's viewpoint to the Rorschach.

Using this model, the first stage in children's mastery of the Rorschach can be conceptualized as one in which there is a relative lack of differentiation within and between the basic constituents of the symbol situation. (1) The symbolic medium is treated in a crude, undifferentiated way. Only one aspect of the blot, and often an only dimly recognized one at that, serves as the basis for the "percept" or representation. (2) The range of concepts represented is similarly restricted. In the pure perseverative protocol, all cards represent only one concept. (3) Symbol and referent are barely distinguishable. As Rorschach (1964) noted, young children have difficulty responding to the test precisely because they treat the task as one of perception "in the strict sense of the word" and do not recognize that stimuli must be "interpreted," i.e., treated as something they are not (p. 17). (4) There is a lack of differentiation between the subject, on the one hand, and the symbolic vehicle and/or referent, on the other. What is represented may depend less on the stimulus material than on children's needs, wishes, and thoughts of the moment; how it is represented may be based as much on an intangible feeling state as on any specifiable characteristic of the inkblot; and the Rorschach task itself is defined in labile, shifting ways, changing from moment to moment as children's moods and inclinations change. (5) There is a similar lack of differentiation between the examiner and the task. The Rorschach test is not perceived as a task governed by its own set of rules, but rather as "an activity done with examiners," an activity which is determined largely by children's experience of that relationship and whose meaning changes as the relationship changes. (6) Finally, there is a relative lack of differentiation between self and other. Young children are typically tested by parents, teachers, and other familiar figures who already "know" them well and are known by them. Although the inquiry process is undoubtedly too difficult for children on purely cognitive grounds, two-year-olds also have no inclination to enter into a dialogue with examiners around their responses because they assume that others "see" the card exactly as they do. Attempts to score early responses or understand their meaning require, of necessity, an intuitive approach on the part of examiners based on empathic attunement to children and the shared context of the testing. Ames et al. (1952), for example, often score the test as it is being given, while their experience of the immediate situation, especially children's movements, expressions, and inflections, is still fresh. To be sure, questions can be raised about such techniques on scientific grounds (Klopfer, Fox, and Troup, 1956); for example, how much of the meaning attributed to responses actually comes from the children and how much from what examiners have read into responses? However, what is significant about the adoption of this seemingly problematic approach to interpretation is that it is not chosen arbitrarily. Rather, the choice of this strategy reflects a recognition of the fact that adults must participate in young children's experience of a situation if they are to understand children's language, gestures, Rorschach responses, or any other form of early symbolic activity.

Successive stages in children's mastery of the Rorschach may be seen to involve increasing differentiation and integration of components of the symbol situation. (1) Progressively more complex rules govern the shaping of the symbolic medium. In confabulatory whole responses, a single aspect of the blot is sufficient to serve as the basis for a representation; in confabulatory combinations, percepts are based on several elements; and, in Stage III, multiple aspects of the blot are integrated within percepts, while discrepant details are eliminated. (2) The range of referents expands, but also becomes subordinate to rules governing the acceptability of concepts. Children progress from giving a single perseverated response to using several content categories to representing a wider and wider range of concepts. At the same time, distinctions are made between proper and improper percepts. For example, whereas in Stage II children are prepared to offer utterly fantastic responses such as "a fireplace with feet," in Stage III, as new criteria are applied in shaping percepts, children describe only the fireplace and ignore the feet. (3) Symbol and referent are now clearly recognized as distinct. In Stage III children achieve what Exner (1978) stresses is a prerequisite for being able to take the Rorschach, "a willingness to identify the blot, or a blot area, as being something that it is not, but to which it has some similarity" (p. 37). In effect, children realize that the inkblot is not to be treated as a picture of a thing, but rather as a medium that is quite different from a picture, one that can be shaped and reshaped to represent many different things. (4) The Rorschach task becomes differentiated from both self and other. In a sense, Stage III is reached when children appreciate that the Rorschach is a task consisting of a set of rules governing the behavior of both tester and testee. The needs and wishes of the subject and the relationship with the examiner continue to have a significant influence on test performance, but this influence operates within a framework established by the Rorschach task and no longer defines the structure of the task itself. (5) Finally, there is a progressive "distantiation" of self and other than can be seen, above all, in the handling of the inquiry process. Children now recognize that examiners do not "know" what they are seeing, and that in order for another person to understand their percepts it is necessary to enter into a dialogue in which they describe what they see and how they see it.

Applications of theories of early mental development to the Rorschach test warrant a more detailed and systematic exposition than can be undertaken here. For now, it is perhaps enough to note the correlation between patterns of handling the test and stages in early mental development and to suggest ways in which developmental theories such as those of Piaget and Werner can be used to explain the phenomena encountered in the Rorschach performance of young children. Such "correlations" and "suggestions" are hardly sufficient to require abandoning traditional theories of the Rorschach response process or adopting alternatives, but they do provide a new perspective on the problems posed by children's Rorschachs and point to directions in which solutions to those problems may lie. For the present, in this regard as in others, the significance of the study of "the Rorschach" and "primitive mental states" in children resides most of all in the possibilities for research and theory it opens up.

REFERENCES

Allen, R. M. (1951), Longitudinal study of six Rorschach protocols of a three-year-old child. *Child Devel.,* 22:61–69.
_____ (1954), Continued longitudinal Rorschach study of a young child for years three to five. *J. Genet. Psychol.,* 85:135–149.
_____ (1955), Nine quarterly records of a young child. *Child Devel.,* 26:63–69.
Ames, L. B. (1959), Further check on the diagnostic validity of the Ames Danger Signals. *J. Proj. Tech.,* 23:291–298.
_____ (1960a), Constancy of content in Rorschach responses. *J. Genet. Psychol.,* 96:145–164.
_____ (1960b), Longitudinal survey of child Rorschach responses: Younger children. *Genet. Psychol. Monographs,* 61:229–289.
_____ (1965), Changes in experience-balance scores in the Rorschach at different ages in the life span. *J. Genet. Psychol.,* 106:279–286.
_____ (1966), Changes in Rorschach responses throughout the human life span. *Genet. Psychol. Monographs,* 74:89–125.
_____ Learned, J., Metraux, R. W., & Walker, R. N. (1952), *Child Rorschach Responses: Developmental Trends From Two to Ten Years.* New York: Hoeber.
_____ Metraux, R. W., Rodell, J., & Walker, R. N. (1974), *Child Rorschach Responses: Developmental Trends From Two to Ten Years.* 3rd ed. New York: Brunner/Mazel.
Bohm, E. (1958), *A Textbook in Rorschach Test Diagnosis for Psychologists, Physicians, and Teachers.* New York: Grune & Stratton.
Exner, J. E. (1969), *The Rorschach Systems.* New York: Grune & Stratton.
_____ (1974), *The Rorschach: A Comprehensive System.* New York: Wiley.

_____ (1978), *The Rorschach: A Comprehensive System: Vol. 2. Current Research and Advanced Interpretation.* New York: Wiley.

_____ & Weiner, I. B. (1982), *The Rorschach: A Comprehensive System: Vol. 3. Assessment of Children and Adolescents.* New York: Wiley.

Flavell, J. H. (1963), *The Developmental Psychology of Jean Piaget.* Princeton, NJ: Van Nostrand.

_____ (1977), *Cognitive Development.* Englewood Cliff, NJ: Prentice-Hall.

Ford, M. (1946), *The Application of the Rorschach Test to Young Children.* Minneapolis: University of Minnesota Press.

Fox, J. (1956), The psychological significance of age patterns in the Rorschach records of children. In: *Developments in the Rorschach Technique: Vol. 2. Fields of Application,* ed. B. Klopfer. New York: Harcourt, Brace & World, pp. 88–103.

Francis-Williams, J. (1968), *Rorschach with Children.* Oxford: Pergamon.

Frank, L. K. (1939), Projective methods for the study of personality. *J. Psychol.,* 8:389–413.

Gesell, A., & Ilg, F. L. (1943), *Infant and Child in the Culture of Today.* New York: Harper.

_____ _____ (1946), *The Child From Five to Ten.* New York: Harper.

Ginsburg, H., & Opper, S. (1979), *Piaget's Theory of Intellectual Development.* 2nd ed. Englewood Cliffs, NJ: Prentice-Hall.

Goldfried, M. R., Stricker, G., & Weiner, I. B. (1971), *Rorschach Handbook of Clinical and Research Applications.* Englewood Cliffs, NJ: Prentice-Hall.

Halpern, F. (1953), *A Clinical Approach to Children's Rorschachs.* New York: Grune & Stratton.

_____ (1960), The Rorschach test with children. In: *Projective Techniques with Children,* ed. A. I. Rabin & M. R. Haworth. New York: Grune & Stratton, pp. 14–28.

Hemmendinger, L. (1953), Perceptual organization and development as reflected in the structure of Rorschach test responses. *J. Proj. Tech.,* 17:162–170.

_____ (1960), Developmental theory and the Rorschach method. In: *Rorschach Psychology,* ed. M. A. Rickers-Ovsiankina. New York: Wiley, pp. 58–79.

Holt, R. R. (1954), Implications of some contemporary personality theories for Rorschach rationale. In: *Developments in the Rorschach Technique: Vol. 1. Technique and Theory,* ed. B. Klopfer, M. D. Ainsworth, W. G. Klopfer, & R. R. Holt. New York: Harcourt, Brace & World, pp. 501–560.

Kay, L. W., & Vorhaus, P. G. (1943), Rorschach reactions in early childhood: Part II. Intellectual aspects of personality development. *Rorschach Research Exchange,* 7:71–77.

Kirkpatrick, E. A. (1900), Individual tests of school children. *Psychol. Rev.,* 7:274–280.

Klopfer, B., Ed. (1956), *Developments in the Rorschach Technique: Vol. 2. Fields of Application.* New York: Harcourt, Brace & World.

_____ Ainsworth, M. D., Klopfer, W. G., & Holt, R. R. (1954) *Developments in the Rorschach Technique: Vol. 1. Technique and Theory.* New York: Harcourt, Brace & World.

_____ Fox, J., & Troup, E. (1956), Problems in the use of the Rorschach technique with children. In: *Developments in the Rorschach Technique: Vol. 2. Fields of Application,* ed. B. Klopfer. New York: Harcourt, Brace & World, pp. 3–21.

_____ & Margulies, H. (1941), Rorschach reactions in early childhood. *Rorschach Research Exchange,* 5:1–23.

_____ Spiegelman, M., & Fox, J. (1956), The interpretation of children's records. In: *Developments in the Rorschach Technique: Vol. 2. Fields of Application,* ed. B. Klopfer. New York: Harcourt, Brace & World, pp. 22–44.

Leichtman, M., & Nathan, S. (1983), A clinical approach to the psychological testing of borderline children. In: *The Borderline Child: Approaches to Etiology, Diagnosis, and Treatment,* ed. K. Robson. New York: McGraw-Hill, pp. 121–170.

————— Shapiro, S. (1980), An introduction to the psychological assessment of borderline conditions in children: Borderline children and the test process. In: *Borderline Phenomena and the Rorschach Test,* ed. J. Kwawer, H. Lerner, P. Lerner, & A. Sugarman. New York: International Universities Press, pp. 343–366.

Levitt, E. E., & Trauma, A. (1972), *The Rorschach Technique with Children.* New York: Grune & Stratton.

Meili-Dworetzki, G. (1956), The development of perception in the Rorschach. In: *Developments in the Rorschach Technique: Vol. 2. Fields of Application,* ed. B. Klopfer. New York: Harcourt, Brace & World, pp. 108–176.

Nordland, E. (1966), Children's Rorschach responses: Developmental trends from three to twenty years. *Pedagogisk Forskning,* 2/3:124–149.

Parsons, C. J. (1917), Children's interpretations of inkblots. *Brit. J. Psychol.,* 9:74–92.

Piaget, J. (1951), *Play, Dreams, and Imitation in Childhood.* London: Routledge & Kegan Paul.

————— (1973), *The Child and Reality: Problems of Genetic Psychology.* New York: Grossman.

————— Inhelder, B. (1969), *The Psychology of the Child.* New York: Basic Books.

Piotrowski, Z. A., & Lewis, N. D. C. (1950), A case of stationary schizophrenia beginning in early childhood with remarks on certain aspects of children's Rorschach records. *Quart. J. Child Behav.,* 2:115–139.

Pyle, W. H. (1915), A psychological study of bright and dull pupils. *J. Ed. Psychol.,* 6:151–156.

Rapaport, D. (1946), *Diagnostic Psychological Testing: Vol. 2.* Chicago: The Year Book Publishers.

Rorschach, H. (1964), *Psychodiagnostics: A Diagnostic Test Based on Perception.* 6th ed. New York: Grune & Stratton.

Schachtel, A. H. (1944), The Rorschach test with young children. *Amer. J. Orthopsychiat.,* 14:1–10.

Schachtel, E. G. (1945), Subjective definitions of the Rorschach test situation and their effect on test performance. *Psychiat.,* 8:419–448.

————— (1966), *Experimental Foundations of Rorschach's Test.* New York: Basic Books.

Schafer, R. (1954), *Psychoanalytic Interpretation in Rorschach Testing: Theory and Application.* New York: Grune & Stratton.

Werner, H. (1961), *Comparative Psychology of Mental Development.* New York: Science Editions.

————— Kaplan, B. (1963), *Symbol Formation: An Organismic-Developmental Approach to Language and the Expression of Thought.* New York: Wiley.

Whipple, G. M. (1910), *Manual of Mental and Physical Tests.* Baltimore: Warwick and York.

Chapter 22
The Role of Primary Process Thinking in Child Development

Sandra W. Russ, Ph.D.

There is at present a movement within the clinical and research literature to identify resources within the child and within the environment that promote adaptive functioning. Much of the work on stress and coping (Murphy and Moriarty, 1976; Garmezy, 1981) and on prevention in at-risk populations is an attempt to identify the important variables in the developing child. Primary process thinking reflects both cognitive and affective processes and is one variable that might contribute to creative problem solving, conflict resolution, and coping in children.

This chapter will review theoretical perspectives and definitions of primary process thinking, cognitive and behavioral correlates in normal populations, and the implications of research findings for normal development. Children's play, a major vehicle for the expression of primary process thinking, will be reviewed as well. A final section will focus on the role of primary process thinking in children evincing borderline and narcissistic features.

PRIMARY PROCESS THINKING

Primary process thinking refers to drive-laden oral, aggressive, and libidinal material and the illogical thinking related to that material (Freud, 1915; Holt, 1977). Freud first conceptualized primary process thought as an early primitive system of thought which is drive-laden and not subject to the rules of logic or oriented to reality. Secondary process thought (logical, reality-oriented thinking) becomes dominant and supplants primary process thinking as the child develops.

Dudek's sophisticated review of primary process ideation (1980) refers to primary process, as originally conceptualized, as "the mechanism by which unconscious instinctual energy surfaces in the form of images or ideas" (p. 520). Primary process thinking discharges tension and is based on the energy model. Initially, as Dudek points out, primary process thinking has an adaptive function for the developing infant in providing tension reduction and wish-fulfillment and in organizing and ordering the world. Rapaport (1950) describes primary process as a drive organization of memory, and secondary process as its conceptual organization.

Psychoanalytic theory has long postulated a relationship between primary process thinking and creativity (Freud, 1915; Kris, 1952; Arieti, 1976). Kris's concept of "regression in the service of the ego" (1952) postulates that the creative individual can regress to this earlier mode of thinking. The creative process would involve access to the primary process in a controlled and adaptive manner. One characteristic of the creative process is the ability to see new relationships among old ideas and to think of alternative solutions to problems (Guilford, 1959). The capacity to see new patterns among old ideas involves a flexibility of search among ideas and associations. Access to primary process thought is hypothesized to facilitate this flexibility in thinking. Primary process thinking is characterized by a "mobility of cathexis" whereby the energy behind ideas and images is easily displaced (Arlow and Brenner, 1964). Ideas are easily interchangeable, and attention is widely and flexibly distributed. This facilitates a fluidity of thought and flexibility of search among ideas and associations, an important component of creative thinking. The concept of "regression in the service of the ego" is consistent with the model of a continuum of primary process and secondary process thinking along which an individual's thinking can regress. Dudek (1980) states that the degree of contact with reality differentiates primary and secondary process.

The traditional view of the creative process in cognitive psychology is Wallas's four-stage model (1926): (1) Preparation stage—information gathering and investigation of the problem. (2) Incubation stage—ideas literally incubate. Thoughts are permitted to roam. The individual is not directly attacking the problem. (3) Illumination stage—solution occurs or artistic plan develops. This is the often cited "aha" experience of the creative scientist. In reality, as Hayes (1978) points out, reaching a solution is probably a more gradual process. (4) Verification stage—idea is tested or plan is carried out.

It is the incubation stage that is thought to be so important in creative problem solving. In that stage, during which thoughts are permitted to roam and attention is dispersed, controlled access to primary process material may aid in the creative process.

Recently, Arieti (1976) and Suler (1980) have suggested that the concept of regression to an earlier mode of thought may not be necessary. Rather, primary process can be thought of as a separate cognitive process whose development parallels that of secondary process thought. Suler stresses that access to primary process by the secondary process is the important point.

Another way of conceptualizing primary process is to think of it as affective content in cognition, a kind of affective residue. Primary process content (oral, anal, phallic) is content around which the child has experienced early intense feeling states, content which at one time was affect-laden. Some intense affect may remain, but what primary process thinking reflects is a style of dealing with intense affective material. Pine and Holt (1960) conceive of primary process thought as a broad cognitive style reflected in many areas of thinking. Bush (1969) and Noy (1969) have advanced similar conceptions. Thus, primary process thinking may refer both to current affective material and to a style of dealing with affective thoughts. These new conceptualizations, which take the construct of primary process thinking beyond the classic psychoanalytic instinctual drive model, prove useful in child development theory and research.

The study of primary process in child development affords insight into cognitive-affective development. Elkind (see Alvin, 1980) views primary process thought as cognition guided by affect, while Zimiles (1981) views it as affect-laden cognition. It may be a variable which, in Werner's terms (1948), reflects a blending of affective and cognitive elements. Although drive-laden primary process thinking does not encompass all affective categories, it does include a wide range of the affective states that children experience and reflects the cognitive integration of affective material.

RESEARCH FINDINGS

Operationalizing primary process thought, a necessary task if it is to be studied, has been difficult. Consequently, it has been largely ignored in the child development literature. The most researched and validated measure of primary process thinking is Holt's scoring system for the Rorschach (Holt, 1977; Holt and Havel, 1960; Suler, 1980). The Holt system is a useful one for teasing out different aspects of primary process thought. It provides measures of frequency of primary process thinking, intensity of the material, and integration of primary process into secondary process thought. The major score is the Adaptive Regression score (AR), which is a combination of intensity and "goodness" of the primary process material. Thus, the response "two fighting, bloody bears" to an appropriate location would be given a high AR score because of the intensity of the aggressive material and the good integration of the response. "Two fighting bears" would earn a lower AR score because the material would receive a lower intensity rating. "Two fighting bears" to an inappropriate location would be given a very low AR score because the primary process material is of poor form quality and is not well integrated into secondary process thought. For children, typical primary process content includes eating, food, mouths, scary monsters, insects, and aggressive animals. Other scores within the Holt system are the Defense Demand score (DD), which measures the intensity of the primary process material, and the Defense Effectiveness scores (DE), which measures the quality of the integration of primary process material, based largely on form quality. The AR score is the product of DD and DE, response by response, summed and divided by the number of primary process responses. Another useful score is the percentage of primary process responses for the entire protocol.

The Holt system measures both access to affect-laden material and the integration of that material into cognition. Can the child think about affective material and is it well integrated into fantasy? Although all affective categories are not included in the Holt system, many of the major categories are. The system encompasses a representative sample of the types of affective states that children experience.

Psychodynamic theory predicts that children who can permit affect-laden material to surface in fantasy and play, and who can cognitively integrate and master that material, will be open to ideas and flexible in their problem-solving approach. Access to internal affect-laden thoughts should facilitate a flexibility of search among ideas and associations, thus aiding in creative problem solving. This formulation has several sources. Freud (1926) states that repression of "dangerous" drive-laden material leads to a more general intellectual restriction. In children as in adults, mobility and flexibility of search should generalize to thoughts and ideas in general. Attention is then widely and flexibly distributed, facilitating a fluidity of thought and flexibility of search among all ideas and associations, affect-laden or not.

In adults, controlled access to primary process thinking (AR score) has been related to divergent thinking (Pine and Holt, 1960), the ability to make remote associations (Murray and Russ, 1981), problem-solving efficiency (Blatt, Allison and Feirstein, 1969), and a variety of creativity measures (Holt, 1977; Dudek, 1980).

There is a growing body of empirical work with children; the major premise of which is that access to primary process thinking, and its integration into secondary process thought, correlates positively with cognitive functioning, flexibility in problem solving, and general coping ability. Well-integrated primary process thinking is an adaptive resource.

Russ (1980) found a substantial relationship ($r = .54$) between AR and reading achievement in second grade children. This relationship remained significant when IQ was partialed out ($r = .45$) and remained consistent over a one-year period (Russ, 1981). Thus, children who expressed primary process material and integrated it well were better achievers, independent of intelligence, than children who had less access to primary process material or who did not integrate it well. An important finding in both the original study and the follow-up was that the relationship between the AR score and achievement was independent of general integrating ability. The overall adaptiveness of all fantasy productions, not just primary process responses, when partialed out, did not significantly lower the correlations. Thus, well-integrated primary process content accounted for a large proportion of the variance in school achievement, independent of both intelligence and general integrating ability. Cognitive integration of affective material was the important variable.

Russ's findings were consistent with Wulach's finding (1977) of a relationship between AR and Piagetian cognitive development in children ages five through eight. By contrast, Dudek (1975) reported a series of studies which found no relationship among primary process integration, achievement, and creativity in fourth grade children. Both Wulach and Russ discuss sample characteristics such as age, sex, and restricted range as possible explanations for the conflicting results.

Achievement and general cognitive development are global criteria. In an attempt to use the more specific criterion of flexibility in problem solving, Russ (1982) investigated the relationship between primary process thinking and flexibility in a problem-solving task. The Luchins' water-jar test (Luchins and Luchins, 1959) was adapted for use with third grade children. The task required the child to break out of an old set in solving a problem and to discover a new and more adaptive approach. This adaptation gives a series of cues to solving the problem. The final score reflects speed of cue utilization and ability to shift sets in solving a problem. The AR score was significantly related to flexibility in problem solving for boys but not for girls. For boys, the relationship remained significant when both intelligence and general integrating ability were partialed out. Flexibility in problem solving also related to school achievement in boys, as did the AR score. One conclusion from the study was that flexibility in problem solving partially accounted for the relationship between AR and school achievement in boys. A similar pattern of correlations emerged in a replication sample. When both samples were combined, the relationship between AR and flexibility in problem solving was $r = .42$ for boys. The higher the AR score, the sooner the child shifted to a new strategy. Also, in both studies, girls had a significantly smaller percentage of primary process responses than did boys.

This same population of children was again tested in the fifth grade (Russ, 1985). In this study, Guilford's Alternate Uses Test (1959) was used as a measure of flexibility of thought. The Alternate Uses Test measures divergent thinking—thinking that goes off in different directions. A typical item is "How many uses for a newspaper?" The test measures the ability to shift categories of uses for common objects. Sex differences again emerged. For boys, both the percentage of primary process ($r = .33, p < .05$) and AR ($r = .34, p < .05$) showed a significant positive relation to divergent thinking ability. There were no significant results for girls. Thus, a pattern of correlations was obtained similar to that yielded by the third grade study, a different task being used to gauge flexibility in problem solving. Zeitlin's Coping Inventory (1980), a teacher's rating scale of general coping ability, was also administered in this study. For boys, divergent thinking ability was significantly and positively related to coping ability ($r = .58$) and remained significant after intelligence was partialed out ($r = .49$). Also, third grade AR scores were predictive of fifth grade coping for boys ($r = .31$). Again there were no significant results for girls. These findings are important because they suggest a link in boys among primary process thinking, flexibility in problem solving, and coping behavior. Consistent with these findings, a study by Kleinman (1984) found that for boys both AR and percentage of primary process responses were negatively related to teachers' anxiety ratings. When AR and percentage of primary process were combined in a multiple regression equation, $R = .57$ $(p < .05)$. Thus, boys who had access to well-integrated primary process material were perceived as less anxious by their teachers. Again there were no significant results for girls.

The sex differences in the pattern of correlations is consistent with the adult literature (Pine and Holt, 1960; Holt, 1977). In general, primary process integration has been related to creativity measures in male subjects, but not in female subjects. In Russ's 1982 study, in the replication sample, percentage of primary process responses (not integration) was predictive of flexibility in problem solving in girls, and percentage of aggressive responses was predictive of their reading achievement. These results are similar to those of Pine and Holt (1960), who concluded from their results with adult samples that the amount of primary process expressed was the better predictor of creativity in female subjects, while integration of primary process was the better predictor for males. Rogolsky (1968), in a study with third grade children, found that a combination of amount of primary process scores and control and integration scores on the Rorschach was significantly related to artistic creativity in boys. The results were not significant for girls. Rogolsky concluded that general cognitive control and perceptual accuracy was an important variable related to creativity in boys. Taken together, these studies suggest that for girls and for boys different aspects of primary process thinking may be important in cognitive functioning.

In several samples of third grade children (Russ, 1982) and one sample of fourth and fifth grade children (Kleinman, 1984), boys have expressed more primary process material on the Rorschach than have girls. In a study of first and second graders by Grossman-McKee (1985) that used ten-minute puppet play sessions, boys again showed significantly more primary process content than did girls, especially aggressive content. These results are consistent with many other studies showing boys to be more aggressive in their behavior and play (Maccoby and Jacklin, 1974). They are consistent also with results showing that girls recall fewer details of aggressive modeling (Bandura, 1965) and that girls require longer tachistoscopic exposure time than do boys for recognition of aggressive scenes (Kagan and Moss, 1962). I have suggested elsewhere (Russ, 1980) that there may be more cultural taboos against the expression of primary process material by girls than is the case for boys, and that in consequence girls may never learn to use primary process thinking for adaptive functioning. This may partially explain the lack of correlation between integration of primary process material and the flexibility and coping measures. However, AR did relate to school achievement in the third grade girls, and third grade AR was predictive of fifth grade reading ($r = .50$) for girls (Russ, 1985).

It is unusual to find such strong correlations between a personality measure and measures of cognitive functioning. One of the reasons that the AR measure has been predictive of cognitive functioning is because it reflects both cognitive and affective components. It is unclear what the mechanisms are that account for the relationships between aspects of primary process and problem solving. Theoretically, access to affective primary process material permits a wide range of associations. Ease of access to internal affective thoughts may generalize to more neutral thoughts. If no affective content areas are forbidden and blocked off, this permits a freer range of association and a more open scanning of the environment. There would be greater breadth-of-attention deployment. An alternative explanation is that easy access to affective material is simply a reflection of good scanning ability. Good scanners are more likely to be aware of affective material as well as of unusual uses for objects. The specific role of affective expression in flexible problem solving needs to be investigated in future studies.

But whatever the mechanism, Holt's scoring system for the Rorschach appears to be useful in tapping an underlying process or structure that reflects both cognitive and affective processes and is predictive of meaningful cognitive and behavioral correlates in children. Although there are definite problems with the measure, it warrants further investigation with a variety of populations. The Holt system is cumbersome both to learn and to use, although interrater reliability has been adequate (Holt, 1977). It has not been normed for children, and its validity with female samples is perhaps suspect. In general, its psychometric properties are in need of further assessment (see Russ, 1987).

PRIMARY PROCESS THINKING AND PLAY

Play is one area in which children learn to express primary process material and to integrate it into fantasy. Freedheim and Russ (1983) state that "through play, the child expresses affect, calls forth forbidden fantasy and feelings, works through and masters developmental problems, and resolves conflicts" (p. 983). Schaefer (1979) points out that both Freud and Piaget thought of play as an adaptive function "to help a young child gradually assimilate and gain mastery over unpleasant experiences" (p. 15).

As Waelder (1933) has noted, play is a leave of absence from reality. It is a time to let go and to allow primary process thinking to occur. A major goal of many forms of therapy with children is to free up their thinking about affective material—to make dangerous thoughts not so dangerous, so that cognitive functioning in general is not so constricted. One of the basic tenets of psychodynamic psychotherapy is that constriction in the affective fantasy sphere will constrict cognitive functioning in other spheres. This was the theoretical foundation of work (Russ, 1980, 1982) which found that children who had greater access to primary process material, and who could integrate it well, were better school achievers and more flexible problem solvers. It is also consistent with Heiniche's finding (1969) that children with reading problems significantly improved in their reading after intensive psychotherapy. There were accompanying changes in "ego flexibility" as measured by Rorschach determinants. This finding is consistent with clinical observations that as anxiety-producing thoughts and feelings surface in psychotherapy, and the child masters and integrates that material, the child often begins to do better in school. The learning process itself is altered. Heiniche's study suggests that the child develops more "ego flexibility," which in turn affects the learning process. It may be that play increases the child's access to primary process and affective material, as well as the ability to cognitively integrate that material into adaptive fantasy. This increased access would in turn facilitate problem solving behavior. This hypothesis remains to be empirically tested.

There have been some relevant studies on play and problem solving. One by Dansky and Silverman (1973) found that children who were given the opportunity to play with objects before testing gave significantly more uses for those objects than did control subjects. Play opportunities increased divergent thinking productions. In a later study Dansky (1980) found that make-believe play was the mediator of the relationship between play and divergent thinking. Free play enhanced associative fluency but only for children who engaged in make-believe play. Also in this second study, the objects in the play period were different from those in the test period. Thus, play was shown to have a generalized effect.

Dansky's theoretical assumption for the hypothesis that make-believe play facilitates associative fluency was that the process of free combination and mutual assimilation of objects and ideas involved in play is similar to the elements involved in creative thinking. Dansky speculated that the free symbolic transformations inherent in make-believe play helped create a temporary cognitive set toward the loosening of old associations. This is consistent with the work of Sutton-Smith (1966), which stresses the role of play in the development of flexibility in problem solving. Play provides the opportunity to explore new combinations of ideas and to develop the capacity to develop new associations for old objects. The object transformations which occur in play help the child develop the capacity to see old objects in new ways. Kogan (1983) suggests that children's play behavior involves a search for alternate modes of relating to the object, a process similar to searching for alternate uses for objects in divergent thinking tasks. Kogan provides an extensive review of the divergent thinking literature.

Play has also been found to facilitate convergent problem solving (Sylva, Bruner, and Genova, 1976). However, Rubin, Fein, and Vandenberg (1983) argue that methodological problems as yet preclude any "firm" statement that play facilitates convergent problem solving.

Sylva and colleagues found that a play condition facilitated problem solving in children ages three to five. Children in the play group required fewer hints than children in other groups. They also were more flexible in their formation of hypotheses. Pepler and Ross (1981) found that divergent play in three- and four-year-olds facilitated divergent thinking as well as performance on convergent thinking tasks. Pepler and Ross concluded that divergent play helped children to be more flexible problem solvers in general. A consistent finding in the literature is that play facilitates flexibility in cognitive functioning.

The two major theoretical variables put forth as mediating between play and flexible problem solving are the capacity to form new combinations of ideas and breadth-of-attention deployment. In all the empirical work on divergent thinking, play, and creativity, the concept of affect is not directly addressed. For example, Dansky's study (1980) did not look at the affective variables involved in make-believe play.

It is important to consider the research findings in the primary process and problem-solving area in conjunction with the research findings on play and problem solving (Russ, 1987). Play facilitates divergent thinking and flexibility in problem solving. Primary process relates to flexible problem solving and divergent thinking. One reason play may facilitate problem solving is its affect-laden primary process component. Play may enable affective material to be expressed and integrated into fantasy, which in turn facilitates problem-solving behavior. Primary process thinking may be an important underlying affective variable partially accounting for the relationship between play and problem solving.

Another function of primary process expression in play may be to aid the child generally in conflict resolution. Expression and integration of primary process material may be central to the "working through" process.

Erikson (1963) has stressed the concept of mastery in play. Children use play to gain mastery over traumatic events and everyday conflicts. Play is a major form of conflict resolution. Waelder (1933) describes the child as repeating the unpleasant experience over and over until mastery over the experience is achieved. Play is a "method of constantly working over and, as it were, assimilating piecemeal an experience which was too large to be assimilated instantly at one swoop" (p. 218). The unpleasant affect associated with the event is no longer unmanageable. The child has turned passive into active and has mastered the event. To use Waelder's metaphor, the child has "digested" the event. Play is an assimilative process. Waelder has described here the "working through" process which is a major mechanism of change in psychotherapy (Freedheim and Russ, 1983). The child gradually gains access to conflict-laden material and plays it out until the conflict has been resolved. It is probable that the working through process helps develop cognitive structure, which aids the child in assimilating future stressful events.

Milos and Reiss (1982) found that experimental play conditions helped young children solve a "real-life" problem—separation anxiety. Three different play conditions were effective in reducing anxiety around separation problems in nursery school. Importantly, quality of play, as measured by amount of emotional themes and attempts to master the problem, was related to the effectiveness of the play in reducing anxiety.

The whole area of play as an aid to coping with life and developmental stresses and problems is ripe for investigation. How play facilitates general problem solving and coping with stress is as important a question as how play facilitates specific cognitive functions such as divergent thinking. One of the major goals of child psychotherapy is to teach children to be good players, so that they may more effectively cope with future life problems.

PRIMARY PROCESS THINKING IN CHILDREN WITH
BORDERLINE AND NARCISSISTIC FEATURES

As Holt (1977) has noted, "we find primary process thinking in conscious subjects either out of strength or out of weakness" (p. 379). In borderline psychotic children, primary process thinking occurs out of weakness. It reflects structural deficits in object relations, self-other differentiation, and ego development. Leichtman and Shapiro (1980) stress the primitive nature of the borderline child's sexual and aggressive wishes. Borderline children experience drives in raw, unmodulated forms. Leichtman and Shapiro point out that primary process content frequently intrudes into thinking and that secondary process is not firmly established.

The blatant expression of primary process material occurs because of the lack of an adequate repressive barrier (Rosenfeld and Sprince, 1963). Given the already intense drive material, especially aggressive and oral aggressive material, primary process thinking periodically breaks through and overwhelms the borderline child. Thus, borderline children frequently act out and have difficulty distinguishing reality from fantasy, especially under stress (Eckstein, 1966; Pine, 1974). Chethik (1979) comments on the tendency for these children to get "lost" in their pretend play and to be unable to stop.

It is very difficult, theoretically, to separate out the dimension of primary process thinking from object relations and self-other differentiation. Urist (1980) has addressed the need for investigation of the relationship between the development of primary process thought and the development of object relations. In order for access to primary process material to work for the child as an adaptive resource, it must be well integrated with secondary process thought. Since secondary process thinking is not well established in borderline children, primary process thinking can easily take over. The development of secondary process thought and the cognitive structure necessary to integrate affect is partially determined by the level of object relations.

As Gilpin (1976) has pointed out, the major role of the therapist with borderline children is to be a stable object which the child can slowly take in. She stresses for the therapist the importance of predictability, consistency, and empathy. The therapist must help the child with self-other differentiation and in separating fantasy from reality. The therapist serves also as an auxiliary ego who helps the child establish cause-and-effect relationships. Gilpin emphasizes the importance of linking outside triggering events with internal feeling states. These processes and interventions should help with the development of internal structure. Only then can primary process thinking be better modulated and integrated.

Children who fall on the borderline continuum can teach us about the relationship between object relations and primary process thinking. In therapy, as the child develops better object relations and firmer self-other boundaries, one can see the development of secondary process thought. Changes often occur in a startling way, with the developing process being "right out there." The immediacy of the therapist-child relationship can show us which interventions are effective. Therapy with these children can reveal, within the therapy hour, the kinds of interactions between child and therapist that effect the development of object relations and the integration of primary process thinking.

Steve, a nine-year-old when first referred for therapy, was diagnosed as being at the severe end of the borderline continuum. He was referred because of hyperactivity, lack of friends, preoccupation with "death, hell, the devil and violence," and periodic bizarre behavior in the classroom. Primary process material on the tests and in the interviews was blatant, intense, and unintegrated. For example, on his Draw-a-Person, he drew a picture of a boy walking on a tightrope that was on fire. Simultaneously, the boy was being shot out of a cannon.

Steve was seen twice a week for three years in individual outpatient therapy. During this time one can trace the markers of developing self-other differentiation and more stable object representations. Integration of primary process thought and firmer secondary process thinking seemed to develop as the therapist worked directly on becoming a stable introject for Steve. Six months into therapy, before the therapist was about to leave for a vacation, Steve asked if he could take home the chalk from the playroom. Writing on the blackboard with the chalk had been his major form of communication with the therapist. When asked why he wanted to take the chalk home, Steve said that he could then draw pictures of me on the sidewalk and remember what I looked like (Steve was at that time unable to hold a mental representation of the therapist on his own). Separations were difficult. After one year of therapy, Steve asked for an appointment book like the therapist's. When asked why he wanted the book, he said, "So I can put the names and phone numbers of my friends in it." He was given an appointment book, which served as a transitional object and as a bridge for developing relationships with other children. As Steve was "taking in" the therapist, his thinking became more logical, reality oriented, and organized. As Steve said at this time, "If your mind knows where it's going, then you know what you're doing."

After two years of therapy, Steve could maintain his internal organization during separations from the therapist. He would now tell the therapist how angry he was that she was there "when I don't need you and not there when I do." During his third year of treatment, the therapy became more like that of a neurotic child. As Gilpin (1976) has noted, "When a child reaches the oedipal stage, the therapy becomes more like that of a neurotic child but with special attention given to the need for defenses" (p. 488).

At termination, precipitated by the therapist's move to a different city, Steve, now twelve, felt that he "could manage" without transferring to a new therapist. He said that he used to be afraid that "this would happen to me," at which point he drew a picture of a boy on the blackboard and erased it. He then said, "I still feel that way sometimes, but I know that it will be all right." Steve was describing the experience of self-annihilation and his now functioning observing ego.

During his therapy one of the best measures of his developing secondary process thought was his description of his annual trip to the Ice Capades. In the first year the description was illogical, hard to follow, with no coherent sequence of events. In the second year the description was clearer, although still fragmented and out of order. By the third year, however, Steve's description was clear, coherent, entertaining, and funny. His use of humor was evident throughout the therapy and, in general, contained primary process themes.

It appeared that Steve had been able to develop a repressive barrier as self-other differentiation and object relations became more developed, and that primary process material was then able to be integrated. Whether primary process thinking became an adaptive resource for Steve, or for other children and adults who have struggled with borderline pathology, is an open question. Theoretically, once the repressive barrier is firmly established, access to and integration of primary process material should aid in creative problem solving and coping. The child can move on to the next developmental task.

Although Holt's scoring system for primary process on the Rorschach has not been used empirically with clinical groups of borderline and narcissistic children, it is a measure that might shed light on the nature of these disorders. It might also be a valuable tool for assessing change in psychotherapy. One would expect the borderline child, in Holt's system, to demonstrate a high percentage of primary process material, high Defense Demand score (high intensity), low Defense Effectiveness score (responses would not be well integrated into secondary process thought), and low AR score. Indeed, in the school populations used in my research studies, the two or three lowest scores in a sample of fifty children were in Rorschach protocols suggestive of borderline pathology.

CONCLUSION

With the refinement of Holt's measure of primary process thinking on the Rorschach and the development of new measures of primary process thinking (as expressed, for instance, in children's play), we can begin to differentiate various aspects of primary process thought. The sex differences noted in the literature suggest that different aspects of primary process thinking are important for boys and for girls. Different aspects may also be related to different clinical diagnoses. Access to primary process content, given even a minimum capacity for integration of primary process, may be important for creativity. The cognitive structure necessary for this integration may be more important for conflict resolution and coping ability.

Therapy with the neurotic child involves helping the child gain access to affect-laden material so that it can be worked through and integrated. By contrast, therapy with children on the borderline continuum involves helping the child build the cognitive structure necessary to repress and integrate primary process material. Empirical investigation of the effects of very specific interventions on different aspects of primary process should be undertaken and may generalize to guidelines for psychotherapy with different clinical populations.

REFERENCES

Alvin, R. (1980), David Elkind: Going beyond Piaget. *APA Monitor,* November, pp. 4–5.

Arieti, S. (1976), *Creativity: The Magic Synthesis.* New York: Basic Books.

Arlow, J., & Brenner, C. (1964), *Psychoanalytic Concepts and the Structural Theory.* New York: International Universities Press.

Bandura, A. (1965), Influence of models' reinforcement contingencies in the acquisition of imitative responses. *J. Personal. & Soc. Psychol.,* 1:589–595.

Blatt, S., Allison, O., & Feirstein, A. (1969), The capacity to cope with cognitive complexity. *J. Personal.,* 37:269–288.

Bush, M. (1969), Psychoanalysis and scientific creativity. *J. Amer. Psychoanal. Assn.,* 17:136–191.

Chethik, M. (1979), The borderline child. In: *Basic Handbook of Child Psychiatry: Vol. II,* ed. J. P. Noshpitz. New York: Basic Books, pp. 304–320.

Dansky, J. (1980), Make-believe: A mediator of the relationship between play and associative fluency. *Child Devel.,* 51:576–579.

———— Silverman, F. (1973), Effects of play on associative fluency in preschool-aged children. *Devel. Psychol.,* 9:38–43.

Dudek, S. (1975), Regression in the service of the ego in young children. *J. Personal. Assess.,* 39:369–376.

———— (1980), Primary process ideation. In: *Encyclopedia of Clinical Assessment: Vol. 1,* ed. R. H. Woody. San Francisco: Jossey-Bass, pp. 520–539.

Eckstein, R. (1966), *Children of Time and Space, of Action and Impulse.* New York: Appleton-Century-Crofts.

Erikson, E. H. (1963), *Childhood and Society.* New York: Norton.

Freedheim, D., & Russ, S. (1983), Psychotherapy with children. In: *Handbook of Clinical Child Psychology,* ed. C. Walker & M. Roberts. New York: Wiley, pp. 978–994.

Freud, S. (1915), The unconscious. *Standard Edition,* 14: 166–215. London: Hogarth Press, 1957.

———— (1926), Inhibitions, symptoms and anxiety. *Standard Edition,* 20:87–174. London: Hogarth Press, 1959.

Garmezy, N. (1981), Children under stress: Perspectives on antecedents and correlates of vulnerability and resistance to psychopathology. In: *Further Explorations in Personality,* ed. A. Rabin, J. Aronoff, A. Barclay, & R. Zuker. New York: Wiley, pp. 196–269.

Gilpin, D. (1976), Psychotherapy of borderline psychotic children. *Amer. J. Psychother.,* 30:483–496.

Grossman-McKee, A. (1985), Affective expression in fantasy play and its relationship to divergent thinking and achievement. Unpublished master's thesis, Case Western Reserve University.

Guilford, J. P. (1959), *Personality.* New York: McGraw-Hill.

Hayes, J. (1978), *Cognitive Psychology: Thinking and Creating.* Homewood, IL: Dorsey.

Heiniche, C. (1969), Frequency of psychotherapeutic session as a factor affecting outcome: Analysis of clinical ratings and test results. *J. Abnorm. Psychol.,* 74:553–560.

Holt, R. R. (1977), A method for assessing primary process manifestations and their control in Rorschach responses. In: *Rorschach Psychology,* ed. M. Rickers-Ovsiankina. Huntington, NY: Krieger, pp. 375–420.

———— Havel, J. (1960), A method for assessing primary and secondary process in the Rorschach. In: *Rorschach Psychology,* ed. M. Rickers-Ovsiankina. New York: Wiley, pp. 263–315.

Kagan, J., & Moss, H. (1962), *Birth to Maturity: A Study in Psychological Development.* New York: Wiley.

Kleinman, M. (1984), Primary process, anxiety, and coping in children. Unpublished master's thesis, Case Western Reserve University.

Kogan, N. (1983), Stylistic variation in childhood and adolescence: Creativity, metaphor, and cognitive styles. In: *Handbook of Child Psychology, Vol. 3,* ed. P. Mussen. New York: Wiley, pp. 631–706.

Kris, E. (1952), *Psychoanalytic Explorations in Art.* New York: International Universities Press.

Leichtman, M., & Shapiro, S. (1980), An introduction to the psychological assessment of borderline conditions in children: Borderline children and the test process. In: *Borderline Phenomena and the Rorschach Test,* ed. J. Kwawer, H. Lerner, P. Lerner, & A. Sugarman. New York: International Universities Press, pp. 343–366.

Luchins, A., & Luchins, E. (1959), *Rigidity of Behavior.* Eugene, OR: University of Oregon Books.

Maccoby, E., & Jacklin, C. (1974), *The Psychology of Sex Differences.* Stanford, CA: Stanford University Press.

Milos, M., & Reiss, S. (1982), Effects of three play conditions on separation anxiety in young children. *J. Consult. & Clin. Psychol.,* 50:389-395.

Murphy, L., & Moriarty, A. R. (1976), *Vulnerability, Cooing and Growth.* New Haven: Yale University Press.

Murray, J., & Russ, S. (1981), Adaptive regression and types of cognitive flexibility. *J. Personal. Assess.,* 45:59-65.

Noy, P. (1969), A revision of the psychoanalytic theory of the primary process. *Internat. J. Psycho.-Anal.,* 50:155-178.

Pepler, D., & Ross, H. (1981), The effects of play on convergent and divergent problem solving. *Child Development,* 52:1202-1210.

Pine, F. (1974), On the concept of "borderline" in children. *Psychoanalytic Study of the Child,* 29:341-368.

———— Holt, R. C. (1960). Creativity and primary process: A study of adaptive regression. *J. Abnorm. & Soc. Psychol.,* 61:370-379.

Rapaport, D. (1950), On the psychoanalytic theory of thinking. *Internat. J. Psychoanal.,* 31:161-170.

Rogolsky, M. (1968), Artistic creativity and adaptive regression in third grade children. *J. Personal. Assess.,* 32:53-62.

Rosenfeld, S., & Sprince, M. (1963), An attempt to formulate the meaning of the concept "borderline." *Psychoanalytic Study of the Child,* 18:603-635.

Rubin, K., Fein, G., Vandenberg, B. (1983), Play. In: *Handbook of Child Psychology: Vol. 4,* ed. P. Mussen. New York: Wiley, pp. 693-774.

Russ, S. (1980), Primary process integration on the Rorschach and achievement in children. *J. Personal. Assess.,* 44:338-344.

———— (1981), Primary process on the Rorschach and achievement in children: A follow-up study. *J. Personal. Assess.,* 45:473-477.

———— (1982), Sex differences in primary process thinking and flexibility in problem solving in children. *J. Personal. Assess.,* 46:569-577.

———— (1985), Primary process thinking on the Rorschach; Divergent thinking and coping in children. Paper presented at the meeting of the Society for Personality Assessment, Oakland, CA.

Russ, S. (1987), Assessment of cognitive affective interaction in children: Creativity, fantasy and play research. In: *Advances in Personality Research,* vol. 6, ed. J. Butcher & C. Spielberger. Hillsdale, NJ: Lawrence Erlbaum Assoc., pp. 141-155.

Schaefer, C., Ed. (1979), *Therapeutic Use of Child's Play.* New York: Aronson.

Suler, J. (1980), Primary process thinking and creativity. *Psychol. Bull.,* 88:144-165.

Sutton-Smith, B. (1966), Piaget on play: a critique. *Psychol. Rev.,* 73:104-110.

Sylva, K., Bruner, J., & Genova, P. (1976), The role of play in the problem solving of children 3-5 years old. In: *Play: Its Role in Development and Evolution,* ed. J. Bruner, A. Jolly, & K. Sylva. New York: Basic Books, pp. 245-257.

Urist, J. (1980), The continuum between primary and secondary process thinking: Toward a concept of borderline thought. In: *Borderline Phenomena and the Rorschach Test,* ed. J. Kwawer, H. Lerner, P. Lerner, & A. Sugarman. New York: International Universities Press.

Waelder, R. (1933), The psychoanalytic theory of play. *Psychoanal. Quart.,* 2:208-224.

Wallas, G. (1926), *The Art of Thought.* New York: Harcourt Brace.

Werner, H. (1948), *Comparative Psychology of Mental Development.* Rev. ed. Chicago: Follet.

Wulach, J. (1977), Piagetian cognitive development and primary process thinking in children. *J. Personal. Assess.,* 41:230–237.

Zeitlin, S. (1980), Assessing coping behavior. *Amer. J. Orthopsychiat.,* 50:139–144.

Zimiles, H. (1981), Cognitive-affective interaction: A concept that exceeds the researcher's grasp. In: *Cognitive and Affective Growth,* ed. E. Shapiro & E. Weber. Hillsdale, NJ: Erlbaum, pp. 49–63.

Chapter 23

Some Thoughts on M in Relation to the Early Structuring of Character in Children

Vera Campo, Ph.D.

This chapter seeks to elaborate some new ideas developed by Campo and Campo (1979) concerning the precocious apparition of human movement responses in children in relation to an early rigidity of character structure. It is well known that M appears relatively late in childhood and does not equal or surpass FM until adolescence. With the exception of a group of "withdrawn" children (Exner, 1978) in whom M equals FM + m at the age of seven and surpasses them from eleven years onward, this has been shown by virtually all normative studies. On comparing Ames, Learned, Metraux, and Walker (1952) with Exner's norms (Exner and Weiner, 1982), it can be observed that at the age of six one human movement, possibly two, constitutes the normal mean until ten years, when 2 M is to be expected. Beizmann (1961), who emphasizes that her results are very similar to those of Ames et al. (1952) and of Romano (1975) in France, also found a mean between 1 and 2 M until the age of ten.

All of the few existing clinical works on children's Rorschachs (Halpern, 1953; Klopfer, 1956; Francis-Williams, 1968; Rausch de Traubenberg and Boizou, 1977; Exner and Weiner, 1982) hold that an increase of M over FM is abnormal before puberty. The excessive presence of M is linked to experiences of affective deprivation and depression (Levi and Kraemer, 1952; Francis-Williams, 1968), to schizophrenia (Thetford, 1952; Halpern, 1953), to delusions and psychosis (Rausch de Traubenberg and Boizou, 1977), or, from another point of view, to reading disability (Vorhaus, 1952).[1]

Nevertheless, with the exception of Exner, Martin, and Mason (1984) none of these authors relate the precocious presence of M directly with character structure. In a discussion regarding "response styles" (in a workshop held in Barcelona) the possibility was raised of considering the more stable elements of the Structural Summary (EB, Afr, FC:CF + C, etc.) as character traits. Exner conceded the point but insisted that he preferred to think in terms of "response styles." Exner pointed out that based on the year-to-year variations observed by him during "normal" development, once an introversive style has formed this style persists, regardless of the age at which it begins. Such persistence before the age of fifteen was not found for the extratensive style. The formation of the introversive style before eleven years (in ideal conditions this would occur between ten and fourteen years of age) implies the danger of greater pathology during adolescence, the interpretive hypothesis being that this early formation becomes a lag, i.e., an obstacle to development, inasmuch as the child tends to establish concrete, oversimple, and infantile relations of cause and effect, thus fostering rigidity. The capacity for abstraction diminishes because ideation remains too primitive; in a more complex world, that of adolescence, the subject can no longer respond adequately.

Therefore, if in the *normative* studies mentioned children tend to be more extratensive, that is to say, more inclined to display emotion as contrasted with reacting ideationally, this implies that an early tendency toward internalization could represent an unusually precocious use of an attitude, trait, or style. This attitude, trait, or style is not an infantile but rather an adult defensive resource, and is in this sense inappropriate in children.

In other words, for a child to resort to attitudes, roles, or identifications (although exactly how identification participates in M responses is still under discussion) that do not correspond to an infantile developmental level, that is to say, to use adult attributes to resolve situations

[1]The author describes a group of children with a high number of M responses (three or more) in the absence or low presence of FM and color responses, as a sign that the subject cannot react deeply and genuinely to the environment and that he lacks spontaneity and vivacity. Thus the creative potential (M) is shut off from the outside world, constituting a merely private source of richness, a secret system of values that must be protected from outside intrusion and that gives place to a successful drive for nonachievement in face of school requirements.

and conflicts, would result in an inflexibility that would be nonadaptive in the face of later developmental changes. At the cognitive level this would be due to the fixation of modes of ideation corresponding to the Piagetian developmental stage of concrete operational thinking prior to the stage of formal thinking that becomes established in puberty. On the emotional level the fixation would refer to already rigid ways of coping with feeling.

Moreover, given the linking between M and object representations and relations (see Mayman, 1967) its ego-syntonic quality could be understood as an identification with aspects of the object mother, father, or their substitutes. This in turn suggests M's function as a character trait (and hence, as part of a defensive armor), accepted and used by the ego in its confrontation with inner and outer reality. In addition, this defensive aspect would imply the fixation or chronification and growing rigidity of certain traits. Herein resides its seriousness in children. Also, the presence of a large number of M responses in children is generally considered a bad prognostic sign.

The case of five-year-old Paula is a good example of this early rigidity of character structure and its vicissitudes. Paula was brought to consultation because her mother felt that "she does not live her age, is superintelligent, very competitive, with an incredible capacity for reasoning; but she lives too much in fantasy. In addition, she is terribly absorbing and she can't stand waiting."

Paula is the youngest of three children; her brother and sister are twelve and eleven, respectively. Her early development was normal except for surgery for piloric stenosis at twenty-eight days and a separation of a month and a half from her mother when she was three months old. According to her mother, the separation was without consequence. Sphincter control was obtained without difficulty around the age of two; she sleeps well and has always eaten well although she rejects milk; she has suffered no serious illnesses. Paula is sociable and generally independent. The mother adds: "The pressing problem is with me: she wants to know whom I love the most, always accuses me of forsaking her when I go out. She is 'fetishistic' about kissing me, saying goodbye, eating the same amount of chocolates as her brother and sister, to have advantage over them. I don't spank her because I could kill her, but I adore her, she fascinates me. I feel guilty for not knowing how to set limits for her. Each morning there is a battle about choosing her clothes; before taking her bath she dances in front of the mirror and tells me to act as her boyfriend. She says she talks with God and scolds us like a Savonarola for not being religious. She is very coquettish and seductive, does the impossible to call attention. She always blames others and feels that they have the best. She is very greedy."

Paula has complete sexual information ("little seed"). About a year ago she was terrified of a friend of her parents, saying that he looked like "the satyr" (a famous rapist). The mother recalls that a short time ago Paula said that "the bottom" of her friend, a girl, was "difficult to open." Two years ago the parents did not get on well together. (Both parents are in psychological treatment.) The father tends to be lenient with her and permits her to dominate him.

Paula's Rorschach Protocol

Free Associations	*Inquiry*
Card I. Like ghosts! A mommy, a daddy, and a little girl [D4]. E: If you look at it a little longer you may find more things. S: I see the ghosts.	E: Repeats R. S: They are ghosts because the heads don't look like—hers are the hands like this [gesticulates and points to D4], they are going to call a taxi and the little girl asked the mommy if she could do like this [waves] and call a taxi; here are the legs, together they are standing.
Card II. Two gentlemen playing.	E: Repeats R. S: Playing pat-a-cake [demonstrates], heads, hands, feet.
Card III. Skeletons!	E: Repeats R. S: Because of the head, the body. E: Please explain the skeletons a bit more. S: They are taking hold of something, two men.
Card IV. Like a monster, a giant.	E: Repeats R. S: The feet, very big! Without tail, nor arms, nor head.

Card V. Like a—a bee.

E: Repeats R.
S: The wings, feelers, this has nothing to do with it, it is not moving.

Card VI. Like a faucet and water coming out, from the bathtub, and water is coming out of the faucet [points to D3].

E: Repeats R.
S: The water is coming out [gesticulates]; they are fixing it because it has broken.
E: Water?
S: Yes, all of this, and the bathtub [D1].

Card VII. Like two little rabbits.

E: Repeats R.
S: They were doing like this and like that [demonstrates], dancing, they are big.

Card VIII. Like a rainbow!

E: Repeats R.
S: Because it has many colors.

Card IX. Hey, like two gentlemen fighting.

E: Repeats R.
S: Fighting with swords.

Card X. Like a —like a rainbow but the colors separated.

E: Repeats R.
S: All the colors.

Testing-the-Limits. Accepts butterfly (1), "prickly" animal skin (VI), spider (X) and adds "Two crocodiles climbing a tree" (VIII).
Liked best. VIII and X because they have colors and are gayer.
Liked least. IV and III because they are scary, the monster and the skeletons.

The protocol shows an ambitendent response style (EB), usual at this age, with 4 M responses—which is most *un*usual—and apparently little disposition to respond to emotional stimulation (low Afr),[2] also quite unusual in children. "Stabilization" (EA between 2.5 and 5 points higher than ep) is clear, as well as cognitive and attitudinal rigidity (a much larger than p) and a tendency toward a ruminative, careful

[2]It must be kept in mind that in protocols with one response per card the Afr will always be low.

intellectual control (Zd and DQ+ are both high). But Paula has little emotional modulation (2 pure C). Contact with reality is low (X+ percentage below 70) in the sense that she tends to twist things according to her personal needs. Her self-esteem, perhaps in relation to the rejection of her more infantile aspects (only 1 FM, low A percentage, M + H high with contents that refer predominantly to adults and to unreal people), is low: 3r+ (2). Her marked interest in the human figure together with the M:FM (4:1) and the EA:ep (7:2) relation, both unusual for her age, show a situation of seeming psychological maturity.[3] This situation creates some stress (1M) but it is probably dissociated as well as acted out (4M, rs, 2C). Characteristically, one sees a mixture of apparently "adult" behaviors (M) with childish (and greedy) attitudes (C). She tries to be the center of attraction, especially in relation to her mother, whom she tries to monopolize, seduce, and dominate.

Paula pays little attention to conventional matters and in the content of her responses one sees a predominance of aggressive fantasies (I ghosts, III skeletons, IV monster-giant, IX gentlemen fighting with swords), idealization (rainbow on VIII and X), seduction (dancing little-big rabbits on VII), and sexual preoccupations (broken faucet with water coming out on VI). Manic and obsessional traits seem prevalent and a general impression is given of an early structuring of a style or character that forebodes future difficulties.

Nevertheless, and in spite of her mother's seeming preoccupation with her, Paula did not enter treatment, as was suggested to the parents. Apparently her mother, perhaps due to her own narcissistic needs, remained too "fascinated" with her. It was as if she had used the psychological consultation and the psychologist as objects in which to deposit her worries, and had then hurriedly left.

The examination of three other protocols with a greater than expected number of M responses before age ten yielded the following common traits: (1) EA equal or higher than ep—a situation associated more with adulthood than with childhood—as an expression of an early *stabilization*[4] of character traits (or "response style"), a stability that

[3]Also shown by the WISC: Verbal IQ = 120, Performance IQ = 101, Full IQ = 112. The unusually high vocabulary level (Weighted = 17) stands in contrast to a rather lower level of efficiency (verbal mean = 13, performance mean = 10).

[4]"In some ways, a much higher EA may signal less flexibility in the psychological behaviors of the person: certainly, it signals less flexibility in the personality structure. Obviously, if a high EA is noted in the record of a young child, it may indicate some potential difficulties for further growth; the organization of resources may have stabilized prematurely, in effect, reducing much of the natural pliability that exists in the personality of the child" (Exner and Weiner, 1982, p. 81).

forebodes a lack of change; (2) low Afr as an expression of *emotional isolation*, contrary to what is expected in children; (3) a marked dissimilarity in the a:p relationship as an expression of *cognitive and attitudinal rigidity;* and (4) overincorporation (Zd higher than +3) as an expression of a ruminative, overly careful processing of perceptual stimuli, suggesting a strong *need for control.* It is my contention that the coexistence of these traits, which appear to reinforce one another, permits one to think of the fixation and chronification usually associated with what is generally understood by the concept of character. Although "character" has disappeared in DSM–III, the entry that seems to touch most closely on it is that for Personality Disorder: "The essential features are deeply ingrained, inflexible, maladaptive patterns of relating to, perceiving and thinking about the environment and oneself. . . ."

These very tentative formulations led me to attempt a broader study involving a greater number of subjects. Specifically, I decided to compare a group of high M children with a group of nonpatient subjects of the same age. Further, I sought to determine if the four traits outlined above could be observed in a larger group of children. From such a study I hoped to determine whether this constellation of indices could throw new light on the early structuring of character.

With this aim in mind, twenty-four child protocols—twelve from subjects five and six years old (six of each), and twelve from seven-year-olds—were obtained[5] and scored according to Exner's Comprehensive System (Exner, 1974, 1978; Exner and Weiner, 1982) by four different psychologists. The only specific criteria were three or more M responses, normal intelligence, and similar socioeconomic level (middle to upper middle class). All were patients referred for psychological consultation.

T tests demonstrated that no differences exist between these two age levels, thus permitting the establishment of means and standard deviations for the group as a whole as regards the main components of the twenty-four Structural summaries (see Table 1).[6] To make the data

[5]They come from my own clinical practice of about thirty years—during which I have seen a very low frequency of such high M records at an early age—and from three Spanish colleagues whose experience confirms mine. The protocols used in this study have been translated into English and proceed from Argentine and Spanish subjects.

[6]The motives for psychological consultation were quite varied: 6 Learning difficulties; 4 Nocturnal enuresis; one tends to overactive behavior; 2 Fears and phobias; one is "too grown up"; 2 Night terrors; 1 Overactive behavior; 1 Difficulty in pronunciation; 1 Lack of physical growth, hearing difficulty, and bouts of asthma; 1 Quadriplegia as sequel to poliomyelitis; 1 Continued allergies and bronchitis, emotionally too mature; 1 Character too adult; 1 Withdrawn; 1 Feels he is "bad" and fear of castration; 1 Depression and temper tantrums; 1 General "fragility" of personality.

TABLE 1

Variables	Mean	Standard Deviation
R	14.91	5.74
W	6.92	2.47
D	6.04	3.21
Dd	1.75	1.65
s	1.25	1.24
DQ: +	5.88	1.31
o	7.75	4.76
v	1.08	0.50
FQx: o	7.04	1.99
w	3.71	2.77
—	3.79	1.87
w — minus	−0.08	2.73
FQf: o	1.83	0.94
w	1.04	1.31
—	1.88	1.09
MQa1: o	2.38	0.68
w	0.88	0.30
—	0.75	0.74
M	4.08	1.21
FM	3.67	2.44
m	0.83	1.09
FM + m	4.50	1.87
FC	1.79	2.02
CF	0.96	1.04
C	0.29	0.55
WSUMC	2.29	1.57
FC − CF − C − Cn	3.04	1.56
CF + C + Cn	1.25	0.75
FC' + C'F + C'	1.29	1.23
FT' + T'F + T	0.38	0.66
FV + VF + V	0.00	0.00
FY + YF + Y	0.29	0.39
Sum Shading	1.96	1.68

TABLE 1 (Continued)

Variables	Mean	Standard Deviation
Fr + rF	0.00	0.00
POP	3.12	1.29
Zf	10.17	3.04
EA	6.37	1.93
ES	6.46	3.81
D	−0.83	0.88
ADJD	0.00	0.78
ACT	6.54	2.58
PAS	2.04	1.83
Ma	3.29	1.52
Mp	0.79	0.98
L	0.53	0.39
XPLUS	0.49	0.12
AFR	0.55	0.24
EGO	0.43	0.17
Contents	4.21	1.38
Bt = Cl + Ge + Ls + Na	2.33	1.16
H + (H) + Hd + (Hd)	4.00	1.38
A + (A) + Ad + (Ad)	7.83	3.58
SCHZI total	2.71	0.47
DEPI total	0.54	0.61

Courtesy of Rorschach Workshops

visually more concrete, a partial Structural Summary of the group profile of the children is presented in Table 2.

When these data are compared with Exner's norms (Exner and Weiner, 1982) for nonpatient children between the ages of five and seven, many differences emerge. The most outstanding of these, apart from a very high M production, is that this group of children are also strikingly "mature." One sees this in the developmental quality of their

TABLE 2
Structural Summary for 24 High M Children

R = 14.92	ZF = 10.17	P = 3.12

Location Features	Determinants
W = 6.92	M = 4.08
	FM = 3.67
D = 6.04	m = 0.83
	C = 0.29
Dd = 1.75	CF = 0.96
	FC = 1.79
S = 1.25	C' total = 1.29
	T total = 0.38
DQ	V total = 0.00
	Y total = 0.29
+ = 5.88	Fr + rF = 0.00
o = 7.75	
v = 1.08	

Form Quality

FQx	FQf	M Qual.
o = 7.04	o = 1.83	o = 2.38
w = 3.71	w = 1.04	w = 0.88
— = 3.79	— = 1.88	— = 0.75

Ratios, Percentages, and Derivations

EB = 4.08 : 2.29	EA = 6.37	L = 0.53	SCHIZ = 2.71
eb = 4.50 : 1.96	ep = 6.46	X + % = 0.49	DEPI = 0.54
	Adjusted D = 0.00		

a : p = 6.54 : 2.04

Ma : Mp = 3.29 : 0.79

FC : CF + C = 3.04 : 1.25

AFR = 0.55

EGO = 0.43

W : M = 6.92 : 4.08

W : D = 6.92 : 6.04

Cont : R = 4.21 : 14.92

Isolate : R = 2.33 : 14.92

H + (H) + Hd + (Hd) = 4.00

A + (A) + Ad + (Ad) = 7.83

concepts (DQ+ high in relation to DQo, while DQv is conspicuously low), and also in relation to their emotional control (FC is much higher than CF + C). Furthermore, their weighted SumC is low but their responsiveness to emotional stimulation (Afr) is even lower. The active-passive ratio is a bit higher than the expected 3:1, indicating cognitive and attitudinal rigidity, Lambda, X+ percentage, and the egocentricity index are also very low.

As regards the comparison with Exner's group of "withdrawn" children between five and seven (1978), the most important differences are: M responses and FM + m are much higher, SumC and FC are about equal but FC is much higher in the FC:CF + C ratio, and Afr is much lower. Sum shading is much lower but C' is about equal. The X+ percentage is much lower and Popular responses also tend to be lower.

As a group these high M children are ambitendent or introversive and tend toward stabilization (Adjusted D = 0.00) in their basic response style (twelve are clearly introversive, ten are ambitendent, and only two are extratensive). Moreover, they shy away from emotionally charged situations (low Afr), and show excessive emotional control (FC:CF + C) reinforced by a need to retain affect (C'). They are not socially isolated (Isolation: R = 2.33: 14.92). They are quite interested in people (H total = 4.00) although they do not feel close to others (T is only 0.38).

In this context, one wonders how these children handle their needs (FM). In fourteen of the protocols M is greater or much greater than FM. This could mean that needs are repressed. As a group, the children all avoid and control affect (low Afr, high FC) or "bite their tongues" (C'). In other words, no adequate outlet exists for their needs.

They appear to be quite intelligent and "mature" (Z frequency = 10.16, Developmental Quality synthesis = 5.88 vs. Developmental Quality ordinary = 7.75 and only 1.08 Developmental Quality vague) yet conservative and limited in their aspirations (W:M = 6.92 : 4.08); that is, they are not using their bright ideational capacity to the full. Although not stereotypic (A percentage is around 50), they cling rigidly to their own ideas and attitudes (a:p = 6.54 : 2.04).

They are much too open to stimuli—except emotionally toned ones—and thus have difficulty in handling complexity. This is shown by their low Lambda (0.53). This could also point to a failure of dissociation and repression in the sense of an inability to back off, keep intellectual distance, "keep things out." They are prone to overrespond, especially on the ideational level (high M and FM + m). A possible potential for acting out is thus suggested, since what has been described in the preceding paragraph corresponds to a lack of adequate channels for discharge. One may surmise that in adolescence these emotionally too "mature" and contained children may develop ideational symptoms (SCHIZ = 2.71) or may become depressed: the low Afr and egocentricity index (0.43) indicates poor self-esteem. They all tend to retain and discharge affect inward (C').

The one other striking and ominous aspect in these children is their poor contact with reality (X+ percentage = 0.49). Actually, for all but two of the twenty-four, perceptual accuracy (F+ percentage) is very low. This poor contact with reality, together with the fact that their minus responses are slightly higher than their weak or unique responses (FQx), points to a tendency toward distortion.

From a diagnostic point of view, six of the twenty-four showed schizoid, paranoid-schizoid, or more paranoid personality organization. Twelve were phobic with schizoid, paranoid, or obsessional traits; two were borderlines; two were depressive; and two were possibly narcissistic with manic defenses. As all but four showed either schizoid, paranoid, or borderline organizations (several in combination with phobic elements), the features so far described might be summarized as a basically withdrawn, guarded, and schizoid attitude.[7] This does not necessarily include depressive features. To my mind, the potential for depression could well be related to their "lost childhood." In many respects these children show traits of an early, rigid, and maladaptive "adultification," which would act as a defense against the depression engendered by that loss. But another, very important possibility is that the "adultification" may represent a defense against basic depression per se, a "flight toward adulthood" when dependency and the experience of loss are too unbearable.

The data raise several interesting questions: A recent review of the Rorschach suicide constellation (Exner, Martin, and Mason, 1984) suggests that a bimodal distribution may exist for the egocentricity index.[8] Because low self-esteem is often related to both suicide and

---

[7]Paula is an exception in this sense, illustrating another way of being "too adult," one oriented much more toward action upon the environment. This goes to show that a high M production, together with the other traits described, can have different clinical expressions, depending on individual personality organization.

[8]"54 of the 101 subjects in this sample do have egocentricity values of less than .30, however, 27 others have egocentricity values that are greater than .45. . . . the possibility exists [of] a different cutoff, or a bimodal cutoff . . ." (Exner, Martin, and Mason, 1984, p. 5).

depression, the egocentricity index among these high M children was examined. The group mean is very low (0.43). In nine the index is even lower, in eleven it is 0.50 or more, and in four it is normal for their age. None gave reflection responses. I therefore wondered whether a bimodal distribution could exist in children. In other words, given other significant findings (low Afr, little use of color, excessive emotional control + C', etc.) could the depressive implication of the low group mean encompass those with a more normal egocentricity index?

Another intriguing and related aspect to be considered is the interpretation of the "pair" response. Most people, children even more so (Exner and Weiner, 1982), react to the symmetry of the Rorschach cards by perceiving and articulating two of a kind. This is understood as related to self-centeredness or egocentricity.[9] Now, what would be the reason for the high M children not perceiving "two"? Would it be possible that to see only "one" may signify that the child is highly narcissistic in the sense that the existence of two cannot be perceived or imagined because the child is involved in a narcissistic object relation? In other words, many pairs as well as too few may point in the same direction, namely, toward self-centeredness of a possibly narcissistic origin. Thus, in relation to self-esteem, either a low or a high index may indicate narcissism or injured narcissism. Might not another possible interpretation of the low egocentricity index be that these children are "other-centered" (i.e., adult-centered) as shown by their M responses? In any case, the flight from their own age level would imply an attitude of rejection toward being a child and thus low esteem for this aspect of themselves. I cannot answer these questions but think they suggest new avenues for research.

Thus far, three of the four expected character traits have been found in this group of high M children (the tendency toward stabilization, emotional isolation, and cognitive and attitudinal rigidity). As regards the fourth, overincorporation, only fourteen were found to be overincorporators. Of these, eleven are either D = +1 or 0, and ten are also cognitively and attitudinally rigid, which would point to a clustering of characteristic traits.

To these four traits two more are added that reinforce the initial three: *excessive affective control* and *inward discharge of emotion.* Thus, as was suggested, both intellectual and emotional rigidity and a fixation of coping styles—character—are to be found in this sample.

---

[9]The pair frequency increases significantly in the most egocentric subjects and is almost nonexistent in the protocols of subjects who have little regard for themselves" (Exner and Weiner, 1982, p. 101; see also Exner, 1978, pp. 290–294).

From an individual point of view, six are evidently "stabilized" ($D = +1$), while in fourteen the tendency toward stabilization is clear ($D = 0$). The striking fact is that this tendency is due basically to the general increase of M and FM + m in face of a low SumC and the low frequency of shading responses, except for C'. From another angle, the experience base (eb) is clearly introversive in fifteen of the children (62 percent). In seven it is ambitendent due to C', only sometimes to Y, and only in two is the right side of the eb slightly increased by the presence of T. Thus, the experience of anxiety (I am referring to the shading responses in very general terms) is apparently absent. Discomfort, if any, tends to be discharged inwardly (C') and coped with ideationally (high M), rigidly (a: p = slightly more than 3:1), and through emotional control (FC > CF + C) and isolation (low Afr)[10]—in other words, by the character traits previously described.

Other interesting characteristics of this group of high M children include the following. Of the five- and six-year-olds, four are introversive, seven ambitendent, and one possibly extratensive. Of the seven-year-olds, eight are introversive, two ambitendent, and one extratensive. This may suggest that the introversive style becomes more marked with age. Finally, of the twelve introversives eleven are also emotionally isolated and show evidence of low self-esteem.

Two individual examples of the picture described so far are Lorenzo and Mara.

Lorenzo is five and a half, his brother two years old. The mother sought a consultation because of the child's night terrors. "During the day he is a lord but at night he has nightmares all the time. More recently, during the day he says that he thinks horrible things and that he cannot go to sleep. He's in a panic. All the time he is asking me why we are not together, that his father and I should marry again [the parents separated six months ago]. Every night he gets into my bed. He asks me to have another baby; a few days ago he even proposed making a baby with him. He cries a lot even if I am a minute late. The relationship with his brother is good and despite his jealousy he protects him. He is extremely careful, too grown-up. He asked if now he is the man of the house. Lately he has been worried about death. We married in order to save our relationship, we were very immature. I had difficulty breast-feeding Lorenzo, the same problems my mother had. At ten months he woke up every night and cried for hours, but otherwise he

---

[10]Actually, Afr is below .70 in twenty of the twenty-four children.

was a quiet baby. Then there were many changes because my husband obtained a scholarship in another country, to which we moved when Lorenzo was sixteen months old. Five months later we left him for four months of travel. He stayed with his grandparents. He had a very bad time, couldn't sleep, had many fears. When he was nearly three and I was pregnant again (after a previous abortion), we returned from abroad. By then our marriage had begun to deteriorate. We lived with my parents until we moved to the house where I live now. I want to do something preventive for Lorenzo because I'm afraid he will explode at any moment."

Lorenzo's Rorschach Protocol

Free Association	*Inquiry*
Card I. Like a monster, is that right? It was a monster. E: If you look a bit longer you may find something more. S: No.	E: Repeats R. S: I found it black, the eyes, the mouth [S] and the ears and a bit of the body, it's the head really, an ugly face.
Card II. A rabbit, a rabbit.	E: Repeats R. S: Eyes and mouth, the face, nose [S].
Card III. A dog, this is a dog or is it three gentlemen? It seems to me that they are two gentlemen, yes, they are two gentlemen, there it is [returns card].	E: Repeats R. S: Here are two apples they are taking away, here a car is coming [D3] and they are going to throw them at it and two gentlemen [D2] who are giving them a kick in the head.
Card IV. This looks like the pants of a gentleman. I don't know what he is doing, he is putting them on and he has very long hair like a girl.	E: Repeats R. S: Yes. E: Long hair? S: [Points to D1] Yes, he has a very small head and little arms, here are the feet.
Card V. Here a bird.	E: Repeats R. S: It's flying.

Card VI. Here I find, it's me, this one who is here is me or is it a butterfly? What is it? It's me or it's a butterfly.

E: Repeats R.
S: Arms, head, and legs [points].

A butterfly.

E: Repeats R.
S: Head and wings [points].

Card VII. Here I see two women looking at each other, two Indians rather, two Indian women.

E: Repeats R.
S: Looking at each other angrily, the feather [points].

Card VIII. Here a picture— of a skeleton. Ugh how ugly! Is it all right, this skeleton?

E: Repeats R.
S: Only skeleton, like that.

Card IX. Here a picture of— a mouse, a she-mouse, a rat.

E: Repeats R.
S: I don't remember what it was here.

Card X. Here a wasp—ouch, I don't like it, it stings!

E: Repeats R.
S: All of it because of the sting [D14] and this way [V] it can be something prettier, a little Christmas tree full of pretty birds. [During the Inquiry he complains more and more of being tired.]

Testing-the-Limits. VIII. Animals? Yes, monkeys climbing. X. Spider or crab? Yes.

Lorenzo appears to be a very isolated, ruminative, rigid, and angry little "gentleman" (no color responses, Afr very low, Zd higher than ±3, a:p, 2S, 3M, 5H, D = 0) who is trying, desperately, to "put on his pants" (IV), i.e., to be "the man of the house." This is consonant with his high aspirations (W:M = childish omnipotence) and need for control (Zf = 11 in 11 responses, Zd), but clashes with his identity confusion: "long hair like a girl" (IV) and "it's me . . . or is it a butterfly?" (VI). Although he is intelligent (the WISC shows an IQ of 119 with little scatter) and conceptually mature for his age (no vagues in the developmental quality), the effort is too great and he distorts reality, (F+ percentage, X+ percentage, minus responses greater) particularly in the face of emotion (F— on the last three cards). He presents himself as "a monster . . . ugly" (I), lifeless like a "skeleton. Ugh how ugly!" (VIII), and feels in danger of being kicked in the head (III), perhaps for his aggressive oedipal fantasies. Because everyday reality becomes dangerous and persecutory in a concrete way—"a wasp—ouch, I don't like it, it stings!" (X)—he regresses to previous levels of perception (CONFAB) and resorts to denial—"this way it can be something prettier" (X), "I don't remember what it was here" (IX). The "adult" fantasy activity (the three M responses) is not enough to absorb the tension and persecution (1 m) (Campo, 1979), and ultimately what is being split off (emotion, i.e., color) and repressed (1 C' only 1 FM and a high Lambda) is acted out and discharged at night by means of the night terrors. Thus, he presents a phobic structure with paranoid traits (Campo, 1982). It is little wonder that with such an internal situation his self-esteem is very low—$3r + (2) = .18$—and the possibility for depression is not far away.

Although his mother wished to put Lorenzo in treatment and readily accepted the psychologist's advice regarding some modifications in the handling of her boy, the father would not pay for it. One year later she sought another consultation, this time for the younger brother. On this occasion she related that with the aid of her parents she was able to enter treatment herself and commented that Lorenzo had "paid dearly" for the lack of treatment: he had hepatitis and was often ill. Nevertheless, his night terrors had abated and he was doing well in school.

Seven-year-old Mara, who has a sister one year younger, was described by her very anxious mother[11] in the following way: "She is the one who has always had problems. She was always fragile, she cried the first three months, and she never smiled until five or six months of age. She was healthy, but after the third month she changed. The constant crying stopped but she was not happy. She had no organic problems. I was ill, I felt as if I was sucked up through a straw, that I couldn't provide enough, I did not understand her, and felt terribly anxious and disconcerted about her desperate crying. I can tell before it begins, it's like a blow or a call in my stomach, like a special communication, and this still happens to me now. I was very confused and desperate. My daughter and I are stuck together, she demands so much that finally I blow up. I can't set clear limits, there are days when I'd kill her. She

---

[11]The mother, to whom the Rorschach was also administered, gave a typical borderline structure, with schizoid and manic features. She is currently finishing her studies in psychology.

always was fragile, very sensitive. I lost my parents. When I was fifteen my mother died suddenly. One day I went to school and when I returned I did not have a mother anymore. My father died seven years after. I felt very bad, like an orphan with my baby, I was like her, we were two children, I couldn't give her tranquility. When she was about three years old she began to constantly masturbate. She is so emotionally fragile, cries with the least frustration. I was going mad, I often beat her and then felt very guilty. There was a difficult period in my marriage, a crisis. I thought of divorce, but a cousin sent us to a therapist and then things got better. When she was five a friend told me to see a psychologist and after a play session Mara had an episode the psychologist thought psychotic. She started to cry desperately, it was at night, she said that something was inside her tummy; then she fell asleep. This forced me to start treatment. She was in treatment (psychoanalytically oriented psychotherapy) for about a year and a half. The crying diminished and she started school very well, but she got desperate when she made a mistake. She is in second grade now and the best pupil, very neat and orderly. She was in several kindergartens and also changed schools. Then we had economic problems and Mara began to resist treatment so it was stopped. Everything is better but her internal demands and fragility persist and with any frustration she cries and screams. About a month ago she had a bad cold and earache, this is frequent, and she came to my bed and said, 'My legs are lazy, I can't control them, can't stand up,' and then this feeling got into her 'birdie' too (that's what she calls her vagina) and into her tummy, and she said that she was very sick. It is because of this that I have come to see you. I want a full personality study, a diagnosis."

Mara's Rorschach Protocol

Free Association	*Inquiry*
Card I. A butterfly.	E: Repeats R. S: Because here was the but [D4] and the two wings, a black one, at night, they are ugly.
Card II. I see two little bears together.	E: Repeats R. S: The ears and snout and half of the body and they are shaking hands like friends.

Card III. [Does not take card right away.] The face of a wolf.	E: Repeats R. S: Snout, ears, eyes, mustaches, it's black, an ugly face.
Card IV. Two feet.	E: Repeats R. S: And these are the spread legs of a gentleman, he's seeing something.
Card V. A fly.	E: Repeats R. S: Head, legs, wings.
Card VI. [Becomes inattentive, thumb in mouth.] A map.	E: Repeats R. S: A map of Paris. Only this part. E: Paris? S: They made it there.
Card VII. Two rabbits.	E: Repeats R. S: Ears, tail, and nothing else.
Card VIII. Two men standing on a rock and pulling a rope.	E: Repeats R. S: They want to see who is stronger. E: Rocks? S: Shape of rocks.
Card IX. A lady with glasses.	E: Repeats R. S: Ears, hat [upper S], eyeglasses, not the green part, and the body, here are the shoulders.
Card X. A dance.	E: Repeats R. S: Here they are dancing, two couples [D1] and two more [D7 + D13 + D14] and this is the ballroom [D9] inside and outside, ladies and gentlemen, because of the colors.

Testing-the-Limits. III. Can you see people here? Yes, two women picking up a pot because it is heavy, wearing white aprons [S]. And here a red bow. V. Bat or butterfly? Yes a bat. VIII. Animals? Yes, two little bears playing. X. Crabs or spiders? Yes, this is a spider.
Liked best. X. Because of the color.
Liked least: V. Don't like it, ugly color.

To judge from the Rorschach, what emerges is an introversive, quite stabilized, isolated, ruminative, cautious, and meticulous but angry girl (EB, D = +1, low Afr + little color, Zd = +4, only 4 W vs. 4D + 2 Dd, increased Hd + Ad, 2S), for whom little spontaneous outlets exist (no FM, only 1 CF—which may even be an FC—). She tends to "bite her tongue" and to discharge affect inward (2FC').[12] She is quite intelligent[13] (4 synthesis in the developmental quality score vs. 6 ordinary and no vagues) but makes little constructive use of her adultlike fantasy life (W:M = 4:4). Her capacity to distort is clear (2M—) and her level of perceptual accuracy and reality contact are weak (F+ percentage and X+ percentage are very low). Like Paula and Lorenzo, she is too preoccupied with adult matters (M contents). She has difficulty handling emotions (poor form level on the last three cards). In consequence, her self-esteem is quite low: "A butterfly . . . they are ugly" (I), "The face of a wolf . . . an ugly face" (III). The bears "shaking hands" (II), the "men . . . pulling a rope" (VIII), and the "dancing . . . couples (X) appear to reflect a flight toward adult attitudes, perhaps as a defense against an early mother-child relationship that must have been confusing for her, judging from the anamnestic data. In this regard, her response to Card VII is interesting ("Two rabbits . . . *and nothing else*"). Perhaps her need to keep the rabbits by themselves reflects her effort and wish to maintain herself separate from mother. However, her central symptom, the crying, shows the underlying desperate loneliness, neediness, and probable depression. Other aspects of the Structural Summary point to a more schizoid organization (in particular, the 2 M—, the large number of minus responses, and the low X + percentage), though her positive responses in Testing-the-Limits militate against this view. Nonetheless it appears at least plausible that the marked distortion of reality in Mara and Lorenzo may be a result of their inadequate attempts to be "grown up," in itself a distortion of reality. (In Paula the distortion is much less serious and has a different aspect: pure C replaces F— in two of the last three cards. It may be surmised that this difference, together with her ambitendent EB and somewhat higher egocentricity index, may reflect her basic recourse to a "solution" of conflict through action (manifest behavior) rather than through symptoms of the type used by the other two children.)

[12]This constellation of traits, i.e., the lack of adequate outlets, may in the absence of Anatomy responses point to dissociation and acting out via the body (Campo and Jachevasky, 1981).

[13]The WISC shows an IQ of 117 (Verbal = 119, Performance = 111), very high on Vocabulary (16), Information (15), and Similarities (16) but very low on Comprehension (6!) and Object Assembly (9).

One last thought concerning Mara's year and a half of treatment. It is possible that the heightened M production and the cautious, ruminative attitude (Zd) are a consequence of psychotherapy. Nonetheless, in spite of the fact that treatment was terminated prematurely, Mara seemed to be better, at least according to her mother. Nevertheless, on the basis of the Rorschach it seems clear that recourse to inadequate ideational activity, together with the characteristic traits described, is not what one would expect as the result of a successful treatment.

Six-year-old Gladys, an only child, is another good example of adultification and its relation to high M production. She was referred for consultation because of continuous allergies and bronchitis. As with Paula, the parents, especially the mother, contributed to the "adultification" through their fascination with the child's intellectual ability. Another reason for including Gladys's protocol is that it relates to the issue of egocentricity discussed earlier.

Her mother describes Gladys as follows: "The pediatrician recommended the examination because she is emotionally too mature. I wish she were more childish but I'm afraid she won't change. It could be a problem in the future, she could be frustrated as an adult for not having had a childhood. She is very jealous of us, can't see us together, won't let us kiss or touch, asks both of us whom we love more. She told me 'in secret' that she loves me more but that I should not tell her father. She is not expressive about her intimate things, she never was, but one day she said, crying, that she was leaving home because she did not want to be with her father any more since 'he yells at me constantly.' This was three months ago. She has suffered from continuous bronchitis and allergic states since the age of six months. She is a girl who is an adult person. We traveled a lot in the past. She is a help, a companion, very close to me. She is not gay, always crying. Until the age of two she did not know how to cry; however, one day she began to rehearse in front of a mirror and since then cries often! Her logic is irrefutable. She is always talking and asking. She is like an encyclopedia and her questions reflect scientific curiosity. She is always thinking. About a year ago she was informed about babies ('little seed') and now she asks how God made the first human beings, how he made himself. She wants to study mythology, to know what gods are like. She has fixed ideas. She wants to see fairies with magic wands, believes in Santa Claus and the Three Kings. She has a great sense of the ridiculous but no sense of humor. She does not accept jokes that are at her own expense. She started kindergarten on her own initiative at two and a half. Last year, in first grade, because she was bored she was allowed to go to second grade. She is sociable but selective, critical of smaller children. She knows rhymes and is a good pupil, a perfectionist. She was never fearful but now she begins to say that she is afraid. We don't know if it is an act or not. For instance, she says that she does not want to go out because 'there is an old crazy man,' or 'my eyes tell me that this is a cat, but my little heart tells me it's something else.' [The mother is afraid of dogs.] She does not like to sleep and has not eaten well since the age of two. [From the age of nine months until she was four and a half she had had her own room; then, due to economic problems—the parents had to move to a smaller apartment (they moved often)—she had to sleep in her parents' bedroom.] She was breast-fed and very greedy in the beginning, so greedy that she often vomited. She gave up the breast on her own at six months, although I wanted to continue. Otherwise her development was normal. The allergies, colds, and bronchitis started at that time."

During another interview the mother related that the father suffers from depressions, which began three years ago and coincided with their economic problems. He is now in treatment. She feels herself to be the dominant figure in their marriage and says her husband feels quite bitter about this. Nevertheless, she wishes that Gladys "would love him more and be closer to him. The other day, on returning from school, she said that she did not want to come home because she did not like men."

Gladys's Rorschach Protocol

Free Association	*Inquiry*
Card I. [She comes with a doll] I don't know—well, to me it looks like, it looks like a, a stick to me, yes, with two bears. Is it?	E: Repeats R. S: They are holding on to the little stick, the hands, the legs down here and tiny hairs are falling off them around there because they are moving so much, they are nearly falling off, only one foot raised, they are going to fall.
E: If you look a while longer you might find more things. S: Little dots.	E: Bears? S: Aren't there black bears? For me they aren't polar bears, these are brown or black, playful ones, the head and the snout [points].

Card II. Well, I don't know, is it this way? Or this? Don't know. Yes, but I don't know if it's that because they have little red spots, two bears holding hands, but why do they have those little red things? Strange pictures!

E: Repeats R.
S: They are spitting water.
E: Spitting?
S: The tongue [D2], snouts, ears, legs, they are playing with their hands.

Card III. I don't know if I'll know—Oh! the bones of human beings.

E: Repeats R, but Gladys interrupts: They are women because one can see that they have high heels, two crooked legs, there's a pair, the bow is pushing them, it pushes them so they won't touch it, if not they'll fall down and get burned in the little red fire [D2], a butterfly down here [D7] they are grabbing.
E: You said two human beings of bone?
S: Yes.

Then, I don't know what the other little red things are, one looks like a bow and the others I don't know. Do you make these? Do you buy them? Each day you buy something new? Two human beings of bone and a bow, nothing more, red.
Madam, what is the blackboard for? If you want me to I'll draw for you, you've got colored chalks.

Card IV. Don't know. This is the most difficult one, don't know. This like shoes.

E: Repeats R.
S: Big ones, giant's shoes, I can tell you that it is a giant butterfly, little wings, little head, it is very strange because next to the head it has shoes! Like when one bends over, a butterfly-giant bending over!

Card V. Uh, a, a butterfly, right? A butterfly but it has a strange shape! [Looks behind card] What does it say here? What it is?

E: Repeats R.
S: Because it has wings with a very strange shape and two arms there and there, backwards, it's flying, head, tiny horns, and feet.

Card VI. Oh! Well, look, for me this way, upside down it looks like a fish, a tiny fish or a fish, whatever you want to write down. This way nothing.

E: Repeats R.
S: Tiny eyes and this is a little bit of river and the fins, it is swimming, a sardfish, long tiny snout. I had fish but they all died [Plays with her doll].

Card VII. Oh, ouch this, two little rabbits on top of earth.

E: Repeats R.
S: They are playing.
E: Earth?
S: Black or gray earth.

What is this? To me it's a monument way back very far away. How pretty they are like this with their tiny paws like this [gesticulates] toward the back [pointing at the rabbits].

E: Repeats R.
S: Far away because it is very small.

Card VIII. A strange whatchamacallit—which way can it be, Madam? The colored stuff I don't know, but the tiny ones are two frogs hanging from something that I don't know what it is. You already finished the page? [Watches what E is writing].

E: Repeats R.
S: These are the little frogs that are hanging from this.

Card IX. Hmm. Oh, how strange this is! Well, the only thing I know is the green, it's tiny grass, maybe the pink is tiny grass too! And the orange too, when it dries it could be, so don't laugh. The pink I don't know, why does it have tiny hands? [Dd21] A cloud,

E: Repeats R.
S: A pink cloud of those fat ones, it is hanging from the tiny green grass.

Madam, it looks like a cloud to me that is hanging from the tiny grass [shows how].

Ah, and the light blue a river and the brown a little path to go to the river. I see nothing more. Here there is a little bit of earth too, it isn't much. [Asks to go to the toilet.]

E: Repeats R.
S: The little path colored brown just like the earth, it's far away.
E: Far away?
S: It's very small.

Card X. Oh look, only one thing I can, ah no, two things: these are tiny sky blue spiders and this is a stick and on both sides of it tiny kangaroos, kangaroos, and these

E: Repeats R.
S: I like them better colored and they are eating the green grass.
E: Repeats R.
S: They are grabbing the stick and playing.

are horses, little horses [pronounces the Spanish word very carefully and pedantically], and these

E: Repeats R.
S: Brown horses jumping among pink clouds [points to D9].

are two green dinosaurs and

E: Repeats R.
S: They are eating the head of a rabbit, poor little rabbit!

these are two tiny flowers, I can't tell you anything more. The spiders have a little grass there, greenish. There are many things more but I can't tell you more.

E: Repeats R.
S: Orange flowers.

Unlike the other cases presented here, Gladys appears to have an extratensive coping style. Nevertheless, certain features of her protocol seem inconsistent with this. For example, the two additional M responses (Card III) may point to a more ambitendent orientation, while her social isolation (47 percent), her limited, quite unrealistic, and mostly fabulized human relations (few and no pure H), and her "Snow White" attitude (MA:Mp = 1:2)[14] seem to emphasize a basic lack of

[14]This must remain hypothetical due to doubts as regards scoring.

real relationships. This is consonant with her very willful, idiosyncratic handling of reality (very low X+ percentage but weak larger than minus responses). Her seemingly easy and spontaneous emotional responsiveness (Afr is within normal limits for her age, CF = 3) is not only often unrealistic (INCOM) but also tends toward overcontrol (FC is unexpected at 6), retention, and inward discharge (2 C′). The overcontrol as reflected by 2 FD's (quite unexpected at age six) is reinforced by intellectualization. In addition, in her language minimization is evident and one sees evidence of denial, idealization, and perhaps hysterical elements.[15]

Gladys is a very complex little girl (8 blends in 17 Responses) who is overwhelmed by stimuli (very low Lambda). The very high FM (9) points to a phobic component (Campo, 1982). Her many needs are not satisfied in close relationships with others (no T) nor are they adequately discharged. Moreover, the absence of Anatomy responses in the presence of somatic symptoms of long duration speaks in favor of splitting and acting out by way of the body (Campo and Jachevasky, 1981). Gladys appears immersed in a prematurely adult but perhaps passive and rather omnipotent fantasy life by means of which reality is both avoided and manipulated (FABCOM) through the omnipotent, unrealistic handling of relations. Again, she is quite intelligent and conceptually sophisticated (Developmental quality synthesis and synthesis/vagues = 9 vs. 5 ordinary and only one vague). She is interested in organizing and keeping control of things (Zf = 13). During the Rorschach administration she attempted to control the examiner. She is good at school, in spite of her very "flaky" thinking (many Special Scores)[16] and poor reality contact (X+ percentage very low).

All of the four children presented, including Gladys, manifest active splitting mechanisms. Despite their very serious pathology, indicated by the "adultification," scholarly achievement is pursued and appears as a logical expression of their need to "get ahead," to move away from childhood, to "know" everything. (This was not true for the entire group of twenty-four.)

[15]In the Spanish language minimization always accompanies the hysteroid style in female subjects. Nevertheless, it occurs also in manic contexts.

[16]Does this aspect, often composed of forced color INCOM's together with the FABCOM's and the conserved egocentricity index, suggest narcissistic and borderline elements?

With respect to self-esteem, for Gladys the egocentricity index was in the expected range. This is one of the features that distinguishes her from Paula, Mara, and Lorenzo, as well as from most of the children in the broader study. What do the contents of her responses tell us about her self-image? In general, she saw "tiny" animals (minimization as probable denial of aggression) that are not particularly dangerous. An exception, however, was the "dinosaurs" eating the head of a "poor rabbit" on Card X. Could this, her only clear oral-aggressive response,[17] reveal the ancient greedy behavior at the breast reported by her mother? Actually, aggression and rage are conspicuously absent from her protocol, which points to denial and possibly reaction formation (high FC). Her human percepts, all unrealistic (H), show that the female image is both "crooked" (III), confused ("butterfly-giant" on IV), and "strange" (V). The male figure is absent from the test except for the bears losing their hair and about to fall (I). This "bear" response, her first one, could refer, at another level, to general feelings of insecurity, threat, and latent depression (Campo, 1979). Gladys keeps moving quickly so that depression cannot catch up with her. In this sense, one may speculate that the normal egocentricity index could be upheld by fundamentally narcissistic object relations based on an omnipotent identification with a combined-confused maternal image.

I fear that the question regarding the generally very low (though in Gladys's case normal) egocentricity index remains unanswered; again, the need for further research is suggested.

SUMMARY

In this chapter I have reported observations of children whose Rorschach records contain several M responses. In these children the manifest symptomatology appears to be little related to the underlying character structure as derived from the Rorschach. In this sense, the Rorschach is immensely useful as a detector of structure and of potential future trouble. In other words, the "flight toward adulthood" is an inner matter, not necessarily observable in manifest behavior. In this sample, learning difficulties, overactive behavior, phobias, enuresis,

---

[17]The bears "spitting water" on II is again a denial, and the "sardfish" on VI is associated to her own fish, which "all died."

and other bodily manifestations "mask" an underlying, rather ominous rigidity. This points once more to the need for deeper and better psychological assessment in childhood in order to clarify the still numerous problems in early psychopathology.

REFERENCES

Ames, L. B., Learned, J., Metraux, R. W., & Walker, R. N. (1952), *Child Rorschach Responses: Developmental Trends from Two to Ten Years*. New York: Hoeber.

Beizmann, C. (1961), *Le Rorschach chez l'Enfant de 3 à 10 Ans*. Neuchatel: Delachaux et Niestlé.

Campo, A. J., & Campo, V. (1979), The Rorschach and the interpretation of play in children: Its use in diagnosis. Paper presented at the Seventh National Symposium of the Sociedad Española del Rorschach y Métodos Proyectivos, Barcelona.

Campo, V. (1979), On the meaning of the inanimate movement response (m), *Brit. J. Proj. Psychol. & Person. Study*, 24.

_____ (1982), On the diagnostic value of FM—animal movement—in phobic children. *Brit. J. Proj. Psychol. & Personal. Study*, 27.

_____ & Jachevasky, L. (1981), Children's bodies: On the meaning of the absence of anatomy responses in children with physical symptoms. Paper presented at the Tenth International Rorschach Congress, Washington, DC.

Dudek, S. Z. (1968), M an active energy system correlating Rorschach M with ease of creative expression, *J. Proj. Tech. & Personal. Assess.*, 32.

Exner, J. E. (1974), *The Rorschach: A Comprehensive System*. New York: Wiley.

_____ (1978) *The Rorschach: A Comprehensive System: Vol. 2. Current Research and Advanced Interpretation*. New York: Wiley.

_____ Martin, L. S., & Mason, B. (1984), A review of the Rorschach suicide constellation. Paper presented at the Eleventh International Rorschach Congress, Barcelona.

_____ Weiner, I. B. (1982), *The Rorschach: A Comprehensive System: Vol. 3. Assessment of Children and Adolescents*. New York: Wiley.

Francis-Williams, J. (1968), *Rorschach with Children*. Oxford: Pergamon.

Halpern, F. (1953), *A Clinical Approach to Children's Rorschachs*. New York: Grune & Stratton.

Klopfer, B., Ed. (1956), *Developments in the Rorschach Technique: Vol. 2*. New York: Harcourt, Brace & World.

Levi, J., & Kraemer, D. (1952), Significance of a preponderance of human movement responses on the Rorschach in children below age ten. *J. Person. Tech.*, 16.

Mayman, M. (1967), Object representations and object relationships in Rorschach responses. *J. Proj. Tech. & Personal. Asses.* 31:17–24.

Rausch de Traubenberg, N., & Boizou, M. (1977), *Le Rorschach en Clinique Infantile*. Paris: Dunod.

Romano, D. G. (1975), *L'Enfant Face au Test de Rorschach*. Paris: Presses Universitaires de France.

Thetford, W. N. (1952), Fantasy perceptions in personality development of normal and deviant children. *Amer. J. Orthopsychiat.*, 22.

Vorhaus, P. G. (1952), Rorschach configurations associated with reading disability, *J. Proj. Techn.*, 16.

Chapter 24

The Representation of Object Relations in the Rorschachs of Extremely Feminine Boys

Susan Coates, Ph.D.
Steven B. Tuber, Ph.D.

The study of extreme boyhood femininity offers the opportunity to shed light on our understanding of childhood and adult gender identity disorders and on the acquisition of normal gender identity.

Both retrospective and prospective studies of adult gender-confused men find that cross-gender interests, behavior, and fantasy are typically reported or observed in their early childhood. Extreme boyhood femininity usually emerges in boys by the age of three or four (Green, 1974; Stoller, 1975; Coates and Person, 1985).

Interestingly, although extremely feminine boys phenotypically most closely resemble adult transsexuals in their interest, behavior, and fantasy, prospective studies have found that extreme boyhood femininity is most often a precursor of adult homosexuality. In Green's prospective study of forty-four boys with boyhood femininity (1985), two-thirds of his sample became either bisexual or exclusively homosexual.

This research was supported in part by a National Institute of Health Biomedical Research Support Grant 1–S07–RR05840 to Dr. Susan Coates. Special thanks are due to Dr. John Fogelman, Director of Child and Adolescent Psychiatry at Roosevelt Hospital, for his generous support of this project. We gratefully acknowledge the assistance of several research staff members including Penny Donnenfeld, Toby Miroff, Robert Sherman, Dr. Nancy Schultz, and several clinical psychology students who routinely administered Rorschachs in the course of their training. Dr. Steven Tuber is sole author of the Appendix.

The DSM–III criteria for Gender Identity Disorder of Childhood for boys are as follows:

A. Strongly and persistently stated desire to be a girl, or insistence that he is a girl.
B. Either 1 or 2
    1. persistent repudiation of male anatomic structures as manifested by at least one of the following assertions:
      a. that he will grow up to become a woman (not merely in role)
      b. that his penis or testes are disgusting or will disappear
      c. that it would be better not to have a penis or testes
    2. preoccupation with female stereotypical activities as manifested by a preference for either cross-dressing or simulating female attire, or by a compelling desire to participate in the games and pastimes of girls
C. Onset of disturbance before puberty

The female stereotypical behavior that these boys typically display includes the following: intense interest in dressing up in girls' clothes and in cosmetics and jewelry; assumption of the role of the mother or another female in playacting; an interest in dolls; a preference for female activities such as jumping rope; a preference for female peers; feminine mannerisms and gait; and the avoidance of rough-and-tumble play. Some boys imitate girls by pushing their penises back between their legs and urinating sitting down.

There are currently two contrasting theories of the etiology of extreme boyhood femininity—a nonconflictual theory proposed by Stoller (1975) and Green (1974) and a conflictual theory proposed by Coates and Person (1985). Stoller (1975) believes that extreme boyhood femininity, which he does not distinguish from childhood transsexualism, emerges when the following five factors simultaneously occur in the boy's earliest years of life:

1. a mother who is chronically depressed
2. a mother who has a bisexual identity with overt penis envy and an only partially suppressed desire to be a male
3. a distant, passive, physically and psychologically absent father
4. a beautiful and graceful son
5. a period of several years in which the mother and son enjoy a blissful symbiosis

Stoller believes that the boy acquires femininity through a form of imprinting: "these boys do not seek femininity but rather receive it passively via excessive impingement of the too-loving bodies of their mothers" (p. 55). Furthermore, he believes that extreme boyhood femininity is a specific dysfunction limited only to the boy's gender identity and that it is not an aspect of a more pervasive psychological disturbance: "These mothers do not cripple the development of ego functions in general or even body ego except in regard to this sense of femaleness. . . . None of these boys has shown the slightest evidence of psychosis or precursors of psychosis" (p. 54). Although Stoller acknowledges that the mothers of feminine boys are disturbed, he believes that the boys' acquisition of a distorted gender identity occurs without trauma or conflict (p. 33).

Green's theory, like Stoller's, views reinforcement as the major force in the acquisition of boyhood femininity. He states explicitly that the prerequisite for the emergence of extreme boyhood femininity is "no discouragement of the behavior by the child's principal caretakers" (1974, p. 238). Green's theory, like Stoller's, is based on the idea that boyhood femininity is not etiologically linked to more pervasive psychopathology.

Coates and Person (1985), by contrast, have argued that extreme boyhood femininity is etiologically linked to a more pervasive psychological disorder. In their study of twenty-five extremely feminine boys (DSM–III diagnosis) they found that 60 percent of their sample had a DSM–III separation anxiety disorder. On the Behavior Problem Checklist of the Revised Child Behavior Profile (Achenbach and Edelbrock, 1983) over 84 percent scored in the range of children referred for psychiatric services. In addition, over half of the sample displayed depressive symptoms. Evidence of pervasive psychopathology in extremely feminine boys has been observed by others as well (Bates, Bentler, and Thompson 1973, 1979; Bates, Skilbeck, Smith, and Bentler, 1974; Bradley, Doering, Zucker, Finegan, and Gonda, 1980). Further evidence of psychopathology was seen in the psychotherapy of these boys, where brief but severe regressions often occurred. Notable, however, was the rapid ability of the boys to reintegrate.

In many of the boys the onset of cross-dressing occurred on the heels of a traumatic withdrawal of the mother from her son during the first three years of life. At times this was a physical withdrawal precipitated by a hospitalization of the mother, while at other times it was a sudden emotional withdrawal precipitated by a psychological trauma to the mother.

In the psychotherapy of these boys severe anxiety often emerged at the end of therapy sessions. In many instances they would handle this anxiety by flipping into the role of a female. In many cases, after the boy had been in therapy for a considerable length of time and had substantially relinquished his cross-gender behavior, it would reappear, often with full intensity if either his parents or his therapist left him for a vacation.

Coates (1985) has described a disturbed family matrix in which this symptom arises. In the majority of cases the father is no longer in the home by the time the son is three. Chronic personality disturbance in the mothers was striking. They tended to be overinvolved with their sons based on their own needs, often had a phobic appraisal of the world, were overprotective, and interfered with the development of autonomy in their sons. Alternating with their overinvolvement was frequent and unpredictable inaccessibility that like the overinvolvement was also based on internal needs. The mothers had great difficulty setting appropriate limits; often they would let things go and then blow up and become extremely harsh disciplinarians. Coates (1985) also noted that many of these mothers feared and devalued men, often viewing them either as ineffective and incompetent or as violent and out of control. Interestingly, they often married men that fit this pattern.

In their attempt to understand the symptom of extreme boyhood femininity based on clinical experience with these boys, Coates (1985) hypothesize that the symptom serves two functions. Withdrawal of the mother from her son, whether chronic, unpredictable withdrawal due to her personality organization or withdrawal due to a sudden trauma, produces severe separation-annihilation anxiety in the child as well as rage. In an effort to maintain an internal tie to the mother, the son confuses *having* Mommy with *being* Mommy and attempts to behave like her (cross-dresses, imitates her, etc.) in order to maintain a fantasy or symbolic connection to her. Since the child's rage at his mother threatens his internal tie to her, he uses a special form of splitting in which rage is projected onto men while women are primitively idealized. By thus identifying with women (specifically, his mother), he dissociates himself from his own rage and protects the internal tie.

We have embarked on a series of Rorschach studies of these boys in an attempt to further understand their internal experience and to explore the meaning of their symptoms.

In our prior Rorschach study (Tuber and Coates, 1985), configurations of these extremely feminine boys' self- and object representations were examined. Of particular interest in that study was the extent to which these children's often dysphoric and chaotic regressions in psychotherapy, and their caricatured feminine behavior and mannerisms, were reflected in the quality and quantity of their Rorschach projections. Fourteen boys meeting the DSM–III criteria for Gender Identity Disorder of Childhood were the subjects of that investigation. The children were aged five to twelve, and had a mean Wechsler full-scale IQ score in the Average range. Verbatim Rorschach protocols, administered by clinical psychology graduate students and interns according to the standard clinical method described by Rapaport, Gill, and Schafer (1945), were the raw data for the study. A standardized inquiry which attempted to rigorously examine responses with animate and/or interactive content in a nondirective manner was employed (Tuber, 1983). Because funds for a matched control group were not available, the normative data published by Ames, Metraux, Rodell, and Walker (1974) were used wherever appropriate as a means of comparison with the present sample.

The results of our investigation revealed a number of significant distortions in the Rorschach content of the extremely feminine boys' group. While their percentage of whole human responses was approximately equal to that of the normative sample of Ames et al., their Rorschach protocols contained about eight times as many quasi-human or (H) responses. These regressed responses are indicative of what Ames et al. called "an immature attitude" (p. 87) toward human representations. They refer to creatures or beings who may perform or pose in a human way but who lack the essential formal characteristics of fully human beings. For these children, the quasi-human response most often took the form of monstrous aggressive creatures such as "Dracula," "demons," or "Frankenstein."

Analysis of the content of the human representations of these extremely feminine boys allowed whole human figure responses to be distinguished from quasi-human responses. Responses were first grouped according to their benevolent, neutral, or malevolent content. Fully human responses were found to be equally represented in the benevolent and malevolent categories. By contrast, quasi-human responses were dominated by malevolent content, 80 percent of these involving the imbuing of the creatures with menacing or threatening intent or action.

Further evidence of impairment in these boys' self- and object representations was manifest in the fluidity and fusion that characterized many of their responses. Blatt's depiction (Blatt and Ritzler, 1974; Blatt and Berman, 1984) of a hierarchy of "boundary disturbances," in which separate percepts and/or fantasies cannot be adequately maintained, was used to characterize the fluidity and/or the fused responses of the extremely feminine boys' group. Eighteen examples of Contamination or Fabulized Combination responses representing the fusion of separate percepts were reported, a figure substantially greater than that reported by Ames et al. (1974) in their normative study. Responses in which the overelaboration of affect produced a disturbance in the "boundary" between fantasy and reality (Confabulation responses) also occurred with significant frequency. All fourteen subjects had at least one response, of either the fused or the overelaborated type, that was indicative of boundary disturbance.

Last, our previous investigation also revealed overt gender confusion and stereotypical feminine responses that paralleled the behavioral phenomenology of these children. Caricatured female representations, accompanied by elaborate depictions of stereotypical female objects, such as jewelry and clothing, including underwear, were commonly found in the records of these children. Responses in which the gender of a percept is fluidly transformed from one to the other, or in which male and female body parts were combined into a single response, were evident.

The following are examples of gender confused percepts:

1. "If it's a girl his (sic) hair goes up . . . or if it's a boy, it needs a haircut." (Card VIII)
2. ". . . this looks like a fat lady, no, looks like a fat man naked with lady's shoes." (Card IV)
3. ". . . she's having a baby . . . Could be a he, too, because he monsters have babies sometimes."
4. "It looks like a lady, looks like a man, turning into Superman . . ." (Card V)
5. "That's a butterfly. That's his (sic) tail where she has her babies through." (Card II)

These boys also frequently confused phallic representations with responses of birth canals and babies, and then could not decide, because of this alternation between phallic and birth content, whether a person was male or female.

The findings in this first study of immature and malevolent Rorschach representations, coupled with lapses in the clarity and bounded nature of the thinking of these subjects, suggested that significant psychopathology was evident. The repeated gender confusions and stereotypical feminine representations also provided a noteworthy analogue in projective material of their behavioral patterns and preoccupations. As we have described earlier, clinical work with these children reveals impairments in the development of an experience of viable autonomy, separate from the mother, with separation anxiety a prominent feature of internal organization (Coates and Person, 1985). The malevolent nature of their quasi-human responses provides corroborative evidence that the template of their inner experience is replete with aggression. The frequency of separation anxiety in these children, however, suggests the need to further elucidate the quality of their malevolent and benevolent responses and to focus more specifically on the nature of the interaction between the responses that they project onto the Rorschach.

In the current study we have therefore used the Mutuality of Autonomy Scale developed by Urist (1977), a measure specifically designed to emphasize the issue of the autonomy of the self vis-à-vis others. A full depiction of the rationale and operationalization of this scale as applied to children's Rorschachs is provided in the Appendix. In brief, this seven-point scale places Rorschach object representation responses along a progressive continuum ranging from mutual, reciprocal, empathic relatedness to themes of malevolent, overwhelming engulfment and destruction. A score is received for each Rorschach response that explicitly or implicitly describes an exchange or interaction between two or more animate or inanimate percepts. Its inclusion of animate and inanimate as well as human movement responses has made it particularly useful in the assessment of children's object representations (Tuber, 1983).

Sixty-five Rorschach responses in this sample were capable of being scored with this scale, an average of 3.93 such responses per child. These scores thus accounted for 58 percent of the total number of human-type responses and 22 percent of the total number of all responses for this sample. Of the boys with more than one such score, all twelve had at least one score in the seriously disturbed range (a score of 5, 6, or 7). All scores in this disturbed range are characterized by an experience of object representations as controlling or dominating interactions at best, and parasitic-attacking or engulfing experiences at worst. Seven of the boys had responses in which one figure was actively destroying the other (a score of 6 or 7). The remaining five had at least one score in which domination or control of one figure by another was paramount (a score of 5). These results provide further evidence, then, of the expectation of malevolence that appears to characterize these boys' inner experience of others.

Importantly, the existence of these destructive self- and object representations, though certainly implying psychopathology, would not of themselves clarify the nature of the gender disturbance these boys present. As depictions of disturbed self and other interactions, the Rorschach responses of these boys are akin to representations seen in borderline or even psychotic children (Leichtman and Shapiro, 1980; Tuber, 1983), but they do not, for example, speak to the idealization of maternal figures described as an essential characteristic of the inner experience of these children's (Coates and Person, 1985). To ascertain whether this commonly seen clinical dichotomy is present in their Rorschach representations of interactive figures, an analysis of all Mutual of Autonomy responses scored 1 or scored 5, 6, or 7 was conducted. Of eleven responses indicative of benign, reciprocal relatedness (a score of 1), nine involved women while the other two were animal figures whose sex was not reported. Thus, for these children, interactive depictions of benign relatedness were linked almost exclusively to female representations.

A review of those Mutuality of Autonomy scores indicative of malevolent content or parasitic interaction was noteworthy for the striking absence of female representations. Of the thirty-four responses scored 5, 6, or 7, only one involved a female; the other thirty-three quasi-human responses involved figures such as "Frankenstein," "Dracula," and other male monsters. These findings suggest that, despite their prominent degree of menacing and malevolent internal representations, these extremely feminine boys have been able to maintain an oasis of benign, high-level relatedness. This oasis almost exclusively involves a depiction of women in reciprocal interaction. This haven of positive female reciprocity, moreover, is further safeguarded by these boys' ability to avoid seeing women in responses characterized by malevolence or destruction. Malevolence is instead attributed almost entirely to more regressed quasi-human male figures, thereby preserving the maternal figure. We view this defensive strategy as a specialized form of splitting whereby women are primitively idealized and men devalued. This mechanism permits the boy to preserve an internal tie to his mother and protects her from his rage. Thus, the pattern seen in the representation of female and male object relations in the Rorschach closely parallels the clinical behavior we have described in these boys (Coates, 1985; Coates and Person, 1985).

APPENDIX: AN EXTENSION OF THE MUTUALITY OF AUTONOMY
SCALE IN THE ASSESSMENT OF CHILDREN'S RORSCHACHS

Urist (1977) and Urist and Shill (1982) have developed a Rorschach scoring system to delineate qualitatively discrete and significant object representational paradigms. Focusing on the thematic content of Rorschach responses, the scale is composed of seven points. It specifically focuses on the progression toward separation-individuation, with particular emphasis given to the "issue of the autonomy of others vis-à-vis the self, and conversely, the autonomy of the self vis-à-vis others." Thus each of the scale points refers to gradations in the "individual's capacity to experience self and other as mutually autonomous within relationships" (Urist, 1977, p. 4).

Urist first developed the scale for use with adults. Because it uses human, animal, and inanimate movement responses as its scoring base, however, it has proved equally promising as a research and clinical assessment tool with children. Recent research (Tuber, 1983; Ryan et al., 1985; Tuber and Coates, 1985) has verified its utility in work with children and adolescents.

In one investigation (Tuber, 1983) the Mutuality of Autonomy Scale was applied to the Rorschachs of children ages six to twelve. That study was a test of the hypothesis that Rorschach measures of object relations could help predict later adjustment. Subjects were seventy patients at a child residential treatment center who were followed up as adults as part of an earlier investigation. Half the subjects were reported at follow-up to have been rehospitalized for at least six months. The other half had no further psychiatric services. The two groups were then compared on a wide variety of preadmission and treatment variables, none of which successfully differentiated the two groups. By contrast, both the single highest object relations score on the Mutuality of Autonomy Scale and the single lowest object relations score meaningfully distinguished the children who were later rehospitalized from those who were not, with the nonhospitalized children having a significantly greater number of high object relations scores and a significantly smaller number of object poor relations scores.

In a study that applied the Mutuality of Autonomy Scale to a nonclinical population, Ryan et al. studied sixty children from grades four through six at an urban elementary school. Rorschach object representation scores were correlated with teacher ratings of child adjustment in the classroom, self-esteem, and locus of control. As predicted, higher mean object relations scores were significantly correlated with higher self-esteem, more positive school adjustment, and an experience of greater control over the environment. Lower Mutuality of Autonomy scores were similarly linked to an experience of being controlled by powerful others.

In the investigations of both Tuber (1983) and Ryan et al. (1985), as well as in a study of normal four- and five-year-olds with imaginary companions by Meyer (1985), the Mutuality of Autonomy Scale was found to be easily applied to children's Rorschachs with good interrater reliability. Exact agreement between raters ranged from .73 to .90, while agreement within one scale point was uniformly above 90 percent.

The following elaborates on Urist's scale, providing information on scoring criteria and nuances derived from earlier use of the scale with children (Tuber, 1983). Urist's initial definitions of each scale point are maintained. It should be noted that Urist calculated five object relations scores from his scale. A mean score was computed, the average of the eight highest and eight lowest scores was calculated, and the single highest and lowest scores were gathered. In work with child populations, it is extremely rare to find Rorschachs with enough object relation scores to warrant the averaging of the eight highest and eight lowest scores. Thus only three object relations scores are routinely calculated for each child: a mode score (M-O-R), the single highest score (H-O-R), and the single lowest (L-O-R). Because the intervals between scale points are not clinically or statistically "equal," the mode, rather than the mean object relations score, is calculated. Research has also shown that failure to generate any Urist scores is noteworthy and often pathognomonic; it should therefore be indicated in any summary of Rorschach scores.

In addition, it is crucial to note that any response in which a relationship is stated or clearly implied, whether between animate or inanimate objects, is scorable. Thus, Rorschach responses in which a relationship is implied, though only one object (animate or inanimate) is actually perceived in the blot, still qualify for a score. Consider the following three examples:

"A fetus with an unbilical cord" receives a score because a relationship is implied between the fetus and a second object. A response of "fetus" would alone be insufficient, as a second object is not implied.

Similarly, "It looks like a bear rug, as if it was cut right down the middle" implies a two-object relationship—something did the cutting to the rug—and is therefore a scorable response.

Finally, "This is a dog and he looks dead. He is squashed and the red looks like blood." This is a scorable response because a relationship is implied in the fact that some thing or person squashed the dog, making him bleed.

The Role of Inquiry

Any Rorschach scoring system is clearly dependent to a significant degree on the manner of inquiry employed to elucidate scores. As the inquiry here is geared toward eliciting from the subject an adequate description of his object representation percepts, any response depicting figures in interaction is given particular scrutiny. Much as in the scoring systems of Klopfer, Ainsworth, Klopfer, and Holt (1954), Beck (1944), and Rapaport, Gill, and Schafer (1945), inquiry is intended to provide the clinician enough data that he may feel reasonably secure in assigning a particular score to a response. Good inquiry elicits this information while avoiding both the Scylla of rote, mechanized "interrogation" and the Charybdis of intrusive, influencing, or shaping "analysis." "You see X as if . . ." or "How do you see the X" or "Tell me more" is almost always sufficient. The key is to be alert to phraseology, behavioral shifts, or sudden changes in the subject's level of articulateness. These nuances should be the focus of the inquiry.

A standardization of the inquiry used in scoring the Mutuality of Autonomy Scale can be formulated as follows. The child is first asked to give the location of the percept. He is then asked "what makes it look like" the percept. At this point an on-the-spot assessment of the child's response is made. If the child describes the relationship between the percepts well enough to produce a Mutuality of Autonomy score, no further inquiry is necessary. If movement or an adjectival description of the percept is given but is too general to score ("people running," "a scary monster"), the salient phrase is repeated to the child, along with the phrase "as if" (i.e., "running as if . . ." or "scary as if . . ."). This "as if" phrase has been found in clinical experience to foster more elaborate depictions of a percept without strongly influencing the content of the elaboration.

If the child's response to the "What makes it look like a . . ." does not provide either movement or a notable adjectival description, the child is asked, "Tell me more." If no further elaboration is provided, the inquiry to that response is dropped. If a vague movement or adjectival response is given to the "Tell me more" inquiry, the "as if . . ." question is also asked, ending the inquiry to that response.

In some cases inquiry may be insufficient to determine precisely what the subject has in mind and therefore what score to apply. Particularly with children, extensive inquiry can be fruitless at best and painfully disruptive to the child at worst. In these cases, subtle turns of phrase are relied on to help establish the quality of the activity or relationship between the two figures. For example, "Two people trying to get *to* each other" may differ in meaning from "Two people trying to get *at* each other." The former may imply more libidinal, perhaps dependent overtones while the latter has more aggressive or destructive features. The first response might receive a score of 1, the latter response a 5.

In rare and extreme cases, when inquiry is insufficient and there is no clue as to the quality of the relationship, even in a turn of phrase, the formal properties of the response may be examined. When form level is poor, indicating that something in the subject's percept has caused a slippage in thought organization, a lower score may be assigned. Here we are speculating that the drop in form level "hides" a more patholog-ical object representation and no "benefit of the doubt" is given. This use of form level should be applied with extreme caution, however, and only with protocols in which the frequency of these scoring ambiguities precludes the more typical content analysis.

Scale Point 1

Scale point 1, the highest level of object relatedness in the scale, reflects the depiction of a figure that is separate, autonomous, but aware of and interacting with another autonomous figure. The conveying of reciprocal acknowledgment of each figure's respective individuality is crucial in achieving such a score. The scale maximizes the "healthi-ness" of this scale point and so should be scored conservatively. Urist gives as an example to be scored a 1 the following response to Card II: "Two bears toasting each other, clinking glasses." The phrase "each other" is often very helpful in deciding whether a response should be scored 1. Other responses scored 1 include:

Card II: Two people dancing, sticking their tongues out at each other.
Card III: Two people greeting each other.
Card VII: Two women turning around to look at each other.
Card VII: Two women about to kiss each other.
Card IX: Two witches (orange). They're laughing, as if sharing a secret about someone.

Scale Point 2

To receive a scale score of 2, the figures should be engaged in some relationship of parallel activity; there is no stated emphasis or highlighting of mutuality, nor on the other hand is there any sense that this dimension is compromised in any way within the relationship (Urist, 1977, p. 4). Urist gives as an example a response to Card III: "Two women doing their laundry."

It should be noted that scale points 1 and 2 are clearly given a positive valence; they are the only scale points in which the autonomy of the figures is not distorted. They may therefore be viewed as representing "neurotic" or higher-level object representations.

A further means of differentiating scores 1 and 2 is as follows. For a response to receive a score of 1, the unique contribution of each individual to the mutual interaction must be highlighted. Thus "Two people dancing" would receive a 2 because there is no stated emphasis on the mutuality of their endeavor. Their activity could be parallel (perhaps they are dancing on opposite sides of the room, with their backs to each other) rather than interactive. However, "Two people dancing a pas de deux" would qualify for a 1. Other responses scored 2 include:

Card II: Two people saluting.
Card III: Two ladies cooking something.
Card VII: Two children waving.
Card X: (Center pink) Two people sleeping.

Scale Point 3

Scale points 3 and 4 reveal an emerging loss of autonomy in interaction. Both points imply a need for another figure to permit a sense of structural cohesion. For a percept to receive a score of 3, the figures must be seen as leaning on each other, or one figure as leaning or hanging on the other. The sense here is that objects do not "stand on their own two feet," that they require an external source of support or direction (Urist, 1977, p. 5). Responses scored 3 include:

Card I: Two animals clinging to a telephone pole, maybe birds.
Card I: A half-man, half-animal (side D) holding on to something.
Card III: (Upper red D's). A fetus tied to mother with its umbilical cord.
Card IV: Two dead trees leaning against each other.
Card VII: Panthers or cats grasping these arms that are attached to these bushes.

Card IX: Beavers (green). They're dead and their heads are hanging up on someone's house, no, just staring somewhere because they're alive.

Card X: Looks like a man dangling out a window.

Scale Point 4

A scale point of 4 on the Urist scale is scored when one figure is seen as the reflection or imprint of another. The relationship between objects here conveys a sense that "the definition or stability of an object exists only insofar as it is an extension or reflection of another" (Urist, 1977, p. 5). Urist suggests that shadows, footprints, etc. would be included here.

While a scale point of 3 implies that autonomy is precariously bound to the availability of an "other," the two figures are still tangible beings, often with no indication that one of them is less fragile or impaired than the other ("Two figures leaning on each other"). By contrast, a scale point of 4 conveys the vivid sense that at best only one solid being is present. Indeed, the essence of this type of percept is often one of a figure gazing into its reflection to validate or actuate itself. Points 3 and 4 do share a depiction of self in which narcissistic issues are pivotal. The difference between the points seems to lie in the extent to which the mirroring, cohesion-building "other" can maintain a degree of physical viability. Responses scored 4 include:

Card III: Double image of a woman.

Card VII: One girl is looking in the mirror and seeing itself [sic] because they are identical.

Card VIII: All these cards are just the same on both sides, two of everything. Two bears, or maybe it's one bear reflected in the water.

Scale Point 5

Points 5, 6, and 7 reflect not only the loss of the capacity for separateness, but increasing malevolence of one figure toward another. While points 3 and 4 may be tentatively linked to "narcissistic" disturbances in Kohut's terms, the final three points of the scale refer to "borderline" or "psychotic" modes of experiencing others. These low scores reflect an experience of object relations where the autonomy of the self is under siege. Representations of self and others are therefore avoided entirely or depicted as experiences of malevolence, depletion, or disintegration.

A scale score of 5 is appropriate when the nature of the relationship between figures "is characterized by a theme of malevolent control of one figure by another. Themes of influencing, controlling, or casting spells may be present. One figure may literally be in the clutches of another. Such themes portray a severe imbalance in the mutuality of relations between figures. On the other hand, figures may be seen as powerless and helpless, while at the same time, others are omnipotent and controlling" (Urist, 1977, p. 5).

Also scorable within this scale point are responses in which fighting between figures becomes a clear violation of both figures' intactness. Thus, a score of 2 is given for "Two cats are fighting" but a score of 5 is given for "Two cats fighting, the red looks like their blood," as the latter response indicates that one or both of the cats' intactness has been violated.

Similarly, figures trying to kill each other are scored 5 because this reflects the effort of one or both to dominate and destroy the other. Thus, "Two bears trying to kill each other" on Card II is a 5, unless the aggression is more malevolently one-sided, in which case a score of 6 would be more appropriate. Responses scored 5 include:

Card III: Puppets. They're just there like someone has them on strings.
Card III: Belly dancers. They've changed somebody into a skeleton.
Card VI: A sea monster ready to attack.
Card VIII: A wolf stalking its pray.
Card IX: Two witches (orange). They've cast a cruel charm against someone.
Card X: A victim.

Scale Point 6

In a scale point score of 6, not only is there a

severe imbalance in the mutuality of relations between figures, but here the imbalance is cast in decidedly destructive terms. Two figures simply fighting is not destructive in terms of the individuality of the figures, whereas a figure being strangled by another is considered to reflect a serious attack on the autonomy of the object. Similarly included here are relationships that are portrayed as parasitic, where a gain by one figure results by definition in the diminution or destruction of another. [Urist, 1977, p. 5]

Responses scored 6 include:

Card II: Looks like two people spitting out blood. They're demons.
Card II: Two people feasting after killing an animal.
Card VI: A dead white bear slit in two by someone.
Card VI: This looks like a jackhammer, splintering through rock. [The autonomy or wholeness of the rock is destroyed by the violent penetration of the jackhammer.]
Card X: A leech, stuck onto that man, sucking up his blood.

As a further clarification of how aggressive interactions of varying intensity and content can be scored with this scale, consider the following:

Score 1: Two people fighting about politics. This one is a liberal and this one is a conservative and they are arguing over whether hunger really exists in this country. It's a heated debate. (Here the response reflects the mutual but independent or differentiated concerns of the two people.)

Score 2: Two people fighting. (Here there is no attempt to hurt, control, or dominate the other.)

Score 5: Two people fighting, they want to kill each other. (The wish or attempt to hurt or destroy is implied.)

Score 6: Two people fighting, blood all over the place, his arm's been broken and he's going to die. (Here the malevolence results in the realization of the wish to destroy one of the figures.)

Scale Point 7

A score of 7 is given when relationships are characterized by an overpowering, enveloping force. "Figures are seen as swallowed up, devoured or generally overwhelmed by forces completely beyond their control" (Urist, 1977, p. 5). The destructive element is "larger than life" in a 7 response. The force is described as overpowering, malevolent, perhaps even psychotic. Frequently the force is described as existing outside the relationship between the figures or objects, underscoring the massiveness of its power, its overwhelming nature, and the complete helplessness of the figures or objects involved. Given the severe level of disturbance evidenced by such a response, the score of 7 should be given conservatively, reserved solely for responses in which the malevolence or aggression is explicitly stated in ahuman, grossly overwhelming terms. Responses scored as 7 include:

Card IX: This is something being consumed by fire, can't even see what it is, just the color of a raging fire.

Card IX: A violent God, up in the sky. He's so angry, he's breathing fire and that's what all the red is, and it's pouring down on the people below. God's wrath. The people are not to survive.

Card X: Debris. It's just scattered things. Maybe a tornado threw everything apart and it's all asunder, just remnants of things. Maybe houses, trees, just parts of them, because everything has been torn apart.

REFERENCES

Achenbach, T. M., & Edelbrock, C. (1983), *Manual for the Child Behavior Checklist and Revised Child Behavior Profile.* Cincinnati: Queen City Printers.

Ames, L. B., Metraux, R., Rodell, J. L., & Walker, R. N. (1974), *Child Rorschach Responses.* New York: Brunner/Mazel.

Bates, J. E., Bentler, P. M., & Thompson, S. K. (1973), Measurement of deviant gender development in boys. *Child Development,* 44:591–598.

——— Bentler, P. M., & Thompson, S. K. (1979), Gender deviant boys compared with normal and clinical control boys. *J. Abnorm. Child Psychol.,* 7:143–159.

——— Skilbeck, W. M., Smith, K. V. R., & Bentler, P. M. (1974), Gender role abnormalities in boys: An analysis of clinical ratings. *J. Abnorm. Child Psychol.,* 2:1–16.

Beck, S. J. (1944), *Rorschach's Test. Vol. 1: Basic Processes.* New York: Grune & Stratton, 1949.

Blatt, S. J., & Berman, W. M. (1984), A methodology for the use of the Rorschach in clinical research. *J. Personal. Assess.,* 48:226–239.

——— Ritzler, B. (1974), Thought disorder and boundary disturbance in psychosis. *J. Consult. & Clin. Psychol.,* 42:370–381.

Bradley, S., Doering, R., Zucker, K., Finegan, J., & Gonda, G. M. (1980), Assessment of the gender disturbed child: A comparison to sibling and psychiatric controls. In: *Childhood and Sexuality,* ed. J. Samson. Montreal: Éditions Études Vivantes.

Coates, S. (1985), Extreme boyhood femininity: Overview and new research findings. In: *Sexuality: New Perspectives,* ed. Z. Defries, R. Friedman, and R. Corn. Westport: Greenwood Publishing Corporations.

——— & Person, E. (1985), Extreme boyhood femininity: Isolated finding or personality disorder? *J. Amer. Acad. Child Psychiat.* 24(6):702–709.

——— ——— (1987), Extreme boyhood femininity: Isolated finding or pervasive disorder. In *Annual Progress in Child Psychiatry and Child Development,* ed. S. Chess, and A. Thomas, New York: Brunner Mazel.

_____ & Zucker, K. (1988). Assessment of gender identity disorders in children. In: *Clinical Assessment of Children and Adolescents*, ed., C. Kestenbaum and D. T. Williams. New York: New York Univeristy Press.

Green, R. (1974), *Sexual Identity Conflict in Children and Adults.* New York: Basic Books.

_____ (1985), Gender identity in childhood and later sexual orientation. Followup of 78 males. *Am. J. Psychiat.* 142(3): 339–341.

Klopfer, B., Ainsworth, M. D., Klopfer, W. G., & Holt, R. (1954), *Developments in the Rorschach Technique, Vol. I, Technique & Theory.* New York: World Books.

Leichtman, M., & Shapiro, S. (1980), An introduction to the psychological assessment of borderline conditions in children. In: *Borderline Phenomena and the Rorschach Test*, ed. J. Kwawer, H. Lerner, P. Lerner, & A. Sugarman. New York: International Universities Press, pp. 367–394.

Meyer, J. (1985), Adaptive uses of imaginary companions. Unpublished doctoral dissertation, City University of New York.

Rapaport, D., Gill, M., & Schafer, R. (1945), *Diagnostic Psychological Testing.* Rev. ed. New York: International Universities Press, 1968.

Ryan, R., et al. (1985), A Rorschach assessment of children's mutuality of autonomy. *J. Personal. Assess.,* 49:6–12.

Stoller, R. J. (1975), *Sex and Gender: Volume II. The Transsexual Experiment.* New York: Aronson.

Tuber, S. (1983), Children's Rorschach scores as predictors of later adjustment. *J. Consult. Clin. Psychol.,* 51:379–385.

_____ Coates, S. (1985), Interpersonal modes in the Rorschachs of extremely feminine boys. *Psychoanal. Psychol.* 2(3):251–265.

Urist, J. (1977), The Rorschach test and the assessment of object relations. *J. Personal. Assess.,* 41:3–9.

_____ Shill, M. (1982), Validity of the Rorschach Mutuality of Autonomy Scale: A replication using excerpted responses. *J. Personal. Assess.,* 46:451–454.

Chapter 25

Adolescence, Self-Experience, and the Rorschach

Arnold H. Rubenstein, Ph.D.

People don't understand teenagers anymore because teenagers are becoming so weird.

—a tenth grade student (1984)

I see no hope for the future of our people if they are dependent on the frivolous youth of today, for certainly all youth are reckless beyond words. . . . When I was a boy, we were taught to be discreet and respectful of elders, but the present youth are exceedingly wise and impatient of restraint.

—Hesiod (c. 700 BC)

The cure for adolescence belongs to the passage of time. . . .

—D. W. Winnicott (1965)

Since its introduction to the literature as a clearly recognized and relatively separate phase of development, adolescence has presented the worker in the field with difficulty. In the effort to address this stage from an investigative, clinical, and therapeutic standpoint problems have persistently arisen. These relate to the dynamic processes and influences that seem so distinctly a part of adolescent development. Not surprisingly, and as a direct consequence, diagnostic precision has eluded the investigator. Recent work by Masterson and his associates (see Rubenstein, 1980) has made considerable headway in this regard.

665

There remain, nonetheless, areas of significant confusion, disagreement, and controversy regarding the diagnosis and treatment of this population.

Problems include a lack of sufficient clarity in distinguishing the normal from the abnormal. Among psychoanalytic workers the prevailing view conceives adolescence as a developmental crisis (Bibring, 1959). Adolescence is seen as a task or set of tasks that must be performed with reasonable success if the individual is to enter adulthood. During this stage, which is characterized by turmoil and upheaval, the individual is judged to be in a state of acute personal crisis.

The work of Anna Freud (1958) is perhaps the most eloquent and influential in this connection. Essentially, she suggests that the relative quiescence of latency, a period of "peaceful growth," is disrupted by the biological, social, and emotional demands of adolescence (p. 275). As a result, the individual is cast into a state of severe psychological disequilibrium, at times bordering on personality disintegration: "The adolescent manifestations come close to symptom formation of the neurotic, psychotic or dyssocial order, and merge almost imperceptibly into borderline states, initial, frustrated or full-fledged forms of almost all the mental illnesses" (p. 267). These indicators speak to the "internal adjustments which are in progress" and which are part of the inevitable and healthy march to adulthood. As one might expect, therefore, "the differential diagnosis between the adolescent upsets and true pathology becomes a difficult task" (p. 267).

The adolescent may suffer with his raging inner battles, his extreme fluctuations in mood, attitudes, and impulses. However, unless his means of coping become "overused, overstressed, or used in isolation" (p. 275) the individual "does not seem . . . to be in need of treatment" (p. 276). Rather, the adolescent "should be given time and scope to work out his own solution" (p. 276). Professional help, if necessary, ought to be directed at the adolescent's parents, in order to enable them to "bear with him."

Several consequences follow from this view of the adolescent condition. Even when things are proceeding according to plan, the adolescent is viewed as turmoil-ridden. This "normal adolescent turmoil" or "craziness of adolescence," noted by Masterson (1972) and Nicholi (1978), can be expected to diminish with the passage of time. A characterization by Rakoff (1967) is gaining some currency on hospital ward rounds: "An adolescent is psychotic, neurotic, and even well-adjusted, in a highly changeable way from minute to minute" (p. 61).

This certainly creates far more confusion than clarity. Perhaps in an effort to resolve this situation, the diagnostic category "adjustment reaction of adolescence" was created (Rubenstein, 1980). If the prevailing view suggested that these reactions were to be expected as part of the normal unfolding of adolescent development, then such reactions would be seen as healthy. Under these circumstances one might, as a professional, steer clear of such an adolescent, not wishing to intervene in a healthy process. However, the absence of such craziness should alert the clinician almost automatically to lurking psychopathology.

Anna Freud's view (1958) is consistent with this notion. An absence of "outer evidence of inner unrest," while perhaps convenient for parents,

> signifies a delay of normal development and is, as such, a sign to be taken seriously. . . . These are children who have built up excessive defenses against their drive activities and are now crippled by the results which act as barriers against the normal maturational processes of phase development. They are, perhaps, more than any others, in need of therapeutic help to remove the inner restrictions and clear the path for normal development, however upsetting the latter may prove to be. [pp. 264–265]

In sum, where the normal individual is concerned, visible signs of upset and upheaval are inevitable.

The influence of this view within traditional psychiatry has been marked. Here clinicians have adopted a somewhat "hands off" approach or, at best, a casual form of intervention where the troubled adolescent is concerned. It is with just cause that parents have viewed psychiatry's stance in this respect with skepticism if not outright derision. Relations between psychiatry and the adolescent's family have been severely strained as a result (Nicholi, 1978). While the service needs of many adolescents and their families were left frustrated, many clinicians were spared the psychological discomfort of exposing their therapeutic wares to this population. In effect, the adolescent in trouble, much like the unwanted patient, evoked a sense of distaste and dislike in the therapist (Eigen, 1977).

The work of Masterson and Rinsley (see Rubenstein, 1980) has gone a long way in challenging these traditional concepts. In their view adolescent turmoil can mask more ominous personality signs suggestive of severe ego pathology. From a different direction, the large-scale longitudinal research cited by Nicholi (1978) has produced other findings contrary to the traditional view. These researchers found that profound and severe inner turmoil was unusual in the adolescents they studied, although evidence was found of mild forms of rebelliousness occurring primarily between the ages of twelve and fourteen. These adolescents were not in the highly disturbed state reflecting the internal psychological drama suggested by Anna Freud. Interestingly enough, these adolescents were found to have relationships with parents that were stable, consistent, and empathic.

Recent conceptual models view the adolescent within a framework of the stressors impinging on the individual at this time (Petersen and Spiga, 1982). Adolescence is regarded as not necessarily a tumultuous, near-psychotic state through which the individual must pass on his way to adulthood. This perspective emphasizes that the individual must encounter a variety of developmental stresses that are frequently interrelated (e.g., change in appearance brought about by pubertal development, parental responses to these changes, and peer group pressures).

Consistent with research already noted, Petersen and Spiga find that effective social supports, particularly parents, can assist in modifying the effects of these stresses and can enhance coping ability. They draw attention to the association between parental support on the one hand and heightened self-esteem and positive emotional tone on the other. This model appears to support the view that the adolescent's coping ability rests emphatically on feelings of effectiveness, self-confidence, and self-esteem. Implicit here is the point that sense of self is central to the success or failure of attempts to meet the challenge of these psychosocial stressors. In their studies of adolescent self-image, Offer, Ostrov, and Howard (1980) found nonsymptomatic adolescents to have a better self-image than symptomatic, psychiatrically disturbed, or delinquent adolescents.

This brief review suggests that the troubled adolescent may in fact be a troubled individual ill equipped to meet the demands of a particular situation. No longer is this situation considered the normal unfolding of adolescent development. Although adolescence is undeniably a period in which stress and major changes are encountered, the majority of individuals are able to meet the challenge successfully without experiencing major psychological problems or developing significant psychopathology. An adolescent manifesting psychotic-like symptoms must be addressed with no less seriousness than would an adult in similar circumstances. The individual is not simply "going through a phase." As Rakoff (1967) has pointedly remarked, "There is no license for the adolescent to be normal and display . . . symptomatology" (p. 60).

SELF-ORGANIZATION AND SELF-EXPERIENCE

If, then, intervention is necessary, what is its structure and content to be? As a related issue, what considerations must therapeutic strategies address? Before offering a preliminary response to these questions, I would like to draw attention to a recurring theme in the work of several clinicians. What is highlighted here is (1) the importance of the self as an organizing structure and (2) the self-experience of the adolescent.

Spiegel (1958) maintains that a "significant task of adolescence is the establishment of a relatively fixed sense of self" (p. 299). The search for identity, the question "Who am I?" is seen to refer to frequent alterations in self-feeling. At the same time, Spiegel (1959) suggests, the question refers to "a need to establish a constancy or steadiness of self-feeling" (p. 97). This is reminiscent of Erikson's later concepts of identity crisis and identity diffusion in adolescence (1968).

Blos (1962) sees a changed quality to the self as a consequence of the adolescent struggle and as the individual enters adulthood. The self has now achieved a relative stability. From a subjective standpoint, the young adult experiences a sense of "unity of inner and outer experiences instead of the fragmented excesses of his adolescence" (p. 192). The quality of the self affects both reality testing and self-evaluation, and provides a base for thinking and action.

Offer, Ostrov, and Howard (1980) advance the view that adolescence is a "transitional stage marked by bodily changes and social changes"; they contend also that such change "must, ipso facto, result in changes in self-concept" (p. 202). Gedo (1979) views adolescence as the transformation of self-organization.

Winnicott (1965a, 1971) regards the self as central to the adolescent's new adaptation to reality. Adolescence, according to Winnicott, is a "time of personal discovery" and has therefore only "one real cure," one which "belongs to the passage of time and to the gradual maturation processes" (1965b, p. 79).

This is a time when the self is vulnerable, when the individual struggles to establish a personal identity. The struggle is aimed at acquiring a feeling of being real. When adolescents undergo "whatever has to be gone through" (p. 84) and when their efforts to feel real have been frustrated, they feel unreal, futile, and in a "doldrums area" of experience. The adolescent, in this respect, is seen as an individual in waiting. He is waiting in the wings without any clearly defined role. In Winnicott's understanding the self is in disarray under the impact of "the new id advance" (1965a, p. 80). The self continues to be experienced as uncertain and vulnerable as the individual grapples with tensions produced by both sexual and aggressive strivings. "Because growing up means taking the parent's place" (1971, p. 144) the fantasy of murder takes a prominent place in the unconscious fantasy of the adolescent. Just as the adolescent requires the availability of adults, of his parents, he is in the throes of rejecting and replacing them. This mixture of dependence and defiance is striking.

INTERVENTION

What are the ingredients of intervention with this population? Suggestions include a willingness to work in a flexible manner; a primary focus on the patient's current functioning, reality testing, and current relationships; support, clarification, and confrontation instead of interpretation; and, little, if any, uncovering of unconscious material (Nicholi, 1978).

There are, of course, differences of opinion. For example, Holmes (1964) states that there are "many times when it is useful . . . to interpret a patient's unconscious wish, defenses, or communicative behavior" (p. 105). In most instances, Holmes suggests, the adolescent "is usually more relieved by having a chance to look the monster in the face than by being left to suffer with the knowledge that the monster is there but nameless" (p. 105).

But even at the very outset of treatment, long before interpretation is an issue, certain technical problems become evident. A rapport must be established, an initial connection by way of which we can involve the adolescent in addressing his need for help. To this one must add immediately that it is most often others whose need it is that the adolescent be helped. Rarely does the adolescent express this need directly or even experience such a need as an organized affective state. Yet, for one reason or another, he does find himself in the professional consulting setting.

The following therapist-patient exchange is taken from a first visit. The adolescent is a seventeen-year-old male.

Therapist: What's your understanding of why we're meeting?
Patient: My mother thinks I'm depressed.
Therapist: What do *you* think?
Patient: Nah! I'm not depressed.
Therapist: Oh.
Patient: Yeah. She's the one that's depressed. You should see her.
Therapist: So why do you think you and I are meeting like this?
Patient: I dunno. She wanted me to see you.
Therapist: Well, are you here then because you might have a problem saying no to your mother?
Patient: (Silence) I dunno. Well . . . maybe . . . yeah . . . maybe something like that.

Of course, following each player's opening gambit the interaction could have proceeded differently. For example, in response to the patient's statement, "My mother thinks I'm depressed," the therapist might have inquired: "Why would she think you're depressed?" or, "What makes her think that?" or "Is there anything you're doing that might lead her to think that?"

However, in my view, confirming or disconfirming the presence of a depression is at this stage of the undertaking not at all the point. Had the therapist proceeded in this manner, little would have been yielded other than mutual frustration. Instead, the therapist rather quickly adopted a quiet but firm confrontational stance which addressed directly the adolescent's opening remarks. In so doing the therapist appeared to respond on the basis of an automatic analysis of the import of the patient's comments. A confrontational stance does not mean that the therapist is unempathic.

Again, to return to the adolescent's rationale for meeting with the therapist ("My mother thinks I'm depressed"), an analysis of this comment might suggest the following subtext: "Being here makes me feel like a child who is told what to do, while I also wish to be an adult who can act on his own." Of course, implicating the mother suggests the ambivalent tie to her and may also be an effort to steer the therapist into adopting a similar transference position. In this respect the therapist is implicitly offered the choice of allying himself with the mother or allying himself with the patient. Either option leads in all probability to losing the patient, who thereby achieves a rather hollow victory over therapist and mother.

Instead the therapist refuses the bait and makes the patient's autonomy a central issue, not only for the therapist but also, very pointedly, for the patient: "What do *you* think?" This tack is absolutely essential, for it reflects to the adolescent his importance in a fashion that carries "here and now" immediacy. The therapist suggests to the boy in a powerful way that his mother's thoughts, feelings, attitudes, and demands are secondary to his own ability to deal with her in an effective manner.

This strategy also models the therapist's focus on the adolescent's need and the apparent lack of importance he assigns to the mother's position in all of this. He crystalizes a problem that the adolescent is having in his development "here and now" in a fashion that makes immediate sense to him.

The therapist must help the adolescent feel like a participant in the intervention process, and this in a manner congruent with the self-oriented needs of the individual. He must do this by shifting the context within which the adolescent is currently operating. This context includes the factual basis of the encounter, the fact that adolescents rarely come for help under their own steam.

Finding himself unable to accommodate to internal pressures and unable to control this inner experience effectively, the adolescent impinges on his interpersonal environment in a disturbing and disruptive fashion. When internal experiences find expression in action, others notice something is amiss. As revealed in the clinical fragment above, the adolescent is sent for treatment by the very people he regards as having the problem. What is syntonic for the adolescent is likely quite dystonic for others (Rubenstein, 1980).

As a backdrop to the referral one sees significant adults, parents who are angry, frightened, and confused. They may want the adolescent "fixed" as a means to relieving themselves of unwelcome thoughts, feelings, and wishes. Family tensions under these circumstances can become intolerable. The adolescent has some sense of this pressure on him to change and resents it. He is, at a fairly accessible level, a hostile partner to the clinical enterprise:

Therapist: What is your understanding of our meeting?
Patient: None of your fucking business!

Though extreme, this example reflects the veto power the adolescent has over the clinical intervention. More generally, it shows the intensity with which he makes efforts at resisting outside interference in his life.

Workers in this area are abundantly, at times painfully aware of the adolescent's negative reactions to therapeutic involvement and the varied resistances mounted to express them. Fraiberg (1955) suggests that the aims of adolescence and the aims of psychotherapy are hostile to each other and that the therapist must walk a tightrope in this work.

According to Winnicott (1965a), adolescents do not want to be understood; but it is also "a prime characteristic of adolescents that they do not accept false solutions" (p. 84). In a typically contradictory fashion the adolescent will at once reject psychotherapy as a false solution for his difficulties while possibly finding in it the help he needs to resume normal growth and development.

If therapy, or the prospect of such an encounter, is formulated as a false solution by the adolescent, the therapist must hold out the possibility that a sense of the real can be achieved—a sense of the real that has at its center a sense of reality about the self. If achieved, these moments can be remarkable experiences for adolescents because for them "everything is in abeyance" and "they feel unreal" (Winnicott, 1965a, p. 84). However, where "cure" is concerned, the adolescent "looks for a cure that is immediate, but at the same time rejects one 'cure' after another because some false element in it is detected" (p. 84).

From Fraiberg's standpoint (1955), "if therapy is to appeal . . . the introduction to treatment must be managed in such a way that the threatened ego is given some measure of control in this new and strange situation, assurance that it will be an active not a passive partner in treatment" (p. 276).

Where consultation with the adolescent is concerned, the task is not restricted to predicting and anticipating therapist-patient paradigms. Since the adolescent is neither child nor adult, adolescent-specific features are added to whatever paradigms emerge. It is important to bear in mind that many of these features are not at all related to pathology but rather are phase-specific and therefore fairly typical.

The task at consultation that holds priority over all others is that of involving the adolescent. Fraiberg (1955) comments pointedly that "a case is more likely to be lost in the early stages of treatment than any other time" (p. 285).

In the context of the dyad one can expect the adolescent to be grappling with issues of loss of autonomy and submission. Within the framework of self psychology (Kohut, 1977), the adolescent is viewed as actively controlling, regulating, and frequently resisting any threat to the self that might emerge in archaic forms of the selfobject transference. When these selfobject transference relationships do emerge in psychotherapy they "tend to be very intense, labile, highly vulnerable to disruption, and extremely taxing of the therapist's empathy and tolerance"; for the patient the focus of threat is to "the central capacity for self-regulation (Stolorow, 1984, p. 48).

According to this view, turbulent transference manifestations are not produced solely on the basis of negative components of the patient's instinctual life. Rather, emphasis is placed on "intersubjective situations in which the patient's self-object needs are consistently misunderstood and thereby rejected" (Stolorow and Lachmann, 1980).

In my view the most important characteristic a therapist can bring to in work with adolescents is the ability to empathize with their archaic emotional experiences, to accept these without challenge, and to protect without controlling. This approach is theoretically and clinically informed by Winnicott's concept of the holding environment (1965b) and Bion's notion of the container and the contained (1977).

In consultations with adolescents the position I try to occupy within the intersubjective field lies somewhere between being the authority/selfobject with whom the adolescent can struggle and the position taken by Aichhorn (1925). In the latter the therapist becomes the adolescent's advocate and takes his part in a strategy designed to win his confidence and draw him into a positive transference.

CONSULTATION WITH THE RORSCHACH

In work with adolescents I have evolved a method of enticing, seducing, and thereby involving the adolescent in the assessment. This is, I believe, a relatively novel approach which confronts some of the difficulties inherent in the patient-examiner paradigm.

Ostensibly, adolescents do not wish to be understood, helped, or otherwise tampered with by adults. Typically they resist invasive and intrusive techniques and approaches. This aggravates a difficulty intrinsic to the patient-examiner relation. The examiner is perceived as being aware of aspects of the individual about which the individual remains in ignorance. The patient has a reality-based notion that the examiner is privy to information outside the patient's scrutiny and control. It is as if the examiner were peering through a one-way mirror in front of which the patient has been asked to disrobe.

In working with adolescents I have used the Rorschach technique not only as a method of collecting data but as a mirror with which to reflect back to the individual that person's self-experience. In describing motivational aspects of the adolescent personality, Holmes (1964) states: "Because he is so uncertain about what he is and what he is supposed to be, he goes about tautly alert to the fleeting, vivid images of himself which other people can reflect back to him. He is extremely interested in himself and in what others can tell him about himself" (pp. 3–4). His deep curiosity about himself and others is an impelling force with which he actively engages in a "testing, experimental examination of the problems of his own life" (p. 4). Should he require the assistance of a psychotherapist to deal with these problems, his curiosity about himself and others becomes a major asset. "Having the support of an interested adult's superior judgment and good counsel can also enable him to indulge his curiosity with greater safety than if he were to attempt this alone" (p. 4). In concise and articulate fashion Holmes captures the essence and aims of my consultation approach using the Rorschach technique with adolescents. The consultation following data collection may take two to three sessions.

The consultation comprises a two-way exploration and interpretation of data. Hypotheses are generated, accepted, dismissed, or deferred as part of a dialogue and not simply as a unilateral exercise by the examiner. My interest is in stimulating and capturing the curiosity and self-interest that are so prominent in adolescence. I invite the individual to examine his Rorschach responses, to interpret them where possible, and then to allow me to broaden these interpretations, which is done in a palatable manner. When this process is successful, the adolescent can peer at himself and into himself with a newfound curiosity, as though he were looking at something vaguely familiar for the very first time. This experience may occur on the basis of one percept or of several— perhaps as the outcome of a response sequence or an awareness of his style of approaching the inkblots. When this process works well, the way is paved for a working relationship in psychotherapy should this be recommended. At an important level the adolescent may sense that the therapist can resonate with his self-experience. If one is to establish moments of rapport with the adolescent this capacity on the part of the therapist is crucial.

THE RORSCHACH AND SELF-EXPERIENCE

In the previous section I outlined a procedure in which the Rorschach can be used to enhance the consultation process. The Rorschach is also a powerful instrument for providing information regarding the adolescent's sense of self and self-experience. Such information has important implications for the therapeutic process. In the following examples one may note several formal aspects of the protocol which may reflect self-experience; in my analysis, however, I have placed exclusive emphasis on the content of responses.

From a clinical perspective Schachtel (1966) has commented on Rorschach responses as an indicator of self-feeling. From a theoretical perspective Spiegel (1959) points out that "the operational significance of the concept 'self' is its function as framework" (p. 96). He suggests that the self "acts as a steadying flywheel to overcome the disturbing discontinuity of intermittent self-representations" (p. 97). This, in his view, "may have a special relevance for those patients with a chronically shaky sense of personal identity" (p. 97).

The question "Who am I?" may then be seen as referring to frequent shifts and alterations in self-feeling in the adolescent. At the same time it may also reflect a need to establish a constancy or steadiness of self-feeling (Spiegel, 1959). An important dimension of the Rorschach in its use with adolescents, therefore, is as an indicator of the relative stability or instability of self-percepts. In the following clinical example I have drawn particular attention to the adolescent's experience of diminished self-esteem associated with deflation of grandiosity.

This older adolescent came for consultation with what he described as a depression he had fallen into some months previous. His description of the circumstances as well as his clinical presentation suggested, at most, a moderate level of depression. However, for this youngster the subjective experience proved frightening and devastating. Ordinarily an excellent student, gifted and talented, he had found himself falling behind academically. As president of his student council, he had administrative and social responsibilities, but it seemed he was no longer able to shoulder the burden placed on him by the admiration of others.

At the time of consultation he seemed to have pulled himself together, at least superficially. He was seeking help, he suggested, to ensure that he would never again be vulnerable to such a disturbing occurrence. In initial interviews he appeared anxious, guarded, and constricted, trying mightily to impress in an off-hand, nonchalant manner. Following administration of the Rorschach he became intrigued by our joint examination and discussion of his responses. He was both reassured and unsettled by what this procedure revealed to him. He was particularly able to appreciate his strategies aimed at eliciting the admiration of others. He was only remotely aware, however, of the consequences when his ability to amaze failed to bring nourishment to his self-esteem.

Card IV is compelling in this respect. His approach to the inkblots was in general ambitious, and here he made a marked effort to give a brilliant performance: "It's like a photograph taken to create the effect of height and dominance of a—I don't know if it's a person or not. It's not. It's a mammal with four extremities anyway. I think he's sitting on a tree stump." He went on to explain various photographic techniques that can be used to make something appear larger than it is. His need to create an effect of dominance, his effort to establish a grandiose sense of self are readily detected here. His need to display special qualities, his need to be admired if not held in awe are plain. His unsuccessful struggle to sustain this self-percept is also evident. He is unable to disguise what ultimately emerges as a rather ordinary response.

His second response to Card IV captures, in a sense, the live action of the process of falling self-esteem: "I think it's the same person but I think he's sky-diving. Different camera angle—the view from the airplane door, legs toward you and diminishing perspective." Again, his efforts to control and ward off feelings of loss of esteem are dramatic.

By Card V one can appreciate that he has run out of energy and is no longer able to keep a grandiose self-structure in place. He is painfully aware of his failure, and his unhappiness speaks for itself: "I'm afraid this is a somewhat conventional answer but it looks like a bat from this angle."

This sequence of responses formed a focus for our work in psychotherapy. This work was particularly useful in helping him identify areas of self-expression which were genuinely satisfying to him, which were not primarily aimed at impressing others.

Another adolescent provided a striking example of how personal talent can be experienced as an affliction. No matter how well this boy performed academically, his efforts were never considered good enough by his parents. His remarkable success, instead of bringing gratification, was therefore experienced as a burden, as persecutory. He functioned in an environment in which his exceptional talents were recognized but in which reinforcement of his self-esteem was scarce. That his ability to maintain and support an adequate sense of self was deteriorating is suggested in his response to Card VI: "I'd say it's a river bed with black tar or black sand shining through at the bottom where the water has eaten away at the surrounding banks." Interestingly enough, further on in the protocol he expressed a wish to be regarded like everyone else, as a way of restoring some sense of self. His response to Card X appeared to reflect this wish: "A flower in a field with other flowers."

Use of the Rorschach as a vehicle for expediting therapeutic involvement does not yield consistently happy results. Sometimes the sense of self is so shriveled, the damage so severe, and the associated lack of interest in the environment so profound, that the therapeutic encounter itself proves too stressful. In these instances the only route to regulating esteem and restoring some ongoing sense of self is through withdrawal from therapy. The notion that therapy might offer relief or resolution of conflict simply cannot be sustained. Therapy becomes an aggravation to an already enfeebled sense of self.

These difficulties are already apparent in the Rorschach responses of a fourteen-year-old boy who had left school. He had taken to spending much of his time isolated in his bedroom, either sleeping or listening to rock music. Fundamental and disturbing aspects of self-experience are evident in two of his responses: (1) "A crushed leaf—a dead one that had cracks in the middle"; (2) "A dead leaf that was just broken." During the course of therapy this boy's functioning improved to some degree. However, he became increasingly avoidant and gradually withdrew from therapy completely. I can only speculate that once a more positive self-feeling began to return, once he had begun to experience glimmers of inner vitality, he was unwilling to expose himself to the possibility that therapy might now undermine this changing sense of self.

A severe degree of disturbance in self-experience and damage to self-esteem is revealed in the protocol of a sixteen-year-old girl. She was brought for consultation only days after a serious suicide attempt. Her dead sense of self is revealed immediately on Card I: "It looks like the skeleton of a butterfly, the bone structure—the fossils left of it." When she reached Card IV she exposed a painfully shattered sense of self left in the ruins of a battered and crippled grandiosity: "If you turn it upside down it looks like some sort of robot. The body's not finished yet. A hole. A strange sort of robot. Yeah. There's the teeth." Following a brief hospitalization the Rorschach proved very successful with this adolescent in discussing her "weird" ideas and inner sense of "craziness." Continuing in psychotherapy, she has responded fairly well and has been able to see it through some very turbulent episodes. At this point she is showing some ability to stand back and reflect on her inner experience, gradually appreciating that it is, in fact, an *inner* experience. She can describe, for example internal images of setting fire to my office; though evidently disturbed by these thoughts, she is far more able to appreciate them as internal events.

REFERENCES

Aichhorn, A. (1925), *Wayward Youth.* New York: Viking, 1948.

Bibring, G. L. (1959), Some considerations of the psychological processes in pregnancy. *Psychoanalytic Study of the Child,* 14:113–121. New York: International Universities Press.

Bion, W. (1977), *Seven Servants.* New York: Aronson.

Blos, P. (1962), *On Adolescence.* New York: Free Press.

Eigen, M. (1977), On working with unwanted patients. *Internat. J. Psycho.-Anal.,* 58:109–121.

Erikson, E. H. (1968), *Identity: Youth and Crisis.* New York: Norton.

Fraiberg, S. (1955), Some considerations in the introduction to therapy in puberty. *Psychoanalytic Study of the Child,* 10:264–286. New York: International Universities Press.

Freud, A. (1958), Adolesence. *Psychoanalytic Study of the Child,* 13: 296–308. New York: International Universities Press.

Gedo, J. (1979), *Beyond Interpretation.* New York: International Universities Press.

Holmes, D. J. (1964), *The Adolescent in Psychotherapy.* Boston: Little, Brown.

Kohut, H. (1977), *The Restoration of the Self.* New York: International Universities Press.

Masterson, J. (1972), *Treatment of the Borderline Adolescent: A Developmental Approach.* New York: Wiley-Interscience.

Nicholi, A. M. (1978). The adolescent. In: *The Harvard Guide to Modern Psychiatry,* ed. A. M. Nicholi, Jr. Cambridge, Mass.: Harvard University Press, pp. 519–540.

Offer, D., Ostrov, E., & Howard, K. I. (1980), The self: Social and psychological perspectives. In: *Advances in Self Psychology,* ed. A. Goldberg. New York: International Universities Press.

Petersen, A. C., & Spiga, R. (1982), Adolescence and stress. In: *Handbook of Stress: Theoretical and Clinical Aspects,* ed. L. Goldberger & S. Breznitz. New York: Free Press, pp. 515–528.

Rakoff, V. (1967), Adolescence as rebirth. In: *Adolescent Psychiatry: Proceedings of a Conference Held at Douglas Hospital, Montreal, Quebec,* ed. S. J. Shamsie. Shering Corporation.

Rubenstein, A. H. (1980), The adolescent with borderline personality organization: Developmental issues, diagnostic considerations, and treatment. In: *Borderline Phenomena and the Rorschach Test,* ed. J. S. Kwawer, H. D. Lerner, P. M. Lerner, & A. Sugarman. New York: International Universities Press, pp. 441–467.

Schachtel, E. (1966), *Experiential Foundations of Rorschach's Test.* New York: Basic Books.

Spiegel, L. A. (1958), Comments on the psychoanalytic psychology of adolescence. *Psychoanalytic Study of the Child,* 13:296–308. New York: International Universities Press.

——— (1959), The self and perception. *Psychoanalytic Study of the Child,* 14:255–278. New York: International Universities Press.

Stolorow, R. D. (1984), Varieties of self-object experience. In: *Kohut's Legacy: Contributions to Self Psychology,* ed. P. Stepansky & A. Goldberg. Hillsdale, NJ: Analytic Press.

——— Lachmann, F. (1980), *Psychoanalysis of Developmental Arrests: Theory and Treatment.* New York: International Universities Press.

Winnicott, D. W. (1965a), *The Family and Individual Development.* London: Tavistock.

——— (1965b), *The Maturational Processes and the Facilitating Environment.* New York: International Universities Press.

——— (1971), *Playing and Reality.* London: Tavistock.

Name Index

Subject Index